IDEOLOGIES

THIRD EDITION

Authors

Douglas Baldwin
Acadia University, Nova
Scotia

Larry Booi
Strathcona Composite High
School, Alberta

David Jones
Writer, Researcher,
Academic International
Press

Thomas Spira
University of PEI, Prince
Edward Island

Douglas Ramsay
Celebration Canada
Committee, Alberta

Bob Berube

Contributing Authors

Matthew Booi
Researcher and Writer,
Alberta

Kim Fraser
Strathcona Composite High
School, Alberta

Gillis Harp
Acadia University, Nova
Scotia

Bob Perrins
Acadia University, Nova
Scotia

John Thomas
Acadia University, Nova
Scotia

Consultants

Mary Friesenhan
Archbishop O'Leary High
School, Alberta

Martin Graham
Archbishop MacDonald
High School, Alberta

Carol Grant
Sundre High School, Alberta

Cordula Paletz
John G. Diefenbaker High
School, Alberta

Lynne Phillips
Viscount Bennett Centre,
Alberta

Peter Sands
Harry Ainlay High School,
Alberta

McGraw-Hill Ryerson Limited

Toronto ▪ Montreal ▪ New York ▪ Auckland ▪ Bogotá ▪ Caracas
Lisbon ▪ London ▪ Madrid ▪ Mexico ▪ Milan ▪ New Delhi
San Juan ▪ Singapore ▪ Sydney ▪ Tokyo

**McGraw-Hill
Ryerson Limited**

A Subsidiary of The **McGraw·Hill** Companies

Ideologies, Third Edition

ISBN: 0-07-552777-4

Printed and bound in Canada

Care has been taken to trace ownership of copyright material contained in this text. The publishers will gladly accept any information that will enable them to rectify any reference or credit in subsequent editions.

Teacher's Resource available.

ISBN 0-07-552778-2

http://www.mcgrawhill.ca

8 9 10 BBM 6

Canadian Cataloguing in Publication Data

Main entry under title:
Ideologies
3rd ed.
Includes bibliographical references and index.
ISBN 0-07-552777-4

1. Political science. 2. Ideology. I. Baldwin,
Douglas, date.

JC348.B34 1997   320   C97-930172-6

PROJECT MANAGER: Geraldine Kikuta
ASSOCIATE EDITORS: Karina TenVeldhuis/Crystal Shortt
SUPERVISING EDITOR: Nancy Christoffer
PRODUCTION EDITOR: Claudia Kutchukian
PERMISSIONS EDITOR: Jacqueline Donovan
PRODUCTION CO-ORDINATOR: Yolanda Pigden
COVER AND INTERIOR DESIGN: Pronk&Associates
COVER IMAGE: Jane Sterrett/The Image Bank

CONTENTS

Preface

The world has undergone tremendous changes since the second edition of *Ideologies* was published in 1992. The Soviet Union disintegrated into a host of smaller countries, and profound changes occurred in Eastern Europe. Civil wars ravaged Yugoslavia, Rwanda, Burundi, Zaire, Haiti, and other African and Asian countries. Apartheid ended in South Africa. Israel signed a peace accord with several Arab countries. Japan's booming economy slowed dramatically, and China further encouraged limited capitalism. Globalization and information technology has advanced at a rapid rate. In Canada, the GST, a second referendum on Quebec separatism, the rise of the Reform and Bloc Québécois parties, and renewed interest in fighting government debts and deficits marked the last half of the 1990s. This edition reflects these and other world economic and political changes.

The major additions to this edition of *Ideologies* include new units on China, the fascist economies of Italy and Germany, nationalism and ethnic conflicts, the Cuban economy, debts and deficits, the American economy, biographies of individuals whose lives made a difference to world affairs, and primary source viewpoints on important issues. End-of-chapter questions have been changed to better meet the needs of students and teachers.

The authors are experienced teachers and authors. Douglas Baldwin has taught in Alberta, Ontario, Prince Edward Island, Japan, and Nova Scotia. This is his thirteenth book. Larry Booi has co-authored several books, and juggles his time between teaching at Strathcona Composite High School and his elected position with the Alberta Teachers' Association. David Jones is an expert on Russian and military history. He has taught at Dalhousie University and the Naval War College in Rhode Island, and has addressed committees of the Canadian Senate and the Congress of the United States. Thomas Spira is the founder and editor of the *Canadian Review of Studies in Nationalism*. He has written several books on Central European history and is editing a multi-volume encyclopedia on nationalism. Douglas Ramsay is on leave from the Calgary Board of Education where he was a Social Studies specialist. Presently he is working on citizenship education projects through the Kahanoff Foundation.

Bob Perrins, who teaches Chinese history at Acadia University and reads Japanese and Chinese, wrote the case studies on Japan and China. Dr. Gillis Harp, who is currently on sabbatical leave at the University of Notre Dame, wrote the case study on the American economy between the wars. Dr. John Thomas, professor of Canadian Studies at Acadia University, wrote the unit on women and Japanese Canadians. Matthew Booi, a recent graduate of the University of Alberta, assisted in the research and writing of the Biographies, and Kim Fraser, a teacher at Strathcona Composite and District Representative on the Alberta Teachers' Association, wrote two Biographies and assisted with others.

Without the hard work and meticulous attention to detail of the following people at McGraw-Hill Ryerson, this book would never have been written: Anne Louise Currie, Nancy Christoffer, Karina TenVeldhuis, Crystal Shortt, Jacqueline Donovan, and Geraldine Kikuta.

Using Ideologies

Key Terms and Concepts appear in boldface when they first appear in the text. Key terms are defined in the margin and in the **Glossary** at the end of the text.

Focus Questions featured in the margin are designed to stimulate critical thinking, debate, and discussion of a key idea or issue.

Biographies profile interesting individuals including, economists, business people, philosophers, writers, and activists who came to different conclusions on critical issues and made an impact on the larger political or economic systems. Biographies are followed by questions of interpretation and analysis.

To make *Ideologies* visually appealing to you, the material is presented in an easy-to-read format. Inviting photographs, cartoons, charts, maps, and literary quotations have been included.

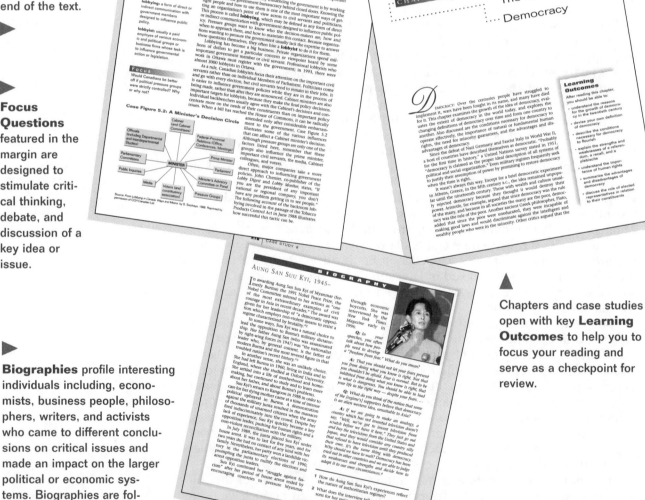

Chapters and case studies open with key **Learning Outcomes** to help you to focus your reading and serve as a checkpoint for review.

Underlying and Emerging Issues provide a systematic way for you to explore the reasons why people disagree on critical issues. You are asked to provide evidence to support various views and conclusions on underlying issues covered within the text.

Focussing Knowledge sections provide content review questions through defining or explaining the significance of important terms, concepts, or historical figures.

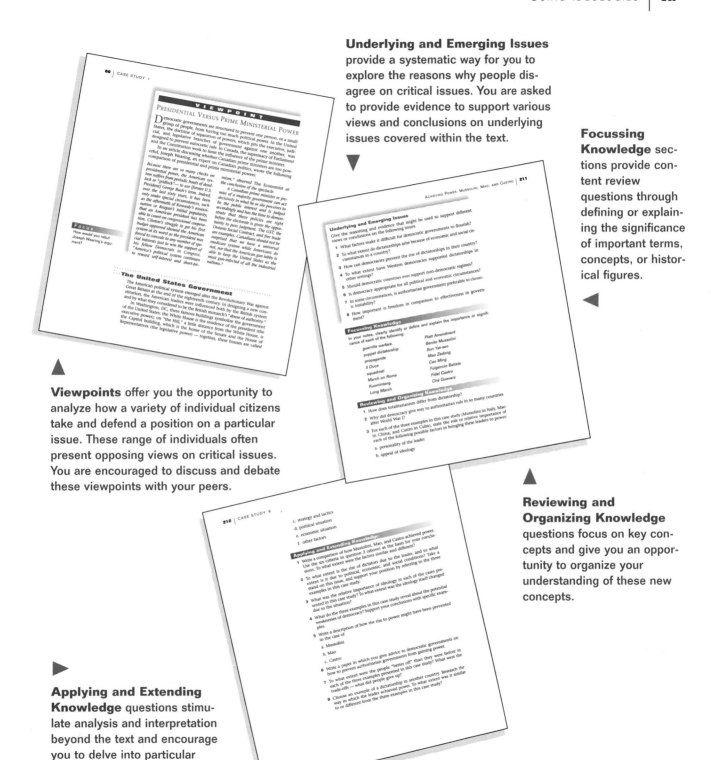

Viewpoints offer you the opportunity to analyze how a variety of individual citizens take and defend a position on a particular issue. These range of individuals often present opposing views on critical issues. You are encouraged to discuss and debate these viewpoints with your peers.

Reviewing and Organizing Knowledge questions focus on key concepts and give you an opportunity to organize your understanding of these new concepts.

Applying and Extending Knowledge questions stimulate analysis and interpretation beyond the text and encourage you to delve into particular issues that are of interest to you.

CHAPTER 1

Values and Political and Economic Systems

*W*HAT IS AN IDEOLOGY and why is it important? This chapter provides an overview of the major themes, content, and approaches of *Ideologies* and discusses the differences between facts and values. You will discover what your values are and the extent to which you are open-minded. As well the major issues and problems that all economic and political systems must address are previewed, followed by a discussion of how an understanding of the past helps to explain current political and economic issues.

World events such as the one pictured on page 2 often occur quite unexpectedly. Although the world is constantly changing, and it is obviously impossible to forecast the future accurately, an understanding of the past can help us make sense of world events. It is also important to be able to place changing events into proper perspective. This book attempts to provide a better understanding of the past, present, and future by examining the major **political** and **economic systems** of the twentieth century and by exploring Canada's relationship to them. It also seeks to provide the analytical tools necessary for you to interpret the world and make informed decisions.

This broad and important field of study is inevitably laden with controversy — in fact, disagreement and controversy are the very essence of politics and economics. Inflation, elections, taxes, and welfare policies are only a few controversial topics. The most brilliant minds in the world have wrestled with these subjects and have been unable to agree on any answers. This means citizens must decide for themselves.

Learning Outcomes

After reading this chapter, you should be able to:

- identify the major issues discussed in *Ideologies*
- distinguish between facts and values
- identify the extent of your own open-mindedness
- define ideology and understand its importance
- understand the concept of a "system"
- appreciate the importance of studying the past for understanding current political and economic issues

political system: an organized way to make, carry out, and interpret laws and rules.

economic system: an organized approach to producing and distributing goods and services.

Protesters wave union banners through the dense fog of tear gas as South Korea's biggest labour strike turns violent in 1996.

Facts and Values

Life is not simply a choice between good and bad alternatives. If each dilemma or problem could be solved by referring only to the facts, then it would be a relatively simple task to resolve conflicts of opinion. In that case, only a lack of knowledge on one or both sides could cause a difference of opinion. Yet we know that this is not always the case. A group of people can be given identical information and still arrive at different conclusions. Some of your classmates, for example, are very concerned about the environment, whereas others are not. Varying opinions often result from the differing values held by each individual. Values are fundamental ideas about what is important in life. They are standards of conduct that cause people or groups to think and act in certain ways. Although we might disagree about what the "facts" are in a situation, a **fact** is simply "what is," whereas a **value** is a deeply held conviction or belief. As people encounter new and different places, ideas, and people, their values are constantly being tested and shaped. Over time, major value changes are much less likely to occur. A disagreement over facts can be resolved on the basis of concrete evidence, but a dispute over values is much more difficult to settle. Three examples illustrate the problem:

fact: an actual occurrence, or a piece of information, presented as having reality.

value: a subjective standard, such as a philosophy or principle, that is deemed valuable or desirable.

- Edmonton is a beautiful city.

- Brian Mulroney was a great prime minister.

- Emily Carr was Canada's best artist.

These three statements combine fact and value judgements. It is possible to verify the factual statements: Edmonton is a city; Brian Mulroney was a prime minister of Canada; Emily Carr was an artist. The words "beautiful," "great," and "best," however, are value-laden terms — what exactly do they mean? Is the whole city of Edmonton beautiful, or just parts of it? Are skyscrapers and large apartment buildings beautiful, or do they signify crowded living conditions? Was everything that Mulroney did great? Did his policies benefit everyone? Is it possible to compare abstract artists to realist artists? Value-laden statements are almost impossible to "prove." To many businesspeople who export goods to the United States, Mulroney was a great prime minister because he helped to pass the Canada–U.S. Free Trade Agreement. Some consumers, however, might take a different view because Mulroney established the GST. A Calgarian might not think Edmonton is beautiful simply because of the rivalry between the two cities.

Since it is impossible not to make value judgements, it is important to know and understand your own values and to ensure that your conclusions are grounded on a solid base of information. If you think that natural areas are beautiful, you could support your **belief** that Edmonton is a beautiful city by referring to the North Saskatchewan River valley or to other scenic areas in the city. It is also essential that you examine other people's values and opinions with an open mind. When faced with different choices, people react with selections that vary largely because they possess different values. It seems inconceivable that only one religion, one country, and one lifestyle could be completely correct. Are all the people in other countries who hold different values from ours wrong?

belief: a conviction that something is true without certain proof.

Differing values help to explain the variety of political and economic systems in the world. Each political and economic system is based upon a set of values on such significant decisions as the importance of the individual versus the rights of the state, the degree of government involvement in the economy, and the method of selecting political leaders. Should everyone's income be similar, or should some people be allowed to amass huge fortunes? Should the country's leaders be chosen in free elections, or should an elite group of people make all political and economic decisions? Such questions as these have been debated for centuries. The basic questions have remained constant, but society's values have not. The answer that each society selects generally reflects its underlying values and assumptions.

Informed analysis occurs when a person is asked to evaluate different points of view, arrive at a conclusion, and support it with facts and value judgements.

What are your political and economic values? To evaluate them, read the above questionnaire. List the numbers 1 to 20 in your notebook, and mark *agree* or *disagree* beside each number. There are no right or wrong answers; you are being asked to make judgements.

This questionnaire has several purposes. The first is to discover whether your ideas and values change over the course of the year. At the conclusion of your course, return to this questionnaire, complete it again, and compare your two sets of responses. The second purpose is to help you discover the

Questionnaire

State whether you agree or disagree with each of the following statements:

1 People should have a say in determining their fate, and the government should be led by people elected by a majority of the citizens.

2 Canadian and Japanese people have almost nothing in common.

3 The Canadian economic system ensures that poverty will be kept to a minimum.

4 Always compromising with our political opponents is dangerous because it usually leads to a betrayal of our own side.

5 A socialist economy is designed to benefit the group, rather than the individual.

6 Even though freedom of speech is a worthwhile goal, it is usually necessary to restrict the freedom of speech of some groups.

7 The average Canadian voter is generally well-informed about election issues.

8 A group that allows a great variety of opinion among its members will not exist very long.

9 One of the beliefs of the private-enterprise system is that if all people were free to do exactly as they wanted, then the whole society would benefit.

10 In this complicated world, the only way we can ensure that the country is governed properly is to rely upon leaders or experts who can be trusted.

11 The major problem with socialism is that it destroys people's incentive to work.

12 There are two kinds of people in this world: those who are truthful and those who are not.

13 There is little difference among socialists, Marxists, and communists.

14 Among all the different philosophies in the world, there is probably only one that is correct.

15 A small economic elite has more influence on the Canadian government than the elected representatives (MPs).

16 Loyal political followers should read only their own party's newspaper.

17 It is impossible to have democracy in a socialist country.

18 I wish I could find someone to solve all my problems and tell me what to do.

19 Dictatorship is not much different from communism.

20 In the history of the world, there have probably been just a handful of really great thinkers.

critical thinking: the ability to subject ideas and situations to a sound estimate of the problems involved.

tolerance: permitting, although not necessarily condoning, particular actions or beliefs that differ from or conflict with one's own standards.

extent to which you are open-minded. Add up the *agrees* you have listed for each even-numbered question (2, 4, 6, 8, etc.). The higher the number of *disagrees*, the more open-minded you tend to be. Do not worry if there are some terms you do not completely understand. By the end of the course, your knowledge of important political and economic words and concepts will have greatly expanded.

If you value **critical thinking** and do not want to accept everything people tell you without first examining its "truth," and you want to be tolerant of other people and receptive to new ideas, then you must attempt to have an open mind toward controversial issues. **Tolerance** means to recognize and respect the rights and opinions of others whether you agree with them or not. Permitting people to follow another religion than your own without condemning them is an example of tolerance. Sometimes, however, a society or an individual can be too tolerant. Should society permit sexism, racism, murder, and violence? There is often a fine line between the need for tolerance and the necessity of imposing restrictions. When, for example, does freedom of speech become the spreading of lies or hatred, and when does government control of free speech become censorship?

People who hold their beliefs so strongly that they will not change them, no matter what, are called closed-minded. This means that their minds are closed to many new and different ideas. Rather than carefully examining information that conflicts with their views, closed-minded people will reject the information without considering its merits. Such people tend to judge issues in black and white terms, and they often evaluate people according to their appearance, occupation, and manner of speaking. Rarely will they question the statements made by figures of authority. As a consequence, they are generally ignorant of the views of those who oppose them.

If democratic governments are to operate effectively, their citizens need to be open-minded. Democratic people must be adaptable to change and receptive to different points of view. Tolerance of divergent ideas is basic to democracy, because one of the most important aspects of democracy is the recognition that people are different. Even more important is the acceptance of these differences. In contrast to the open-mindedness of the democratic personality, the closed-minded personality is often intolerant, distrustful, conforming, and rigid.

No individual is completely closed- or open-minded. One of the purposes of this book is to expose you to different ideas. Do not accept anything you read without first questioning it, and do not reject new opinions without first considering their merits. The more open-minded you attempt to be, the more you will learn.

One way to discover your biases is to jot down your reactions to a photograph before reading the caption, and then to record your reactions after reading it. How do you react to this photograph? With sympathy? Curiosity? Indifference? Jot down your feelings before reading on.

How does your response change if you discover that the photograph shows

a. London, England, after a German attack during World War II?

b. Detroit, Michigan, after a riot in 1967?

c. Berlin, Germany, after a combined British-American-Canadian attack in 1945?

Try this test on your friends and family. Then give them the true identity of the photograph, as found on page 9.

··· Ideologies

Our beliefs are influenced by everything we do. As we grow up, we are pushed and pulled in one direction or another by family, teachers, friends, and the media. At times we consciously choose among competing religious, scientific, social, and political ideas, but in many cases, we simply accept the current beliefs in society without making a conscious choice. Gradually we adopt a set of values that we accept as being true. This set of values about the world is called an *ideology*.

An ideology is a systematic set of beliefs that provides a fairly thorough picture of the world that a group of people accepts as true. Although the word "ideology" has many different definitions and meanings, it generally has the following characteristics:

- a set of basic assumptions about human nature and society;

- an interpretation of the past;

- an explanation of the present;

- a vision of the future;

- a goal for which to strive, and a strategy to achieve this goal;

- heroes (martyrs, founders, leaders), rituals (pledges, anthems, salutes), and sacred religious documents (Talmud, Koran, Bible) or political declarations (manifestos, constitutions);

- a strong emotional appeal that is designed to win converts and encourage action;

- a simple, easily understood picture of the world, which is claimed to be the truth.

Although many people are not aware of their own basic beliefs, all contemporary societies have their own ideologies. Few societies, however, are so dominated by a single ideology that there are no alternatives available within the system. Because each ideology is a blend of facts and values and is intended to have an emotional appeal, people often perceive it in terms of black and white, or good and bad, without making the effort to understand what such words as democracy, communism, socialism, nationalism, capitalism, fascism, terrorism, or fundamentalism really mean. This is largely due to their unconscious acceptance of one or more of these ideologies.

Ideologies are important because they enable people to understand their environment and order their lives accordingly. An ideology provides a way of judging and evaluating a confusing variety of issues and world events. It makes the future seem more predictable and imparts a feeling of security. An ideology also binds people together by providing them with a common value system and a way of looking at the world, which contribute to a feeling of belonging. Finally, an ideology promises a good life and provides a method of attaining it.

This book examines some of the major economic and political ideologies of the contemporary world. Although it is true that an ideology is not always an accurate depiction of reality, people base their actions upon what they believe is true. It is therefore important to examine the underlying values and assumptions of every major political and economic system in order to better understand each country's actions.

Societies and Systems

People often talk about "the social system," or "the political system," or "the education system." What do they mean by the word "system?"

A **system** is an orderly combination or arrangement of parts, elements, facts, or concepts into a whole. It is helpful to think in terms of comparisons. In biology, whole series of body parts and processes make up the respiratory system, the digestive system, and the nervous system. Biology can be better understood by studying these various systems, each of which is designed to meet a particular bodily need (oxygen, nutrients, etc.). A car has an enormous number of parts, which are all elements of various systems needed to make it work (fuel system, cooling system, braking system, etc.). Each of these systems is focussed on a particular need that must be met if the car is to function properly (energy, dispersing heat, stopping, etc.)

system: an orderly combination or arrangement of parts, elements, facts, or concepts into a whole.

For similar reasons, societies have systems to organize and meet society's needs. For example, every society must prepare its children to function effectively as adults. Agricultural societies need people with different skills than those of industrial societies, so they develop an educational system that is appropriate to their needs (training in agricultural skills).

In addition, every society develops ways of meeting people's spiritual needs to deal with such important questions as the purpose of life, a supreme being, the afterlife, and moral conduct. A society's organized way of providing these needs can be called its religious system. Some societies enforce a strict conformity to one religion or belief system, whereas others tolerate a wide range of beliefs.

In a similar manner, political and economic systems are methods of arranging society's resources to meet the political and economic needs of the people.

Political and Economic Systems

The fundamental political and economic problems of every country resemble those problems facing every family in the world. Members of each household must decide how their income will be used, who will perform what chores, and how such decisions will be made. In many families with young children, the parents jointly decide what will be done (or one parent makes the major decisions), and the children are told what to do. As the children mature, they are given greater responsibilities, but not always more say in family decisions. A major source of disagreement in many households is how the family's income should be used. Because there almost never seems to be enough money to satisfy everyone's needs, most families choose to budget their income. The purchase of a new car might mean fewer restaurant meals and no summer holiday, or it might require one member of the family to take a second job.

resources: in economic theory, the basic items (land, labour, and capital) used in all types of production.

The family income is comparable to a country's total production or income derived from such **resources** as farmland, factories, and minerals, and such human resources as trained scientists, factory workers, and teachers. These factors of production, as they are called, are limited. Each country must decide how best to use them. Should farmland be employed to produce food, or should it be subdivided into suburban housing? Should universities concentrate on training computer programmers or producing surgeons?

scarcity: in economic theory, the condition that results from an excess of wants over resources.

This relative **scarcity** of resources is the central economic problem of the world. It involves making choices and sacrifices. Each country must decide

- what goods will be produced;
- how they will be produced;
- who will own the means by which these goods will be produced;
- how these goods will be divided among the people.

As in the family analogy, someone or some group must make these decisions. The central political problem is determining who should govern. A study of a country's political structure must examine who exercises power, how power is maintained, who makes the important decisions, and why these decisions are made.

Although it is impossible to completely divorce politics from economics, to better understand each topic this book is divided into two major sections: political and economic. In the political section, separate chapters examine the theory and ideology underlying democratic and non-democratic governments. Individual case studies then explore how such political ideologies as democracy, communism, and fascism work in practice. In the economic section, separate chapters explain the ideology underlying private enterprise, centrally planned economies, and mixed economies, and case studies investigate how well they work in real-life situations.

All political and economic systems are artificial — they are made by human beings and can be altered by them. These are the central questions posed in this book:

1 How can each country's resources be distributed most fairly and efficiently?

2 What political system can cater to the needs and wishes of its people most effectively?

3 What are the basic values and beliefs underlying each political and economic system?

4 Why have people chosen different political and economic systems?

Your answers to these questions depend upon which goals or values you think are most important. No system is perfect, and society's needs change over time. The more we know about the goals and values of each, as well as the advantages and disadvantages of our own economic and political systems, the better equipped we will be to make appropriate decisions regarding these systems.

Why Study the Past?

To understand our current political and economic systems and ideologies, it is important to study past events. Just as travel broadens the mind, so too does journeying into the past. A trip into history allows us to step outside the beliefs and customs of our society and view the world from a different perspective, which can help us to understand and appreciate other cultures. Glimpses of earlier times also stimulate our imaginations and illustrate the range of choices available on any single issue.

It is difficult for Canadians to understand their own country, and more so other places, unless they know something of its past. Existing social customs, institutions, or current events cannot be properly understood without considering their history. Everything that exists today is rooted in the past. The latest popular songs are the result of evolving musical styles. The problems of the Middle East can be better understood by examining Arab and Jewish historical claims to Israel. Similarly, the present French–English conflict in Canada had its beginnings in the British Conquest of 1760, the Riel Rebellions, and the World War I conscription crisis.

History is to society what memory is to the individual. It helps us to answer the following questions: Who are we? How did we get here? What is our purpose? Where are we going? And how should we get there? In making decisions about the most appropriate political and economic systems in today's world, we need to know what various other peoples and their governments have tried before, and with what success. Much of this book discusses the diversity of economic and political decisions that various

The photograph on page 5 shows Hiroshima after the atomic bombing of August 6, 1945.

countries have made in structuring their societies. After exploring the ideologies underlying these decisions, and how they operate in practice, you will be better equipped to make the important decisions that will face you as a citizen of a complex and changing society.

This book critically examines the various ideologies. Each political and economic system is subjected to a thorough and probing analysis. If a democratic country is to operate effectively, its citizens must understand not only how its institutions operate but also their limitations. Throughout this book, you will be asked to analyze different ideas, evaluate opposite points of view, and judge issues based on their merits. To approach such hotly debated topics as political and economic systems in any other way would be indoctrination, not education.

Our lives are constantly complicated by the necessity of choosing between two or more options. We have to solve conflicts where a choice must be made among a variety of "good" solutions, rather than simply between good and bad. Every day, problems are becoming more complex and difficult to understand, let alone solve. The ability to make reasoned choices among different competing values and ideas is an essential skill for solving the dilemmas and problems of everyday life, and for being an effective citizen.

Underlying and Emerging Issues

Give the reasoning and evidence that might be used to support the different views or conclusions on the following issues.

1 On what basis can we say that one "value" is superior to another?

2 At what point should our desire for individual freedom give way to our need for order? Are there some things that no society should control?

3 To what degree are "ordinary people" capable of giving direction to government?

4 Is it more important for a society to provide the opportunity for individuals to become wealthy, or to meet the basic needs of all its people?

5 How important is it that members of a society share certain views in common? How important is a diversity of opinions?

6 What are the limits to tolerance? At what point, and for what reasons, should society restrict certain views, actions, or ideologies?

7 Should everyone have an equal say in determining what happens in society?

8 On what basis should people make decisions about competing ideologies, political systems, and economic systems?

9 To what degree can or should past experience be a guide to present and future decisions?

10 To what degree can the experience of people in other societies be useful in our decisions?

Focussing Knowledge

In your notes, clearly identify or define and explain the importance or significance of each of the following:

political system	*tolerance*
economic system	*diversity*
fact	*ideology*
value	*system*
factual judgement	*resources*
value judgement	*scarcity*
belief	*decision-making*
critical thinking	*history*

Reviewing and Organizing Knowledge

1 Why should ordinary citizens study the major political and economic systems of the twentieth century?

2 Why are disagreement and controversy important to politics and economics?

3 What is the difference between

a. facts and values?

b. factual judgements and value judgements?

4 How do values help to explain the existence of a great variety of political and economic systems in the world?

5 Why is some degree of tolerance important in a study of political and economic systems?

6 Why is some degree of open-mindedness necessary in a democratic society?

7 a. What is the difference between a belief and an ideology?

b. What are the main features of an ideology?

c. Why are ideologies important?

8 a. What is meant by a society's systems?

b. What needs are met by a society's education system? What needs are met by its religious system?

9 a. How do scarcity, resources, and choices result in the need for an economic system?

b. What questions must every economic system answer?

10 What are the important qualities of a political system?

11 What are the central questions in the study of political and economic systems?

12 How can studying the past help us to make decisions about present-day political and economic issues?

Applying and Extending Knowledge

1 Choose a current issue from the news. Write a paragraph in which you describe the dilemma of making a choice from among several good solutions regarding the issue.

2 Select a current issue that is of interest to you. In a paragraph, describe which aspects of the issue are caused by disagreements over facts, and which stem from disagreements over values.

3 Choose a newspaper article (an editorial or letter to the editor) that illustrates a position taken on an issue. What values underlie the position taken by the author?

4 Find a newspaper article that illustrates one of the Underlying and Emerging Issues on pages 10–11. In a paragraph, explain how the article illustrates the issue. What are the different sides to the issue? Why do people disagree? What values are involved?

5 Find newspaper articles that illustrate each of the following terms: political system, economic system, ideology, scarcity. Briefly explain how the articles illustrate these terms.

CHAPTER 2

Introducing Government

WHY DO WE NEED GOVERNMENT? The ideas of three famous philosophers, Thomas Hobbes, John Locke, and Jean Jacques Rousseau, are explored for their views of why humans established governments, the essential nature of moral rights, human nature, and the right to rebel against authority. The ideas of free will, biological drives, and basic human needs are further explored by examining the conclusions of psychologist Abraham Maslow. The chapter also discusses the terms left, right, radical, reactionary, moderate, liberal, and conservative and outlines various methods of classifying political ideologies.

Why do governments exist? On the surface, this appears to be an easy question to answer. You might be familiar with the "island analogy," in which shipwrecked travellers on a desert island are faced with the problem of survival. It quickly becomes apparent to them that some form of **government** is required to solve such problems as theft, defence, and the distribution of chores.

Why do we need governments, and upon what grounds can government be justified? There are at least five different answers to this question:

1 Anarchists believe that all governments should be abolished because they restrict individual freedom. Moral human beings do not need laws, they state, because human goodness will create order.

2 In contrast, some people believe that the possession of power is all the justification that government needs. Leaders can compel others to do their bidding by their strength and intelligence alone.

government: a system of ruling or controlling the affairs of a specific geographic area.

3 Other people justify government on the grounds that it is ordained or sanctioned by God.

4 Still others believe that government is justified because it is established by an agreement among the people to surrender their rights to the government in return for security and order. This is the idea of the "social contract."

5 Finally, some individuals approve of government as long as it works for the general good.

In the following section, three of history's most eminent philosophers present their views on the purpose and origin of government.

Thomas Hobbes' Views on Government (1588–1679)[1]

In the early days of civilization, there were no laws and no government. Because it is the nature of humans to be selfish and to care nothing about others, this was a period of complete **anarchy,** *chaos, violence, and destruction. It was a war of all against all, as everyone sought to improve his* own material condition of life. The security of an individual depended upon his own strength and intelligence. In this natural state of war, there was no time for beauty, knowledge, fine buildings, art, industry, or culture. There was continual fear and danger of violent death; an individual's life was solitary, poor, nasty, brutish, and short.*

anarchy: the absence of a system of government and law.

Individuals are born with both passions and reason. Their passions bring about this state of war, and their desire for a better life persuades them to seek peace — if only for their own selfish interests. Reason shows people that the only solution is the establishment of a society with a stable government. But since agreements without the sword are but words, it is necessary that the government be backed by force. The bonds of words are too weak to control people's ambition and greed without the fear of some coercive power. Individual security thus depends upon the formation of an all-powerful government that can curb people's selfish and aggressive nature.

The establishment of a government commences when every person agrees to relinquish his right to govern himself and gives all power to a man (or to a group of men) who will legislate peace and common defence. The people must promise complete obedience in return for order and security. The only choice is between **absolute power** *or complete lawlessness. Freedom is possible only if the people surrender their liberty to an all-powerful* **sovereign.**

absolute power: the doctrine or system of government that bestows unlimited control on a ruler.

The sovereign's power is absolute, whether the sovereign is an individual or a group of people. Self-interest will persist in this new society, but destructiveness, violence, and war will be prevented by fear of the sovereign's power. Society is established and maintained out of fear.

sovereign: a person who exercises supreme (but not necessarily unlimited) power; to be independent of any other authority; free.

---

* At this time in Western history, it was generally believed that women were incapable of participating in government. The writings of Hobbes, Locke, Rousseau, and other male writers reflect this belief.

Thomas Hobbes (1588–1679)

*Resistance to the sovereign is almost never justified; obedience must last as long as, and no longer than, the ruler is able to protect the people. Sovereigns can maintain peace only if they have complete and unlimited **authority**. If a sovereign loses power, he ceases to be sovereign and the people are thrown back upon their own devices for self-protection, until they agree to give their allegiance [obedience] to a new sovereign who can protect them.*

authority: the power or right to command, enforce obedience, or make final decisions.

F o c u s

What assumptions does Hobbes make about human beings?

How would Hobbes define freedom?

How would Hobbes justify the sovereign using force against his subjects?

John Locke's Views on Government [1632–1704][2]

Originally, all men were in the state of nature. They remained so until they voluntarily agreed to become members of a society. Everyone is obliged by the natural moral law (which can be discovered by reason) not to harm another person or take his possessions. This freedom from harm is one of man's natural rights, given to him by God. Fortunately, men are fundamentally reasonable and are inclined to respect these natural rights. Although in theory everyone should obey these laws, it does not follow that everyone will obey them in practice. Some will try to take advantage of others, and sometimes two people, both believing they are right, will come into conflict. In such situations, strength, rather than justice, will prevail. Judges, written laws, and fixed penalties are thus needed to ensure that man's natural rights are preserved.

Society is not unnatural to man. The family, for instance, is natural to man; society is also natural because it fulfills human needs. It is in man's interest to form an organised society in order to protect his property and his other natural rights.

*Political society and government must rest on the consent of the people. Because man is by nature free and independent, no one can rule him without his own consent. The purpose of government is to protect and foster the **individual's rights** and liberties. This means that it should interfere as little as possible in man's activities. People are most free when they are governed least. In voluntarily relinquishing the power to protect their own property and maintain their rights, people curtail their liberty. But men relinquish these powers in order to enjoy their liberties more securely, and nobody is obliged to obey unless he has freely agreed to do so.*

All laws must rest on the will of the majority, and they must be designed for no other end than for the good of the people. Society can be dissolved only by the

F o c u s

What assumptions does Locke make about human nature?

How does Locke justify the establishment of government?

individual's rights: the natural or lawfully delegated power of an individual to enjoy certain privileges or powers.

agreement of its members. When government does not live up to its trust, rebellion is justified — and the people shall judge when such rebellion is warranted. Government is obligated to rule by the natural and moral laws. Any government that destroys life, liberty, and prosperity has thus forfeited its right to rule.

Jean Jacques Rousseau's Views on Government [1712–1778][3]

Before the existence of society, man roamed the forests and lived like the animals. He drank from the nearby brook and made his bed at the foot of the nearest tree. This man of nature was without speech, culture, and mature thought, yet life was peaceful. There were no wars or suffering because humans generally lived apart from each other and were reluctant to inflict pain upon others. Natural man was neither moral nor vicious; he was not unhappy, but neither was he happy. Selfishness, culture, war, affection, vice, and love can exist only in sociable beings who live together in groups.

Natural man differed from the animals in his ability to improve himself. At some point, men united in a society in order to improve themselves — only within society do men become human, developing their mental and moral abilities, their freedom, and their individuality. Justice is substituted for instinct. Instead of stupid and unimaginative animals, men become intelligent, moral beings.

*The problem is to establish a society that will protect everyone, and in which every man will remain as free as he was before. The solution is for all men to conclude a **social contract** and agree to place themselves under the direction of the general will. The general will is always right because it functions in the best interests of the entire group — it stands for the universal good. It follows, therefore, that any government whose object is the good of its people must conform to this general will. A government deserves to be obeyed only if its actions follow the general will.*

The general will is simply the common good; it is not necessarily the majority opinion. The will of just one person, for instance, might be the general will if its object was the common good. Those who do not agree with the general will must be forced to obey — they must be forced to be free. The general will is, in reality, the will of everyone (although some might not realize it at the time), and to follow one's own will is to act freely. Therefore, to be forced to conform to one's own will is to be forced to be free. Man serves his own good by serving the common good.

social contract: the theory that a government cannot wield its authority by force alone but must have the written consent, such as a constitution, of the governed.

Focus

What assumptions does Rousseau make about human nature?

How does Rousseau justify the establishment of government?

How would Rousseau define freedom?

Government and Human Needs

Hobbes, Locke, and Rousseau each reasoned that humanity had once lived in a **natural state** without government. They also believed that people were capable of creating a government that served their interests better than the natural state did, and as we have seen, some people argue that government is justified only if it meets the people's needs. Psychologist Abraham Maslow (1908–70) classified human needs into seven groups and arranged them from basic biological needs at birth to complex psychological needs

natural state: a condition under which people are not organized under a social contract.

that emerge only after the basic needs have been satisfied. At each developmental level, needs must be at least partly fulfilled before the requirements at the next level become important. As Figure 2.1 illustrates, physical needs are at the base of this pyramid. Humans need food, shelter, water, and sleep for survival. Unless these needs are satisfied, we do not have the time or the motivation to proceed to the next stage.

Once these physical needs are satisfied, the next concern is safety — the need to feel secure and safe from harm. Safety needs dominate during times of crisis, war, and natural disaster.

Figure 2.1: Maslow's Hierarchy of Human Needs

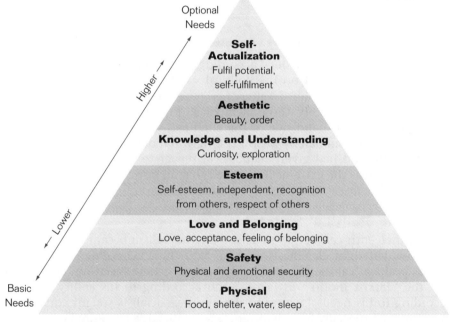

Source: *Motivation and Personality*, 3rd Edition by Abraham H. Maslow. Copyright © 1954, 1987 by Harper & Row Publishers, Inc. Copyright © 1970 by Abraham H. Maslow. Reprinted by permission of Addison-Wesley Educational Publishers Inc.

The third category consists of the need for love and belonging. Maslow believed that humans are social beings, so we need to feel accepted, to have friends, and to love and be loved. These needs can be fulfilled through marriage, by having children, and by membership in clubs and other groups.

Esteem needs are next in the hierarchy. The drive for success and the need to have self-respect and the respect of others are in this category. People seek awards, compliments, recognition, and appreciation for their abilities and actions.

Higher-level needs include people's desire for knowledge and understanding. People need to learn, experiment, inquire, and philosophize. Humans also have aesthetic needs. They need to surround themselves with what they regard as beautiful objects.

Only a few people reach the highest category of self-actualization. Self-actualized individuals develop themselves to their highest potential. They are open, creative, and spontaneous, and are capable of deep reflection.

Although not everyone accepts Maslow's theory about human needs, which he believed to be relevant to individuals in all cultures, it is widely used as a way of explaining people's actions, be it voting behaviour, employee job satisfaction, or aggressive conduct.

The theories of Hobbes, Locke, Rousseau, and Maslow illustrate the importance of the connection between human needs and government. Our assumptions or conclusions about the nature of human beings and how best to meet their needs have enormous implications for our views about what government can and should do.

The Political Spectrum

left: political groups representing the radical or liberal wing of socio-political reform parties.

right: political groups representing the conservative or reactionary wing of socio-political parties.

Governments are often classified according to whether their underlying ideologies are **left** or **right** on the political spectrum. These words were first used as political labels shortly after the French Revolution in 1789. In the French National Assembly, those members who wanted democratic government sat on the left-hand side of the chamber, while those members who favoured a strong monarchy sat on the right-hand side. The extreme right believed that God had given all political power to the monarch through heredity, whereas the extreme left argued that all power came from the people. The "moderates" in the centre sought a compromise.

Economic–Political Spectrum

In the nineteenth century, as socialism and liberalism became more prominent, this left–right classification came to include economic ideologies as well as political values. Figure 2.2 illustrates this new spectrum. On the far left, the Marxist motto was "From each according to his ability, to each according to his needs." Closer to the middle, socialists sought equality of opportunity, especially for the lower classes. Liberals also desired equality of opportunity, but emphasized middle-class rights. On the right of centre, conservatives staunchly defended private property and supported private charity. On the extreme right, fascists in the twentieth century believed that abilities were inherited, and equality was thus impossible — as well as undesirable.

Figure 2.2: An Economic–Political Spectrum

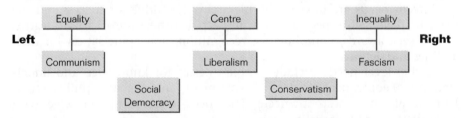

Ideologies may also be classified according to how much control the government has over the economy and society in general. As Figure 2.3 shows, in theory, communists and fascists favour total government control, whereas anarchists believe that society can best exist without government. Liberals desire government regulation in order to promote greater economic and social equality. Socialists tend to believe in government control of vital industries and agencies, whereas conservatives want to limit government control to only essential activities.

Figure 2.3: Government Control Over Society and the Economy

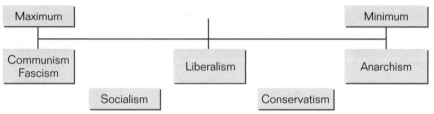

Although anarchists are generally seen as "left wing," on this economic spectrum they are on the "right." Similarly, fascists are usually characterized as "right wing," but it depends on what the spectrum is measuring.

The conventional left–right spectrum does not apply to all issues, and it varies according to what is being measured. Left and right are only convenient labels. They should not be substitutes for a detailed understanding of each group's point of view. In many cases, the extremes of the spectrum end up working together — although for different reasons and objectives. Left- and right-wing groups might become temporary allies, for example, to protest government censorship laws. The left wing might argue in favour of freedom of speech; the right wing might argue its case from the perspective that the government has no right to interfere with private business.

Change and the Political Spectrum

She's a radical feminist.
Isn't there a more moderate solution?
That's too liberal for me.
If he was any more reactionary, he'd be Attila the Hun.
That's a rather conservative comment.

These terms — **radical, moderate, liberal, conservative,** and **reactionary** — are among the most commonly used words in politics.* Unfortunately, they are also among the most misunderstood and misused terms in political science. In everyday language, these terms usually have a

___
* There is a difference between a small "l" liberal (or a small "c" conservative) and a large "L" Liberal (or large "C" Conservative). The small "l" or "c" refers to an ideology, and the large "L" or "C" refers to a political party.

radical: a political extremist.

moderate: a political middle-of-the-roader, who believes in balance or compromise.

liberal: a person who favours reform, especially in government, economics, and religion, and who prefers democratic forms of government in a constitutional state.

conservative: a person who favours the retention of traditional values, especially in government, economics, religion, and morals.

reactionary: a person who favours a return to narrow, traditional values of the past, especially in government, economics, religion, and morals.

value attached to them (which serves to further complicate debate), but in political analysis they are value-free. Figure 2.4 indicates their location on the left—right political spectrum.

Figure 2.4: The Political Spectrum

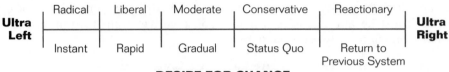

This classification examines people's attitudes toward change in the political system. Almost every group desires some degree of change. Those people who wish to adopt new political institutions or values can be placed on the left of the status quo (the existing state of affairs), and those who want to return to past ways are to the right of the status quo. The extent of the desired change is also important in this spectrum. The further people find themselves from the status quo, the more dissatisfied they are with the existing situation and the more drastic their proposed changes. Such people are more likely to demand immediate, revolutionary "improvements."

The word "radical" comes from the Latin word *radix,* or root, indicating a desire for profound change. Radicals of both the left and the right are extremely unhappy with the status quo and favour instant, fundamental change in society. Radicals on the extreme left end of the political spectrum believe that society is so corrupt that it can be cured only through violence. Compromise is impossible! Radicals a little further to the right are also frustrated with the system, but prefer relatively peaceful methods of enacting change where possible. Political scientist Leon Baradat suggests that such famous political activists as Mahatma Gandhi and Martin Luther King, Jr. can be found at the far right of the radical group. They proposed immediate and profound changes in India and the United States, but opposed violence.

Liberals are less dissatisfied with the existing political system, generally abide by the law, and seek change only by legal methods. They do, however, advocate rapid and far-reaching changes if the status quo is of the extremist type. The word "liberal" comes from the Latin word *liber,* meaning free. Liberals are optimistic about people's ability to solve their own problems. They believe in the power of reason. Since nothing is sacred, theoretically everything can be changed for the better. As a result, the ideals and objectives of liberalism have changed over the last three centuries. In the seventeenth and eighteenth centuries, such original liberals as John Locke, Adam Smith, and Thomas Jefferson argued for personal freedom and fewer government restrictions, and in favour of private property. Today, such ideas are associated with conservatism. Liberals viewed people as being essentially good and were optimistic about humanity's ability to improve the world. Contemporary liberals still maintain these ideals, but prefer to use the government to improve society, even if this means placing restrictions on people, such as on how much private property one person can own.

Moderates are generally satisfied with the status quo. They believe that some changes are needed, but these are only minor adjustments that should be gradually adopted. Conservatives also support the status quo, although for different reasons. Conservatives are cautious about change — they favour upholding tradition. As a result, they believe that change ought to be both gradual and minimal. Conservatives tend to be less optimistic than liberals about people's ability to solve their own problems. Thus conservatives tend to prefer authoritarian rule to democracy. In the eighteenth century, Edmund Burke provided a philosophical base for conservatism. In a well-governed society, Burke stated, everyone knew his or her place. The wealthy, intelligent, and "well-born" should govern in the best interests of everyone, while the people of lower rank should recognize their betters and submit to their rules.

Modern conservatives believe that government should intervene as little as possible in human affairs. Compulsory seat-belt legislation is the type of regulation conservatives oppose as being an invasion of individual freedom. Conservatives believe strongly in the rights of private property, prefer political order, and tend to be elitist and authoritarian.

Only reactionaries wish to return to an earlier time. They are just as frustrated by the status quo as are the radicals, but instead of proposing a brand new world, they seek to replace the present system with old institutions and values. As with radicals, reactionaries range from those who believe in the necessity of violence to the more peaceable proponents of traditional government.

Few people retain the same viewpoint on the political spectrum on every issue. Most people are happy with at least some aspects of society and do not want to change them (conservative), but can think of several areas that need adjustment (liberal). In general, however, it is possible to locate individuals in one of these five positions on the spectrum.

Examining Your Political Ideology

Testing Conservative Views

To what extent are you an ideological conservative? Take the following test and note whether you agree or disagree with each statement. Remember, these questions examine *your* political beliefs, so there are no right or wrong answers.

1 Those of us who are better off have a responsibility to provide assistance for the less fortunate.

2 We should address inequalities in political and economic power through affirmative action programs.

3 It is important to condemn divorce, illegitimate childbirth and homosexuality in order to protect the family unit.

4 We need to crack down on crime if we are to solve social problems.

5 One person's actions, provided they affect only that individual, are of no concern to anyone else.

6 Social norms are relative, dependent on time and place; what was unacceptable 200 years ago is of no relevance to what is appropriate today.

7 Over time, humans will be able to eliminate poverty, intolerance, war ... the problems we have suffered throughout history are progressively being eradicated.

8 The problem with today's society is that there is a lack of responsibility; individual needs are put before the needs of the family, the community and the nation.

9 The entrance of women into the work force has disrupted the natural balance of society, and has caused more harm than good.

10 Progress is inevitable, and we should do everything we can to hurry it along.

Score one point for each "agree" on questions 1, 3, 4, 8 and 9, and one point for every "disagree" on questions 2, 5, 6, 7 and 10. Low scores reflect little support for conservatism; high scores indicate strong conservative leanings.

The left believes more in rational thought and human equality, whereas the right believes in natural inequalities among people and the need for order. On the far left, Karl Marx's communist theories pictured a future society in which ordinary people held all political power and shared equally in material goods. On the far right, Fascist leader Benito Mussolini appealed to people's emotions and declared, "Feel, don't think!" The masses were expected to obey their leader without question.

Combining the Economic and Political Spectrums

It is important to remember that the meaning of the terms left and right depend on which spectrum is being used. In a communist system, a person who favoured rapid, fundamental change to the system would be a left-wing communist, whereas someone who wished to keep the status quo would be a right-wing communist. As a society changes, so do its values and its vocabulary. Such terms as neo-liberal and neo-conservative are in common usage. *Neo* means new. Rather than be trapped by labels, to better understand another person's views and ideology it is preferable to discover what economic and political approaches this individual favours.

In the real world, it is impossible to separate completely economic and political systems and ideologies. Communism, for example, includes both political and economic beliefs. Figure 2.5 employs quadrants to better explain the connection between economic and political systems. Do not be alarmed if you do not understand some of the words or names in this chart. The important point to grasp is the theory, not the details. Future chapters will examine in depth such terms as fascism, communism, and capitalism, as well as look at the ideas of some politicians, philosophers, and economists. You might want to return to this chart at a later time.

The Importance of Government

Government is an integral part of every society. It makes laws (legislative powers), interprets them (judicial powers), and carries them out (administrative or executive powers). Its basic function is to help a community achieve its collective goals. Government affects almost every aspect of our lives — from taxes and transportation, to schools and traffic lights. It can prevent us from achieving our most cherished goals, and it can require us to sacrifice our lives in times of war. The political system might therefore be viewed as the master control system of society. The economy is affected by government laws that restrict unfair employment practices, regulate labour relations, and establish tariffs, as only a few examples. Family activities are limited by school regulations, medical requirements, and marriage laws. The rules of a society can range from a few simple traditions that are passed down orally from one generation to another, to a complex, bureaucratic state.

Figure 2.5: The Connection Between Economic and Political Systems

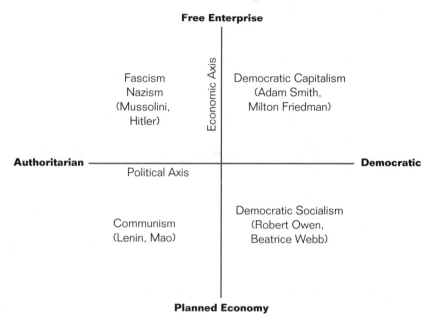

Sometimes it is difficult to distinguish between a society's economic system and its political system. In fact, in the past (and still in some countries), students studied "political economy." In general, the economic system is society's method of producing and distributing goods and services. The political system makes, carries out, and interprets society's laws and regulations.

The study of politics, which is usually called *political science*, was born when people began to speculate about the rules of society. Should these rules be obeyed? Why do different countries have dissimilar governments? Is there one set of rules that every society should adopt? This inquiry has been going on for thousands of years.

Each generation is faced with deciding whether to accept the rules made or accepted by the previous generation, or whether to modify or replace them with others. The ordinary citizen, faced with the decision of voting for a political party, may be trying to answer the question that Greek philosophers tried to answer over 2000 years ago: what is the best form of government? Of course, most citizens are more likely to attempt merely to decide which party will help them the most. Even so, the voter is really asking a similar question: which candidate or political party will pass laws that will best reflect my views?

Government and Power

Monarchy, democracy, dictatorship, fascism, theocracy, constitutional monarchy, communism, aristocracy, oligarchy — the number of different types of governments seems endless. In the fourth century B.C., the Greek philosopher Aristotle attempted to simplify the choice by classifying governments according to their distribution of political power. He arranged them in terms of governments in which only one person ruled; countries where more than one, but not many, ruled; and states where the majority of the people governed. Although the distribution of power is only one method of categorizing governments, power is an essential ingredient in almost every type of organization. In particular, it is the way in which governments gain and use their power that distinguishes them. Absolute monarchs do not usually have to listen to the wishes of their subjects. When King Louis XIV of France said, "I am the State," what he meant was, "I am the Government, and what I say goes." In a democracy, the people themselves, through their elected representatives, decide how the government should use its power.

The principle of one-person rule is rooted in a philosophy or ideology that supports and justifies the use of power. A street gang in Calgary or Vancouver, for example, may be controlled by one person. A successful assumption of power is thought to show that the leader is superior to other people. Organized crime is only one example of the success of this philosophy.

The leadership principle, however, is too limited to attract or hold many followers for a long period of time. Ideas are needed to recruit supporters and encourage loyalty. Hitler did this by adopting the belief that the German people were the master race. In North America, the Ku Klux Klan's ideology states that its members are appointed by God to protect white Protestant society from Catholics, blacks, and Jews. Historically, most governments based their power upon religious arguments. This was true of the Egyptian pharaohs, the Russian tsars, and the Chinese emperors. Communist states justify their actions by referring to the doctrine of class warfare against capitalists and to the belief that under communism all property will be administered for the benefit of the working class. Likewise, the belief in "majority rule" is employed by democratic governments to justify their use of power.

ARISTOTLE

Classifying Governments

The Greek philosopher Aristotle (394–322 B.C.) lived in Athens, which was the most democratic of the 158 Greek city-states he examined. The following table illustrates Aristotle's final classifications of political systems.

Number of rulers	Rule for the general good	Rule for own good
One	Monarchy	Tyranny
Few	Aristocracy	Oligarchy
Many	Polity (constitutional democracy)	Democracy

Aristotle's classification system has become part of Western thought, and he is considered the founder of comparative politics. The following selection is from his masterpiece of political philosophy, *Politics:*

Where ought the sovereign power of the state to reside? With the people? With the propertied classes? With the good? With one man, the best of all the good? With one man, the tyrant? There are objections to all these. Thus suppose we say the people are the supreme authority, then if they use their numerical superiority to make a distribution of the property of the rich, is not that unjust? It has been done by a valid decision of the sovereign power, yet what can we call it save the very height of injustice? Again, if the majority, having laid their hands on everything, distribute the possessions of the few, they are obviously destroying the state. But that cannot be goodness which destroys its possessor and justice cannot be destructive of the state.

So it is clear that this process, though it may be the law, cannot be just. ... If it is just for the few and wealthy to rule, and if they too rob and plunder and help themselves to the goods of the many, is that just? If it is, then it is just in the former case also. The answer clearly is that all these three are bad and unjust. The fourth alternative, that the good should rule and have the supreme authority, is also not free from objection; it means that all the rest must be without official standing, debarred from holding office under the constitution. The fifth alternative, that one man, the best, should rule, is no better; by making the number of rulers fewer we leave still larger numbers without official standing. ...

At the moment it would seem that the most defensible, perhaps even the truest, answer to the question would be to say that the majority ought to be sovereign, rather than the best, where the best are few. For it is possible that the many, no one of whom taken singly is a good man, may yet taken all together be better than the few, not

Focus

What criteria does Aristotle use to classify governments?

What criticism do you think Aristotle might have had of democracy?

individually but collectively, in the same way that a feast to which all contribute is better than one given at one man's expense. For where there are many people, each has some share of goodness and intelligence, and when these are brought together, they become as it were one multiple man with many pairs of feet and hands and many minds. So too in regard to character and powers of perception. That is why the general public is a better judge of works of music and poetry; some judge some parts, some others, but their joint pronouncement is a verdict upon the whole.[4]

Conclusion

Which is the "best" system of government? How is it possible to answer such a value-laden question? To do so, we must examine the ideology and the strengths and weaknesses of the various available choices. Some important questions to ask are

- How is power achieved?

- Who controls power?

- How is power maintained and passed on from generation to generation?

- Upon what basis are decisions made? What are the government's goals and ideals?

- What role does the individual citizen play in the political system?

- To what extent are people free to express their opinions?

The next chapter examines the theory and ideology of democracy. It is followed by six case studies that explore how the ideals of democracy are practised in such countries as Canada, the United States, and Sweden. The next section of this book examines the theory and ideology of non-democratic governments, followed by real-life examples from Germany, Russia, Italy, Cuba, and China. At the conclusion of the political section of the book, you will be asked to evaluate these political systems and to come to your own conclusions about political systems.

SIMONE DE BEAUVOIR, 1908–1986

Philosopher, novelist, intellectual, feminist, political activist — Simone de Beauvoir's life reflected the range of her interests and her intense commitment to both ideas and action. She played a central role in founding the philosophical approach of existentialism, but probably is more famous as an international symbol and inspirational role model for women in their struggle for equality and identity.

Early in life, de Beauvoir rejected the upper-middle-class, conservative religious and social values of her family and society. At age 15, she decided to become an author, stating prophetically, "By writing a work based on my own experience, I would recreate myself and justify my existence. At the same time I would be serving humanity."[5] She also asserted her lifelong need to exercise her freedom of choice and to make her own way in the world; at age 19 she wrote, "I don't want my life to obey any other will but my own."[6]

While in university in Paris, de Beauvoir met the writer Jean-Paul Sartre, whom she said "corresponded exactly to the dream companion I had longed for since I was fifteen." She refused his offer of marriage, and they established an unconventional "union of independent togetherness" that lasted for 51 years, until Sartre's death in 1980.

De Beauvoir's novels, writings, and political actions all were shaped by her existentialist philosophy, an affirmative view that emphasized individual freedom, choice, commitment, and action: "The meaning of life is not some pre-determined, God-given or universal quality, but a responsibility which each human being has to take upon him- or herself."[7]

The publication of her book *The Second Sex* in 1949, described as her "greatest and most enduring achievement," created an uproar.

First, that man, conceiving of himself as the essential being, the subject, has made woman into the unessential being, the object, the Other; second, that there is no such thing as feminine nature and that all notions of femininity are artificial.[8]

De Beauvoir's later writings dealt with a wide range of other social issues. Her 1970 study of old age was described as "a scathing exposé and indictment of Western civilization's cruel neglect of the elderly." She concluded that the shameful treatment stemmed from capitalist society's judging the elderly as useless because of their limited productive capacity.

She became more involved in political action in her later life, pressing for measures to aid battered wives, working women, single parents, and people in developing countries. Her activism and her writing had two consistent purposes: to "raise the consciousness" of others, and to provoke social change. Always a controversial figure, de Beauvoir played a central role in forcing modern Western political and economic systems to confront issues related to women, and "inspired a generation of women to change the course of their lives to their own advantage."

---

1 How do Simone de Beauvoir's life and ideas provide a challenge to traditional views of political and economic systems?

2 To what extent are her criticisms relevant to Canada's society today?

Underlying and Emerging Issues

Give the reasoning and evidence that might be used to support different views or conclusions on the following issues.

1 To what degree are people "naturally" good, bad, selfish, or kind?

2 Do people need a government to curb selfish and aggressive tendencies?

3 What should be the limits to the powers of government? How much control should government have over people's daily lives?

4 Are people born with natural rights? If so, what are they?

5 To what degree are people born equal? To what degree should they receive equal treatment?

6 To what degree should individuals be free to oppose the will of the majority?

7 Is there a point at which people are justified in using force to overthrow a government?

8 To what degree are particular human needs best met through actions by individuals or by government?

9 How important is individual freedom in comparison to equality and security?

Focussing Knowledge

In your notes, clearly identify or define and explain the importance or significance of each of the following:

government	left
anarchy	right
absolute power	centre
sovereign	spectrum
authority	radical
individual rights	moderate
social contract	liberal
general will	reactionary
natural state	conservative
hierarchy of needs	neo
political science	

Reviewing and Organizing Knowledge

1 Compare the ideas of Hobbes, Locke, and Rousseau in a chart using the following headings:

a. human nature

b. purpose and power of government

c. natural or individual rights

d. use of force

e. type of political system likely to be associated with him

2 a. According to Abraham Maslow, what is the rank order of the seven groups of human needs?

b. What is the importance of Maslow's view of "levels" of needs?

c. What are the implications of Maslow's work for questions about government?

3 a. What was the political meaning of left, right, and centre at the time of the French Revolution?

b. What are the different bases for classification in Figures 2.2 and 2.4? What is meant by "left" and "right" in each case?

c. How does Figure 2.4 differ from the previous spectrums? What do "left" and "right" mean in this case?

d. Referring to Figure 2.4, give the reaction of each of the following to the prospect of change: radical, liberal, moderate, conservative, reactionary.

4 a. What are the basic powers of government in a political system?

b. How do we distinguish between a society's political system and its economic system?

5 How can a person arrive at a conclusion to the value-laden question, "Which is the 'best' system of government?"

Applying and Extending Knowledge

1 Explain how Hobbes, Locke, and Rousseau might respond to one or more of the following:

   a. the French Revolution (1789);

   b. the Russian Revolution (1917);

   c. the internment of Japanese Canadians during World War II;

   d. the Canadian government's use of the War Measures Act during the FLQ Crisis of 1970;

   e. the Tiananmen Square Massacre in China in 1989;

   f. laws restricting the use of heroin and cocaine.

2 Write a dialogue in which you describe an imaginary discussion among Hobbes, Locke, and Rousseau

   a. on the topic "the best form of government"; or

   b. on their possible reactions to a current issue.

3 Research the life of either Hobbes, Locke, Rousseau, Aristotle, or Maslow. Identify the extent to which that person's views were influenced by particular events in his life and times.

4 Draw up a complete list of all of your activities yesterday. Identify the various ways in which government had an impact on your situation or actions.

5 Find newspaper articles that illustrate the meaning of at least three of the following terms: left-wing, right-wing, radical, liberal, moderate, conservative, reactionary. In a paragraph for each, explain how the articles illustrate these terms.

6 Choose a newspaper editorial or letter to the editor that takes a clear position on an issue. Select a term from question 5 to describe the article's position, and explain why you chose that term.

7 Select a newspaper article that illustrates Canada's political system, and one that illustrates its economic system. Explain how the articles illustrate these terms.

8 Find a newspaper article that illustrates one of the Underlying and Emerging Issues on page 28. In a paragraph, explain how the article illustrates one or more sides of the issue.

CHAPTER *3*

The Ideals of

Democracy

D EMOCRACY! Over the centuries people have struggled to implement it, wars have been fought in its name, and many have died for it. This chapter examines the growth of the idea of democracy, evaluates the extent of democracy in the world today, and explores the changing definitions of democracy over time and from one country to another. Also discussed are the conditions necessary for democracy to operate effectively, the importance of natural or fundamental human rights, the need for minority guarantees, and the advantages and disadvantages of democracy.

Since the defeat of Nazi Germany and Fascist Italy in World War II, a host of countries have described themselves as democratic. "Probably for the first time in history," a United Nations survey stated in 1951, "democracy is claimed as the proper ideal description of all systems of political and social organization." Even military regimes frequently seek to justify their assumption of power by promising to restore democracy when the time is right.

It wasn't always this way. Except for a brief democratic experiment in Athens, Greece, in the fifth century B.C., the idea remained unpopular until the nineteenth century. Those with wealth and culture usually rejected democracy because they thought it would destroy their power. Aristotle, for example, argued that since democracy was the rule of the many, and because in all societies the many are the poor, democracy was the rule of the poor. Another ancient Greek philosopher, Plato, added that since the poor were uneducated, they were incapable of making good laws and would discriminate against the intelligent and wealthy people who were in the minority. Other critics argued that the

Learning Outcomes

After reading this chapter, you should be able to:

- understand the reasons for the growth of democracy in the twentieth century

- devise your own definition of democracy

- describe the conditions necessary for democracy to flourish

- explain the strengths and weaknesses of a referendum, a recall, and a plebiscite

- understand the importance of human rights

- summarize the advantages and disadvantages of democracy

- discuss the role of elected representatives in relation to their constituents poor were incapable of understanding what was in their own best interests, and that government should be left to the educated and wealthy citizens who could govern in the real interest of the entire community.

Nearly every educated person from the earliest historical times down to the second half of the eighteenth century accepted these basic criticisms of democracy. Then, with the flourishing of capitalism in the eighteenth and nineteenth centuries, democracy gradually became an acceptable system of government. According to Freedom House, a non-profit organization devoted to promoting global democracy, in 1995 there were 117 democracies (although 40 of them restricted their citizens' rights to a considerable extent), containing 54 percent of the world's population.

Even non-democratic governments call themselves democracies, and communist countries tend to employ terms such as "people's democracies" and "democratic centralism." President Sukarno of Indonesia called his dictatorship a "democracy with leadership," Nasser's Egypt was a "democratic dictatorship," and Castro's Cuba is a "true democracy."

A Definition of Democracy

The fact that such politically different countries as Canada, Mexico, Cuba, Germany, the United States, and China all claim to be democracies indicates that "democracy" is interpreted in many different ways. According to communist theory, democracy is rule by and for the working class. Under communist control the country's resources are shared equally, and private property — the source of class exploitation — is abolished. In communist terms, democracy means material or economic equality, not necessarily political liberty. If the state must restrict individual freedom in order to achieve an equal distribution of the country's wealth, then it will do so. Communists use the term **formal democracy** for such democratic ideas as freedom of speech, freedom of the press, freedom of association, and equality before the law. Western liberal democracies, on the other hand, place a higher value on civil liberties.

formal democracy: the term applied by communists to the ideas of freedom of speech, freedom of the press, freedom of association, and equality before the law.

Disagreements about the meaning of democracy reflect fundamental differences in values and ideologies. *Democracy* is a very broad concept. Viewed as a political system, it is a method of conducting government and making laws. As a decision-making process, it is a way of reaching policy decisions in which all adult citizens are entitled to participate. As a social system, it exists to promote and protect individual freedom and equality. But democracy is much more than this — it is a vision of a way of life in which all people are free to develop their potential as human beings.

Supporters of democracy believe that people are by nature rational, moral, and just. Given a chance, they can live in peace, discuss issues rationally, make wise decisions, and improve the world.

The word "democracy" is a combination of the Greek words *demos* (the people) and *kratein* (to rule), meaning rule by the people. In simple terms, democracy is a political system that provides for free and open competition for power among various individuals and groups, as well as a significant degree of accountability to the people by those who hold the formal positions of power.

It is important to remember that democracy is not an "either/or" question. A country's political system is better viewed as being on a continuum, or spectrum (see Chapter 2), from highly democratic to highly undemocratic. Rather than trying to determine whether a country is either democratic or undemocratic, it is more appropriate to ask *how* democratic is its government.

Fundamental Rights

All democratic countries believe that certain human rights are essential. Some rights have been considered so important that they are called **natural rights** (or fundamental rights), meaning that they are beyond argument.

However, what people in one country believe are fundamental rights are not necessarily the beliefs of people in another country. Natural rights not only have different meanings to different people, but they have also changed with the times. In the eighteenth century, rights were discussed almost exclusively in political terms. A number of social or economic rights, which today are believed to be natural or normal, were not even thought of a century and a half ago. The United Nations' Universal Declaration of Human Rights, for example, acknowledges the right of an individual to work for a living, to earn equal pay for equal work, to join a trade union, to obtain education, and to be cared for by the state in times of sickness.

Most Western countries now assume that political rights alone cannot achieve individual equality and liberty. The concept of fundamental rights is therefore subjective. Rights are "self-evident" only in their own time and place, and even then they are often interpreted in widely different ways.

natural rights: a political theory, according to which all people are born with certain inalienable privileges — rights that cannot be taken away.

Are You Satisfied With Democracy?

In 1995, The International Gallup Poll asked citizens in 17 countries whether they were satisfied with the way democracy was working in their country. The results were as follows:

Table 3.1: Satisfaction With the Way Democracy Works

Country	% Satisfied	% Dissatisfied	% Net satisfaction*
Canada	62	24	38
United States	64	27	37
Iceland	54	23	31
Germany	55	27	28
Costa Rica	52	25	27
Thailand	54	27	27
Chile	43	31	12
France	43	32	11
Taiwan	25	18	7
Japan	35	32	3
Dominican Republic	40	38	2
Spain	31	30	1
United Kingdom	40	43	–3
India	32	43	–11
Venezuela	28	59	–31
Hungary	17	50	–33
Mexico	17	67	–50

*Net Satisfaction = % Satisfied minus % Dissatisfied

Source: The International Gallup Poll, Vol. 55, No. 51, Gallup Canada Inc.

Focus

Is there any connection between democracy and geographical location?

Direct and Representative Democracy

polis: in ancient Greece, a city and its surrounding countryside.

Democracy arose many centuries ago in the *polis* of Athens, Greece. A **polis** consisted of a small city and its immediate surrounding countryside. Because of its size, every citizen had the opportunity to participate in government decisions. At that time, only men who had been born in the polis were considered citizens; women and slaves were excluded. In an average year, approximately 15 to 20 percent of the populace served in some governmental capacity. These positions were usually filled by drawing lots. The most important government jobs were rotated every year or two. Once a week (or when necessary), the citizens gathered in the marketplace to decide upon matters of policy. All citizens had the opportunity to speak, and then a decision was reached by majority vote.

direct democracy: a state in which all political decisions are made directly by qualified voters.

This method of government is called **direct democracy,** because the people themselves make the laws. Today, although several New England towns in the United States and some Swiss cantons practise it, no country has adopted direct democracy.

Although democracy is often defined as government by the people, no country has ever allowed all of its inhabitants to participate in decision-making. At different times, age, gender, literacy, wealth, colour, ethnicity, and religion have been used to prevent certain people from voting or holding public office. Today, some of these restrictions, such as not allowing children or people declared legally insane to vote, seem logical. Only recently in Canada have prisoners in jails been allowed to vote in federal elections. However, at one time or another, society considered each of the preceding limitations self-evident. In the nineteenth century, for instance, every country took it for granted that women should not be allowed to vote. In Canada, women did not have full **suffrage** (the right to vote) until 1918; British women gained the vote in 1929, French women in 1945, and Swiss women not until 1971. Likewise, for a long time the United States limited the political rights of African Americans. In Canada, Japanese Canadians, First Nations peoples, and poor people were denied the vote at various times. Yet all of these countries have long been recognized as democracies.

suffrage: the right to vote in an election.

As times changed, so did the definition of democracy. Beliefs that were inconceivable in one period of history were taken for granted at a later time. Not so long ago, Canadians under 21 years of age were not allowed to vote. The age limit is now 18. What might it be 30 years in the future? Such changes are evident almost everywhere. In the nineteenth century, most people defined democracy solely in terms of political and legal equality. Today, governments place more importance on reducing economic and social inequalities.

representative democracy: a state in which the legislative powers are delegated by qualified voters to their representatives in a legislative body, such as a parliament, senate, or congress.

Canada, like most other Western countries, is a **representative democracy.** This means that the citizens elect people to represent their interests. These elected representatives then meet and pass laws on behalf of the whole country. Figure 3.1 illustrates the differences between direct and representative democracy.

Figure 3.1

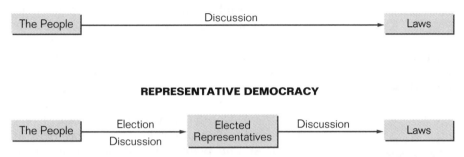

DIRECT DEMOCRACY

| The People | —— Discussion ——→ | Laws |

REPRESENTATIVE DEMOCRACY

| The People | Election / Discussion →| Elected Representatives | Discussion →| Laws |

··· **The Elected Representative**

In a representative system of democracy, the people are one step removed from government decisions. Western representative democracies believe that a political system is democratic if the people have effective control over their representatives. During the last two centuries, liberal reformers in such countries as Canada, Great Britain, France, Germany, Sweden, Switzerland, Italy, and the United States have succeeded in gaining a reasonable degree of control over their governments. Just what constitutes a "reasonable degree of control," however, has been a matter of debate.

One such discussion centres around the role of the elected representative. Should representatives make decisions based on their own judgements or according to the wishes of their constituents? Supporters of the first viewpoint argue that most of the people either know very little about the issues or are not interested in them. Constituents elected the representatives because they trusted their judgement. If politicians make unpopular decisions, citizens can vote them out of office at the next election. This ensures that the representatives are accountable to the public. The second viewpoint asserts that the representatives are the people's agents. The legislators, according to this argument, are obligated to discover their constituents' views and to act upon them.

To provide citizens with more control over their elected representatives, some political thinkers have advocated such democratic procedures as a recall, a referendum, and a plebiscite. In general, a **recall** means that if a certain percentage of citizens in a constituency disapprove of how their elected representative voted in parliament, they can "recall" that person and hold a by-election to appoint a new representative. This idea was particularly popular in Western Canada in the 1920s and 1930s and is advocated by the Reform Party today.

recall: the ability of citizens to replace one elected representative with another through a by-election.

The **referendum** is quite popular in Switzerland and the United States. Canadian governments have occasionally asked the people for their opinions on important questions before reaching a final decision through the use of a **plebiscite.** In 1898, Wilfrid Laurier's Liberal government conducted a plebiscite to discover whether the public wanted to prohibit the sale of alcohol. During World War II, the Mackenzie King government asked the people if they would release the government from its election promise that there would be no conscription. Every province but New Brunswick has held at least one plebiscite. The last plebiscite in Alberta was conducted in 1971, when the province voted on whether or not to adopt Daylight Savings Time.

The difference between a referendum and a plebiscite is that the results of a referendum are binding on the government, whereas a plebiscite is merely an attempt to discover what the public is thinking. In the 1898 plebiscite on prohibition, for example, although a majority voted in favour of prohibition, Laurier decided not to implement it. Although the two Quebec votes on whether to separate from the rest of Canada (1980, 1995) were called referendums, they were really plebiscites.

A major advantage of referendums and plebiscites is that they allow more direct decision-making by citizens. However, they can also require citizens to have a solid background in and knowledge of the issue. Although a topic such as whether to allow Sunday shopping is a relatively simple one, an issue such as free trade is extremely complicated and requires a much broader base of knowledge. Another disadvantage of referendums and plebiscites is that they may allow the government to avoid taking a stand on controversial issues.

In an attempt to reduce complex problems to a yes/no question, referendums must simplify the issues. In 1992, for example, the Charlottetown Accord referendum on Canada's Constitution involved extremely complex matters that the people were asked to settle by a single yes or no vote.

Parliamentary Recall—Your Call

In February 1994, Gallup Canada asked a random sample of Canadians, "Would you favour or oppose Parliamentary recall, where voters could recall their Member of Parliament and hold a by-election if a certain percentage of the riding's voters, say 50%, signed a petition?" The results were as follows:

Table 3.2: Do You Favour Parliamentary Recall?

Region	Yes	No	No opinion
Atlantic	60	23	18
Quebec	70	14	16
Ontario	78	13	9
Prairies	77	14	9
British Columbia	81	12	8
Total*	75	14	11

*Due to rounding off, the figures do not always total 100 percent.

Source: Gallup Canada, Inc. March 3, 1994.

Focus

Why do you think recall has not been used in Canada?

referendum: the submission of a planned law to a direct vote of the people.

plebiscite: a direct ballot by all qualified voters on an issue of national importance.

PRESTON MANNING

Recalls and Referendums

In the following selection, Preston Manning, the leader of the Reform Party of Canada, explains why he supports the adoption of recalls and referendums. This excerpt is taken from his 1992 book, *The New Canada:*

Because Canada is a federal state with an unevenly distributed population, most national referendums should be subject to the "double majority" principle. By this I mean that a referendum ballot should be decided in favour of the position receiving 50 percent plus one of the votes cast overall, and a majority in more than half of the jurisdictions affected.

Because governments may abuse referendum legislation ... Reformers support provisions for "citizens' initiatives." This provides the people with an opportunity to place an issue or question on the referendum ballot by filing a petition with a certain number of names with the chief electoral officer.

The number of names required to launch a citizens' initiative should be high enough to prevent frivolous use of the exercise. In the American states, citizens' initiatives require signatures from between 5 and 10 percent of the electorate. Switzerland uses a fixed total of signatures rather than a percentage. We propose a 3 percent minimum for Canada. In 1991, this means approximately 780,000 names.

Reformers also advocate a special initiative generally known as the "recall petition." If a sufficient number of electors in a federal constituency file a recall petition with the chief electoral officer, they can force their elected member to stand down; a by-election would then be held. ... We advocate these measures as a necessary complement to parliamentary democracy, to make the government more representative and responsible than at present. The aim is to achieve a better balance and to ensure that one set of abuses (the constant ignoring of majority opinion by elected officials and special interests) is not replaced by another set of abuses (the use of referendum votes by majorities to run roughshod over minority rights or special interests). ...

As for the criticism that Canadians are not well enough informed to make important decisions by referendum, Reformers agree with that old Democrat, Thomas Jefferson, who said, "I know of no safe depository of the ultimate powers of society but the people themselves, and if we think them not enlightened enough to exercise control with a wholesome discretion, the remedy is not to take it from them, but to inform their discretion."[1]

Focus

What are some of the disadvantages of recalls and referendums?

Political Decisions—Your Decision

In late 1995, *Maclean's* asked Canadians: "If there are to be changes to the Constitution how should they be done?" The answers to this question reveal much about Canadians' attitudes toward direct democracy, representative democracy, and referendums. Which choice would a believer of direct democracy make? Which areas of the country seem to have the least faith in Canada's politicians?

Table 3.3: Who Should Make the Important Political Decisions?

	Canada	B.C.	Prairies	Ont.	Que.	Atlantic
By the prime minister and premiers	30%	21%	32%	27%	37%	27%
By an assembly of elected officials and people representing different groups	24	22	23	23	25	28
By community groups that submit ideas to the government for approval	23	35	22	22	18	20
By national referendum	19	15	18	23	14	22

Source: *Maclean's* Magazine, Maclean Hunter Publishing Limited, January 1, 1996.

The Prerequisites of Democracy

Democracy involves more than elections. For democracy to work effectively, citizens must become involved in the issues of the day, and politicians must discover what the people think about these issues. This means that there must be freedom of access to information, and government secrecy must be kept to a minimum. Just how much freedom of information there should be, however, is a matter of constant debate, as are such topics as limits on free speech and freedom of dissent (see Case Study 4).

Several conditions are necessary to ensure effective popular control over government decisions. These include the following:

1 The people should be able to remove their leaders and replace them with more suitable representatives. This requires that

a. Elections be held at relatively frequent and guaranteed intervals.

b. There is a real choice among different candidates and parties.

c. Elections are free of fraud, bribery, and intimidation. This usually implies the use of a secret ballot to protect voters from being punished for their political opinions.

d. There is **universal suffrage** (all qualified adult citizens may vote). The broader the franchise (the right to vote), the greater the degree of democracy.

e. There are democratic procedures for changes in leadership.

universal suffrage: a political system that grants the right to vote to all qualified citizens, regardless of political or religious beliefs, gender, race, or ethnic affiliation.

f. There is freedom of association. It would be impossible to present the electorate with an alternative choice unless those people who want to run for election had the freedom to organize.

2 Formal equality before the law. Every citizen must have similar political and legal rights.

3 To ensure legal equality, judges should be free from political or other control.

4 Such civil liberties as freedom of speech, freedom of the media, protection for minority groups, and freedom from arbitrary arrest and prosecution must be guaranteed.

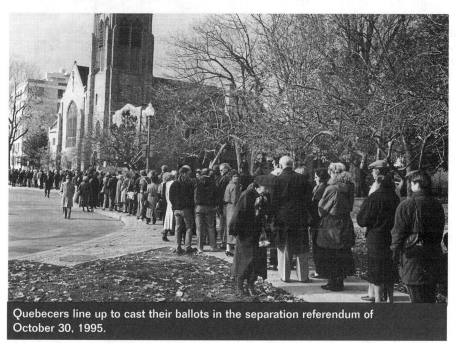

Quebecers line up to cast their ballots in the separation referendum of October 30, 1995.

Human Rights

In 1988, over 100 000 teenagers screamed at the top of their lungs as Bruce Springsteen belted out "Born in the U.S.A." This was no ordinary rock concert — it was the beginning of a 15-country tour designed to promote the fortieth anniversary of the United Nations' Universal Declaration of Human Rights. The 30 articles in this document state that everyone should be treated with dignity and respect. The Declaration includes the right to life, liberty, and security; the right not to be held in slavery, tortured, or arbitrarily arrested; and the right to freedom of thought, religion, and expression. Although many countries have agreed to these ideas, **human rights** are still ignored in many parts of the world.

human rights: the rights of all people to enjoy certain basic freedoms and protection against such dangers as hunger and disease.

Democracies must be particularly alert to ensure that the
rights of their minorities are
protected. When a minority
comes to believe that the majority is continually treating it
unfairly, the minority will ultimately refuse to abide by government laws. Faced with the
threat of disturbance, anarchy,
or even civil war, the state will
be tempted to resort to repressive measures. Democracies
thus need to operate on the
bases of consensus and compromise. Majority rule is most
effective when the minority
agrees with its decisions.
Majority rule (50 percent plus 1)
is not a synonym for democracy. According to the Equality
Rights section of the Canadian
Charter of Rights and Freedoms,
"Every individual is equal
before and under the law and
has the right to the equal protection and equal benefit of the
law without discrimination

Sue Rodriguez, who had amyotrophic lateral
sclerosis, unsuccessfully challenged the
laws against assisted suicide, claiming they
violated her Charter rights.

and, in particular, without discrimination based on race, national or ethnic
origin, colour, religion, sex, age or mental or physical disability." The passage of this amendment to the Constitution in 1982 gave more power to
individuals and the courts, while taking some power away from elected legislatures. An average of 1000 Charter cases are decided by the courts each
year, which reflects the increased importance of the courts as a forum for
political change and the importance of human rights issues in Canadian
society.

The Advantages of Democracy

Because democracy can be defined in many different ways, the arguments in
its favour have been posed in a variety of forms. One of the most persistent
defences of democracy is that government policies are made in the interest
of the people. The argument is as follows: the rule of a few will produce a
government that passes laws for the benefit of the few; the rule of the many
will create a government that legislates on behalf of the majority. In other
words, those people who hold political power will use it for their own benefit. Therefore, if the wishes of the entire community are to be followed, *all*

Human Rights Violations

Peter Benenson founded Amnesty International in England in 1961 to expose flagrant global violations of human rights — government-sanctioned killing, torture, and imprisonment of citizens. The organization now has over 41 chapters around the world. The following excerpt is from the summary of the detailed 1993 *Amnesty International Report:*

Appalling human rights catastrophes shocked the world in 1992. In the former Yugoslavia and in Somalia, the carnage was on a terrifying scale, with thousands of men, women and children tortured, killed or unaccounted for. In countries such as Chad, China, Iraq, Liberia, Peru and Sri Lanka, human rights violations and abuses continued at horrifying levels. The scale of these crises, and others that barely made the news, was almost beyond comprehension and seemingly beyond control....

The report exposed scores of governments that let their police and soldiers get away with beating, inflicting electric shocks or raping prisoners just to humiliate them or force them to sign false confessions. There are descriptions of gruesome torture sometimes leading to death. There are stories of some of the thousands of people who have "disappeared" or were brutally murdered at the hand of security forces or government-linked "death squads." ... This report also shows that armed political and opposition groups commit sickening abuses, including torture, mutilation, deliberate and arbitrary killing and hostage-taking....

So how have governments around the world responded to such atrocities? Most are quick to proclaim that human rights abuses must be ended ... despite this, politically motivated selectivity has continued to be the norm for governments when dealing with human rights issues, and international treaty obligations have been cynically ignored when convenient.[2]

Focus

What are Amnesty International's major goals?

How could these goals be achieved?

Are these goals unrealistic in the present world climate?

must rule. Government *of* the people is most likely to be government *for* the people.

Another argument in favour of democracy emphasizes its ability to safeguard individual liberties. Free competition among political parties provides a check against possible governmental tyranny and oppression, just as periodic elections provide a powerful antidote to the corrupting effect of political power. This essentially negative view of democracy assumes that democratic government will be less arbitrary in its actions than will other political systems.

Another group of political theorists believes that democracy is more than just a method of arriving at decisions. To them, the democratic process is a means of developing or moulding a democratic-minded citizenry. The democratic environment, they assume, will promote the creation of self-governing, confident, inquiring, intelligent human beings who are willing to compromise and are respectful of different opinions and values. Because decision-making in a democracy relies upon voluntary co-operation and the arts of verbal and written persuasion, physical violence is replaced by peaceful coercion, and force is replaced by intelligence. By actively taking part in elections and voluntary organizations, citizens will develop a cooperative, public-spirited character that will place the good of the entire society above narrow, self-interested goals.

A riot police officer tries to stop human rights activists unfurling a banner in Paris, France.

···Defining Democracy in Practice

Since the early 1970s, political scientist Raymond D. Gastil has monitored the extent of democracy in the world. To determine how democratic each country is, Gastil rates its performance in preserving political and civil rights on a scale from one (best rating) to seven (worst). Gastil's checklist for political rights includes the following questions:

- Has there been a recent election?

- Is there more than one political party?

- Are the elections run fairly?

- Is there an effective opposition?

- Are the candidates freely selected?

- What role does the military play in the political process?

- To what extent do other countries control the government?

- Do minority groups have a say in government?

- Are there periodic changes in the ruling party?

- How wide is the franchise?

Since political liberties cannot exist without civil rights, Gastil also evaluates each country according to the following criteria:

- Is the media free of political censorship?

- Is there freedom of association and religion?

- Is the judiciary free of corruption?

- Is there freedom from torture and arbitrary imprisonment?

- Does the government ever lose in court in political cases?

- Is there freedom to join a trade union?

- Is there freedom to travel, own property, and marry?

- What is the degree of economic inequality?

Not surprisingly, Gastil discovered that countries that had a high degree of civil liberties also provided full political rights. Since Gastil first began this study in 1973, some parts of the world have exhibited frequent changes. Since the fall of the Soviet Union in 1991, for example, democracy has spread in Eastern Europe. On the other hand, Nigeria dropped to the lowest level when its government executed human rights activist Ken Saro-Wiwa in 1996.

Table 3.4: Measures of Democracy, 1995–1996

Country	Political rights	Civil liberties	Country	Political rights	Civil liberties
Australia	1	1	Iraq	7	7
Brazil	2	4	Israel	3	1
Canada	1	1	Japan	2	1
China	7	7	Mexico	4	4
France	2	1	Russia	4	3
Germany	1	2	South Africa	1	2
Greece	1	3	Sweden	1	1
Haiti	5	5	Switzerland	1	1
India	4	4	United Kingdom	1	2
Iran	7	6	United States	1	1

1 represents the most free and 7 the least free category.

Source: Reprinted with permission from *Freedom in the World: The Annual Survey of Political Rights and Civil Liberties* 1995-96 (Freedom House, 1996).

F o c u s

What do the highly rated (or lowly rated) countries have in common?

Becoming Democratic

Today, as slightly over one-half of the world's population lives in a democratic country, it should be remembered that many of the African countries that have tried democracy since World War II have reverted to authoritarian rule. For democracy to work, the people must be familiar with their democratic rights and willing to fight for them. Democracy usually requires high literacy rates, national unity, a consensus on national goals and values, relative economic equality and equality of opportunity, and the absence of passionate religious, racial, ethnic, or political differences. Many of the countries without democratic governments are educationally and economically less developed.

In some parts of Asia, South America, and Africa (the three areas with the least amount of democracy) there is only a small middle class, and the people are more likely to be split into two major groups: the wealthy and the poor. It should also be remembered that the evolution of democracy in Western Europe took centuries and was frequently accompanied by revolutions. Democracy cannot be achieved overnight. Once it is in place, citizens must have faith in the system and be ready to defend it.

Democracy and Controversy

Several years ago, an influential British member of Parliament visiting Canada stated, "What is wrong in my country — and I have a suspicion it is wrong over here as well — is the contrast between the reality of how we politicians behave, and the legend of how we behave." Textbooks are full of descriptions about how democracy works. According to popular belief, there is an all-competent citizenry that is capable of settling any public problem. The media provides people with all the facts, and after people listen to the pros and cons of each issue, they make up their minds. Prior to an election, political parties decide upon their policies and nominate candidates to run in the contest. The **electorate** decides not only which people (or party) it wants to run the country, but also what policies it desires the new government to implement. The elected representatives know that if their actions do not please the majority of the people, they will not be re-elected. This power to reward and punish decision-makers is the guarantee that ultimate political power rests in the hands of the people.

electorate: the body of citizens that have the right to vote.

The contrast between this idealized view and the reality of politics has undermined many citizens' confidence in democratic government and in the integrity of politicians. Polls have shown that over the past two decades, Canadians' confidence in their elected leaders has consistently declined. In the early 1980s, Canadians described politicians as principled (63 percent) and competent (57 percent). By the 1990s, this confidence had declined dramatically. In March 1996, over 1000 Canadians were asked how they would rate the honesty and ethical standards of members of a variety of professions. Twelve percent of those people surveyed gave Members of Parliament a high rating, whereas 42 percent gave them a low rating. Another poll in 1996 asked Canadians how much respect and confidence they had in the federal government. Twenty-nine percent answered a "great deal/quite a lot," and 26 percent responded "very little."[3] In January 1995, according to a *Maclean's* poll, 77 percent of Canadians believed that "too many people seek public office for financial gain."

Perhaps these people are being too critical of elected officials. For example, another *Maclean's* poll discovered that less than half of 1201 Canadians surveyed agreed with the following statement: "If I could, I would welcome the chance to serve my country or community by becoming an elected official."

To admit that there is a difference between the theory and practice of democracy does not mean that democracy is a sham or that we should discard it completely. This admission, in fact, should help to strengthen our democratic system of government, because we can then concentrate our efforts upon improving its defects. The remainder of this chapter outlines some of the major criticisms of democracy. Subsequent case studies will explore some of these criticisms in greater depth.

Tyranny of the Majority

Most democracies rely upon a simple parliamentary majority (50 percent plus 1) in making policy decisions.* This is based on the assumptions that the majority is more likely to be correct than the minority, and that the majority is entitled to have its own way. Unfortunately, this has frequently led to what is called the **tyranny of the majority,** which means that the minority is deprived of its rights. Historical examples of such tyranny include white domination of African Americans in the southern United States, the mistreatment of Aboriginal peoples all over the world, and Protestant oppression of Roman Catholics in Northern Ireland. (Apartheid in South Africa was an example of tyranny by the minority.)

tyranny of the majority: a condition under which the ruling majority oppresses minorities of any type.

This raises the important question of how we can rely upon the majority to protect the minority. To shield the minority from the majority, some countries entrench (or guarantee) minority rights in a constitution, which is much more difficult to change than an ordinary law. In this way, individuals are protected from governments (and majorities). Canada's Charter of Rights and Freedoms and the American Bill of Rights are two such examples, and they illustrate why democracy is often described as majority rule with minority rights.

Inefficiency

Some critics claim that technology has progressed too fast for democracy. The phenomenal growth of economic, scientific, and technical information in the twentieth century makes it impossible for the average person to remain well-informed on political and economic issues. Members of Parliament find it difficult to cope with the increasing size and complexity of government activities. As a result, some people claim that democratic government is too slow and inefficient to meet the demands of a rapidly changing world.

Other people believe that technology can strengthen democracy by

---

* In democracies with three or more political parties, such as Canada, the United Kingdom, and Sweden, the winning party seldom receives as much as 50 percent of the vote. This situation is discussed in Case Study 2.

improving communication between policy-makers and the public. In the United States, Speaker of the House Newt Gingrich arranged for all House documents to be placed on the Internet so that anyone with a modem can access them. In the future, he stated, Americans can "begin to have electronic town-hall meetings." Already, politicians use the latest technology to keep in touch with the public through opinion polls and radio talk shows. In addition, public feedback pours into politicians' fax machines and electronic mailboxes. Interactive television promises even greater citizen–politician communication.

Elite Groups

Some political scientists argue that in all large organizations, power and political influence gradually fall into the hands of a few leaders who soon lose touch with the rank and file. As a result, the minority imposes its opinion upon the majority. Democratic governments, they argue, are no exception. In Western democracies, this minority usually consists of wealthy citizens who have the time, influence, and money to ensure that their needs are satisfied by the government.

Another form of undue influence is the existence of lobbies and pressure groups, which put enormous political pressure upon the government in power to do their bidding. Examples include the Canadian Manufacturers' Association, Greenpeace, pro- and anti-gun lobbies, labour unions, and pollution and medicare activists.

According to some writers, however, the existence of such **interest groups** within society actually serves to strengthen democracy, because these groups enable concerned citizens to express their opinions about legislation that directly affects them. In theory, competition between interest groups representing different concerns allows people to exert greater control over decisions of the government. This theory is called **pluralism.**

There are, however, several serious criticisms of pluralism. As Figure 3.2 illustrates, the people are another step removed from the decision-making process. Active participation in pressure groups requires more time, money, and knowledge than most people possess. Many citizens do not have organizations to represent their interests, nor is every pressure group equal in terms of finances, power, or access to influential people. As a result, some critics believe that Canada and other Western democracies are ruled by a small number of people who control the economy and unduly influence government decisions.

interest group: an organized or informal group representing a specific political, social, or economic position in society.

pluralism: a theory that states that diversity of ideas and competition among interest groups allows citizens greater control over government decisions.

Figure 3.2

PLURALISM

An Apathetic Electorate

According to some critics, democracy expects too much from citizens. Democratic reformers, they argue, have concentrated so much of their effort on providing democratic institutions that they have forgotten that most people are more interested in family and friends, sports, movies, or their work than they are in politics. This lack of interest is aggravated by the growing size and complexity of government — and the civil service — which leaves the average citizen feeling powerless and alienated from government.

One of the assumptions underlying the importance of elections in a democracy is that the average voter is "rational." This means that voters understand the major campaign issues, are aware of the relationship of the issues to themselves, know each candidate's stand on these issues, and vote for the candidate or party that comes closest to their own beliefs. Yet, in recent years, some political scientists have argued that voting behaviour is more closely related to the voter's social and economic position in society than to the issues. Ethnicity, religion, occupation, education, and social class, they believe, generally determine how people vote. One study has shown that whereas nearly 60 percent of Canadians had identified themselves with a political party by the time they entered grade 8, very few of them even knew the names of the leaders of each political party.

Bureaucracy

As democratic governments expanded the scope of their activities in the twentieth century, the civil service, or **bureaucracy,** became enlarged to handle the increased, and more technical, workload. In Canada, from 15 to 20 percent of the labour force consists of government employees, including military and law enforcement personnel, hospital workers, social welfare employees, teachers, and Crown corporation employees. Recent government cutbacks and deregulation (see Case Study 15), however, continue to reduce the number of civil servants each year.

The bureaucracy's role is to advise elected government officials and to administer the laws decided upon by the government. Without a bureaucracy, government programs could not be carried out. In theory, politicians make choices from the options presented to them by trained and specialized civil servants. The central problem is to ensure that the bureaucracy is accountable to the people through their elected representatives. Civil serv-ants are relatively permanent; politicians come and go. And, whereas bureaucrats soon come to possess a specialized knowledge of their area, Cabinet ministers are often switched from one area (portfolio) to another. Since politicians depend upon the advice of their experts, civil servants wield a great deal of power and may dominate elected members who do not have the needed technical knowledge.

The civil service can be a barrier between the people and their elected representatives that increases the voters' sense of remoteness from the decision-making process. In addition, some people fear that the bureaucracy has too much political clout. In recent years, governments have appointed ombudsmen to investigate claims by individual citizens that the bureaucracy has treated them unfairly. Almost every Canadian province has appointed its own

bureaucracy: a system that administers the affairs of a government or business enterprise through employed officials; in government, this is also called the civil service.

ombudsman. Investigative news reporting, the courts, and well-organized interest groups can also mount effective opposition to unpopular bureaucratic measures. Despite these criticisms of government bureaucracy, the government could not operate effectively without a trained, efficient civil service.

Evaluating Democracy

Democracy is founded on faith in the people. Its future rests on the citizens' commitment to making it work. This means ensuring that the democratic machinery is functioning properly and that the needs of the majority and the minority are respected. As British Prime Minister Winston Churchill declared, "It has been said that democracy is the worst form of government except all those other forms that have been tried from time to time."

In this introduction to democracy, we have examined its origins, goals, prerequisites, and fundamental principles. In the real world, each democrat-ic country has adopted its own variation of democracy, based upon its history, culture, values, and goals. It is unrealistic to believe that one particular political system can satisfy every country's needs, just as it is unrealistic to believe that any one method of government is without flaws.

Although democratic governments (and the methods and institutions each country adopts to maintain them) vary from place to place, they can be evaluated according to the extent to which

- government decisions are subject to popular control;

- the ordinary citizen is involved in the running of the country;

- individual liberties are upheld.

What's Coming Next

The case studies that follow this chapter examine the political institutions of Canada, the United States, and Sweden before turning to several important issues that challenge the ultimate viability of democracy. Case Study 1 compares the Canadian and American political systems. How do they differ? What are the merits and disadvantages of each? Case Study 2 explores proportional representation by examining the Swedish system of electing people to Parliament. Is the Canadian single-member constituency a better method? Case Study 3 outlines the history of Canada's political parties and discusses the extent to which our multi-party system is accountable to the public. Case Study 4 deals with the extent to which citizens in a democracy should obey the law, and whether civil disobedience is justified. Case Study 5 explores the political power of the media and lobby groups and their role in a democracy. Do they exert too much influence on elected officials? Case Study 6 discusses the problems women and minorities face in democracies. To what extent does Canada protect these groups? As you read these case studies, decide what changes, if any, you would like to have implemented in Canada.

BIOGRAPHY

FRIEDRICH NIETZSCHE, 1844–1900

In his book *The Passion of the Western Mind,* philosopher Richard Tarnas wrote, "By all accounts the central prophet of the postmodern mind was Friedrich Nietzsche." Given Nietzsche's profound impact upon the twentieth century, it would be difficult to disagree with this assessment; his influence on modern Western culture is almost impossible to overestimate. The symphonies of Strauss, the novels of Mann, the poetry of Yeats and Rilke, the plays of Shaw, the psychology of Freud and Jung, the philosophy of Camus and Sartre — it seems that every field of intellectual endeavour was affected by Nietzsche's views. While he directed most of his energies to attacking what he characterized as the steady decline of Western culture, Nietzsche was also vitally concerned with issues of politics and government, reserving some of his fiercest criticisms for the institutions of democracy and socialism.

Nietzsche was born in 1844 in Rocken, a village in what was then Prussian Saxony. After an excellent classical education at one of Germany's leading Protestant boarding schools, he studied theology and classical philology (linguistics) at the University of Bonn and Leipzig. Despite the fact that he had not finished a doctoral thesis, he so impressed the staff at the University of Basel with his intellect and writings that he received an appointment as a professor of philology in 1869 at the age of 25.

Nietzsche's declining health — he had contracted dysentery and diphtheria during wartime service as an orderly, and was rumoured to have contracted syphilis as a student — and the strains of academic life led him to resign his post in 1879. Having lost most of his interest in philology following the indifferent reception of his work *The Birth of Tragedy,* Nietzsche increasingly turned his attention to philosophy. During the remainder of his life, he produced a series of explosively written but little-read works (until his madness and death in 1900, he languished in virtual obscurity), which bitterly attacked the "nihilistic and decadent" tendencies he felt characterized his society.

While Nietzche's philosophy is perhaps most famous for these attacks on culture and his powerful criticism of Christian morality, it also contains a scathing critique of democracy. He maintained that democracy, by ensuring that all individuals have a voice in government, would increasingly lead to a mediocre and intellectually bankrupt society. Under such a system, the government would be forced to pander to the more uneducated masses rather than to the nation's intellectual elite. To Nietzsche (who "subordinated everything to culture" and regarded the entire concept of equality as a means by which "the weak chained the strong"), such a political system was akin to committing cultural and artistic suicide.

In his book *Beyond Good and Evil,* he stated that democracy waged a "common war upon the higher duty, the higher responsibility, the higher man … and all that is rare, strange and privileged." He believed that a democratic society would be incapable of rising above the desires of the "mediocre herd, " and would turn its back on the "voices in the wilderness" that were so essential to advances in culture.

Nietzsche's attacks on democracy and socialism were later to endear him to the Nazis and other fledgling fascist movements, but despite surface similarities, there are vast differences between Nietzsche and those who appropriated his views. Nietzsche denounced anti-Semitism as "scabies of the heart," attacked wars of expansion and imperialism as "vile and insipid," and called for the end of nationalism and the creation of the "Good European." In writing on the Nazis' "hijacking" and misrepresentation of Nietzsche's ideas and the resulting public misperception of his work, the French philosopher Albert Camus said, "We shall never finish making reparation for the injustice done to him."[4]

In his book *The Story of Philosophy*, Will Durant offers this synopsis of Nietzsche's great distrust of democracy:

Democracy means drift; it means permission given to each part of an organism to do just what it pleases; it means the lapse of coherence and inter- dependence, the enthronement of liberty and chaos. It means the worship of mediocrity, and the hatred of excellence. It means the impossibility of great men — how could great men submit to the indignities and indecencies of an election? ... How can the superman arise in such a soil? And how can a nation become great when its greatest men lie unused, discouraged, perhaps unknown. ... Not the superior man but the majority man becomes the ideal and the model; everybody comes to resemble everybody else.[5]

---

1 What are Nietzsche's criticisms of democracy?

2 Explain the basis for Albert Camus' statement about the "injustice" done to Nietzsche.

Underlying and Emerging Issues

Give the reasoning and evidence that might be used to support different views or conclusions on the following issues.

1 To what degree can genuine democracy exist in a society with great extremes of wealth and poverty?

2 Is it more important to guarantee civil liberties or to reduce social and economic inequalities?

3 Should representatives make decisions based on their own judgements or according to the wishes of their constituents?

4 Should important and controversial issues be settled by referendums?

5 What are the best ways to ensure popular control over government decisions?

6 Should all people be guaranteed fundamental rights, including political, economic, and social rights?

7 Are rights "absolute"? If not, what are the reasonable limits to rights?

8 At what point does majority rule become majority tyranny?

9 How should we protect the minority from the majority?

10 How do we decide between self-interested goals and the good of the whole society?

11 Is changing technology giving more power to elites, or is it enhancing democracy?

12 Do interest and pressure groups enhance minority rights, or lead to control by elites?

13 What should be done about political alienation or apathy of voters?

14 To what degree is bureaucratic power a problem?

Focussing Knowledge

In your notes, clearly identify and explain the importance or significance of each of the following:

democracy	*human rights*
formal democracy	*Amnesty International*
natural rights	*political rights*
direct democracy	*electorate*
suffrage	*tyranny of the majority*
representative democracy	*minority rights*
recall	*elites*

referendum　　　　　　　　*interest group*

plebiscite　　　　　　　　　*pluralism*

universal suffrage　　　　　*bureaucracy*

*Universal Declaration
of Human Rights*

Reviewing and Organizing Knowledge

1 Why was democracy not popular before the nineteenth century?

2 What are the various meanings that people have given to the term "democracy"?

3 a. What restrictions have countries placed on participation in decision-making in the past?

　　b. How does representative democracy differ from direct democracy?

4 a. How do recalls, referendums, and plebiscites provide citizens with more control over elected representatives?

　　b. What are the suggested drawbacks to referendums and plebiscites?

　　c. What conditions are necessary to ensure popular control over government decisions?

5 How has the concept of "natural rights" changed through time?

6 What are the conclusions of the *Amnesty International Reports* regarding the present state of human rights in the world?

7 What is the role of the Canadian Charter of Rights and Freedoms with respect to minority rights?

8 What are the advantages of democracy?

9 What are the disadvantages of democracy?

10 On what bases did Raymond Gastil monitor the extent of democracy in different countries?

11 What factors have been commonly associated with successful adoption of democracy?

Applying and Extending Knowledge

1 Examine the issue of technology and democracy. Research the arguments that suggest that technological advances will enhance democracy, and those that suggest that these changes will be harmful. Take a position and defend it.

2 Choose one of the Underlying and Emerging Issues on page 51. Research the issue in terms of present-day Canada; take a position and defend it.

3 Select another of the Underlying and Emerging Issues. Find newspaper articles that illustrate the issue. Explain how each article illustrates the reasons for people's disagreement or differing conclusions about the issue.

4 Select newspaper articles that illustrate some of the Focussing Knowledge terms on pages 51–52. Explain how each article illustrates the terms.

5 Draw up a constitution for your school, defining the rights of the students and the extent and limits of the power of teachers, administrators, and others. When this is complete, design a Declaration of Responsibilities to accompany the statement of rights.

6 Use Raymond Gastil's criteria (see page 43) to examine the political system of a selected country today. In terms of both political rights and civil rights, how democratic is the country?

Democratic Institutions in Canada and the United States

Learning Outcomes

After reading this case study, you should be able to:

- better understand how the Canadian government operates
- compare the Canadian and American systems of government
- debate the advantages of either system
- understand the American political system

*T*HERE ARE MANY DIFFERENT TYPES of democracies in the world. Two of these—the Canadian and the American styles of democracy—are examined in this case study. This includes exploring government bodies and practices, the roles of key participants, and the passage of legislation. A comparison of the two systems highlights the strengths and weaknesses of each.

Democratic governments are based upon the principle that the wishes of the people should be law. This means that the legislature must be accountable to the electorate. Although few people argue with the theory, almost every country disagrees on the best method of achieving this system of government. Some democracies are **parliamentary**, or **constitutional**, **monarchies**, while others are **republics**. In a constitutional monarchy, the head of state is a monarch (usually a king or queen who inherited the throne) who is mostly a figurehead. A constitution gives effective political power to an elected parliament. Canada, Belgium, Great Britain, Denmark, Norway, Spain, the Netherlands, Sweden, Japan, and New Zealand are examples of countries that have constitutional monarchies. A republican government, such as that of the United States, has no monarch, and all political power resides in the people's elected representatives, usually headed by a president or prime minister.

Most governments have a **bicameral legislature** (an upper house and a lower house), but a few countries have only one house (unicameral). In Canada, the House of Commons (the lower house) is more powerful than the Senate (the upper house). In the United States, both houses — the House of Representatives and the Senate — have considerable political power.

Elected officials are usually chosen for periods ranging between two and six years. Members of Parliament (MPs) in the Canadian House of Commons are elected for a maximum of five years, whereas members of the House of Representatives in the United States remain for two years. The time between elections varies from variable terms that are subject to change (as in Canada and Great Britain) to fixed terms (as in the United States and Sweden). History, tradition, and convenience often have had more to do with each country's choice of options than have logic or political theories.

Governments can be classified according to their degree of centralization. In a **unitary system**, law-making power is concentrated in one central government. There might be municipal, regional, or other governments, but the central body can veto their actions. In a **federal system**, government powers are divided between the central government and regional or provincial governments. A written **constitution** assigns different functions to each governing body. The central government usually has control over such national concerns as defence, foreign affairs, and currency. Regional governments are often responsible for such local matters as education, roads, and hospitals. A constitutional or Supreme Court arbitrates disputes between the two branches of government and interprets the constitution.

Federal Systems of Government

Although only approximately 20 of the current 185 member countries of the United Nations have federal governments, 5 of the 6 largest countries by area are federal (China is the exception). The American Constitution of 1789 created the first modern federal government. This model was later copied and modified by Canada, Brazil, Mexico, Australia, Czechoslovakia, Austria, Argentina, India, West Germany, the USSR, Switzerland, and Indonesia. Federal systems are usually created in geographically large countries and in states with a variety of culturally distinct groups. Switzerland is geographically small, but it has a diverse religious and linguistic population. Canada opted for a federal system in 1867 to allow Quebec to retain its cultural distinctiveness, and because the Maritime colonies did not want local matters to be decided by Ottawa. One of the reasons why the United States created a federal system was to ensure that one level of government could act as a check on the other and to prevent any one body from becoming too powerful.

Practically all federal governments have a bicameral legislature to ensure that each regional government has a voice in the central government. In most cases, each region has equal representation in the upper house. The selection of the regional representatives may be based on appointment by the central government or on popular election. The powers of regional rep-

parliamentary (constitutional) monarchy: a political system in which the head of state is a king or queen, but political power resides in an elected parliament.

republic: a political system in which the head of state is a non-hereditary official, usually a president.

bicameral legislature: a legislature that consists of two houses of parliament.

unitary system: a political system under which all geographic regions are governed directly by the central government.

federal system: a political system under which legislative and administrative powers are divided between national and regional governments.

constitution: a legal document that outlines the basic rules for government and assigns different functions to each governing body of a country.

resentatives vary from relative powerlessness to equality with the lower house. Canada's first prime minister, John A. Macdonald, desired a weak Senate, partly because he believed that the American Civil War in the 1860s had been caused by the individual states having too much power.

The most important question democracies have to decide upon is the distribution of power among the legislature (which makes the laws), the executive or administration (which carries out the laws), and the judiciary (which interprets the laws). In deciding this distribution, democracies have adopted either the British parliamentary system or the American presidential or republican system. This is a major difference between the Canadian and American governments.

A country's system of government is a product of its history, values, and goals. The differences between Canada and the United States, for instance, are partly the result of their different relationships with Great Britain. Both were colonies of Great Britain, but whereas Canada achieved its freedom peacefully, the United States had to fight for it. It is thus no wonder that Canada's government more closely resembles the British system.

The Canadian Government

Focus

Do you think the monarchy should be abolished in Canada?

minority government: a government in which no one party has the majority of the seats in the legislature.

coalition government: a government that stays in power by combining with another political party or parties to form a majority.

The British monarch is Canada's head of state, and is represented by the governor general. The governor general has little political power and serves more of a symbolic than a political role. For example, he or she is appointed by the government in power, must act on the advice of the Cabinet, and performs such ceremonial duties as greeting visiting dignitaries and signing all legislation. Only in times of emergency, when the government is deadlocked over an issue, can the governor general act on his or her own initiative.

An important component of our parliamentary system is the House of Commons, which is the effective ruling body. Following a federal election, the leader of the political party with the majority of elected representatives in the House of Commons becomes prime minister. If no party wins a majority, then the leader who can gather a majority of the MPs' support becomes prime minister. Such a situation leads to the formation of a **minority government**, or less often, a **coalition government**, in which two or more parties temporarily unite to achieve a majority.

The most important group within the House of Commons is the Cabinet. It consists of the prime minister and the heads of such government departments as finance, national defence, and immigration, who are chosen by the prime minister from among Members of Parliament. Using the senior civil service as a source of information and advice, the Cabinet draws up bills (proposed laws) and submits them to the House for approval. Cabinet solidarity prevents Cabinet members from criticizing government bills in public or disclosing private Cabinet discussions. Individual Members of Parliament may introduce a bill (termed a private member's bill), but since they do not have the undivided support of the government, few are passed into law. Although the Cabinet is extremely powerful, it is ultimately responsible to the House of Commons. If the Cabinet loses the support of the majority of the members in the House on a vital piece of legislation, especially a money bill, then the prime minister and the executive must resign. In such cases, either an election will be held or another party will attempt to gain majority support and make its leader the new prime minister. This system is called **responsible government** — the prime minister and Cabinet are responsible to the elected representatives in the House of Commons and must resign if they lose this support. This is a major difference between the Canadian and American political systems.

responsible government: a system of parliamentary government in which the executive functions at the will of the legislative body.

This is the theory. In practice, the immense control exerted by political parties generally prevents individual MPs from voting against their party's policies. To date, the only examples at the national level of a government losing office as the result of a defeat in the House occurred in 1873, when Alexander Mackenzie defeated John A. Macdonald as a result of the Pacific Railway Scandal; in 1926, when W.L. Mackenzie King defeated Arthur Meighen; and in 1979, when the combined vote of the Liberals and the NDP overthrew Joe Clark's government on a budget issue. In the last two cases, the defeat was made possible by the presence of a minority government.

Case Figure 1.1: Government of Canada

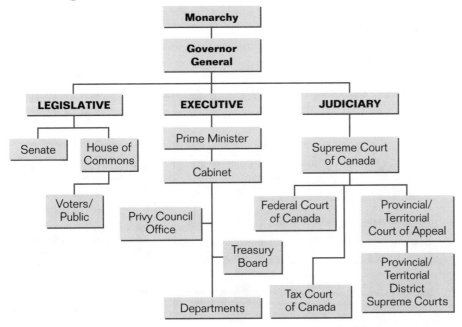

Creating a New Law in Canada

A new policy or law is usually devised by a Cabinet minister in conjunction with the civil servants of her or his particular department. This proposal is then submitted to the Cabinet for discussion. If the idea is approved, the Cabinet committee on legislation drafts the bill and resubmits it to the Cabinet for final approval. Only now is the bill presented to the House of

Commons, where it must pass through three readings. (All bills that require spending public money must originate in the House of Commons.) During the first reading, the title of the bill is announced to House members and the text of the proposed legislation is distributed to them. During the second reading, the members debate and vote on the principle of the bill. From here, a parliamentary committee examines the bill clause by clause. It might invite expert witnesses and interested groups to comment upon the proposal. The membership in these committees is based upon each political party's strength in the House. Although the governing party controls each committee, the latter sometimes amends a proposal before returning it to the House. During the second and third readings, the opposition parties have the opportunity to criticize and amend the proposed legislation. The bill is then introduced into the Senate, where it goes through a similar process of three readings and committee reports. If the Senate does not object in principle to the proposal, it will often process the bill at the same time as it is being examined in the lower house. Amendments made by the Senate must receive approval by the House of Commons. When the governor general signs the bill, it becomes law.

Case Figure 1.2: How a Bill Becomes Law in Canada

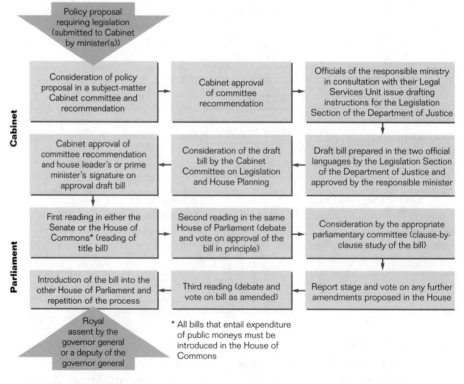

Source: Statistics Canada

Since the government must maintain the confidence of the House of Commons to remain in office, loyalty to the party usually takes precedence over the MPs' personal beliefs. Party members, however, have the opportunity to influence government bills and policies at party caucus meetings. At these gatherings of the party's elected representatives, the prime minister informs and consults with party members. When a government measure reaches the floor of the House of Commons, it is almost certain of success. This explains why the debates in the House often take place before a half-empty chamber.

Debating Senate Reform

Another important component of the Canadian parliamentary system is the Senate. Although its members supposedly represent the interests of the provinces, senators are appointed by the federal government. Senators must be at least 30 years old and live in the province they represent. They may serve until they reach the age of 75 or miss two consecutive sessions of the Senate. Although the Senate can amend bills and delay legislation (except money bills), it cannot permanently stop government measures.

In September 1990, the question of Senate reform came to the forefront of Canadian politics. When the Liberal-dominated Senate refused to approve the Goods and Services Tax (GST) that had been passed by the Conservative-dominated House of Commons, Prime Minister Brian Mulroney successfully appealed to Queen Elizabeth under section 26 of the British North America Act to create eight new Senate positions. Naturally, the new senators whom Mulroney had appointed all supported the GST. Although the Conservative Party now had a majority in the Senate, the Liberal members blocked a final vote on the GST. The prime minister claimed that the Senate was acting undemocratically. An appointed body, he argued, should not block the wishes of the elected House of Commons. Liberal Senators, however, pointed to opinion polls indicating that the majority of Canadians opposed the GST and supported the Senate's actions. Since the House of Commons is the more powerful body, the GST became law.

Various influential people and many provinces have suggested radical changes to the composition, powers, and selection of senators. The comments range from abolishing the Senate to greatly expanding its powers, and from popular election to provincial control over appointments. Reform Party leader Preston Manning, for example, has championed the Triple E Senate — an *E*lected Senate with *E*ffective powers and *E*qual provincial representation. The basic debate is whether senators should be elected or appointed (and by whom); what regions, groups, or people they should represent; and what powers they should have.

Focus

What reasons are given by those who think the Senate should be abolished in Canada?

VIEWPOINT

PRESIDENTIAL VERSUS PRIME MINISTERIAL POWER

Democratic governments are structured to prevent one person, or a small group of people, from having too much political power. In the United States, the doctrine of separation of powers, which pits the executive, judicial, and legislative branches of government against one another, was designed to prevent autocratic rule. In Canada, the supremacy of Parliament and the Constitution work to limit the influence of the prime minister.

In an article discussing whether Canadian prime ministers are too powerful, Joseph Wearing, an expert on Canadian politics, wrote the following comparison of presidential and prime ministerial powers:

Because there are so many checks on presidential power, the American system suffers from periodic bouts of deadlock or "gridlock"— to use [former U.S. President] George Bush's term. Indeed, over the last sixty years, it has been only under special circumstances, such as the aftermath of Kennedy's assassination or Reagan's initial popularity, that an American president has been able to count on congressional cooperation. Clinton's struggle to get his first budget approved showed the American system at its worst as the president was forced to concede to any number of special interests just to win the support of his fellow Democrats in Congress. "America's political system continues to reward self-interest and short-ter-

mism," observed The Economist *at the conclusion of the spectacle.*

A Canadian prime minister or premier of a majority government can act decisively in what he or she perceives to be the public interest and is judged accordingly and has the time to demonstrate that these policies are right before the electorate is given the opportunity to pass judgment. The GST, the Ontario Social Contract, and free trade are examples. Canadians should not be surprised that we have a universal medicare system while Americans do not, nor that the American gun lobby is able to keep the United States as the most gun-infected of all the industrial nations.[1]

Focus

How would you rebut Joseph Wearing's argument?

···The United States Government

The American political system emerged after the Revolutionary War against Great Britain at the end of the eighteenth century. In designing a new constitution, the American leaders were influenced both by the British system and by what they considered to be the British monarch's "abuse of authority."

In Washington, DC, three famous buildings symbolize the government of the United States: the White House is the residence of the president (the executive power); on "the Hill," a little distance from the White House, is the Capitol building, which is the home of the Senate and the House of Representatives (the legislative power) — together, these houses are called

Congress; still higher on the Hill is the Supreme Court building (the judicial power). These separate buildings symbolize the division among the executive, legislative, and judicial branches of the U.S. government. To prevent any one group or party from becoming too powerful, the American Constitution divided the powers of government among these three branches and established a system of checks and balances designed to prevent any one branch from controlling the state. This separation of executive, legislative, and judicial powers is one of the most important differences between the Canadian and American government systems.

The chief executive, or head of state, of the United States is the president. This person is responsible for the enforcement of laws and for the negotiation of treaties with foreign countries. The president is commander-in-chief of the armed forces and appoints federal judges and ambassadors, subject to the approval of the Senate. The president recommends laws to Congress and signs or vetoes measures passed by Congress.

Case Figure 1.3: How a Bill Becomes Law in the United States

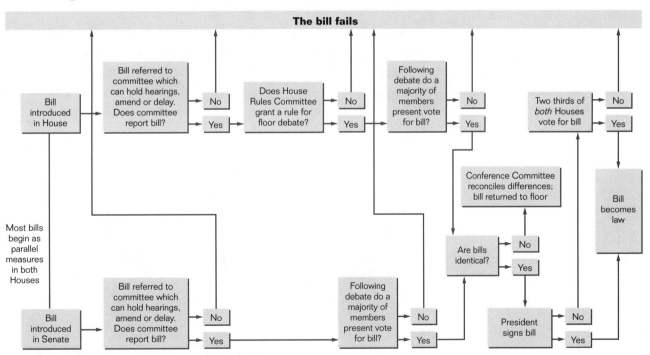

Source: David McKay, *American Politics and Society* (Cambridge, MA: Blackwell, 1993), p. 158.

separation of powers: a political system in which the executive, legislative, and judicial powers of government are distinctly divided.

checks and balances: a system of government in which the executive, legislative, and judicial branches of government are constitutionally vested with the right to check one another's actions in order to prevent concentration of power.

Separation of Powers in the American Government

It should now be evident what Americans mean by the terms **separation of powers** and **checks and balances**. Each of the three branches of government has distinct powers and acts as a check on the freedom of the others. The president commands the armed forces, but only Congress may declare war or vote money for troops. All bills passed by Congress must be signed by the president before they become law; Congress, however, can override the president's veto by passing the same bill again with a two-thirds majority in each house. Congress can also refuse to vote the money required by the president to implement policies. The Supreme Court, through its right to interpret the Constitution, can check both the executive and legislative branches by declaring a law unconstitutional. Yet even the Supreme Court's powers are not absolute — new judges can be appointed by the president with the Senate's approval, and the existing judges can be impeached (removed from office) by the House of Representatives.

Case Figure 1.4: Checks and Balances in the American Political Structure

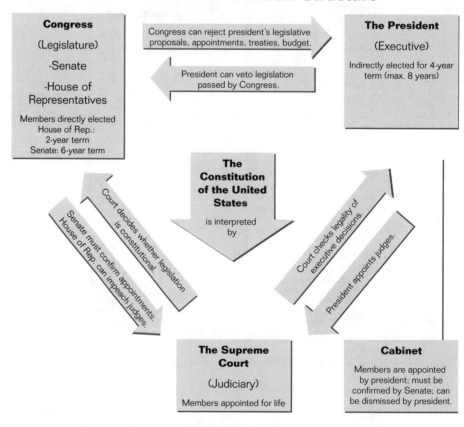

Source: Reprinted with permission from *Canadians and Their Government* by Allen S. Merritt and George W. Brown, 1985, Fitzhenry & Whiteside, Markham, Ontario.

···Comparing the Canadian and American Executive Branches

There are two major differences between the Canadian parliamentary system of executive power and the American congressional system of executive power. The executive power in Canada is controlled by the prime minister and the Cabinet, who are jointly responsible for government decisions. In the United States, the executive power is largely in the hands of one person, the president.

The second difference is even more significant. In the parliamentary system, Cabinet ministers are Members of Parliament, and they retain their office only as long as they have the support of the majority of the House of Commons. The executive is therefore responsible to the elected Members of Parliament. The U.S. president, on the other hand, is not a member of Congress and is not responsible to that body. He or she is elected for a four-year period and holds office for the duration of this term, even if his or her party does not have a majority in Congress. This executive independence was founded on the belief that the president should not be a servant of the two houses of Congress. The prime minister's position, on the other hand, is based upon the belief that the executive should be responsible to the House of Commons.

This difference is illustrated by the manner in which prime ministers and presidents are chosen. The prime minister is not elected separately, but is usually the leader of the political party with the largest number of supporters in the House of Commons and can retain that position as long as the support of Parliament is secured. In Canada, a national election must be called within five years of a government attaining office, but it can be held at any time within the five-year period at the government's discretion. U.S. presidential elections are held on the Tuesday following the first Monday in November of any year that can be divided evenly by four — such as 1988, 1992, 1996, and 2000. A president cannot be elected for more than two consecutive terms.*

In Canada, the head of state is the governor general, while the head of government is the prime minister. In the United States, the president is both the head of state and the head of government. Because in the United States the president represents both of these positions, Americans may revere the office of the president but may not politically support the person in that office.

Focus

Should the head of state be the same person as the head of government? Give reasons for your answer.

---

*Prior to 1952, there was no limit on how many terms a president could serve, although only President Franklin D. Roosevelt was elected for more than two four-year terms. In presidential elections, Americans vote for state "electors," who then select the president and vice president.

Comparing the Canadian and American Legislative Branches

One of the first observations that a Canadian visitor to the American Congress would make is that the seating arrangement, as seen in these two photographs, is quite different from that of the House of Commons (left). Note how the Canadian system includes a clear division between government members and members of the opposition. The executive is absent from the American House of Representatives (right), but is present in the "front benches" in the Canadian House of Commons. Do you see any other differences?

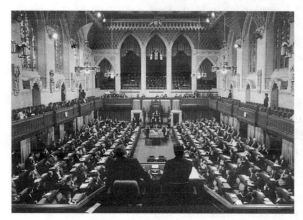 

In a parliamentary system, most of the important bills are drawn up by the Cabinet and are introduced into the House of Commons as "government measures," which means that the executive must resign if they are defeated. In the American government, the president recommends legislation, but Congress does not have to pass it. In fact, each House usually writes its own bills and then holds extensive negotiations with the other before reaching a final agreement.

The legislative branches in both countries consist of two Houses. Unlike the Canadian Senate, which has little power, the American Senate is far more important and in some ways is more powerful than the House of Representatives. This is because it has the right to approve or reject the president's appointments of judges to the Supreme Court, ambassadors to foreign states, and all Cabinet ministers. Treaties made by the president with other countries must also be ratified by a two-thirds majority of the Senate. Each state elects two senators for six-year terms. One-third of the Senate positions come up for re-election every two years.

The Canadian House of Commons is elected for a flexible term of up to five years, while the U.S. House of Representatives is elected for a two-year term. Both lower Houses may initiate bills dealing with money matters. The House of Commons can reverse any executive decision by a simple majority vote and may also remove the Cabinet if it wishes. The House of Representatives, however, in cooperation with the Senate, can override the president's veto if a two-thirds vote of both houses is secured.

Comparing the Canadian and American Judicial Branches

In Canada and the United States, the judicial system is responsible for interpreting and applying the country's laws. Canada has a unitary system of shared courts for both federal and provincial laws. Although the different levels of courts in Canada (superior, county, and district) are created and maintained by the provinces, their judges are appointed by the federal government. Civil laws are primarily governed by the provinces, and criminal laws are controlled by the federal government. The United States has what is known as a dual court system, which includes federal courts for federal laws, and state courts for state laws.

Two additional tiers of courts complete Canada's judicial system. Provincial courts are maintained and staffed by the provincial governments and deal with lesser criminal matters. They are the workhorses of the judicial system and hear 90 percent of the criminal cases in Canada.

In both Canada and the United States, the **Supreme Court** stands at the top of the judicial system. Supreme Court judges in Canada are appointed by the federal government and hold their positions until retirement at age 75. In the United States they are appointed for life by the president, subject to approval by the Senate. As the final courts of appeal, Supreme Courts interpret and clarify the law so it will be uniformly applied across the country. Since 1982, the Supreme Court of Canada has had the power to overrule any government action if it infringes on or denies anyone any of the fundamental rights recognized in the Charter of Rights and Freedoms.

Supreme Court: the highest court of appeal; the final authority in the interpretation of laws.

Case Figure 1.5: Canada's Court System

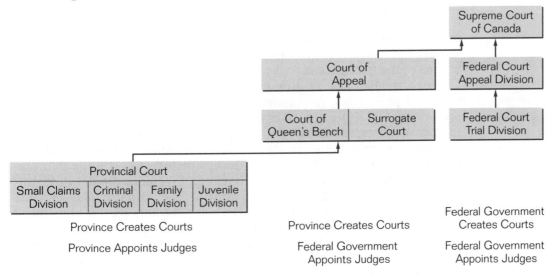

Source: E.L. Morton, ed., *Law, Politics and the Judicial Process in Canada*, 2nd ed. (Calgary: University of Calgary Press, 1992), p. 64.

Case Figure 1.6: The American Court System

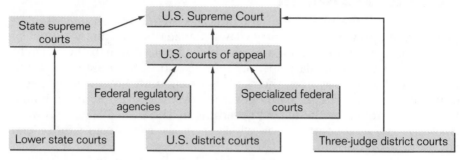

Source: John H. Aldrich, Gary Miller, Charles Ostrom and David Rohde,
American Government: People, Institutions, and Policies.
Copyright © 1986 by Houghton Mifflin Company. Used with permission.

Comparing the Canadian and American Constitutions

Some level of political order and stability is the goal of virtually every society. To achieve this end, modern societies create a fundamental framework of rules and regulations, which are referred to as a constitution. A constitution might be thought of as the frame of the engine of government, or as the rules of the game of politics and government.

Constitutional laws differ from ordinary laws in several ways. First, they "take precedence." If an ordinary law conflicts with a constitutional law, the constitutional law prevails. To ensure that the basic rules of society are protected from the whim of the majority, constitutional laws are usually much more difficult to change than ordinary laws. Finally, constitutions usually include individual human rights, and protect citizens from the arbitrary actions of the government.

The Canadian Constitution is a combination of written and unwritten rules and procedures. For example, neither the Cabinet nor the office of prime minister are mentioned in the British North America Act, now called the Constitution Act of 1867. Formal written documents play a large role in the constitutions of both Canada and the United States. Americans even call their most important constitutional document "The Constitution." It outlines the American system of government and includes the Bill of Rights, which defines the rights of individuals. The Canada Act and the Constitution Acts of 1867 and 1982, the two most important documents of the Canadian Constitution, outline the Canadian system of government. The Constitution Act of 1982 includes an amending formula that enables Canadians to change their Constitution. The Charter of Rights and Freedoms defines the democratic, mobility, legal, equality, and language rights to which Canadians are entitled.

Although many similarities exist between the constitutions of Canada and the United States, there are important differences. The U.S. Constitution reserves for the states all powers not directly assigned to the federal government, whereas the Canadian Constitution gives these powers, called "residual powers," to the federal government. Also, unlike in the United States, criminal law became a federal responsibility in Canada.

Nevertheless, most commentators conclude that the Canadian Constitution is becoming more like the American. The Charter of Rights and Freedoms is an example. Although the Charter contains distinctly non-American elements such as the notwithstanding clause, which allows governments to disregard the Charter in particular instances, it also contains language similar to that of the U.S. Bill of Rights. Because the Charter now takes precedence over ordinary legislation, the role of the Supreme Court of Canada in interpreting the Charter has become crucial, just as it is in the United States.

Case Table 1.1: Comparing the Canadian and American Systems

	Canada	United States
Government system	• Parliamentary or constitutional monarchy • Federal • Responsible (executive part of legislature)	• Presidential or congressional • Republic • Federal • Separation of powers with checks and balances
Head of state	• Governor general	• President
Head of government	• Prime minister – Member of Parliament – Leader of party that controls the majority of seats – May be re-elected indefinitely – Selects Cabinet – Must resign if he or she loses support of House of Commons	• President – Not member of Congress – Selected by presidential election – May be re-elected once – Selects Cabinet – Retains position even when he or she loses congressional support
Time of elections	• Within 5 years	• Set terms from 2 to 6 years
Executive	• Responsible to legislature (Parliament)	• Not responsible to legislature (Congress)
Cabinet	• Appointed by prime minister from among members of legislature	• Appointed by president • Not members of Congress
Bills	• Passed by majority in House of Commons and Senate	• Passed by majority in Congress and must be signed by president
Constitution	• Written and unwritten	• Written

Strengths and Weaknesses of the Two Systems

In Canada, amendments can be made to bills only if they are directly related to the subject of the proposed legislation. By contrast, in the American Congress all kinds of additions are made to a bill in order to obtain enough votes for passage. A proposal for gun control legislation, for example, might have amendments tacked on relating to taxation, pig farming, and credit card controls. Case Figures 1.2 and 1.3 illustrated the sometimes tortuous route a bill must take before becoming law in both countries.

The Canadian principle of responsible government involves cooperation between the legislature and the executive, but can lead to successive changes in government and instability. This is particularly true for a minority government. Critics also claim that the need for party discipline and the dominance of the House of Commons has made the Cabinet much too powerful. In fact, as noted earlier, non-confidence motions have overturned the national government only three times in Canadian history.

In the United States, the staggered terms of office tend to reduce popular control of elected officials. House members serve for two years, the president for four years, and senators for six years. It thus takes at least six years to completely change the government. The fact that these terms of office are fixed and almost unchangeable further reduces the electorate's control over the government. Direct control is limited to election day. As a result, the government does not change suddenly during times of crisis. Whereas some people consider this stability an advantage, critics argue that it fosters an unresponsive government.

Another possible problem in U.S. government is the checks and balances system. Although it prevents one government body from becoming too powerful, it can also lead to political deadlock when the president's political party does not control the Congress. In 1995, for example, many civil servants were put out of work temporarily and some government departments were shut down when the Congress and the president could not agree on government policies. If the Democratic and Republican parties are divided along ideological lines, then the possibility exists for long-term instability. In addition, since the legislature cannot topple the executive by a vote of non-confidence, there is no need for party solidarity, and no reason for the president's fellow party members to support the executive's proposed bills. Although this freedom allows elected representatives to vote according to their conscience or their constituents' wishes, it means that to secure enough votes for a bill to pass Congress many compromises must be made.

Some political scientists rate the Canadian system as more democratic and the American system as more liberal. By more democratic, they mean that the parliamentary system more effectively expresses the will of the majority. By more liberal, they mean that it is difficult for one group of people to control the government.

Focus

Which system of government do you think is more democratic? Why?

BIOGRAPHY

BERTHA WILSON, 1923–

In a 1990 speech Bertha Wilson, the first woman appointed to Canada's Supreme Court, highlighted two central concerns: the question of the role of the judiciary in promoting justice and social change in Canada, and the issue of gender bias in Canada's legal system.

Born and educated in Scotland, Wilson and her husband emigrated to Canada, where she earned a law degree in 1958. After serving as a partner and research director of a large law firm, she became the first woman named to a provincial supreme court with her appointment to the Ontario Court of Appeal in 1975.

Wilson's appointment to the Supreme Court in 1982 coincided with a substantial increase in the power of the judiciary with the passage of the Charter of Rights and Freedoms as part of the Constitution in that year. The effect was to make judges the "watchdogs of Parliament"; the Supreme Court had the final say on whether laws violated the constitution, and could strike down legislation or invalidate government actions if they went against the Charter. A dramatic example was the Abortion Ruling of 1988, in which the Supreme Court declared Canada's abortion law unconstitutional. Bertha Wilson was at the centre of the issues and was "not afraid to innovate." She played a central role in the Supreme Court for nearly a decade, and became known as "the most activist judge on the high court."

A "moderate feminist," Wilson has been a strong advocate of human rights and has stirred some controversy. Her statements on gender bias in the legal system (see opposite) prompted the conservative women's organization, REAL Women, to call for her removal from the Supreme Court, but a judicial council found no basis for the charge. Wilson has said that she has no patience with people who demand that she use her position to advance women's rights: "If I displayed bias, it would make me totally useless as a judge."[2]

Described as a "genuinely private person" (she had never given an interview before 1985), she has become increasingly outspoken and involved in issues since her retirement. Her actions are reflected in newspaper headlines: "Ex-judge favors Natives' own legal system" (1992); "Ex-justice urges women to fight for rights" (1993); "Retired judge not retiring type in battle against bias in legal system" (1994).

Wilson's views are reflected in the following excerpts from a 1990 speech:

In my view there are probably whole areas of the law on which there is no uniquely feminine perspective. … In some other areas of the law, however, I think that a distinctly male perspective is clearly discernible and has resulted in legal principles that are not fundamentally sound. … Some aspects of the criminal law in particular cry out for change since they are based on presuppositions about the nature of women and women's sexuality that in this day and age are little short of ludicrous. …

If women lawyers and women judges through their differing perspectives on life can bring a new humanity to bear on the decision-making process, perhaps they will succeed in infusing the law with an understanding of what it means to be fully human.[3]

---

1 Why does Bertha Wilson maintain that a woman's perspective is essential in Canada's justice system?

2 To what extent should the courts be involved in promoting "justice and social change" in Canada?

Underlying and Emerging Issues

Give the reasoning and evidence that might be used to support different views or conclusions on the following issues.

1 How should governments deal with the problem of differences among regions?

2 Should Canada change the present division of power between the federal and provincial governments?

3 How can constituents ensure the accountability of elected officials?

4 Should the executive be responsible to, or separate from, the legislature?

5 To what degree do political parties enhance or undermine the principles of democracy?

6 What are the best ways to avoid too much power being concentrated in too few hands?

7 To what degree do our governments listen to the people?

8 Is it more important to have efficiency and effectiveness in government, or to limit the power of government?

9 How important is it to have stability in government?

10 Do we have enough protection for individual rights?

11 Is the emphasis on individual rights undermining the unity of society?

Focussing Knowledge

In your notes, clearly identify or define and explain the importance or significance of each of the following:

parliamentary monarchy	Senate
republic	Goods and Services Tax (GST)
bicameral legislature	separation of powers
unitary system	checks and balances
federal system	Supreme Court
constitution	Congress
House of Commons	House of Representatives
Parliament	government measure
minority government	notwithstanding clause
coalition government	residual powers
Cabinet	Preston Manning
responsible government	Bertha Wilson

Reviewing and Organizing Knowledge

1 What factors account for the different length of terms for elected officials in Canada and the United States?

2 a. In a federal system, what is the usual basis for dividing power between the central and regional governments?

b. Why have some countries chosen a federal system?

c. Why do countries with federal systems usually have bicameral legislatures?

3 Define the relationship between the executive and the legislature.

4 a. How does responsible government allow the legislature to control the executive in Canada?

b. How is responsible government tied to the operation of political parties?

c. Where do Members of Parliament have the chance to influence government bills and policies?

5 What are the main issues in the question of Senate reform in Canada?

6 a. How does the U.S. system of separation of powers and checks and balances prevent individuals or groups from becoming too powerful?

b. What are the main differences in executive power between Canada and the United States?

c. How do the Canadian and U.S. systems differ with respect to the head of state and the head of government?

7 How do the Canadian and U.S. legislatures differ in principle?

8 a. What are the major differences between the judiciaries in Canada and the United States?

b. How is the U.S. Supreme Court similar to Canada's?

9 a. How does a constitution differ from "ordinary law"?

b. What are the key differences between the constitutions of Canada and the United States?

10 How does the U.S. system of checks and balances take some power away from each of the three branches of government?

11 What are the advantages and disadvantages of the Canadian and American systems of government?

Applying and Extending Knowledge

1 In two columns, list the similarities and differences between the Canadian and American systems of government. When you have finished, rate each item on a scale of 1 to 5 (where 1 is "not important" and 5 is "very important"). Use this analysis as a basis for a paper describing the similarities and differences between the two systems.

2 In 1996, Israel moved to a direct election of its prime minister as well as the legislature. If Canada were to adopt this approach, how would it affect the rest of our system? What other changes would be necessary? What would be the advantages and the disadvantages?

3 Which aspects of the U.S. system would you like to see adopted in Canada? Why? What would be the trade-offs, costs, and benefits?

4 Which aspects of the Canadian system do you think Americans should adopt? Why?

5 Select one of the Underlying and Emerging Issues on page 70. Research the issue in the context of Canada's present situation, then take a position and defend it.

6 Choose several newspaper articles that illustrate differences between the Canadian and American systems. Explain how the articles illustrate the differences.

7 Find newspaper articles that illustrate problems in the Canadian or American political systems; explain how the articles illustrate these problems.

Democracy in Sweden

*S*WEDEN'S POLITICAL PARTIES gain their seats through proportional representation. What are the advantages and the disadvantages of this system? This case study briefly discusses Sweden's political parties and explores the importance of the general consensus that exists in Sweden among the various political parties and non-government organizations. Two opinion pieces comparing the different methods of electing members of Parliament debate the merits of Sweden's system of proportional representation versus Canada's system of single-member constituencies.

In many ways, Sweden's government is similar to Canada's. Both countries are constitutional monarchies in which the monarchs have so little effective power that they perform more of a public relations function than anything else. The effective political power in Sweden lies with the **Riksdag** (Parliament), the prime minister, and the Council of State (Cabinet). In 1971, Sweden abolished its upper house; in most other matters, however, Swedish government functions resemble those of Canada. The prime minister is the leader of the political party that has the support of the majority of the elected members of the Riksdag. The prime minister and the appointed Cabinet can be voted out of office by Parliament, although (as in Canada) party solidarity prevents this from happening very often. Each Cabinet minister is in charge of a separate department, such as finance or national defence, and is responsible for preparing legislation for the approval of the Riksdag. Unlike the American system of separation of powers, the governing political party in Sweden combines both executive and legislative functions.

Learning Outcomes

After reading this case study, you should be able to:

- understand and explain Sweden's system of government
- debate the benefits of the Swedish "politics of compromise"
- differentiate among different methods of electing representatives to Parliament
- evaluate the strengths and weaknesses of proportional representation
- summarize the similarities and differences between the Canadian and Swedish systems of government

Riksdag: the Parliament of Sweden.

Since 1994, general elections in Sweden are held every fourth year on the third Sunday in September. If the government is defeated by a non-confidence vote, another election must be held when the original four-year term expires — even if the deadline is only one year away. At election time, each party provides lists of its candidates for office. Voters select the lists of their choice and place them in the ballot box.

Sweden has eight major political parties. The Social Democratic Labour Party is the largest. It favours social welfare policies and draws most of its support from blue- and white-collar workers. Since 1932, it has been in power, either alone or in coalition with other parties, for all but nine years. The Centre Party, which appeals to farmers, has generally opposed the high taxes needed to fund the country's comprehensive welfare policies (see Case Study 14). The Conservative Party, which was in power from 1991 to 1994, has close ties with big business and with people in upper-income brackets. The Liberal Party is struggling to retain its middle-class support. The Communist Party gets scattered votes from those workers who believe in nationalizing industry and erasing all class differences. Following the collapse of the Soviet Union, support for the Communist Party declined and the party failed to elect any members in 1991. Under Gudrun Schyman (the second female leader of a Swedish party), the Communist Party reorganized itself as the Left Party and won over 6 percent of the popular vote in 1994. The Green Party, formed in 1988, attracts voters concerned with industrial pollution and other environmental problems. The New Democracy Party represents the far right of the political spectrum.

Politics of Consent

Despite the number of political parties and their differences, political discussions and parliamentary debates lack the fire and the conflict of Canadian or American politics. The 1994 election is a good example. Several major issues had the potential for confrontation: the economy was in a major recession, with 14 percent of the population unemployed; in addition, Sweden was scheduled to hold a referendum in November on whether to join the European Union, which some observers termed one of Sweden's greatest decisions of the twentieth century. Despite the important nature of these issues, the *Scandinavian Review* reported that the election was "a relatively undramatic affair,"[1] and the Social Democratic Labour Party under Ingvar Carlsson returned to office after a three-year absence.

Unlike in Canada, where political parties are usually reluctant to work together, in Sweden opposition parties do not oppose the government as much as they negotiate, bargain, and compromise with it. The Social Democratic Labour Party held power continuously from 1932 to 1976, yet only twice did it have a majority of the seats in the Riksdag. All members of the Riksdag, even those in opposition, can introduce a bill that requires government action. Trained specialists within the civil service are then assigned the task of researching and designing needed legislation. Part of this research involves consulting with all the groups that might be affected by the legislation. The final draft is submitted to these groups for their comments, and then the draft and the comments proceed to the Riksdag for discussion.

Parliament itself consists of a combination of interest groups. Most of the important labour leaders, businesspeople, and representatives from other important segments in society are elected to the Riksdag. This multi-level office-holding blurs the distinction between public and private interests in Sweden and provides another check on unpopular legislation. In Sweden, politics are thought of in terms of cooperation rather than conflict. Since the largest political party rarely wins a majority of the seats in Parliament, it usually rules by forming a coalition with one or more parties to fashion a majority.

···Different Methods of Electing MPs

All modern democracies are representative democracies in which the elected politicians make decisions on behalf of the people. Most democracies divide their country into geographic areas, called **constituencies** (ridings or electoral districts), in order to elect representatives to Parliament.* How these politicians are elected varies from country to country. "Anglo-American" democracies such as Canada, the United Kingdom, New Zealand, and the United States use the simplest system: in each constituency, the candidate who receives the most votes is elected. These countries all have **single-member constituencies** in which each riding elects only one person to represent the citizens in that particular geographic area. The winning candidate is the person who receives the largest number of votes. When three or more candidates compete in the same constituency, the successful person often receives less than a majority of the votes.

Australia uses a slightly different system. There, the voters rank the candidates in their constituency in order of preference (they place a "1" beside their favourite candidate, a "2" beside their second choice, and so on). If no candidate receives a majority of first-place votes, the person with the lowest number of ballots is eliminated and his or her ballots are distributed among those candidates who placed second on the ballots. This continues until one candidate has a majority. This method was also used in provincial elections in British Columbia in 1952–53.

France and Russia use a **run-off system**. If no candidate receives a majority of the votes, all but the top two vote-getters are dropped from the ballot, and another election is held a week or two later. As a result, the winning candidate is ensured of receiving a majority of the ballots cast.

Other countries, such as Sweden, Germany, Austria, the Netherlands, Denmark, Norway, and Israel use some form of **proportional representation** to determine who is elected. In its simplest form, citizens vote for political parties rather than for individuals. Seats are given to each party in proportion to their share of the popular vote. If the party earns 40 percent of

Focus

What do you see as the primary differences between how interest groups operate in Sweden and how they operate in Canada?

constituency: an electoral district used to elect members to Parliament.

single-member constituency: an electoral district in which one person is elected to represent the citizens of that district.

run-off system: an election system in which, if no candidate receives a majority of the votes, the top vote-getters are placed on another ballot and a second election is held to determine the majority winner.

proportional representation: a political system under which parties gain their seats in the legislature based on the percentage of votes they receive in an election.

* Ideally, each constituency contains an equal number of people. This is called representation by population — each member of Parliament "represents" the wishes of an equal number of people.

the ballots cast, it receives 40 percent of the seats in Parliament. Before the election, each party publishes a list of candidates in order of preference, and if a party receives 20 seats, for example, the top 20 names on the list are elected.

In Japan, most constituencies elect from two to six representatives, and the maximum number of candidates that each party may run in each constituency cannot exceed the number of members who can be elected. Since each person can vote for only one candidate, the Japanese electoral system sometimes encourages competition among members of the same party. The candidates with the most popular support are successful. For instance, in a five-member constituency, the five individuals with the most votes are elected members of Parliament.

multi-member constituency: a political subdivision from which more than one person is elected.

In Ireland, which also has **multi-member constituencies** (more than one candidate is elected from each riding), the voters rank the people running for office in order of preference. Candidates who are the first choice of only a few electors may still be able to gain a seat in Parliament if they are ranked second or third by a sizable portion of the constituency's voters. In the late nineteenth century, several Canadian cities had dual-member constituencies, in which one riding elected two Members of Parliament. Voters in Hamilton and Ottawa, for example, cast their ballots for two candidates.

Which is the better system — proportional representation or single-member constituencies? There is no easy answer. Your choice will depend upon your values, goals, and knowledge. The following sections clarify the debate over the merits of proportional representation versus single-member constituencies by giving the arguments on both sides.

Advantages of Proportional Representation: An Argument

Single-member constituencies, like those in Canada, can create parliaments that do not accurately reflect the nationwide strength of each party. As Case Table 2.1 illustrates, each party's popular vote does not match its number of seats. In addition, the party with the most votes receives more seats than its support warrants. This phenomenon results from the **first-past-the-post** voting.

first-past-the-post: selection of the winning candidate by the largest number of votes (not necessarily a majority).

Case Table 2.1: Canadian Federal Election Results, 1974–1988*

Year	Conservative Party		Liberal Party		New Democratic Party	
	% Seats	% Vote	% Seats	% Vote	% Seats	% Vote
1974	36	35	53	43	6	15
1979	48	36	40	40	9	18
1980	37	33	52	44	11	20
1984	75	50	14	28	11	19
1988	57	43	28	32	15	20

* Because of rounding and other political parties, the numbers do not total 100 percent.

Because single-member constituencies force candidates to win the single largest number of votes cast in order to get elected, political parties are discouraged from directing their appeal at a narrow segment of the electorate (such as senior citizens, farmers, schoolteachers, or Quakers, for example). Only when that segment is concentrated in a particular region would this strategy be successful. Proportional representation, whereby a party receives the same proportion of the seats in government as its percentage of the popular vote, allows different sectors and ideas to gain representation in Parliament. In Sweden and Germany, environmentalists can vote for the Green Party, and in Israel, Orthodox Jews have their own party.

In Canada, such parties would never elect a candidate, although they might receive a relatively sizable percentage of the popular vote. As Case Table 2.1 indicates, third parties such as the NDP generally receive fewer seats than their popularity warrants. In 1993, NDP candidates captured 7 percent of the total votes cast but won only 3 percent of the seats (nine MPs). The Progressive Conservative Party, which was reduced to third-party status in this election, won 16 percent of the vote, but elected only two candidates (0.6 percent). In contrast, political parties whose strength is concentrated in particular sections of the country often elect more members to Parliament than their percentage of the popular vote warrants. In 1993, for example, the Bloc Québécois elected 18 percent of Canada's MPs (all 54 members were elected in Quebec) with only 13 percent of the popular vote.

The winner-take-all system that is used in Canada can lead to some very

Voting in Provincial Elections

The first-past-the-post system also exists in Canadian provincial elections. In 1935, for example, the Liberal Party of Prince Edward Island captured all 35 seats. In New Brunswick, the Liberal Party under Frank McKenna had similar success in 1987, winning all 58 seats. In 1996, Gordon Campbell's Liberal Party in British Columbia won more votes than Glen Clark's New Democratic Party (42 compared with 39 percent), but ended up in second place (33 compared with 39 seats).

Alberta has had one of the most diverse voting systems. In 1909, the province employed the single-member constituency system everywhere but in Calgary and Edmonton. Each voter in these cities cast two votes to elect two members from each area. In 1913, only Edmonton kept this dual-member voting system. Eight years later, Calgary and Edmonton each elected five members, and Medicine Hat elected two members to the provincial legislature. The voters in these three cities cast as many ballots as there were members to be elected.

From 1926 to 1959, Calgary and Edmonton had several multi-member constituencies that varied in size from five to seven members. Instead of selecting the candidates who won the most votes (as had been the situation earlier), a variation of Sweden's system of proportional representation was used to determine the winners. The voters in the single-member constituencies in the rest of the province ranked the candidates in their ridings in order of preference. If no individual received a majority of first-preference votes, the person with the lowest number of ballots was eliminated and his or her ballots were distributed among those candidates who had placed second. This process continued until one candidate had a majority. In 1959, Alberta adopted the single-member constituency system it had used from 1905 to 1909.

strange results. Examine the election results in Case Table 2.2 for two different Alberta constituencies in the 1993 federal election. Candidates Bethel and Ramsay were both elected, although in Edmonton East, only one-third of the voters cast their ballots for Bethel. Many more people did not want Bethel as their representative than wanted her. Robertson received a mere 115 votes fewer than the winning candidate, yet she will have no official say in government policies. In addition, the majority of the people in the constituency will be represented in Ottawa by a person for whom they did not vote. Some hold the view that it is only because the single-member constituency favours the major parties that no changes have been made.

Case Table 2.2: 1993 Election Results

Edmonton East Riding				Crowfoot Riding		
Candidate	No. of votes	% of votes		Candidate	No. of votes	% of votes
Bethel, Judy (L)	11 922	32.96		Ramsay, Jack (R)	23 611	65.98
Robertson, Linda (R)	11 807	32.64		Heidecker, Brian (C)	6 431	17.97
Harvey, Ross (N)	7 976	22.05		Sandford, Darryl (L)	4 506	12.59
Kovacs, Kevin (C)	2 672	7.39		Wilting, Berend (N)	860	2.40
Musson, Jim (NA)	1 049	2.90		Two others	377	1.01
Five others	745	2.05				

L—Liberal Party, R—Reform Party, N—New Democratic Party, C—Progressive Conservative Party, NA—National Party

Proportional representation is often criticized for creating minority governments. It should be noted, however, that in the 13 Canadian federal elections held between 1957 and 1993, only six minority governments were elected. To the complaints that the large number of parties lead to numerous elections and ever-changing governments, it should be remembered that Sweden, Austria, Germany, and the Netherlands have had very stable governments.

GETTING WHAT YOU VOTE FOR

In the 1979 and 1980 federal elections, the Liberal Party won almost no seats in the West and the Progressive Conservative Party elected very few candidates in Quebec. Since political parties are supposed to bridge the gap between regional differences and provide a forum for representatives from all over Canada to resolve regional problems, this situation disturbed many people. A closer examination, however, revealed that each party had received considerable support from every part of Canada. The problem seemed to lie with the first-past-the-post electoral system. The results of the 1993 election, which saw the emergence of political parties that were based on regional support, sparked similar complaints about Canada's electoral system. The following excerpt from political scientist John Hiemstra was in response to the question: "Should a system of proportional representation be adopted in Canada?"

In contrast to FPTP [first-past-the-post], a PR [proportional representation] electoral system would strengthen Canada's political system by encouraging a new dynamic. PR would continue to rely on political parties and party discipline, but would force parties to define how they are distinct from the others in order to attract votes. Parties would be encouraged to develop clearer principles and to define their policy platforms. This would allow political parties to become vehicles for voters to give mandates to MPs and to hold them accountable between elections. MPs would clearly be obliged to act in accordance with the principles and policies that they agreed to with their supporters. This would include serving the individual voters according to these principles, if the parties want to maintain electoral support. MPs with a sense of obligation to voters would be a clear advance over FPTP, which limits voters to rubber stamping or jettisoning representatives at election time.

While PR would encourage a sense of obligation between representatives and their supporters, it would not guarantee this outcome. ... [PR] has increased the parliamentary representation of women, ethnic groups, and cultural minorities. ... PR has also allowed parties to increase the overall quality of individual MPs on their lists. ...

PR allows parties and governments to be as good or as flawed as the people they represent. It leaves the public free to decide which groups or principles or approaches they want represented, by creating parties to reflect these concerns. PR ultimately leaves the voters to decide which parties they want to be represented by in the House of Commons. For example, if 7 percent of Canadians support the Green Party's approach to environmental issues, PR will give that party 7 percent of the seats, no more and no less.[2]

Focus

How would you rebut each of Hiemstra's arguments?

In the 1993 federal election in Canada, more than 20 political parties fielded candidates and 5 elected at least one member, yet the Liberal Party easily formed a majority government. Is it not better that parties represent specific ideological positions that the voters can distinguish than be faced with the task of voting for parties that seem to represent nothing or everything? Both theory and experience suggest that the closer a party gets to holding power, the more moderate it becomes. The next section explains how proportional representation operates in Sweden.

The Swedish System of Proportional Representation

In Sweden, each constituency is allotted several seats and voters cast their ballots for the political party (not the candidate) of their choice. Within every electoral district, the parties may nominate as many candidates as the number of seats in the riding. The party ranks these representatives in order of preference. If the party wins three seats, then the first three names on its list of candidates are elected to the Riksdag. These seats are won according to the proportion (percentage) of the vote received by the parties per constituency. In this way, 310 members are elected from the individual constituencies to Parliament.

Another 39 seats are distributed on the basis of each party's share of the total votes cast nationally. This compensates for any differences between the percentage of seats held by the parties and their general popularity. To prevent too many smaller political parties from participating, each party must obtain at least 12 percent of the total vote in a single riding, or 4 percent of the nation-wide vote, to obtain representation in the Riksdag. In 1991, for example, both the Green Party and the Communist Party were shut out of the Riksdag because they received less than 4 percent of the vote. In 1994, the New Democracy Party failed to win enough votes to elect any of its candidates. Without proportional representation, such parties would not exist, and the electorate would have fewer choices.

Advantages of Single-Member Constituencies: An Argument

In Sweden, citizens vote for political parties rather than for individuals. Proportional representation allows the political party to exert more control over its members than is possible in a single-member constituency. The candidates are usually chosen by party officials. If the candidates do not "toe the line," they might be listed at the bottom of the slate of candidates, thereby virtually ending all chances of election. In this system, according to its critics, there is not much of a connection between the constituency and individual MPs, and there is thus no incentive for elected members to build up a personal following by their actions in favour of the riding.

If the Swedish system is so good, its critics ask, why did a government decide to allow voters to state their preference for individual candidates, rather than the party, beginning in 1998? As the following official explanation illustrates, proportional representation can also be very difficult to understand.

Seats are distributed between parties by the "odd-figure" transferrable vote method, with the first divisor set at 1.4. Under this method a seat is awarded, in a certain order of preference, to the party with the highest comparative ratio in each round. The first comparative ratio is the number of votes divided by 1.4. Having the first divisor greater than 1 makes it more difficult for a party to gain its first seat. This, therefore, can be termed a bar to small parties. The subsequent comparative ratios are obtained by dividing the number of votes won by a party with the figure corresponding to twice the number of seats allotted to that party plus 1 — that is, 3, 5, 7 and so on. This method is used when allocating both the fixed constituency mandates and the equalising seats. Where the latter are concerned, however, a modification comes into play whereby, in a constituency where the party has not been allotted a fixed constituency mandate, the comparative ratio in connection with the first equalising seat equals the number of votes polled by the party. In other words, an odd-figure method is used. This reduces the risk of a party being completely unrepresented in a constituency.[3]

Countries with single-member constituencies, such as Canada and the United States, generally produce stable majority governments with only a few political parties. However, countries with proportional representation, such as Italy and Belgium, have so many parties that the government seldom lasts longer than one year. This makes long-term planning almost impossible. The advantage of the first-past-the-post system is that it usually guarantees that one party will have a majority.

Case Table 2.3: Results of the 1994 Election in Sweden

Party	% of vote	No. of seats	% of seats
Social Democratic Labour Party	45.3	162	46.4
Conservative Party	22.4	80	22.9
Centre Party	7.7	27	7.7
Liberal Party	7.2	26	7.4
Left (Communist) Party	6.2	22	6.3
Green Party	5.0	18	5.2
Christian Democratic Party	4.1	14	4.0
New Democracy Party	1.2	0	0

The problem with minority governments is that following an election, a coalition has to be formed. An examination of Case Table 2.3 shows seven different combinations of parties that could be made to form a government (50 percent of votes or more). It is possible to make up a ruling coalition even without the Social Democratic Labour Party. More distressing is the possibility that the party one votes for might join a coalition with a party one detests. Because such coalitions may consist of people who have very different ideologies, there is a greater likelihood of paralyzed decision-making and frequent elections.

Opponents of proportional representation feel that it encourages the creation of numerous minor parties that represent narrow interests and undermine the development of broadly based national parties that attempt to bridge sectional rivalries and differences. It also fosters parties on the extreme ends of the ideological scale and enables such parties to share in power. A single-member constituency system is the best way to ensure stable government according to the advocates of this approach.

BIOGRAPHY

ALVA MYRDAL, 1902–1986

Alva Myrdal was a Swedish sociologist, diplomat, Cabinet minister, and leader in the international movement for nuclear disarmament. In 1982, at the age of 80, she was named co-winner of the Nobel Peace Prize in recognition of her two decades of work in United Nations disarmament negotiations and for influencing international opinion through her writings and speeches.

As a child in Stockholm and later on a farm outside the city, Myrdal had strong ambitions and longed for a good education. However, only boys were admitted to the public high school. Fortunately, her father was sympathetic to her goals and formed a little study group using the curriculum of the boys' school. This was all Myrdal needed to set her on the path of higher education, and she never looked back.

A deep humanitarian interest was evident in every stage of Myrdal's diverse career. At first, she studied religious and literary history at the University of Stockholm, and led study circles in the Workers Education Association. This led to studies in psychology and pedagogy in London and Leipzig, where she became intensely interested in education and child welfare. She founded a Training College for Pre-school Teachers in 1936 and promoted many reforms and novel ideas, such as the creation of "adventure playgrounds."

Myrdal was 15 when she met her future husband, Gunnar. The attraction was immediate, and they were married just before her graduation from the University of Stockholm. They had three children, and their remarkable partnership of mutual respect and love continued to the end of their lives. Gunnar himself became a successful and influential economist who also won a Nobel Prize in 1974. They are the only husband and wife to have both won the prize in completely independent fields.

In 1934, the public was shocked by the publication of the Myrdals' book, *Crisis in the Population Question*, because of its daring proposals for voluntary parenthood, sex education, contraception, abortion, generous maternity benefits, free school lunches, and rent subsidies for large families. These ideas were to have a profound effect on the shaping of Sweden's new social policy. (See Case Study 14.)

Alva Myrdal was also a leader in the movement for political and economic equality for women. She was secretary of the Government Commission on Women's Rights from 1935 to 1938, edited a monthly magazine for women, and served as the president of the Swedish Federation of Business Women. Her commitment to sexual equality was a consistent focus throughout her life not only in the public realm, but also in her personal life as she struggled to combine motherhood and a career.

During World War II, Sweden remained neutral. However, the Myrdals worked with an international group of Social Democrats, assisting refugees from Fascist Europe who were living in Sweden. Countless hours of study and discussion were conducted in the Myrdals' living room with this circle of intellectuals, many of whom later became important in the postwar economic and cultural reconstruction of Europe. For example, Willy Brandt, who later became Chancellor of Germany, and Bruno Kreisky, later Chancellor of Austria, were in this group.

Alva Myrdal served on some important government commissions during the war as well, which made her a prime candidate, in 1949, for a job with the United Nations as principal director of the Department of Social Affairs. This was the highest position of any woman at the UN. After a stint with UNESCO (the United Nations Educational, Social and Cultural Organization) in Paris, she made another career shift, this time to diplomacy, when she became ambassador to India from 1955 to 1961.

Myrdal's work for peace and disarmament began in 1961 when she became Sweden's chief delegate to the disarmament conferences in Geneva. She founded the Stockholm International Peace Research Institute in 1964, was elected to Parliament, and was named minister in charge of disarmament in 1966. Sweden's formal renunciation of nuclear, chemical, and biological weapons was largely due to her enormous influence.

Though she retired from government at the age of 71, Myrdal continued to write and lecture in Europe and America, tirelessly campaigning for peace. Her best-known book, *The Game of Disarmament*, was published in 1977 and provided the theme of her acceptance speech for the Nobel Peace Prize in 1982. The advice she offered the world in that book reflects her own approach to life: "It is not worthy of mankind to give up. We win nothing by doing only wishful thinking. There is always something one can do!"[4]

Alva Myrdal fell ill with heart disease in 1984 and died two years later. Her daughter, Sissela Bok, is now a noted philosopher teaching at Brandeis University in the United States. In her biography of her mother she writes

Alva and Gunnar made clear that it was possible to come to grips with world problems, that one ought to have the courage to speak out critically when the need arose, and that boundaries — national, ethnic, professional, and most others — were there to be crossed. ...

To grow up in a home where the adults truly felt the full attraction of the Enlightenment ideals of reason and human potential could give a nearly dizzying sense of the depth and the scope one can experience if only one dares to think freely.[5]

---

1 How do Alva Myrdal's experiences reflect important aspects of Sweden's approach to government?

2 What are the consistent principles or themes that underlie the wide range of Alva Myrdal's actions?

Underlying and Emerging Issues

Give the reasoning and evidence that might be used to support different views or conclusions on the following issues.

1 Are the principles of democracy threatened by "first-past-the-post" elections?

2 Should representatives represent *all* of their constituents — even those who voted against them?

3 How important is it that a party's popular vote correspond to its number of representatives?

4 Is it more important to vote for the individual representative, the party, or the leader?

5 What system of representation best balances majority rule and minority rights?

6 What is the most effective way to ensure that minority opinions and groups are represented in legislatures?

7 Should political parties try to represent particular interests and positions, or should they try to appeal to a wide variety of groups?

8 Is it more important to have stability in government, or more effective representation?

9 Should Canada adopt a system of proportional representation?

Focussing Knowledge

In your notes, clearly identify or define and explain the importance or significance of each of the following:

Riksdag	*proportional representation*
Social Democratic Labour Party	*multi-member constituency*
constituency	*first-past-the-post*
single-member constituency	*preferential ballot*
run-off system	*Alva Myrdal*

Reviewing and Organizing Knowledge

1 a. In what general ways is Sweden's government similar to that of Canada?

b. Describe the main features of Sweden's democratic system.

2 What are the problems with the first-past-the-post system?

3 What approaches have been tried as alternatives to first-past-the-post and single-member constituency systems?

4 What are the main features of Sweden's system of proportional representation?

5 What are the main arguments in favour of Sweden's proportional representation?

6 What are the main arguments against Sweden's system of representation?

Applying and Extending Knowledge

1 Research the experience of one or more countries that have used a form of proportional representation (for example, Germany, Austria, the Netherlands, Denmark, Norway, Israel). How is it similar to or different from Sweden's approach? What positive and negative features emerge?

2 Research France's run-off system and Australia's preferential approach. What are the advantages and disadvantages of each?

3 Make two lists, one for everything that Canada would gain by adopting proportional representation, and a second for everything that Canada would lose. Rank each item in terms of its importance on a scale from 1 to 5 (where 5 indicates "very important"). What do your lists and rankings suggest about what position you would favour on the issue?

4 Identify the questions that you would need answered before you could come to a conclusion about proportional representation. Devise a research plan for answering the questions.

5 Write a letter to your Member of Parliament in which you outline your conclusions on issues related to proportional representation.

The Role of Political Parties in a Democracy

Learning Outcomes

After reading this case study, you should be able to:

- debate the ideal number of political parties

- discuss the strengths and weaknesses of the Canadian party system

- outline the functions of political parties

- evaluate the extent to which Canada's political parties are accountable to the people for their actions

- explain the origins of political parties in Canada

- discuss the importance of third parties

- understand the differences among Canada's political parties

*H*OW DID CANADA'S POLITICAL PARTIES evolve and how powerful are they? This case study discusses the strengths and weaknesses of one-party, two-party, and multi-party systems and considers which method provides the greatest degree of accountability to the electorate. It also analyzes the functions, strengths, and weaknesses of the Canadian political party system.

Democracy was defined earlier as a political system in which there is free and open competition for power among various individuals and groups, with a significant degree of accountability to the people by those who hold formal positions of power. This case study examines the extent to which Canada's political parties are accountable to the people for their actions.

Definition and Origin

A political party is composed of people with similar beliefs who have united to accomplish specific goals. To achieve these goals, the party attempts to elect sufficient members to public office to gain control of the government.

Although it is difficult for us to imagine democratic politics without organized political parties, they are essentially a modern phenomenon. Parties existed in Great Britain as early as the eighteenth century, but organized political parties were not fully established there until the early nineteenth century. The first Canadian political parties began to emerge in central Canada in the 1820s and 1830s, but since the governor and his appointed councils did not have to obey the wishes of the people's elected representatives, organized political parties did not emerge until after responsible government was granted in the 1840s.

Responsible government required the governor to sign bills passed by the people's elected representatives. Political parties emerged to ensure that the people's wishes were presented to the governor. However, party ties remained loose for another half-century, and politicians freely switched parties from issue to issue. The secret ballot was not adopted until 1874, and simultaneous balloting was not completely established until 1908. With open balloting and non-simultaneous elections, candidates did not need to commit themselves to a party until it became evident who would win. Before the western provinces went to the polls, for example, they usually knew which party would win the election. To assure themselves of some influence in the government, they often voted for this party.

Until the beginning of the twentieth century, candidates often knew all the voters personally. Because the population was small, they could canvass the people without outside help. As a result, they had less need for the support of a party. All this was changed with the extension of the franchise to women and poor people in the early twentieth century.

At Confederation, each MP represented approximately 750 voters; 130 years later, the average MP represents approximately 95 000 citizens. Candidates can no longer canvass more than a small proportion of the people, yet the votes of these citizens are necessary for victory. The obvious solution is to rely upon a party to supply scores of tireless workers, campaign literature, and media coverage.

Another reason for the growing reliance on political parties has been the rise in campaign costs. In the 1993 general election, for example, the parties (and the 2155 candidates) combined spent over $37 million — of which the Conservatives spent $11.4 million, the Liberals $9.9 million, and the NDP

Case Table 3.1: How Much Do Federal Politicians Earn?

Salaries of Federal Political Figures
(as of Sept. 30, 1995)

Governor General	$97 400
Senators $64 400 plus $10 100 tax-free expense allowance and 64 travel points[2] per year	
The following senators receive as extra salary on top of their Senate salaries:	
Leader of the Government	$49 000 plus $2000 car allowance
Leader of the Opposition	$23 800
Speaker of the Senate	$31 000 plus $3000 residence allowance and $1000 car allowance
Deputy Leader of the Government	$14 900
Deputy Leader of the Opposition	$ 9 400
Government Whip	$ 7 500
Opposition Whip	$ 4 800
Members of Parliament $64 400 plus $21 300 tax-free expense allowance[1] and 64 travel points[2] per year.[3]	
The following members of Parliament receive as extra salary on top of their MP salaries:	
Prime Minister	$69 920
Cabinet Ministers	$46 645
Speaker of the House	$49 100
Secretaries of State	$34 984
Deputy Speaker	$25 700
Official Opposition Leader	$49 100
Other Opposition Party Leaders	$29 500
Opposition House Leader	$23 800
Other House Leaders	$10 500
Government and Opposition Whips	$13 200
Other Party Whips	$ 7 500
Government and Opposition Deputy Whips	$ 7 500
Deputy Chairman, Committees of the Whole House	$10 500
Assistant Deputy Chairman, Committees of the Whole House	$10 100
Parliamentary Secretaries	$10 500

(1) 24 MPs representing remote or distant ridings receive $26 200 tax-free expense allowance; 2 MPs representing NWT ridings receive $28 200 tax-free allowance. (2) One travel point represents a first-class return air trip anywhere in Canada and can be used by representatives or their spouses or a designated family member. (3) Members who travel in Canada on official business and are at least 100 km from their principal residences may claim $6000 in food, accommodation, and incidental expenses.

Source: From *The 1996 Canadian Global Almanac* by John Robert Colombo. Reprinted by permission of Macmillan Canada.

Focus

Should professional athletes, musicians, and business executives earn more than the prime minister of Canada?

$7.5 million. Despite laws in this country designed to reduce the amount of money each candidate may spend on election campaigns, the costs of becoming an MP are still beyond the limits of most Canadians. It is the modern political party with its national organization and tireless fundraisers that provides the money needed to get elected. As a result, the political party is usually more powerful than the individual MPs, and wealthy individuals and corporations can wield considerable political power.

Case Figure 3.1: Political Party Election Expenses, 1993

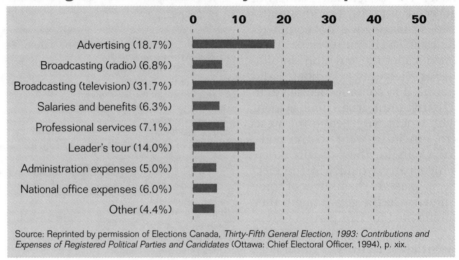

Source: Reprinted by permission of Elections Canada, *Thirty-Fifth General Election, 1993: Contributions and Expenses of Registered Political Parties and Candidates* (Ottawa: Chief Electoral Officer, 1994), p. xix.

One-Party Versus Two-Party Versus Multi-Party Systems

What is the ideal number of political parties needed to ensure the greatest degree of accountability to the people? The three basic types of party systems are one-party (as in Mexico, although several parties contest elections), two-party (as in the United States), and multi-party (as in Italy and Sweden). A possible fourth type of party system, a hybrid, is a combination of two strong parties with one or more weaker, yet still significant, parties (as in Canada prior to the 1993 election).[1]

On the surface, it appears that a **one-party system** is incompatible with democracy because it does not present the electorate with a real choice between candidates or policies. However, such a system can perhaps be called democratic if no one is excluded from membership, if everyone is permitted to express an opinion within the party, and if members are free to organize themselves within the party to push for particular policies.

The supporters of the **two-party system** claim that it is superior to other systems because it presents voters with a definite, clear-cut alternative that allows them to evaluate how well the party of their choice did in carrying out its promises. The counter-argument, however, is that the two-party

one-party system: a system in which only one political party wields all the constitutional power.

two-party system: a system in which two political parties dominate the politics and legislation of a country.

system reduces the alternatives presented to voters. In addition, the two parties tend to become alike on important matters of policy. Let us use the issue of capital punishment as an example. Assume that public opinion is evenly divided between those who support capital punishment and those who oppose it. If one party moderately favours capital punishment (point A in the first diagram), the other party merely has to position itself at point B to attract enough support to win power. Assuming that the first party is willing to modify its beliefs to gain power, it would now move to point C to be successful. Ultimately, the drive to find the middle ground will reduce the differences between the two parties. Supporters of the two-party system claim that this argument is based upon the false assumptions that both parties will do anything to win and that they have no firm, unshakable beliefs of their own. Any party that constantly changed its opinions would soon lose the confidence of the electorate

Opinions on Capital Punishment

Oppose   C   B   A   Support

The same pressures to conform do not operate in a **multi-party system.** As the following diagram illustrates, a move to the right or to the left by any party might result in a loss of part of its original support to one of the other parties. For example, if party C moves to point X, it might steal some of party B's support, but it also runs the risk of losing followers to party D. In a multi-party system, therefore, the parties maintain their distinctiveness, which allows them to present the electorate with a clear choice of policy alternatives.

multi-party system: a system in which more than two parties dominate politics and legislation, usually by means of coalition governments.

Opinions on Capital Punishment

Oppose   A   B   C   D   E   Support
                 ▲   ▲ X ▲   ▲   ▲

The disadvantage of having multiple parties is that one party seldom wins a majority and the government usually consists of a coalition of two or more parties. This makes it less easy for the voters to know which party is responsible for the government's actions. Even if a party is part of the ruling coalition, it can deny responsibility for individual governmental policies. A coalition government may force the parties either to compromise their principles or to withdraw their support, thus causing a series of unstable governments. On the other hand, a coalition usually means that the majority of the electorate voted for its members. In Canada, by contrast, less than 50 percent of the electorate usually votes for the victorious political party.

A hybrid of the two-party and multi-party system is the existence of significant third parties within the two-party system. Third parties arise because one segment of the electorate believes that neither of the two original parties is concerned with its special needs. Certainly, it seems virtually impossible for two political parties to continuously satisfy the varied demands and interests of modern countries, which are often separated by geographic boundaries, language, religion, ethnicity, and conflicting economic interests.

Although third parties strive to win, their significance in the past has been primarily to keep the other two parties "on their toes." They help to bring fresh ideas into politics, and if these ideas prove popular, they are usually adopted by the older parties. For example, near the end of World War II, when the Cooperative Commonwealth Federation (the forerunner of the NDP) began to have political success by promising social welfare policies, the ruling Liberal Party adopted many of the CCF's ideas, including unemployment insurance, to stay in power. In 1926, the Liberal Party established an old age pension program because it needed the support of the Progressive Party to remain in power.

Third parties also allow neglected and frustrated people to vent their grievances and bring their demands to the attention of the country. In 1993, for example, the Reform Party provided a voice for many western Canadians who believed that the federal government was ignoring their interests. Finally, by stirring up popular interest, third parties tend to bring democracy closer to the people. Whereas in the normal course of events the major parties tend to dominate the news, election campaigns expose Canadians to a variety of ideas. In the 1993 election, some Canadians had the opportunity to learn about and to vote for over 20 parties, including the Abolitionist Party, the Green Party, the Libertarian Party, the Marxist-Leninist Party, the Canadian Party for Renewal, the Natural Law Party, the Parti Rhinoceros, the Confederation of Regions Western Party, and the Christian Heritage Party.

Focus

What do you see as the primary importance of third parties?

The Caucus

Once elected, representatives are expected to look after the interests of their constituencies. This includes voting on proposed legislation in Parliament and discussing policies at **caucus** meetings when the elected members of the party gather to discuss strategy. In parliamentary democracies such as Canada and the United Kingdom, the House of Commons is the major democratic agency in the government because it has final say on all laws and can force the executive to resign. It is in this body that the country's different ethnic groups, occupations, and classes are represented. "No Cabinet which keeps in constant touch with this body," argues R.M. Dawson in *The Government of Canada*, "can be very far removed from fluctuations in public opinion, for the House is always acting as an interpreter ... conversely, a Cabinet which grows out of touch with the Commons is courting disaster."

caucus: the plenary (full) meeting of a political party in which party policies are discussed and approved, often by consensus.

Within the governing political party, the caucus provides another forum for individual MPs to exert their influence. At caucus meetings, the party discusses general policies and strategy, and the Cabinet submits its proposed legislation for approval. The meetings are private and the members are expected to express their views without restraint. It is at this time that they are able to modify government policies to reflect the interests of their constituencies. As Canadian Prime Minister William Lyon Mackenzie King told the House of Commons in 1923:

[The caucus] is the means whereby a Government can ascertain through its following what the views and opinions of the public as represented by their various constituencies may be. It is not a means of over-riding Parliament. It is a means of discovering the will of the people through their representatives. ... [The caucus] is simply coming into closer consultation with the people's representatives in a manner that permits of the greatest freedom of expression on their part.

In return for this opportunity to express their feelings, the elected party members agree to accept the decisions of the caucus as final and to support these government measures when they come before the House of Commons for approval.

The Strengths of Political Parties in Canada

Political parties, state their defenders, fulfil a variety of important functions in a democracy. First, they provide a channel of communication between the people and the government. In order to compete for the electorate's support, each party must attempt to discover what the people want, and then try to satisfy these wishes when elected. By offering candidates for re-election, the party provides the people with a way of expressing their opinions and of holding the governing party accountable for its actions.

Second, political parties recruit and train political leaders. Parties interest people in politics, persuade them to accept minor political offices, choose candidates to run for elections, and provide them with financial and organizational support.

Third, political parties organize and educate the public and provide alternative choices for the electorate. In their attempts to win elections, political parties propose a series of social, economic, and political policies — which together make up the **party platform** — designed to gain broad support. The election campaign then attempts to mobilize citizens to vote for these platforms. Between elections, parties keep the electorate informed about government actions — either to gain support for these actions, or to convince the people not to vote for the same government at the next election. Parties that are not in power thus provide a useful check on government actions.

party platform: a plan of action or statement of policies and principles of a political party.

To achieve power in a country such as Canada, a political party must obtain substantial support from a population that is divided by ethnicity, religion, income levels, values, and regional differences. Faced with divisions, a party must be flexible. It must avoid issues that divide the country and soften those that do exist. It is no mere coincidence that two Canadian party leaders with long terms in office — John A. Macdonald and W.L. Mackenzie King — were always willing and able to make concessions, to post-

Focus

How well does the Canadian party system work in practice?

pone contentious decisions, and to bring people of different beliefs together.

Finally, parties provide a method for changing leaders peacefully, and create a forum for dissent. Dissatisfied citizens can attempt to change the direction of government by working for the party of their choice, or even by organizing their own political parties.

Politicians often make promises during an election campaign that they are unable to keep after the election. For example, in the 1993 federal election, Liberal candidate Sheila Copps stated that she would resign her seat in Parliament if her party did not abolish the GST within three years. When this time elapsed and the GST was still in operation, Copps initially argued that she had made the statement in "the heat of battle" and refused to resign. Eventually, public pressure forced Copps to resign her seat in Hamilton and run in a by-election — which she won easily.

...WE'RE SENDING OUT A STRONG MESSAGE...

...ANY ATTEMPTS TO FOLLOW THROUGH ON ELECTION PROMISES WILL NOT BE TOLERATED!!

During what stage in the Copps' resignation issue was this cartoon drawn?

The Weaknesses of Political Parties in Canada

The most sweeping criticism of Canadian political parties concerns their relationship with elected representatives. The first loyalty of the representatives, critics charge, is to the party rather than to the people who elected them. In other words, political parties make government less accountable to the people.

This has arisen, critics argue, because of the rapid growth in the size of the electorate. Because the average MP now represents so many people and requires tens of thousands of dollars to get elected, he or she must rely on a party organization to provide the canvassing and money necessary to run a successful campaign. This has increased party control over candidates who run for political office. A survey of first-term MPs revealed that the vast majority of them believed they would not have been elected had they run as independents. The decision to allow a party to place its name on the ballot opposite its candidate's name has further diminished the chances of independent candidates being elected.

As a result, individual MPs have become increasingly more dependent upon the party and its leader. After an election, say the critics, **party loyalty** becomes a prime political virtue for successful candidates. All members are expected to support their leader, whether or not they agree with the party's policies. Canadian MPs almost never vote against their own party lest they run the risk of being expelled from the party caucus. Occasionally, on controversial issues such as capital punishment and abortion, party solidarity is relaxed so that MPs may vote according to their conscience. In 1996, for example, the government allowed a free vote on its proposed bill to add gay rights to the Human Rights Act after some Liberal MPs expressed concern that the party's position on this issue might put them in conflict with the wishes of their constituents.

Party members have a natural tendency and willingness to accept the control of their leader, whom they selected at a party convention. Sometimes, it is said, the only glue holding a party together is the members' allegiance to the leader. The media has also increasingly concentrated its attention on party leaders, and in many cases, individual members owe their victory directly to their leader's popularity. This serves to reduce members' independence. In addition, a prime minister has at least 100 important positions, such as Cabinet posts, to distribute among the party faithful. An MP who votes contrary to party instructions has little hope of political advancement. As a last resort, the prime minister can withdraw the party's support from a rebellious member. The following article in *The Chronicle-Herald* (Halifax) illustrates this situation:

Rebel MP John Nunziata has been turfed from the Liberal caucus, putting his political future in doubt. Prime Minister Jean Chrétien appeared to slam the door on any chance of Nunziata rejoining the party, suggesting in the Commons that he would not sign Nunziata's nomination papers if he chose to seek a fourth term as a Liberal MP. Chrétien said, "He will sit as an independent member of Parliament and I wish him good luck to be elected as an independent candidate." The prime minister later said: "You have to support the government which helped you get elected."

People interviewed on the streets of Nunziata's riding were split: "I voted for the Liberals, not him as a person, so I think he should do what Jean Chrétien says," said Kelly-Ann Carver.

Ray Moore Jr. said he likes Nunziata's reputation as a troublemaker, "I like him, I voted for what he said, not which party he's with."[2]

According to some critics, the belief that the people's representatives have ultimate control over government legislation is a myth. Laws, they argue, are decided upon by the Cabinet and

party loyalty: the obligation of elected members of a political party to cast a vote in the legislature in their party's favour, even if they disagree with the party's position.

Focus

Do you think an MP should owe allegiance to the party leader or to the party only? Explain.

How does the message of this cartoon relate to this case study?

backbencher: a Member of Parliament who is not a member of Cabinet or one of the leading members of an opposition party.

then passed, seemingly without question, by a government majority in the House of Commons. The only substantial criticism comes from opposition parties, and they generally have too few members to prevent a bill from passing. The House of Commons merely refines the legislation; it polishes but does not control policy.

Critics also charge that the caucus has become merely a place for the Cabinet to inform **backbenchers** of what it is planning to do. The influence MPs might have on policy decisions varies according to their prestige and knowledge. But because almost half of the members lose their bid for re-election, and since first-year representatives often lack the time and the expertise to effectively critique legislation drawn up by Cabinet ministers (who have whole departments of experts to advise them), the people's representatives usually have little control over public policies.

In December 1995, *The Toronto Star* examined how often the 24 Toronto MPs who were not Cabinet members rose in the House of Commons to ask a question or take part in discussions in the previous 281 days of Commons meetings. Participation varied from Paul Szabo who spoke 211 times, to Jim Karyglannis who took part only 6 times. The average Toronto backbencher (Cabinet members and party leaders sit in the front rows) spoke every fourth day. The Toronto backbenchers, however, stated that there are other ways of serving their constituents. Jim Karyglannis noted, "I'm voicing my opinions in caucus. ... I'm a riding person. My time is better spent in the riding, not in Ottawa. If a constituent needs me, I'm here to solve a problem in Scarborough, not up in the House making a speech about Bosnia." Szabo, on the other hand, noted, "If I don't do anything, then I know nothing will get done. As a backbencher, I get very few opportunities to influence public policy, so I take every advantage."[3]

party discipline: obeying party decisions, which is a stronger feature of Canadian politics than loyalty to constituents or a politician's personal views.

In some democracies, representatives are less restricted by party discipline than are Canadian MPs. American politicians usually owe their first loyalty to their constituency rather than to the party. While the citizen may be better represented by such a system, this lack of **party discipline** also slows the pace at which legislation is passed and implemented. In the United States, there are few restrictions on how much money a candidate may spend during an election campaign. Wealthy politicians such as Ross Perot have spent millions of their own money to finance their campaigns. This reduces the control that American parties have over their candidates, and encourages only the extremely wealthy to participate in politics.

The Evolution of Canada's Political Parties

The origins of Canada's two oldest political parties — the Conservatives and the Liberals — can be traced to the 1840s in Central Canada. What became the Conservative Party was a coalition of French- and English-Canadians under John A. Macdonald and George-Étienne Cartier. Except for the period from 1873 to 1878, Macdonald was prime minister from 1867 until his death in 1891. During this time, the Conservatives ran on a platform of nation-building, which included building a transcontinental railway (the Canadian Pacific Railway), protecting Canadian manufacturers with a high tariff (tax) on imported goods, and bringing settlers to Western Canada. The Conservatives emphasized the British connection and received most of their support from French Canada, urban areas, and big business.

V I E W P O I N T

THE NECESSITY FOR PARTY DISCIPLINE

The Canadian parliamentary system requires that the party in power maintain the support of the majority of the members in the House of Commons. Without this support, the government would find it difficult to carry out the promises it made at election time. Party discipline is a means of ensuring that the MPs of the winning party are united in carrying out these objectives. In the United States, members of Congress are freer to vote according to personal conscience. Political scientists Robert Jackson and Paul Conlin discuss this issue in answering the question "Should party discipline be relaxed?"

Calls for the relaxation of party discipline in Canada are not a recent phenomenon. Like the perennial cure for the common cold, the topic of parliamentary reform provides exaggerated hopes for optimists, then later gives way to despair when it fails. As early as 1923, for example, the MP from Calgary, William Irving, introduced a motion in the House of Commons that would have allowed for the relaxation of party discipline by reducing the number of votes considered to be votes of confidence. The motion was defeated, but to this day "reformers" still look to the United States and see the relaxation of party discipline as the panacea [cure] for perceived parliamentary inadequacies. Simplistic prescriptions such as the relaxation of party discipline, while seductive, fail to take into account the complexity of the parliamentary system. ...

Imagine a scenario where party discipline in Canada was significantly relaxed. Issues formerly resolved along party lines, based on consensus and accommodation in caucus, would be decided on much narrower grounds.

Regionalism and special interests would dominate decision-making in the House of Commons, and political parties would cease to serve their function as institutions that bind the country together. The decision-making model now in place, which requires political parties to produce nationally acceptable compromises, would be replaced by an increase in confrontation. MPs liberated from the yoke of party discipline would be saddled by the demands of lobbyists and others representing narrow special interests and regional interests. This scenario is especially disquieting when taken in conjunction with the fact that there are now five and possibly six parties legitimately competing for seats in the House of Commons, instead of only two or three. The prospect of minority governments has been greatly enhanced following the growth of the Reform Party and the Bloc Québécois. ... A lack of party discipline during a minority government would result in a chaotic situation where no prime minister could maintain the confidence of the House.[4]

Focus

Select up to 10 individual words that summarize the arguments presented in the Viewpoint.

The Liberals, who did not become a cohesive party until after Wilfrid Laurier became leader in 1887, favoured freer trade with the United States and greater provincial rights, and gained support from Ontario and from farmers. However, it was not until Laurier accepted the necessity of a tariff that the Liberals came to power in 1896. Laurier promptly initiated his own railway building program and attracted millions of immigrants to Western Canada.

Early in the twentieth century, the Wilfrid Laurier Liberals and the Robert Borden Conservatives clashed frequently on issues of Canadian nationalism. In general, Laurier wished to avoid involvement with the British Empire, whereas Borden wanted to have a say in Empire foreign policy. Major issues included Canada's involvement in the Boer War, the creation of a Canadian navy, and conscription in World War I.

Politics Between the World Wars

World War I reshaped Canadian politics. Prime Minister Robert Borden's decision in 1917 to make military service compulsory alienated French Canada from the Conservative Party. Except for John Diefenbaker's victory in 1958, Quebec voted solidly Liberal until Brian Mulroney's Conservative Party swept to power in 1984 and began a new trend. The Liberal Party's practice of alternating French- and English-Canadian leaders also strengthened that party's appeal in Quebec.

World War I alienated many Western Canadian farmers from both parties. These farmers believed that Central Canadian businesspeople and politicians dominated Canadian political and economic life. Thus, when Borden drafted farmers' sons for the war despite promises not to do so, and the economy went into a severe recession, the Western provinces formed their own party in 1919 — the Progressive Party. In contrast to the two major parties, the Progressives wanted the people to have more control over their representatives and advocated such policies as recalls and referendums. Based in Alberta, Manitoba, Saskatchewan, and rural Ontario, the Progressive Party captured 65 seats in the 1921 election — more seats than the Conservative Party. Five years later, however, better economic times and more favourable Liberal policies meant the virtual end of the Progressive Party.

With two short breaks (three months in 1925, and from 1930 to 1935), Liberal leader William Lyon Mackenzie King was prime minister from 1921 until his retirement in 1948. Like Macdonald and Laurier, King was a master at compromise and delay. He rarely initiated new legislation unless the country was wholeheartedly in favour of it. King tended to cater to French Canada, looked favourably upon the United States, adopted social welfare measures, sought to separate Canada from British ties, and wished to keep Canada out of all foreign commitments. The Conservatives went through four different leaders during this period. The party generally favoured closer connections with Great Britain, wanted Canada to play a larger role in world affairs, and was associated by most people with big business.

The Rise of Third Parties During the Great Depression

When neither political party proved able to end the Great Depression of the 1930s, some Canadians joined either the right-wing fascist party of Adrien Arcand or the left-wing communist party of Tim Buck. Both parties were outlawed at the start of World War II, and Arcand was jailed.

Two other third parties were more successful. William Aberhart founded the Social Credit Party, which assumed power in Alberta in 1935. Although Social Credit, with its emphasis on reforming the banking system, never fared particularly well in national politics, it achieved considerable provincial success in Alberta, British Columbia, and Quebec.

The Cooperative Commonwealth Federation (CCF) was also a product of the hard times of the 1930s. Founded in 1933 and led by J.S. Woodsworth, the CCF was a democratic socialist party that sought "to replace the present capitalistic system with its inherent injustice and inhumanity" with economic planning and nationalization of major industries to create a more egalitarian society. In 1956 the CCF dropped its opposition to capitalism. Five years later, it changed its name to the New Democratic Party and became affiliated with the Canadian Congress of Labour. The NDP favoured improved social welfare measures and a reduction of American economic control over Canada, and was against Canada acquiring nuclear weapons.

Postwar Politics

In 1948, William Lyon Mackenzie King was succeeded by Louis St. Laurent, who was followed by Lester Pearson. Although these two prime ministers involved Canada in world events, they generally followed King's isolationist policies. Conservative Prime Minister John Diefenbaker, however, wished to strengthen Canada's connection to Great Britain, distrusted the United States, and did not look as favourably on Quebec's desire for special treatment. These sentiments arose particularly over the Liberals' adoption of the Maple Leaf flag in 1965 and the controversy over whether to accept nuclear weapons on Canadian soil.

When Pierre Trudeau came to power in 1968, the Liberals strengthened the central government, advocated economic nationalism, and

Focus

Which political party has held power the longest?

Case Table 3.2: Canadian Prime Ministers

John A. Macdonald	Conservative	1867–73
Alexander Mackenzie	Liberal	1873–78
John A. Macdonald	Conservative	1878–91
John C. Abbott	Conservative	1891–92
John S. Thompson	Conservative	1892–94
Mackenzie Bowell	Conservative	1894–96
Charles Tupper	Conservative	1896
Wilfrid Laurier	Liberal	1896–1911
Robert Laird Borden	Conservative	1911–20
Arthur Meighen	Conservative	1920–21
W.L. Mackenzie King	Liberal	1921–26
Arthur Meighen	Conservative	1926
W.L. Mackenzie King	Liberal	1926–30
Richard B. Bennett	Conservative	1930–35
W.L. Mackenzie King	Liberal	1935–48
Louis St. Laurent	Liberal	1948–57
John G. Diefenbaker	Conservative	1957–63
Lester Boyles Pearson	Liberal	1963–68
Pierre Elliott Trudeau	Liberal	1968–79
Charles Joseph Clark	Conservative	1979–80
Pierre Elliott Trudeau	Liberal	1980–84
John N. Turner	Liberal	1984
Martin Brian Mulroney	Conservative	1984–93
Kim Campbell	Conservative	1993
Jean Chrétien	Liberal	1993–

initiated bilingualism. However, after the Brian Mulroney Progressive Conservative Party came to power in 1984, it decentralized federal power, adopted free trade with the United States, and privatized Crown corporations (see Case Study 15).

The 1993 election witnessed a major political shift. The Progressive Conservative Party under Kim Campbell almost disappeared as it fell from 157 seats in Parliament to 2 seats. NDP support also declined drastically, from 44 to 9 seats. Although Jean Chrétien's Liberal Party swept to power with 177 members, the big story was the success of two new parties — the Bloc Québécois, with 54 seats, and the Reform Party, with 52 seats.

The Bloc Québécois was formed in the early 1990s when Lucien Bouchard and several other Quebec MPs left the Conservatives to form their own party. The failure of the Meech Lake Accord and its proposal to give Quebec "distinct society" status had convinced them that Quebec's future lay in independence. Focussing on separatism, the BQ won 49 percent of the popular vote in Quebec and elected 54 of the province's 75 members. In a touch of irony, since the BQ had the second-largest number of MPs, it became Her Majesty's Loyal Opposition.

Lucien Bouchard giving a speech to Parliament.

The Reform Party, led by Preston Manning, opposed recognizing special status for Quebec. The party began in 1987 as a vehicle for Western discontent. Its unofficial slogan at this time was "The West Wants In." The Reform Party promised looser party discipline over its members, more free votes in the House, and such democratic measures as recalls, a "Triple E" Senate, and referendums. During the 1993 federal campaign, Manning opposed official bilingualism, multiculturalism, and special privileges for any province; suggested limiting immigration; promised to reduce the size of government; and pledged to eliminate Canada's national debt. As a result, the Reform Party captured 18.7 percent of the popular vote, most of it coming from west of Quebec.

It is unclear as yet whether the 1993 election marked the beginning of a multi-party system, with regional parties as the norm. It has certainly raised questions about whether the basis for national parties has fundamentally changed.

BIOGRAPHY

SHEILA COPPS, 1952–

Colourful, flamboyant, controversial, "a populist with a feisty approach to politics" — all of these descriptions have been applied to Sheila Copps. In her years on the federal opposition benches, she was described as "queen of the party's Rat Pack, the Liberals' most feared lip, who terrorized Brian Mulroney and his government for nine years with her high-decibel denunciations."[5] With her appointment as Deputy Prime Minister after the Liberal election victory of 1993, Copps became "the most powerful woman in Ottawa" — and the controversy continued.

Copps' roots in Hamilton politics make her own involvement a continuation of a family tradition: her father was Hamilton's popular mayor for 13 years, and her mother served as a Hamilton municipal councillor for a decade. After graduating from university Copps began a career as a journalist, but soon moved to politics. Her 1981 election as a Liberal MPP made her the only woman on the opposition benches in the Ontario legislature. After placing second in the provincial Liberal leadership contest, she switched to federal politics. Her 1984 election as an MP marked the beginning of nine years of opposition to Brian Mulroney's Conservative government.

The dramatic shift from opposition to power came with the Chrétien Liberals' overwhelming defeat of the Conservatives in 1993.

Copps continued some aspects of her outspokenness even in Cabinet. When as Environment Minister she was criticized by animal rights activists for wearing a black leather coat trimmed with fur, she responded, "I'm pro-fur. It's a renewable resource. I've always said, if people are vegetarians I appreciate their views. Otherwise, if you wear leather shoes or a leather belt, it's a farce."[6] Despite being a strong advocate for women's issues, she stated, "I'm not there just to be a watchdog for women, because you get pigeonholed — and again, marginalized."[7]

But unquestionably the greatest controversy stemmed from Copps' 1993 campaign promise to resign if the Liberal government failed to scrap the Goods and Services Tax (GST).

In an early memorable incident, Conservative Justice Minister John Crosbie said to her in Parliament, "Just quiet down, baby." Copps' response, "I'm nobody's baby," provided the basis for the title of her 1986 book about women and politics, from which the following selection is taken:

Women see the need for our national health care system most clearly. Because we bear and raise children, and since we outlive men, women are the greatest users of the system. We see the effects of a national education policy with public access for all. And in our daily lives, we experience first hand the benefits of our way of life — a lower crime rate, less personal violence, clean and lively cities. …

Maybe we've been led too long by "masculine" ideals of conquest and aggression rather than by "feminine" urges to nurture and protect. Each of us, man and woman, has aspects of both. But in the political process as in society at large, we have allowed those aggressive, overpowering instincts to suppress the attributes of harmony and growth. Those masculine qualities are needed. But they must be balanced by benevolence and cooperation, traditional female characteristics which have been so absent from political life.[8]

1 How does Sheila Copps' career reflect important aspects of Canada's party system?

2 Why would Sheila Copps attract both widespread support and criticism?

Underlying and Emerging Issues

Give the reasoning and evidence that might be used to support different views or conclusions on the following issues.

1 To what degree does the growing cost of election campaigns undermine the principles of democracy?

2 What system of political parties is most likely to result in accountability in government?

3 What type of party system best accommodates a country's diversity in people and views?

4 Should political parties appeal to specific groups and interests, or should they attempt to gain broad support?

5 Does Canada's present party system undermine the principles of democracy?

6 Should Canada move to a system that involves less party discipline?

Focussing Knowledge

In your notes, clearly identify or define and explain the importance or significance of each of the following:

political party	party loyalty
simultaneous balloting	backbencher
one-party system	party discipline
two-party system	Conservative Party
multi-party system	Liberal Party
third parties	Progressive Party
Cooperative Commonwealth Federation (CCF)	New Democratic Party
	Bloc Québécois
Reform Party	W.L. Mackenzie King
caucus	Sheila Copps
party platform	Robert Borden

Reviewing and Organizing Knowledge

1 What historical developments led to the rise of political parties in Canada?

2 How has the rise in campaign costs contributed to the growing reliance on political parties?

3 List the advantages and disadvantages of each of these government systems: one-party system; two-party system; multi-party system; hybrid (with third parties).

4 What is the importance of the party caucus to the operation of government?

5 What are the advantages and disadvantages of Canada's system of political parties?

6 a. List the main policies of the Liberals and the Conservatives before World War I.

b. How did the Liberals and the Conservatives differ during the time of Mackenzie King?

c. What factors and policies led to the rise of each of the following third parties: Progressives, Social Credit, CCF/NDP?

d. What were the main policies of the Liberals under Trudeau, and of the Conservatives under Mulroney?

7 a. What factors and policies led to the rise of the Bloc Québécois?

b. What factors and policies led to the rise of the Reform Party?

Applying and Extending Knowledge

1 Choose one current political issue (such as privatization of Crown corporations, health care, deficit and debt reduction, immigration, crime, or any one that seems important to you). Contact a representative of each political party in your area to obtain information on the party's position on the issue. Write a description of the extent to which the parties are similar and different in their views on the issue.

2 Identify the five issues that are most important to you as a citizen in terms of deciding which party to support. Contact the parties for their positions on these five issues. Construct a chart that allows you to compare the parties' positions. Which party, overall, comes closest to your own views on the issues?

3 Contact the MP for your area through her or his constituency office, and arrange for a brief interview.

a. Ask your MP about her or his position on key issues that you have identified.

b. Determine your MP's position on issues related to Canada's present party system. (You might wish to use the Underlying and Emerging Issues as a basis for discussion.)

4 Do research on one of Canada's main political parties. How have its policies and the groups that it appeals to changed over time?

5 Look into one of Canada's lesser-known (or "fringe") parties. What are its policies? To what groups does it appeal?

6 Do research into one of the past leaders of one of Canada's political parties. To what extent did the leader shape the party, and what effect did the party have on the leader?

7 Examine the issue of gender in Canada's party system. To what extent have parties tried to appeal to women? What roles have women played in the various parties? What positions do the present parties take on women's issues, and on the involvement of women in the party?

8 Select newspaper articles that illustrate one or more of the Underlying and Emerging Issues on page 100. What do the articles contribute to your understanding of the issues?

Individual Freedom

Versus Group Welfare

*H*OW MUCH CONTROL should a democratic government have over an individual's freedom of action? This case study explores the delicate balance between individual freedom and the need to obey the law. U.S. President John F. Kennedy's argument that all citizens are obligated to obey the law is contrasted with Martin Luther King, Jr.'s statement that civil disobedience is sometimes justified. The case study then examines the life of Indian leader Mohandas Gandhi and his ideas and activities regarding civil disobedience. The views of anti-apartheid leader Nelson Mandela are then examined before concluding with brief examples of violent and non-violent protests in Canada.

In the spring of 1974, a group of police officers conducted a drug raid in a small Fort Erie hotel. By the time they finished, they had searched virtually all of the 115 patrons on the premises; in the case of the 35 women patrons, the police had them herded into washrooms, stripped, and subjected to [comprehensive physical] examinations.

Despite all of the searching, stripping, and inspecting, the police found nothing more incriminating than a few grains of marijuana. And most of these few grains were found not on articles of clothing or within body orifices, but rather on the floor and tables of the lounge.

The ensuing public outrage forced the government of Ontario to create a special Royal Commission to assess the propriety of the raid. After listening to the evidence of the police, the patrons, and other interested parties, the Commission issued the inevitable verdict: the intrusive aspects of the raid were described as "foolish" and "unnecessary," but, cautioned the Commission, they were not unlawful.

Learning Outcomes

After reading this case study, you should be able to:

- appreciate the problems related to preserving order in a democratic society

- decide upon how much control the government should have over its citizens

- debate the issue of public order versus individual freedom

- demonstrate your understanding of the philosophy behind non-violent protest

- discuss the merits of civil disobedience

- understand the views of Mohandas Gandhi, Martin Luther King, Jr., and Nelson Mandela

- recognize the actions of some Canadians who protested government actions

Under the Narcotic Control Act, if the police have reasonable grounds to believe that places other than dwelling houses contain illicit drugs, they are entitled, without warrant, to enter forcibly and conduct a search. ... According to the Commission's interpretation of the Act, the police, in such circumstances, may search everyone found on the premises whether or not each search is accompanied by reasonable suspicion. All it takes to render a person lawfully vulnerable to such intrusions is the coincidence of being innocently present on suspicious premises.[1]

Democracy and Freedom

This incident illustrates the theme of this case study — how much control should a democratic government have over an individual's freedom of action? Democratic societies are based on the belief that people should decide for themselves how to worship; what to read, write, and say; where to work; and with whom to associate. This is one of the basic differences between a democratic and a non-democratic state. In a dictatorship the ruler usually decides how the citizens should live, whereas in a democracy the objective is for the citizens to decide for themselves how they will live.

The survival of the democratic system depends upon the preservation of these freedoms. Many democratic countries (as we shall see in Chapter 4) have been turned into dictatorships without the shedding of a drop of blood when people no longer cared enough, or were powerless to preserve their freedom. It is easier to let someone else make the decisions that we ought to make as responsible citizens, but it is never easy to regain what has been lost. Perhaps the most eloquent warning of the perils to freedom emerged from the ruins of World War II. Recounting his experience with the Nazi regime in his country, Reverend Martin Niemöller, a German Protestant clergyman, made the following statement:

First they arrested the Communists — but I was not a Communist, so I did nothing. Then they came for the Social Democrats — but I was not a Social Democrat, so I did nothing. Then they arrested the trade unionists — and I did nothing because I was not one. And then they came for the Jews and then the Catholics, but I was neither a Jew nor a Catholic and I did nothing. At last they came and arrested me — and there was no one left to do anything about it.

Here is the everlasting problem of democracy: the very freedoms that democracy gives us — such as freedom of speech — can be used against democracy by its enemies. Yet we cannot preserve freedoms by destroying them — if freedoms are denied to one person, they can just as readily be taken away from every citizen. At the same time, we must recognize that freedom is not absolute. If people are to live peacefully together, there have to be some limits on what individuals can and cannot do. The problem is deciding what are "reasonable" limits to individual freedom.

The Need for Order

If freedom is defined as the absence of restraint, then freedom is impossible to maintain. We are constantly restricted and controlled by the religious and moral beliefs of society, by government rules and regulations, by our need to make a living, and by the actions of other individuals. These and other restrictions prevent us from always doing what we want — even Robinson Crusoe was limited by his environment and his own abilities.

There are two aspects of freedom: the first is the freedom to do what one wants, and the second is the freedom from being interfered with by others. Together, these two aspects of freedom present a paradox — does individual freedom include the right to injure others? If so, then the victims are deprived of their rights. The paradox is that the victims and the attacker cannot both have absolute freedom. If cigarette smokers have the right to smoke, do they also have the right to contaminate the air in an elevator? If a chemical company has the freedom to operate as it wants, does it have the right to pollute the rivers and destroy the livelihood of the fishers who depend upon those rivers? Similarly, the freedom to let your front lawn become overgrown conflicts with your neighbour's freedom not to have to contend with dandelions or an unpleasant view.

The preamble to the 1960 Canadian Bill of Rights states that people and institutions "remain free only when freedom is founded upon respect for moral and spiritual values and the rule of law." The state, in other words, protects your freedom by restraining mine. If I steal your car, the state will put me in jail and I will lose my freedom because I restricted your freedom to own property.

An important problem that each democratic society must solve is how to achieve the proper balance between **public order** and **individual freedom**. How much power should the state have over the individual? A balance must be struck between our freedom to associate with whomever we wish and to speak, write, and worship as we please, and the government's duty to preserve the peace and protect the general welfare. Section 1 of the Canadian Charter of Rights and Freedoms "guarantees the rights and freedoms set out in it only to such reasonable limits prescribed by law as can be demonstrably justified in a free and democratic society." But what are "reasonable limits"?

Asked whether the federal government had "become so large and powerful that it poses an immediate threat to the rights and freedoms of ordinary citizens," 32 percent of 1016 Canadians surveyed in May 1995 said yes and 60 percent replied no. A similar survey of Americans discovered that 39 percent agreed with the statement and 58 percent did not.[2] (Some respondents had no opinion.)

To what extent should the individual be bound by the law? Are there circumstances under which citizens are justified in disobeying the law, or in using violence to achieve their goals? This is an issue that has been debated for centuries. The following box presents the arguments for both sides of this dispute.

public order: a state in which law and order are maintained by governments either by law or by extraordinary powers vested in them.

individual freedom: the constitutional or traditional right of individuals to be protected against illegal actions launched against them by their government.

Freedom Versus Security

In the summer of 1996, the explosion of a TWA Boeing 747 jet in the skies over New York City and a bomb blast during the Summer Olympics in Atlanta generated a debate in the United States about whether personal security or personal liberty should be the priority. President Clinton immediately reacted to both events by expanding the authorities' ability to wiretap the telephones of suspected terrorists. Spectators going to Olympic events were delayed by searches of all items they were carrying, from diaper bags to camera cases.

The fourth amendment to the U.S. Constitution guarantees protection against unreasonable search and seizure. Speaker of the House Newt Gingrich stated that "As much as we want to get the terrorists, we want to do it in a methodical way that preserves our freedoms. The goal here is not to allow the terrorists to pressure us into suspending the very freedoms that make America precious." Other politicians noted that unlimited freedoms might be luxuries that Americans could no longer afford. The issue of allowing the police greater freedom to use wiretapping had emerged the year before, following the bombing of a government building in Oklahoma City in 1995. The wiretapping clause in the subsequent anti-terrorist bill, however, was removed on the grounds that it encroached too much on personal liberties.

Police consider wiretapping and other forms of electronic surveillance necessary to prevent crime. They justify this view with four major reasons: first, crime is on the increase and every reasonable technique available to them is needed to combat it; second, fighting organized crime (such as the Mafia) presents the police with very different problems than does apprehending individual criminals; third, criminals use technology to aid their crimes, and the police should not be handicapped by having the same technology denied them; fourth, only criminals have anything to fear — wider police wiretapping powers, it is argued, will be used only against organized crime.

However, other people believe that neither the police nor the justice system is perfect. Even with the best intentions, it is impossible to ensure that law enforcement efforts are directed only toward those who are guilty of crimes, and will not invade the privacy and freedom of law-abiding citizens.

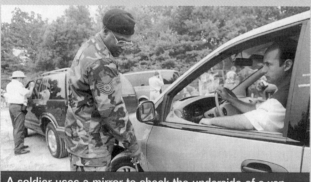

A soldier uses a mirror to check the underside of a van during the Atlanta Olympics.

The Obligation to Obey the Law

Violence is not justified in a democracy because a democracy offers alternatives to it. Violence is counter-productive because it nourishes repression, not justice. American democracy, declared President John F. Kennedy, *is founded on the principle that observance of the law is the eternal safeguard of liberty and defiance of the law is the surest road to tyranny. ... Americans are free, in short, to disagree with the law, but not to disobey it. For in a government of laws and not of men, no man, however prominent or powerful, and no mob, however unruly or boisterous, is entitled to defy a court of law.*

If this country should ever reach the point where any man or group of men, by force or threat of force, could long deny the commands of our court and our Constitution, then no law would stand free from doubt, no judge would be sure of his writ and no citizen would be safe from his neighbours.

According to this argument, individuals in a democracy are not justified in disobeying a law because there is no guarantee that they will disobey only unjust laws. This, in turn, will undermine the willingness to obey all laws, and the collapse of society will follow. Furthermore, if one person is allowed to disobey one law, everyone must then be allowed to disobey other laws when the circumstances seem to be justified. This will only make the situation worse. As soon as we give the right to disobedience to everyone, we can be sure that many just laws will be disobeyed. The choice is between social order and chaos.

The Right to Disobey the Law: Martin Luther King, Jr.

Although disobedience usually should not be condoned, some political philosophies maintain that there are times when it is justified. Disobedience, for better or worse, does settle some problems, often for the better. The best example is the success of the Civil Rights Movement in the United States during the late 1950s and early 1960s. Using legal challenges, civil disobedience, passive resistance, and mass demonstrations, the Civil Rights supporters eventually ended legal segregation of African Americans.

In the first half of the 1900s, segregation laws in some parts of the United States forbade African Americans from using the same hospitals, theatres, buses, trains, parks, and other public facilities as whites, or required African Americans to stay in separate sections of those facilities. African Americans were excluded from the best jobs and schools. Lynching and other kinds of violence still occurred in the southern states. When legal and political appeals in the 1950s produced only small gains, some African-American leaders turned to civil disobedience. Martin Luther King, Jr., a Georgia-born, northern-educated Baptist minister, became a key leader of the Civil Rights Movement.

In 1955, in Montgomery, Alabama, Rosa Parks was arrested and fined for refusing to give up her seat on a bus to a white passenger. In protest, King and other black leaders encouraged African Americans in Montgomery to boycott the city's bus company. In retaliation, the Ku Klux Klan bombed King's house and burned several black churches. Some African Americans wanted to meet violence with violence, but King said, "We must love our white brothers, no matter what they do to us."

King argued that it was permissible to disobey unjust laws that were immoral and broke God's laws. Segregation, for example, was "morally wrong and sinful." Unjust laws, he believed, were usually passed by undemocratic governments that did not consult the people they affected the most. Other unjust laws seem fair on the surface, but are applied in unfair ways. For example, King was taken to court for marching in favour of civil rights without a licence. The unjustness of the law was that the city refused to grant him such a licence. "Like a boil that can never be cured so long as it is covered up but must be opened with all its ugliness to the natural medicines of air and light," King wrote from his jail cell, "injustice must be exposed, with all the tension its exposure creates, to the light of human conscience and the air of national opinion before it can be cured."[3]

King's eloquence, courage, and leadership eventually contributed to the removal of legal segregation. But on April 4, 1968, James Earl Ray, an escaped white convict, shot and killed King in Memphis, Tennessee.

Focus

How does King distinguish between a just and an unjust law? How does he justify breaking the law?

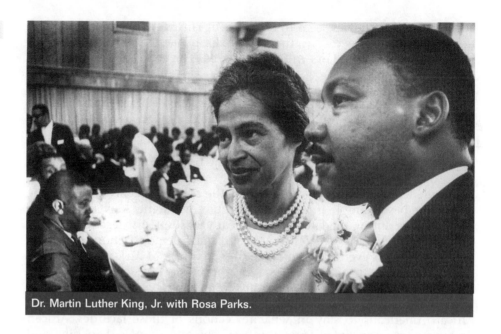
Dr. Martin Luther King, Jr. with Rosa Parks.

Mohandas Gandhi and Non-Violence

The U.S. Civil Rights Movement based its non-violent protest activities on the philosophy and actions of Mohandas Gandhi (1869–1948), who successfully used non-violent political protests in India and South Africa to counter colonialism, racism, poverty, religious bigotry, and economic exploitation. The following discussion of Gandhi's career as a social activist focuses on the importance an individual can have on world events and presents his views on non-violent, **passive resistance** to government authority.

Gandhi was born in India in 1869. To achieve his ambition of becoming a lawyer, he went to school in England at the age of 17. After five years of lonely study, Gandhi became a lawyer and returned to India. As a debater in court, however, he was unsuccessful. Once he even broke down in court, cried, and was unable to proceed. Just when it appeared that his life as a lawyer was a failure, the Indian government sent Gandhi to South Africa to represent an Indian firm in a legal dispute with the South African government. Here, Gandhi was moved by the injustices that his compatriots endured. Asians were denied legal status in South Africa. They were registered and fingerprinted, had to pay a special tax for living in the country, and could not be legally married. Gandhi spent much of the next 21 years attempting to improve their position.

Gandhi gave up all worldly ambitions and began his campaign of passive resistance in South Africa. Although the government had Gandhi and some of his Indian followers arrested and thrown into jail, the agitation they created forced authorities to grant limited legal status to Indians in South Africa.

passive resistance: the systematic, non-violent refusal by individuals or groups to obey the laws and regulations of a state, and their refusal to cooperate with government officials and their representatives.

Returning to India in 1914, Gandhi took up the cause of overworked and underpaid Indian mill workers who lived in terrible poverty. When a labour strike failed, Gandhi refused to eat until the owners remedied the workers' grievances. Gandhi got thinner and thinner. Finally, the mill owners gave in and granted his requests. At this time, Gandhi acquired the title "Mahatma" (Great Soul), for championing the causes of the poor and the oppressed.

In 1920, Gandhi turned his attention to improving the lot of India under British rule. Great Britain had ruled India since 1857. Although the British united the country and improved India's economy, they discouraged local Indian industries. Britain's most significant contribution to India's economic development was the railroad system. This transportation network increased raw-material exports, such as cotton, from India and accelerated India's shift from subsistence food to commercial agricultural production. The high demand for raw cotton continued through the American Civil War, but ceased when the Civil War ended. As a result, millions of Indians were unable to convert the agricultural surplus back into food. From 1865 through 1900 India experienced several famines and the bubonic plague. By the 1900s Indian nationalists were calling for an end to British rule. Nationalist leaders such as Gandhi and Jawaharlal Nehru sought self-rule and independence for India.

Gandhi organized a non-cooperation movement and encouraged Indians not to work for the British in any capacity. No one was to pay taxes or attend government schools, hospitals, or law courts. Police officers and soldiers were not to go to work. Although Great Britain granted some reforms, it still denied India self-rule. Following a series of bloody riots in 1921, for which Gandhi spent two years in jail, he decided that Indians were not yet trained for non-violence and began to teach the virtues of peaceful opposition. He preached self-restraint and instructed protesters to act calmly and cheerfully despite beatings, shootings, and imprisonment. Non-violence was not meant to be passive. When faced with cowardice or violence, Gandhi recommended action:

Mohandas Gandhi, later called Mahatma, or Great Soul.

When my eldest son asked me what he should have done, had he been present when I was almost fatally assaulted in 1908, whether he should have run away and seen me killed or whether he should have used his physical force which he could and wanted to use, and defended me, I told him that it was his duty to defend me even by using violence.

In the mid-1920s, Gandhi protested the British tax on salt, which weighed particularly heavily on the poorer classes, and the law that forbade people from making their own salt from sea water. In a 386-km symbolic march to the coast, Gandhi was joined by thousands of supporters. To stop the growing opposition, the British government arrested him. When the civil disobedience continued, the British released Gandhi from jail and allowed him to participate in negotiations with British officials in England. After these discussions failed, Gandhi, who was now back in jail, announced that he would "fast unto death" unless his demands were met. Gandhi was in his early sixties and many people feared that another fast might kill him. Anxious crowds waited outside the prison for news of his condition. Several days later, the government agreed to compromise, and Gandhi broke his fast.

Gandhi now decided to abandon mass disobedience because he believed that the Indian people were not yet ready for it. He adopted individual disobedience and began a country-wide march throughout India with his followers. Once again, the British imprisoned him. He fasted once more, and the British released him.

Frail and thin, with large eyes, and wearing only a loincloth, Gandhi was hardly a visually striking person. He was nevertheless determined when basic principles were at stake. Non-violence was one such belief:

War with all its glorification of brute force is essentially a degrading thing. It demoralizes those who are trained for it. It brutalizes men of naturally gentle character. Its path of glory is foul with the passions of lust, and red with the blood of murder. This is not the pathway to our goal. ... Self-restraint, unselfishness, patience, gentleness, these are the flowers, which spring beneath the feet of those who accept but refuse to impose suffering.

At a prayer meeting in Delhi in 1948, Nathuram Godse, a Hindu extremist, sat in the front row of the congregation with a small pistol in his pocket. "I actually wished him well and bowed to him in reverence," Godse recalled at his trial. When Gandhi touched his palms together, smiled, and blessed the congregation, Godse pulled the trigger, killing Gandhi. Indian Prime Minister Jawaharlal Nehru declared over the radio, "The light has gone out of our lives and there is darkness everywhere."

NELSON MANDELA, 1918–

The Issue of Violence

As a young black lawyer in South Africa, Nelson Mandela worked with the African National Congress (ANC) to help end the system of racial segregation known as **apartheid**, in which the minority group of white people in South Africa dominated the majority group of black people. When the all-white government banned the ANC in 1960, Mandela went underground to oppose apartheid. From there, he arranged a three-day stay-at-home protest in 1961 and organized acts of sabotage in several South African cities. Mandela was arrested in 1963, tried for treason, and sentenced to life imprisonment.

When Frederick W. de Klerk became president of South Africa 26 years later, he sought to end apartheid by working with the ANC. De Klerk showed his good will by freeing prominent black prisoners, including Nelson Mandela, whose reputation had grown stronger during his long years in prison thanks largely to the efforts of his wife Winnie. Mandela emerged from prison in January 1990 as a hero in South Africa, Europe, and North America. Reassuming leadership of the ANC, Mandela suspended the organization's armed struggle and met with de Klerk to end apartheid.

The following excerpt is from Mandela's 1964 defence against the charge of treason before an all-white court:

apartheid: apartness, in Afrikaans; a political system in South Africa under which blacks had to live in segregated Bantustans, or townships, where they were supposedly permitted to develop their own culture. Apartheid was abolished in 1993.

Firstly, we believed that as a result of Government policy, violence by the African people had become inevitable, and that unless responsible leadership was given to direct and control the feelings of our people, there would be outbreaks of terrorism. ... Secondly, we felt that without violence there would be no way open for the African people to succeed in their struggle against the principle of White supremacy. All lawful modes of expressing opposition to this principle had been closed by legislation, and we were placed in a position in which we had either to accept a permanent state of inferiority, or to defy the government. ...

The African National Congress was formed in 1912 to defend the rights of the African people which had been seriously curtailed. ... For thirty-

seven years — that is until 1949 — it adhered strictly to a constitutional struggle. ... But White Governments remained unmoved, and the right of Africans became less instead of becoming greater.

In 1960 there was the shooting at Sharpeville [the police killed 69 and wounded 178 anti-apartheid demonstrators], which resulted in the proclamation of a state of emergency and the declaration of the ANC as an unlawful organization. My colleagues and I, after careful consideration, decided that we would not obey this decree. The African people were not part of the Government and did not make the laws by which they were governed. We believed in the words of the Universal Declaration of Human Rights, that "the will of the people shall be the basis of authority of the Government," and for us to accept the banning was equivalent to accepting the silencing of the Africans for all time. The ANC refused to dissolve, but instead went underground. ...

Four forms of violence were possible. There is sabotage, there is guerrilla warfare, there is terrorism, and there is open revolution. We chose to adopt the first method and to exhaust it before taking any other decision. ...

Attacks on the economic life lines of the country were to be linked with sabotage on Government buildings and other symbols of apartheid. These attacks would serve as a source of inspiration to our people. In addition,

they would provide an outlet for those people who were urging the adoption of violent methods and would enable us to give concrete proof to our followers that we had adopted a stronger line and were fighting back against Government violence. ...

During my lifetime I have dedicated myself to this struggle of the African people. I have fought against White domination, and I have fought against Black domination. I have cherished the ideal of a democratic and free society in which all persons live together in harmony and with equal opportunities. It is an ideal which I hope to live for and to achieve. But if need be, it is an ideal for which I am prepared to die.[4]

Resisting Authority in Canada

Focus

How did Mandela justify the use of violence?

How would you compare the views of Mandela and Martin Luther King, Jr.?

Although in Canada we have had fewer violent and non-violent protests than most industrial democracies, over the years, Canadians' reactions to "unfair" laws have run the gamut from such passive resistance as the women's suffrage movement (see Case Study 6) and environmentalists chaining themselves to trees in British Columbia, to such violent resistance as the 1837 rebellions in Central Canada. Read the following examples of resistance and decide whether Mandela, King, or Gandhi would have approved of them.

- In 1869, when Canada bought present-day Manitoba from the Hudson's Bay Company, no one thought to inform the Métis people who were living there what would happen to them. Led by Louis Riel, the Métis sent delegates to Ottawa to negotiate with Prime Minister Macdonald. They eventually succeeded — Manitoba entered Canada as a separate province in 1870, and the Métis received guarantees for their language, religion, and land. But the Manitoba confrontation opened old wounds between the French and the English communities of central Canada. During the crisis, a Protestant called Thomas Scott was executed for treason by Riel's men. The hostilities sparked a new round of accusations between French and English during which Riel fled to the United States, where he spent the next 15 years. Upon his return, the Aboriginal peoples of Western Canada were starving, and the Métis were again worried about their language, culture, and land ownership. Riel sent petitions to Ottawa, but they were ignored. In trying to take control of the West, the Métis attacked an RCMP detachment. This time, Macdonald sent troops to the West, violence erupted, and Riel was captured and executed for treason.

- Following World War I, unemployment, inflation, low wages, and terrible working conditions angered many labourers. In Winnipeg in 1919, when the employers would not negotiate with the metal work unions, the workers called a strike. Soon the entire city was on strike, and unions held sympathy strikes in several other Canadian cities. Finally, government troops ended the strike with force.

- In 1929, the Saskatchewan government decreed that all children "should have an adequate knowledge of the English language and the training necessary for good Canadian citizenship." This legislation was aimed at the Doukhobors, members of a religious sect who wanted to teach their children their own language, religious beliefs, and community traditions. When the government insisted on school attendance, a radical Doukhobor sect resisted by burning down school buildings and by demonstrating in the nude. As a result, 55 men and 49 women were convicted of indecent exposure.

- In 1935, Canadians had suffered through six years of the worst depression in history. Frustrated at government inaction, 800 unemployed men in British Columbia jumped on freight trains intending to travel to Ottawa to present their complaints to Prime Minister Bennett. This On-to-Ottawa Trek ended in tragedy in Regina. On July 1, Mounted Police officers set off a riot when they arrested the leaders. Four days later, the trekkers were put on trains and sent to work camps in Western Canada.

- In the 1960s, the Front de Libération du Québec (FLQ) sought to gain Quebec's independence by bombing symbols of the federal government and of English "domination." In 1970, two cells of the FLQ kidnapped British trade commissioner James Cross and Quebec Cabinet minister Pierre Laporte (who was later killed). To end the FLQ threat, Prime Minister Trudeau imposed the War Measures Act, which allowed the federal government to suspend normal civil liberties while it hunted for the FLQ. Over 450 people were arrested and jailed, most of whom were never charged with any offence.

Aboriginal Land Claims and Civil Disobedience

Aboriginal land claims and demands for self-government have sparked violent and non-violent protests. The 1990 Oka crisis in Quebec triggered protests across the country — Aboriginals blocked highways, occupied government offices, shut down railway lines, and blew up hydro towers. Violence flared again in 1995 from Eel Ground in New Brunswick to Gustafsen Lake, British Columbia.

A common theme in these confrontations was the belief of some Aboriginals that they are — or should be — exempt from Canadian law. According to Ovide Mercredi, National Chief of the Assembly of First Nations, "We have pre-existing rights as indigenous people that supersede the rights of Canada as a nation and that even their claims to our land are subject to our prior title."

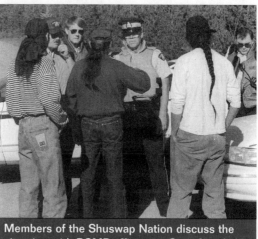

Members of the Shuswap Nation discuss the situation with RCMP officers at Gustafsen Lake.

At Gustafsen Lake, members of the Shuswap Nation along with some non-Natives seized control of disputed land, stating that it had deep spiritual meaning. In the ensuing tense showdown between the RCMP and the militants, two RCMP officers were shot in the back, escaping injury only because of their bullet-proof jackets. The protesters' lawyer denied that the defenders of the Shuswap Nation had committed a criminal act. "Definitely not," he stated, "they are resisting treason, fraud and genocide. The RCMP are engaged in a criminal act just by being here. ... Canadian laws do not apply here."[5]

B I O G R A P H Y

ROSA PARKS, 1913–

Now referred to as "the first lady of civil rights" and "the mother of the Civil Rights Movement," Rosa Parks became famous for her refusal to give up her seat to a white man in Montgomery, Alabama, in 1955. Her action and subsequent arrest triggered the Montgomery Bus Boycott, the first of the major civil rights actions and non-violent civil disobedience that led to the eventual end of segregation laws in the United States.

But as one writer observed, "There is much more to Rosa Parks's story than just one act of defiance." She was heavily involved in activities in the National Association for the Advancement of Colored People (NAACP) long before the Civil Rights or women's movements were established, and continued to work in civil rights for decades after 1955.

Parks' early life was deeply affected by the legalized racial discrimination that pervaded the southern United States during her youth. Schools for black children often closed three months earlier than those for whites, to allow for full-day employment of black children. The Ku Klux Klan operated openly, but as Rosa Parks observed, "Whites would accuse you of causing trouble when all you were doing was acting like a normal human being, instead of cringing. You didn't have to wait for a lynching. You died a little each time you found yourself face to face with this kind of discrimination."[6]

In 1943, Parks attempted to register to vote, a process that was made very difficult for African Americans by the authorities. She was turned down, but continued her attempts, and was finally successful two years later.

But of all the aspects of legalized segregation (which included separate restaurants, drinking fountains, and public restrooms), one of the worst indignities facing African Americans in Montgomery was the public transportation system.

African Americans had to pay their fare at the front of the bus, get off and enter by the rear door, and sit in the black section. Rosa Parks describes the events of December 1, 1955, in her autobiography *My Story*:

One evening in early December 1955 I was sitting in the front seat of the colored section of a bus in Montgomery, Alabama. The white people were sitting in the white section. More white people got on, and they filled up all the seats in the white section. When that happened, we black people were supposed to give up our seats to the whites. But I didn't move. The white driver said, "Let me have those front seats." I didn't get up. I was tired of giving in to white people.

"I'm going to have you arrested," the driver said. "You may do that," I answered. Two white policemen came. I asked one of them, "Why do you all push us around?" He answered, "I don't know, but the law is the law and you are under arrest."

For half of my life there were laws and customs in the South that kept African Americans segregated from Caucasians and allowed white people to treat black people without any respect. I never thought this was fair, and from the time I was a child, I tried to protest against disrespectful treatment. But it was very hard to do anything about segregation and racism when white people had the power of the law behind them.

Somehow we had to change the laws. And we had to get enough white people on our side to be able to succeed. I had no idea when I refused to give up my seat on that Montgomery bus that my small action would help put an end to the segregation laws in the South. I only knew that I was tired of being pushed around. I was a regular person, just as good as anybody else. There had been a few times in my life when I had been treated by white people like a regular person, so I knew what that felt like. It was time that other white people started treating me that way.[7]

Her arrest triggered the Montgomery Bus Boycott. Headed by a local minister, the 26-year-old Dr. Martin Luther King, Jr., the 13-month boycott united the African-American community in political action, and finally resulted in the U.S. Supreme Court desegregating public transportation. It also served as a spark for the Civil Rights Movement and the national leadership of Dr. King.

Rosa Parks and her husband faced continued threats and harassment. She eventually moved to Detroit, where she continued her work in civil rights, particularly in providing leadership training for minority youth. Her importance in bringing about change is summarized in the following statements by two American civil rights leaders:

When Mrs. Rosa Parks boarded that bus in Montgomery, Alabama, on that December afternoon in 1955, she sparked a revolution that would transform America. As Martin Luther King Jr. said, her refusal to cooperate with racism on that historic day was based on "her personal sense of dignity and self-respect … by the accumulated indignities of days gone by and the boundless aspirations of generations yet unborn." (Coretta Scott King)

Rosa Parks's life story makes it clear that her 1955 refusal to surrender to segregation on a Montgomery city bus was no impulse born of tired feet; it was instead the natural response of a woman who can trace her family history to an African slave, who saw Klansmen ride past her door as a child, who realized the damage done to blacks by racism at age 6, and whose life's work has been civil rights. (Julian Bond)[8]

---

1 What factors led to Rosa Parks' historic action in 1955?

2 How do her actions reflect important issues considered in this case study?

Underlying and Emerging Issues

Give the reasoning and evidence that might be used to support different views or conclusions on the following issues.

1 How much control should a democratic government have over an individual's freedom of action?

2 What are the "reasonable limits" to freedom in a democracy?

3 Is it justifiable to use violence against an undemocratic government?

4 Does one have a moral responsibility to disobey unjust laws?

5 Are individuals ever justified in disobeying the law in a democratic society?

6 Can the use of violence ever be justified in a democratic society?

7 If one believes that civil disobedience can sometimes be justified, what are the limits to its uses?

8 Is a democratic society ever justified in suspending democratic rights?

9 Is Canada's present system of government fair and democratic in its treatment of minorities?

10 Does Canada's present system provide enough protection for individual rights?

11 Is our protection of individual rights interfering with our ability to deal with crime?

Focussing Knowledge

In your notes, clearly identify or define and explain the importance or significance of each of the following:

absolute freedoms	Martin Luther King, Jr.
rule of law	Rosa Parks
Civil Rights Movement	Mohandas Gandhi
civil disobedience	Nelson Mandela
passive resistance	Louis Riel
African National Congress (ANC)	public order
Métis	individual freedom
On-to-Ottawa Trek	apartheid
War Measures Act	

Reviewing and Organizing Knowledge

1 How does the Fort Erie incident recounted on page 103 illustrate the theme of this case study?

2 What important point about individual rights is illustrated by Niemöller's statement on page 104?

3 a. Why are freedoms not "absolute"?

   b. What are the two meanings of the term "freedom"?

   c. How does the Canadian Charter of Rights and Freedoms limit the rights and freedoms set out in it?

4 What arguments are raised in favour of an obligation to obey the law and refrain from violence?

5 What arguments in favour of the right to civil disobedience emerge from the examples of Martin Luther King, Jr.? Mohandas Gandhi? Nelson Mandela?

Applying and Extending Knowledge

1 In an essay, describe how Hobbes, Locke, or Rousseau (from Chapter 1) would view the actions of King, Gandhi, and Mandela.

2 Examine in detail how the courts have interpreted the Canadian Charter of Rights and Freedoms, with respect to Section 1, the "reasonable limits" clause. On the basis of what you find, decide whether the Charter gives enough protection for individual rights.

3 Examine the use of the War Measures Act in the FLQ Crisis of 1970. After your research is completed, write a position paper in which you take a stand on the question of whether the suspension of civil liberties was justified.

4 Research one of the five incidents listed on pages 112–13, or Aboriginal land claims. To what extent do you agree with the actions of the government and the groups involved?

5 Research the present situation in India, South Africa, and the southern United States with respect to racial segregation and minority rights. How have circumstances changed (or not) since the situations described in this case study?

6 Research the emergence of right-wing "militias" in the United States. What is the basis for their assertions about an all-powerful government and a new world order that seeks to eliminate individual rights?

7 Choose one of the Underlying and Emerging Issues on page 117. Research the issue in the context of Canada today, then take a stand and defend it.

The Media, Pressure Groups, and Lobbyists

*T*HE MEDIA, PRESSURE GROUPS, and lobbyists play an important role in the democratic process. The media and public opinion polls influence the electorate; pressure groups and lobbyists attempt to influence government policy. This case study examines the strengths and weaknesses of pressure groups in general.

The Media

In 1787, future American president Thomas Jefferson declared, "Were it left to me to decide whether we should have a government without newspapers, or newspapers without a government, I should not hesitate a moment to prefer the latter." Indeed, the existence of a "free press" that provides the public with information, conveys what the government is doing, and criticizes its actions has long been considered a necessary ingredient for democracy. One of the first steps taken after a non-democratic coup is to seize control of all the media — either to shut it down, or use it to distribute propaganda supporting the new regime. In fact, when the newspapers began to attack Jefferson, he moved to control the press.

In more recent times, media critics have questioned whether the media is an impartial observer of political events. Does it present the voters with enough accurate information to make informed decisions? Let us examine some evidence bearing on this question.

The media defines reality for its audiences and shapes the public's perception of the political world. Because the media selects certain

Learning Outcomes

After reading this case study, you should be able to:

- understand the importance of the media in a democracy
- discuss the importance and influence of public opinion polls
- evaluate the extent to which the media is biased
- conduct research using newspapers and other media
- identify the variety of pressure groups operating in Canada
- evaluate the advantages and disadvantages of pressure groups

Focus

What role does the media play in determining how people think?

events over others to discuss, it directs and influences public opinion. Although it may not tell us what to think, it tells us what to think *about*.

Some observers believe that the media is at least as powerful as the opposition parties in keeping tabs on the government, and it has been termed the "taxpayers' watchdog," and the "citizens' surveillance team." Politicians sometimes refer to reporters as the "police." Yet the media can often be the politician's best friend. According to one Canadian MP:

Ninety per cent of the people in the constituency hardly ever, if ever, have met their member. You try to meet as many as you can and deal face-to-face with as many as you can, but for a very large percentage of the population, all they know of their politicians is what they see in the paper and what they hear and see on television and radio and it's just vital to try and keep as positive a profile in the media as one can.[1]

Critics claim that the growing role of the media in election campaigns has emphasized public relations, physical appearance, and personality over party platforms and campaign issues. During the last 70 years, politicians have had to develop new techniques to keep pace with the invention of the radio in the 1920s and television in the 1940s. In Canada, William Aberhart demonstrated the effectiveness of radio campaigning when he became premier of Alberta in 1935 — after entering politics only two years earlier. Twenty-two years later, John Diefenbaker effectively used television to capture the prime ministership of Canada. Other party leaders, such as Joe Clark and John Turner, were much less successful in using the media to their political advantage. Clark's chin and Turner's speaking quality often seemed to be the main focus of media attention.

New communications technology, such as computers, websites, interactive pay-TV services, electronic kiosks, interactive voice-response systems, electronic banking, and a 200-channel television universe herald future changes, including the possibility that political parties will be able to by-pass the traditional media and communicate more directly with voters. The Clinton administration, for example, has created a service on the Internet for individuals to send messages directly to the White House. Canadians are also active on the Internet. Government documents and papers can be accessed electronically from the comfort of your own home.

Television, however, is still the most important medium in politics. The benefits and pitfalls of television campaigning are vividly portrayed in the following review of the first televised leadership debate in North America:

In 1960, two candidates for the U.S. Presidency, John Kennedy and Richard Nixon, made history when they appeared face-to-face in live television debates. The election vote was extremely close (Kennedy eventually winning by 0.2 percent) and most observers agree that the televised debates made the difference. However, there are indications that Kennedy came out on top not so much because of what he said but because of how he "performed."

Just before the first debate, Nixon learned that Kennedy was not going to use makeup. Nixon decided he would also go in front of the camera without makeup. Kennedy, sporting a deep suntan, did not need makeup, but Nixon, who was extremely tired after campaigning and had a fever, did. A good makeup job could have masked Nixon's pale, drawn appearance. Nixon also suffered from a tendency to perspire, and the beads of sweat on his face made him look nervous and ill-at-ease.

All of this affected the viewers' image of the two men. Kennedy, an accomplished television performer, appeared cool, self-assured and confident. Nixon appeared nervous and under pressure.

When analysing the reaction of the estimated 101 million viewers, researchers found that Kennedy came out of the debates a clear winner. However, some people who only listened to the debates on radio, and therefore did not see Nixon's haggard appearance, thought Nixon was the winner.

Following the TV debates, many undecided voters made their choice of candidate. The Gallup Poll showed that Kennedy picked up three percentage points, while Nixon only got one point. The net effect was that Kennedy picked up just enough votes to win the election.

The merit of the live television debate is that voters are able to see how candidates react under intense pressure, and in situations they cannot control or anticipate. The danger is that an accomplished television performer can easily defeat a more able, honest and potentially better, leader who is uncomfortable in front of the cameras.[2]

Despite the popularity of this debate between presidential hopefuls, the next televised debate was not held until 1976. In Canada, Prime Minister Trudeau avoided all such debates between 1968 and 1979. Now, televised leadership debates are regular features of elections. About 70 percent of Canadian and American voters watch them, and approximately 50 percent claim that debates help them decide how to vote.

To ensure that politicians "perform" well, each party has a team of public relations people who are skilled in the arts of communication. Catchy tunes, cartoons, and sophisticated advertising techniques have taken centre stage. Politicians recognize that television provides many people with much of their campaign information, so they plan campaigns with careful attention to the media. Newspapers are no different — one study of newspaper election coverage revealed that 42 percent of newspaper reports dealt exclusively with party leaders, and only 12 percent discussed the issues.

> **Focus**
>
> To what extent does the media accurately convey campaign issues?

Is the Media Biased?

The media is the "gatekeeper" of modern society's ideas and information — which is one reason why freedom of the press and freedom of expression are protected by the Canadian Charter of Rights and Freedoms. Of course, the media can never be completely unbiased. Everyone has a perspective, or way of looking at issues and events in their own particular manner. In the 1993 election, the Quebec media concentrated attention on the activities of the Bloc Québécois, whereas Western Canadian media focussed on the rise of the Reform Party. Two years later, during the Quebec referendum, English-language coverage of the benefits and drawbacks of separatism was radically different from that of the French-language media.

Canadians obtain the vast majority of their information from the media. Ninety-nine percent of Canadian households have at least one radio and one television, and most homes also receive a daily newspaper. Since the media provides us with what we know about current politics, it is important that the media be as unbiased as possible, that it present all sides of an issue in a balanced way. Newspapers and television and radio stations, however, are owned and operated by businesspeople whose primary aim is to earn profits. Advertising accounts for over 75 percent of daily newspapers' revenues and almost all of private radio and television income. Theoretically, this gives wealthy advertisers considerable control over media coverage. Some critics argue that because a few corporations control the vast majority of Canada's media, "the freedom of the press belongs to those who own one." In 1996, Conrad Black went on a buying spree that saw his corporation, Hollinger Incorporated, become the world's third-largest newspaper chain by circulation. Hollinger controls approximately 170 daily and 475 non-daily newspapers in Canada, the United States, Great Britain, Australia, and Israel. Case Figure 5.1 illustrates the small number of corporations that control Canada's newspaper industry. In television, 5 companies provide the programs that 62 percent of Canadian viewers watch, and in radio, 10 companies account for 55 percent of all revenues. The media claims to be as unbiased as possible and points to the fact that the CBC is a dependable source of relatively bias-free news.

But, is it reasonable to expect any newspaper or television station to be unbiased? Many media critics state that people must recognize that every news source has a perspective, and that to achieve a balanced coverage of events voters should consult a wide variety of sources. However, if the media is controlled by large corporations, alternative opinions are more difficult to locate.

Case Figure 5.1: Who Owns Canadian Dailies?

Alberta
9 dailies
Toronto Sun: 4
Hollinger: 3
Thomson: 1

Manitoba
5 dailies
Thomson: 2
Toronto Sun: 1
Quebecor: 1

Quebec
11 dailies
Power: 4
Quebecor: 3
Hollinger: 2

Newfoundland
2 dailies
Southam: 2

British Columbia
17 dailies
Hollinger: 12
Thomson: 5

Prince Edward Island
2 dailies
Hollinger: 1

Saskatchewan
4 dailies
Hollinger: 4

Ontario
42 dailies
Hollinger: 23
Thomson: 8
Toronto Sun: 5

New Brunswick
5 dailies
Irving family: 4

Nova Scotia
6 dailies
Southam: 8
Dennis family: 2

Source: *The Globe and Mail*, Toronto, November 1996.

Media companies are usually owned by corporations with extensive holdings in the business world. The Thomson family corporate empire, for example, has interests in retailing, real estate, oil and gas, and insurance and finance, in addition to its media holdings. It controls about 400 companies with assets of up to $8 billion. Internationally, Rupert Murdoch's News Corporation has media holdings on five continents. It controls 66 percent of the metropolitan newspapers in Australia and 33 percent of those in Great Britain. Murdoch's satellite broadcasting service reaches more than 13 million homes in 22 countries, and Murdoch is the largest owner of television stations in the United States.

In 1974, the New Brunswick government sued K.C. Irving's company for using its control of the media against the interests of the province. The trial judge agreed with the government. He stated that free competition in New Brunswick had been "absolutely stifled," and that Irving's monopoly was detrimental to the public. He ordered Irving to sell two of his newspapers. Irving appealed this ruling, and the appeal judge upheld the appeal, finding no evidence of any direct interference by Mr. Irving with the decisions of the newspapers' editors or publishers.

What is the message of this cartoon?

Polls and the Electorate

Opinion polls play an increasingly important role in Canadian election campaigns. Governments use them to help decide when to call elections, and during actual election campaigns, parties employ private polls to determine which policies voters prefer. Some critics consider this to be a surrender of leadership, but other people ask what is wrong with finding out what the people think.

There is debate over whether polls taken during election campaigns assist or hinder the democratic process. Proponents of polls claim that they give citizens greater input into party policy. Polls are a means by which vot-

opinion poll: a survey conducted by a public opinion firm or political party to test the public's attitude concerning certain events, conditions, or leaders.

pollster: a person employed by a public opinion firm or political party to canvass public opinion.

Focus

Do you favour polls during election campaigns? Why or why not?

electoral process: the system of organizing and administering the voting process.

bandwagon effect: joining what appears to be the winning side in a political campaign.

ers may express their favour or displeasure with a party's platform or actions. Most parties are extremely wary of supporting measures that are opposed by a large section of the general public. Although they are not a substitute for direct democracy, polls are one of the few means by which the Canadian public can make its collective will known to politicians.

Polls are much more accurate today than they were years ago. In the 1936 American presidential election, for instance, several newspapers in the United States predicted that Alf Landon would win a landslide victory over Franklin Roosevelt, and some erroneously announced the morning of the election that Landon had won. The actual result was quite the contrary. The problem was that **pollsters** had limited their surveys to those individuals who owned telephones. Since few Americans during the Depression could afford telephones, the polls predicting a Landon victory reflected only the opinions of wealthy citizens.* Today, pollsters use more scientific and accurate means to measure public opinion. Even if one poll during an election campaign is inaccurate, other polls will generally correct this situation.

Polls may, in certain circumstances, encourage voters to participate in elections. If poll results indicate that the election outcome will be close, voters feel that their vote will be more significant, and they will make a special effort to vote. Some political analysts claim that if a particular party is trailing badly in the polls, its supporters will be more likely to cast ballots. In this way, polls may have a positive influence on the operation of democracy.

Still, many political scientists and politicians claim that polls have a detrimental impact on the **electoral process**. They suggest that polls be banned or severely restricted during election campaigns. A standard nationwide poll uses a sample of 1000 people who are supposed to be representative of the entire Canadian population. In reality, this is not always the case. A poll based on 1000 interviews is accurate within plus or minus four percentage points 19 out of 20 times. If 30 percent of Canadians actually support a particular policy or party, then 19 out of 20 polls should have results between 26 and 34 percent. One poll would not fall within this range.

This margin of error may substantially alter poll results. Suppose that an opinion poll measured party preference as follows: Liberal — 38 percent, Conservative — 35 percent, and Reform — 27 percent. Liberal support could actually range from 34 to 42 percent, Conservative support from 31 to 39 percent, and Reform support from 23 to 31 percent. The Liberal advantage over Reform could be a high as 19 percent or as low as 3 percent. Polls are seldom completely accurate; rather, they provide only a general indication of public opinion at a particular time.

During election campaigns, according to some experts, voters might support a particular party because it is leading in the polls. Such individuals would rather vote for a winner than a loser. This tendency for parties to benefit from their leading position in the polls is known as the **bandwagon effect**. In this way, polls may contribute to landslide election victories.

---

* A similar situation emerged during the 1996 presidential election in Russia. The pollsters underestimated the Communist Party's strength because its support tended to be in rural and farming areas where few people had telephones.

One new disturbing polling tactic emerged during the U.S. 1996 Republican leadership contest to determine which candidate would run for the presidency. When Bob Dole's campaign began to lose ground to Pat Buchanan, *Time* magazine reported that Dole's advisers

quietly added some new and pointed questions to its routine polling. Its telephone polltakers began asking hundreds of voters in New Hampshire whether they would be more or less inclined to vote for Buchanan if they knew he once said that women lacked "ambition and the will to succeed," and that South Korea, Taiwan and Japan should be armed with nuclear weapons. … Dole deputy campaign manager William Lacy defended the practice as standard and says he has used it regularly to test opponents' vulnerabilities.[3]

Pressure Groups

A group of people with a common interest or cause, voluntarily working together to influence the government to adopt a specific policy, is known as a **pressure group**. Unlike a political party, pressure groups are interested in influencing political decisions, not in holding political office. Because pressure groups communicate the views of specific groups of people to the government, they are an important feature of democracy. But, do pressure groups, which represent only certain groups of people, exert too much influence over government policies?

Almost every imaginable type of interest seems to be represented by an organization. There are, for example, approximately 1000 environmental groups, over 2000 business associations, almost 500 organizations representing agricultural interests, and about 200 associations that focus on Aboriginal issues. The National Action Committee on the Status of Women represents several hundred women's associations across Canada. There are pressure groups that represent labour (the Canadian Labour Congress), agriculture (Canadian Federation of Agriculture), professionals (Canadian Medical Association), religious groups (Canadian Council of Churches), ethnic groups (Canadian Jewish Congress), and the environment (Greenpeace), among others. New technologies have greatly aided the growth and influence of pressure groups. Computerized mass mailings, the Internet, e-mail, and fax machines all provide faster and more efficient communications.

pressure group: a group with a special interest that is aggressive and activist in its efforts to achieve a certain objective.

Methods of Influencing Government Policies

Pressure groups attempt to influence government policy either directly through contact with the government, or indirectly by influencing public opinion, which in turn might affect government decisions.

Direct Methods

Direct influence by pressure groups can be accomplished in many ways. They may, for example, urge their members to write letters to the prime minister, send petitions to a Member of Parliament, submit briefs to government committees, conduct protest marches, or establish contact with important civil servants and politicians.

One effective means of directly influencing the government is by working quietly within the government bureaucracy behind closed doors. Knowing the right people and how to use them is one of the most important ways of getting an organization's point of view across to civil servants and politicians. This process is called **lobbying**, which may be defined as any form of direct or indirect communication with government designed to influence public policy. Pressure groups want to know who the decision-makers are, how and when to approach them, and how to maintain this contact. Because organizations wanting to pressure the government usually lack the expertise to answer these questions themselves, they often hire a **lobbyist** to do it for them.

Lobbying has become a big business. Private organizations spend millions of dollars to get a particular concern or viewpoint heard by some important government member or civil servant. Professional lobbyists who work in Ottawa must register with the government; in 1993, there were almost 3000 lobbyists in Ottawa.

As a rule, Canadian lobbyists focus their attention on the important civil servants rather than on individual Members of Parliament. Politicians come and go with every election, but civil servants tend to remain in their jobs. It is easier to influence government policies while they are in the process of being made, rather than after they are announced. Cabinet ministers are also important targets for lobbyists, because they make the final policy decisions. Individual backbenchers usually agree with the Cabinet's decisions and concentrate more on the needs of their constituents than on important policy issues. When a bill has reached the House of Commons, it can be radically amended only after considerable embarrassment to the government. Case Figure 5.2 illustrates some of the various influences that can affect a Cabinet minister's decision. Although pressure groups are only one of the factors listed here, remember that these groups also influence the prime minister, important civil servants, the media, Cabinet colleagues, and voters.

Often, major companies take a more direct approach to influencing government policies. John Chenier, co-publisher of the *Lobby Digest* and *Lobby Monitor*, states, "If you are the president of any important national or regional company, you don't have any problem getting in to see people." The following account of the backroom lobbying involved in the passage of the Tobacco Products Control Act in June 1988 illustrates how successful this tactic can be.

lobbying: a form of direct or indirect communication with government members designed to influence public policy.

lobbyist: usually a paid employee of various economic and political groups or business firms whose task is to influence governmental action or legislation.

Focus

Would Canadians be better off if political pressure groups were strictly controlled? Why or why not?

Case Figure 5.2: A Minister's Decision Circle

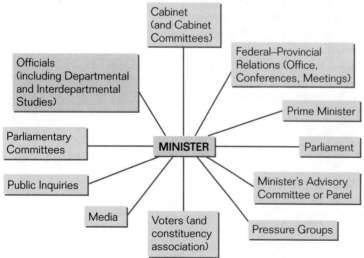

Source: *From Lobbying in Canada: Ways and Means* by S. Sarpkaya, 1988. Reprinted by permission of CCH Canadian Ltd.

The final regulations for the Act were only published in January 1989, and in the interim the Canadian Tobacco Manufacturers' Council, through its president and lobbyist, Bill Neville, managed to bring about a number of significant changes. Documents obtained by the Non-Smokers Rights Association showed that officials in the Department of Health and Welfare originally wanted warnings on tobacco packages that covered 30 percent of the surface, and that stated that tobacco is addictive, and a cause of lung cancer, heart disease and birth defects. Attention would be drawn to this warning by means of a prominent circle and arrow displayed on the package. According to The Globe and Mail, *Neville wrote a long memo protesting these proposed regulations in August 1988, claiming that it was wrong to say that tobacco is addictive. A meeting was sought on August 23, and the next day a departmental memo was written weakening the regulations, and removing any reference to addiction. By November the regulations were further weakened when the size of the warning was reduced. It is not clear how much impact Neville's personal connections had on this process, though during the fall election campaign he acted as a senior adviser to the government and worked on speeches for the Prime Minister. Neville clearly had access to the draft regulations at an early stage, and even requested that the CTMC's participation be kept secret until after the regulations were finally published. Health groups that had opposed the CTMC were not so privileged, and were kept in the dark about the regulations until they were published.[4]*

Indirect Methods

Indirect influence by pressure groups on government policy is becoming more significant. Politicians are very aware of public opinion polls, and the major political parties use their own public opinion companies to provide feedback on how Canadians feel about various issues. Pressure groups know this, and many of them spend a great deal of time and effort to influence public opinion, both between and during elections. According to one survey of federal MPs in 1995, 56 percent considered "mobilizing public opinion" to be the most effective method of influencing government policy. During the American Congressional hearings on tax reform, for example, lobbyists armed with cellular phones closely watched the debate. The minute a senator suggested a change that did not favour a particular group, its lobbyist immediately alerted interested parties, who saw to it that the senator was deluged with telephone, letter, and fax complaints.

When governments have to make decisions, they often discover that several pressure groups are actively pushing for different proposals. For example, conflicting interests can occur when a company wants to build a manufacturing plant that might harm the environment. The company may lobby the government directly for permission to build the plant. An environmental group may attempt to stop the project by launching a media campaign or by holding rallies against the construction of the plant.

V I E W P O I N T

GREENPEACE
Environmental Pressure Group Tactics

Greenpeace, an international environmental protection organization founded by Canadian David McTaggart in 1971, is a good example of a pressure group that uses a variety of methods to exert direct and indirect pressure on governments and companies. During its first 25 years, Greenpeace led campaigns on such issues as toxic waste, acid rain, nuclear weapons, whaling, and kangaroo slaughter. Its strategy was to call the public's attention to an issue through bold, and often dangerous, behaviour. Greenpeace activists glided small Zodiac boats beneath the bows of huge whaling ships, climbed New York skyscrapers, sailed into areas where nuclear bomb tests were to be held, and filmed outrageous activities by governments and companies, and sent the films to the media.

Case Figure 5.3: Greenpeace Activity

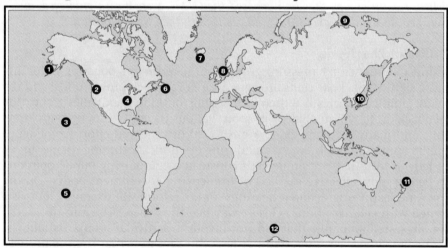

Source: © 1996 Time Inc. Reprinted by permission

1 Amchitka, Alaska, 1971
Greenpeace is founded. The ship *Phyllis Cormack* opposes a U.S. nuclear test site, leading to its closing.

2 Seattle, 1995
Protesting wasteful catches of squid and other fish killed unintentionally, activists prevent a trawler from leaving port.

3 Pacific Ocean, 1982–83
The *Rainbow Warrior* demonstrates against dolphin slaughter by U.S. tuna fleets and against the 10-mile-long [16-km] drift nets used by Japanese salmon-fishing fleets.

4 Mississippi River and Great Lakes, U.S., 1988
Protests are mounted against pollution at 75 toxic "hot spots."

5 Mururoa Atoll, South Pacific, 1972–95
Last year the French navy seized a Greenpeace ship campaigning against nuclear tests.

6 Newfoundland, 1978–85
Activists protest hunting of baby seals, prompting the European Economic Community to ban imports of seal pelts.

7 Iceland, 1986–89
The ship *Sirius* challenges Iceland, Norway, and Japan. Persuades Iceland to end all whaling.

8 North Sea, Britain, 1995
Demonstrators occupy the Shell oil platform Brent Spar, causing Shell to decide against dumping the out-of-service rig in the ocean.

9 Kara Sea, Russian Arctic, 1992
The ship MV *Solo* documents Russian radioactive-waste dumping, forcing the government to acknowledge it.

10 Sea of Japan, 1992
The ship MV *Greenpeace* exposes Russia's discarding of radioactive waste, in violation of worldwide moratorium.

11 Auckland, New Zealand, 1985
En route to protest French nuclear tests, the *Rainbow Warrior* is bombed by the French secret service.

12 Cape Evans, Antarctica, 1988–90
Polar ships *Greenpeace* and *Gondwana* set up a base to highlight environmental abuse.

In 1996, executive director Thilo Bode decided to modify Greenpeace's methods. In the following interview with *Time* magazine, Bode outlines the new strategy of this powerful pressure group.

Bode: *To be effective, Greenpeace needs to use different campaign styles in different cultures. In some cases, we will push the limits in campaigns that provoke debate and reaction. Before we do anything, we must first identify the best method for achieving change. The Chinese authorities would not understand confrontational tactics or civil disobedience. So we adapt our strategy to the particular culture. It would certainly make our task far easier if China were a partner rather than an adversary.*

Time: *What lessons has Greenpeace learned from last year's protest against the French nuclear testing in the Pacific Ocean? Your boat was impounded, and the tests went ahead. ...*

Bode: *The protests reminded us of the nonviolent nature of the organization and of the fact that we are not a military power. They also demonstrated what a huge impact we can have. Despite the difficulties, we were successful. [French President] Chirac is now pushing for a nuclear test-ban treaty. ...*

Time: *You have said that "the ecological fate of mankind will be decided in Asia." What do you mean by that?*

Bode: *During a recent visit to Asia, I was struck by both the enormity of the task in this region and our near absence from the arena. We are still a very long way from being a truly international organization. We are simply not present, or not strong enough, in the areas of the world where our environmental fate will be determined. ...We have to concentrate on a few issues and do them well. Right now those issues are the forest, the oceans, toxic pollution and excessive energy consumption. And of course nuclear disarmament will remain a classic component of Greenpeace campaigning.*

Time: *How will you tackle these?*

Bode: *We must reaffirm Greenpeace as an important international environmental pressure group providing a counterbalance to the purely commercial interests of society. ... Our challenge is to get this message across while inspiring people, not turning them off.*[5]

F o c u s

What new strategies does Bode envision this pressure group using?

Business as a Pressure Group

Large corporations often have their own public affairs departments to influence government policies. Corporations have also been a traditional source of party revenue for both the Liberal and the Conservative parties. The New Democratic Party, on the other hand, receives most of its funds from labour unions and from individual donations. The first major scandal in Canadian politics occurred after the 1872 election, when Prime Minister Macdonald promised to give the contract to build the Canadian Pacific Railway to a Montreal businessman if he contributed funds to the Conservative Party. Macdonald won the election, but when the public learned about this "Pacific Scandal," the prime minister resigned and lost the next election.

To prevent wealthy groups or individuals from unduly influencing government policies, the government limits the amount of money that individual candidates and parties are permitted to spend during an election campaign. In addition, radio and television stations must provide both paid and free broadcast time for each party during election campaigns.

Corporations often have extensive personal links with government. Business is a major recruiting ground for public office. Paul Desmarais of Power Corporation is one of Canada's most powerful businesspeople. Here is how columnist Peter C. Newman described Desmarais' political connections as of 1993:

No businessman in Canadian history has ever had more intimate and more extended influence with Canadian prime ministers than Desmarais. He was a good friend and financial supporter of Lester Pearson, who became prime minister in 1963; he was one of the chief backers of Pierre Trudeau's leadership bid and acted as one of his main confidants for his 16 years in office. Desmarais had meanwhile become one of Brian Mulroney's chief mentors, and during the nine Mulroney years, no one outside the prime minister's immediate family had as much influence. ... The chain remains unbroken with this election. The daughter of the man who will become Canada's 20th prime minister is married to Paul Desmarais' son.[6]

Pressure Groups — For Better or For Worse

To what extent do pressure groups help to make governments more responsive to citizens' needs, and to what extent are they vehicles through which minority groups attempt to subvert the wishes of the majority?

Freedom of speech and freedom of assembly are basic democratic rights. When a group of citizens organizes to demand a speed bump on a residential road and meets with its local city councillor to express its concerns, it is as much an example of lobbying as is a labour union asking for a higher minimum wage. The question to be asked is: Was "undue influence" used by the lobby group to achieve its objectives?

Pressure groups are a fact of life in the Canadian democratic process. They are the principal mechanism by which interested groups make their preferences known to government policy-makers. Some people argue that pressure groups provide a necessary communications link between the governed and the governors. Pressure groups provide decision-makers with information about the "real world," including technical information as well as an assessment of the feelings and attitudes of the organization's members. In this way, pressure groups provide opportunities for meaningful political activity and help government to identify areas of dissatisfaction.

Pressure groups identify, arouse, express, and represent the views of people who share a common interest. By providing an opportunity for their members to express their wishes or defend their ideas, pressure groups also act as an escape valve for people's frustrations. And, by acting as mediators between government and individuals, these groups provide another mechanism for political representation.

The communication flow is two-way. Governments often use pressure groups as a means of testing their proposals before taking them to Parliament; they request advice and assistance before finalizing their policies. Pressure groups are also used to help explain government policies to the public and to obtain support for them. Finally, lobbyists act as a check on the government, advising, warning, and providing alternative courses of action for the legislators.

The basic flaw in this view, according to some political scientists, is that some segments of society are better organized than others and can mobilize greater resources in support of their interests. These resources include money, available time, organizational skills, and political connections. In fact, some areas of society remain unorganized or poorly organized at best. By and large, the most active pressure groups represent producers rather than consumers; although there are many labour unions, consumer associations, charitable societies, and church groups, the most influential pressure groups represent business. In addition to their contacts with the media, business groups maintain continuous contact with important government agencies. As a result, when the desires of a multinational oil company (to take one example) come into conflict with an environmental group, the oil company has the advantage.

The very fact that pressure groups work behind closed doors, argue their detractors, means that at best they are undermining the idea of open government. At worst, they have something to hide. Civil servants and politicians naturally wish to work with the most powerful pressure groups because they do not want to antagonize these groups and jeopardize important political support. What tends to happen is that wealthy groups, which can afford to hire teams of lawyers, lobbyists, and publicists, are more able to influence government decisions. There are always more poor people than rich people, yet the existence of pressure groups has the potential to enable the minority to dominate the majority — the very antithesis of democracy.

OVIDE MERCREDI, 1946–

The most prominent leader of Canada's Aboriginal peoples in the 1990s, Ovide Mercredi was hailed in 1992 as "the country's eleventh premier and the most powerful native politician of his generation." But the failure of the Charlottetown Accord in October of that year left him with the difficult task of attempting to find new solutions to the problems and aspirations of Canada's Aboriginal peoples in his role as National Chief of the Assembly of First Nations (AFN).

Because Mercredi's Cree mother married a man of mixed Aboriginal and European descent, she was stripped of her Indian status under the Indian Act. The family lived outside the Native reserve near Grand Rapids, Manitoba, where Mercredi's father fished and trapped. Painfully shy as a boy, Mercredi dropped out of school at age 16; he later returned, and eventually received a law degree from the University of Manitoba in 1977.

His criminal law practice opened the door to more political activity on behalf of Aboriginal peoples, first through Mercredi's appointment to the Manitoba Human Rights Commission. In 1989, he became vice-chief for Manitoba in the AFN; by 1991, he had become president of the organization, which represents 633 chiefs from First Nations bands across Canada.

Much of Mercredi's approach was centred on gaining a constitutional guarantee for "Natives' inherent rights to self-government." He worked successfully with Aboriginal leaders and other politicians to overturn the 1987 Meech Lake Accord on the grounds that it ignored Aboriginals' interests and aspirations. He played a high-profile role in representing Aboriginal people in the successful negotiations for the 1992 Charlottetown Accord, which resulted in the proposed constitutional recognition of distinct status for Native peoples through the right to self-government.

But the Charlottetown Accord was defeated in a national referendum in October 1992. There were many reasons for its rejection, but one had to do with the vagueness of the concept of Aboriginal self-government. In fact, despite Mercredi's active support of the Accord, over 60 percent of Aboriginal voters rejected it, often on the grounds that it contained too many obstacles to achieving self-government.

The rejection of the Charlottetown Accord has had an enormous political impact in Canada, but for Aboriginal peoples it has meant the apparent failure of the path of obtaining self-government through constitutional change. Mercredi was re-elected head of the AFN in 1994 by a narrow margin and faces the task of leading a diverse and often divided group in a new direction.

He has always admired the non-violent approach of Gandhi and Martin Luther King, Jr., and played the role of mediator in the confrontations at Oka, Quebec, in 1990 and at Gustafsen Lake, British Columbia, in 1995. Recently, Mercredi has advocated a more activist stance, including the establishment of an Institute for Aboriginal Non-violence to teach successful civil disobedience techniques. He discussed his ideas in an interview with *Maclean's*:

Q: [Y]ou yourself have also recently advocated a more aggressive stance for Canadian natives.

A: [The protest leaders accuse] people like myself and the elected chiefs of being collaborators with the federal government. Well, we are not collaborators. But the fact remains that the federal government disregards our authority to deal with issues affecting our people, and the current minister of Indian affairs has done everything to bypass the duly elected leaders of the

Indian people. That's why I've been saying recently that, as a leader, I have to become more aggressive in dealing with the government and that we may have to resort to acts of civil disobedience as a means of getting a resolution to our grievances.

But when it comes to civil disobedience, there are four conditions that I place on any act. One is that the elected leaders — that means the chief and council elected by their own people — must be in a leadership role and must be in control. The second condition is that the people themselves in the communities affected support that civil disobedience. The third is that there must not be any resort to violence, no use of weapons whatsoever. The final condition is that there must be no loss of life and no destruction of property. ...

Q: *What can governments do to repair the relationship between native and non-native Canadians?*

A: *They must be prepared to work with us as equals, not as subordinates. They have to work with us as having a right to represent our peoples as heads of governments. And they should not look upon us as their citizens to rule, because that is the relationship of dominance that we have been fighting and trying to overturn.[7]*

---

1 How do Ovide Mercredi's actions reflect important concepts and issues examined in this case study?

2 How do you react to Mercredi's proposals for civil disobedience? Why?

Underlying and Emerging Issues

Give the reasoning and evidence that might be used to support different views or conclusions on the following issues.

1 How powerful is the news media in shaping public opinion?

2 To what degree does the news media give a balanced view of events and issues?

3 Is the news media in Canada dominated by business interests?

4 To what degree do opinion polls promote or hinder democracy?

5 Do pressure groups in Canada have too much influence on government actions?

6 Should there be more control over the practice of professional lobbying?

7 Do business interests have too much influence on or control over government in Canada?

8 Should we limit the amount of money that individuals and parties can spend during election campaigns?

9 Is the Canadian government dominated by wealthy groups?

Focussing Knowledge

In your notes, clearly identify or define and explain the importance or significance of each of the following:

bias	lobbying
perspective	lobbyist
opinion poll	Greenpeace
pollster	Conrad Black
electoral process	Paul Demarais
bandwagon effect	Ovide Mercredi
pressure group	

Reviewing and Organizing Knowledge

1 Identify the main criticisms and strengths of the recent roles of media in Canadian democracy.

2 How did the 1960 Nixon–Kennedy TV debate reflect positive and negative aspects of the role of news media in politics?

3 What are the potential problems with the ownership of most news media by a small number of corporations?

4 a. What are the main arguments in favour of the extensive use of opinion polls in politics?

b. Why do some people maintain that polls have a detrimental effect?

5 a. What are the main direct methods that pressure groups use to influence government?

b. Why do lobbyists tend to focus their attention on civil servants and Cabinet ministers?

c. What indirect methods are used by pressure groups?

6 How do large corporations attempt to influence government policies?

7 How do the examples of the tobacco manufacturers and Greenpeace reflect important aspects of pressure groups?

8 What are the main arguments for and against the present role of pressure groups in Canada?

Applying and Extending Knowledge

1 Follow the news reporting and editorial position in one newspaper for two weeks. What is the newspaper's perspective? How would you describe the newspaper in terms of balance and bias?

2 Compare the treatment of an issue or event by two different newspapers. How are they similar or different? Use the concepts of bias, balance, and perspective in your analysis.

3 Compare the treatment of a specific event by a television station and a newspaper. How are they different? What are the strengths and weaknesses of each?

4 Choose a newspaper article that deals with the results of an opinion poll. How does the article reflect concerns raised in this case study?

5 Research one of the pressure groups described in this case study. What strategies and tactics are used? How successful are the results?

6 Read a newspaper thoroughly for three successive days, and make a list of all the pressure groups mentioned. What are the goals and tactics of the groups?

7 Choose one of the Underlying and Emerging Issues on page 134 and write an essay that outlines your opinion on this topic.

Issues of Equality
in Canada

HE STRUGGLE OF WOMEN AND MINORITIES for equality in Canada illustrates many of the themes of the previous case studies, including non-violent disobedience, individual freedom and group welfare, and the media and lobbying. This case study examines the notion of equality and the status of women in the nineteenth and twentieth centuries and reviews the campaign waged for the right to vote. The nature of racism as it was experienced by Canadians of Japanese origin and their struggle for redress are explored.

"That's not fair!" We have all used this phrase when we think that we are not being treated equally. While the main focus in this case study is on political equality, the issues are closely tied to questions of social and economic equality. Equality may be analyzed from both an individual-rights perspective and from a collective-rights perspective. For instance, are you guaranteed the right to work in any province, or do provinces have the right to reserve jobs for their own residents? Are your neighbours free to hire their friends and relatives to work for them, or must they open those jobs to anyone? Does your first language enjoy official status in Canada, or is that status reserved for particular languages? Equality is a complex and sometimes contradictory notion.

In Canada today we generally express our commitment to **equality** by recognizing that individuals and groups have specific rights, including the right to be treated equally under the law and not to be discriminated against on the basis of gender, race, or age. At the very least we understand the term to mean a responsibility to treat everyone with respect and dignity. It may also include our commitment to ensure that all people are paid a fair wage and have health care, decent housing and food, and opportunities for personal development. Canada's multicultural policy discusses "removing barriers to full participation" in Canadian society.

equality: treating people the same in terms of human and political rights.

Suffrage in Canada

Suffrage—the right to vote—is an important first step toward achieving political equality. Who has the right to vote and who does not indicates how open society is to sharing political power. Today, approximately 70 percent of Canada's population has the right to vote. The remaining 30 percent comprises young people under the age of 18 and immigrants who are not Canadian citizens. Compare these percentages with those of 100 years ago. In the province of Quebec, for instance, only 15 percent of the population had the right to vote. As the following box indicates, democracy as we understand it is a relatively recent arrival to Canada.

The Right to Vote in Federal Elections

1867: Only male citizens aged 21 or older who owned or rented a specific amount of property could vote.

1885: Only "persons" could vote. A "person" was defined as a male, excluding those of Mongolian or Chinese "race." Aboriginal peoples living east of Manitoba and not living on a reserve could vote.

1917: Wives, sisters, and mothers of Canadian men serving overseas in the army were enfranchised, as were Aboriginals serving in the armed forces. In this wartime election year, conscientious objectors and men born in enemy countries lost the right to vote. (These rights were restored after the war.)

1918: Women were given the same right to vote as men.

1921: Japanese Canadians who served in World War I were enfranchised.

1947: Canadians of South Asian and Chinese ancestry were enfranchised.

1949: Canadians of Japanese ancestry were enfranchised; Inuit were given the vote.

1960: Aboriginal Canadians living on reserves were enfranchised.

1987: Judges eligible to vote.

1988: Canadians with mental disabilities eligible to vote.

1992: Prison inmates eligible to vote.

Focus

Why do you think male property holders were the first group to hold the right to vote?

The Women's Suffrage Movement

Sexism can be defined as the intentional or unintentional refusal of one gender to share power and resources fairly with the other gender. When the struggle for women's rights began in earnest during the nineteenth century, sexism was a major feature of Canadian society, although the term was vir-

sexism: the intentional or unintentional refusal to practise gender equality.

No Occupation

She rose before daylight made crimson the east
For duties that never diminished.
And never the sun when it sank in the west
Looked down upon work that was finished.
She cooked an unending procession of meals.
Preserving and canning and baking.
She swept and she dusted,
She washed and she scrubbed.
With never a rest from it taking
A family of children she brought in the world.
Raised them and trained them and taught them.
She made all the clothes and patched, mended and darned
'Til miracles seemed to have wrought them.
She watched by the bedside of sickness and pain
Her hand cooled the raging of fever.

Carpentered, painted, upholstered and scrapped
And worked just as hard as a beaver.
And yet as a lady-of-leisure, it seems,
The Government looks on her station
For now, by the rules of census report
It enters her—No Occupation.[1]

tually unknown. Most people assumed that men and women had quite distinct natures and thus had different responsibilities. Men were fathers and breadwinners, women were mothers and homemakers, and each gender had a "separate sphere," or area of influence, in which it was considered superior. Under this notion of separate spheres, boys were educated for duties in the public sphere (professionals, politicians, businessmen), while girls were prepared for duties in the domestic sphere (homemakers, seamstresses). Class as well as gender determined women's role in society. Their social standing depended in large part on the status of their fathers and husbands. These beliefs were held by many males *and* females.

According to one view, the "separate sphere" argument was simply a rationalization for male dominance. In any event, this idea of separate spheres meant that women had very little power or influence outside the home during the nineteenth century. Although a few women, usually widows, had the right to vote in certain situations during the early and middle decades of the century (which they later lost), the vast majority of women were officially excluded from politics. Canada's Election Act stated that "no woman, idiot, lunatic, or criminal shall vote." Women were not eligible to run for federal or provincial office. If women spoke out about their absence of formal political power, they were considered aggressive and bold. The wife of a lieutenant–governor of Quebec expressed a commonly held opinion when she wrote: "I consider that the role of a woman is to govern her home and to direct the education of her family. In my opinion she would gain nothing by descending into the political arena in becoming an elector."

As industrialization transformed the Canadian economy in the second half of the nineteenth century, opportunities increased for women to work outside the home. Domestic service was the most common form of employment. Factory work was another possibility, as were such "nurturing" professions as teaching elementary school and nursing. By the turn of the century, clerical work was another alternative. For women, such employment meant a measure of independence and an income with which they could help their families. But the pay was almost universally meagre; domestic servants were often lonely and were exploited by their employers; factories had dreadful working conditions; office work was strictly regimented; and the "nurturing" professions received little recognition or status.

Out of these changes emerged a form of feminism that historians call "first-wave feminism," "social feminism," or "maternal feminism." Unlike equal rights feminists, who argued that men and women were equal and therefore ought to have equal rights, first-wave feminists argued that because women's sphere was growing and society increasingly required their nurturing skills outside the home, women's rights and powers should also be expanded. The maternal feminist demand for the vote was therefore linked closely to the desire to purify society and rid it of the evils of poverty, disease, drunkenness, and prostitution that seemed to accompany industrialization.

Suffragists faced considerable obstacles in their struggle for political reform. Those people who opposed the suffragists had an endless collection of reasons for denying women the vote: women were too irrational and emotional to participate in the world outside the home; an active role in politics would humiliate and corrupt women; wives might vote against their husbands and destroy the harmony of the home; since wives would vote as their husbands wished, there was no reason to give them the vote; women were already represented in the political process by their fathers and brothers; women's brains were smaller than men's, therefore they should not have the right to vote. The assumption underlying most of these reasons was that women and men were different. Because maternal feminists agreed that women and men had distinct natures, it was difficult for them to effectively challenge these arguments. Thus, the first-wave feminists confronted enormous challenges.

Each province had unique conditions that needed to be met before the vote could be won. Initially, the suffragists adopted a low profile. In 1876, for instance, some suffragists formed the Toronto Women's Literary Club. The name was deliberately misleading as the club's main concern was getting women the vote. Gradually, other women's groups formed throughout Canada. These suffrage clubs joined in 1889 to form the Dominion Women's Enfranchisement Association. "Votes for Women!" was the cry. The battle was on.

A suffrage member campaigning for votes.

Nellie McClung

Perhaps the most important figure in the suffrage movement was Nellie McClung. Born in Ontario and raised on a Manitoba farm, McClung started her career as a schoolteacher but made her name as a writer and journalist. She gained national attention in 1908 when her novel *Sowing Seeds in Danny* became a bestseller. McClung showed strength and poise in the toughest situations. While she was speaking against liquor at a temperance meeting, for instance, a male heckler yelled, "Don't you wish you were a man right now, Nellie?" She quickly replied, "Don't you wish you were?" A fiery and eloquent speaker, McClung devoted herself to getting women the right to vote.

Rodmond Roblin, the premier of Manitoba in 1914, opposed the suffragists. "I don't want a hyena in petticoats talking politics to me," he once told McClung, "I want a nice gentle creature to bring me my slippers." Later, the premier addressed a delegation of female suffragists:

Let it be known that it is the opinion of the Roblin government that woman suffrage is illogical and absurd as far as Manitoba is concerned. Placing women on a political equality with men would cause domestic strife. Sex antagonism would be aroused. It is an easy flame to fan. I believe that woman suffrage will break up the home. It will throw the children into the arms of servant girls. The majority of women are emotional, and if given the franchise they would be a menace rather than an aid.

The next evening the women staged a mock Parliament in the Walker Theatre. This time, however, the women were the politicians and the men were pleading for the vote. McClung played the role of premier. Mimicking Roblin's gestures, she proclaimed:

The trouble is that if men started to vote, they will vote too much. Politics unsettles men, and unsettled men means broken furniture, broken vows, and divorce. If men were to get into the habit of voting — who knows what might happen — it's hard enough to keep them home now. History is full of unhappy examples of men in public life — Nero, Herod, King John.[2]

Her performance "brought the house down" and probably convinced many in the audience of the justice of female suffrage.

A year later, Roblin was defeated by the Liberals under T.C. Norris. The suffragists had campaigned for Norris, and in January 1916, Manitoba became the first province to grant women the vote. Saskatchewan and Alberta passed similar laws that year. Ontario and British Columbia followed suit in 1917, Nova Scotia in 1919, and Prince Edward Island in 1922. Newfoundland extended the franchise to women in 1925, as did Quebec in 1940.

Emmeline Pankhurst (left) and Nellie McClung (right) fought to get women the vote.

World War I and the Suffrage Movement

World War I was the single most important event in promoting women's suffrage. Great Britain, France, and Russia went to war against Germany and Austria-Hungary in 1914. As a British colony, Canada was also at war. Many Canadians believed that this was a struggle between democracy and dictatorship. If this was true, reasoned the suffragists, how could Canadians justify losing thousands of lives in Europe defending freedom and democracy when half the population at home was denied the right to vote?

As thousands of young men volunteered for the army, wives were left to fish and run the farms themselves, and new factory jobs opened up for women. Women knitted socks for the soldiers, raised money for the war, and served as nurses. They were convinced they had earned the right to vote.

The most important reason for the federal enfranchisement of women, however, was party politics. Conservative Prime Minister Robert L. Borden was worried that his party would lose the federal election of 1917 to the Liberal Party led by Wilfrid Laurier. Many people were unhappy with the Conservative government. During the war, the cost of food had risen faster than wages. Many workers believed that their bosses were taking advantage of the war situation to make very large profits. The worst discontent was in Quebec. Many French Canadians objected to fighting in a war that they thought did not concern Canada.

Women doing "men's work" in a World War I munitions factory.

The Borden government was in trouble. To make matters worse, the Canadian troops in Europe were receiving insufficient reinforcements. In the spring of 1917, for example, more than 20 000 Canadian soldiers were killed or injured, but only 3000 new men were added to the forces.

Borden decided to conscript Canadians to fight overseas. The Liberals opposed conscription, but the prime minister was convinced that it was essential to win the war. He was determined to win the election at any cost. The Military Voters Act was passed in August 1917, and the Wartime Elections Act was introduced the following month. The first law gave the vote to members of the Canadian armed forces, no matter how long they had lived in Canada. The second act granted the vote to all mothers, wives, sisters, and daughters of Canadian soldiers. It also took the vote away from immigrants born in enemy countries who had settled in Canada after 1902, as well as from all men who refused to fight for religious reasons.

The intention of these bills was obvious. As one politician remarked, "It would have been more direct and at the same time more honest if the bill simply stated that all who did not pledge themselves to vote Conservative would be disenfranchised." The Conservatives won the 1917 election and the next year women received the vote.

Modest Gains

Despite this victory, change came slowly for women during the half-century to follow. Male domination and the "separate spheres" concept remained. In 1921, just four women (0.6 percent) were nominated to run in the federal election. Agnes Macphail was the only woman elected to the House of Commons. This 31-year-old schoolteacher from rural Ontario defeated 10 men to win the nomination, and then spent two months persuading her constituents that her gender would not diminish her ability to look after their interests. In the House of Commons, Macphail felt very isolated and lonely. "I couldn't open my mouth to say the simplest thing without it appearing in the papers," she once wrote, "I was a curiosity, a freak. And you know the way the world treats freaks."

Macphail's limited success mirrored the fortunes of the women's movement. Her constituents did not always share her concerns, nor did all women. When she supported Glace Bay miners in their strike for better working conditions, several groups spoke out against her. One issue that unified the women's movement was the exclusion of women from the Canadian Senate because the Constitution said that only "persons" could be senators. The result was the famous "Persons Case" of 1929, in which Nellie McClung and four other Alberta women—Irene Parlby, Louise McKinney, Henrietta Edwards, and Emily Murphy—helped to change the law to recognize women as "persons." Cairine Wilson subsequently became Canada's first female senator.

Later Developments

In the 19 federal elections held between 1921 and 1980, a total of only 67 women were elected to the House of Commons. In 1993, 53 women were elected to the House of Commons. Although this was the highest total ever elected, it still represented less than 18 percent of the membership of the House of Commons.

While women do a great deal of behind-the-scenes work as policy analysts, organizers, and fundraisers, relatively few women reach the upper levels of politics. Government legislation on health concerns, abortion, pay equity, rape, and divorce are critical issues affecting women, but male politicians generally make the final decisions. In 1993, Kim Campbell became leader of the Conservative Party and prime minister of Canada before being defeated in the federal election of that year. In 1996, the leader of the federal New Democratic Party and the premier of Prince Edward Island were women. Although this suggests that women can and will be taken seriously as future leaders of this country, the vast majority of the leaders of Canada's political parties are males.

Case Table 6.1: **Percentage of Women in Canadian Federal and Provincial Legislatures**

Legislature	1975	1980	1984	1988	1993
Federal	3.4	5.0	9.6	13.4	18.0
All provinces	3.7	4.8	7.2	11.8	18.4
Newfoundland	1.0	3.8	5.8	1.9	5.8
Nova Scotia	2.2	0.0	5.8	5.8	9.6
Prince Edward Island	6.3	3.1	6.3	9.4	25.0
New Brunswick	3.4	6.9	6.9	12.1	17.2
Quebec	0.9	5.5	6.6	14.8	18.4
Ontario	5.6	4.8	4.8	15.4	21.5
Manitoba	0.0	1.8	12.3	15.8	19.3
Saskatchewan	3.3	1.6	7.8	7.8	18.2
Alberta	2.7	7.6	7.6	12.0	19.3
British Columbia	10.9	10.5	10.5	13.0	25.3

Source: Donley T. Studlar and Richard E. Matland, "The Dynamics of Women's Representation in the Canadian Provinces: 1975–1994," *Canadian Journal of Political Science,* Vol. 29, No. 22 (June 1996), p. 273.

Focus

Which provinces have the most impressive increases over the period shown? What factors might account for these?

Second-Wave Feminism

The issue of political equality cannot be separated from larger developments and issues. Major economic, technological, scientific, and attitudinal changes in society during the past 30 years have helped to foster, and have in turn been affected by, what has come to be known as "second-wave feminism." The second wave emerged in the 1960s and focussed on achieving social, legal, and economic equality for women in society. Although they are divided into moderate and radical camps, second-wave feminists seek equal rights for women as an absolute minimum goal. Pressure from women's groups led to the establishment of the Royal Commission on the Status of Women in 1967, and six years later to the creation of the National Action Committee for the Status of Women to lobby for gender equality. One major area of debate focussed on the issue of equality of access to education and employment for women and for minorities. In particular, the question of "affirmative action" or "employment equity" programs to ensure the representation of adequate numbers of women and minorities in the workplace was hotly contested. The impact of second-wave feminists has been immense, and has been particularly evident in the number of women enrolling in university, entering the professions, and joining the work force. The accomplishments of second-wave feminists include the recognition of equal rights for females in the Charter of Rights and Freedoms, and the 1986 Employment Equity Act, which limits employment discrimination.

Women still face barriers that limit their full social, political, and economic equality. Negative attitudes, little time and money, and male networking all continue to discourage women from seeking political office and achieving economic equality. According to a recent study, 62 percent of single mothers and 47 percent of single older women live below the poverty line. One-quarter of all women can expect to experience sexual assault in their lifetime, and every second female will be sexually harassed. Although women are widening their choice of occupations, many professions are still considered either female or male occupations. In 1915, Nellie McClung penned words that are still relevant today:

At the present time there is much discontent among women and many people are seriously alarmed about it. They say women are no longer contented with woman's sphere and woman's work. We may as well admit that discontent is not necessarily wicked. Discontent may mean the stirring of ambition, the desire to spread out, to improve and grow. Discontent is a sign of life, corresponding to growing pains in a healthy child.[3]

Minorities in Canada

At Confederation, only 10 percent of the Canadian population was of non-British or non-French origin. By 1991, 31 percent of the population was neither British nor of French ancestry. This dramatic shift illustrates the growing importance of immigrants from around the world to the development of Canada. As Case Figure 6.1 indicates, Canada is part of the global village.

Earlier, you learned that for many years Canada withheld voting and citizenship rights from several minority groups. Many of these groups are what are called "visible minorities." As non-Europeans, such minorities were denied their civil rights on the basis of ethnic, racial, or cultural characteristics. This denial of rights is an example of racism. Like sexism, racism is a term that has come into popular usage only in this century but most societies have traditionally been both sexist and racist.

Racism includes the notion that one race or ethnic group has the inherent right to exercise power over another race or group. Racial discrimination that stems from personal prejudice is called *individual discrimination*. Any law or policy that excludes racial or ethnic groups is called *systemic discrimination* because the discrimination is part of the legal, political, or social system. When the social beliefs, habits, and attitudes of one culture encourage individual and systemic discrimination against another culture, the result is called *cultural discrimination*.

Japanese Canadians

The history of Japanese Canadians contains illustrations of individual, systemic, and cultural discrimination. It is also the story of how Japanese Canadians and their supporters overcame that discrimination and won redress from the Canadian government for the worst systemic discrimination: the abolishment of their civil and human rights during and after World War II.

Case Figure 6.1: Sources of Immigration to Canada, 1981–1991

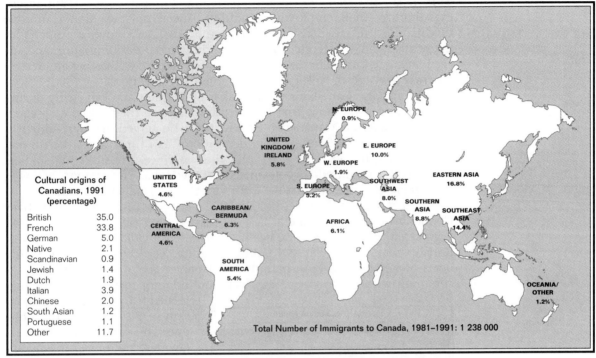

Cultural origins of Canadians, 1991 (percentage)	
British	35.0
French	33.8
German	5.0
Native	2.1
Scandinavian	0.9
Jewish	1.4
Dutch	1.9
Italian	3.9
Chinese	2.0
South Asian	1.2
Portuguese	1.1
Other	11.7

Total Number of Immigrants to Canada, 1981–1991: 1 238 000

Source: Reproduced by authority of the Minister of Industry, 1996, Statistics Canada, adapted from *Canada's Changing Immigrant Population*, Catalogue No. 96–311, 199, page 23.

Like most immigrants, Japanese came to Canada because it offered them more economic opportunity than their homeland. The first Japanese immigrants arrived in 1877, but it was not until the mid-1890s that immigration began in earnest. By 1911 there were more than 9000 Japanese immigrants in Canada. Known among themselves as *Issei*, this first generation of Japanese Canadians comprised mostly young men who began businesses in Vancouver and Victoria, settled on farms in the Fraser Valley, or took up fishing, logging, mining, railroad, and factory work, usually in British Columbia.

In 1895, British Columbia barred Japanese Canadians, both naturalized and Canadian-born, from voting in provincial or federal elections. In 1907, following a riot in Vancouver during which whites attacked Japanese and Chinese, Canada and Japan agreed to restrict immigration to 400 males per year. Because of this systemic discrimination, after 1911 the number of young female immigrants increased dramatically so that many children, called *Nisei* or second generation, were soon born in Canada. By 1941, the Japanese-Canadian population had grown to 23 450, 75 percent of whom were Canadian-born or naturalized.

The impact of racist laws and practices was one important reason why the economy of the Japanese Canadian community failed to grow more rapidly than it did. Many white workers feared economic competition from Asians because discriminatory labour laws and practices permitted white employers to pay Asians lower wages than whites received for the same work. Japanese Canadians were also barred from most professions and teaching, limiting their employment options. Social practices and restrictive caveats also prevented Asians, blacks, and Jews from buying property in many areas. Such systemic, cultural, and individual discrimination encouraged Japanese Canadians to live in close proximity to each other and to create their own social, cultural, and economic organizations.

Yet Japanese Canadians served valiantly in the Canadian Army during World War I in the hope that by defending Canada they would earn equal rights for Japanese Canadians. Of the 184 who served, 54 were killed in action and another 91 were wounded—more than three times the normal casualty rate. In 1931, 13 years after their sacrifice, the surviving soldiers were finally permitted to vote in federal elections. The cartoon below is more representative of Canadian attitudes toward Japanese Canadians.

Japan's aggression in China in the 1930s, its alliance with Hitler's Germany in 1940, and the attack on Pearl Harbor on December 7, 1941 aggravated the racist rhetoric against Japanese Canadians that was part of British Columbia's social and political culture. The confiscation of fishing boats owned by Canadian nationals of Japanese ancestry, the arrest of 38 community leaders in December 1941, and inflammatory press reports that fuelled fears of a Japanese invasion of B.C. resulted in public pressure to intern male Japanese nationals. In January 1942, the federal Cabinet responded by ordering the internment of all male Japanese nationals of military age and the confiscation of all motor vehicles, cameras, and radios owned by Japanese Canadians, actions that only served to confirm public fears. Although Canadian military and police leaders told the federal Cabinet that Japanese Canadians posed no threat to national security, politicians from British Columbia saw the war as an opportunity to rid British Columbia of all Japanese Canadians. On February 24, 1942, in response to pressure from B.C. Members of Parliament and the information that U.S. President Roosevelt had ordered the relo-

Despite the fact that the Japanese-Canadian population actually declined between 1931 and 1941, anti-Japanese feeling ran high in the years leading up to World War II.

Focus

What is the cartoonist's message, and what "facts" does he use to support this message?

cation of Japanese Americans away from the U.S. Pacific coast, the federal Cabinet ordered the uprooting and detention of everyone of Japanese ancestry who resided within 60 kilometres of the coast of British Columbia.

For the next seven years, Japanese Canadians were exiles with civil liberties in their own country. By November 1942, 21 881 men, women, and children had been shipped to detention camps in the interior of British Columbia or to sugar beet farms in Alberta and Manitoba. Some 700 males were confined in the Petawawa and Angler internment camps for refusing to be separated from their families. In 1943, all Japanese-Canadian businesses, farms, and personal property left in the care of government was sold without the owners' consent. The proceeds were taken to repay any welfare

A street scene at Tashme Detention Camp, British Columbia. Most of the camps were crude and provided only basic necessities.

accepted by the owner. In 1945, Japanese Canadians were forced to choose between moving east of the Rocky Mountains or deportation to Japan. Despairing of re-establishing themselves in Canada, 3964 Japanese Canadians—half of them children—deported to Japan. Not until April 1949, were full civil rights restored and Japanese Canadians granted the right to vote. Immigration from Japan did not resume until 1962.

The treatment of Japanese Canadians stands in stark contrast to that accorded German, Ukrainian, and Italian Canadians. While some male community leaders with connections to fascist or communist organizations were interned or kept under surveillance, German, Ukrainian, and Italian Canadians were not subject to loss of their civil liberties or the confiscation of their property. Japanese Canadians were deprived of their civil liberties solely on the basis of their common ancestry with an enemy nation and regardless of their Canadian nationality.

The Redress Campaign

For Japanese Canadians, the 30 years after World War II were characterized by hard work and educational achievement as the *Issei* and *Nisei* rebuilt their lives and raised the third generation of Japanese Canadians, the *Sansei*. In the late 1970s and early 1980s, access to government documents and the publication of new historical studies reopened the question of Canada's wartime actions against Japanese Canadians. The now successful and politically well-connected *Nisei*, their well-educated children, the *Sansei*, and concerned *Issei* began questioning the official claims that Japanese Canadians had been uprooted for their own good to protect them from mobs in British Columbia. They rejected the rationale that the uprooting was a "blessing in disguise" and the cause of their postwar prosperity. In 1981, the National Association of Japanese Canadians (NAJC) began educating the Canadian

---

In 1942 Canada Sent a Lot of Kids to Camp

You were born in Canada. Your parents were Canadian citizens. But that didn't stop the government.

Family property was seized and sold for a fraction of its worth. Your father was assigned to forced labour. You and your mother were transported to flimsy tarpaper shacks in the middle of nowhere, and left to cope with –30° winters.

Because you were a Canadian of Japanese descent, this would be your life for the next four years.

This, you discovered, was Canadian "democracy" at work.

WAS IT NECESSARY?

Were these drastic measures implemented against some 22,000 men, women and children necessary for national security?

The RCMP produced strong evidence to the contrary, but were overruled by the government.

Two tragic years later, this same government would publicly admit that no act of subversion by a single Japanese Canadian had ever been found before or during the war.

THE WRONG REMAINS

After the war they were left with little but the feeble utterances of succeeding governments. And for 41 years nothing's changed.

The present government proposes a unilateral quick fix in the name of "Multiculturalism" that does nothing to redress the real injuries suffered by these Canadians of Japanese ancestry.

It is time to right the wrong once and for all. Time, in the eyes of the world, to redress this long-standing failure of Canadian democracy itself.

WHAT YOU CAN DO

Join us in petitioning the Government of Canada to: (1) negotiate solely with the National Association of Japanese Canadians, the community's elected voice for over 38 years, (2) formally acknowledge government wrongs during and after WW II, (3) establish a just formula for compensation, and (4) insure through appropriate legislation that no future government can similarly mistreat another minority.

Please sign this ad and send it to:
**The Canadian Council of Churches
40 St. Clair Ave. East
Toronto, Ont. M4T 1M9**
It will accompany our formal petition to Ottawa.
Toronto Ad Hoc Committee for Japanese Canadian Redress.

A tax-deductible donation toward the cost of this ad would also be greatly appreciated. Please make cheque payable to "Canadian Council of Churches (Redress)".

RIGHT THE WRONG
Support Japanese Canadian Redress

"Right the Wrong" is an example of the support the Redress Campaign received from Canadians from all walks of life.

public about the wrongs done to Japanese Canadians and their causes. They collected evidence of the true extent of their property losses ($400 million in 1986 dollars) and lobbied the federal government for an apology, group and individual redress, and legislative changes to prevent similar discrimination ever happening again to any Canadian.

By 1988, backed by overwhelming public and media support, the NAJC succeeded. In June, the *War Measures Act* under which Japanese Canadians were uprooted was revoked and replaced with the *Emergencies Act*, which prohibits emergency orders that discriminate on the basis of race, national or ethnic origin, colour, religion, sex, age, or mental or physical ability. On September 22, 1988, Prime Minister Brian Mulroney officially acknowledged the wrongs done to Japanese Canadians. Over the next five years, 16 000 survivors accepted a symbolic redress payment of $21 000 for the loss of their civil rights. The Mulroney government also authorized a $12 million fund for rebuilding the Japanese-Canadian community destroyed by the uprooting and pledged a further $24 million to fund a Canadian Race Relations Foundation to fight all forms of racism in Canada and to foster racial harmony.

V I E W P O I N T

MARYKA OMATSU

A Father's Tragic Past

Maryka Omatsu's family was among those whose lives were shattered by the Canadian government during World War II. In the 1980s, she was part of the movement to win redress from the government, and was one of the negotiators of the final agreement. Omatsu's book *Bittersweet Passage* is a moving account of the Japanese-Canadians' struggle to come to terms with their painful history in Canada and of the author's own journey to discover her family's past. In the following passage, the author discovers hidden parts of her father's past.

Shortly after his death I returned to his small sunlit bedroom in our family house in Hamilton, Ontario, to go through his personal effects. ... Going through his wallet, I found his plastic Canadian citizenship card, his Hamilton senior citizens transit card, and—tucked away in a back compartment and neatly folded—his worn World War II government-issued "enemy alien" identification card, complete with his photo and thumb print. During the war and for a time after, all Japanese Canadians were legally required to carry these numbered identification cards. They had to produce them upon request by police and government officials.

Sitting on his bed, with his lifetime spread out around me, I felt anger and sadness upon seeing that tattered document—anger at the government that had "tattooed" my father and sadness for the man who had always lived in fear. It wasn't until years later that I would understand why. ...

During and after the war, Japanese Canadians were held in detention camps, denied freedom of movement, and made subject to a dawn to dusk curfew. My father had applied to the RCMP for a permit to travel to another town to look for work. The officer, unfamiliar with Japanese names, had misspelt his name and instead of writing "Omatsu" had written something approximating it. Later on, when officials asked my father to show his identification papers and found the wrong name, my father was thrown into jail, without a trial, for "travelling without authority." My father, apparently shamed by this episode, went to his grave with the secret. ...

In 1948 you were almost fifty, an "enemy alien," homeless, unemployed, with a dependent wife and children. You were virtually penniless because

the government had made you spend all of your life's savings to pay for your five years of captivity. Did you know how difficult it would be to start over? ...

[Even when the war was over] you and all other Canadians of Japanese ancestry were still denied freedom of movement. You were prohibited from returning to the "one-hundred mile zone" along the west coast where most of the community had lived until 1942. Throughout the years of forced relocation and detention you had wondered what had happened to your restaurant and dreamed of suddenly waking up surrounded by the hustle and bustle of customers and the smell of freshly made coffee. In 1948 the federal and B.C. governments did not want homeless, unemployed, and destitute Japanese Canadians returning to their homes, farms, and businesses, which were by then owned by veterans or persons who had benefitted from the 1942 government-held fire sales. But in 1980 no one thought to stop a small, white-haired Japanese Canadian from staring wistfully at a dream that had faded with time.[4]

Focus

What parts of this account indicate that Maryka Omatsu would later be one of the leaders for redress?

Conclusion

The issues of gender equality and the internment of Japanese Canadians raise fundamental questions about the existence of sexism and racism in Canada and about the safety of individual rights during times of crisis. How can the rights of minority groups be best protected? Is Canadian society changing?

B I O G R A P H Y

David Suzuki, 1936–

In *Current Biography*, David Suzuki is described in a capsule summary as "Canadian broadcast journalist; geneticist; writer; educator; environmentalist; civil rights activist."[5] This range of activities reflects Suzuki's passionate commitment to science, the environment, and the need for citizens to be involved in decisions that affect their future.

Suzuki is internationally known for his work, in both print and broadcast journalism, in popularizing science issues. In *Quirks and Quarks* on radio; television programs such as *Science Magazine* and *The Nature of Things* (CBC), and *Secrets of Life* (PBS/BBC); as well as in newspaper columns, books, and speeches, Suzuki has constantly worked to raise interest and awareness in science issues that affect people's lives. One writer described him as "passionate, driven, irreverent, brilliant, charismatic, and controversial, usually all in the same sentence."[6]

When Suzuki was 5 years old, his family was removed from their home in Vancouver and interned in a single room in a run-down building in Slocan City, a remote ghost town in the interior of British Columbia. His parents lost nearly all of their possessions, including insurance policies for their children's education. Suzuki described the internment as an experience that "seared his soul." It left him with a desire to prove his own worth, and a lasting sensitivity to human rights issues.

As a university student, Suzuki progressed rapidly in biology and genetics. He became a full professor at the University of British Columbia at the age of 33 and won awards for his research. But increasingly he devoted his activities to broadcast journalism in an effort to focus public attention on crucial issues in science and the environment. "Science alone can never provide answers to important questions like what is right and wrong," Suzuki stated. "If we are to control science, we must all learn how to think and to assess informa-

tion for ourselves."[7]

Suzuki has put much of the blame for current environmental problems on the developed world's political and economic systems, with special criticisms reserved for corporate and political elites and capitalist growth models. He draws particular attention to the developed world's consumption of 80 percent of the world's resources with only 20 percent of the population, and to the role of media in encouraging the message, "Consume, consume, consume."

Suzuki's contributions have been recognized in Canada and internationally with such awards as the Order of Canada, UNESCO's Kalinga Prize, and the UN Gold Medal. With his wife Tara, he has established the David Suzuki Foundation for sustainable development to promote "a vision of sustainable communities living within the planet's carrying capacity ... a strategy for communities to work toward that vision, and a communications plan to help work through the strategy."[8]

Suzuki's books include *Wisdom of the Elders*, *It's a Matter of Survival*, *Metamorphosis*, and *The Secret of Life*. The following excerpt is from his 1994 book, *Time to Change*.

To bring about the economic and societal changes needed to provide a sustainable future, we will need vision, courage, and leadership. People in positions of power must be persuaded to change their values and actions.

Right now the people who wield power and influence in society are politicians and business leaders. But they are severely constrained by the priorities of their respective professions: maximum profit and short-term results in the case of business and party loyalty, electoral constituents, and financial donors for politicians.

Those who are not part of the power elite often see issues with greater clarity. So when a broad base of grass-roots support grows, leaders who emerge will express the values that must be acquired in business and politics. ...

In 1989 when I interviewed [later U.S. vice president] Al Gore, I was profoundly influenced by what he said: "If you want real change, don't look to politicians like me for leadership. You must sell your ideas to the grass roots, empower them with a vision and the means to achieve it. When the public really understands it and demands it, we politicians will fall all over ourselves to climb on board."

Reflecting on Gore's advice, I realized that politicians and business leaders are severely limited by the rules that delineate the games they are playing. There is nothing evil or stupid about the participants; they are simply constrained by the definition of success as reelection or profit.

There was no better example of the limits imposed by politics than Lucien Bouchard when I interviewed him in 1989 while he was federal minister of the environment. He told me he believed global warming was the major problem we faced and that it threatened "the survival of our species." Yet when I asked whether that meant he would try to stop all oil megaprojects, he replied: "We can't annihilate the past. Those are political decisions already made."

Real change can only come from the grass roots up, and the change is already happening. In North and South, local environmental groups are sprouting up like mushrooms. They will not go away, because they are rising in response to the planet's distress.[9]

---

1 Why does David Suzuki put so much emphasis on ordinary citizens coming to their own conclusions on important issues?

2 How does his view of sustainable communities relate to his criticisms of our present political and economic systems?

Underlying and Emerging Issues

Give the reasoning and evidence that might be used to support different views or conclusions on the following issues.

1 To what extent is there equality of opportunity for individuals and groups in Canada?

2 To what degree are there barriers to full participation in Canadian society, based on gender and race?

3 To what extent are sexism and racism problems in Canada?

4 Should combatting sexism and racism be a high priority of Canadian governments?

5 Do males and females differ in abilities and aptitudes?

6 Does Canada's political system reflect systemic discrimination against women?

7 Should Canadian governments pursue policies of affirmative action and employment equity?

8 Is Canada's political system run by wealthy, older white males?

9 Are cultural or religious values and beliefs a justification for denying people equality?

10 Should governments have the right to limit civil liberties during times of war?

11 Should governments provide compensation for mistakes made by governments in the past?

12 To what extent is cultural diversity an advantage or a disadvantage?

13 To what extent should governments promote common values, and to what extent should they promote respect for diversity?

14 Should Canada pursue a policy of official multiculturalism?

Focussing Knowledge

In your notes, clearly identify or define and explain the importance or significance of each of the following:

equality	*racism*
multicultural policy	*systemic discrimination*
suffrage	*cultural discrimination*
sexism	*internment*
"separate spheres"	*Redress Agreement*
maternal feminism	*Nellie McClung*
enfranchisement	*Wartime Elections Act*

"Persons Case"

Royal Commission on the Status of Women

Agnes Macphail

Kim Campbell

second-wave feminism

National Action Committee on the Status of Women

affirmative action

Reviewing and Organizing Knowledge

1 What are the different approaches to analyzing the concept of equality?

2 a. How did the "separate spheres" view contribute to sexism?

b. How did it contribute to first-wave feminism?

c. What factors limited the success of the early suffragists?

3 Describe the factors that contributed to Nellie McClung's successes.

4 To what extent has women's participation in the political system changed since 1921?

5 a. How did the concerns of second-wave feminists differ from those of earlier groups?

b. What accomplishments resulted?

c. What remaining factors act as barriers to equality?

6 Describe the factors that work against equality for women in less-developed countries.

7 a. To what extent did Japanese Canadians face discrimination before World War II?

b. Why did the federal government take action against Japanese Canadians during World War II?

c. Describe the federal government's actions against Japanese Canadians during the war.

8 a. Why did Japanese Canadians press for redress?

b. What fundamental questions are raised by the treatment of Japanese Canadians during World War II?

Applying and Extending Knowledge

1 Research the role played by an individual woman in the early suffrage movement. To what extent were her motivations and actions similar to those of the women described in this case study?

2 Research one other country regarding the attainment of women's right to vote. Describe the extent to which the situations and actions were similar to and different from the Canadian experience.

3 Write a position paper in which you take and defend a stand on the following statement: "Canada's present political system reflects widespread systemic sexism."

4 Interview a woman over the age of 65. Ask her to describe the changes in the role and status of women that she has witnessed in her lifetime, and the degree to which she approves of those changes.

5 Research the issue of affirmative action and employment equity policies. In a position paper, describe your view of what actions should be taken.

6 Feminist theory is sometimes divided into three branches: liberal feminism, Marxist feminism, and radical feminism. Research these three approaches, and describe their similarities and differences in an essay.

7 Write a dialogue in which representatives from REAL Women and the National Action Committee for the Status of Women debate the need for action on women's issues.

8 Research the circumstances surrounding the treatment of Japanese Canadians during World War II. Write a position paper on the topic "To what extent was the wartime treatment of Japanese Canadians the result of cultural discrimination?"

9 Examine the experiences of another ethnic group in Canada. To what extent did or does this group experience systemic or cultural discrimination?

10 Investigate the position of the various political parties on the present policy of official multiculturalism. Defend one of the positions in a paper.

11 Select newspaper articles that reflect some of the Underlying and Emerging Issues on page 153. Explain how the articles illustrate the issues.

12 Choose one of the Underlying and Emerging Issues. Explain the complexity of the issue by outlining the arguments and evidence on the different sides.

Authoritarian Forms of Government

*W*HAT ARE THE BASIC PRINCIPLES underlying authoritarian states? This chapter discusses the origins and variety of authoritarian governments; reviews the writings of Carlyle, Nietzsche, Arendt, Hitler, and Machiavelli; and explores the "Great Man" theory, divine right, dictatorship, military coups, fascism, and totalitarian regimes. The chapter outlines the major characteristics of totalitarian and fascist states and evaluates the various theories that explain the attractiveness and success of such regimes. The conclusion compares fascism and communism and provides a critique of authoritarianism.

We have defined "democracy" as a system of government under which the ultimate power rests with the people, who elect lawmakers and government representatives from among themselves. Elections are held either when an administration or Cabinet chooses to dissolve government or loses the support of the majority of the elected lawmakers (as in Canada or Great Britain), or at the end of a legally defined term of office (as in the United States). The government thus derives its authority from the "will of the people" as expressed through elections.

Abuse of governmental authority is limited by the fact that all citizens enjoy a number of basic civil rights, or individual liberties. These are guaranteed either by tradition or by a bill of rights. The concept of such rights and the belief that the protection of the individual enjoying them is a prime responsibility of the state have become hallmarks of the ideology of modern liberalism and of liberal democratic forms of government.

Leaders of **authoritarian governments** see matters differently. They tell the people what to do and expect the people to obey. This obedience is usually justified in the name of some higher value (crown, state, nation, or race) to which an individual's interests and rights may be sacrificed. Such governments are commonly termed "authoritarian" and represent the opposite extreme to a pure democracy.

In one sense, democracy means rule by *all* of the people and is characterized by political equality. Authoritarianism or dictatorial regimes are based on rule by *some* (or only one) of the people, and are characterized by political inequality. The most extreme form of authoritarian rule is **dictatorship** (one-person rule).

Just as there are different types and degrees of democracy, there are also different versions of authoritarian regimes. In some cases, they may be one-person (often military) dictatorships, ruled by an authoritarian parental figure. A more common situation is rule by a small group, which is termed an **oligarchy**. Oligarchies controlled by the military are called **juntas**. The leader may either permit the expression of a broad range of dissenting views or demand total submission. When authoritarian governments seek to dominate and control all facets of public and private behaviour, they are generally referred to as **totalitarian**. Under this type of rule, all opposition is banned and the citizens surrender all rights to the ruling dictator, elite, or party.

Dictatorship

The term "dictator" comes from ancient Rome, where it referred to a position created to deal with national emergencies. When the Roman Republic was threatened by an invasion or other crisis that the regular authorities could not solve, one man was given absolute powers to rule the republic until the emergency was over. At that point, his authority reverted to the republic and he again became a private citizen. In the modern world, however, few dictators have shown a willingness to give up their powers voluntarily.

The idea of rule by one person is very old. In the ancient world, one-person rule usually took the form of an absolute monarchy. For example, in about 3000 B.C., a single king, or pharaoh, emerged in Egypt. By conquering smaller territories, he forcibly united the region along the Nile River into a single state under his absolute rule. His authority and that of future pharaohs was strengthened by the claim that they were gods. Their power was symbolized by the massive pyramids built to house the pharaohs' bodies after death.

Similar developments occurred in China, the Middle East, and India. In China, for example, the emperors were viewed as the "sons of heaven." The first Ch'in ruler, Shih Huang Ti, who united China around 221 B.C. and built the largest section of the famous Great Wall, erected a burial tomb that rivalled any structure found in Egypt. All such regimes were non-democratic and were dominated by powerful individuals holding political, military, and religious powers. Such states were typical of the ancient world. The democracies of Athens and the Roman Republic stand as marked exceptions. Even in Athens, the philosopher Plato argued for rule by an oligarchy of "guardians." Rome eventually abandoned its republican principles for rule by an emperor.

authoritarian government: a political system in which those in power are not controlled by the people but rather dictate to the people.

dictatorship: absolute rule by one person.

oligarchy: a government conducted and controlled by a relatively few influential members.

junta: an oligarchy controlled by the military.

totalitarian: relating to a political system in which the ruler or ruling body has established total control over all aspects of society.

European monarchs continued to enjoy religious and political authority throughout the Middle Ages. In the seventeenth century, for example, Russian rulers claimed complete power as tsars and **autocrats**. Western European political thinkers developed the theory of the "divine right" of kings. Monarchs, they claimed, were appointed by God and were responsible to God alone. Their subjects, therefore, must obey them unquestioningly. God's will was present in the birth of a new monarch, and any rebellion was thus a revolt against God.

autocrat: a person who rules as an authoritarian.

VIEWPOINT

JACQUES BENIGNE BOSSUET, 1627–1704
Divine Right of Kings

Jacques Bossuet, a Roman Catholic bishop, was one of the most prominent speakers and writers of his time. When King Louis XIV of France appointed him to tutor his son, Bossuet wrote *Treatise on Politics, Based on the Very Words of Holy Writ* (1678) to instruct the young heir to the throne on his divine rights and on his God-appointed duties when he became king of France:

ON THE NATURE AND THE PROPERTIES OF ROYAL AUTHORITY

Firstly, royal authority is sacred; secondly, it is paternal; thirdly, it is absolute; fourthly, it is subject to reason. ... God establishes kings as his ministers, and reigns through them over the peoples. We have already seen that all power comes from God. ...

Princes act as ministers of God and his lieutenants on earth. It is through them that He rules His empire. This is why we have seen that the royal throne is not the throne of a man, but the throne of God Himself. ...

It appears from all this that the person of the king is sacred, and that it is a sacrilege to attack him. ... Kings must be guarded as being sacred; and he who neglects to guard them deserves to die. He who guards the life of the prince, *places his own [life] in the safe-keeping of God. ...*

The service of God and the respect for kings are one; and Saint Peter puts these two duties together: "Fear God; honour the king."

The kings must respect their own power and use it only to the public good. Their power coming from above, as we have said, they must not believe that it belongs to them to be used as they please; but they must use it with fear and restraint, as a thing which comes from God and for which God will call them to account. Kings should therefore tremble when using the power that God has given them, and think how horrible is the sacrilege of misusing a power which comes from God.[1]

Focus

How do Bossuet's ideas compare with those of Thomas Hobbes in Chapter 2?

Liberal democratic ideas arose in opposition to monarchical rule. Although their initial victories came in the English revolutions of the 1600s, the American Revolution (1775–83), and the French Revolution (1789–99), only in the later 1800s did democratic forms of government become common throughout Western Europe. The end of World War I in 1918 was widely regarded as marking the victory of the liberal democratic ideal, the principles of which spread into Eastern and Central Europe. But this liberal triumph was short-lived. During the 1920s and 1930s, many democratic regimes — both old and new — rapidly reverted to authoritarian forms of rule as citizens grappled with the economic collapse and political instability that followed World War I and that were intensified by the Great Depression (1929–39). Hungary, Italy, Poland, Germany, and Spain, along with Japan and many Latin American countries, turned to dictatorial forms of government. In Russia, meanwhile, Vladimir Lenin's "dictatorship of the proletariat" had been transformed into the personal dictatorship of Joseph Stalin.

Unlike most monarchs of the past, the new dictators of the twentieth century were not chosen because of blood ties with past rulers. Rather, their power depended on the support of important segments of society, including the army.

President Harry Truman, centre, poses with British Prime Minister Winston Churchill, left, and Soviet Premier Josef Stalin during the Potsdam Conference, 1945.

Military Coups

Many of the world's governments are military dictatorships. In most of these countries the leaders gained their positions of power by a ***coup d'état.*** "I came in on a tank," said Saddam Hussein of Iraq, "and only a tank will evict me." Or, as Salvador Allende declared prior to the 1973 coup in Chile, "It won't cost you much to get a military man in. But by heaven, it will cost you something to get him out."

coup d'état: an attempt, whether successful or unsuccessful, to overthrow the government of a state.

Latin American Dictatorships Between the Wars

The Great Depression spawned dictatorships throughout Latin America. Only seven South American countries escaped dictatorial rule during the interwar period. As the following list indicates, dictatorships also thrived in Central America and the Caribbean.

Bolivia — Alternated between civilian and
              military dictatorships

Brazil — G. Vargas, 1930

Cuba — F. Batista, 1933

Dominican Republic — R. Trujillo, 1930

Ecuador — Political turmoil, 1931

El Salvador — M. Martinez, 1932

Guatemala — J. Ubico, 1930

Honduras — T. Andino, 1932

Nicaragua — A. Somoza Garcia, 1936

Peru — A. Leguia, 1919

A *coup d'état* is a sudden, violent, or illegal replacement of one government for another. The leaders of a coup are usually army officers, or public officials who infiltrate the army, who use the armed forces to seize power. For a coup to be successful, the leaders must gain the support of the majority of army officers. Officers with similar ethnic or religious affiliations or political views may be most easily swayed. The leaders may also look for officers with frustrated career ambitions who may be eager to participate in forming a new order. If the officers cannot be won over, civilian leaders of a coup attempt to immobilize the army, or at least distract it, while the coup is being executed by their own paramilitary forces. The essential elements of a successful takeover have included seizing the presidential palace, if only for symbolic reasons; disrupting communications and transportation by controlling the media, closing the airport, and setting up roadblocks around the capital; and arresting important political opponents.

Once the coup leaders have gained power, or at least control of communications, they address the people. Depending on what the previous regime was like, they may promise equality to all, an end to political terrorism, the dawn of a new era, or freedom from external control. Once the leaders have consolidated their power, there is no need to fulfil these promises. The final step is to transform the regime from a military to a quasi-democratic government. As political scientist Luttawak wrote in 1969, "Generals who fail to become politicians very soon cease to be either."

In some Latin American countries, coups became the established way to change governments. Bolivia, for example, has had 68 coups in 65 years. In general, coups differ from revolutions, which are usually more broadly based and far-reaching in their effects.

The "Great Man" Theory

Most authoritarian regimes throughout history have been based on the belief that a small elite is best able to govern a country. Faced with growing pressures for liberal reforms in the nineteenth century, many conservative political thinkers presented this argument in a new way. Impressed with Napoleon Bonaparte's laws in France (dating from 1799–1815) and the career of Julius Caesar (dating from 101–44 B.C.) in ancient Rome, they advocated rule by a talented and "enlightened" leader. British writer Thomas

"Great Man" theory: a theory that perfect government demands rule by a man possessing extraordinary abilities.

---

* The "Great Man" theory reflected the prevailing belief that men were best suited for such public positions as doctors, politicians, generals, and entrepreneurs, whereas women were better suited to remain at home and tend to their husbands and children. This view has been challenged effectively in the twentieth century in ways documented in this textbook.

Carlyle, for example, claimed that perfect government demanded rule by a "great man."* Carlyle detested democracy because it threatened to destroy the elitist social and economic order he so admired in Great Britain. According to Carlyle,

The history of what man has accomplished in this world is at bottom the history of the Great Men who have worked here. They were the leaders of men, these great ones; the modelers, patterners, and in a wide sense creators of whatever the general mass of men contrived to do or to attain.

By the early twentieth century, many other political theorists had popularized such ideas. Especially influential were the views of German philosopher Friedrich Nietzsche (1844–1900), who envisaged a future society run by a "superman" who set his own morality. Nietzsche believed that, while democracy created equality for all, it also bred conditions in which the spirits of superior people were crushed in the interests of the mediocre. This was a disaster, he argued, because only the superior person could achieve anything worthwhile. While his views were later distorted, they influenced many people, including Adolf Hitler, who claimed,

Iraqi President Saddam Hussein waves to supporters in 1995 after being sworn in as president for another seven years.

In all ages it was not democracy that created values, it was individuals. However, it was always democracy that ruined and destroyed individuality. It is madness to think and criminal to proclaim that a majority can suddenly replace the accomplishment of a man of genius. ... Every people must see in its most capable men the greatest national value, for this is the most lasting value there is. ... The will of the nation ... is of most use when its most capable minds are brought forth. They form the representative leaders of a nation, they alone can be the pride of a nation — certainly never the parliamentary politician who is the product of the ballot box and thinks only in terms of votes.[2]

In 1933, after 10 years of struggle, Hitler became chancellor of Germany and, inspired by these convictions, immediately began transforming that country into the Third Reich, one of the most powerful totalitarian states of the modern world.

Totalitarianism and Ideology

Following World War II, a number of American political scientists, among whom Karl Friedrich and Hannah Arendt were prominent, developed the theory of totalitarianism to explain the success of authoritarian regimes such as Mussolini's Fascist Italy, Hitler's Nazi Germany, and Stalin's Soviet Union.

Focus

Why would a totalitarian government want to dictate musical tastes, architectural styles, and literary themes?

They believed that such governments were unique in terms of the degree of control the state exercised over its citizens. The term "totalitarian" referred to these regimes' apparent desire to control *totally* all aspects of human life. Authoritarian governments, on the other hand, were content to control only the state's political life. Total control, political scientists argued, was made possible by the advances in communications (radio, cinema, telegraph, airplanes, railroads, cars) achieved during the nineteenth and twentieth centuries. These changes enabled the state to control almost all access to information and thereby attempt a systematic indoctrination of the populace.

Unlike earlier non-democratic leaders, modern totalitarian leaders sought to indoctrinate the people and restructure society to fit their ideological vision of the world. State propaganda sought to wipe out opposition, promote mass solidarity, and prepare for war. In this effort, the rulers devoted special attention to the youth, because if the system was to endure, it had to prepare future leaders who believed in the regime's methods and ideology. Hitler, for instance, talked of a "thousand-year Reich."

In this context, the term "ideology" means a prescribed set of beliefs about human nature, society, and the ideal state. These ideas often simplify the world to present citizens with clear-cut choices and easily identified enemies, and build on religious or other prejudices. Such is the case, for example, with the fundamentalist Muslim leadership in Iran (for whom the United States, "the Great Satan," is the enemy), or with groups such as the Ku Klux Klan, North American white supremacist groups, and some American "militia" movements.

Previous anti-democratic leaders, as well as some modern ones, were usually content to maintain the status quo. As long as their authority and desires remained intact, they frequently left the people alone to act and think as they chose. But the ideologies inspiring modern totalitarian leaders — whether of the left or the right — more often than not condemn the existing order as selfish and corrupt and seek to replace it with a morally and spiritually more strict social and economic system. To achieve this ultimate goal, the regime uses its monopoly of education and the media to convert the citizenry to its beliefs. In the process, liberal-democratic individual rights are rejected as obstacles to building the new and perfect world.

Modern totalitarian regimes share many characteristics: a desire to control and shape society; rule by one political party; control by a charismatic leader; a lack of individual rights; internal repression; censorship of the media; an extensive network of propaganda agencies that pay special attention to youth; control of the economy for the needs of the state and its rulers; preparation of society for war; and the spread of an ideology that justifies these measures.

Totalitarianism regards the nation as a living organism in which the individual is only a single cell. Each person has value only as a part of the larger whole and therefore can be sacrificed freely for the greater good of the social organism. Totalitarian ideologies justify the need for such sacrifices by maintaining a perpetual atmosphere of crisis, which demands continued vigilance to ensure that the enemy does not somehow rob the group of its victory in the struggle between good and evil. This same sense of ongoing struggle and the biological view of the nation as a living organism that is healthy only as long as it is growing and expanding demands expansionist policies. The only alternative is decline and eventual death.

Origins of Totalitarianism

Why would the citizens of a democratic state give up their voice in government and surrender their **civil liberties**? One common answer is that often they simply have no choice. From the beginning, most dictatorships enjoy at least the passive support of the police and armed forces, which permits them to use violence against their opponents. Once in power, totalitarian leaders usually escalate the levels of terror and violence to consolidate their rule and expand their authority throughout all levels of society. An environment of censorship, secret police, death squads, and concentration camps is used to exert physical and psychological control over the populace. This fear helps to promote conformity with the regime's directives. In Hitler's Germany, for example, the secret police (Gestapo), the Nazi party's private army of Brownshirts (SA), and the elite guards of the *Schutzstaffel* (SS) performed these functions. In the Soviet Union, this was the work of such state agencies as the KGB (Committee for State Security) and the Internal Troops of the Ministry of the Interior (MVD).

The situation in Chile from 1973 to 1989 provides a typical example of the use of terror by a right-wing regime. In 1973, the democratically elected socialist government of President Salvador Allende was overthrown by a military coup that brought General Augusto Pinochet to power. To ensure continued dominance, the military immediately launched a campaign of terror. During the first year of Pinochet's rule, some 60 000 people were arrested and held for at least 24 hours for interrogation. Some of these people were subsequently tortured, executed, or simply disappeared.

Even admitting the effectiveness of terror, it is clear that totalitarian regimes cannot exist without substantial support from the populace. Pinochet came to power at a time when there was considerable discontent with Allende. Mussolini was revered by numerous Italians. Many Germans remember the first years of Hitler's rule as the best years of their lives, and one can still hear Russians mourning the days when "Boss" Stalin maintained order with an iron fist. The question remains: why have authoritarian and totalitarian ideas been so attractive to so many people?

Theories of Causation

One widely accepted explanation for totalitarianism is the **crisis theory**.[3] This theory states that conditions of acute distress, such as economic depression or war, may produce such intense feelings of resentment, frustration, insecurity, and outright fear that people are willing to accept drastic political solutions. If the government seems incapable of solving these problems, people turn to totalitarianism with its **charismatic** leaders, simplistic solutions, easily defined enemies, emphasis on action, and promises of future well-being and glory. A number of historical examples seem to support this

civil liberties: the lawful freedoms of action and belief enjoyed by citizens of a democratic state.

crisis theory: the political science theory that all historical events in human society are triggered by various crises, such as war and economic depression.

charismatic; charisma (n.): having the ability to capture the attention and gain the support of people through the force of one's personality.

explanation: Mussolini took power in 1922 when Italy seemed to be on the brink of civil war brought about by social, political, and economic tensions; Lenin came to power in 1917 when Russia was in the midst of severe economic hardships; and Hitler emerged victorious in 1933 during the depths of the Great Depression.

Since not all countries have sought escape from their problems by turning to dictatorship or totalitarianism, we must answer the question of why some countries are less immune to the lures of this ideology. There is no universal agreement on this issue. American political sociologist Seymour M. Lipset argued that Nazism in Germany appealed to the middle classes, whereas communism appealed to the working classes. Lipset believed that the working classes were basically inclined toward authoritarian and totalitarian values. Their lack of education, he believed, prepared them for action rather than words, and toward accepting simple, uncomplicated answers. Since the working classes also earned lower wages, they were more likely to be dissatisfied and willing to blame their problems on others (the capitalists in Russia or the Jews in Germany). Other scholars have argued that the lifestyles in working-class families, which are often characterized by frustration and friction, produce authoritarian parent–child relationships, which further incline workers to accept totalitarian appeals.

Psychologist T.W. Adorno identified a personality type that he believed was especially open to totalitarian values. In his view, authoritarian parent–child relationships tend to produce adults who blame others for their misfortunes. They are dependent upon others for their strength and dislike people or groups they consider to be inferior. A person possessing an **authoritarian personality** thinks in stereotypes, conforms to majority opinions, admires power and strength, wants to punish "evil," sees people in terms of black and white, and is satisfied with superficial solutions. (See the questionnaire in Chapter 1.)

According to psychologist Erich Fromm (1900–80), modern industrial society has created feelings of personal isolation (alienation) and a lack of power that cause some people to seek direction from a strong leader who will give meaning to their lives and rescue them from their sense of helplessness. "The principal avenues of escape in our time," he wrote, "are the submission to a leader, as has happened in fascist countries, and the compulsive conforming, as is prevalent in our own democracy."

Fascism

Fascism is a right-wing nationalist ideology with a totalitarian structure. The term came from ancient Rome, where government authority was symbolized by the *fasces*, a bundle of rods (representing popular unity) containing an axe with the blade projecting (symbolizing leadership). Mussolini used the term fascism to label the movement he led to power in Italy in 1922. This term was later used to describe such groups as Hitler's Nazi movement in Germany, the Arrow Cross in Hungary, the Falangists in Spain, and the National Social Christian Party in Canada in the 1930s.

Focus

What can non-democratic governments do that democratic governments cannot? How would this be attractive to the populace?

authoritarian personality: a personal trait in which people are governed by the need to dominate everyone with whom they interact.

fascism: a political ideology characterized by an extreme right-wing view and support for totalitarian government.

Fascists attribute simple causes to complex events and offer simple remedies. They believe that the world is divided into good and evil with nothing in-between, and that there is a secret worldwide conspiracy against their nation by a hostile group. These extreme nationalists believe that their nation was once a powerful country that went into decline when it lost its racial purity. A common feature of fascist regimes is their belief that a nation is like a biological organism; each of the separate parts is necessary for the whole to survive, but separately the individual parts cannot survive. Human beings, they believe, are inherently sociable and divide themselves into distinct societies. Each society possesses a life of its own and is generally defined by unity of language, culture, religion, traditions, customs, and a feeling of territory. Each society is also united in pursuit of spiritual goals. Since these spiritual goals are superior to individual goals, and as workers act instinctively and emotionally (not rationally), the people need a strong leader who best understands and represents the nation's characteristics and goals. The creation of a sort of national family allows individuals to overcome the sense of personal loneliness and alienation of modern society.

Although fascism is often used as a synonym for Nazism, these two ideologies are in some ways quite distinct. Joseph Goebbels, Hitler's minister of propaganda, stated that fascism is "nothing like Nazism." However, there are substantial similarities. Case studies 8, 9, and 17 further explore the ideas of Hitler and Mussolini.

Communism and Fascism

The Marxists were obvious foes of fascism. Not only were they rivals for support from the masses, but their doctrine of class warfare and workers' internationalism was a clear threat to national unity. In addition, the Marxists' claim of rationalism threatened the very basis of the fascists' ultra-nationalism.

It is thus a mistake to equate Soviet Russia with Nazi Germany. It is true that Soviet Russia, especially under the rule of Joseph Stalin, shared many totalitarian traits with fascist dictatorships. All were regimes based on mass movements, dominated by a single leader who attempted to exert total control over the populace by propaganda and terror. The same may be said of theocratic regimes, such as the fundamentalist Muslim government in Iran.

However, there are also vast ideological differences among the various fascist, Marxist, and theocratic dictatorships of our century. Fascism uses myths, emotions, and hate, rather than reason, to motivate people. It looks to the past for its models and rejects reason and science as means of solving social and economic problems. As a result, fascist regimes tend to maintain themselves by external expansion. Theocratic Iran seems to share many of these traits, but proclaims an ideology based on a more deeply rooted religious doctrine that has wide appeal beyond Iran's borders. Communists, on the other hand, believe in human rationality and accept technology and the physical sciences as the means to build a brighter future. This belief probably encouraged internal change and allowed the Soviet Union to progress slowly from the Stalinist police state to the less autocratic state of Mikhail Gorbachev (see Case Studies 7 and 12).

Neo-Fascism

neo-fascist: a term used to
describe contemporary movements or persons advocating
white superiority and racial
purity.

The authoritarian challenge did not end with the defeat of Hitler in 1945, or
with the breakup of the Soviet Union in 1991. Aspects of totalitarianism
exist in a number of countries, especially in developing countries. The term
neo-fascist (*neo* means new) is used to describe contemporary movements
that preach white superiority and believe that immigration of ethnic groups
other than their own is a plot to dilute their race. Neo-fascist groups include
the Heritage Front in Canada, the Italian National Alliance, the National
Front in France, the Falange in Spain, Aryan Nations in the United States,
and the Ku Klux Klan in North America.

···What's Coming Next

The following four case studies examine how non-democratic governments
behaved in the past. To what extent does the theory presented in this chapter explain these real-life examples? Case Study 7 describes the causes of the
Russian Revolution in 1917, the subsequent Soviet system of government,
and the collapse of the Soviet Union. Case Study 8 explores how authoritarian regimes achieve power by examining how Mussolini, Mao, and Castro
seized power in Italy, China, and Cuba, respectively. Case Study 9 on Nazi
Germany asks you to evaluate a variety of primary documents to determine
how Hitler maintained control of Germany in the 1930s. Case Study 10 on
nationalism and ethnic conflict explores how well the rights of people are
protected.

Table 4.1: Communism Versus Fascism in Practice

	Communism	Fascism
Method of gaining power	• violent revolution	• abuse of the electoral system and terror (coup)
Method of rule	• single-party dictatorship	• single-party dictatorship
Source of beliefs	• writings of Marx, Lenin, Mao	• writings of Mussolini, Rocco, Sorel
Goals	• triumph of the working classes, world revolution, the overthrow of capitalism	• national greatness, constant expansion
Economy	• state-controlled, no private property, favours proletariat, emphasis on equality	• state regulation of private enterprise, favours capitalists, natural inequalities
Appeal	• working class, peasants, intelligentsia	• lower middle class, some upper class and clergy
Scope	• a worldwide movement, opposed to nationalism	• a series of national movements, stresses nationalism
Belief in reason	• humans are basically rational	• humans are basically irrational

HANNAH ARENDT, 1906–1975

According to some philosophers and historians of the twentieth century, human agents have little or nothing to do with the unfolding of history. These writers claim that world events such as wars, revolutions, and other major upheavals are brought about by complex political, economic, and social forces rather than by the actions of individuals. Political scientist and philosopher Hannah Arendt provides a powerful challenge to these views with her insistence that individual actions ultimately help to drive the engines of the historical process. At the same time, she provides important and controversial insights into the nature of totalitarian regimes.

Born in Germany and educated primarily at the University of Heidelberg, Arendt showed her considerable intellectual talents at an early age, earning a PhD in philosophy under the reknowned Karl Jaspers by her twenty-second birthday. Because of her Jewish background and her hatred of Nazism, Arendt fled to France and then the United States after Hitler's rise to power in 1933.

Although she had some initial difficulty in obtaining an academic post in the United States, this all changed with the publication of Arendt's highly regarded 1951 book, *The Origins of Totalitarianism*, a work that won for her both critical praise and a position as the first female professor at Princeton University. The book, the first important formal academic study of the roots of totalitarianism, advanced the contentious thesis that such systems were the natural outgrowth of anti-Semitism and imperialism.

Arendt is perhaps best known for *Eichmann in Jerusalem: A Report on the Banality of Evil*, her highly controversial account of the trial of Adolf Eichmann, a Nazi war criminal who was kidnapped by the Israelis and forced to stand trial in Israel in 1961. The work went against the common conception of Eichmann as a monumental monster who was almost solely responsible for the murder of 6 million Jews, and instead portrayed him more as a clerk in a broad anti-Semitic movement that existed throughout Germany and much of Europe. According to Arendt, Eichmann was no archvillain bent on the systematic destruction of an entire race, but rather an "ignorant and self-centred bureaucrat" who was so blinded by his ambition and devotion to the party that he failed to see the horror and consequences of his actions.

The work also alerted readers to a new and completely modern form of evil: according to Arendt, contemporary atrocities are no longer always accomplished through "sword or siege"; increasingly, they are committed by bureaucrats with the stroke of a pen, hundreds of kilometres away from those whom they consign to death. Aided by modern state structures and technology, men like Eichmann are able to murder millions with chilling speed and efficiency.

Arendt's description of Eichmann reveals much about the appeal of totalitarian movements to some individuals:

[H]e had been an ambitious young man who was fed up with his job as travelling salesman even before the Vacuum Oil Company was fed up with him. From a humdrum life without significance and consequence the wind had blown him into History, as he understood it, namely, into a Movement that always kept moving and in which somebody like him — already a failure in the eyes of his social class, of his family, and hence in his own eyes as well — could start from scratch and still make a career.

And if he did not always like what he had to do (for example, dispatching people to their death by the trainload instead of forcing them to emigrate), if he guessed, rather early, that the whole business would come to a bad end, with Germany losing the war, if all his cherished plans came to nothing ... he never forgot what the alternative would have been. Not only in Argentina, leading the unhappy existence of a refugee, but also in the courtroom in Jerusalem, with his life as good as forfeited, he might still have preferred — if anybody had asked him — to be hanged as Obersturmbannfuhrer a.D (in retirement) rather than living out his life quietly and normally as a traveling salesman for the Vacuum Oil Company.[4]

1 What contributions does Hannah Arendt make to your understanding of totalitarianism?

2 Why would Arendt have referred to modern evil as "banal"?

Underlying and Emerging Issues

Give the reasoning and evidence that might be used to support different views or conclusions on the following issues.

1 To what extent do most people "need to be led"?

2 Are dictatorships more efficient and effective than democracies?

3 Should we give more powers to governments during times of national crisis?

4 Are governments justified in using immoral means in order to achieve good ends?

5 Should we entrust government to people of superior ability?

6 Does democracy result in mediocrity?

7 Do advances in communications and technology make authoritarianism more likely?

8 Does modern industrial society create alienation?

9 How important is the individual when compared with the whole society?

10 What should be the role of emotion and reason in decisions about political and economic systems?

11 What should be the role of religion in political and economic systems?

12 To what extent is nationalism a desirable quality or value?

13 Is it more important to improve people's material conditions, or their liberties and freedoms?

14 To what extent should democratic societies tolerate racist or authoritarian movements?

15 How should Canada's government deal with white supremacist movements?

Focussing Knowledge

In your notes, clearly identify or define and explain the importance or significance of each of the following:

authoritarian government	crisis theory
political inequality	charismatic, charisma
dictatorship	authoritarian personality
oligarchy	fascism
junta	neo-fascist
totalitarian	Jacques Bossuet

autocrat	*Thomas Carlyle*
"divine right" of kings	*Friedrich Nietzsche*
coup d'état	*Augusto Pinochet*
"Great Man" theory	*Hannah Arendt*
civil liberties	

Reviewing and Organizing Knowledge

1 a. What are the fundamental features of authoritarian or dictatorial approaches to governing?

b. What forms can authoritarianism take?

c. How does totalitarianism differ from other forms of authoritarianism?

2 How prevalent has authoritarianism been in history? Why?

3 How does Jacques Benigne Bossuet's writing support autocracy?

4 What factors contributed to the decline of liberal democracy after 1918?

5 a. What factors contribute to the success of coups?

b. How do coups differ from genuine revolutions?

6 What were the views of the following writers regarding authoritarianism:

a. Thomas Carlyle?

b. Friedrich Nietzsche?

7 a. How do totalitarian systems differ from previous non-democratic regimes?

b. Why do people in some societies surrender liberties to totalitarian regimes?

8 Explain the views of each of the following regarding reasons for the success of totalitarian ideologies:

a. crisis theorists

b. Seymour Lipset

c. T.W. Adorno

d. Erich Fromm

9 On what basis does totalitarianism reject liberal-democratic beliefs?

10 a. What are the common features of fascist regimes?

b. What are the areas of disagreement between fascists and communists?

Applying and Extending Knowledge

1 Make a thorough list of all the arguments in favour of, and against, authoritarian approaches to government. Rate each of the items on your list on a scale from 1 to 10 (where "1" means "very weak argument" and "10" means "very strong"). On this basis, choose the three strongest arguments in favour of authoritarianism, and the three strongest arguments against it. Using these conclusions, write an essay outlining why people would both support and reject authoritarian forms of government.

2 Write a dialogue between an advocate of democracy (such as Martin Luther King, Jr., or Nellie McClung) and an advocate of authoritarianism or totalitarianism (Mussolini or Hitler).

3 Research a Latin American, Asian, or African country that has had a long history of authoritarian rule. What factors have contributed to the success of authoritarianism in the country?

4 Costa Rica has been democratic for an extended period of time, while many of the countries surrounding it have been authoritarian. What factors led to the success of democracy in Costa Rica?

5 Find newspaper articles that reflect aspects of authoritarianism in the world today. Explain how the articles illustrate elements of authoritarianism.

6 Select newspaper articles that illustrate some of the Underlying and Emerging Issues on page 169. Explain how the articles reflect the issues.

7 Choose one of the Underlying and Emerging Issues. In an essay, outline the arguments and evidence that might lead people to differing conclusions on the issue.

The Rise and Fall
of the Soviet Union

*T*HE GOVERNMENT of the Union of Soviet Socialist Republics (USSR) evolved from the Russian Revolution of 1917. This case study examines the post-revolutionary political system created by Lenin and Stalin and compares how this system was intended to operate in theory with how it worked in practice. It also discusses the origins of the Communist Party and its membership, functions, and powers. The next section examines the rise of Mikhail Gorbachev, his attempts to democratize the Communist Party, and his liberalization of the political system. The study concludes with an analysis of the fall of the Soviet Union, the power struggle that emerged in the wake of Gorbachev's fall from power, and Russian government under Boris Yeltsin.

The history of the world contains numerous examples of dictatorships, monarchies, oligarchies, and military juntas, as well as the more recent fascist and communist totalitarian states. There are more models of non-democratic than of democratic governments, and we should not assume that the record is complete.

This point is immediately evident if we look at Russia and the former Soviet Union. On the one hand, events since 1985 suggest that even the totalitarian state created by Joseph Stalin might evolve into a liberal democracy. On the other, during the 1996 election, there was a real possibility that the Russians might democratically elect a new Communist government (as was the case in several former communist states), and that this might lead to a return to totalitarianism.

How did this happen? This case study examines this question. As you read this study, keep the following questions in mind: Who made the decisions, and how did they maintain power? How and why has this system evolved since Stalin's death, especially since 1985? What were the basic values and assumptions of each type of government? Where does Russia seem to be headed?

The Russian Revolution of 1917

According to Marxist theory, in 1917 Russia was an unlikely place for a communist revolution to take place. Karl Marx had rejected the possibility that a socialist revolution could occur in a non-industrial country. Even Lenin at times became discouraged about ever seeing such a revolution in Russia in his lifetime, but he modified Marx's view in important ways. The resulting revolution changed the history of the world.

Under the tsars, Russian government was authoritarian, inefficient, and repressive. Compared with that of other Western European countries, agriculture in Russia was out of date and unproductive. Russia's economy was in the early stages of industrialization and the standard of living was low. With the spread of famine in the early part of the twentieth century, the tsar's iron hand had trouble controlling the people, and radical movements advocating a variety of solutions grew in popularity.

World War I triggered two revolutions. As the German army pushed farther into Russia, soldiers and civilians began to starve, inflation skyrocketed, and the cities became overcrowded with refugees. In late February 1917, women demonstrated against the high prices of goods, striking workers clashed with troops, and some soldiers deserted their regiments. These spontaneous demonstrations against the government eventually resulted in Tsar Nicholas II's abdication on March 15.* As the new government continued the war, the economy worsened. Subsequent military defeats increased inflation and produced more hardships. An attempted coup in September failed. Two months later, riots erupted on food lines and soldiers refused to stop the rioting. Promising "peace, land, and bread," the Communists (Bolsheviks) seized control of telephones, railways, banks, electric plants, and other vital utilities in Petrograd on November 7, 1917.

To end the war and begin rebuilding, Lenin made peace with Germany. Russia surrendered much of Ukraine, Finland, Poland, the Baltic states, and territories in Asia. Combined, these areas contained approximately 25 percent of Russia's population and cultivated land, and 73 percent of its iron and steel industries. In addition, Lenin had to crush a civil war in which Canada, Great Britain, the United States, and 10 other countries supported his enemies in Russia. By 1921, however, the Communists were victorious and turned their attention to governing the largest country in the world.

---

*Prior to 1918, Russian dates did not correspond with those in the Western world. The Gregorian calendar, which is now in general use in most parts of the world, was designed by Pope Gregory XIII in 1582. The Julian calendar, which was designed by Julius Caesar and used in Russia, was in error one day in every 128 years. (It is now 13 years behind the Gregorian calendar.) In 1918, the Soviet Union switched from the Julian to the Gregorian calendar, and the day after January 31, 1918, officially became February 14, 1918.

VLADIMIR ILICH ULYANOV (LENIN), 1870–1924

The Communist Party

Vladimir Ulyanov, who adopted the name Lenin, dedicated his life to overthrowing the Russian government after his brother Sasha was executed for plotting to assassinate Tsar Alexander III. In February 1897, Lenin was sentenced to a three-year exile in Siberia for revolutionary activity. He was released in 1900 and continued his revolutionary work.

Lenin was living in exile in Switzerland when Tsar Nicholas II fell from power in 1917. The Germans, wishing to promote chaos in Russia, arranged to transport Lenin to Russia in a "sealed" train. Lenin led the Soviet Union until his death in 1924.

Although Lenin was a Marxist, he differed from Marxist ideology in several important respects. In the following excerpt from his 1902 pamphlet, "What Is to Be Done," Lenin explains his views of the composition and duty of the Communist Party.

I assert: (1) that no revolutionary movement can endure without a stable organization of leaders maintaining continuity; (2) that the broader the popular mass drawn spontaneously into the struggle, which forms the basis of the movement and participates in it, the more urgent the need for such an organization, and the more solid this organization must be...; (3) that such an organization must consist chiefly of people professionally engaged in revolutionary activity; (4) that in an autocratic state, the more we confine the membership of such an organization to people who are professionally engaged in revolutionary activity and who have been professionally trained in the art of combating the political police, the more difficult will it be to unearth the organization; and (5) the greater will be the number of people from the working class and from the other social classes who will be able to join the movement and perform active work in it. ...

To concentrate all secret functions in the hands of as small a number of professional revolutionaries as possible does not mean that the latter will "do the thinking for all" and that the rank and file will never take an active part in the movement. On the contrary, the membership will promote increasing numbers of the professional revolutionaries from its ranks. ...

The only serious organizational principle for the active workers of our movement should be the strictest secrecy, the strictest selection of members, and the training of professional revolutionaries.[1]

Focus

How do Lenin's ideas differ from those of Karl Marx?

Values, Assumptions, and Myths

The Soviet government wished to convey the appearance that it was a democracy. Article 2 of the final (1977) Soviet constitution reads

All power in the Soviet Union belongs to the people. The people exercise state power through Soviets of People's Deputies, which constitute the political foundation of the USSR. All other state bodies are under the control of, and accountable to, the Soviets of People's Deputies.

In the West, these statements were dismissed as propaganda. But millions of Soviet citizens regarded their government as "democratic." This raises the issue of what social scientists often call "mythology." By this they do not mean tales from the past, but rather the generally accepted view of history that underlies any government and justifies its existence.

The history expressed in these "myths" is not necessarily false, but it is usually not the whole truth. For example, while it is true that the American Revolution was a revolt against the seemingly unfair policies of the British government, it is not true that all Americans were rebels. About one in three Americans supported Great Britain, and many eventually became the United Empire Loyalists who helped to settle Canada.

Two kinds of myths are important to know when analyzing any country's history. The **founding myth** explains why the government came to power. The **sustaining myth** reinforces the founding myth by explaining why the system of government continues in power. Together they justify the existence of that regime. If they are undermined, the government's existence becomes threatened.

founding myth: the underlying "story" that explains why a government came to power.

sustaining myth: the underlying "story" that explains why a government continues in power.

Democratic Forms

Article 2 of the Soviet constitution expressed the democratic aspect of the founding myth of the USSR. According to this myth, the 1917 revolutions overthrew the autocratic government of the tsar and replaced it with the democratic Soviets. And to some extent, this is true. "Soviet" is the Russian word for "council." The first modern soviet appeared as a strike council in St. Petersburg during the 1905 revolution. Similar "grass-roots" councils sprang up throughout Russia after the fall of the monarchy in February–March 1917. These democratic organizations coordinated policies through country-wide congresses, which elected a national committee to represent them between meetings. By seizing power in the name of the national Congress of Soviets, the Bolshevik Party, led by Vladimir Lenin and Leon Trotsky, formed the first Soviet government. Thereafter, the soviets became an important element of the official founding myth that the Communist Party used to justify its tenure in power.

In January 1918, the national Congress of Soviets proclaimed Russia to be a republic of workers', peasants', and soldiers' soviets. The Congress of Soviets was declared "the highest organ of power." A Central Executive Committee managed its affairs between sessions, while a Council of People's

Commissars, which was also elected by the congresses, served as the state's Cabinet or executive.

When the Union of Soviet Socialist Republics was created as a federal state in 1922, the other republics adopted a similar structure. The Congress of Soviets of the USSR, along with their Central Executive Committees, became the highest legislative body, and a Council of People's Commissars (later changed to Ministers) of the USSR emerged as the supreme executive body. Although subsequently renamed, these three bodies (congress, executive committee, and ministerial council) remained in place until Mikhail Gorbachev's constitutional reforms of 1988–89.

Clearly, the Soviet Union's formal structure of government was theoretically democratic. The Soviet Union also pointed with pride to the peaceful manner in which its many ethnic groups worked together and enjoyed equal rights. Since 1924, every new constitution formally guaranteed the democratic nature of this federation by stating that "each of the union republics preserves the right to freely secede from the Union."

. . . .

···**Authoritarian Essence**

Despite such statements, the Soviet regime was not democratic in the sense understood in the West. Between 1918 and 1989, no Soviet government willingly permitted any region to secede, and those that escaped (Finland, Lithuania, Latvia, and Estonia) did so by force of arms. Furthermore, as soon as it could (1939–40), the Soviet Union captured parts of Poland, Ukraine, Lithuania, Latvia, and Estonia, again by force.

Inside the Soviet Union, the democratic nature of the soviets was undermined immediately by the creation of a one-party state. Under the pressures of civil war and internal reconstruction, Lenin and his colleagues became increasingly intolerant of opposition. By 1922, the Communist Party of the Soviet Union (CPSU) was the only legal political party in the USSR.

Marxist–Leninists provided two main arguments to justify the Communist Party's monopoly of power. First, since Marxism teaches that political parties represent the interests of economic classes (such as the bourgeoisie and the proletariat), a state with only a proletariat needs only one party. Secondly, Lenin viewed the Communist Party as the "vanguard of the proletariat," the protector of the "true" doctrine of communism. This being the case, the presence of other political parties was at best an unnecessary irritation, and at worst a dangerous obstacle to the proper development of Soviet society. For these reasons, Communist thinkers considered the USSR a one-party "people's democracy." The Marxists viewed elections in capitalist countries as a sham in which the people chose among various members of the wealthy ruling classes, thereby creating the illusion of real choice.

As Case Figure 7.1 illustrates, the Communist Party was theoretically democratic. Initially it was democratic, but in 1921, Lenin banned all opposition and adopted the principle of **democratic centralism**. Issues were to be discussed thoroughly from the bottom up until they were decided upon at the top by a party congress. Then all discussion and protest were to stop,

democratic centralism: a political approach under which issues are discussed from the bottom up, then resolved by the party congress with the expectation that all party members will obey the policy.

and all party members were expected to obey the "party line" and implement the policies without question.

Case Figure 7.1: Theoretical Structure of the Communist Party

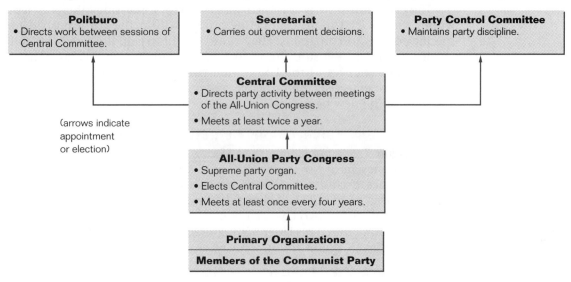

It is essential to bear these concepts in mind when attempting to understand the manner in which the Communist Party functioned. Also, remember that its purpose was quite different from that of Canadian political parties. The CPSU was responsible for supplying leaders for almost every organization in the country, for providing political and economic guidelines for mobilizing the people to fulfil the party's commands, and for public indoctrination.

Stalin and the Communist Party

General Secretary Joseph Stalin ruthlessly used the police and the courts to purge all opposition within the party. Once Stalin had concentrated power in his hands, the principle of democratic centralism became a justification for stifling all opposition by censorship, imprisonment, and executions. In this way, Stalin ensured complete personal control over the party. Subsequent leaders possessed similar powers. As a result, the party's general secretary was the most powerful figure in the USSR. The government controlled the USSR, the party controlled the government, and Stalin controlled the party.

Under Stalin, the Communist Party's policies were made by a small group of about 15 leaders who formed the **Politburo**, which was under the supervision of the **Secretariat**. In practice the Politburo, whose discussions were kept secret, was the country's supreme policy-making body. The Communist Party was the elite, and the Politburo was the elite within the elite. The general secretary and his assistants supervised all government and state appointments and implemented policies throughout the Soviet Union.

Politburo: the supreme executive agency of the Communist Party in the former USSR that was responsible for making and enforcing policy.

Secretariat: the supreme administrative agency of the Communist Party that managed the daily activities of the Party.

In 1989, General Secretary Gorbachev had at his disposal in the Secretariat 6 commissions and 29 departments that were responsible for such areas as agriculture, defence, ideology, transport and communications, culture, the chemical industry, and propaganda.

The Communist Party was the major arena for discussing different views within the Soviet Union. Competing groups within the party pushed for specific policies and programs. They either sought to gain the ear of the leaders or attempted to ensure the victory of sympathetic candidates. Indeed, major policy changes in the USSR often parallelled changes in leadership. Once a victor emerged, the principle of democratic centralism ensured the adoption of the new party line.

The Party and Government Structure to 1988

As Case Figure 7.2 demonstrates, the USSR's government retained all the basic institutions present in November 1917 until 1989. The constitutions of 1936 and 1977 gave exclusive legislative power to a parliament known as the Supreme Soviet of the USSR. A direct descendant of the Congress of Soviets, this body consisted of two co-equal houses, the Soviet of the Union and the Soviet of Nationalities. This latter body contained representatives from the 53 states of the Soviet Union and in some ways resembled the American Senate.

Case Figure 7.2: Theoretical Structure of the Soviet National Government to 1988

(closest Canadian equivalent in parentheses)

Although this system appeared both democratic and federal, in practice the Supreme Soviet seldom met more than twice a year, and then for only a few days. Real decision-making occurred elsewhere. Almost all laws were passed first by the Presidium and later approved by the Supreme Soviet. The Presidium was elected by a joint session of both houses of the Supreme Soviet. So too was the Council of Ministers (formerly the Council of People's Commissars), which acted as the highest executive and administrative organ of state power. It was headed by a first minister or premier who theoretically was the most powerful figure in the state. The Chairman of the Presidium meanwhile served as president, but he was mostly an ornamental head of state.

The real purpose of the Supreme Soviet was not to maintain a careful watch over the executive but to help spread its messages. Since reports of its proceedings received wide coverage in the media, its sessions served as publicity events for the unveiling of new laws. Despite the government's theoretically separate and parallel position beside the Communist Party, the CPSU transformed the Supreme Soviet into its own agency. Indeed, in many respects the two were integrated, and it was the CPSU that made government policy. In practice, the CPSU's control of the government was even tighter than this suggests, as the overwhelming majority of ministers and senior state officials were also party members.

The Soviet system was thus designed to allow a small group of people to control the government, supposedly for the benefit of all. Given the ban on other political parties until the latter 1980s, Soviet elections were ritualistic affairs. Like the sessions of the Supreme Soviet, they usually served as occasions for spreading the party's new policies rather than as opportunities for the people to make meaningful choices among various leaders and policies. At the polls, the voters were told to mark an "X" through every name on the secret ballot except for the person they supported. But since there was seldom more than one name on the ballot, there was no real choice. Even in local elections, the CPSU nominated 60 percent of all candidates.

Despite the fact that the results of such elections were a foregone conclusion, the party made vigorous efforts to ensure a high voter turnout. In districts in which prominent party and state officials ran, special efforts were made to meet local needs (a new bridge, for example). Elsewhere, local party leaders made frequent speeches, party workers distributed pamphlets and conducted door-to-door canvassing, invalids were transported to polling booths, voters often found free buffet lunches awaiting them, and so on. As a result, the Soviet Union boasted a 99.8 percent voter turnout for elections.

Other considerations cast further doubt on Soviet claims that the USSR was a true constitutional democracy. In theory, there seemed much to justify the claim that Stalin's 1936 constitution was "the most democratic constitution in the world." It included a bill of rights that guaranteed freedom of speech, association, religion, organization, and the press. Other provisions promised gender equality as well as protection against arbitrary arrest. All discrimination was prohibited, and everyone was granted the right to employment, education, leisure time, and support in sickness and in old age. However, this new constitution did not establish a means to enforce these rights, nor did it limit the government's power over citizens. Further, along with the list of citizens' rights, there were also citizens' obligations, which included the duties to abide by the law, maintain labour discipline, perform all public duties honestly, and safeguard public "socialist" property.

Ironically, the adoption of this constitution coincided with the beginning of Stalin's "Great Purges," when millions of Russians were arrested and many of them executed as "enemies of the people." Despite attempts to

Focus

Why was the Soviet Union so concerned with the appearance of democracy?

minimize the numbers executed in these purges, in February 1990 the CPSU publicly admitted the errors of the Stalinist regime.

Communist Party Membership

Given the important role of the Communist Party in governing the Soviet Union, the quality of its membership was a matter of priority. Membership was restricted only to those who were worthy in terms of political consciousness, honesty, ability, and dedication. It took approximately two years to become a member. Each applicant had to be nominated by a party member and undergo a thorough investigation. As a result, only about 20 percent of those over the age of 18 were full members. As of January 1991, approximately 6 percent of the population were members of the CPSU (about 16 million people). As Communists, they were expected to be dedicated, accept the party's right to make basic decisions affecting their lives, undertake whatever tasks were assigned, and adhere to strict rules of personal conduct. Members failing to meet these standards, or who disobeyed party directives, lost their membership, along with the privileges and advantages it offered for career advancement.

The Communist Party represented the educated elite. Factory directors were Communists, as were journal editors and almost all army and navy officers. So too were most judges, attorneys, senior police officers, 40 percent of engineers, and roughly half of the USSR's scholars. Nevertheless, the party took pride in stressing that the majority of its members were employed in industry and agriculture (72 percent in 1989). Of these, the overwhelming mass were urban workers. Farmers and women (30 percent) were underrepresented.

Even with these drawbacks, the CPSU membership was diverse enough to ensure that it penetrated all aspects of Soviet life. Backed by the authority of the state (and the secret police), the Communist Party ensured that the official founding myths of party and state were the only views mentioned in either the media or the schools. Similarly, literature and history presented accounts that agreed with the official party line.

Victory in World War II, in which 25 million Soviet citizens died, provided the sustaining myth of the importance of the Communist Party. Thereafter, Communism and nationalism combined to sustain Soviet morale through the first decades of the Cold War.

Gorbachev's Constitutional Reforms

Despite some modifications by Nikita Khrushchev, the political system changed very little after Stalin's death in 1953. By the mid-1970s, however, the Stalinist system showed signs of strain. Economic growth had slowed sharply, while new ideas began to surface among the Soviet elite. No changes were made under the leadership of Leonid Brezhnev (1964–82), a period now called the "period of stagnation." Signs of real change became evident only under the brief rules of Yuri Andropov and Konstantin Chernenko. A full program of restructuring (***perestroika***) seemed possible only with the emergence of Mikhail Gorbachev as general secretary of the CPSU in the spring of 1985.

perestroika: a program of economic and political restructuring introduced in the USSR by Mikhail Gorbachev in 1985.

While economic restructuring was the essential aspect of Gorbachev's effort (see Case Study 12), he felt that he would need widespread popular support for such changes and thus sought to make the government more democratic. To do this, he first had to strengthen his position within the CPSU. In 1987, Gorbachev allowed discussion of major political issues and strengthened citizens' rights of appeal against unjust government decisions and violations of civil rights. More significant was the new openness (*glasnost*) allowed in the debates within the Communist Party and in the activities of the Supreme Soviet of the USSR.

Substantial political restructuring finally came in 1988. New laws provided greater protection for civil liberties, and the Soviet of People's Deputies was given greater powers. To achieve this last goal, Gorbachev demanded the creation of an active Supreme Soviet under the direction of an elected president. A second group of measures dealt with the Communist Party—it too was to be democratized to allow "free discussion of all topical questions of policy and practice." However, Gorbachev remained committed to communism's basic elements, convinced that it was possible to make the necessary reforms from within.

By the end of 1988, Gorbachev had succeeded in implementing the first stage of his reorganization. He also had emerged as president of the USSR as well as general secretary of the CPSU. When the Supreme Soviet approved these innovations, Gorbachev felt secure enough to introduce a number of amendments to the constitution that radically changed both the electoral system and the structure of the central government (Case Figure 7.3).

glasnost: a policy of openness that allowed increased freedom of expression of political opinions within the Communist Party and the USSR under Mikhail Gorbachev.

Case Figure 7.3: Structure of the Central Government and Administration, 1989–1991

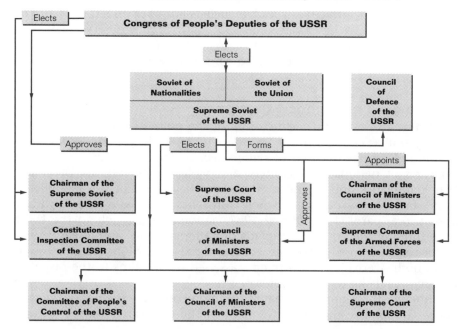

Congress of People's Deputies: a government body, comprising 2250 members, introduced by Mikhail Gorbachev to wield full authority in the USSR.

Under Gorbachev, the **Congress of People's Deputies** became the most important political body. Its 2250 members, who met only once a year, elected 542 of their number to serve in the two houses of the Supreme Soviet. The Supreme Soviet acted as a permanent legislature and elected its own Presidium (under the Chairman) to conduct its business between sessions; appointed the Chairman of the Council of Ministers (the Premier); approved that council's membership, examined the annual budgets; approved all major diplomatic, military, and judicial appointments; declared war; ratified treaties; and called and monitored elections.

The public's interest in these more democratic governing bodies was indicated by the fact that during the first six months of 1989 the government received some 680 000 letters and telegrams. The Supreme Soviet itself was swamped by 38 000 visitors. Nevertheless, Gorbachev remained dissatisfied with the rate of progress, and in early 1990 he won approval for further reforms. His new program aimed at the complete transfer of real power from the CPSU to the government. The party now was to surrender its privileged position and compete with other political parties. Additional measures separated the regime's executive, legislative, and judicial functions.

At first glance, these changes seemed to signal the introduction of liberal democratic ideals and institutions to the Soviet political system. In reality, the Communist Party remained powerful. The new system offered the Communist elite distinct advantages as compared with its rivals. The CPSU was given significant representation in the new Congress and its two Soviets. The same was true of Communist Party groups such as the Young Communist League, the armed forces, and the trade unions. In fact, of the 2250 People's Deputies elected in 1989, 1957 were party members and only 160 deputies could be called "non-party." True, membership in the CPSU was becoming less attractive as leaders such as Boris Yeltsin left the party to pursue other approaches. Even so, as 1990 dawned, few observers believed that the CPSU was in any immediate danger of being swept from the political stage, and Gorbachev still wielded considerable authority as its general secretary.

The Dangers of Democratization

The democratization and restructuring of the political system were parallelled by similar changes in the economy (Case Study 12) and by less censorship and greater freedom of public debate. These reforms opened the floodgates of nationalist discontent and violence. As early as December 1986, nationalist riots engulfed Alma-Ata, the capital of the republic of Kazakhstan. These riots began when Gorbachev replaced a Kazakh with a Russian local party chief. During 1987, nationalists throughout the USSR began forming their own movements or national fronts, and in early 1988 violence again erupted. This time it assumed the proportions of a small-scale war as both Azerbaijan and Armenia asserted their claims to the disputed Nagornyi-Karabakh region by force of arms.

Although these uprisings shared common concerns, their aims differed widely. Groups like the Volga Germans or the Crimean Tartars, exiled to

Central Asia during World War II, now wanted to be restored to their ancestral lands. Georgians, Abkhazians, and Ossetians sought greater political and cultural autonomy. Lithuanians, Latvians, and Estonians demanded separation from the USSR.

In making their demands, the nationalists offered different interpretations of Soviet history. For example, claims for the independence of the Baltic republics forced a reassessment of Stalin's agreement with Hitler in 1939, which had led to these three states' annexation to the USSR. This then forced a re-evaluation of Stalin's wartime leadership that revealed his mistakes. As more and more of the so-called "blank pages" in Soviet history were filled in, faith in both the founding and the sustaining myths of the Soviet Union and the Communist Party began to crumble.

Case Figure 7.4: Distribution of the Nations and Nationalities of the USSR

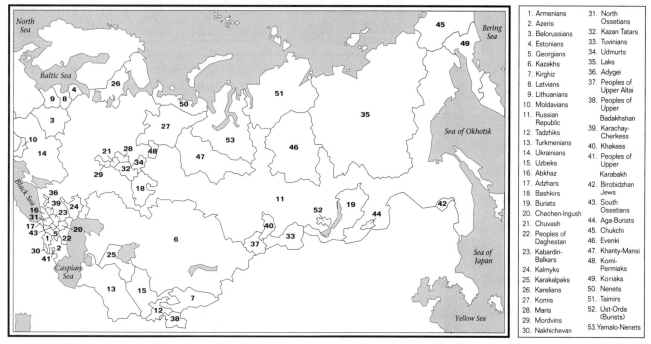

1. Armenians	31. North Ossetians
2. Azeris	
3. Belorussians	32. Kazan Tatars
4. Estonians	33. Tuvinians
5. Georgians	34. Udmurts
6. Kazakhs	35. Laks
7. Kirghiz	36. Adygei
8. Latvians	37. Peoples of Upper Altai
9. Lithuanians	38. Peoples of Upper Badakhshan
10. Moldavians	
11. Russian Republic	39. Karachay-Cherkess
12. Tadzhiks	40. Khakass
13. Turkmenians	41. Peoples of Upper Karabakh
14. Ukrainians	
15. Uzbeks	42. Birobidzhan Jews
16. Abkhaz	
17. Adzhars	43. South Ossetians
18. Bashkirs	44. Aga-Buriats
19. Buriats	45. Chukchi
20. Chechen-Ingush	46. Evenki
21. Chuvash	47. Khanty-Mansi
22. Peoples of Daghestan	48. Komi-Permiaks
23. Kabardin-Balkars	49. Koriaks
24. Kalmyks	50. Nenets
25. Karakalpaks	51. Taimirs
26. Karelians	52. Ust-Orda (Burists)
27. Komis	53. Yamalo-Nenets
28. Maris	
29. Mordvins	
30. Nakhichevan	

···Gorbachev's Executive Presidency

Faced with growing ethnic violence, economic discontent, and political opposition, Gorbachev sought to strengthen his position. In March 1990, the Third Congress of People's Deputies created an "executive" president who would have the combined powers of a U.S. president and a Canadian prime minister and governor general. Although Gorbachev was elected to this position by the Third Congress, all future elections were to be conducted by direct popular vote.

Gorbachev's new powers included the right to introduce legislation; to veto other bills; to appoint the prime minister, ministers, and senior judicial figures; to declare martial law and war; and to negotiate treaties. The Congress of People's Deputies retained the power to approve all presidential decrees and appointments and could overturn the president's veto or fire him by a two-thirds vote. Even so, by holding the posts of general secretary and president, Gorbachev had acquired more personal power than any Soviet leader since Stalin.

The extent to which the CPSU had lost its authority became evident in July 1990. Armed with his new powers, Gorbachev faced a hostile majority of delegates. Most delegates disliked many aspects of Gorbachev's reforms, but they failed to win election to the Secretariat. The delegates had little alternative but to watch as Gorbachev changed the Soviet empire by preparing a new all-union treaty of federation. In a sense, Gorbachev (termed "the man of half-measures" by his critics) alienated both groups. Those who favoured democracy felt that he had not gone far enough; hard-line Communists regarded him as the agent of dangerous changes.

Key opposition to Gorbachev's power came from Moscow's former Communist Party leader Boris Yeltsin. Expelled as leader of Moscow's section of the Communist Party in 1987, Yeltsin was elected chair of Russia's Parliament in June 1990. A year later he was elected president of the Russian Republic, becoming the first democratically elected head of the Russian people. From this position, Yeltsin set out to undermine Gorbachev. Despite brief periods of cooperation, the feuding continued through the first half of 1991 and did much to weaken Gorbachev's struggle to preserve the USSR. Nonetheless, the new all-union treaty of federation was drawn up and scheduled for signing on August 20, 1991.

End of the Soviet Union

The attempted pro-Communist coup of August 19–21, 1991, sounded the death knell for both Gorbachev and the Soviet Union. It began as an attempt by hard-line Communists to regain control. On the previous day, a group of dissatisfied military men, conservative officials, and embittered Communists placed Gorbachev under house arrest at his summer house in the Crimea. At 6:00 a.m. the next day, Moscow Radio announced that he was incapacitated, and that power had passed to an emergency committee. For the next three days the world watched while Yeltsin took centre stage and urged the public to defend the White House (the parliament building). In the end, the rebels withdrew and were arrested.* Although Gorbachev was released and returned to Moscow, he was now totally dependent on Yeltsin.

The plotters wanted to prevent the signing of a new agreement that would give more power to the regions. But instead of regaining power, the opposite occurred. All hopes of implementing the new treaty of federation

---

*See Chapter 4 for a discussion of the elements of a successful coup.

were dashed, and real power now lay in the hands of Yeltsin and the presidents of the republics. Events moved rapidly. On August 23, Yeltsin banned the CPSU and seized its assets. On the 24th, he recognized the independence of the Baltic states (Latvia, Lithuania, and Estonia), and the Ukraine declared itself a separate country. The governments of the other republics quickly followed suit. By September, the Congress of People's Deputies had little choice but to formally dissolve the USSR. Additional negotiations led to a series of agreements that culminated in a treaty creating the Commonwealth of Independent States (CIS), a loose association of most of the former republics, on December 8, 1991. But the CIS was a face-saving measure: the end was clearly in sight. On December 25, Gorbachev formally resigned as Soviet president. When all Soviet flags were officially lowered on the night of December 31, the Soviet Union ceased to exist.

Case Figure 7.5: The Impact of the Fall of Communism on Eastern Europe and the Soviet Union, 1989–1991

Source: From *A History of Modern Europe, Vol. 2: From the French Revolution to the Present* by John Merriman. Copyright © 1996 by John Merriman. Reprinted by permission of W.W. Norton & Company, Inc.

In the place of the Soviet Union was left a Russian Federation and a host of other new states: the three Baltic republics, Belarus, Ukraine, Moldovia, the central Asian republics, and those of the Caucasus. As for democracy, prospects varied widely from republic to republic. In Russia, President Yeltsin quickly came into conflict with his new parliament, now known as the State Duma. After two years of turmoil, in October 1993, Yeltsin responded to the opposition's seizure of a television station by sending in tanks to attack the same White House he had defended two years earlier, and then dispersing the deputies.

In October 1996, Communist demonstrators mark the third anniversary of clashes between the Yeltsin government and opposition hard-liners.

In December, Yeltsin introduced a new constitution that concentrated power in his hands as president, left the Duma an ineffective debating society, and relegated the judicial system to the fringe of public life. The 1995 elections to the Duma resulted in gains for more extreme parties. In the summer of 1996, Russians went to the polls in a presidential election to decide upon the country's future. The basic choice was between Boris Yeltsin and Gennady Zyuganov. Yeltsin had been extremely unpopular in 1995, particularly after the Chechnya war, but he had recovered much of his support, in part through manipulation of the media. Zyuganov promised a return to the Communist past (with some changes), including more food and jobs, an end to crime, and a return to national greatness. He pointed to the recent ills of democracy: hyperinflation, industrial collapse, civil war in Chechnya, rampant crime and corruption, and a decline in the people's standard of living. Yeltsin offered personal freedom and warned of renewed repression if the Communists were successful. "We have come too far," he said, "to suddenly change everything back to the old ways." Although the 1996 election was about Russia's future, it was also about its past. Was the Soviet era a time of repression, mass murder, purges, empty store shelves, and endless line-ups, as Yeltsin argued, or were Zyuganov's claims true that it was a period of economic security, national pride, military power, industrial might, and international respect?

Despite some of Yeltsin's less democratic actions, many people portrayed the election as a choice between moving forward to a more market-oriented economy and democratic society, or moving backward to a more moderate brand of communism. Although Yeltsin was successful in 1996, few observers are willing to predict how the next regime will tackle the economic and political problems that still reign throughout much of the Russian Federation. Yeltsin's poor health only compounds the problems.

Soviet Leaders Since Stalin

Georgi M. Malenkov	Premier	1953–55
Nikita S. Khrushchev	General Secretary	1953–64
	Premier	1958–64
Nikolai A. Bulganin	Premier	1955–58
Leonid I. Brezhnev	General Secretary	1964–82
	President	1977–82
Aleksei N. Kosygin	Premier	1964–79
Yuri V. Andropov	General Secretary	1982–84
Konstantin U. Chernenko	General Secretary	1984–85
Mikhail S. Gorbachev	General Secretary	1985–91
	President	1988–91
Boris N. Yeltsin	President of Russia	1991–

Conclusion

For many citizens of the former USSR, the years since 1991 have brought little if any improvement, and the concept of democracy itself has been badly tarnished. In their view, economic reforms have brought chaos and stagnation rather than an improved standard of living. Crime has increased dramatically, and the so-called "mafia" often seems more powerful than the government; civil war has engulfed Chechnya; in Russia's Asian regions, Islamic fundamentalism has gained widespread support; Russia has lost much of its once-powerful role in international politics. Consequently, extreme Russian nationalism has gained popularity, and many Russians apparently have lost their enthusiasm for democratic and economic ideologies based upon those found in the West.

There is profound disagreement in Russia about both the past and the future. Some Russians look back to the communist past as a time of stability, order, economic security, and national greatness. Other people see a legacy of dictatorship, repression, terror, and restrictions. These judgements of the past will play a critical role in the Russian peoples' political and economic decisions about their future.

ALEKSANDR SOLZHENITSYN, 1918–

"Admired by some as a modern saint and prophet and dismissed by others as an egoist and a fanatic,"[2] Aleksandr Solzhenitsyn is a controversial figure in twentieth-century literature and politics. For nearly four decades in his novels, non-fiction books, and speeches, he fearlessly challenged the Soviet view of life under Communist rule in the USSR. While Solzhenitsyn's courageous defiance of the Soviet state earned him the approval of many in the West, some of these supporters have been alienated by his more recent attacks on the moral decline of North America.

Born into relative poverty in Kislovodsk, a small community in the Caucasus in the former USSR, it is said that Solzhenitsyn knew by the time he was 9 years old that he would be a writer. Although he enrolled in mathematics at the University of Rostov, the desire to write was always at the back of his mind. Following his graduation in 1941, he was hired as a mathematics teacher in a small southern Russian town, but soon was drafted into the army after the German invasion of Russia.

In what was to become the defining moment of his life, Solzhenitsyn was arrested for writing "anti-Stalinist sentiments" in 1945 after one of his private letters was intercepted by the secret police. Taken before a three-man tribunal and denied the right to a fair trial, he was sentenced to eight years in a Soviet labour camp. While he had been an ardent supporter of communism in his youth, Solzhenitsyn's experiences in the brutal *gulag* ended any sympathy for the Stalinist system.

Following his release in 1954, Solzhenitsyn was not allowed to return to his home and was forced into permanent exile in Kazakhstan. However, this exile was short-lived when Khrushchev initiated liberalization after Stalin's death. Solzhenitsyn was allowed to publish his novel *One Day in the Life of Ivan Denisovich* in 1962, shortly before the return of repression under the Brezhnev regime. The work, an account of the harshness of life in a Soviet prison camp, earned Solzhenitsyn international fame, and ironically even the gratitude of government officials.

But with the return of hard-line communism in the mid-1960s, Solzhenitsyn was once again regarded as a renegade. His manuscripts and archives were confiscated by the secret police; probably only his international fame (in 1970, he won the Nobel Prize for Literature) saved him from more severe punishment. His continued defiance and open attacks on the government finally culminated in his forced exile in 1974. After a brief stay in Germany, Solzhenitsyn emigrated to Vermont, where he lived until the collapse of the USSR.

In a move that surprised some, Solzhenitsyn was equally critical of Western society, focussing on what he regarded as the increasing spiritual and moral decay of the West. In his view, Westerners had become like spoiled children "who had turned their backs on the Spirit, and embraced all that is material with excessive and unwarranted zeal." By their disregard for religion and morality, the Western democracies had abdicated their positions as world leaders. While such claims did little to endear him to many Western intellectuals, most would still agree that Solzhenitsyn must be regarded as one of the most important writers of the twentieth century.

---

1 How does Aleksandr Solzhenitsyn's life reflect important elements of the rise and fall of the Soviet Union?

2 What factors have led to his status as a controversial figure in the West?

Underlying and Emerging Issues

Give the reasoning and evidence that might be used to support different views or conclusions on the following issues.

1 Why is democracy not widespread in the world?

2 To what extent are political systems based on mythologies?

3 To what extent is Canada's system based on a mythology?

4 Is material progress a justification for denying individual rights?

5 To what degree can one-party systems reflect elements of democracy?

6 How can countries with cultural and ethnic diversity achieve national unity and consensus?

7 Are democracy and economic growth related?

8 Should political and economic reform be gradual or rapid?

9 Can democracy succeed in countries that lack democratic traditions?

10 To what degree do economic difficulties limit chances for democracy?

11 How important is the success of democracy in Eastern Europe to Canadians?

12 Should Western countries give substantial aid to republics of the former Soviet Union in order to promote democracy?

13 How important are order and stability as compared with freedom?

14 To what degree were people "better off" under communism in the USSR?

15 Is it justifiable to use undemocratic practices to bring about democracy in the long run?

Focussing Knowledge

In your notes, clearly identify or define and explain the importance or significance of each of the following:

Union of Soviet Socialist Republics (USSR)	Commonwealth of Independent States (CIS)
tsar	Duma
soviet	Chechnya
proletariat	Vladimir Lenin
democratic centralism	Joseph Stalin
Great Purges	Leonid Brezhnev
perestroika	Mikhail Gorbachev
glasnost	Boris Yeltsin
Congress of People's Deputies	Gennady Zyuganov
Executive Presidency	

Reviewing and Organizing Knowledge

1 a. Describe the characteristics of Russia under the tsar before the 1917 Revolution.

b. How did World War I contribute to the Revolution?

2 How did Lenin's ideas on government differ from those of Marx?

3 Distinguish between the two kinds of myths that underlie political systems.

4 a. What was the early role of the soviets?

b. How did the Bolsheviks use the soviets?

5 a. In what ways was the formal structure of the government of the USSR theoretically democratic?

b. What early factors undermined the democratic elements?

c. How did Lenin justify the Communist Party's monopoly of power?

d. How did the political system change under Stalin?

6 Describe the role of each of the following in the Stalinist political system:

a. Politburo

b. Secretariat

c. Supreme Soviet

d. Presidium

7 a. Describe the factors that allowed a small group of people to control the government of the USSR.

b. To what extent did the membership of the Communist Party reflect the diversity of the society?

8 a. What factors led Gorbachev to attempt political reform?

b. Describe the main elements of Gorbachev's early reforms.

c. What were Gorbachev's main changes to the structure of government?

d. Describe the factors that worked against Gorbachev's success.

9 a. What factors prompted the attempted coup of August 1991?

b. How did the unsuccessful coup result in Gorbachev's loss of power and the dissolution of the USSR?

c. Describe the structure that replaced the USSR at the end of 1991.

10 a. Describe the state of democracy in Russia under Yeltsin after 1991.

b. How did the presidential elections of 1996 reflect fundamental choices and differing views in Russia?

c. What problems may affect the future of democracy in Russia?

Applying and Extending Knowledge

1 Research and compare the policies and actions of Lenin and Stalin. To what extent were they similar and different in their approaches?

2 Investigate the Great Purges. To what extent were they motivated by Stalin's paranoia, or by a desire to consolidate power?

3 Explore the life and writings of Leon Trotsky. To what extent might Russia have developed differently with Trotsky rather than Stalin in charge?

4 You have examined the mythology underlying the USSR's political system. To what extent do liberal-democratic systems have founding and sustaining myths? Answer this question by referring to Canada and the United States.

5 Research and compare the USSR's political system under Stalin and Brezhnev. To what extent was Brezhnev's regime a continuation of Stalinism?

6 Write a position paper on the following topic: "Gorbachev's policies were too little, too late."

7 Write a dialogue between one of the following pairs that develops one or more of the themes or issues covered in this case study:

a. Stalin and Gorbachev

b. Gorbachev and Yeltsin

c. Yeltsin and Zyuganov

8 Take and defend a position on the following statement: "Once he got into power, Yeltsin became another Russian dictator."

9 Research the developments in Russia's political system since the 1996 presidential election. To what extent have prospects for democracy improved or diminished?

10 Find newspaper articles that illustrate recent developments in Russia's government. How do the articles contribute to your understanding of the situation?

11 Select newspaper articles that reflect some of the Underlying and Emerging Issues on page 189. Explain how the articles illustrate the issues.

12 Choose one of the Underlying and Emerging Issues. Describe the arguments and evidence on the different sides, and explain why the issue is complex.

Achieving Power:

Mussolini, Mao,

and Castro

USSOLINI'S SUCCESS IN ITALY in the 1920s is attributed to a combination of the political and economic turmoil in the country after World War I, the problems faced by the Italian government, and Mussolini's personality, fascist ideology, and tactics. Mao's success in China after World War II is explained by the country's chaotic political and depressed economic situation, and by Mao's philosophy and strategy. The case study concludes with an examination of Fidel Castro's successful revolution in Cuba.

Non-democratic governments have achieved power in a variety of ways. Such totalitarian leaders as Benito Mussolini in Italy and Adolf Hitler in Germany manipulated the democratic electoral process in the 1920s and 1930s to gain political office. Once in power, they used their position to impose one-party rule. In a monarchy, power is passed on through inheritance. Most non-democratic leaders gain power by such violent means as revolutions, **guerrilla warfare**, and military *coup d'états*. It is also not unusual for such countries to install **puppet dictatorships** in conquered countries.

Historical and contemporary examples of non-democratic regimes are almost endless. Dictatorships continue to flourish in Latin America, Africa, and Asia. In the twentieth century, communist regimes emerged in Asia, Europe, and some developing countries. More often than not, one dictatorship merely replaced a previous non-democratic government, but in several instances, democracies fell victim to non-democratic regimes.

What made this period different from earlier times was the rise of totalitarianism. Generally, totalitarianism refers to a form of government that rejects individualism, and is controlled by a single political party that controls almost all aspects of life, from the economy to cultural institutions. The governing party possesses a revolutionary ideology, and uses terror, **propaganda**, and mass communication to gain and retain power.

One of the best methods of analyzing the underlying beliefs of a political system is to examine how political power is achieved and what provisions are made for the continuance of the regime. Are the people consulted? To what extent are individual rights and freedoms subordinated to the demands of the state? Who are the political leaders? What role does the individual citizen play in the political system? Keep these questions in mind as you read the following accounts of the rise to power of Benito Mussolini, Mao Zedong, and Fidel Castro.

guerrilla warfare: small-scale fighting, mostly hit-and-run raids, by small groups of often non-professional soldiers.

puppet dictatorship: a dictatorship in which the leader is under the control of a person, group, or country.

propaganda: systematic attempts to manipulate opinions or beliefs, often through the mass media, to maintain control over or to intimidate a populace.

The Decline of Democracy

Immediately following World War I, democracy appeared ready to sweep through Europe. But as the map illustrates, during the 1920s and 1930s, country after country turned to some type of authoritarian or dictatorial rule. In Turkey, Poland, and Iran, military officers assumed control. Yugoslavia, Romania, and Albania established monarchical dictatorships. Dictatorships also emerged in Bulgaria, Hungary, Greece, Austria, Latvia, Lithuania, Estonia, Portugal, and Spain.

The peace treaties that came out of World War I were partly to blame for this situation. Their harsh terms angered the defeated countries and left two countries on the victorious side, Italy and Japan, particularly unhappy. The hard economic times following the war and the devastating depression of the 1930s also served to discredit democracy. Unhappiness seemed to exist everywhere. During the 1930s, Japan witnessed the assassination of two prime ministers, two failed military coups, and the rise of military personnel to key political positions. In the Caribbean and in South and Central America, many countries fell under dictatorial rule between the 1920s and the 1950s. Confused, bitter, and unemployed, many people turned to energetic and dynamic leaders who promised to solve their problems.

Italy After World War I

World War I (1914–18) had a traumatic effect upon Europe, including Italy. Soldiers returned from the battlefront to find no jobs available because munitions factories and other war industries had been closed. The continued decline of Italy's economic production and a decrease in overseas trade resulting from the war added to the country's economic problems. Unemployment rose from 90 000 in the summer of 1920 to over half a million by the end of the next year. The cost of living increased by 50 percent, and the middle classes soon found that their meagre savings were consumed by inflation. For example, one Italian lira in 1919 could buy only one-tenth of the amount of food it had in 1913. Most urban workers and rural peasants had no savings to lose and remained mired in poverty.

Case Figure 8.1: Dictatorships in Europe, 1932–1937

Source: From *A History of Modern Europe, Vol. 2: From the French Revolution to the Present* by John Merriman. Reprinted by permission of W.W. Norton & Company, Inc.

What made the situation even worse was that Italian politicians had promised the people prosperity after the war. Disillusionment began to set in, and many Italians became increasingly unhappy with the country's democratic rulers. In the countryside, rich landlords had their houses burned and their livestock slaughtered when they opposed several left-wing groups attempting to redistribute their land among the poorer peasants. Although not much land actually changed hands, the mayhem convinced large landholders that stronger government action was necessary to prevent a communist revolution.

In the large industrial cities, strikes became more and more frequent. Industrial strife reached a peak in the fall of 1920, when workers seized 600 factories in a series of sit-in strikes. Although the crisis soon passed and the factories were returned to their owners, occasional strikes continued to disrupt Italian industry. These rural and urban conflicts revealed the weakness of the government. Paralyzed by divisions within Parliament, the coalition governments lacked the power to intervene and re-establish order.

One of the Italian government's promises to the people had been that participation in World War I would bring national honour to the country. Italy entered the war to secure additional territory and emerged from the war with high hopes of obtaining the western part of Yugoslavia, including the ports of Trieste and Fiume, a strip of Dalmatia on the eastern Adriatic shore, and some of Germany's colonies in Africa.* The middle and upper classes considered Italy's failure to secure most of these possessions a blow to Italian national prestige. Once again, the government was accused of inaction and ineffectiveness.

The Italian Government

Italy was a constitutional monarchy. As in Great Britain, the king had limited powers and the Chamber of Deputies (similar to the Canadian House of Commons) was the most important legislative branch of government. Clearly defined political parties had been slow to emerge in Italy, partly because it had become a fully unified country only in 1870, and partly because the people were not used to democratic procedures. Italy had a Parliament, but no parliamentary traditions. The party system was extremely fragmented. There were at least 10 different political parties, and the two largest ones — the Socialists and the Christian Democrats — were unable to cooperate because of ideological differences. In addition, elected representatives frequently switched from one party to another.

The result was chronic political instability. On the average, governing coalitions changed every year and a half. When the people turned to the government for help, they saw a divided Parliament engaged in endless debates, bickering, name-calling, "buck passing," and procrastination. Faith in democracy dwindled as the political regime seemed incapable of defending Italy's interests abroad, solving the country's economic woes, or providing law, order, and efficient government at home. Into this confused situation stepped Benito Mussolini.

Mussolini's Early Career

Benito Amilcare Andrea Mussolini was born in northern Italy in 1883, the eldest in a family of three children. His father was a poor blacksmith with socialist beliefs that he tried to instil in his children. Mussolini was named after the Mexican revolutionary, Benito Juarez, and his middle names were taken from two prominent Italian socialists.

Mussolini attended a Catholic high school from which he was expelled for stabbing a rich schoolmate with his penknife. Despite another knifing incident at the next school, Mussolini graduated in 1902 with an elementary school teaching certificate. A year later, he travelled to Switzerland to

---

* Italy's lack of ideological commitment to the war was evident when the country chose the winning side partway through the conflict in return for promised territorial gains.

further his education, but soon became so involved in encouraging strikes and establishing trade unions that he was deported. Returning to Italy, Mussolini continued his socialist preachings and in 1908 was imprisoned as a dangerous revolutionary. Once out of prison, Mussolini became editor of *Avanti* (Forward), the official newspaper of the Italian Socialist Party, and for the next few years he threw himself behind the socialist cause with total commitment.

When World War I erupted in 1914, Mussolini termed it a bourgeois or middle-class war and urged Italy to remain neutral — which was acceptable socialist doctrine. It was not long,

Why would Mussolini have approved of this picture?

however, before he changed his mind and began urging Italy to participate. As a result, Mussolini was forced to resign from *Avanti* and break with the Socialist Party. A short while later, he was drafted into the army, where he was wounded, discharged, and exempted from further duty. Mussolini was now ready to begin a new phase in his career.

Following a failed attempt to found a separate labour party, Mussolini decided to create a movement that was both "material" and "socialist." In March 1919, about 300 journalists, former Socialists, war veterans, and revolutionaries met with Mussolini and organized themselves into combat groups. Mussolini was now ready to enter the political fray.

Mussolini the Leader

Before describing Mussolini's rise to power, let us first examine the character of the man who was to rule Italy for over two decades. He did not cut an imposing figure — he was rather short and was balding, and his round face was marked by a jutting jaw, a large mouth, and dark, protuberant eyes. To disguise his short stature, Mussolini always stood ramrod straight, pushed out his lower lip and jaw, and tilted his head back so that he always seemed to be looking down at the person to whom he was talking. Once in power, he enjoyed standing next to the king, whom he dwarfed in size.

Mussolini and the Fascists wanted to stand for virility and strength. His poor health and ulcer, which prevented Mussolini from eating meat and drinking wine, were therefore hidden from the public. Likewise, his fondness for playing the violin, which was considered effeminate, was seldom mentioned. Instead, he was pictured as a horseman, a pilot, and a driver of fast cars. Although he also liked to pretend that he was a cultured, well-read intellectual, he had little interest in art, and he usually skimmed a book as quickly as possible to obtain its highlights. His one love was politics, and his goal was to achieve power and influence.

In personal relationships, *Il Duce* (The Leader, as he liked to be called) was a vain egotist who was insensitive to the feelings of those around him. His only real friends were his father and brother. He was ready to sacrifice everyone else, including his wife, who bore him five children, and his many mistresses, in his pursuit of power.

Mussolini appears to have suffered from an inferiority complex. In times of crisis, he was afraid to take action. Lacking self-confidence, he tended to follow the advice of whoever spoke to him last. Complex problems were ignored or reduced to a simple matter of black and white.

Rhetorical skill was Mussolini's major asset. With a voice that was both powerful and flexible, *Il Duce* was able to establish a rapport with a crowd — and stimulate it to action. He spoke in a series of sharp, often unconnected statements. In short, he had charisma. Following World War I, he was ready to put his talents and his ambition to work.

Mussolini's Rise to Power

In March 1919, Mussolini began to gather around him a small group of ex-Socialists and former armed servicemen who were having difficulty adjusting to civilian life. Initially, the movement was nationalistic, anti-clerical, and anti-capitalist. Attempting to appeal to the workers, Mussolini advocated an eight-hour workday, universal suffrage, and an end to class privilege. In the election of that year his party received fewer than 5000 votes, and his old Socialist friends paraded in front of his house carrying a coffin bearing Mussolini's name.

Mussolini changed course once again. Rather than continue to appeal to the apparently unresponsive lower classes, he decided to cater to wealthy businesspeople. He drafted a less radical platform that offered something for everyone. This sudden reversal did not appear to bother Mussolini, and he subsequently told the people, "We permit ourselves the luxury of being aristocratic and democratic, conservative and progressive, reactionary and revolutionary, legal and illegal, according to the circumstances of the moment, the place and the environment."

In 1920, following an abortive attempt by workers to seize the factories, *Il Duce* threw his whole weight against the Socialists and the Communists. Groups of young men called **squadristi** were outfitted in black shirts and sent into the streets to combat the Communists. They broke strikes, raided trade union offices, vandalized the offices of left-wing newspapers, and terrorized anyone who opposed them. It was not long before this violence spread throughout Italy. If, as sometimes happened, a Fascist member was murdered, within hours truckloads of Fascists would come rumbling into town on a punitive expedition. The government, which also disliked left-wing groups, did nothing to stop the violence. In fact, it quietly supplied the Fascists with weapons and gave them free railroad transportation. The police, too, often aided them in their battles against the leftists, or did nothing to stop them. The *squadristi* attacks created a sense of camaraderie among Mussolini's supporters. More important, they helped to mobilize widespread support. In the process, a private army, answerable only to Mussolini, was created.

Il Duce: Benito Mussolini, "The Leader" of Fascist Italy between 1922 and 1945.

squadristi: in Mussolini's Italy, groups of young Fascist men sent into the streets to combat the Communists.

The March on Rome

In the 1921 general election, Mussolini's Fascist Party captured 35 seats in Parliament, and party membership grew to 300 000. This was an indication of the growing success of Mussolini's tactics. By the next year, almost every segment of society was ready to cooperate with the Fascists. Merchants, skilled workers, professionals, and intellectuals all wanted a strong leader who could rebuild Italy's national prestige and restore law and order in the streets. To landowners, Fascism meant protection against further land seizures. To employers, it meant fewer strikes and the possibility of lower wages. Mussolini's deliberate attempts to increase violence and anarchy in the streets served to keep property owners in a state of alarm. With the government unable to do anything, Fascism seemed to be the only solution. Moreover, the Socialist Party's success in appealing to the labouring class made the middle and upper classes uneasy. Mussolini played on their fears by prophesying that a communist revolution similar to the 1917 Russian Revolution would happen in Italy if he were not elected.

Although *Il Duce* had been anti-clerical and anti-monarchist, by 1922 he was on cordial terms with Pope Pius XI, and Italy's Queen Mother herself was an avid Fascist. The Pope, distrusting the parliamentary system, which he thought was incapable of preventing the growth of socialism, believed he could work with Mussolini. King Victor Emmanuel's younger brother supported the Fascists, whom he hoped would place him on the throne. The fear that the Fascists might replace Victor Emmanuel with his brother was enough to keep the king from obstructing the spread of Fascism. Finally, the civil service and many politicians supported *Il Duce* because they believed they could control his actions. Given power, Mussolini would become more responsible — or so they thought.

By 1922, Mussolini felt strong enough to challenge the government. When the government ignored his threat to seize control of the state if he was not given power immediately, he ordered the *squadristi* to isolate the government offices in Rome from the rest of Italy by capturing strategic railway and telegraph offices. At the same time, the Fascists, approximately 26 000 strong, began their "march on Rome."

After a period of indecision and confusion, the government decided to call out the army. In retrospect, this was the correct decision. The Fascists were outnumbered and had no cannons, and some were armed only with clubs. They were trained for street fighting, not for a full-scale military campaign. In fact, the Fascist troops were instructed to avoid conflict with the army, and where the authorities did offer resistance, the marchers fell back without putting up a fight. The king, however, did not know this. He used his authority to cancel the government's order to call out the army. Two days later, the king invited Mussolini to become the new premier — the change in government was thus constitutional.

Italy's Fascist Government

For the first few years, *Il Duce* lived up to the expectations of the upper and middle classes. He took lessons in protocol and manners. He wore conventional clothes for public appearances, and he reported twice weekly to the king. In Parliament, Mussolini established a conventional ministry and was given a vote of confidence by the Chamber of Deputies. It is true that he demanded and was granted dictatorial powers until the end of 1923, but this was not unusual in Italy at this time, and was perfectly legal.

Gradually, Mussolini gained more and more power. Although the Chamber of Deputies continued to function, the Fascist party selected all candidates and presented them to the electorate for approval. The ballot read: "Do you approve of the list of deputies chosen by the Fascist Grand Council?" Civil servants who disagreed with the Fascist philosophy were dismissed. *Il Duce* was given permanent control of the military forces, which swore personal allegiance to him. Local municipal elections were abolished, and municipal officials were appointed by the government in Rome. Newspapers were censored, and Socialist and Catholic trade unions were prohibited. Mussolini placed dedicated Fascists in charge of the schools, created a Fascist youth movement, Fascist labour unions, and many other Fascist organizations. He abolished divorce, and told women to stay home and produce children. In 1934, Mussolini passed a special tax on bachelors, and four years later, women were limited to a maximum of 10 percent of the better-paying jobs in industry. "Italy wants peace and quiet, and calm in which to work," Mussolini declared, "This we shall give her, by love if possible, by force if need be."

By the end of 1926, Mussolini was the undisputed Fascist dictator of Italy. He would remain so until successive military defeats forced him out of office in July 1943. Unlike Hitler, *Il Duce* did not persecute Jews and did not establish a truly ruthless police state. In 1945, Mussolini was caught by his enemies and hanged.

The Chinese Revolution

China's revolution of 1911–12, which overthrew the 2000-year-old Manchu dynasty, opened an era of unprecedented change for Chinese society. Dr. Sun Yat-sen, the leader of the **Kuomintang** Party that toppled the Manchu dynasty, was an idealistic man who wished to restore China's national pride and economy after years of foreign domination. Convinced that only large-scale reforms would achieve this goal, Sun Yat-sen based his government upon a three-fold program of nationalism (the unification of China and the expulsion of all "foreign devils"), democracy (a popularly elected government), and socialism (nationalization of all basic industries and redistribution of land to the starving peasants). However, Sun Yat-sen failed to gain complete control of the army, and warlords in nearly every province continued to dominate and oppress the people.

When Sun died in 1925, the Kuomintang comprised two major groups. Sun was succeeded by his lieutenant, Chiang Kai-shek (Jiang Jieshi), who led the conservative faction. The Communist Party formed the second group. Having failed to successfully provoke revolution in Europe, the Soviet

Focus

How would Mussolini justify one-man rule?

How could the Italian government have prevented Mussolini's rise to power?

Kuomintang: Chinese political party that toppled the Manchu dynasty in 1911–12.

Union's Stalin and Lenin aided in creating the Chinese Communist Party in 1921, and suggested that the party ally itself temporarily with the Kuomintang. In 1927, Chiang Kai-shek broke with the Communist Party and attempted to destroy it. His troops killed thousands of Communist supporters. The survivors fled from the cities and hid in the countryside.

Chiang's suppression of Communist activity in the cities, and China's small urban and industrial base, forced Communist leaders such as Mao Zedong (Tse-tung) to modify Lenin's and Marx's reliance on the industrial workers for help. In 1927, Mao retreated into the countryside and turned to the peasants, who, he wrote, were like the "raging winds and driving rain. … No force can stand in their way. … They will bury beneath them all forces of imperialism, militarism, corrupt officialdom, village bosses and evil landlords." This "mighty storm" would sweep all opposition before it. Mao insisted that the civilian population be treated with respect. Force was to be used only on the enemy. In their mountain strongholds, the Communists redistributed the land to the people; paid for the food and supplies they took; reduced taxes; eliminated child slavery, prostitution, and opium smoking; and began mass political education programs. Since the "richest source of power to wage war lies in the masses of the people," Mao issued the following instructions to his men:

- Speak politely.
- Pay fairly for what you buy.
- Return everything you borrow.
- Pay for anything you damage.
- Don't hit or swear at people.
- Don't damage crops.
- Don't take liberties with women.
- Don't ill-treat captives.

As the peasantry became friendlier, Mao's ragged band of followers grew larger, and Mao expanded his bases.

Mao's other major contribution to Marxist–Leninist revolutionary theory was the belief in guerrilla warfare. Lenin believed that power must be achieved at a single stroke, in as little time as possible. Chiang's immense power and China's tremendous size, however, meant that any revolutionary struggle would take many years. Mao argued that the Communists would have to become mobile and harass their enemy, rather than engage in major conflicts. They should confuse their foes, disrupt their lines of communication, force them to disperse their strength, and, most important, undermine their morale. Never destroyed, the guerrillas would provide the appearance of invincibility and would thus humiliate those who could not defeat them. To Mao, guerrilla warfare meant "The enemy advances, we retreat; the enemy camps, we harass; the enemy tires, we attack; the enemy retreats, we pursue."

During the first phase of the guerrilla warfare, Mao's soldiers concentrated on securing safe bases for rest and training. No other territory was worth losing lives over. In the second phase, numerous small groups ambushed and otherwise harassed the enemy. "The first law of war," Mao wrote, "is to preserve ourselves and destroy the enemy." The final phase would begin only when victory was certain and involved conventional warfare with large troop movements.

In 1930, Chiang mobilized his forces against the Communists, and four years later his larger and better-equipped army had surrounded them. Faced with destruction, Mao's Red Army left its mountain base, broke through Chiang's lines, and fled northward. Thus began one of the twentieth century's most dramatic adventures — the **Long March**. For over a year, Mao and some 130 000 supporters trudged through uncharted territory, crossed 18 mountain ranges, and fought 10 warlords before establishing a separate base in Yenan. Their snake-like route was the equivalent of crossing Canada on foot from Halifax to Vancouver and returning to Winnipeg. Since it was more a running battle than a march, only about 35 000 people survived. From 1949 until the early 1980s, almost every important Chinese leader was a survivor of the Long March.

Long March: the 9600 km journey of Mao Zedong and his Red Army to their eventual base in Yenan.

When Japan attacked China in 1937, Chiang reluctantly agreed to join forces with Mao to fight their common enemy. In fact, Chiang agreed to a truce only after he had been kidnapped by one of his own officers. Their combined forces were overwhelmed by the Japanese, who gained control over most of China's cities by 1939. Several times the uneasy truce between the two Chinese forces broke down, and they fought each other rather than the Japanese. Whenever possible, Chiang's forces held back and allowed the Red Army to bear the brunt of the fighting, while they stockpiled American weapons in preparation for the final battle with Mao. This allowed Mao to portray himself as a patriotic leader. Corruption within Chiang's government, its brutal and overpaid officers, and its reluctance to fight the enemy, increased support for the Communists. While Chiang's forces deteriorated from inactivity, Mao built respect for the Red Army. By reducing rents and promising to give land to the poor, Mao seemed to be the true patriot.

Following the United States victory over Japan in 1945, the two Chinese forces engaged in a final struggle for control of China. The Soviet Union and the United States tried to convince the combatants to form a coalition government, but both sides were confident of victory. The Communists' fair treatment of the peasantry now paid dividends. Mao's cause was also aided by Chiang's inept and corrupt dictatorship, which was by now quite unpopular. Mao's promises to restore China's pride and revive an economy that was in tatters found fertile ground. Eventually, although the United States supported Chiang, Mao forced him to retreat to the island of Formosa (now Taiwan) in 1949, and Mao proclaimed the creation of the People's Republic of China.

Following this victory, Mao hoped to export his brand of revolutionary communism to Asia, Africa, and Latin America — all of which suffered from uneven economic development and ruthless governments. According to

Communist troops march through Beijing along with propaganda trucks to fan enthusiasm.

Focus

How did Mao adjust his revolutionary theories to fit Chinese conditions?

Mao, success depended upon establishing bases in the most rugged areas, protracted military conflict, peasant guerrilla warfare, winning the support of the local population, and appealing to the people's patriotism or nationalism. Communist parties in Burma, Cambodia, Laos, Malaysia, the Philippines, and Thailand copied Mao's liberation policies. In Vietnam and Korea, Chinese military assistance helped to establish new Communist states.

VIEWPOINT

CAO MING, 1913–

Literature as Propaganda: Maoism

Cao Ming was born to a poor rural family in 1913. Her early writing consisted largely of anti-Japanese propaganda that described Japan's capture of Manchuria in 1932. Five years later, she became a member of the Communist Party in Yenan, where she worked with the peasants and wrote stories that promoted Mao's beliefs. Following Mao's victory in 1949, Ming held various government posts and continued writing short stories and novels.

A Native of Yan'an, written in 1947, is one of Cao Ming's best-known short stories. The story begins in 1937. The main character is an old, illiterate peasant woman named Granny Wu. In the following excerpt, Granny Wu is talking with her daughter-in-law:

The younger woman shaded the sun from her eye with her hands and looked carefully in the direction indicated by her mother-in-law. She exclaimed in surprise:
"Ma, that's him. Ma, that's him!"
Granny Wu was alarmed; she stood up slowly:
"Who is he?"
"He is Chairman Mao, Ma, that's him. I heard him speak at the May Day celebration; I've also heard him speak at the mobilization meeting." ...
"That's Chairman Mao!"

"That's Chairman Mao!"

"There's no mistake, it's really him!"

The shopkeepers all ran out of the houses, trying hard to identify the tall shape as that of their beloved leader. A few intellectuals who had just come here from the south, eagerly joined the masses, and confirmed what the people were saying. One of them even said that once he had seen Chairman Mao have a long chat with the peasants in the fields. By now there were about ten people all watching with rapt attention as the group was getting farther and farther away. Chairman Mao had crossed the Yan River on horseback and had slowly made his way to Yangjialing. His mighty figure as he went farther away and his genius and solemn appearance seemed to become a tangible brilliance which shone with the sun. ...

The old woman straightened her back and continued with her description. It seemed as if she had become over ten years younger. "Moreover, I noticed that his forehead was rather broad, what an intelligent head! He can solve problems which have baffled hundreds and thousands of people. ...

"Did you hear that during the 8000 mile Long March, Chairman Mao met an old woman who was about to freeze to death? He immediately took off his goat-fur-lined waist coat and put it on her. Have you ever seen anyone serving the people so wholeheartedly? ..."

[Ten years go by and Chiang Kai-shek's army invades Yenan. The Communists flee, but Granny Wu, who is sick, refuses to leave her home. When the enemy captures Granny, they ask her in which direction the Communists have fled. Granny tricks them into taking the wrong path, which results in 50 soldiers being killed by buried land mines.]

One of the soldiers aimed his gun at her, but was stopped by the low-ranking officer who walked up to her and asked in a muddle-headed way:

"Did you know that this meant death for you?"

"Yes, I knew," she stopped laughing.

"What did you do it for? I don't understand. Is there anything more precious than life?"

"What for? For him!" she answered solemnly. "The benefactor who leads us!"

"He has fled! You'll die here in his stead!"

"No, he's forever with us, he'll never die, we'll win!" ...

The officer nodded his head and finally understood the strong willpower of the people of northeast China. After he had finished his questioning, he took up his pistol and fired three shots at Granny Wu's chest.

This old woman destroyed some of the enemy's strength with her patriotic honesty and wisdom. In her dizzy semiconsciousness before death the wave-like songs of the northwest people who were prepared to sacrifice everything to defeat the savage assault of the enemy sounded once more.[1]

Focus

Why is this short story considered propaganda?

What images of themselves did the Communists want to present to the people?

⋯ **The Cuban Revolution**

Cuba is the largest island in the West Indies. It measures about 1245 km long and from 35 km to 208 km wide. The island is located at the entrance to the Gulf of Mexico, only 150 km off the Florida coast. Because of its size and strategic location, Spain colonized Cuba and enslaved its indigenous peoples shortly after Christopher Columbus landed on the island. During the following four centuries, Cuba remained a colony of Spain, which profited from the island's abundant sugar plantations.

Cuban nationalistic feelings erupted in 1868, but it was not until 1898 that Cuba, with American help, freed itself from Spanish control. Following the defeat of Spain, American troops remained in Cuba for four years. During this time, the United States ran the government and American businesspeople took the opportunity to consolidate their holdings and acquire more property on the island.

In 1902, the United States withdrew its troops, contingent upon Cuba's acceptance of the **Platt Amendment**. This document literally made Cuba an American protectorate. It allowed the United States to intervene in Cuban affairs for "the preservation of Cuban independence, the maintenance of a government adequate for the protection of life, property and individual liberty." The United States Navy was given specified coaling and naval stations at which to resupply its ships, and a trade agreement opened Cuba to American agricultural and industrial products. Most Cubans felt humiliated by the Platt Amendment.

Platt Amendment: a United States law of 1901 that made Cuba an American protectorate. It was abolished by the Cuban Treaty of 1934.

Case Figure 8.2: Map of Cuba

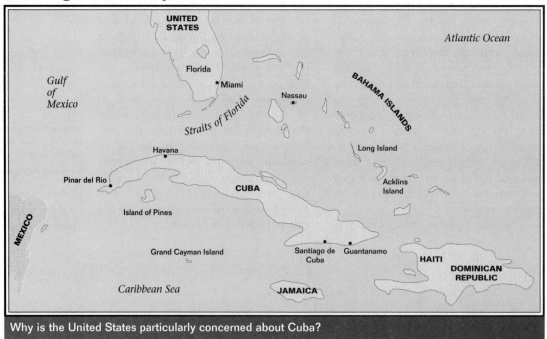

Why is the United States particularly concerned about Cuba?

The Revolution of 1933

Soon after the American withdrawal from Cuba in 1902, Cubans' dissatisfaction with their country's political system turned into strikes, protest marches, and riots. A few small uprisings were brutally crushed, and political prisoners were tortured. Near the end of July 1933, a nation-wide strike brought industry and communications to a standstill. When several revolts within the army broke out a few days later, the army allied with politicians to appoint Carlos Manuel de Céspedes as president. The violence continued. On September 4, rank-and-file soldiers led by Sergeant Fulgencio Batista rebelled against their officers. After a meeting with university students, a group of five men formed a provisional government. Former university professor Ramón Grau San Martin headed the government, and Batista (now a colonel) remained in control of the army.

Once again, however, the government was overthrown by the army. After only 120 days in office, Grau was removed by the Batista-led army. The United States almost immediately recognized the new regime, which promised to protect foreign investments and provide a stable government. The 1933 revolution marked the entry of the army into politics. From this point onwards, every Cuban civilian regime lay at the mercy of military leaders.

The Batista Era

From 1934 to 1940 Batista, as head of the army, ruled Cuba through a series of puppet presidents. Although Batista sought to broaden the base of his support, the army remained the source of his power. The army was enlarged and modernized, and its living standards were greatly improved. The United States supplied the army with the best in weaponry and trained many of the Cuban officers. It was this army that Batista employed to rout his enemies. During the general strike of 1935, for example, hundreds of people were injured, union offices were raided and destroyed, and opposition newspapers were closed. The strike was ruthlessly suppressed. Although this kind of terrorism did not continue for very long, the Batista-controlled government reinstated the repression and corruption of pre-1933 Cuba. The army shared in the fruits of this corruption. In fact, soldiers were recruited from the ranks of demoralized Cuban youth who had no hesitation about joining in the spoils of office.

After spending time in and out of power, Batista overthrew the government in 1952, adopted more gangster-like tactics, and increasingly relied on corruption, which angered the propertied classes that had originally welcomed him. Although the Cuban economy was generally prosperous during the late 1940s and early 1950s, the increased wealth of plantation owners, ranchers, hotel owners, and utility companies was not passed on to the workers, who had one of the lowest standards of living and the highest illiteracy rates in Latin America. Outside the capital of Havana, for example, there were very few medical doctors. Unemployment was a chronic problem. The workers had no organizations through which they could express their frustration. The most obvious source of help would have been the trade unions, but Batista had won their leaders over through bribery and intimidation.

The Roman Catholic Church, which had played an important role in the overthrow of several other Latin American dictatorships, was generally conservative in nature and did not oppose Batista until 1958. Even then, the Church had no deep roots in Cuban society because most of the priests were still Spanish, and because the Church catered largely to the urban middle class.

Opposition to the regime was thus disorganized and leaderless. There was no alternative around which the people could unite. Several attempts at opposition were met with fierce brutality, the leaders jailed and exiled. The Communist Party was driven underground. Appeal to the United States appeared hopeless because Washington had just granted recognition to several other Latin American dictatorships.

Fidel Castro

From 1952 to 1956, the burden of opposition was carried by university students. Dissent took the form of student demonstrations, terrorism, armed assaults on military garrisons, and assassination attempts on Batista's life. Although this opposition was defeated, the flame was kept alive. There was no charismatic national leader around whom the students could unite. Certainly, the older generation of politicians had proven itself unworthy of trust.

Opposition to Batista's regime came from university students and recent graduates of the University of Havana. One of these was Fidel Castro. Born in 1926, Castro came from a wealthy landowning family. He was brought up in the country, where his playmates were children of the poorer families. Castro attended a Catholic high school in Santiago de Cuba, where he obtained good marks and was named Cuba's best school athlete in 1944. Tall, good-looking, athletic, and articulate, he entered politics as soon as he began university. Although he was a good debater and a courageous, active thorn in the side of the Batista regime, Castro was never the leader of more than a handful of followers. In 1950, he graduated from law school and joined a small law firm, but was never happy as a lawyer and took little interest in the firm. Most of his clients were poor widows or labourers whom he charged very little for his services.

Fidel Castro (1985)

Castro's Rise to Power

When it became apparent that Batista could not be deposed by legal action, Castro decided to organize an armed uprising. His first target was the army barracks in Santiago de Cuba. Success here would provide his supporters with badly needed weapons and, Castro hoped, act as a catalyst in arousing Cubans to take up arms against the government.

Secrecy was critical. Castro divided his supporters into cells of about 10 each. No one was told where the target was or when they would strike. Contact among the cells involved only cell leaders, and then only through intermediaries. The date of the uprising was set for the morning of July 26, 1952. This was Carnival night, and a large group of strangers would likely go unnoticed. Success depended upon surprise.

Despite meticulous planning, the raid ended in failure and Castro was forced to flee. Many of those who were caught in the raid were tortured and murdered. Five days later, Castro and the rest of the conspirators were apprehended, and Castro was given a 15-year prison sentence.

Despite its failure, the attack captured the imagination of Cubans and gave Castro national publicity and prestige. While in prison, he worked out the strategy and tactics he would later use to overthrow Batista. He also wrote articles for a popular Cuban magazine and succeeded in having 10 000 copies of *History Will Absolve Me* (a reprint of his defence in court) printed. This material was smuggled out of prison in matchboxes with false bottoms, or by using lemon juice to write between the lines of his regular letters.

Castro was freed from prison in May 1955 as part of a general amnesty designed to improve Batista's public image. Castro had been offered freedom earlier, in exchange for a promise not to cause anymore problems, but he apparently replied: "We do not want amnesty at the price of dishonour. ... Better a thousand years in prison before the sacrifice of integrity." Shortly after he was released, Castro became convinced that the government was plotting his assassination, and he fled to Mexico.

In Mexico, Castro met Dr. Ernesto ("Ché") Guevara, who had fought against the Guatemalan and Argentinean dictators and was now searching for another Latin-American war of liberation in which to participate. Castro and Ché began to plan for an invasion of Cuba. The liberation movement had begun. Despite harassment from the Mexican authorities, some 80 men were trained in guerrilla warfare. They were taught how to shoot, make bombs, use camouflage, attack, withdraw, disappear, and attack again. When Castro thought that his men were ready, he announced that he would return to Cuba in 1956. "I want everyone in Cuba to know I am coming," Castro replied to one of his men who questioned the wisdom of disclosing their plans. "I want them to have faith in the 26th of July Movement. It is a peculiarity all my own although I know that militarily it might be harmful. It is psychological warfare." When Castro proved true to his word, the movement gained a great deal of political currency in a country used to broken promises and disappointments.

The invasion was planned for November 30, 1956. It was to coincide with a wave of locally organized sabotage in Cuba, and with an attack on the island's military installations. The two forces were then to join to overthrow the government.

It didn't work that way. Rough seas, an overcrowded, leaking boat, and seasickness combined to delay Castro's landing by two days. By the time the boat arrived, the uprising had been crushed and most of its leaders were dead or in jail. The rebels would have to fend for themselves. To make matters worse, the ship landed off course and the 82 revolutionaries had to wade through 3 km of swamp and quagmire. By that time, a government plane was flying over their heads and a naval vessel had begun to fire into the surrounding bush. A short while later, a group of soldiers surprised them, killing 21 men. The surviving members divided into small groups and headed for the rugged Sierra Maestra mountain range. Two weeks later, they re-formed in the mountains. Besides Castro, his brother Raul, and Ché Guevara, only nine members survived the trip. Although they were physically exhausted and without weapons, Castro announced, "And now we're going to win."

The first rebel victory was in La Plata, where a small army post of about 12 soldiers was seized early in 1957. Castro now had more weapons than men, but this problem was partially solved in February of that year, when Herbert Matthews of the *New York Times* was invited to the Sierra Maestra mountains to interview Castro. The Cuban government had reported that Castro had been killed, and the interview was arranged to let Cubans know that he was alive and fighting. While Matthews was interviewing Castro, his brother Raul paraded back and forth with the same men to give the impression that they had more than the 18 supporters they did have. When the interview was published, it created a sensation. Castro was pictured as a romantic figure combatting a wicked tyrant. This won him the sympathy of many Americans as well as the support of the Cuban people.

Batista ordered the army to destroy the guerrillas, but army action served only to reinforce Matthews' newspaper account of Castro as a formidable force. Unable to capture the rebels, the army decided to remove the farmers in the Sierra foothills from their homes and then bomb the depopulated area — a tactic that also failed.

The number of Castro's volunteers grew with each success. Peasants lent their assistance partly because the friendly and considerate guerrilla force was quite different from the arrogant and brutal soldiers; also, the rebels paid for everything, provided free medical care, and promised to redistribute land once they had overthrown the government. The high standard of morality maintained by the guerrillas helped to shake people's cynicism.

By April 1957, the guerrilla camp had grown to approximately 80 volunteers, and Castro was ready to expand his attacks. Enemy detachments were ambushed and small army posts were attacked. In May, a stunning victory in the Battle of Uvero proved the rebels' fighting ability. In December, army troops were pulled out of the Sierra Maestra and a ring of army posts was erected surrounding Castro's headquarters in the mountains. If the government could not destroy the rebels, perhaps it could isolate them.

In the summer of the following year, the guerrillas broke out of the encirclement and moved farther west. By winter, they controlled almost the whole eastern half of the island, and this with fewer than 2000 fighters. The army had not been trained in guerrilla warfare and was no match for the rebels. As desertions increased, the army became demoralized. Corruption and brutality, not warfare, were their strong points. By December, they were in no mood to resist the guerrillas.

Part of Castro's strategy was to keep the people constantly informed of his progress. Early in 1958, *Radio Rebelde* began broadcasting. Its policy was to tell the truth, which contrasted markedly with government propaganda. Castro's followers also proved to be apt propagandists. They placed a two-page advertisement for cigarettes in Havana newspapers, showing a man with a pack of cigarettes in one hand and a book entitled *High **Fidelity*** in the other.

The army's reprisals against this propaganda were so violent that Batista lost the loyalty of many of his supporters, and citizens were repulsed by the sight of the bullet-riddled bodies of young men left in the streets with bombs tied to them as a warning to the rebels. Batista's picture on movie screens began to provoke catcalls, and when musicians played the dictator's favourite song at dances, couples stood still.

The government's morale was further weakened by the United States' decision to stop all shipments of weapons and munitions to Cuba. Although these supplies were not of crucial military importance, the action indicated that Washington was losing patience with the regime. Castro, on the other hand, was careful not to alienate America. He promised to protect foreign investments, maintain the private enterprise system, and promote freedom. In fact, Castro was successful partly because no one knew his future plans. The period of rebellion had been so brief that he had not alienated any large group from his movement.

Batista's regime was built on terror and fear. Once Castro showed that he had a good chance of defeating the dictator, the people — particularly peasants who wanted the land reforms Castro promised — flocked to the guerrillas. The government finally collapsed and Batista fled the country, leaving the capital open to the guerrillas. In December 1958, 33-year-old Fidel Castro became the leader of Cuba.

Although Castro was influenced by such Marxists as Ché Guevara, he did not become a Communist until after the revolution. American hostility toward his policies of providing Cuban peasants and workers with a better standard of living at the expense of large American companies operating in Cuba apparently drove Castro into Soviet arms. Although he hoped to export his revolutionary techniques to other Latin American states, the absence of suitable mountainous terrain in most of these countries made rural guerrilla warfare almost impossible. Castro's success, however, showed that revolutionary leaders need not begin as committed Communists to be successful. Chapter 8 examines the present situation in Cuba.

BIOGRAPHY

AUNG SAN SUU KYI, 1945–

In awarding Aung San Suu Kyi of Myanmar (formerly Burma) the 1991 Nobel Peace Prize, the Nobel Committee referred to her actions as "one of the most extraordinary examples of civil courage in Asia in recent decades." The award was given for her leadership of "a democratic opposition which employs non-violent means to resist a regime characterized by brutality."[2]

In some ways, Suu Kyi was a natural choice to lead the opposition to Burma's military dictatorship. Her father Aung San (who was assassinated by right-wing forces in 1947) was "the nationalist leader who, by general consent, is the father of modern Burma and the most revered figure in that troubled nation's recent history."[3]

In another sense, she was an unlikely choice. She had left Burma in 1960, living in India and in England, where she studied at Oxford University. She settled into a life of motherhood and homemaking, but continued to study and to learn more about her father, and about Burma's problems.

Suu Kyi's return to Rangoon in 1988 in order to care for her dying mother came at a time of intense political upheaval in Burma. A demonstration against the military junta resulted in the massacre of thousands of unarmed citizens when the army fired indiscriminately into the crowd. Despite her lack of experience, Suu Kyi quickly became a key opposition leader, pushing for human rights and a non-violent reconciliation with the military.

In July 1989, the junta placed Suu Kyi under house arrest. It was to last for five years, and for two years she had no contact of any kind with her family. Nevertheless, her party won a landslide victory in the parliamentary elections of 1990, prompting the junta to nullify the elections and arrest opposition leaders.

Suu Kyi continued her "struggle against fascism" after her period of house arrest ended by encouraging countries to pressure Myanmar through economic boycotts. She was interviewed by the *New York Times Magazine* early in 1996:

Q: In your speeches, you often talk about how people need to develop a "freedom from fear." What do you mean?

A: That you should not let your fears prevent you from doing what you know is right. Not that you shouldn't be afraid. Fear is normal. But to be inhibited from doing what you know is right, that is what is dangerous. You should be able to lead your life in the right way — despite your fears. …

Q: What do you think of the notion that some of the [regime's] supporters believe that democracy is an alien western idea, unsuitable to Asia?

A: If we are going to make an analogy, a country which has not invented television doesn't say, "Well, we've got to invent television from scratch before we have it here." They just go out and buy the televisions from the United States and Japan, and they would consider any country silly that refused to have television until they produced their own. It's the same thing with democracy. Why should we have to wait? Democracy has been tried out in other countries and we are able to judge its weaknesses and strengths and decide how to adapt it to our own circumstances.[4]

---

1 How do Aung San Suu Kyi's experiences reflect the nature of authoritarian regimes?

2 What does the interview tell you about the reasons for her resistance to the regime?

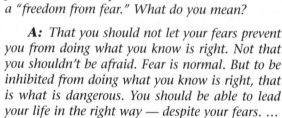

Underlying and Emerging Issues

Give the reasoning and evidence that might be used to support different views or conclusions on the following issues.

1 What factors make it difficult for democratic governments to flourish?

2 To what extent do dictatorships arise because of economic and social circumstances in a country?

3 How can democracies prevent the rise of dictatorships in their country?

4 To what extent have Western democracies supported dictatorships in other settings?

5 Should democratic countries ever support non-democratic regimes?

6 Is democracy appropriate for all political and economic circumstances?

7 In some circumstances, is authoritarian government preferable to chronic instability?

8 How important is freedom in comparison to effectiveness in government?

Focussing Knowledge

In your notes, clearly identify or define and explain the importance or significance of each of the following:

guerrilla warfare	*Platt Amendment*
puppet dictatorship	*Benito Mussolini*
propaganda	*Sun Yat-sen*
Il Duce	*Mao Zedong*
squadristi	*Cao Ming*
March on Rome	*Fulgencio Batista*
Kuomintang	*Fidel Castro*
Long March	*Ché Guevara*

Reviewing and Organizing Knowledge

1 How does totalitarianism differ from dictatorship?

2 Why did democracy give way to authoritarian rule in so many countries after World War I?

3 For each of the three examples in this case study (Mussolini in Italy, Mao in China, and Castro in Cuba), state the role or relative importance of each of the following possible factors in bringing these leaders to power:

a. personality of the leader

b. appeal of ideology

c. strategy and tactics

d. political situation

e. economic situation

f. other factors

Applying and Extending Knowledge

1 Write a comparison of how Mussolini, Mao, and Castro achieved power. Use the six criteria in question 3 (above) as the basis for your conclusions. To what extent were the factors similar and different?

2 To what extent is the rise of dictators due to the leader, and to what extent is it due to political, economic, and social conditions? Take a stand on this issue, and support your position by referring to the three examples in this case study.

3 What was the relative importance of ideology in each of the cases presented in this case study? To what extent was the ideology itself changed due to the situation?

4 What do the three examples in this case study reveal about the potential weaknesses of democracy? Support your conclusions with specific examples.

5 Write a description of how the rise to power might have been prevented in the case of

a. Mussolini

b. Mao

c. Castro

6 Write a paper in which you give advice to democratic governments on how to prevent authoritarian governments from gaining power.

7 To what extent were the people "better off" than they were before in each of the three examples presented in this case study? What were the trade-offs — what did people give up?

8 Choose an example of a dictatorship in another country. Research the way in which the leader achieved power. To what extent was it similar to or different from the three examples in this case study?

Maintaining Power:
Nazi Germany

*U*P TO THIS POINT, we have examined how several non-democratic governments achieved power, and we noticed that violence and extra-legal tactics were common practice. Most authoritarian regimes, however, must rely upon methods other than force and intimidation if they hope to remain in power. This case study analyzes how Adolf Hitler maintained the support of the German people in the 1930s.

After briefly outlining Hitler's rise to power, this case study employs primary documents to explore how he was able to maintain his control over Germany. His methods included control of the legal and judiciary system, economic achievements, his magnetic personality, extensive propaganda, mass rallies, indoctrination of young people through education and youth groups, and the use of violence and terror.

In the two decades following World War I, many recently created democratic countries turned to some type of authoritarian or dictatorial rule. In general, those countries that remained democratic were satisfied with the peace treaties, were industrialized, and had long traditions of democracy. Germany was one of the many countries that exchanged democracy for authoritarian rule. This case study requires you to analyze a series of primary documents in order to explain how this happened.

Learning Outcomes

After reading this case study, you should be able to:

- recognize the value of original documents

- explain why Hitler was able to maintain power

- write an essay evaluating the different techniques Hitler used to keep power

- understand why so few people opposed Hitler's regime

- identify the major tactics used by authoritarian states once in power and the importance of propaganda and control of the media

Case Figure 9.1: The Spread of Authoritarian Governments, 1917–1938

Source: Dennis Sherman et al., *World Civilizations: Sources, Images, and Interpretations, Vol. 2* (New York: McGraw-Hill, 1994), p. 263. Reprinted by permission of The McGraw-Hill Companies.

The Rise of Adolf Hitler

In many ways, Hitler's rise to power in Germany resembled Mussolini's success in Italy a decade earlier. Both countries had only recently been unified, and neither had a long tradition of democratic government before they were overthrown by a semi-legal coup. The results of World War I left the people of Germany and Italy dissatisfied, and this disillusionment was turned against the governing democratic regimes that had signed the peace treaties. Hitler and Mussolini both used economic problems and fear of a communist revolution to further their own ends.

After centuries of autocratic rule, a democratic government — the **Weimar Republic** — was established in Germany at the end of World War I. Unfortunately, the leaders of the new Weimar Republic had signed the Treaty of Versailles peace settlement (which many Germans believed imposed unjust measures on their country), and the former autocratic government escaped blame for its role in the war. Because the German people had not seen the approaching collapse of the army at the front, they deceived themselves into believing that the liberals and socialists had betrayed them. Other Germans blamed their defeat either on the communists or on the Jews, or on both.

The Treaty of Versailles at the end of the war was harsh. The victorious Allies blamed the war on Germany and demanded that it pay for the costs of the war. To make these reparations, which totalled $33 billion, Germany printed more paper money. Unfortunately, this caused rapid inflation. As prices rose, people's savings became worthless. Germans went shopping with bags full of paper money and returned with only a handful of groceries. Hitler skilfully blamed these problems on communists and Jews and promised to solve these problems if he were elected to office.

Weimar Republic: the republican type of parliamentary democracy, with its capital located in Weimar, which ruled Germany from 1919 to 1933.

The Weimar government was soon threatened by both left- and right-wing groups that wished to overthrow it. In 1919, a Marxist group failed in an attempt to establish a communist regime (the Spartacist Revolt). The following year, a right-wing revolution also failed (the Kapp *Putsch*). Three years later, Adolf Hitler jumped onto a table in a beer hall in Munich and proclaimed a revolution. This Munich Beer Hall **Putsch** was poorly organized and easily crushed. Hitler was sent to prison for six months, where he wrote his book **Mein Kampf**. Despite the fact that there were over 20 political parties competing for power, the Weimar Republic limped on until the Great Depression hit the Western world in 1929. By 1932, over 20 percent of the German labour force was unemployed, and there seemed no hope in sight.

Putsch: *a coup d'état*, loosely translated into German.

Mein Kampf: *My Struggle*, Adolf Hitler's autobiographical and philosophical book, which outlines his objectives.

"Our Last Hope." What emotions did this poster hope to arouse?

Nazi Party: the National Socialist German Workers' Party that governed Germany under Adolf Hitler, 1933–45.

Storm Troopers: a paramilitary force of Brown Shirts, also known as the SA, who were the Nazis' private army.

Reichstag: the lower legislative chamber of Germany's Parliament in the Weimar Republic.

Enabling Act: the act passed by Adolf Hitler in 1933 that gave him absolute dictatorial powers in Germany for four years.

Nuremberg Laws: the laws passed by Adolf Hitler in 1935 that took away German Jews' citizenship rights and prohibited Jews from marrying non-Jews.

Hitler spent this time strengthening the National Socialist German Workers' Party (**Nazi Party**). Party members wore badges and uniforms, gave victory salutes, and marched like robots through the streets. His private army, the *Sturmabteilung* (SA), or **Storm Troopers**, also known as Brown Shirts, was patterned after Mussolini's Black Shirts. Financed by wealthy industrialists who feared a communist revolution, the Nazi Party made rapid political gains. From only 7 seats (out of 608) in the 1928 *Reichstag* (the lower house of Parliament), the party gained 230 seats in the 1932 election. Political chaos continued as Nazi and left-wing paramilitary groups fought in the streets. Conservative elements in the government calculated that they would be able to control Hitler, and in January 1933, they persuaded President Hindenburg to appoint the Nazi leader as chancellor.

They miscalculated. Hitler quickly outmanoeuvred the moderates and called a snap election for March 1933. A month before the election, the *Reichstag* building was destroyed by a fire that Hitler blamed on the communists — although many historians suspect that Hitler was responsible. Hitler filled the jails with the Nazis' left-wing opponents, and the Nazi Party subsequently captured the largest number of seats in the *Reichstag*. In March 1933, claiming (falsely) that there was a threat of a communist revolution, Hitler passed the **Enabling Act**, which gave him absolute dictatorial powers for four years, and he immediately moved to smash all opposition and outlaw other political parties. The Nazis were now free to consolidate their power. In 1935, the passage of the **Nuremberg Laws** began Hitler's persecution of German Jews.

Similarities Between Hitler's and Mussolini's Rise to Power

- unhappiness with Treaty of Versailles
- economic depression and high unemployment
- fear of communism
- dissatisfaction with democratic government's actions
- use of violence and paramilitary forces
- appeal to upper and lower middle classes
- weak democratic resistance

- ideology that stressed strong leaders, nationalism, and race
- Hitler and Mussolini invited to take over leadership of country legally
- used language of socialism to broaden appeal
- people tired of violence demanded order
- promises of territorial expansion

Popular Opinion

After his attempted revolution failed in 1923, Hitler realized that he would have to achieve power by more democratic means. His National Socialist German Workers' Party sought to attract enough popular support to gain political control of Germany. The following table illustrates Hitler's success in this respect. Which parties suffered the most from the Nazis' growth in popular support, and what does this indicate about the type of people who voted for the Nazis?

Case Table 9.1: Elections to the German *Reichstag*, 1924–1933 (percent of the vote)

Party	May 1924	Dec. 1924	May 1928	Sept. 1930	July 1932	Nov. 1932	Mar. 1933
National Socialist German Workers' Party (Nazi)	7	3	3	18	37	36	45
German Nationalist People's Party (conservative, democratic)	20	21	14	7	6	9	8
Center Party (Catholic, democratic)	13	14	12	12	12	12	11
Social Democratic	21	26	30	25	22	20	22
Communist	13	9	11	13	14	17	13
Numerous Other Democratic Parties	26	25	30	25	9	6	1

Hitler was the first dictator to make full use of modern technology. Mass-circulation daily newspapers, with their potential for shaping public opinion, became possible in the twentieth century with the invention of the linotype machine, which mechanized typesetting. Modern advertising techniques quickly followed. By 1920, motion pictures, phonographs, radios, microphones, and public address systems provided new methods of influencing the public. By the mid-1930s, for example, three out of every four German households owned a radio. At the same time, psychology provided new insights into the way people thought. Sigmund Freud, for example, claimed that human behaviour was basically irrational. As subsequent documents and photographs show, Hitler used mass propaganda to win over the people's hearts, rather than their minds.

But this case study is not about how Hitler achieved power; rather, it examines how one totalitarian state was able to maintain control over the country. The following documents illustrate some of the methods employed by the Nazis that enabled them to rule Germany for 12 years — a period during which Hitler threatened the very survival of Western European civilization, and heaped death, destruction, and terror on Germany and the rest of the world. At the conclusion of this case study, you should be able to decide how Hitler retained control over Germany. The questions at the end of each section are designed to help you analyze the documents.

Why would this photograph be good propaganda for the Nazis?

ADOLF HITLER, 1889–1945

Opinions About Race

Adolf Hitler was born in an Austrian farming village near the Bavarian border. His father wanted Hitler to became a civil servant like himself, but Hitler wanted to become an artist. Unable to gain admission to the Vienna Academy of Fine Arts, Hitler eked out an existence in the city's hostels. World War I offered an escape from life in the slums, and Hitler volunteered for what he later called his greatest experience. Bitter about Germany's defeat in the war, he entered politics after the war.

In 1923, Hitler took part in an unsuccessful political uprising — the Munich *Putsch*. While in jail, he wrote *Mein Kampf* (My Struggle) from which the following quotation, which illustrates his ideas about race, is taken:

The struggle for daily bread allows all those who are weak, sick, and indecisive to be defeated, while the struggle of the males for females gives to the strongest alone the right or at least the possibility to reproduce. Always this struggle is a means of advancing the health and power of resistance of the species, and thus is a means to its higher evolution.

As little as nature approves the mating of higher and lower individuals, she approves even less the blending of higher races with lower ones; for indeed otherwise her previous work toward higher development perhaps over hundreds of thousands of years might be rendered useless with one blow. ...

All the great civilizations of the past died out because contamination of their blood caused them to become decadent. ... In other words, in order to protect a certain culture, the type of human who created the culture must be preserved. ...

Whoever would live must fight. Whoever will not fight in this world of endless competition does not deserve to live. Whoever ignores or despises these laws of race kills the good fortune that he believes he can attain. He interferes with the victory path of the best course and with it the precondition for all human progress. ...

What we see before us today as human culture, all the yields of art, science, and technology are almost exclusively the creative product of the Aryan race [descendants of Nordic stock]. Indeed this fact alone leads to the not unfounded conclusion that the Aryan alone is the founder of the higher type of humanity, and further that he represents the prototype of what we understand by the word MAN. ...

If we were to divide mankind into three groups, the founders of culture, the bearers of culture, the destroyers of culture, only the Aryan could be considered as the representative of the first group. From him originate the foundations and wall of all human creation. ... He provides the mightiest building stones and designs for all human progress.[1]

Focus

What evidence does Hitler provide to support his argument?

Use of the Law

The following three proclamations, which were part of the Enabling Act, reveal how Hitler legally established his control over the German government and sought to maintain it.

1 *Decree of the Reich's President for the Protection of the People and State — February 28, 1933*

In virtue of Section 48(2) of the German Constitution, the following is decreed as a defensive measure against Communist acts of violence endangering the state:

Restrictions on personal liberty, on the right of free expression of opinion, including freedom of the press, on the right of assembly and the right of association, and violations of the privacy of postal, telegraphic, and telephonic communications, and warrants for house-searches, orders for confiscations as well as restrictions on property, are also permissible beyond the legal limits otherwise prescribed.

2 *Law Against the New Establishment of Parties — July 14, 1933*

(1) The National Socialist German Workers' Party constitutes the only political party in Germany.

(2) Whoever undertakes to maintain the organizational structure of another political party or to form a new political party will be punished with penal servitude up to three years or with imprisonment of from six months to three years, if the deed is not subject to a greater penalty according to other regulations.

3 *Law to Safeguard the Unity of Party and State — December 1, 1933*

(1) After the victory of the National Socialist revolution, the National Socialist Workers' Party is the bearer of the German state-idea and indissolubly joined to the state.

*(2) The **Führer** determines its statutes.*

Führer: "Leader" in German. Specifically, Adolf Hitler.

During the first few years after his assumption of power, Hitler held a series of elections and plebiscites to give citizens the appearance of a voice in government and to show that the people approved of his actions. The results were usually close to 100 percent in his favour. The following document illustrates one method that was used to achieve these results.

Police supervision of plebiscites. Subject: Plebiscite of 10 April 1938

Copy of a schedule is attached herewith enumerating the persons who cast "No" votes or invalid votes at Kappel, district of Simmern. The invalid votes are listed first, ending with —; thereafter come the "No" votes.

Third Reich: the name given to the period in Germany of 1933–45 by the ruling Nazi Party.

The control was effected in the following way: some members of the election committee marked all the ballot papers with numbers. During the ballot itself, a voters' list was made up. The ballot papers were handed out in numerical order, therefore it was possible afterwards with the aid of this list to find out the persons who cast "No" votes or invalid votes. One sample of these marked ballot papers is enclosed. The marking was done on the back of the ballot papers with skimmed milk.[2]

Justice in the Third Reich

Judges were often reminded of what the regime expected of them. The following command is a typical example of Nazi attitudes toward justice:

The judge has no right to scrutinize decisions made by the Führer and issued in the form of a law or a decree. The judge is also bound by any other decision of the Führer which clearly expresses the intention of establishing law.[3]

In the following extract, a German defence attorney describes the problems of gaining a fair trial in Nazi Germany:

At that moment I intervened and asked permission to question the defendant, before the hearing of evidence, about ... whether he had been beaten by the officers of the Secret State Police in connection with the signing of these statements.

I had hardly finished the question when the State prosecutor jumped up excitedly and asked the President of the court to protect the Officers of the Secret State Police against such attacks by the defence.

Appeal Judge — rose from his chair, leant on his hands on the court table and said to me: "Council for the defence, I must draw your attention to the fact that even though the trial here is conducted in camera [in secret] a question such as you have asked can lead to your being arrested in the courtroom and taken into custody. Do you wish to sustain the question or not?"

These details are still fresh in my memory because they made an extraordinary impression on me. Also, subsequently I have repeatedly discussed this case because it seemed to me typical of National Socialist justice.[4]

Portrait of a Dictator

How much of Hitler's success was due to personality and charisma? The following extracts help to answer this question.

Physically, Hitler weighed about 150 pounds and was five feet nine inches in height. His skin was pale, and his physique generally unprepossessing. ...

In his own private circle, Hitler's behaviour was generally genial. No one crossed him, and he was liked by his intimates for the usual reasons — kindliness and cordiality. He was especially friendly toward children and older people. He had a great understanding for the little pleasures and in his dealings with women displayed a positive charm.[5]

One of his most bitter critics, Otto Strasser, wrote:

I have been asked many times what is the secret of Hitler's extraordinary power as a speaker. I can only attribute it to his uncanny intuition, which infallibly diagnoses the ills from which his audience is suffering. ... Adolf Hitler enters a hall. He sniffs the air. For a minute he gropes, feels his way, senses the atmosphere. Suddenly he bursts forth. His words go like an arrow to their target, he touches each private wound on the raw, liberating the mass unconscious, expressing its innermost aspirations, telling it what it most wants to hear. ...

When he wanted to persuade or win someone over he could display great charm. Until the last days of his life he retained an uncanny gift of personal magnetism which defies analysis, but which many who met him have described. This was connected with the curious power of his eyes, which are persistently said to have had some sort of hypnotic quality. Similarly, when he wanted to frighten or shock, he showed himself a master of brutal and threatening language.[6]

What feelings would Hitler evoke in a sympathetic crowd?

Focus

What aspects of his personality contributed most to Hitler's success?

Propaganda

As Minister for Propaganda and Public Enlightenment, Joseph Goebbels controlled art, motion pictures, sports, the celebration of national holidays, radio, newspapers, music, museums, tourism, the post office, libraries, and the national anthem. The documents that follow illustrate the purpose and activities of the Propaganda Ministry.

These selections were typical instructions to German newspapers:

General Instruction No. 674

In the next issue there must be a lead article, featured as prominently as possible, in which the decision of the Führer, no matter what it will be, will be discussed as the only correct one for Germany. ...

What is necessary is that the press blindly follow the basic principle: The leadership is always right! Gentlemen, we all must claim the privilege of being allowed to make mistakes. Newspaper people aren't exempt from that danger either. But we all can survive only if, as we face the world, we do not put the spotlight on each other's mistakes, but on positive things instead. What this means in other words is that it is essential — without in principle denying the possibility of mistakes or of discussion — that it is essential always to stress the basic correctness of the leadership. That is the decisive point. ...

The Propaganda Ministry asks us to put to editors-in-chief the following requests, which must be observed in future with particular care:

Photos showing members of the Reich Government at dining tables in front of rows of bottles must not be published in future, particularly since it is known that a large number of the Cabinet are abstemious. Ministers take part in social events for reasons of international etiquette and for strictly official purposes, which they regard merely as a duty and not as a pleasure. Recently, because of a great number of photos, the utterly absurd impression has been created among the public that members of the Government are living it up. News pictures must therefore change in this respect.[7]

Mass Rallies

In this selection, Hitler discusses the psychological importance of evoking the public's emotions through the use of mass demonstrations:

The mass meeting is also necessary for the reason that in it the individual, who at first, while becoming a supporter of a young movement, feels lonely and easily succumbs to the fear of being alone, for the first time gets the picture of a larger community, which in most people has a strengthening, encouraging effect. The same man, within a company or a battalion, surrounded by all his comrades, would set out on an attack with a lighter heart than if left entirely on his own. In the crowd he always feels somewhat sheltered, even if a thousand reasons actually argue against it.

But the community of the great demonstration not only strengthens the individual, it also unites and helps create an esprit de corps. … When from his little workshop or big factory, in which he feels very small, he steps for the first time into a mass meeting and has thousands and thousands of people of the same opinions around him, he is swept away by three or four thousand others into the mighty effect of suggestive intoxication and enthusiasm, when the visible success and agreement of thousands confirm to him the rightness of the new doctrine and for the first time arouse doubt in the truth of his previous conviction — then he himself has succumbed to the magic influence of what we designate as "mass suggestion."[8]

In the following account, American correspondent William Shirer describes his reaction to a 1934 Nazi Party rally at Nuremberg:

I'm beginning to comprehend, I think, some of the reasons for Hitler's astounding success. Borrowing a chapter from the Roman church, he is restoring pageantry and colour and mysticism to the drab lives of twentieth-century Germans. The hall was a sea of brightly coloured flags. Even Hitler's arrival was made dramatic. The band stopped playing. There was a hush over the thirty thousand people packed in the hall. Then the band struck up the Badenweiler March, *a very catchy tune, and used only when Hitler makes his big entries. Hitler … strode slowly down the long centre aisle while thirty thousand hands were raised in salute. It is a ritual which is always followed. Then an immense symphony orchestra played Beethoven's* Egmont Overture. *Great Klieg lights played on the stage, where Hitler sat. … When the music was over, Rudolf Hess, Hitler's closest confidant, rose and slowly read the names of the Nazi "martyrs" — brownshirts who had been killed in the struggle for power — a roll-call of the dead, and thirty thousand seemed very moved.*

In such an atmosphere it is no wonder, then, that every word dropped by Hitler seemed like an inspired Word from on high. Man's — or at least the German's — critical faculty is swept away at such moments, and every lie pronounced is accepted as high truth itself.[9]

Focus

To what extent does Shirer's account indicate that Hitler was correct about mass meetings?

Education

Schools were considered important agents in creating proper citizens, and thus in maintaining power. In the following excerpt, a brother and sister recall their early school days in Nazi Germany.

Every subject was now presented from the National Socialist point of view. Most of the old lecture books were replaced by new ones which had been written, compiled, and censored by government officials. Adolf Hitler's Mein Kampf *became the textbook for our history lessons. We read and discussed it with our master, chapter by chapter, and when we had finished we started again from the beginning. Even though we were supposed to know the contents of the book almost by heart nothing much ever stuck in my mind.*[10]

How would William Shirer have described this scene?

In this excerpt, a critic of the regime remembers his feelings about Nazi education.

Our school had always been run on very conservative lines and I am sure the situation was difficult for our teachers. Most of them had been doubtful about Hitler, but unless they wanted to lose their jobs they had to make a violent turn in his direction. Even if they sympathized with my attitude towards politics, they could not afford to let me get away with it. Some of the children in each class would not hesitate to act as informers. The Government was probing into the past history of every teacher, exploring his political background. Many were dismissed and it was dangerous to act as anything but a National Socialist.[11]

German students were required to recite the following prayers at lunch:

Before meals:
Führer, my Führer, bequeathed to me by the Lord,
Protect and preserve me as long as I live!
Thou hast rescued Germany from deepest distress,
I thank thee today for my daily bread.
Abideth thou along with me, forsaketh me not,
Führer, my Führer, my faith and my light!
    Heil, mein Führer!

After meals:
Thank thee for this bountiful meal,
Protector of youth and friend of the aged!
I know thou hast cares, but worry not,
I am with thee by day and by night.
Lay thy head in my lap.
Be assured, my Führer, that thou art great.
    Heil, mein Führer![12]

Focus

Analyze the picture of the Nazi rally. What atmosphere did these rallies create, and would this help to win the people's support?

Focus

What feelings were the prayers designed to evoke?

Why did the Nazis place so much emphasis on educating the youth of Germany?

Youth

Hitler Youth clubs were established to gain greater control over the activities and thoughts of Germany's young people. In 1935, only those people who had participated in such clubs were eligible to enter the civil service. The following speech was read to new members when they joined the youth club:

Dear boy!/Dear girl!

This hour in which you are to be received into the great community of the Hitler Youth is a very happy one and at the same time will introduce you into a new period of your lives. Today for the first time you swear allegiance to the Führer which will bind you to him for all time.

And every one of you, my young comrades, enters at this moment into the community of all German boys and girls. With your vow and your commitment you now become a bearer of German spirit and German honour. Every one, every single one, now becomes the foundation for an eternal Reich of all Germans.

When you too now march in step with the youngest soldiers, then bear in mind that this march is to train you to be a National Socialist conscious of the future and faithful to his duty.

And the Führer demands of you and of us that we train ourselves to a life of service and duty, of loyalty and comradeship. You, ten-year-old cub, and you, lass, are not too young nor too small to practise obedience and discipline, to integrate yourself into the community and show yourself to be a comrade. Like you, millions of young Germans are today swearing allegiance to the Führer and it is a proud picture of unity which German youth today presents to the whole world. So today you make a vow to your Führer and here, before your parents, the Party and your comrades, we now receive you into our great community of loyalty. Your motto will always be:

"Führer, command — we follow!"

(The cubs are asked to rise.) Now say after me: "I promise always to do my duty in the Hitler Youth in love and loyalty to the Führer and to our flag."[13]

Violence, Oppression, and Fear

Hitler wrote in *Mein Kampf* that terrorism was an effective political tool. "I shall not deprive myself of it merely because these simple-minded bourgeois 'softies' take offense," he stated. "People will think twice before opposing us if they know what awaits them in the camps."[14] In the following account, Austrian Bruno Bettelheim describes his experiences in the concentration camps at Dachau and Buchenwald:

During their initial transport to the camp, prisoners were exposed to nearly constant torture. The nature of the abuse depended on the fantasy of the particular SS man in charge of a group of prisoners. Still, they all had a definite pattern. Physical punishment consisted of whipping, frequent kicking (abdomen or groin), slaps in the face, shooting, or wounding with the bayonet. These alternated with attempts to produce extreme exhaustion. For instance, prisoners were forced to stare for hours into glaring lights, to kneel for hours, and so on.

Focus

How would the Hitler Youth have helped to maintain Hitler's power?

From time to time a prisoner got killed, but no prisoner was allowed to care for his or another's wounds. The guards also forced prisoners to hit one another and to defile what the SS considered the prisoners' most cherished values. ...

The purpose of this massive initial abuse was to traumatize the prisoners and break their resistance; to change at least their behaviour if not yet their personalities. This could be seen from the fact that tortures became less and less violent to the degree that prisoners stopped resisting and complied immediately with any SS order, even the most outrageous. ... Most of them were soon totally exhausted; physically from abuse, loss of blood, thirst, etc. ... before it could lead to a suicidal resistance.[15]

Focus

To what extent is the use of terror an important tool for the maintenance of power in a non-democratic regime?

How did the existence and nature of these camps reflect the theory and practice of fascism?

· · · A Personal View

We have now examined some of the methods used by the Nazi regime to ensure continued support. How did the people react to these measures? Two German teenagers recall their feelings after Hitler's assumption of power in 1933:

One morning, on the school steps, I heard a girl from my class tell another: "Hitler has just taken over the government." And the radio and all the newspapers proclaimed: "Now, everything will improve in Germany. Hitler has seized the helm."

Hans at the time was fifteen years old; Sophie was twelve. We heard a great deal of talk about Fatherland, comradeship, community of the Volk, and love of homeland. All this impressed us, and we listened with enthusiasm whenever we heard anyone speak of these things in school or on the street. For we loved our homeland very much. ... We loved it, but were hardly able to say why. Until that time we had never lost many words over it. But now it was written large, in blazing letters in the sky. And Hitler, as we heard everywhere, Hitler wanted to bring greatness, happiness, and well-being to this Fatherland; he wanted to see to it that everyone had work and bread; he would not rest or relax until every single German was an independent, free, and happy man in his Fatherland. We found this good, and in whatever might come to pass we were determined to help to the best of our ability. But there was yet one more thing that attracted us with a mysterious force and pulled us along — namely, the compact columns of marching youths with waving flags, eyes looking straight ahead, and the beat of drums and singing. Was it not overwhelming, this fellowship? Thus it was no wonder that all of us — Hans and Sophie and the rest of us — joined the Hitler Youth.[16]

LENI RIEFENSTAHL, 1902–

Who has had a life like Riefenstahl's? Whose films were so brilliant, yet achieved under such a cloud? And who has paid for political naivete with so long and rancorous an exile? ... Riefenstahl is still the world's most controversial director; her name summons the conflicts of defiant artistry and compromised morality.[17]

Denounced by some observers as a Nazi collaborator whose films served the cause of Hitler, celebrated by others as perhaps the greatest female director in the history of cinema, the life and art of German filmmaker Leni Riefenstahl continue to be controversial more than half a century after the end of the Nazi regime.

Born in Berlin in 1902 to a moderately wealthy family, Riefenstahl displayed her considerable artistic talent at an early age, rising to the top of the German dance world by her mid-teens. While convalescing in 1924 from a knee injury that effectively ended her dance career, she happened to catch a film directed by Dr. Arnold Fanck, a pioneer of films set in the mountains of Europe. Captivated, she travelled to Switzerland to meet the director. In a scene that might have been taken from a Hollywood movie, Fanck was so impressed with Riefenstahl's audacity and potential that he gave her the main role in his film *The Holy Mountain* — which promptly turned Riefenstahl into a star.

She made a series of films with Fanck, performing all of her own stunts (many of which were dangerous), and becoming steadily more popular. But Riefenstahl's desire to write and direct her own feature films led to the formation of her own motion picture production company. Her first attempt, *The Blue Light*, won a gold medal at the prestigious Venice Film Festival in 1932.

One of the film's admirers was Adolf Hitler, who reportedly said, "This woman will one day make the films of the National Socialist Party." When Hitler eventually asked her to film the 1934 Nazi Party Congress at Nuremberg, Riefenstahl is said to have accepted on condition that she be given complete independence, particularly from the control of Propaganda Minister Josef Goebbels. The resulting film, *Triumph of the Will*, is almost universally considered a landmark in documentary filmmaking, and established Riefenstahl's reputation — but it also inspired the controversy that has surrounded her career. One film historian wrote that while it is "cinematically dazzling it must be regarded as ideologically vicious";[18] another stated, "It could never have been made by anyone not fanatically at one with the events depicted."[19]

Olympia, Riefenstahl's innovative and memorable film of the 1936 Berlin Olympics, was made over the objections of Goebbels; she rejected his demand to play down the achievements of "non-Aryan" athletes, including the black American track star Jesse Owens (whose performances are among the highlights of the film).

Riefenstahl's high-profile image and work during the Nazi regime had enormous consequences after the defeat of Germany in World War II. The Allies confiscated her property and film equipment, and imprisoned her. While she was officially cleared of any wrongdoing by a Baden denazification court in 1948, Riefenstahl's past made her a pariah in the postwar world; she was "blacklisted," and cut off from filmmaking at the height of her artistic powers.

Riefenstahl has constantly made the case that she was not a Nazi, that she abhorred their racist and violent ways: "I made one film for [Hitler], which had three parts, and out of that the press wove a legend."[20] But she has been unable to convince everyone, or to end the controversy.

Prevented from making feature films, Riefenstahl turned her attention to still photography, and soon received high acclaim in that field. Now in her nineties, she continues to work, devoting most of her time to photographic documentation of marine life in the Mediterranean and Caribbean seas.

In his book *Inside the Third Reich*, Albert Speer (see Case Study 17) recalls the first time he met Leni Riefenstahl:

During the preparations for the Party Rallies I met a woman who had impressed me even in my student days: Leni Riefenstahl, who had starred in or had directed well-known mountain and skiing movies. Hitler appointed her to make films of the rallies. As the only woman officially involved in the proceedings, she had frequent conflicts with the party organization, which was soon up in arms against her. The Nazis were by tradition antifeminist and could hardly brook this self-assured woman, the more so since she knew how to bend this men's world to her purposes. Intrigues were launched and slanderous stories carried to Hess, in order to have her ousted. But after the first Party Rally film, which convinced even the doubters of her skill as a director, these attacks ceased.[21]

1 How does Leni Riefenstahl's life reflect some of the dilemmas facing individuals in authoritarian societies?

2 Riefenstahl has defenders and critics. Which of her actions would each group point to in support of its position?

Underlying and Emerging Issues

Give the reasoning and evidence that might be used to support different views or conclusions on the following issues.

1 Should people accept elements of dictatorship in some instances in order to prevent a more totalitarian government?

2 Is it more important to preserve freedom or to promote prosperity?

3 How can people prevent governments from using modern technology to abuse power?

4 To what extent should governments attempt to win over people's hearts or minds?

5 Can democracy flourish in difficult economic times?

6 Should democratic societies ever suspend individual rights in order to deal with national emergencies?

7 To what extent do different ethnic and cultural groups have different characteristics?

8 How important is the right to disagree with government policies?

9 Is popular support a justification for restricting liberty?

10 To what extent should we look for charisma in our political leaders?

11 How important to democracy is an independent judiciary?

12 To what degree is nationalism a legitimate value, and to what degree is it a threat to democracy and peace?

13 If schools teach students the values of democracy, are they engaging in political indoctrination?

14 How important is it for citizens to speak out on injustice that does not affect them personally?

15 How should an ordinary citizen attempt to deal with a brutal and tyrannical government?

Focussing Knowledge

In your notes, clearly identify or define and explain the importance or significance of each of the following:

primary source	*Enabling Act*
Weimar Republic	*Nuremberg Laws*
Treaty of Versailles	*Führer*
Putsch	*Third Reich*
Mein Kampf	*National Socialism*
Nazi Party	*mass rallies*
Storm Troopers (SA)	*Hitler Youth*
Reichstag	*Joseph Goebbels*
anti-Semitism	

Reviewing and Organizing Knowledge

1 Based on the map on page 214, which European countries did not adopt authoritarian governments in the years 1917–38?

2 a. How were the factors in Hitler's rise to power in Germany similar to those of Mussolini in Italy?

b. What other factors contributed to Hitler's rise to power?

3 Hitler and the Nazis used a variety of techniques to maintain and consolidate their hold on power. Explain how the primary documents in each of the following sections illustrate one or more of these techniques:

a. Popular Opinion

b. Viewpoint: Opinions About Race

c. Use of the Law

d. Justice in the Third Reich

e. Portrait of a Dictator

f. Propaganda

g. Mass Rallies

h. Education

i. Youth

j. Violence, Oppression, and Fear

4 Refer to the documents in the section "A Personal View." Why did Hans and Sophie join the Hitler Youth?

Applying and Extending Knowledge

1 Choose the five factors that seem most important in Hitler's control over the German people, and in an essay explain why you chose these factors.

2 Select another twentieth-century dictator, and research how he or she maintained power. To what extent were the techniques similar to and different from those used by Hitler?

3 "Without World War II, Hitler would have remained in power indefinitely." In an essay, take a position on this statement, and defend your stand.

4 Research the attempt to assassinate Hitler in July 1944. Discuss the issue of whether this action was morally justified.

5 Examine the history of anti-Semitism in Europe before Hitler. To what extent was Hitler's anti-Semitism a departure from, or a continuation of, what had gone on before in Europe?

6 Choose one of the techniques used by Hitler to maintain power (for example, racism or youth movements), and research how this technique has been used by other authoritarian governments in the twentieth century.

7 Can you find evidence of the use of any of these dictatorial techniques discussed in this case study in Canadian society during this century? At present?

8 At what point does education become indoctrination? Write a paper in which you distinguish between the two terms.

9 Select newspaper articles that illustrate one or more of the techniques of dictatorship at present somewhere in the world. Explain how the article illustrates the technique.

10 Choose newspaper articles that illustrate one or more of the Underlying and Emerging Issues on page 228. Explain how each article illustrates the issues.

Nationalism in the Contemporary World

CEASEFIRE PROCLAIMED BY TUTSI REBELS

(The Vancouver Sun, November 5, 1996)
Canada

ABORIGINALS OFFER LAST CHANCE

(The Gazette, November 22, 1996)
Canada

UN STEPS UP PEACE HUNT AS AFGHAN FOES HAGGLE OVER POWER

(The Times, October 19, 1996)
England

5000 U.S. TROOPS TO LEAVE FOR BOSNIA

(New Straits Times, October 3, 1996)
Malaysia

These headlines from around the world have one common characteristic—nationalism. During the last two centuries, nationalism has played a major role in world events and has competed for people's loyalties throughout the globe.

In general, nationalists believe that people who share a common language, culture, history, and territory should govern themselves and should seek to maintain their unique cultural identity. In the past, these sentiments helped to create such countries as Italy, Germany, the United States, Israel, Poland, India, and Algeria. Today, nationalist feelings in such locations as Quebec, Russia, Spain, the Balkans, Sri Lanka, and Burundi make the headlines almost every day. This case study explains the origins of nationalism and examines its role in world events by focussing on Russia and the Balkans.

The Origins of Nationalism

Nationalism is partly a question of who or what possesses the supreme loyalty of a country's inhabitants. In the Middle Ages (c. 500–1500), the Roman Catholic Church claimed the loyalty of Western Europeans. Although some European monarchs, especially those of England and France, tried to limit the Church to spiritual control, they were largely unsuccessful. A number of events helped to alter this situation.

Johann Gutenberg: a mid-fifteenth-century printer noted for pioneering movable type.

secular: worldly or non-religious.

In the mid-fifteenth century, **Johann Gutenberg** invented printing from movable type. This development launched an educational revolution that benefitted the professional and commercial middle classes the most. The nobility, which largely rejected the new technology, rapidly lost much of its influence. The clergy, unable to hold back **secular** knowledge and progress, also felt its influence decline. Western European monarchs engaged the services of educated middle-class experts and administrators, who gradually replaced the clergy and nobility. The foundations were laid for a dynamic middle class to take charge of political events in many Western European countries. This new ideology was based on the principle of national unity and the reduction of class and religious distinctions.

Protestant Reformation: the sixteenth-century religious revolution that resulted in the splitting of the Roman Catholic Church.

In 1517, the **Protestant Reformation** began in Germany. In numerous European countries, Protestant revolts overthrew the Roman Catholic Church and weakened its authority and prestige. This religious revolution influenced even those European countries that remained Roman Catholic. The resulting religious, economic, and social transformation profoundly affected the loyalty of Western Europe's inhabitants, particularly the middle classes.

The new Protestant religions proclaimed that secular rulers should be the leaders of the state (in England and many German states, they also headed the state church). Armed with these powers, a number of European monarchs seized the Catholic Church's properties and became much wealthier through its assets and income. As these monarchs assumed increased power, they proclaimed themselves to be the spiritual, political, and economic masters of their realms. They demanded, and received, the undivided loyalty of their subjects and gradually established highly centralized nation-states, which became the forerunners of the nationalist revolution in late-eighteenth-century France.

The glory and the might of these absolute monarchs was reduced first in England and then in France. In England, a revolution overthrew the absolute monarchy with the execution of Charles I in 1649. An English "nation" was born. This was only a prelude to the full-fledged nationalism that would emerge in France in the next century.

France had a relatively ethnically homogeneous population but was socially divided. The First Estate (clergy) and the Second Estate (nobility) enjoyed exclusive economic and social privileges and tax-free status but were frustrated with their lack of political power. The Third Estate, especially the bourgeoisie (middle classes), occupied important commercial, professional, and administrative positions, but they lacked social prestige and paid a large share of the country's tax load. The seeds of a major revolution were present. Every authority needs the support of at least one major faction in the country. In 1788, King Louis XVI had lost most of his support from every Estate.

What occurred in France in the next few years had a profound effect in every corner of the globe. In 1789, when Louis XVI forbade Estates-General representatives to meet, discuss, and vote together, the Third Estate members withdrew to an empty indoor tennis court. There, in what is historically known as the Tennis Court Oath, they proclaimed themselves to be the sole representatives of the French nation and invited the members of the First and the Second Estate to join them in a "National Assembly." The flustered Louis XVI, when informed of these events, turned to an adviser and asked: "Is this a revolt?" The reply was: "No, Sire, it is a revolution!"

This, indeed, was a revolution. In the Middle Ages, the Roman Catholic Church had decided who was or was not a legitimate member of the community. This judgement was based on an individual's obedience to church regulations. Following the Protestant Reformation, secular heads of state decided whether or not a person had the right to live under the protection of the government, based on that individual's loyalty to the monarch. After the Tennis Court Oath, only those people who accepted the legitimacy of the National Assembly were considered French subjects, thereafter called citizens.

People who advocate this type of popular sovereignty that is centred on the nation are called *nationalists*, and they expect all citizens to conform to established national standards. Governments pursuing policies based on this ideology are called *nationalistic*.

Language and Nationalism

Before the nationalistic ideas unleashed by the English and French revolutions could become a global reality, one more component had to be added. A few decades prior to the outbreak of the French Revolution, **Johann Gottfried von Herder** (1744–1803), a German Protestant minister and philosopher, introduced an idea that became a central theme of nationalist ideology. Herder argued that language best expressed the unique nature of each of the world's nations, and that each nation should preserve its native language at all cost. When a people stop using this language on a day-to-day basis, he stated, their nation will crumble. This "God-given" gift must therefore be preserved, together with folk tales, folk songs, and folk customs.

Johann Gottfried von Herder: an eighteenth-century German philosopher who advocated the preservation of native language from foreign influence.

Herder's theory had a profound impact on people's views about the importance of language. Within his lifetime, scores of philosophers, professors, popular writers, and national leaders proclaimed the importance of linking language with political loyalty. They reasoned that people—whether they were Swedes, Serbs, Czechs, Romanians, or anyone else—could be certain of preserving their beloved language only if everyone lived under a government of his or her own nationality.

These new nationalists believed that humanity should be politically organized on the basis of language, and that only people who spoke the same language could truly understand and love one another. This ideology of nationalism spread rapidly throughout Europe, and from about 1815 onward, the following changes were desired:

1 People living in small countries (for example, the various Italian and German states) where nearly everyone spoke the same language wanted to be unified in one big state, led by fellow nationals who spoke their language.

2 People who were ruled by a group that used a different language from theirs (for example, Poles living in Russia or in the Austrian Empire) wished to be liberated and to form their own country, with leaders from their own language group.

3 People who belonged to scattered linguistic groups that were too small to form their own sovereign government (for example, Wends in Eastern Europe, or Basques in southern France) wanted special rights, or autonomy, that would enable them to maintain their own language and culture, undisturbed by the "alien" ruling majority nationality.

The Rise of Modern Nationalism

Herder's ideas on language appealed to the numerous nationalities who lived under alien rule, while the French Revolution and the subsequent Napoleonic Wars spread the ideologies of liberalism and nationalism throughout Europe. In addition to introducing other peoples to these concepts, France's often harsh treatment of its conquered peoples sparked nationalist feelings in Spain, Russia, Italy, and Germany. From 1858 to 1871, Germans and Italians engaged in a series of wars to unify themselves and gain independence. Italy was united in 1870 and Germany in 1871. These changes upset the balance of power in Europe by adding two major nation-states with a combined population of some 100 million people.

In Germany, the new national government used pro-German propaganda to erase regional, religious, and political differences, and by the late 1880s, Germany was sufficiently unified to launch the next phase of its nationalistic program: European and overseas expansion. The Italians eagerly followed suit. Germany and Italy forged a military alliance in 1883, which France and Great Britain perceived as a threat. The subsequent nationalistic rivalry was one of the sparks that started World War I in 1914. This period introduced a new word into the vocabulary: **jingoism**, which means an excessive nationalism that has no regard for other people and wishes to wage war to prove national superiority. The word "jingo," found in the song "We Don't Want to Fight," was invented by W.G. Hunt in 1878 when Britain was on the verge of a war with Russia.

World War I intensified nationalist sentiments. When the war concluded in 1918, the Allies carved out several new countries (supposedly based on language and ethnic similarities) from the defeated countries of Austria-Hungary, Germany, and Turkey. Maps from before and after the war illustrate the changes in political borders. Russia, which had withdrawn from the war in 1917 and signed a separate peace with Germany and Austria-Hungary, lost its Poles, Finns, Ukrainians, Lithuanians, Latvians, and Estonians. Germany lost most of its Poles to the new country of Poland. Austria was forced to surrender some of its German and Czech-speaking citizens to Czechoslovakia, and nearly all of its Italians to Italy. Hungary had to surrender large tracts of territory inhabited by Magyars to Czechoslovakia, Romania, and Yugoslavia. Poland received a large share of Ukrainians, Lithuanians, and Jews. Italy was unhappy because a significant number of Italians came under Yugoslav rule, which violated a wartime agreement that had brought Italy into the conflict on the Allied side. The Turkish (Ottoman) Empire lost its entire Arab-speaking population. This distribution of the spoils of war fed nationalistic feelings among those people who were separated from their own ethnic groups and became one of the causes of World War II.

jingoism: a nationalistic attitude that favours an aggressive foreign policy.

Case Figure 10.1: Europe in World War I

Anti-German Coalition

Germany and Its Allies

Italy, though a member of the German Alliance System, remained neutral at the beginning of the war and joined the Anti-German Coalition in 1915. Albania did not "officially" take part in the war, although it was occupied by both sides.

Source: From *The Twentieth-Century World: An International History*, Third Edition, by William R. Keylor. Copyright © 1996 by William R. Keylor. Used by permission of Oxford University Press, Inc.

Case Figure 10.2: Europe After World War I

Source: From *The Twentieth-Century World: An International History,* Third Edition, by William R. Keylor. Copyright © 1996 by William R. Keylor. Used by permission of Oxford University Press, Inc.

Defining Nationalism

The word *nationalism* has three main meanings. As a process it refers to nation-building. As a sentiment, it means a consciousness of belonging to a nation. As an ideology, the nation is placed at the centre of all concerns. The ideology of nationalism holds the following beliefs:

1 The world is divided into nations that have their own distinctive characteristics;

2 All political power emanates from the nation;

3 A person's first loyalty must be to the nation;

4 Freedom can be achieved only through membership in one's own nation;

5 A nation can be free only if its citizens have their own sovereign country, which is ruled by a member of their own nationality.

Nationalism and Communism

Beginning with the 1917 Communist Revolution in Russia, and continuing with the rise of Fascism in Italy and Nazism in Germany in the 1920s and 1930s, totalitarian governments grew rapidly in Europe (see Case Studies 8, 9, and 17). Fascism/Nazism and nationalism were comfortable bedfellows. In fact, their brand of nationalism has been referred to as "ultranationalism." Marxism, on the other hand, argued that people were divided according to class, not language, and discouraged nationalism. Lenin believed that capitalism encouraged nationalism among the workers in order to divide them and prevent organized attempts to improve wages and working conditions. As a result, Russia's new leaders promoted internationalism. The Soviet Union was a multi-ethnic state, and many non-Russian citizens turned a deaf ear to Lenin's pleas for a Russian-dominated unity.

To prevent the growth of ethnic nationalism, the Soviet Union under Joseph Stalin encouraged the development of a "New Soviet Person" who could speak Russian fluently. However, many non-Russian citizens were unwilling to give up their language and separate ethnic identity. In the interwar years, when the USSR used force to recapture Ukraine (1920), the Caucasus region (1923), and Moldavia, Latvia, Lithuania, and Estonia (1940), Stalin eliminated their national and ethnic leaders; made Russian the sole language of higher education, national politics, and the armed forces; and uprooted entire nationalities from their homelands and transplanted them elsewhere. In 1944, for example, the Crimean Tatars were moved to Central Asia, and the Chechens were moved to Siberia.

Nationalism and Independence

In the late nineteenth and early twentieth centuries, European imperial powers exploited non-white peoples in Africa and Asia. Few areas of the world escaped Western occupation. World War I weakened the hold of imperialism and strengthened the determination of indigenous leaders throughout the colonized world to seek sovereignty for their peoples. World War II intensified their desire for freedom and independence. Starting with India and Pakistan in 1947, dozens of colonies demanded, fought for, and received their freedom from reluctant Western governments. Case Figure 10.3 illustrates the rise of nationalism and the growth of independence in Africa. By 1997, only St. Pierre and Miquelon (France), Samoa (United States), and a few other states remained colonial possessions.

In many of these former colonial countries there are now serious stirrings among peoples who were liberated from colonial rule, but who do not belong to the ruling ethnic majority. The Karens of Myanmar (formerly Burma), the Tamils of Sri Lanka (formerly Ceylon), Muslim separatists in the Philippines, the Kurds in Iraq, and Kashmir secessionists in India are prominent examples. There are separatists of some sort in many of the world's approximately 200 sovereign states, and all invoke nationalism as their battle cry.

Case Figure 10.3: Decolonization of Africa, 1956–1986

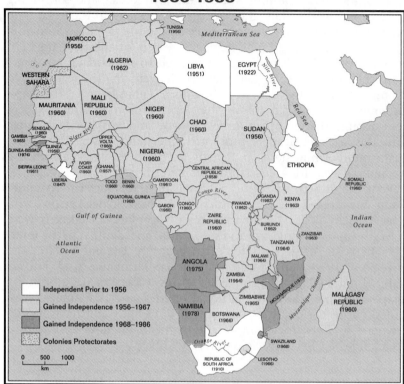

Source: Douglas Baldwin, et al., *The Rise of the Global Village* (Toronto: McGraw-Hill Ryerson, 1988), p. 203.

Nationalism and the End of the Soviet Union

Following the Allied victory in World War II, the Soviet Union imposed Soviet-style governments on its European satellite states, partly to establish a security zone that would protect the Soviet Union against an expected attack by capitalist Western countries. As a result, Poland, Czechoslovakia, Romania, Bulgaria, and the German Democratic Republic (East Germany) lost most of their independence and became buffer states to protect the larger Soviet Empire. But by the late 1980s, a remarkable transformation began to occur.

Throughout 1988, headlines such as the ones on page 239 alerted the world that an explosive mixture of nationalist and ethnic resentments raged beneath the seeming conformity of Soviet life. The USSR contained some 200 ethnic groups whose members spoke 96 distinct languages and used 75 distinctive alphabets. The rise of Mikhail Gorbachev in 1985 and his policies of *glasnost* and democracy opened the floodgates of nationalist violence. The aims of the various national groups ranged from total separation from the USSR (the Baltic countries), to greater political autonomy (the Abkhazians), to the restoration of lost homelands (the Volga Germans and the Crimean Tatars).

SOVIET CITY PUT UNDER NEW CURFEW AS RIOTERS BURN HOMES, CARS

(The Globe and Mail, September 22, 1988)

RAMPAGING MOBS KILL THREE SOVIET SOLDIERS

(Halifax Chronicle-Herald, November 24, 1988)

THOUSANDS FLEE HOMES IN ARMENIA, AZERBAIJAN

(New York Times, December 2, 1988)

In Eastern Europe, the withdrawal of Soviet troops opened the way for independence. The first step toward freedom came in Poland, where poor economic conditions provoked a series of strikes in 1988. The following year, without Soviet opposition, Poland formed Eastern Europe's first non-Communist government since 1948. In quick succession, Hungary, East Germany, Czechoslovakia, Romania, and Bulgaria asserted their freedom. This was followed by the unthinkable: the collapse of the USSR itself. The disintegration of the Soviet Union in 1991 opened the door for various dissatisfied ethnic groups within the old USSR to gain their freedom.

As the *New York Times* stated, "[1989] produced a new map where the sense of regional identity is more fragile [than ever]. It is an Eastern Europe defined not by ideology but by national character, and one in which the flames of nationalism continue to burn throughout the region." It was this sense of nationalism that led to the reunification of Germany at the end of 1990, the division of Czechoslovakia into Slovakia and the Czech Republic in 1993, and the renewal of ethnic conflicts in Romania, Hungary, Bulgaria, and Yugoslavia. But the breakup of Yugoslavia best illustrates the continuing power of nationalism in today's world.

The Balkan Conflicts

Yugoslavia was, in some way, a "sociological laboratory" of different national and religious groups. This country of 24 million people had three official languages (Serbo-Croatian,* Macedonian, and Slovenian). Its ethnic compo-

---

*Serbo-Croatian is written in two ways. Serbs and Muslim South Slavs use the Cyrillic alphabet, and the Croats use the Latin alphabet. The spoken language, allowing for regional differences, is essentially the same.

sition included Serbs (36 percent), Croats (20 percent), Bosnians (9 percent), Slovenes (8 percent), Albanians (8 percent), Macedonians (6 percent), and considerable numbers of Germans, Magyars, and Bulgarians. In religion, 50 percent of the population were Eastern Orthodox, 32 percent Roman Catholic, and 12 percent Muslim.

Yugoslavia was created after World War I. The war began when Austria-Hungary invaded Serbia, the core country of the future Yugoslav state. Final victory ensured the promised creation of a Greater South ("Yugo" means south) Slav state composed of mainly three South Slavic peoples: Serbs, Croats, and Slovenes. Contrary to expectations, the three founding partners were incompatible in many respects, with their different ethnic backgrounds, religions, history, and expectations. The Serbs had been under harsh Turkish Muslim rule for centuries. Those Serbs who converted to Islam, and who lived in the provinces of Bosnia and Herzegovina, were often hated by the Christian Orthodox Serbs. Because of its domination by the Turkish Empire, Serbia missed many of the technical and economic advances made by Western Europeans; it remained predominantly agricultural.

Case Figure 10.4: Yugoslavia's Ethnic/Religious Mix

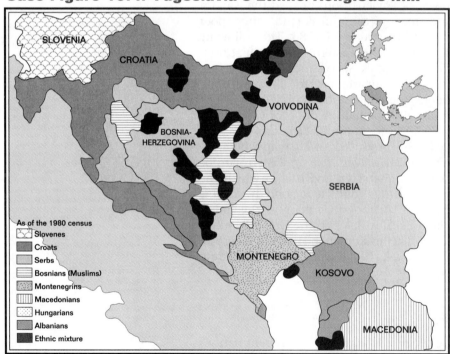

As of the 1980 census
- Slovenes
- Croats
- Serbs
- Bosnians (Muslims)
- Montenegrins
- Macedonians
- Hungarians
- Albanians
- Ethnic mixture

Source: From *Russia, Eurasian States and Eastern Europe*, 26th Edition. Reprinted by permission of Stryker-Post Publications.

The Roman Catholic Croats had lived under the thumb of the Western-oriented Austro-Hungarian Empire. Since the Croats participated in the political, commercial, and educational life of this empire, they were economically advanced compared with the Serbs, although they still lagged behind most Western European countries technologically. The Roman Catholic Slovenes, like the Croats, were firmly grounded in Western European culture. The Serbs, who were the largest ethnic group in the new state, were the only ones among the South Slavs who had an independent state of their own (since 1878 in modern times) and were toughened by centuries of fighting against the Turks and the Bulgarians.

When Yugoslavia was created in 1918, the Serbs dominated the direction of the new country by controlling the administration, the armed forces, and the civil service. They pursued assimilationist policies, trying to eradicate the native languages and customs of the other ethnic groups. The Croats retaliated by assassinating high-ranking Serb politicians, including King Alexander I (1934). The numerically weak Slovenes kept a low profile. Tensions were heightened during World War II with the murder of hundreds of thousands of Serbs by pro-Axis Fascist Croats.

Two non-Slavic peoples, who inhabited large and strategically vital areas of Yugoslavia, also posed a problem for the survival of the new country. The province of Kosovo, located near Muslim-ruled Albania, had a largely Muslim population composed of ethnic Albanians. The Serbs, who composed only about 10 percent of the population, often disliked and distrusted Muslim Albanians. Both Serbs and Albanians considered Kosovo sacred soil. Macedonia, where the predominantly Orthodox population had the majority, posed similar problems. The third ethnic sore point was Yugoslavia's Magyar population. These people lived close to Hungary's southern boundary. The Magyars were made up of Roman Catholics and Protestants, and they traditionally held the Serbs in low esteem.

Yugoslavia's Communist leader, Marshall Tito, attempted to promote national unity after World War II, but after his death in 1980, Yugoslavia began to disintegrate into its separate ethnic/religious parts. Brief but vicious wars fought in 1991 following independence declarations by Slovenia and Croatia resulted in the eventual independence of these states. Kosovo declared its independence in July 1990, but the presence of a large Serbian army prevented its freedom. In January 1991, Macedonia became independent. But the most serious upheaval was still to come.

In the spring of 1992, Bosnia-Herzegovina, with its population of Orthodox Serbs, Roman Catholic Croats, and Muslim Serbs, declared its independence. The ensuing war was fought among these three ethnic groups. Each of the three groups seized as much territory inhabited by their own people as they could and held the other two sides' populations hostage. The Serbs in Yugoslavia supported the Bosnian Orthodox Serbs, Croatia supported the Roman Catholic Croats in Bosnia-Herzegovina, and the Muslims were left to fend for themselves.

After years of fighting and "ethnic cleansing," untold massacres, torture, and other horrors, the combatants tentatively agreed to settle their territorial and other disputes in the 1995 Dayton (Ohio) Accord. This agreement divided the disputed areas into two parts—a Muslim-Croat Federation and a Serb area—united in a loose federal structure. Serbia and Montenegro (another former province of Yugoslavia) continued to call their combined territory Yugoslavia. The tensions remained, especially in areas where minorities were dissatisfied with the new situation.

CAN WORLD PEACE BE IMPOSED?

In 1995, there were ongoing conflicts in over 30 different parts of the globe. The countries involved included Afghanistan, Algeria, Angola, Azerbaijan, Bangladesh, Myanmar, Kampuchea, Colombia, Georgia, Guatemala, Kashmir, Indonesia, Iraq, Israel, Peru, Rwanda, Somalia, Sri Lanka, Sudan, and Northern Ireland. While some of these conflicts were relatively new, others had been smouldering for decades. When one war stops, another seems to begin. The causes of these wars vary widely. Many are fuelled by ethnic or religious hatreds, while others are personal struggles among rival factions for political power.

What should the "great powers" such as the United States, France, and Great Britain do, if anything? In the following excerpt, *Time* correspondent George J. Church discusses how successful outside pressure has been in the past in solving such conflicts.

Diplomacy has had some successes, but is difficult in situations where hated rivals have for decades talked only with guns. Often, too, there are many more than two sides to bring together. The Sudanese war began as a rebellion of black Christians and animists in the south against a government dominated by Muslims of Arab descent in the north, but the rebels have since splintered into seven factions that fight one another as well as the government. [Former U.S. president] Jimmy Carter persuaded all parties to agree to successive cease-fires that lasted from March through July, but warfare promptly resumed at the beginning of August. No surprise. Sally Burnheim, spokesperson for a United Nations relief operation in Sudan, notes that the combatants have often used cease-fires to regroup and prepare for new offensives.

Intervention by armed peacekeepers has usually been futile or worse. Since the U.S.-led UN force pulled out of Somalia [in 1995], the country has reverted to warlord-vs.-warlord combat

strikingly similar to preintervention 1992. African peacekeepers led by Nigerian troops became shooting participants in the Liberian war. Some old Africa hands think intervention might have prolonged the conflict.

Perhaps the worst failure was the attempt of the Indian government to end the struggle between majority Sinhalese and minority Tamils in Sri Lanka. After four years of war, India in 1987 brokered an agreement under which the Sri Lankan government granted some autonomy to the Tamils in the northeast, and New Delhi sent a peacekeeping force to disarm the so-called Liberation Tigers of Tamil Eelam, who insisted on complete independence. The Indians found themselves fighting a full-scale war against the Tigers, but that did not win the hearts and minds of the Sinhalese. In fact, a Sinhalese rebellion broke out against the government, which the rebels contended had no business inviting Indian troops onto the island for any purpose. The Indians pulled out in March 1990, and the war goes on.[1]

Does Church advocate outside intervention? What solution would you propose?

Guest Workers

In addition to ethnic and nationality problems inherited from the distant past, many countries also have nationalism-related problems with so-called **guest workers**. After World War II, an economic boom swept over most industrialized countries. Short of labour, these countries invited citizens from some of the poorer states to perform the more dangerous, low-prestige, and poorly paying jobs that most of their own citizens turned down. In this way, countries such as Germany, Switzerland, and Sweden acquired millions of Turkish, Greek, Yugoslav, and Italian denizens—people who live legally in a place but who lack the possibility of acquiring citizen status. Similarly, Singapore and Japan attracted workers from poorer Asian countries. When the economic boom was over, these people were established in their new locations; many had children who attended the schools of that country and spoke its language. What to do with these unwanted individuals, most of whom do not wish to return home and whose presence in their native countries is no longer desired, is a continuing problem.

guest workers: people from poorer countries who legally settle in a richer country in order to work, but who have no possibility of gaining citizenship in the new country.

Conclusion

Yugoslavia illustrates the central dilemma for the world: nationalist ideologies can create terrible wars as well as feelings of togetherness. Ironically, in this age of globalization, members of ethnic groups in many countries demand independence. Examples include some Scots and Welsh in Great Britain, Bretons and Corsicans in France, Sicilians and Sardinians in Italy, Basques in Spain, Tamils in Sri Lanka, Chechens in Russia, and Québécois in Canada.

Occasionally, demands for independence have been satisfied by granting more autonomy. An example is Belgium's decentralization of power to areas controlled by its two main ethnic groups, the Dutch-speaking Flemings and the French-speaking Walloons. In other situations, nationalism has led to a peaceful division into independent countries, such as Czechoslovakia's split into the Czech Republic and Slovakia. But in many instances, the result is a civil war, such as in Bosnia-Herzegovina and Chechnya. Ironically, at a time when Western Europe is moving toward greater unity through the European Union and many other parts of the world seek freer trade (e.g., NAFTA), the flames of nationalism are igniting conflicts in many other areas.

GEORGE SOROS, 1930–

George Soros occupies a unique position in the world of international finance—he is known equally for making billions and for giving them away. In September 1992, he was called "the man who broke the Bank of England" when he made a profit of over $1 billion through speculation in currency trading in the British pound. At the same time, he has given away close to $1 billion to promote freedom and development, mainly in Eastern Europe.

These two sides of Soros' life are inseparably linked. On the 32nd floor of a New York office building is the centre of the Quantum Fund, the main vehicle of Soros' $11 billion investment empire. According to *Time* magazine, "This is where George Soros, billionaire speculator, makes his money."[2] One floor below is the headquarters of the Soros Foundations, which give his money away.

Born to a Jewish family in Hungary, Soros was shaped by his experiences in World War II, particularly in 1944 when over 400 000 members of the Hungarian Jewish community perished in the Holocaust. He survived through the efforts of his father, who paid for false identity papers that enabled his son to hide from the Nazi SS by posing as the godson of an official of the Hungarian government responsible for confiscating Jewish properties. Soros developed a lifelong aversion to totalitarianism, and a corresponding passion for "open societies."

After the war, Soros made his way to London, where for a time he lived a life of loneliness and poverty. He graduated in philosophy from the London School of Economics and worked for a while in an investment bank. Eventually he moved to New York, where he became increasingly adept at "arbitrage" ("the buying and selling of securities among different markets and grabbing narrow profits through marginal price differences"[3]), especially in world currency markets. Soros left the security of his job and in 1969 formed his Quantum Fund, with spectacular success.

Soros' large-scale philanthropy began in 1979 with the establishment of the Open Society Fund, which was created to give college scholarships to black students in South Africa. But Eastern Europe has been his central concern, particularly since the collapse of the Soviet Empire. In the mid-1980s, he donated hundreds of photocopiers to Hungary on condition that they not be controlled. The result greatly aided the underground press.

Soros points to the vital need to "shape history" at this critical time and worries that the West will miss the opportunity presented by the collapse of communism. He recently donated $250 million for educational programs in Russia and the former Soviet republics, and another $230 million to develop the Central European University in Prague and Budapest.

Soros' foundations donated $335 million for humanitarian purposes in 25 countries in 1994, more than any other private foundation and more than many Western governments, who are generally cutting back on aid. He has also promoted investment in developing countries; $3 billion of the $11 billion that Soros manages is directed to projects and markets in developing countries.

Soros is highly controversial and is criticized by some for making his fortune in currency speculation and thus "betting on the demise of others." But, according to one Macedonian, "I believe that he has saved our country. He put up two $25 million loans at a time when we were in deep crisis and nobody else, not even the U.S. government, would help us."[4]

Soros' views on the situation in Russia are reflected in the following interview with *Business Week:*

Q: *You recently called Russian President Boris Yeltsin "a spent force." Is the same true for his country's economy?*

A: *I was hoping to see an orderly transition to an open society, a market-oriented democratic system based on the rule of law. That attempt has basically failed. But you do have the emergence of a new system: robber capitalism. It is very raw and ugly, but it is a very vital, self-organizing system. It can succeed. There are now economic interests that know how to defend themselves. You have tremendous natural resources in Russia in which it is worthwhile to invest. You could have new growth to offset the continuing decay of the old. But the system is creating a tremendous sense of social injustice and a decline in civilized values. There is a great and pervasive sense of corruption.*

There is a grave danger that the sense of frustration and disorientation will lead to a political backlash and a xenophobic, nationalistic mood. To contain the growing resentment, two things need to be done. One is to sustain cultural and intellectual life, which is very important to the sense of identity of Russians. This is what my foundation is seeking to accomplish. But more important, you need to provide a social safety net for the large masses who are very badly hurt. This is where the International Monetary Fund and World Bank can play an important role.[5]

1 In what ways are George Soros' efforts an attempt to deal with the problems of nationalism, especially in Eastern Europe?

2 Why is Soros worried about the present global situation and related Western policies?

Underlying and Emerging Issues

Give the reasoning and evidence that might be used to support different views or conclusions on the following issues.

1 To what extent should individuals seek fulfilment through identification with others who share their language and culture?

2 To what extent do national groups have the right to an independent country?

3 Does the desire for national independence justify the use of violence?

4 How should nation-states deal with the issue of ethnic minorities?

5 How should democratic societies deal with ethnic diversity?

6 Why do differences among peoples lead to war in some cases, but not in others?

7 To what extent can different cultural groups learn to live in harmony in a shared political system?

8 What kinds of political structures and policies are most likely to promote harmony among different cultural groups?

9 Can the desires of ethnic minorities be accommodated through decentralized federalism?

10 Should Canada seek to accommodate Quebec nationalism through increased decentralization of power?

11 Is nationalism a more important value than democracy?

12 Is nationalism consistent with the values of democracy?

13 To what extent does nationalism encourage intolerance?

14 To what extent is nationalism responsible for large-scale conflict in the world?

15 Does the increasing number of small countries contribute to economic instability?

16 To what extent does the European Union offer an alternative to the appeal of nationalism?

17 Should Canada encourage an increased sense of nationalism in its citizens?

Focussing Knowledge

In your notes, clearly identify or define and explain the importance or significance of each of the following:

nationalism	Serbo-Croatian
Protestant Reformation	Magyar
nation-state	Bosnia-Herzegovina
jingoism	"ethnic cleansing"
satellite states	autonomy
Chechnya	guest workers
Slavic	Johann von Herder
South Slav	Marshall Tito

Reviewing and Organizing Knowledge

1 Explain the role of each of the following in the origins of nationalism:

a. the rise of the nation-state

b. the Protestant Reformation

c. the French Revolution

2 a. Describe Herder's contribution to the rise of nationalism.

b. What were the desired changes that stemmed from the increase of nationalism after 1815?

3 Describe the impact of the following developments on nationalism:

a. late nineteenth-century imperialism

b. World War I

4 Outline the main beliefs that underlie the ideology of nationalism.

5 a. How does Marxism view nationalism?

b. How did Stalin deal with ethnic nationalism in the USSR?

6 What factors led to the rise of nationalism and independence in former colonized countries?

7 Describe the impact on and involvement of nationalism in

a. the collapse of the Soviet Empire;

b. the disintegration of the USSR.

8 a. Describe the factors that led to the breakup of Yugoslavia.

b. How has the Yugoslav conflict been resolved?

9 How does the problem of guest workers relate to the issue of nationalism?

10 Describe the three main approaches to dealing with the issue of nationalism and ethnic minorities.

Applying and Extending Knowledge

1 Albert Einstein said, "Nationalism is an infantile disease. It is the measles of mankind." Stephen Decatur said, "Our country, right or wrong." In an essay, explain which of these two views you favour. Support your position with arguments and evidence.

2 Research a developing country on issues that are related to nationalism. Describe

a. how it achieved independence;

b. how it deals with the issue of ethnic nationalism.

3 In an essay, examine the political system of Switzerland. How has this country been able to achieve peace and prosperity despite the presence of substantial ethnic and linguistic differences among its citizens?

4 Write a paper comparing the approaches of Canada and Belgium in dealing with the aspirations of their French-speaking minorities. To what extent are their situations and policies similar and different?

5 In a paper, compare the experience of Ukraine with one of the other newly independent former Soviet republics. How have the two countries dealt with issues related to nationalism and ethnic minorities?

6 Choose two former satellite states of the USSR to research. How have they handled the questions related to nationalism and ethnicity?

7 In a research paper, examine in depth the causes of the wars in Yugoslavia in the early 1990s. Could they have been prevented? To what extent were these conflicts the result of historic ethnic and cultural differences, and to what extent were they caused by specific developments in the late 1980s?

8 Research the Chechnya conflict. Compare the rationale and actions of the Russian government and the Chechen rebels in an essay.

9 Choose one of the Underlying and Emerging Issues on page 246. Describe the various sides, and explain the complexity and importance of the issue.

10 Choose newspaper articles that illustrate issues related to the role of nationalism in the world today. Explain how the articles illustrate the issues.

CHAPTER *5*

Political Systems and World Developments

*T*HIS CHAPTER REVIEWS THE MAJOR DIFFERENCES between authoritarian and democratic beliefs and uses the political ideology of Saudi Arabia as an example of the wide range of political systems that exist outside the Western world. After examining the importance of studying each country's political ideology, the chapter discusses the impact of a number of world events related to political systems. These developments include the emergence of Islamic fundamentalism, conflict in the Middle East, the increasing importance of multinational corporations, and the rise of environmental groups such as the Greens.

Our study of political ideologies has concentrated mainly on the relationship between people and their leaders. In an ideal democracy, government functions in obedience to the desires of the governed. In an authoritarian state, however, government functions in obedience to the desires of the rulers, and the people obey this authority.

In the real world, governments lie somewhere between the two ends of this spectrum. Even the most democratic government demands a certain obedience to authority for the protection of everyone, whereas in an authoritarian state the government must take care not to demand more of its citizens than they are prepared to give.

We should also remember that the concepts of authoritarianism and democracy that we have been examining were formulated either in Western Europe or by the descendants of Europeans in other parts of the world. These concepts fit most easily when we examine governments that are influenced by Western civilization. Although it is useful to analyze all governments in relation to these concepts, this must be done with care to avoid applying inappropriate categories to non-Western governments.

Learning Outcomes

After reading this chapter, you should be able to:

- discuss ongoing political changes in the world

- decide about your own political ideology

- explain the connection between environmentalism and ideology

- understand the growth of Islamic fundamentalism

- appreciate the importance of maintaining an open mind when evaluating politics

- hypothesize about future political directions

- understand that not every country holds the same values as the Western world

- explain the growth and power of multinational corporations

hereditary monarch: any ruler who inherits the right to rule a country, based usually on family (dynastic) affiliation.

Let us briefly consider one example of this potential danger. Saudi Arabia is ruled by a **hereditary monarch** assisted by an extensive network of hereditary princes. Even so, any male citizen can approach the monarch directly with a personal petition. Certain times and places are set aside to allow people access to the ruler, who is required by custom to listen to the lengthy recital of his subjects' needs and might well decide to investigate the matter personally and remedy the situation.

This suggests that Saudi citizens have more effective access to their government than do the citizens of Canada, who sometimes may have difficulty getting the attention of government clerks. However, the Saudi monarchy is not required to do what the male citizens ask, and Saudi women have no right to launch political petitions. In addition, the monarch and his princes make all major government decisions without consulting the people. Saudi Arabia has no constitution and no elected parliament. Some analysts suggest that a better understanding of Saudi government can be gained by examining the traditions of desert nomads, from which the political system came, than by comparing it with Western forms of government. The Saudi government, they suggest, is a traditional government superficially adapted to twentieth-century conditions.

Governments of developing nations need to be examined individually, in the light of their history and their present political and economic situation in the world. A study of many African countries, for example, should pay attention to tribal alliances that hold them together or tribal rivalries that threaten to split them apart. Sometimes developing countries adopt Western ideologies, but often they try to avoid such identification.

How can studying ideologies help us when we are examining governments? In the first place, an ideology explains the basis on which all governments exist. An examination of ideologies introduces us to the study of government at its fundamental level. Once we have thought about government in general, we are in a better position to examine specific governments.

Ideologies can also be used to evaluate our own governments. Assuming that no government is ever a perfect expression of the ideology it sets forth, political ideals can be used to suggest ways to improve government: ideologies give us a goal to strive toward. Finally, a careful study of ideologies helps us to identify our most deeply held values and enables us to maintain or change them based on how well they are serving us.

Political Changes

It is important to note that political systems are not static—they tend to change as circumstances change. One relatively recent change has been the growth of democracy. In response to citizens' demands, a number of countries have cast off dictatorships in favour of multi-party systems and free elections. This revolution occurred gradually in Latin America, where many countries finally rid themselves of generals and military dictatorships in favour of democratic governments. The process began in Ecuador in 1979, spread to Peru (1980), and then emerged in Bolivia (1982), Argentina (1983), Uruguay (1984), and Brazil (1985). Since then, several countries in Central America have experienced democratic triumphs. Cuba is the only country that remains defiantly communist and retains an uncompromising one-party state system in Latin America.* As well, the military still plays a dominant role in El Salvador and elsewhere in Central and South America.

Changes in Africa

Most African countries continue to be dominated by military or one-party dictatorships. An alarming trend in Africa is the revival of tribal hostilities. European colonization of Africa resulted in the formation of countries that contained a variety of ethnic/tribal groups. When Western imperialist countries left or were forced out of Africa after World War II, the former colonies attempted to create either Western-style capitalist or Marxist states. More recently, many of these attempts have been crumbling under the weight of tribal hatred. The underlying causes of this situation are historical, psychological, and sociological.

Since tribal units are based on loyalty to extended families or clans, many people are not prepared to accept the formation of a modern state that would incorporate numerous clans and tribes under the direction of a single, centralized authority that would then represent the entire nation. Age-old rivalries persist, and many Africans are deeply suspicious of the motives of neighbouring tribes, especially if they are larger and more powerful. Religious differences among the various tribes, divided as they are by Christian, Muslim, and more traditional beliefs, as in Nigeria and Sudan, merely heighten potential conflict in some countries.

In several African countries, religious and tribal hostilities have had tragic consequences. In some cases, a dominant tribe has assumed political control over a country and then slaughtered fellow citizens who are members of a hostile tribe. Tribal massacres have claimed the lives of hundreds of thousands of victims, and some countries have fallen into anarchy and chaos; Eritrea, Liberia, Burundi, and Rwanda are some examples. Elsewhere, bitter civil wars have been fought, such as those in Nigeria and Zaire. In the Republic of South Africa, democracy is threatened by the potential for civil war between two major tribes, the Zulus and the Bantu (Xhosa), who have been enemies for centuries.

The Growth of Democracy

One method of studying the growth of democracy is to chart the percentage of the world's population that has lived in a democracy at different times in the past. Although it is impossible to divide the world's countries into simple categories of democratic and non-democratic (since there are many shades of grey), the following table provides a rough indication of the growth of democracy since 1840.

Table 5.1: Democracy Over the Years

Year	Number of countries	Percent democratic
1840	3	3.9
1900	13	12.3
1920	29	20.6
1940	15	11.4
1950	29	34.4
1970	37	36.4
1990	55	43.2
1995	117	54.0

Sources: Mary Hawkesworth and Maurice Kogan, eds., *Encyclopedia of Government and Politics*, Vol. 2 (London: Routledge, 1992), p. 1360; *International Living*, Canadian ed. (January 1996), p. 13.

Focus

Explain the decline in democracies between 1920 and 1940, and their growth between 1990 and 1995.

---

* See Chapter 8 for a detailed discussion of events in Cuba.

The continuation of these problems suggests hard times for the future peace and prosperity of the African continent and for its prospects for democracy.

Changes in Europe and the Balkans

Balkans: a large peninsula in southeastern Europe.

In Eastern Europe and the **Balkans,** an area dominated by the Soviet Union until 1990, the collapse of communist, one-party, totalitarian governments was unexpected, sudden, and convincing. The collapse was associated with the Soviet Union's weakness, which was caused by the unsettling economic consequences of *perestroika* (the restructuring of the Soviet economy) under General Secretary Mikhail Gorbachev (see Case Studies 7 and 12). By 1990, every country in the Soviet Bloc—East Germany, Czechoslovakia, Poland, Hungary, Romania, and Bulgaria—had experienced grass-roots democratic revolutions that easily overthrew the communist regimes. Only in Romania and Bulgaria did the former communists retain a toehold, but at the heavy price of abandoning their communist labels and permitting opposition groups to compete in the political marketplace. Only Albania, an independent Marxist state, has thus far refused to abandon its dictatorial and repressive ways. However, "reformed" communist parties achieved electoral success in Poland, Hungary, and Lithuania in the early 1990s.

An important consequence of these revolutions was East Germany's wish to reunite with West Germany. This impulse was so powerful that neither the Western allies nor the Soviet Union, with its 350 000 troops stationed on East German soil, could stop or slow German reunification. A reunited Germany became a reality in October 1990.

Ethnic, religious, and historic differences have destroyed Yugoslavia, a country whose people had been held together by leader Marshal Tito (Josip Broz). Tito, a wartime Marxist guerrilla, liberated his homeland from German and Italian military occupation after World War II. After his death in 1980, Yugoslavia gradually disintegrated into its various ethnic, religious, and ideological divisions, each ethnic-religious people looking after its own interests. In 1991, Western-oriented Roman Catholic Slovenians and Croatians, who speak different languages, founded their own independent states (Slovenia and Croatia), as did Greek Orthodox Macedonians. Bosnia-Hercegovina, with a population composed of Muslims, Roman Catholic Croats, and Russian Orthodox Serbs, most of whom speak the same language, erupted in a fero-

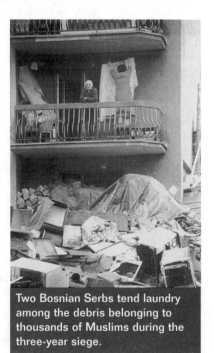

Two Bosnian Serbs tend laundry among the debris belonging to thousands of Muslims during the three-year siege.

cious civil war that ended with a three-way ethnic and religious territorial division in 1996. Only the massive military presence of the Russian-oriented Orthodox Serbs in the province of Kosovo has thus far prevented the Muslim Albanian-speaking population from leaving Serbia and joining its neighbouring Muslim-ruled Albania. The Serbian Russian Orthodox territory has lost nearly all of its non-Serbian population. Each new state has sworn to uphold democratic principles and ideals, but whether these diverse peoples can do so in the long run remains to be seen, particularly in light of the ethnic and religious hatreds that seem so dominant.*

Movement toward democracy and capitalism in Eastern Europe has been uneven. In some countries there has been virtually no movement, whereas in others it has been unexpectedly rapid. Most countries fall somewhere in the middle.

A vitally important by-product of the movement toward democracy has been the division of the Soviet Union into 15 smaller countries based largely on ethnicity and religion, such as the three Baltic republics of Lithuania, Latvia, and Estonia. The Islamic republics are caught in the grip of a worldwide Islamic fundamentalist revival.

Islamic Fundamentalism

Fundamentalism is the belief that all statements made in a holy book should be taken literally. In the case of Muslims, this holy book is the Qur'an (or Koran). Muslims believe that the word of God was revealed through the archangel Gabriel to Muhammad (c. A.D. 570–632) and that God, not Muhammad, is the author of the Qur'an.

While Islam was founded in Arabia, the Muslim world population today is estimated at more than 935 million. Islamic fundamentalism experienced a dramatic resurgence in the 1970s and 1980s as a reaction against modernism. It has had a tremendous impact on world events. Islamic fundamentalists believe that Western morality has corrupted their governments and way of life, and they advocate a return to the dictates of the Qur'an. These include modest dress for women (including wearing veils), sexual segregation, compulsory tithes (fees paid to the mosques), and harsh punishments for crimes such as robbery and promiscuity.

Islamic fundamentalism, which began in the nineteenth century, intensified between the end of the 1967 Arab–Israeli war, in which Arab forces suffered a crushing defeat, and the successful Iranian revolution 12 years later. **Shiite Muslims** are one of the two major groups in Islam (the other being Sunni Muslims). When the Shiite spiritual leader, the Ayatollah Khomeini, overthrew the Shah of Iran in 1979, he created a **theocracy** based on the laws of the Qur'an. Today, Iran is governed largely by *mullahs*, or religious leaders, who conduct the affairs of state along strict Islamic fundamentalist principles.

fundamentalism: the belief that the words of a holy book (such as the Bible or the Qur'an) are the words of God and therefore should be taken literally.

Shiite Muslims: an Islamic sect that broke away from Sunni Muslims in the late seventh century, largely on doctrinal grounds.

theocracy: a system of government in which God is recognized as the supreme ruler and religious laws are regarded as the laws of the state.

---

* For a more detailed description of recent events in the Balkans, see Case Study 10.

According to fundamentalist ideology, religious authorities should regulate the political, economic, social, and moral activities of the people. Since the fundamentalist victory in Iran, this ideology has spread into Islamic countries ranging from Pakistan to Saudi Arabia to West Africa, and has led to a virtual civil war in Afghanistan and Algeria. The Persian Gulf War (1990–91), which saw Western armies use Saudi Arabia, the protector of the Islamic holy cities of Mecca and Medina, as a military base only increased fundamentalist vigour. Many people regard the Muslim world as the West's only real ideological competitor. In the Middle East, Muslim and Jewish fundamentalism meet head to head.

Figure 5.1: Map of Islamic States

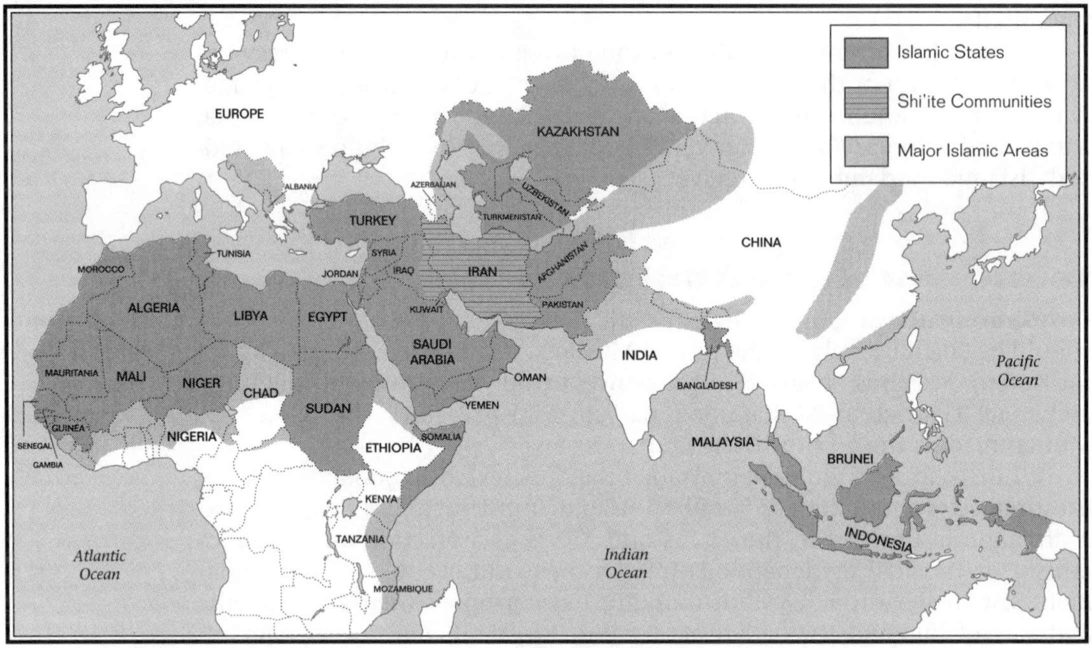

Source: D. Baldwin, et al., *The Rise of the Global Village* (Whitby, ON: McGraw-Hill Ryerson, 1988), p. 223.

Changes in the Middle East

The end of the Cold War—the hostility between the United States and the Soviet Union and their respective allies that followed World War II—brought hopes of peace in the Middle East. A first step on the road to a settlement came when Russia suspended its financial and diplomatic aid to the Arab world. Next, the United States persuaded Israel to negotiate peace with the Arabs. This involved surrendering control over the Israeli-occupied West Bank of the Jordan River and the Gaza Strip to the Palestinians, who were persuaded to accept the agreement by vague promises of autonomy.

The prospect of Israeli–Palestinian peace had two startling ideological consequences. In Israel, the Jewish population split over the terms of the peace agreement. The majority of secular-minded Israeli Jews accepted the "peace for land" agreement. More fundamentalist, mainly Orthodox, Israeli

Jews rejected the agreement, citing Israel's spiritual claim to all of Israel's "sacred soil," which goes beyond Israel's present borders. The Mid-East struggle has created a gulf between secular and spiritual forces—both Jewish and Muslim—that could spill over into the Western world.

The ideological split in the Jewish community, which numbers approximately 15 million people globally, is minor in comparison with the violent reaction to the Israeli–Palestinian agreement in the Arab world, which numbers nearly 200 million people. The Arabs had already split along religious–secular lines during the Iranian revolution in 1979, and the Israeli–Palestinian agreement only aggravated the problem. Some Palestinian Arabs, mainly composed of Muslim religious extremists, have sworn to overturn the Israeli–Palestinian peace by violence if necessary. In Israel, a right-wing Jewish extremist assassinated Prime Minister Yitzhak Rabin, who had promoted peace with the Arab world. The 1996 election brought Binyamin Netanyahu to power. He promised to "go slow" on further peace agreements and the peace process was once again in doubt. In the Middle East, the choice among political ideologies is made even more difficult by religious and cultural differences, as well as ancient hatreds.

The Impact of Multinational Corporations

Every time you eat a Big Mac, wash it down with a Pepsi, fill the car with gas, withdraw money from the bank, or purchase a tennis racquet and a pair of running shoes, you are probably dealing with a multinational corporation that has stores and factories in many countries around the world.

Multinational corporations (MNCs), also called transnational corporations, are business firms that operate in a number of different countries and tend to adopt a global rather than a national perspective. They function along the lines of the large business corporations that emerged after the American Civil War in the 1860s. Such famous examples as Standard Oil and Wrigley's were thriving by 1914. They began by monopolizing a certain industry, such as steel, and then acquired control over other industries that were directly or indirectly related. In the case of steel production, steel corporations bought coal mines, iron foundries, and railway systems.

Using mass-marketing techniques, these large corporations expanded overseas, sometimes merging with similar foreign business firms, to form multinational corporations. While the MNCs marketed their products in Europe and North America, they acquired the necessary raw materials in Latin America (copper, sugar, bananas), and the Middle East and Africa (oil and gold). Between 1946 and 1989, American MNCs alone increased their investments in foreign **subsidiaries** from $7.2 billion to $373.4 billion. In the twentieth century, European and Asian MNCs, such as Volkswagen, Shell Petroleum, and Sony, entered the race. Japanese firms concentrated their early investments in Asia, and by the 1970s were producing transistor radios, televisions, cameras, and pocket calculators using cheap raw materials and labour from Taiwan, Malaysia, and Thailand. The emergence of European

multinational corporation (MNC): a business organization that functions on a global basis and so is not subject or loyal to any particular government or state.

subsidiary: a company that is more than half owned or controlled by another company.

and Japanese MNCs marked the age of global business in an interdependent world.

Initially, these corporations remained residents of their home countries, where they paid taxes and obeyed state laws. Following World War II, the MNCs developed new techniques to escape from political control. Often they moved to countries that imposed fewer controls. From there, the companies treated the world as one big market, coordinating activities across political boundaries to reap immense profits. In the early 1990s, MNCs employed over 70 million people worldwide, and their total production represented about 40 percent of gross world production.

Table 5.2: The World's Largest Corporations, 1995

Company	Originating country	Revenues $millions	Profits $millions	Number of employees
1. Mitsubishi	Japan	184 365.2	346.2	36 000
2. Mitsui	Japan	181 518.7	314.8	80 000
3. Itochu	Japan	169 164.6	121.2	7 182
4. General Motors	U.S.	168 828.6	6 880.7	709 000
5. Sumitomo	Japan	167 530.7	210.5	6 193
6. Marubeni	Japan	161 057.4	156.6	6 702
7. Ford Motor	U.S.	137 137.0	4 139.0	346 990
8. Toyota Motor	Japan	111 052.0	2 662.4	146 855
9. Exxon	U.S.	110 009.0	6 470.0	82 000
10. Royal Dutch/ Shell Group	Neth./Brit.	109 833.7	6 904.6	104 000
11. Nissho Iwai	Japan	97 886.4	(259.5)	17 005
12. Wal-Mart Stores	U.S.	93 627.0	2 740.0	675 000
13. Hitachi	Japan	84 167.1	1 468.8	331 852
14. Nippon Life Insurance	Japan	83 206.7	2 426.6	89 690
15. Nippon Telegraph & Telephone	Japan	81 937.2	2 209.1	231 400

Source: *Fortune* (August 5, 1996), p. F-1. © 1996 Time Inc. All rights reserved.

Focus

Do you think these MNCs should be ranked by revenues, profits, number of employees, or some other criterion?

MNCs act like separate countries. They sell in more than one country, obtain their raw materials and capital from varied sources, and produce goods in several countries, preferably where labour costs are cheap and natural resources are plentiful. The impact of MNCs, especially in developing countries, is debated. Their defenders claim that in this age of modern technology that seems to have shrunk the world, MNCs are the most efficient form of doing business. They provide technology and jobs in developing nations. Some small countries have learned to play one MNC against another, and have forced them to conform to local needs. In the past, several Middle East countries simply nationalized foreign oil companies.

On the other hand, MNCs often act like old imperialist countries, forcing their values, tastes, and products on the consumers of developing nations. Some global companies have sold goods to these countries that were not suited to local conditions. For example, mothers in some developing countries were urged to stop breast-feeding their infants and to buy powdered baby formula. However, with no way to sterilize baby bottles or obtain clean water, hundreds of infants died.

Through their purchasing and production, MNCs affect a country's economic life. They now have the potential to rival the governments of nation-states for global superiority. Critics fear a time when multinational corporations might openly force the world's governments to do their economic bidding, based upon the belief that the economic experts employed by the corporations know how to govern a state best. Other people maintain that market forces, competition, and economic necessity will increase the trend toward multinational corporations, and argue that nation-states will become obsolete. Will these economic changes result in more fundamental changes to our political systems? The implications for the future are profound.

Environmentalism

MNCs may be an efficient form of doing business, but they also play a major role in one of the world's most pressing problems—destruction of the natural environment. At the core of the environmental movement is a concern for preserving the natural environment and a belief in the intrinsic value of all living things. Although environmentalism covers such wide-ranging concerns as global warming, the ozone layer, air and water pollution, nuclear non-proliferation, deforestation, and whaling, the movement offers a world view that includes ethical principles and recommendations for promoting a better world for all.

The environmental movement includes a wide range of groups and organizations. Greenpeace International (see Case Study 5), for example, has a worldwide membership of close to 2.9 million people, 6 ships, and an annual budget of $153 million. Other organizations, such as the World Rainforest Movement and the Sierra Club, cut across national boundaries and propose political action on a global scale.

Although environmentalism has its roots in the Industrial Revolution, not until the twentieth century did people realize that unchecked economic growth was polluting our water, making our air toxic, and rendering much of our land unusable. Some experts warn that life as we know it is in jeopardy unless we do something to halt harmful economic activities.

This crisis has spawned many powerful political groups in all Western countries. Called by different names in different places, they are generally labelled **Greens**. The German Greens, which formed a political party in 1980, were the most successful, taking 8.2 percent of the national vote and

Greens: political activists who are functioning in many countries to save the environment.

46 seats in the 1987 German election. Environmentalists in other countries also established "green" parties, such as the Ecology Party in Great Britain and the Values Party in New Zealand. Jonathan Power, a London-based journalist, described the impact of the environmental movement on Göteborg, a Swedish industrial centre with a population of nearly half a million: "There are no expressways slicing up the neighbourhoods. Transportation is by fast, nonpolluting streetcars first, bicycles second, and cars third. ... There are no slums. Nor are there any homeless, and there is barely any unemployment."[1] Similar attitudes and conditions exist in the other Scandinavian countries of Norway, Denmark, and Finland.

During the 1990s, the popularity of nearly all the green parties declined. Part of the problem stemmed from globalization and competition, which led companies and countries to keep costs down—often at the expense of the environment. Others wanted to create jobs, regardless of the environmental impact. According to Robert Paehlke, however, environmentalism "provides a very useful base from which to make individual life choices, from which to take collective political action, and from which to decide a surprisingly broad range of public policy issues. In short, environmentalism is a political ideology, and one that is likely to endure."[2] While some people believe that recent trends toward deregulation of business could lead to less protection for the environment, others believe that the important nature of the environmental challenges that face humanity ensure that the environmentalist movement will continue to be a force into the twenty-first century.

Major Political Systems: Conclusions

The survival of our world as we know it depends on the knowledge, wisdom, forbearance, and diplomatic skills of individuals throughout the globe. They will need a vast range of practical know-how, supported by strong ideological convictions of their own, paired with a knowledge of people's practical needs and ideological requirements. In order to accept or reject an ideology, it is essential that we first understand it. This means keeping an open mind, learning about contemporary world affairs, analyzing the issues, and separating fact from opinion. It is equally important that we understand the beliefs, practices, and institutions of our own country. It is difficult to chart future directions without knowing where we have been, and how others got to where they are.

What's Coming Next

Chapter 5 concludes our discussion of politics. The remainder of this book focuses on economic theories, systems, and ideologies. To provide a general framework for this discussion, Chapter 6 explains the important terminology and economic tools that you will need to explore the benefits and drawbacks of the world's major economic systems. Although we have separated political systems from economic systems in this textbook, it is important to remember that in the real world the two are intertwined.

BIOGRAPHY

AYATOLLAH RUHOLLAH KHOMEINI, 1900–1989

The Iranian revolution led by Ayatollah Khomeini in 1979 did much more than overthrow the Shah of Iran's leadership and establish a theocracy in Iran. It ushered in a time of turmoil that included the spread of Islamic fundamentalism, dramatic shifts in Middle Eastern and world politics, and a clear challenge to the trends of Westernization and modernization that had dominated the century.

The person at the centre of the storm began his career as a religious scholar in the Shiite branch of Islam in the Iranian holy city of Qom. Khomeini gradually rose in power and influence in religion, attaining the title of *ayatollah* (or major religious leader) in the 1950s, and grand *ayatollah* by the early 1960s.

At the same time, Khomeini's opposition to the policies of Shah Mohammed Riza Pahlevi became more intense. Many in the West were willing to tolerate the Shah's dictatorship and often-brutal secret police (SAVAK) because of his pro-Western stance and his modernization of Iran. Khomeini completely rejected the Shah's "white revolution," particularly in its provisions for women's rights and agricultural reforms, which took power away from the clergy. Above all, he despised the Western, secular nature of the Shah's rule, referring to him openly as an "American stooge," and to America as "the Great Satan."

Khomeini's rebellious activities led in 1964 to his 15-year exile, first in Iraq, and later in Paris. Increasingly he became the centre of the Iranian opposition, and when his forces finally overthrew the Shah in 1979, his triumphant return to Iran's capital city of Tehran was greeted by a crowd of 3 million people.

In contrast to Western views on the separation of church and state, Khomeini believed in the absolute inseparability of religion and politics. He quickly established a theocratic Islamic Republic, with himself as lifelong "spiritual adviser." He soon alienated his more secular followers with his enforcement of rigid traditional practices for women and his ruthless suppression of all opposition. "According to his son Ahmad he would weep if you killed a fly but would not shed a tear if you killed 2000 unbelievers."[3]

The Iranian takeover of the U.S. embassy in Tehran, accompanied by holding Americans from the embassy hostage for a year, alienated many Western nations, and Iran's eight-year war with Iraq drained the country's resources. However, Khomeini continued to defiantly promote his revolutionary fundamentalism throughout the Muslim world and beyond. When Indian-born British author Salman Rushdie's satirical book *The Satanic Verses* offended many Muslims in 1989, Khomeini encouraged his Islamic followers around the world to kill Rushdie and his publishers. Rushdie is still forced to live in hiding.

Khomeini's death in 1989 brought the same conflicting responses as his life: many in the West welcomed the end of a tyrant, while his followers mourned the passing of a fearless saint who changed the history of their world.

---

1 Why did Khomeini reject both international communism and the Western world?

2 Why might Khomeini be seen as a hero to some people in less developed countries?

Underlying and Emerging Issues

Give the reasoning and evidence that might be used to support different views or conclusions on the following issues.

1 Can culture and tradition be a legitimate basis for denying rights to individuals or groups?

2 To what extent should the political system reflect the culture and traditions of a society?

3 To what extent should a political system reflect the dominant religious beliefs in a country?

4 To what degree should Canada's political system reflect the multicultural make-up of Canadian society?

5 On what basis should we come to conclusions about the desirability of different approaches to political systems?

6 Could a one-party system be the best approach for some countries in some situations?

7 To what extent should countries have the right to determine their own political and economic systems?

8 Are there circumstances in which one country has a right to intervene in the internal affairs of another country?

9 Should Canada actively encourage the growth of democracy around the world?

10 Should Canada trade with countries whose governments deny human rights to some of their citizens?

11 Should governments make environmental protection a higher priority than job creation?

12 Is it more important to be globally competitive or to protect national interests?

13 Do multinational corporations represent a threat to national sovereignty? To democracy?

14 How should nation-states deal with the increasingly international nature of corporations?

15 Should we have international laws to control multinational corporations?

Focussing Knowledge

In your notes, clearly identify or define and explain the importance or significance of each of the following:

hereditary monarch	*theocracy*
Balkans	*secular*
environmentalism	*multinational corporations*
fundamentalism	*subsidiaries*
Islamic fundamentalism	*Greens*
Qur'an	*Muhammad*
Shiite Muslims	*Ayatollah Khomeini*

Reviewing and Organizing Knowledge

1 a. Why do most political systems lie somewhere between the ends of a spectrum that has democracy and authoritarianism at either end?

   b. What are the limitations or dangers of using this democracy/authoritarianism spectrum to analyze a country's political system?

2 How can we get a more thorough understanding of non-Western or developing nation governments?

3 How are ideologies useful for examining governments?

4 How have recent developments affected the political systems of the following areas:

   a. Latin America?

   b. Africa?

   c. Eastern Europe (including the Balkans and the former USSR)?

5 How have each of the following affected political systems in the world?

   a. Islamic fundamentalism

   b. the Middle East

   c. multinational corporations

   d. environmentalism

Applying and Extending Knowledge

1 On the basis of your study of political systems, write an essay in which you describe your views on what needs to be done about Canada's political system. What changes would you recommend? What aspects of the present system should be retained? Support your answer by referring to specific examples from your study of political systems.

2 Write a description of your own political ideology. Clearly outline the main elements of the approach to political systems that you favour, and support your position with arguments and evidence that reflect your study of political systems.

3 Select a country and analyze its political system. To what extent are the main elements of democracy and authoritarianism present or absent? What factors (such as tradition, culture, religion, economics, or history) have led to the emergence of the particular nature of the country's present political system?

4 Choose two countries and compare their political systems in terms of democracy and authoritarianism. What factors might have led to the differences in the two systems?

5 Choose one of the following areas: Africa, Asia, Latin America, Eastern Europe, Western Europe. Research and describe the changes that have occurred in the political systems in the area over the last decade.

6 Research one of the following topics: Islamic fundamentalism, the environmental movement, multinational corporations. Evaluate the impact of the development: What are its positive and negative results?

7 Choose one of the Underlying and Emerging Issues on page 260. Outline the arguments and evidence on the various sides of the issue. Take a position, and explain why you arrived at that position in light of the arguments and evidence.

An Introduction to Economic Systems

HAT SHOULD A COUNTRY PRODUCE? How should it be produced? How should these goods be divided among the people? There are four ways to answer these questions: by traditional methods, through central direction, by the market forces of supply and demand, and through a mixture of central planning and the market economy. To help you analyze national economies, this chapter explains such economic terms as Gross National Product and productivity. It concludes with a discussion of various methods of evaluating different countries' standard of living and the growth of global interdependence.

Although most people talk a lot about the economy, often they actually do not know much about it. Many people are less concerned with how the economy functions, or with competing economic theories, than they are with how the economy relates directly to their lives. However, it is extremely important to get a broader picture of economic systems in order to have a foundation on which to base the more specific decisions required of us as individuals and citizens.

Every day, we make hundreds of economic decisions that affect our own lives and the lives of thousands of people we don't even know. Did you have cereal or eggs for breakfast? Did you watch television last night or go to a movie? What clothes did you wear to school today?

If you ate eggs, then in some small way you encouraged farmers to raise chickens rather than plant cereal crops. By going to the movies, you contributed money to the theatre owner, the movie producer, the actors, the ushers, and probably the popcorn and soft drink industries.

Similarly, we are affected by the economic decisions of others, which are beyond our personal control. The construction of a large

Learning Outcomes

After reading this chapter, you should be able to:

- understand basic economic concepts
- distinguish among the various types of economic systems
- analyze statistical charts and graphs
- explain the extent of global economic interdependence
- discuss the significance of the three basic economic questions
- understand the differences in income distribution among countries

shopping mall in the suburbs might undercut your family's downtown business and result in bankruptcy and the loss of your car and home. An increase in the price of gasoline and oil might reduce the number of kilometres you drive or lead to the purchase of a wood-burning stove.

Economic issues also form an important part of most political decisions. Should the government delay repairing roads in order to reduce taxes? How can unemployment be reduced and inflation lowered? Can working conditions be improved? Are welfare payments necessary? What role should the government play in the economy? How should we deal with the national debt and deficit? The answers to such questions are extremely important not only in themselves but also because, as history has shown, economic depression and unemployment have contributed to discontent, revolution, and wars.

Scarcity

Despite a rapid improvement in the standard of living in the Western world during the last century, most people still do not have everything they desire. You might find, for example, that you do not have enough money to buy a compact disc player or new clothes. In other words, when it comes to satisfying all your desires, you don't have enough money. There are never enough available resources to satisfy everyone's demands. This scarcity is a fundamental fact of economics—it is the fact from which the study of economics originates. According to one popular definition, economics "is the science that investigates problems arising from the scarcity of resources and goods that can be used to satisfy human wants. It studies how people allocate and develop their scarce resources to satisfy their wants and needs in a way that is compatible with the basic values of their societies."[1]

Of course, few people would term economics a "science" in the way that physics is a science. Former American president Herbert Hoover, for example, was said to have wished for a one-armed economist—so that he would not have had to listen to his financial experts begin sentences with the phrase, "On the one hand...".

Scarcity is, of course, a relative term. For many people in Asia, Africa, and South America, it can mean not having enough food to eat, whereas for many North Americans, it can simply mean not having a personal computer. Most Canadians have the basic necessities of life (food, shelter, and clothes); what they desire are often more consumer goods, such as cellular telephones, cameras, stylish clothes, and cars. Because of the discrepancy between these desires and the resources necessary to supply them, people must choose which goods they want. Hence, economics is also called the science of choice.

Focus

Why is economics considered a social science rather than a pure science?

Figure 6.1: The Problem of Scarcity

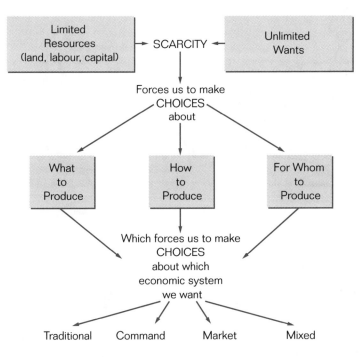

Source: Adapted from P. Saunders, L. Silk, and A.H. MacDonald, *The World of Economics*, 2nd Canadian ed. (Toronto: McGraw-Hill Ryerson, 1979), p. 24.

Basic Economic Questions

To satisfy their wants, people must decide how best to use their time, skills, and energy; what to purchase; how much money to save for future needs; and how to increase their incomes. Similarly, because no society can avoid the problems created by the scarcity of resources, each country must decide how its limited resources can best be used to meet its needs. Every society (even those that do not use money) must confront these three questions:

1 *What goods should be produced?* To what extent should we grow wheat, manufacture machinery, educate the populace, or defend the country?

2 *How should these goods be produced?* By what people, using which resources and what techniques, will goods be produced? Who should farm? Who will work in the factories? Should we grow wheat with a few people and many machines, or should we use more people and machinery but less land?

3 *How much should everyone get of what is produced?* Should a few people receive most of the goods, or should the country's resources be divided evenly? On what basis should these decisions be made?

How does this cartoon depict the science of choice?

Canada, Sweden, the United States, Cuba, Egypt—indeed, every country in the world—must solve the three basic economic problems of "what," "how," and "for whom." The institutions and practices that each country establishes to meet these questions form an economic system that is based upon the country's economic ideology. Although many methods have been used in the past to organize an economy, three broad categories can be distinguished: economies run by tradition, economies run by the market, and economies run by central direction. Although none of these three types exists in pure, undiluted form, it is useful to examine the theory underlying each system.

In traditional economic systems, the customs and natural environment of the people determine how society will function. To the question of what to produce, the **traditional economy** answers, "Produce what has always been produced." Similarly, a traditional economy solves the question of how to produce by replying, "As we have always done it." Children, for example, are expected to follow in their parents' footsteps. The distribution of goods is also determined by custom and force of habit.

The **market economy** solves the problems of production and distribution by allowing individuals to make their own economic decisions based on prices and markets. In this system—also called private enterprise or capitalism—the country's resources are privately owned and the government does not intervene in the economy (see Chapter 7).

In a centrally planned economy—often called a socialist, communist, or **command** system—the country's resources are owned and controlled by the government, which makes all major economic decisions (see Chapter 8).

traditional economy: an economic system largely practised by people in a pre-industrial stage of development, based mostly on agriculture or fishing and on a division of labour decreed by custom and tradition.

market economy: an economic system in which the basic questions of what, how, and for whom to produce are resolved by the interaction among buyers and sellers.

command economy: an economic system in which the basic questions of what, how, and for whom to produce are resolved by the government, which makes all major economic decisions.

No society relies exclusively on the traditional, market, or centrally planned system, although most societies depend more heavily on one type than on the other two. In most modern industrial countries, the market and the centrally planned systems have merged into a hybrid form called the **mixed economy** (see Chapter 9). In Canada, for example, resources are generally privately owned, but the government intervenes in the economy in an attempt to correct such social ills as poverty and unemployment and to deal with economic problems such as inflation.

While it may be useful to establish categories, it is not an easy task to label the different economic systems existing in the world today. In the real world, economies are complex and dynamic. Every country's economic system has undergone tremendous changes over the last century. Moreover, capitalism in Canada is not the same as capitalism in Japan, the United States, or Great Britain, and Cuban communism differs from Chinese communism. Finally, the values or ideology of each economic system affect all aspects of a society, tending to become confused with politics and political ideologies. It is impossible to separate political systems completely from economic systems.

> **mixed economy:** an economic system that combines the market and centrally planned systems; private enterprise is subject to some government regulation.

⋯ Comparing Countries' Economies

A car salesperson closes a deal at 9:30 a.m. in St. Albert, Alberta. At the same time (three hours later) off the coast of Lunenburg, Nova Scotia, a small fishing boat returns with the morning's catch. Both of these activities are examples of production. Production is the major purpose of all economies. Economies must produce goods such as steel or fish, or provide services such as those of the car salesperson, in order to satisfy the needs and wants of the population. How many cars are sold and how many fish are caught is called **productivity**. Productivity is a simple way to measure how many goods and services a firm or a country is producing. Normally, when productivity increases, the economy is considered to be growing, and therefore healthy. Measuring productivity also allows economists to compare one firm or country with other firms or countries and to measure their relative **efficiency.** Economists rate efficiency according to how technologically advanced an economy is, how well the economy distributes its goods and services, and the rate of innovation and invention in the economy.

When dealing with a country's economy, the economist must consider everything that is produced by its citizens. The **Gross National Product (GNP)** of a country is the final value of all goods and services produced in a given year. Another way of saying this is the sum of the price tags of all goods and services produced in a year is that country's GNP. The growth or decline of an economy can be charted by comparing its GNP over a span of years.* The higher the productivity of individual workers, the greater the GNP. A farmer who plants 100 ha of wheat is bound to be more productive

> **productivity:** in economic theory, the rate of labour output by individual workers and machinery.
>
> **efficiency:** maximizing the amount of output obtained from a given amount of resources or minimizing the amount of resources used for a given output.
>
> **Gross National Product (GNP):** in economics, the sum total of a country's annual economic production.

---

* Of course, inflation must be taken into account when comparing one year's GNP with another year's GNP. The term "real GNP" is used when inflation has been taken into account.

Are productivity and GNP the best ways to compare economies?

GNP per capita: the average amount of goods and services produced each year by every individual in a country.

Gross Domestic Product (GDP): the total income generated within a country.

standard of living: the relative level of material goods, comfort, and well-being in a society.

than a farmer who plants only 10 ha, just as a car salesperson who sells five cars per day is more productive than one who sells only one car.

GNP per capita (per person) is the average amount of goods and services produced each year by every individual in the country. To find GNP per capita, simply divide GNP by the population. GNP per capita provides a better measure of the standard of living in a country than does GNP. India, for example, has a much larger GNP than Canada, but because its population is so much larger and its productivity is lower, India's GNP per capita is lower than Canada's. To illustrate with a specific example, in 1993, China's GNP of $2047 billion dwarfed Canada's $526 billion, but as Canada's population was 28 million compared with China's 1.2 billion, Canada's GNP per capita was $18 940 compared with China's $1738.[2]

Economists also use the term **Gross Domestic Product (GDP)**. To determine the GDP of a country, subtract the income earned from property and companies abroad from the GNP, and add income earned by foreign firms operating in the country. GDP is thus the income generated within a country, whereas GNP is the total value of all income received by the residents of a country. "National" refers to production by the country's citizens, wherever they may live, and "domestic" refers to production within the country's borders, regardless of citizenship. In practice, the two values are almost identical and are used interchangeably.

Generally, the more productive a country, the higher its **standard of living.** How well a country creates wealth from its natural and human resources depends on a variety of factors, including its infrastructure (roads, telephones, and similar facilities), scientific and technological research and development (R&D), supply of skilled workers, financial resources, and the strength of its educational system. The 1994 *World Competitiveness Report* ranked 41 countries according to 381 such criteria. The top 5 countries were the United States, Singapore, Japan, Hong Kong, and Germany.

Another common method of comparing countries is by examining how industrialized they are. With few exceptions, the greater the rate of industrialization, the higher the standard of living. The 27 most developed countries, which occupy 25 percent of the world's land mass but account for only 15 percent of the world's population, generate 77 percent of the world's production. At the other end of the scale, the 162 less developed countries, which occupy 58 percent of the world's land mass and house 77 percent of its population, account for only 19 percent of global production. Figure 6.3 divides world economies into three categories of development: start-up, emerging, and mature.

Of course, standard of living involves more than a country's income per person, and development means more than industrialization. For example, wealth might be unevenly distributed, some groups might face discrimination, or modern health facilities could be lacking.

If you could live anywhere in the world, where would you live? To answer this question, you would have to decide what was most important to you. Would you want to live in the United States, where almost every individual has a motor vehicle, or in Ecuador, where there is one vehicle for

Figure 6.2: Global Economies: A Comparison of Development

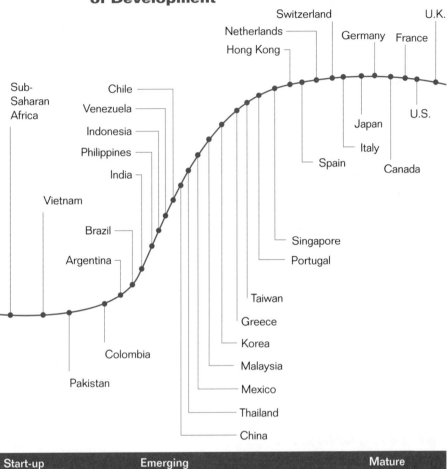

Start-up   Emerging   Mature

Source: Riley Moynes, *The Money Coach* (Toronto: Copp Clark, 1995), p. 55. Reprinted by permission of Addison-Wesley Publishers Ltd.

every 41 inhabitants? In Canada, there are 640 television sets for every 1000 people, whereas in Peru there are 100 televisions for every 1000 people. In Japan, the average person can expect to live until the age of 79; in Ethiopia, average life expectancy is 50. Since 1990, the United Nations has measured **quality of life** by considering such factors as income, education, doctors per person, political freedom, racial and gender equality, average life span, crime rate, and pollution. Table 6.1 lists the countries that have the highest and lowest well-being based on the UN's findings for 1995.

Of course, not everyone would select similar factors, nor would they agree on how to measure such topics as pollution and education. *International Living*, for example, chose to measure the economy (GNP per capita), health care (life expectancy, daily kilojoule intake, doctors and hos-

quality of life: the standard of living of a country measured in terms of income, available education and health care, political freedom, life expectancy, and other such factors.

pital beds per person), culture (literacy rates, newspapers, museums, and movie theatres per capita), freedom (civil liberties), ecology (pollution, deforestation, population density), cost of living, and infrastructure (motor vehicles, telephones, railroad tracks, telecommunications). Its fifteenth survey in January 1996 listed Liechtenstein, the United States, San Marino, Canada, and Finland (in that order) as the countries with the best quality of life. Eritrea, Rwanda, Somalia, Angola, and North Korea had the worst quality of life.[3]

Table 6.1: Quality of life of the Global Population, 1995

The highest	The lowest
1. Canada	174. Niger
2. United States	173. Sierra Leone
3. Japan	172. Somalia
4. Netherlands	171. Mali
5. Norway	170. Burkina Faso
6. Finland	169. Afghanistan
7. France	168. Ethiopia
8. Iceland	167. Mozambique
9. Sweden	166. Burundi
10. Spain	165. Angola

Source: *UN Human Development Report, 1995* (New York: United Nations, 1995).

Interdependence

interdependence: in economics, the need for individuals and business firms to interact with one another for the mutual benefit of all parties involved.

The last half of the twentieth century has seen a growing trend toward international trade and **interdependence**. Each country's economy has become increasingly integrated through trade, foreign investments, satellite communications, and global computer networks. The availability of McDonalds' hamburgers, IBM computers, and Calvin Klein jeans around the world is visible evidence of the growing globalization of the world's economy. Since few countries possess all the resources they need, they are forced to trade with other countries to obtain them. The map of Canada's major trading partners illustrates Canada's economic connections with the rest of the world. By subtracting the imports from the exports, it is possible to determine with which countries Canada has a positive (or negative) balance of trade.[4]

A country wishing to obtain or maintain a high standard of living for its people seeks world markets for its products. Canada, for example, depends a great deal on world markets because its domestic market is too small to generate enough wealth to maintain the standard of living to which most Canadians aspire.

Figure 6.3: Canada's World Trade, 1990 and 1994

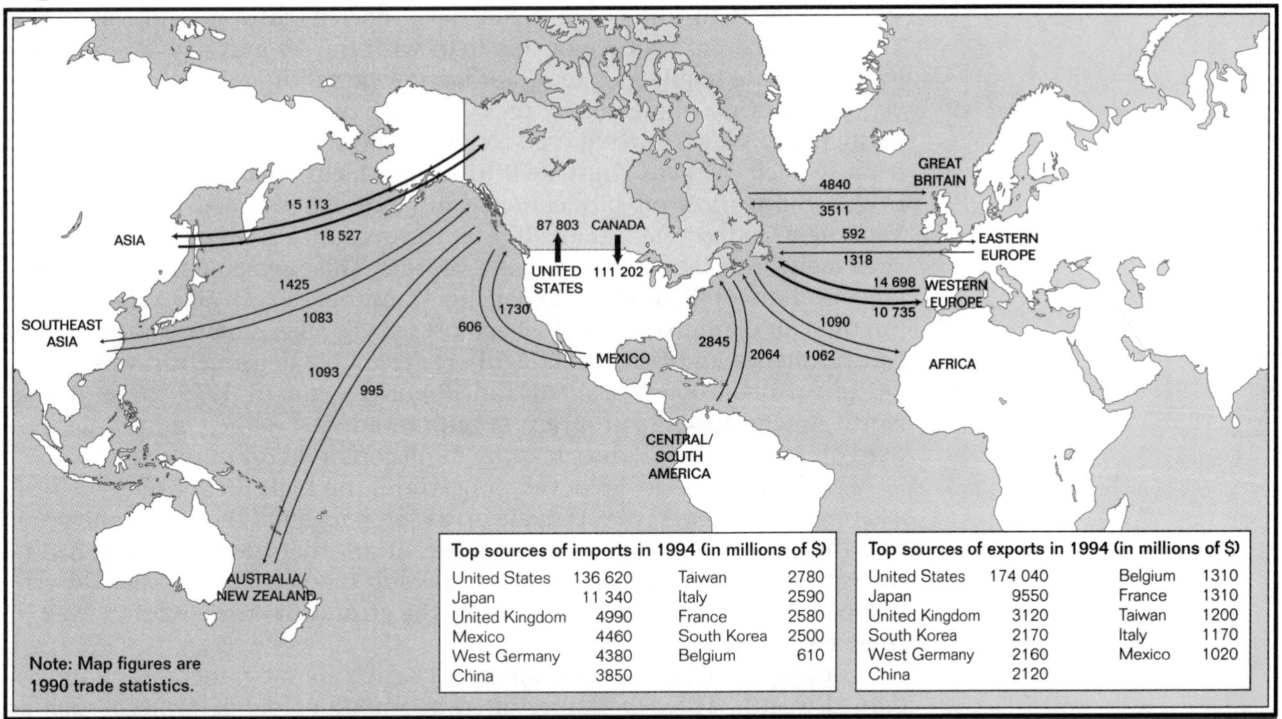

Top sources of imports in 1994 (in millions of $)			
United States	136 620	Taiwan	2780
Japan	11 340	Italy	2590
United Kingdom	4990	France	2580
Mexico	4460	South Korea	2500
West Germany	4380	Belgium	610
China	3850		

Top sources of exports in 1994 (in millions of $)			
United States	174 040	Belgium	1310
Japan	9550	France	1310
United Kingdom	3120	Taiwan	1200
South Korea	2170	Italy	1170
West Germany	2160	Mexico	1020
China	2120		

Note: Map figures are 1990 trade statistics.

With which of these countries does Canada have a favourable balance of trade?

Source: John Robert Colombo, *The 1996 Canadian Global Almanac* (Toronto: Macmillan, 1996), pp. 208–9. Based on *The Integrated Atlas: History and Geography of Canada and the World* (Toronto: Harcourt Brace, 1996), p. 119. Reprinted with permission.

Another factor that promotes interdependence is the growth of multinational corporations (see Chapter 5). They promote trade by establishing offices and plants in many different countries and shipping their products and services to markets around the world. Mobil petroleum company, for example, has its headquarters in New York City but operates in over 100 countries. Siemens, the German electronics corporation, does business in more than 120 countries.

The new "Information Age" has fuelled global demand for information, which further promotes interdependence. International telephone calls increased dramatically from 13 billion minutes in 1983 to 47 billion minutes a decade later, and the number of minutes is expected to reach 100 billion by the year 2000. More than 100 000 computers are sold worldwide every 24 hours. The world's large computer networks can move data over telephone lines, cable TV, and satellite lines. Few people knew about the Internet in 1987, but by 1995 there were over 35 000 area networks, each ranging from a few dozen computers to tens of thousands.

Focus

How has interdependency changed the world in your view?

World Dependence on Oil

What happens in one country can have repercussions around the world. There is no better example of this than with the oil industry. The modern industrial state requires oil to power its transportation, lubricate its machinery, and provide numerous by-products such as cosmetics, medicines, and plastics. The Western world used to take its oil supply for granted, probably because such Western firms as British Petroleum, Texaco, and Shell controlled the world's oil production. This monopoly ended in 1959 when Venezuela and several Arab oil-producing countries signed an informal agreement regulating the supply of oil. This agreement created the Organization of Petroleum Exporting Countries, or OPEC. When OPEC imposed an oil embargo in 1973 against Israel's allies, the world, especially North America and Europe, suddenly realized how dependent it was on oil. Oil prices quadrupled in 1973 and doubled again in 1979. In response, North Americans and Europeans began rationing gasoline, and people who used oil to heat their homes became more conservation-minded.

For the non-industrial developing world, the high fuel prices were devastating because energy costs made up a high portion of the cost of the products they produced. Higher energy prices meant that these countries had to increase the price of their exports in a world market that was already very competitive. This was the beginning of the great debt crises that followed in these countries.

For oil-producing countries, many of which are Arab, there was unprecedented wealth. This windfall resulted in ambitious public projects such as universities, hospitals, highways, and water systems, as well as greater military expenditures.

But what goes up often comes down. Oil prices plummeted in the 1980s. By 1986, the price of oil had declined from $40 to $10 per barrel. This reflected the effectiveness of conservation, the search for alternative supplies, such as Great Britain's off-shore oil discoveries, and the difficulty OPEC encountered in controlling its own members. Getting all of its members to agree on limiting oil production became OPEC's greatest problem. Members such as Iran and Iraq, which needed oil revenues to finance a war against each other, were reluctant to limit oil sales. Once again, these effects were felt around the globe. The interdependence map in Figure 6.5 illustrates the relationship among oil producers and oil consumers.

Figure 6.4: OPEC and the World Oil Trade

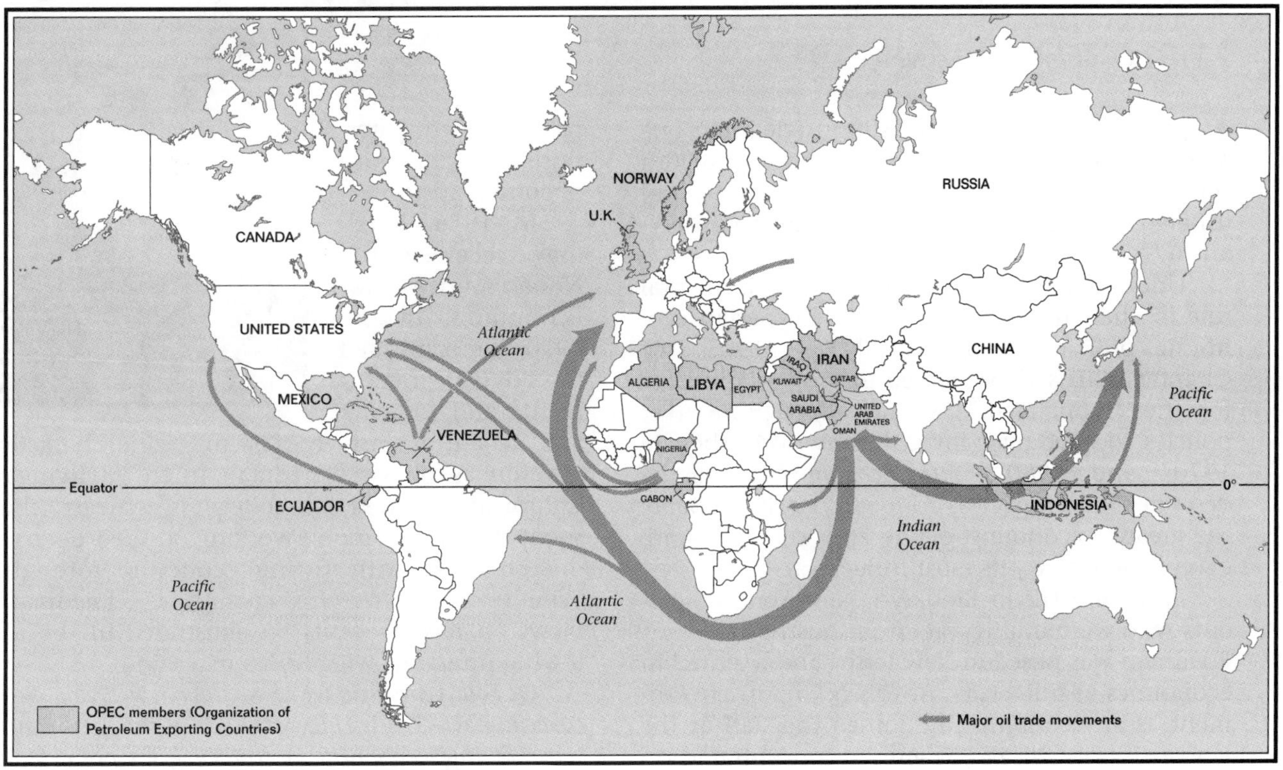

Source: McKay, John P., Bennett D. Hill, and John Buckler, *A History of World Societies*, third edition.
Copyright © 1992 by Houghton Mifflin Company. Reprinted with permission.

What's Coming Next

Now that we have discussed the general principles underlying economic systems, it is time to examine the underlying beliefs of the three major economic ideologies. The following chapters outline the theory supporting private enterprise, centrally planned economies, and mixed economies. The seven accompanying case studies provide in-depth examples of how each system decides *in practice* what goods will be produced, how they will be produced, and how these goods will be distributed.

BIOGRAPHY

MILTON FRIEDMAN, 1912–

Life magazine, in naming Milton Friedman one of "the most important Americans of the 20th century," described him as "the economist [who] ushered in a new 'trickle down' era of conservatism."[5]

Unquestionably, Friedman played a pivotal role in challenging the prevailing Keynesian economic policies of the world after 1945 (see Chapter 9). His views helped to provide the basis for the "monetarist," "supply-side," pro-market policies adopted by many governments in the late 1970s and 1980s. *The Economist* magazine described his impact as follows: "He is probably the greatest economist of the 20th century—and, except for Keynes, its most influential."[6]

Born in 1912 in Brooklyn, New York, to parents who were immigrants from Austria-Hungary, Friedman was raised in New Jersey and majored in economics at university. After working in government as an economist, he joined the staff at the University of Chicago, where he concentrated on research and writing.

Friedman increasingly rejected Keynesian economics' reliance on fiscal policy—with its use of government spending, taxation, and budgets—to manipulate the economy. He became famous as the chief advocate of the monetarist approach, which emphasized the role of monetary policy. Friedman contended that the government instead should use a gradual, controlled expansion of the money supply to assure a steady rate of economic growth without inflation.

Not content merely to challenge fiscal policy, in his books *Capitalism and Freedom* and *Free to Choose* Friedman attacked government economic intervention in general, calling for a dramatic shift to laissez-faire capitalism. He stated that the marketplace should be the determining factor in every economic situation, and that "there is no such thing as a free lunch." He soon became known as the "champion of free enterprise" and "the guru of conservatism."

In 1976, Friedman received the Nobel Prize for Economics. In the 1990s, he continued to advise governments and to write and debate extensively. *Life* magazine characterized him as follows: "Friedman, [then] 78, living in California, married his college sweetheart (they spent their honeymoon working on their doctoral dissertations) with fitting economic foresight: Wife Rose is often his co-author."[7] Friedman's views on recent events are illustrated in the following interview with *Forbes* magazine:

Q: Four years ago, when we interviewed you, our cover line was "Why Liberalism"—in the American sense of interventionist government—"is obsolete." Well, if liberalism is dead, why won't it lie down?

A: There are too many good jobs at stake. You have this enormous bureaucracy in Washington, and also in every city and state, all dependent upon the continuation of New Deal and Great Society kinds of programs. Instead of Lincoln's government of the people, by the people, for the people, we have government of the people, by the bureaucrats, for the bureaucrats—including among the bureaucrats the elected bureaucrats. …

Indeed, right now it looks as if the East European countries are trying to move to where we were 50 years ago, while we are trying to move to where they were 50 years ago.

And not only Eastern European countries. Look at Latin American countries. Fifteen years ago or so I was being picketed and harassed for supposedly running Chile from my office at the University of Chicago. Today Chile is a great success story. You've got a politically free as well as an economically free country. Mexico is trying to follow. Argentina too.

In the Far East you have the four "Little Tigers." Hong Kong is the purest case of the free market approach. Taiwan, Singapore and South Korea have large elements of authoritarian paternalism. But all of them stress the market as opposed to central planning. The same thing is now happening in Indonesia. It's certainly happening in Malaysia. It's happening all over the place.

Q: Your life's work, to some extent, has been demonstrating that Roosevelt's economic policies were actually perverse in that they probably [worsened] the Depression. But politically, Roosevelt's policies were immensely successful.

A: I agree. The government's failure in managing the economy from 1929 to 1933 produced, ironically, the public perception that only the government could manage the economy. The long-run effects of the Depression were far more severe than the economic effects. ...

What bothers me is not so much the historical debate, but what's ahead. The combination of polit-ical and technological change opens up a vast amount of low-cost labor. There may be half a billion workers in China, Eastern Europe, and Latin America. And that constitutes a real revolution in possible cooperation between capital-rich and labor-rich countries. It could give us the equivalent of another Industrial Revolution. ...

But what bothers me is this: Not only the U.S. but other countries seem to be missing this enormous opportunity. The capital-rich countries are going in a protectionist direction, building walls around their blocs. Fortress Europe. The U.S. with Canada and Mexico. ... I would prefer unilateral, multilateral free trade.[8]

---

1 In general, what answers does Friedman propose to the "basic economic questions"?

2 How does the interview reflect Friedman's basic approach to economic issues?

Underlying and Emerging Issues

Give the reasoning and evidence that might be used to support different views or conclusions on the following issues.

1 To what extent should societies attempt to meet present needs, and to what extent should they try to provide for the future?

2 On what basis can we say that one economic system is "better" than another?

3 How important is the security and stability offered by traditional economic systems?

4 In moving away from traditional economic systems, has modern society given up things of importance?

5 How important are individual freedom and equality in decisions about economic systems?

6 How important should market forces be in different economic decisions?

7 What is the appropriate role for government in the economic system?

8 To what extent does development mean more than economic growth?

9 How can we measure development? How can we measure quality of life?

10 Has the move toward industrialization resulted in the loss of important or valuable aspects of our society?

11 Does increasing global interdependence mean the loss of national sovereignty?

12 To what extent might different kinds of economic systems be appropriate to different societies?

Focussing Knowledge

In your notes, clearly identify or define and explain the importance or significance of each of the following:

scarcity	Gross Domestic Product (GDP)
traditional economy	standard of living
market economy	development
capitalism	quality of life
centrally planned economy	interdependence
productivity	Information Age
efficiency	OPEC
Gross National Product (GNP)	Milton Friedman
GNP per capita	

Reviewing and Organizing Knowledge

1 How are economic decisions related to

a. personal decisions?

b. political decisions?

2 a. How are scarcity, resources, allocation, values, and economics related?

b. What are the three basic economic questions that every society must confront?

3 a. What are the major characteristics of each of the three basic types of economic systems?

b. Why do real-world economic systems not exist in any of the three pure forms?

c. Why are economic systems dynamic?

4 a. How is GNP related to productivity, standard of living, and infrastructure?

b. What other factors besides income, industrialization, and GNP are used to determine quality of life?

5 a. What factors have contributed to the acceleration of global interdependence?

b. How does the example of petroleum illustrate interdependence?

6 If countries all face the same three basic economic questions, why are there so many different types of economic systems in the world?

Applying and Extending Knowledge

1 Find newspaper articles that illustrate each of the three basic economic questions in Canada. Explain how each article illustrates the question.

2 Locate two newspaper articles that illustrate the concept of scarcity. One article should be about a Canadian situation, the other about a non-Canadian situation. Compare the idea of scarcity in the two situations.

3 In economics, when we make choices, we give up one thing for another. Keep careful track of the money that you spend in one week. Describe the cost in terms of what you had to give up because of your choices— that is, what did you *not* buy because of your choices?

4 Choose two newspaper articles to illustrate aspects of the market and central-planning approaches in Canada's present economy. Explain how the approach is reflected in the article.

5 Read the business section of a newspaper and select several articles that reflect economic interdependence. Explain how the articles illustrate this term.

Private Enterprise

HOW DOES THE PRIVATE ENTERPRISE SYSTEM answer the three basic economic questions. To answer this question, the chapter begins with a brief history of the origins and growth of capitalism, including the ideas of Adam Smith, David Ricardo, Thomas Malthus, and Charles Darwin. Concrete examples illustrate the role of prices, competition, supply and demand, and profits in the functioning of private enterprise, and the major values and beliefs of capitalism are summarized. Primary documents that discuss the merits of the private enterprise system and the relationship between capitalism and political ideologies are also included.

As pointed out in Chapter 6, each country must decide which goods it would most like to have, what resources will be used in their production, and how these goods will be distributed among the people. These decisions are difficult to make, because each one opens up a whole range of overlapping problems that must be coordinated for the economy to run smoothly and efficiently. What type of work should each Canadian do? What will their salaries be? How many cars should be produced, and what proportion of them should be mini-vans? Should Prince Edward Island concentrate on growing wheat or potatoes or on raising livestock? This chapter describes how, in theory, the economic system known as private enterprise* or capitalism answers these

---

* The term *private enterprise* refers to the fact that most economic concerns are operated by private groups rather than by government agencies. This system is also called *free enterprise* (because the individual is free to conduct business without interference), *capitalism* (because of the importance of individual ownership of capital goods), and the *price system* or *market economy* (for reasons that will soon be evident).

three basic problems. It also examines some of the criticisms levelled at capitalism.

··The Origins of Capitalism

The prevailing economic system in Europe prior to the nineteenth century was **mercantilism**. Under this system, a country's international strength was directly related to its supply of gold and silver. Individual states sought to accumulate precious metals and thereby become more powerful. To achieve this objective, countries attempted to export more goods than they imported and geared their economies to achieve this end.

Economic activity was believed to be too important to be left to the discretion of individuals. Mercantilist governments regulated almost every aspect of their economies (although they seldom owned any enterprises). They established **protective tariffs** to limit imports from other countries and protect local industries. England forbade imports of French and Italian silk, and France prohibited imports of cotton from England. For similar reasons, skilled workers were forbidden to leave their countries. Government restrictions were everywhere. The state fixed the size, weight, and quality of many goods. Overseas colonies were created to supply raw materials for the mother country and to provide a market for manufactured products. Goods produced in the colonies could be exported only to the mother country, and then only in ships belonging to that state. The government gave local monopolies, or even entire overseas colonies, to individuals. In 1670, for example, England gave much of present-day Northern Ontario, Quebec, Saskatchewan, Manitoba, and Alberta to the Hudson's Bay Company. Craft guilds controlled specific trades in every town. These guilds limited competition by controlling who and how many could enter a trade. They also regulated prices and quality.

During this time, the Roman Catholic Church condemned usury (lending money at high interest rates), sought to set a "just price" for every commodity and service, and took a dim view of commercial professions. Under these conditions, commercial banks and large-scale business enterprises had difficulty developing.

The Protestant Reformation in the sixteenth century slowly changed the negative image of business. The Calvinists, in particular, extolled the qualities needed for capitalism by stressing the value of hard work, thrift, and material growth. They believed that business profits should not be spent on high living but reinvested in the business, that wealth should be used to produce more wealth, and that prosperity gained by honest means brought entry into heaven.

In the sixteenth century, the discovery of precious minerals in the Americas and riches in China and India provided more capital for enterprising businesspeople. The expanding population and improved transportation system created new markets for consumer goods such as textiles, spices, and furs. Entrepreneurs emerged to buy and sell goods from foreign lands. They kept themselves informed of changes in fashion and fluctuations in demand

mercantilism: an economic system widely practised in Europe until the end of the eighteenth century, in which private enterprises were permitted to function only by submitting to detailed intervention and supervision in their business activities by the government.

protective tariff: a tax imposed on imports to protect domestic producers.

from year to year, and were always ready to switch their priorities according to the supply of and demand for goods. Rather than seeking to restrict trade, they favoured free trade.

Toward the end of the seventeenth century, merchants in the Netherlands, France, and England began to complain about their governments' economic restrictions. Mercantilism also ran counter to the newly emerging ideas of liberalism (see Chapter 2). Liberals believed that the economy, like the state, should be free to follow natural laws, not the arbitrary rules of governments. In their view, an economy that was free of government regulation was just as important as political freedom was to individual well-being. They believed that when people were motivated by self-interest, they worked harder and achieved better results. Competition spurred economic activity. To liberals, the best government was one that interfered as little as possible with the economic activities of its citizens.

Adam Smith

In the late eighteenth century, British philosopher David Hume insisted that government should not interfere with foreign trade. In France, a school of economic philosophers called the physiocrats developed the slogan "Laissez-faire," meaning "Hands off," or "Let the government leave the economy alone." Laissez-faire thinking culminated in Scottish professor Adam Smith's book *An Inquiry into the Nature and Causes of the Wealth of Nations* in 1776.

Although many people have disagreed with Smith's ideas, his book remains one of the great classics of economic thought. Two centuries later, the economic system he described in 1776 is still defended by many economists. Reacting to the restrictive economic laws, Smith advanced this novel viewpoint:

Every individual is continually exerting himself to find the most advantageous employment for whatever capital he can command. It is his own advantage, indeed, and not that of society, which he has in view. But the study of his own advantage naturally, or rather necessarily, leads him to prefer that employment which is most advantageous to the society. ... In this case, as in many other cases, he is led by an invisible hand to promote an end which was no part of his intention. I have never known much good done by those who affected to trade for the public good.[1]

Unlike mercantilist supporters, Smith declared that the strength of a country rested on the value of the goods it produced, not on the amount of gold and silver it possessed. Government laws and restrictions hindered, rather than promoted, economic growth. There was no need to plan the economy. If people were free to pursue their own self-interest (which Smith believed to be a basic psychological drive), the sum of their individual actions would automatically work for the betterment of society. To ensure that such a "natural" economic law would operate effectively, government should not interfere in the economy except to protect the country against foreign enemies, ensure competition, maintain law and order, and protect individual property rights.

This was the doctrine of private enterprise—an economic system based on private property, competition, profit, and the freedom to buy and sell. It was another generation before the British government slowly adopted the doctrine of laissez-faire.

The development of modern capitalism is usually associated with the **Industrial Revolution** and the emergence of large-scale factory production. By 1860, Great Britain was the workshop of the world, retaining few traces of the old economic order. With the success of British capitalists and inventors, the ideas of free enterprise spread throughout Western Europe and on to North America. It was

Adam Smith (1723–90)

Industrial Revolution: the transformation, which occurred first in mid-eighteenth century England, of a traditional agricultural economy into an urban, factory system of production.

the work of British inventors and capitalists in the late eighteenth and early nineteenth centuries that provided the strongest argument in favour of private enterprise. Through a series of inventions, especially the steam engine, British inventors created new methods of large-scale production. British capitalists invested vast sums of money to purchase these machines and create factories in which large-scale production could take place. In addition, improvements in agriculture made it possible to feed the large numbers of factory workers, while changes in transportation and communication opened up new markets for manufactured goods. These changes transformed Great Britain during the nineteenth century, bringing about an Industrial Revolution.

Belgium was the first country to follow Great Britain's example. Then, between 1840 and 1860, France, the United States, and various German states began to industrialize. Sweden, Russia, and Japan followed suit after 1870.

Laissez-Faire Capitalism

The new science of political economy, founded near the end of the eighteenth century by such men as Adam Smith and David Ricardo, preached that the world's economy was controlled by natural economic laws that regulated production and distribution. An **invisible hand** ensured that the common good would be enhanced if all people sought to serve their own personal self-interests. These natural laws operated efficiently only if government did not interfere in the economy. When this doctrine of laissez-faire was combined with the ideas of Thomas Malthus (1766–1834), the "logical" conclusion was that the state should not distribute charity to the poor.

invisible hand: the expression used by Adam Smith to explain the fact that the selfish economically governed actions of all individuals of a society ultimately combine to benefit all of society.

In his now famous book, *Essay on Population* (1798), Malthus wrote that the world's population was advancing at a faster rate than the world's ability to produce food. Population growth in the past had been checked by wars, disease, and famine. According to Malthus, poverty was nature's way of limiting population, and any interference would disrupt nature's plan. Charity would interfere with nature's way of killing off the weak and leaving the fit to carry on the race. Economist David Ricardo used Malthus's ideas to argue that poverty was inescapable. Higher wages, he stated, led to larger families, too many workers, and even lower wages than before. He believed that poverty was a law of nature that governments should not challenge.

Natural Selection

These ideas were provided with additional support when Charles Darwin (1809–82) published his *On the Origin of Species* in 1859. The laws of science, Darwin concluded, applied to plants and animals. Through the process of natural selection (survival of the fittest), nature ensured that only those physical characteristics that were suited to the environment would survive. Darwin's theories were later modified by such men as Herbert Spencer and William Sumner. **Social Darwinism**, as their ideas came to be known, provided additional support for the belief that government should meddle neither in the lives of its citizens nor with the economic system. Competition among individuals was declared to be the best method of ensuring that only the fittest would survive. Because the most efficient producers would obviously win, competition would eventually result in the progress of the human race as a whole.

Such arguments were accepted by the economic elite because they provided justification for its business practices and for the vast differences in wealth between the rich and the poor. "Big business," said American tycoon J.D. Rockefeller, "is merely the survival of the fittest, the working out of the law of nature and the law of God." People received what they were worth, based on the demand for their talents. If labourers were paid $2 a day, that was because they produced only $2 worth of goods, whereas the salaries of engineers were 10 times higher because the value of their work was 10 times higher than that of labourers. According to this view, employers would violate natural economic laws if they paid employees more than they were worth. Entrepreneurs had done more than their share in contributing to the workers' welfare by providing them with jobs. True, some tinkering and adjustments to the system were necessary from time to time, but on the whole, businesspeople and politicians of the nineteenth century believed that the economic system was working well.

Social Darwinism: the misguided adaptation of Darwin's biological theories to aspects of human society.

Charity and Laziness

In the view of these thinkers, poverty was a sign of biological and social inferiority. The doctrine of evolution implied that human society, like nature, must be harsh to its "weaklings" or the wheels of progress would be stopped. Charity, in other words, would slow humanity's evolution.

According to this analysis, people were poor because they were lazy, immoral, uneducated, and thoughtless. They wasted their energies and threw away their earnings in the taverns. Individual weakness was the problem—not the system or the employers. One had to work for what one got. "If thou dost not sow," warned the Bible, "thou shalt not reap." Idleness was a sin, whereas prosperity was the earthly reward for living a moral life. If people failed, it was their own fault. All people, it was argued, could be successful if they worked hard, saved their money, and lived respectable, moral lives. Authors such as Horatio Alger Jr. wrote children's books about penniless orphans who rose from rags to riches through hard work, ability, thrift, and good moral character—this was the gospel of work.

Charles Darwin (1809–82)

Basic Beliefs

The private enterprise system, also referred to as capitalism, stresses economic freedom—freedom of trade (no monopolies or government regulations) and freedom of choice (where to work, what to produce, what price to charge, what to buy). Capitalism also stresses the importance of the individual. Individual goals are emphasized over the needs of society because capitalism assumes that when each person carries out these goals, the society as a whole will benefit.

Finally, the system is based on a belief in the virtues of self-reliance, initiative, hard work, progress, and production — the more, the better. The following list summarizes the major characteristics of the private enterprise system:

- private property
- the price system, based on supply and demand
- competition
- freedom to buy and sell
- the profit motive
- little government intervention in the economy
- inequalities of wealth

SAMUEL SMILES, 1812–1904

Self-Help: The Capitalist Ethic

Samuel Smiles' father died early, leaving his 11 children to make their own way in the world. Apprenticed to a doctor, Smiles worked hard and became a physician himself. Later, he worked as an editor for a London newspaper, managed two railways, and became a famous author. Smiles wrote *Self-Help* in 1859. It was an instant success and was translated into several languages.

Smiles' writings reflected and encouraged the capitalist ideas of his time. He hoped to cure people's problems by educating the working class in the benefits of hard work, thrift, and morality. He practised these values in his own life and eventually suffered a stroke from apparent overwork. The following selections are from *Self-Help* and *Thrift* (1875).

SELF-HELP

The spirit of self-help is the root of all genuine growth in the individual; and, exhibited in the lives of many, it constitutes the true source of national vigour and strength. ... Whatever is done for men* or classes, to a certain extent takes away the stimulus and necessity of doing for themselves; and where men are subjected to over-guidance and over-government, the inevitable tendency is to render them comparatively helpless.

Even the best institutions can give a man no active help. Perhaps the most they can do is to leave him free to develop himself and improve his individual condition. ... [N]o laws, however stringent, can make the idle industrious, the thriftless provident, or the drunken sober. Such reforms can only be effected by means of individual action, economy, and self-denial; by
better habits, rather than by greater rights. ...

National progress is the sum of individual industry, energy, and uprightness, as national decay is of individual idleness, selfishness, and vice. ... [T]he highest patriotism consists, not so much in altering laws and modifying institutions, as in helping and stimulating men to elevate and improve themselves by their own free and independent individual action.[2]

THRIFT

Industry enables men to earn their living; it should also enable them to learn to live. Independence can only be established by the exercise of forethought, prudence, frugality, and self-denial. To be just as well as generous, men must deny themselves. The essence of generosity is self-sacrifice.

---

* Since many women were working in the mines and factories at this time in Great Britain, Smiles (as was the custom) probably meant "men and women" when he wrote "men." The only book that the famous political economist, John Stuart Mill, wrote that was not a commercial success was *The Subjugation of Women* (1869). Two years earlier, Mill had proposed that the word "person" be substituted for "man," but this bill failed miserably in Parliament.

The object of this book is to induce men to employ their means for worthy purposes, and not to waste them upon selfish indulgences. Many enemies have to be encountered in accomplishing this object. There are idleness, thoughtlessness, vanity, vice, intemperance. The last is the worst enemy of all.
...

All that is great in man comes of labour—greatness in art, in literature, in science. Knowledge — "the wing wherewith we fly to heaven"— is only acquired through labour. Genius is the power of making great and sustained efforts. ... Of all wretched men, surely the idle are the most so—those whose life is barren of utility [usefulness], who have nothing to do except to gratify their senses. Are not such men the most miserable, and dissatisfied of all, constantly in a state of boredom, alike useless to themselves and to others,
who, when removed, are missed by none, and whom none regret?

Who have helped the world onward so much as the workers; men who have had to work from necessity or from choice? All that we call progress — civilization, well-being, and prosperity — depends upon industry. ... All useful and beautiful thoughts, in like manner, are the issue of labour, of study, of observation, of research, of diligent elaboration. ...

But a large proportion of men do not provide for the future. They do not remember the past. They think only of the present. They preserve nothing. They spend all that they earn. They do not provide for themselves; they do not provide for their families. They may make high wages, but eat and drink the whole of what they earn. Such people are constantly poor, and hanging on the verge of destitution.[3]

Focus

How did Smiles define success?

In what ways did Smiles' ideas support the private enterprise system?

Figure 7.1: Features of the Private Enterprise Economy

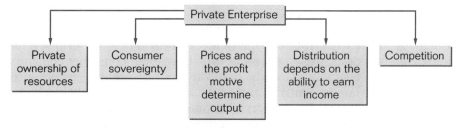

The Market Economy

Allowing businesspeople to do what they want does not seem like a "system," and freedom from government intervention is not much of an economic plan. To discover how the private enterprise system is supposed to work, let us examine how it determines what is produced, how it is produced, and to whom the goods are distributed.

The private enterprise economy is sometimes described by its supporters as a miracle because it coordinates the decisions and activities of millions of individuals and enterprises in a reasonably orderly and efficient manner, without the help of a central coordinating authority. Nobody designed it — it just evolved.

The system can best be understood by examining how traditional marketplaces were organized. In pre-industrial villages, an open space was set aside where sellers presented their goods for sale. When a buyer wished to purchase an item, she or he bargained with the seller until a mutually agreeable price was established. If the seller charged too much, the buyer went to another merchant. If the buyer was not willing to pay what the seller believed was fair, the merchant sold to someone else. The selling price, therefore, was a compromise between what the buyer was willing to pay and what the seller considered a fair return. Similar markets still exist in such countries as Indonesia, Malaysia, and Thailand. The theory of the private enterprise economy is an extension of this mechanism. Each buyer attempts to buy at the lowest possible price, and each seller tries to sell at the highest possible price. Their interactions determine the final price of each item and how much of each item is sold.

It is naturally more profitable to make and sell goods and services that people are interested in purchasing. If there is little demand for a particular item, its producers will stop making it and turn to manufacturing goods that people want. If an enterprise is not able to adjust to people's shifting demands, it will go out of business, whereas its more adaptable competitors will survive. Entrepreneurs enter an industry when it is profitable and leave it when it becomes unprofitable. In order to sell its products and make a profit, each enterprise will try to produce goods more cheaply and offer them for sale at a lower price than its competitors. To do this, the businessperson must either cut costs by producing more efficiently, or accept a smaller profit. The system thus ensures that the economy is both responsive to the demands of consumers and uses the most efficient means of production.[4] Clearly, competition is crucial to this model.

price system: the mechanism that coordinates the multitude of economic decisions carried out in the marketplace.

The mechanism that coordinates the multitude of economic decisions carried out in the marketplace is the **price system**. Prices perform several interrelated functions: they transmit information about consumer demands and the available supply of goods; they provide an incentive to produce those goods that are in demand, and to do so by the least costly methods; and they determine the distribution of income. The following two examples illustrate how the price system performs these functions.

1. Hamburgers Versus Fried Chicken

Imagine what would happen if a fast-food hamburger chain devises a catchy new advertising campaign that persuades a large number of teenagers to switch from buying fried chicken to eating hamburgers. As the number of people wanting to buy hamburgers increases (the demand), the number of available hamburgers (the supply) will decrease until there will be a shortage of hamburgers. At the same time, there will be more chickens available than there will be people wanting to buy them. This situation will allow the hamburger chain to increase the price of hamburgers, whereas those restaurants selling chicken will be forced to lower prices in order to sell their surplus supply of chicken. The increase in the price of hamburgers might

- reduce the number of people willing to buy hamburgers at the new price;

- encourage farmers to raise cattle rather than chickens;

- lead to the production of substitutes for hamburger meat, such as soybeans or minced pork;

- encourage other firms to enter the hamburger business and share in the high profits.

In the long run, these four changes would combine to reduce the shortage of hamburgers and lower their price. The same circumstances would influence the production of chicken — only in reverse. As the supply of chickens fell below the demand for them, their price would increase, and ultimately more chickens would be raised.

In this way, the price system determines what will be produced (hamburgers or chicken), how human and natural resources will be allocated (the farmer's land and labour), and who will get what (those who can afford hamburgers will buy them). In summary:

- An increase in price removes shortages by reducing the demand and increasing the supply;

- A decrease in price removes a surplus by discouraging production and encouraging people to buy more.

The price system thus creates a balance between **supply** and **demand**. If there is a scarcity of one particular item and consumers want it badly enough, they will be willing to pay such a high price that others will be encouraged to supply it. Supply and demand together determine relative scarcity. This system of rewards (profit) and punishments (losses) ensures that the wants of consumers are taken into account, and that unwanted items will not be produced.

supply: the relationship between various possible prices of a product and the quantities of the product that businesses are willing to supply.

demand: the relationship between the various possible prices of a product and the quantities of the product that consumers are willing to purchase.

2. Lead Pencils

Suppose that there is an increased demand for lead pencils, perhaps because a baby boom increases school enrolment. Retail stores will order more pencils from their wholesalers. The wholesalers will order more pencils from the manufacturers. The manufacturers will, in turn, order more wood, more brass, more graphite — all the products used to make pencils. In order to encourage the suppliers to produce more of these raw materials, the manufacturers will have to offer higher prices for them. Higher prices will influence suppliers to increase their work force to meet the higher demand. To hire more workers (assuming no unemployment), they will have to offer higher wages or better working conditions. In this way, the effects spread in ever-widening circles, transmitting the message to people all over the world that there is a demand for pencils — or, to be more precise, for the materials needed to produce pencils.

Prices not only transmit information from prospective buyers to retailers, wholesalers, manufacturers, and owners of resources, they also transmit information the other way. Suppose that a forest fire or a labour strike reduces the availability of wood. The price of wood will increase. This will inform pencil manufacturers that it will be wise to use less wood, and it will not profit them to produce as many pencils as before unless they can sell them at a higher price. Lower production of pencils will enable the retailer to charge a higher price for them, and the higher price will inform consumers that it would be economical to wear pencils down to a stub before discarding them or to switch to pens.

The price system also operates with respect to workers and owners of resources. An increase in the demand for wood will tend to produce higher wages for loggers; this is a signal that labour of that type is in greater demand than before. Higher wages give workers the incentive to act on that information, with the result that some workers may now choose to become loggers, and more young people entering the labour market may also become loggers.

Profit and Competition

competition: rivalry among entrepreneurs engaged in the same business enterprise, each of whom is trying to capture as large a share of the market as possible.

profit motive: the desire of business entrepreneurs to accumulate capital by engaging in a commercial venture.

Belief in private property and **competition** is central to the private enterprise system. Profit, whether measured in terms of land, money, or factories, is the reward (or incentive) for those who are successful in the business world. Without private ownership, there is no incentive for individuals to do their best. By permitting people to accumulate private wealth, the economic system encourages them to save money and invest it in profitable areas of the economy. Although the **profit motive** may appear selfish, free enterprise supporters argue that it promotes research and savings and leads ultimately to greater productivity and wealth for all. Those who provide these services receive their reward based on their ability to satisfy people's desires.

Personal income in a private enterprise economy is largely determined by the supply and demand for a person's talents, skills, and possessions. People with abilities or resources that are in great demand receive higher incomes than those without such abilities or resources. The owner of a lot in a busy downtown city will make more money than the owner of a lot of the same size in the country. A top hockey goal scorer will earn more than a checker on the third line. According to this view, poor people in a private enterprise economy are people without highly valued talents and resources.

The private enterprise system is based on people's materialistic nature. In the desire to accumulate goods, individuals have unconsciously created the mechanisms of private enterprise. According to the theory, although some people may have more ability to acquire material wealth than others, the system ensures that even the most selfish people serve society by trying to get ahead. The same price is established whether the buyer's motives are selfish or not. Whatever the motive, the system supposedly translates individual economic actions into the greater good.

For private enterprise to function smoothly, individual businesses must seek to maximize their profits, consumers must know the different prices of each item offered for sale, both must make buying and selling decisions based on self-interest, and no individual or group should be able to control or manipulate the price of any item. Buyers and sellers are brought together in **markets**. Car manufacturers, for example, should attempt to make as much money as possible, and no small group of suppliers should agree on a set price—otherwise consumers would be forced to pay more than they should. At the same time, if prospective car buyers do not shop around to compare the price and quality of different cars, and if they do not base their decisions on the merits of each car, then there would be little reason for the companies to compete with one another by lowering prices or by manufacturing better cars.

market: any arrangement for bringing buyers and sellers together.

The system also requires a great deal of competition for jobs, customers, and goods. If, for example, there was only one hockey stick manufacturer, that company could simply increase the price and everyone who wanted a stick would have to pay the higher price. In a competitive situation with several dozen manufacturers all producing a similar product, each company would attempt to sell more hockey sticks by lowering the price or by improving the quality. This competition ensures that hockey players pay a "fair" price for their sticks, and that the manufacturer produces them in the most efficient way.

The company that fails to make the best use of the available human and natural resources will be forced into bankruptcy, because the high costs of production will increase the price of its products. Similarly, if large numbers of workers are looking for jobs — and they have not made an agreement among themselves (a union) — the competition for work will prevent wages from rising above an "acceptable" level.

The private enterprise system answers the three basic economic problems in the following manner:

- *What* goods are produced is determined by the demands of consumers. If consumers will pay enough money for fried chicken, then chicken will be raised. If consumers shift their preferences to hamburgers, then more cattle and fewer chickens will be produced.

- *How* goods are produced is determined by competition among producers to sell their goods. To earn the greatest possible profit, producers will select the cheapest possible method of production. If it is cheaper to dig a tunnel using labourers equipped with picks and shovels than to use a bulldozer, then this is how it will be done. However, if the cost of gasoline drops and the wages of labourers increase, then bulldozers will replace the picks and shovels.

- *Who* gets what share of the goods that are produced is determined by supply and demand. If the demand for a person's skill or property is greater than the supply, then that person will command a larger income than someone whose skill or property is in less demand relative to its supply.

Focus

Why are competition and private property crucial to the private enterprise system?

A Real-Life Case Study of Private Enterprise

The following history of the ballpoint pen industry illustrates the advantages and disadvantages of the market economy for consumers. In 1945, Milton Reynolds acquired a patent on a new type of pen that used a ball bearing in place of the old nib-tipped fountain pens that had to be dipped into inkwells. He formed the Reynolds International Pen Company and began production on October 6, 1945.

The Reynolds pen was introduced with a good deal of fanfare by Gimbels, the New York department store, which guaranteed that the pen would write for two years without being refilled. The price was set at $12.50. Production costs were only about 80 cents per pen. Gimbels sold 10 000 pens on October 29, 1945, the first day they were on sale.

The Reynolds International Pen Company quickly expanded production. By early 1946, it was employing more than 800 people in its factory and was producing 30 000 pens per day. After six months, it had $3 million in the bank. Not to be outdone, Gimbels' traditional business rival, Macy's department store, introduced an imported ballpoint pen from South America that sold at $19.98. Other pen manufacturers also entered the field. Eversharp produced its first ballpoint in April, and Sheaffer followed with its pen in July. So far, however, Reynolds still sold the cheapest pen on the market at $12.50, and its costs had declined to 60 cents per pen. The first signs of trouble emerged when the Ball-Point Pen Company of Hollywood (disregarding a patent infringement suit) put a $9.95 model on the market, and a manufacturer named David Kahn announced plans to introduce a pen selling for less than $3. A price war had begun.

Reynolds responded with a new model, priced at $3.85, that cost about 30 cents to produce. By Christmas of 1946, approximately 100 manufacturers were in production, some of them selling pens for as little as $2.98. The next year, Gimbels decided to purchase its ballpoint pens from the Continental Pen Company and reduced its price to 98 cents. Reynolds had introduced a new model priced to sell at $1.69, but Gimbels sold it for 88 cents in its continuing price war with Macy's. Reynolds then designed a new model listed at 98 cents. By this time, ballpoint pens had become economy items rather than luxury items, but they were still highly profitable.

Table 7.1: Advantages and Disadvantages of the Market Economy

Advantages	Disadvantages
• The market gives producers an incentive to produce goods that the public wants.	• Consumers may be manipulated by advertising.
• The market provides an incentive to acquire useful skills.	• Prices and incomes might not reflect what is best for society.
• A wide variety of goods and services is available.	• The economy experiences many ups and downs, with considerable unemployment during the downs.
• There are incentives to use resources efficiently.	• Monopolies and oligopolies can emerge that charge unreasonable prices.
• Competition encourages good quality and lower prices.	• Extreme income inequality results.
• Productivity is rewarded by higher profits.	• Industry cost-cutting can lead to environmental problems.
• The market economy fosters self-reliance.	• Insecurity is present on a large scale.
• It is possible to become very wealthy.	• It is difficult to break out of a cycle of poverty.

In 1948, ballpoint pens selling for as little as 39 cents cost about 10 cents to produce. In 1951, prices of 25 cents were common. Today, there is a wide variety of models and prices, ranging from 19 cents upwards, and the market appears stable, orderly, and only moderately profitable.

As this example illustrates, the ideal circumstances for the operation of the market economy includes many producers making and selling an identical product that many people are willing to buy. In this situation, no individual buyer or seller can control the price of the product. The resulting competition ensures that the product will be sold at a "fair" price.

Private enterprise does have its limitations. In situations of extreme competition, some sellers lower their costs by producing goods of such inferior quality that they are not worth the price. Manufacturers will also resort to frequent product changes ("new and improved," as their advertisements proclaim) to persuade customers to buy their product. Although these changes are usually minor, they add to the cost of the product. Competition can also lead to secrecy. As the ballpoint pen example showed, the first firm to produce the new pens made fantastic profits. The Reynolds International Pen Company did not announce its new design until the pens were ready for sale. As a result, many customers bought the old fountain pens just before they became obsolete. At the same time, each pen company was conducting its own research — much of which was wasteful duplication.

Debating the Merits of Free Enterprise

The critics of free enterprise accuse capitalism of undermining society's values. The profit motive, they claim, creates an abnormal interest in competition and materialism at the expense of morality. The scramble for the "all-mighty dollar" encourages unethical business practices. Critics argue that human worth is all too often measured in terms of a person's wealth, that the search for profits has led to ecological disasters, and that while some people are millionaires, many families live in poverty.

Supporters of capitalism disagree. Some people contribute more to society than do others. The inventors of insulin, for example, were more important than the doctors who administered it. Average people add very little to civilization, yet they benefit greatly from advances made by a relatively few people in such fields as medicine, technology, and the arts. These geniuses actually receive very few rewards in relation to their contribution to society.

To the complaint that entertainers such as Madonna earn much more than they contribute to society, supporters of capitalism like Ayn Rand and Milton Friedman claim that people are entitled to spend their money on whatever they wish — including expensive concert tickets. Those who don't like her music do not contribute to Madonna's income.

Other Criticisms and Responses

Another frequent criticism of the capitalist system is that money creates power — not only economic power but also political power. Through the use of skilful lobbying, expensive lawyers, contributions to political parties, and control of the media, businesspeople are able to influence government legislation. The chart of Westinghouse's business interests (Figure 7.2) illustrates this interconnection among business, media, and government. Thus, the "competition" quickly becomes unfair. Supporters of private enterprise disagree. They believe that political freedom, even with all its flaws, is probably the most important benefit of capitalism. Ayn Rand, for example, stated that capitalism is the only system that allows people to be free. All human relationships are voluntary and, most important, because everyone has private property, all are free to disagree.

Figure 7.2: Westinghouse's Connections with Business, Media, and Government

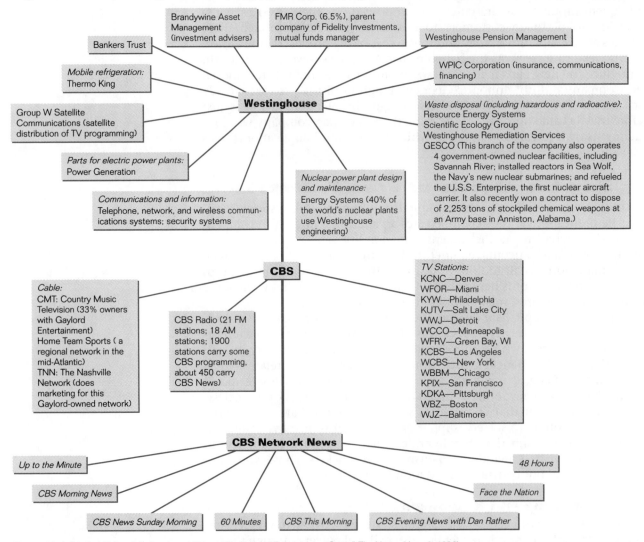

Source: Mark Crispin Miller and Janine Jaquet Biden, "The National Entertainment State," *The Nation* (June 3, 1996).

Milton Friedman expands upon Rand's ideas:

*It is widely believed that politics and economics are separate and largely uncon-
nected; that individual freedom is a political problem and material welfare an economic problem; and that any kind of political arrangements can be combined with
any kind of economic arrangements. But such a view is a delusion. There is an intimate connection between economics and politics, and only certain combinations of
political and economic arrangements are possible. A society which is Marxist cannot also be truly democratic.*

*In addition to providing economic freedom, capitalism promotes political free-
dom by separating economic power from political power and in this way enables
the one to offset the other. This prevents power from being concentrated in only a
few hands. ...5*

*A free society releases the energies and abilities of people to pursue their own
objectives. It prevents some people from arbitrarily suppressing others. It does not
prevent some people from achieving positions of privilege, but so long as freedom is
maintained, these positions of privilege are subject to continued attack by other
able, ambitious people. Freedom preserves the opportunity for today's underprivi-
leged to become tomorrow's privileged and, in the process, enables almost everyone,
from top to bottom, to enjoy a fuller and richer life.6*

Capitalism, Liberalism, and Conservatism

Capitalism and liberalism emerged together during the nineteenth century.
Both ideologies promoted individualism—that everyone should have freedom of choice. They wished to maximize individual liberty by limiting government intervention in human affairs. The government's role was to
protect its citizens from internal interference (a police force) and external
interference (a national defence).

Nineteenth-century British political thinker John Stuart Mill (1806–73)
provided the classic defence of liberalism. In his famous essay *On Liberty*
(1859), Mill argued that the only justification for government action was to
protect individuals from being harmed by others. The state should not
attempt to regulate moral standards, provide economic benefits, protect
individuals from harming themselves, or provide charity. If individuals
wished to hurt themselves or do something stupid or immoral, that was
their own business.

Each individual, Mill wrote, tended to be the best judge of his or her
own interests and happiness. Thus, the decisions made *by* individuals tended to be superior to those made *for* them. Although some people might suffer from a poor decision, this was the price society had to pay for economic
and political freedom.

In the late nineteenth century, supporters of liberalism began to accept
the need for more government involvement in the economy and sought to
limit the economic freedoms of entrepreneurs in order to guarantee greater
economic freedom for the poorer members of society. John Stuart Mill, for
example, later supported laws against child labour and unsafe working conditions. In the twentieth century, liberalism supported social welfare measures.

classical (traditional) liberalism: the early nineteenth-century version of liberalism, which opposed almost all government intervention of any kind, including social welfare measures.

To distinguish between these two types of liberalism, the nineteenth-century variety is now called **classical** (or **traditional**) **liberalism**.

Today, the ideological support for capitalism springs from free enterprise conservatism, also called neo-conservatism. One of its intellectual defenders is Milton Friedman. Some elements of neo-conservatism can be seen in the policies of politicians Preston Manning, Ralph Klein, and Mike Harris in Canada, and Newt Gingrich in the United States. Neo-conservatism is suspicious of anything that interferes with the economy, individual freedom, or private property. It opposes most government regulations, and demands that state enterprises be sold to private owners. Private enterprise, neo-conservatives argue, is the most democratic way to organize the economy, and capitalism is necessary for democracy to flourish.

What's Coming Next

We have examined the theory supporting private enterprise, but how well does this ideology operate in practice? No country has ever had a pure capitalist system. Perhaps the closest example of pure capitalism existed in the United States prior to the Great Depression of the 1930s. Case Study 11 outlines the American economy in this period and examines why the government decided to play more of a role in the economy.

AYN RAND, 1905–1982

Born Alice Rosenbaum to Jewish parents in St. Petersburg, Russia, novelist Ayn Rand occupies a prominent and controversial position on the right wing of American political and economic thought. Revered by her admirers as a "prophet and seer" and derided by her critics as a "peddler of almost laughably bad philosophical novels," Rand continues to be a powerful figure in American ideological debates in the decades following her death.

Educated at the University of St. Petersburg (she received a degree in history in 1924 at the age of 19), Rand's hatred of the repressive nature of the fledgling Bolshevik regime led her to jump at the opportunity to join relatives in Chicago in 1925.

After living briefly with her aunt, Rand moved west in the following year to Hollywood, where she found work as a movie extra and wardrobe assistant. After several years of working at odd jobs in the movie industry, her writing skills so impressed a Hollywood executive that in 1931 she was hired by RKO Pictures as a junior screen writer. Even though her early scripts were not produced, the money she received for them gave her the financial security to devote herself to her writing full time.

Rand's philosophy, which she called "Objectivism," emerged in two novels. *The Fountainhead* gives an account of an architect who destroys his own building when he learns that changes have been made without his approval; *Atlas Shrugged* is a mammoth examination of a wretched world of the future. Both were "rhapsodies to the superior individual who successfully resists engulfment by the common herd."[7]

In an appendix to *Atlas Shrugged*, Rand succinctly described the heart of her philosophy: "[T]he concept of man as a heroic being, with his own happiness as the moral purpose of his life, with productive achievement as his noblest activity, and reason as his only guide." She maintained that both individual and societal happiness could be gained only through the fostering of a "rational egoism," and a rejection of anything that was collectivist or altruistic in nature. The motto of the Objectivist movement is reflected in a declaration by Rand's protagonist in *Atlas Shrugged:* "I swear—by my life and my love of it—that I will never live for the sake of another man, nor ask another man to live for mine."[8]

Rand maintained that this fundamental individualism could occur only under a government that stayed out of both business and the private lives of its citizens, essentially restricting its actions to keeping the peace. She argued that big business was "America's persecuted minority," and stated, "Every government interference in the economy consists of giving an unearned benefit, extorted by force, to some men at the expense of others."[9]

---

1 How does Rand's philosophy of Objectivism reflect the basic principles of private enterprise?

2 According to Rand, who could jeopardize fundamental individualism?

Underlying and Emerging Issues

Give the reasoning and evidence that might be used to support different views or conclusions on the following issues:

1 To what degree should the prices of goods and services be determined by market conditions?

2 Under what circumstances should governments intervene to protect consumers?

3 If all individuals act in their own self-interest, will the best interests of society be served?

4 Is the presence of poverty in society inescapable?

5 To what degree are poor people responsible for their own situation?

6 How important is individual freedom as compared with the well-being of society?

7 To what degree should society accept responsibility for the well-being of individual citizens?

8 Does the price system lead to the most efficient use of scarce resources?

9 Should the presence of unemployment and inflation be accepted as a natural result of a free-enterprise system?

10 Is competition the best mechanism to ensure quality, fair price, and variety of goods and services?

11 Is the possibility of becoming wealthy more important than the risk of economic insecurity?

12 Does capitalism create a "cycle of poverty"?

13 Do people need individual incentives in order to work hard?

14 Does competition and the need to cut costs lead businesses to take actions that harm the environment?

15 Does capitalism foster undue selfishness?

16 How can people be protected from the emergence of monopolies and oligopolies?

17 Do capitalism and democracy reinforce each other?

18 Should Canada actively promote global free trade?

19 Should Canada move closer to the model of private enterprise?

Focussing Knowledge

In your notes, clearly identify or define and explain the importance or significance of each of the following:

private enterprise	competition
mercantilism	profit motive
protective tariffs	classical liberalism
usury	Adam Smith
just price	Thomas Malthus
invisible hand	Charles Darwin
Social Darwinism	price system
Ayn Rand	supply
John Stuart Mill	demand

Reviewing and Organizing Knowledge

1 What were the main characteristics of the system of mercantilism that preceded capitalism?

2 How did developments in the sixteenth and seventeenth centuries undermine mercantilism and promote the rise of capitalism?

3 What contributions to emerging capitalist theories were made by

a. Adam Smith?

b. Thomas Malthus?

c. David Ricardo?

d. Social Darwinists?

4 How does the writing of Samuel Smiles illustrate the early capitalists' view of poverty and charity?

5 What important features of the private enterprise system eventually emerged?

6 How do the examples of "Hamburgers versus Fried Chicken" and "Lead Pencils" illustrate how the market economy and price system operate?

7 What role in private enterprise is played by

a. the profit motive?

b. competition?

8 How does the model of private enterprise answer the three basic economic questions?

9 Make a thorough list of

a. advantages/arguments in favour of private enterprise;

b. disadvantages/arguments against private enterprise.

10 How are the terms capitalism, liberalism, conservatism, and neo-conservatism related?

Applying and Extending Knowledge

1 Choose articles from the newspaper that illustrate the advantages and disadvantages of private enterprise, and explain how the articles illustrate these points.

2 Select articles from the newspaper that illustrate important aspects of private enterprise (such as markets, supply and demand, competition, profit motive, price system.) Explain how the articles illustrate these terms.

3 Write an essay in support of one of the following statements:

a. Economic freedom is necessary for political freedom;

b. Economic planning and political freedom are perfectly compatible.

4 Research one industry in Canada. Describe the degree to which the industry is affected by government regulations or other interventions.

5 Write a dialogue between Ayn Rand or Milton Friedman and a representative of a group that works on behalf of children living in poverty.

6 Find newspaper articles that illustrate some of the Underlying and Emerging Issues on page 296. Explain how the articles illustrate the issues.

The American Economy

*T*HIS CASE STUDY ANALYZES the relationship between the federal government and the economy in the United States during the 1920s and 1930s. It outlines how ideas about state intervention in the economy changed over time and how these changes were reflected in government policy. After examining the causes of the stock market crash of 1929, the case study analyzes how President Franklin Delano Roosevelt responded to the Great Depression that followed and explains how the present limited welfare state and mixed economy of the United States grew out of Roosevelt's New Deal reforms.

United States at a Glance

Area: 9 372 610 km²

Population (1995): 263.8 million (world's third-largest country)

Life Expectancy in Years (1994): Males 72.6, Females 79.4

GDP (1994): $6638.2 billion (U.S.)

GDP per Capita (1994): $24 300 (U.S.)

Doctors per 1000 People (1993): 2.38

Hospital Beds per 1000 People (1993): 4.4

Health Expenditures as Percentage of GDP (1990): 12.7

Telephones per 1000 People (1994): 590

Televisions per 1000 People (1992): 814

Sources: John Robert Colombo, ed., *The 1996 Canadian Global Almanac* (Toronto: Macmillan, 1996); Marlita A. Reddy, ed., *Statistical Abstract of the World* (New York: Gale Research, 1994).

Learning Outcomes

After reading this case study, you should be able to:

- explain the Republican economic policies from 1921 to 1929

- understand the weaknesses in the economy in the 1920s and the causes of the 1929 stock market crash and the subsequent depression

- understand how the stock market operated

- explain the reasoning behind the New Deal

- debate the achievements and failures of the New Deal

- understand the historical roots of the American welfare state

Case Table 11.1: Presidents of the United States in the Twentieth Century

Name	Years in Office	Party
Theodore Roosevelt	1901–9	Republican
William H. Taft	1909–13	Republican
Woodrow Wilson	1913–21	Democrat
Warren G. Harding	1921–23	Republican
Calvin Coolidge	1923–29	Republican
Herbert C. Hoover	1929–33	Republican
Franklin D. Roosevelt	1933–45	Democrat
Harry S. Truman	1945–53	Democrat
Dwight D. Eisenhower	1953–61	Republican
John F. Kennedy	1961–63	Democrat
Lyndon B. Johnson	1963–69	Democrat
Richard M. Nixon	1969–74	Republican
Gerald R. Ford	1974–77	Republican
Jimmy Carter	1977–81	Democrat
Ronald Reagan	1981–89	Republican
George Bush	1989–93	Republican
William F. Clinton	1993–	Democrat

The United States was born in part out of a mistrust of government authority. Most Americans believed that governments should intervene as little as possible in people's lives. In the late nineteenth century, although corporations and farmers' groups sought (and often achieved) government aid and protection on their behalf, most American economists believed that the government should play a passive role in the economy, and that the government's main function was to respond to problems rather than to take the initiative in promoting economic growth. Economic ups and downs were such an accepted fact of life that President Harding stated in 1921, "There has been vast unemployment before and there will be again. There will be depressions and inflation just as surely as the tides ebb and flow."[1] This case study examines the extent to which this mentality changed.

The Harding Administration

During World War I, the American government intervened in the economy as never before, and its powers considerably expanded. After the social, economic, and emotional upheaval of the war, many Americans hoped to return to an earlier, quieter, more stable life. The popular image of prewar America may have owed more to myth than to reality, but voters were attracted to politicians who promoted this idealized picture. One such politician was Republican Warren G. Harding, who became president of the United States in 1921. Harding was a handsome man (an important factor according to some contemporary commentators) who spoke in reassuring tones that appealed to the popular mood. He set the tone for the era when he called for a return to "normalcy."

But what did "normalcy" mean with regard to economic policy and the relationship between the state and the economy? For Harding (who was not an economic theorist), it is difficult to say exactly what this meant. For many key people within the Republican Party, however, normalcy meant discarding the business controls that remained from World War I.

Although the United States had seen considerable economic growth during the war years, Harding's administration found itself in a serious recession in the spring of 1921. The traditional economic response to hard times was to reduce government expenditures and allow the "natural" business cycle to restore prosperity. Andrew W. Mellon, Secretary of the Treasury, pursued this approach by cutting federal expenditures by over 20 percent. To stimulate growth, Mellon reduced federal taxes, particularly for wealthy

Americans. Harding's administration also reversed the wartime trend of government involvement in the economy, and even offered naval ships to private business at bargain basement prices. The administration continued its support of business. Federal troops, for example, broke a coal strike in West Virginia in 1921, and the courts ended a railway strike the following year. Harding's standard response to union demands for protection was that traditional **individualism** needed to be revived. Labour unions represented a barrier to this individualism.

individualism: an ethical, economic, or political theory that emphasizes the importance and responsibility of individuals over groups.

The Coolidge Administration

Harding's successor as president, Calvin Coolidge, was in many ways an even more enthusiastic cheerleader for the non-interventionist state than Harding had been. The new president declared that "the business of America is business" and set about constructing a "businessman's government." Coolidge's vision was laissez-faire. He was a firm believer that the economy would prosper solely on the basis of business leadership, not as the result of state intervention. This vision also applied to the presidency itself. As Irving Stone wrote, Coolidge "aspired to become the least President the country ever had; he attained his desire."[2]

Reductions to the graduated income tax continued under Coolidge. With Mellon still in charge of the Treasury, the tax on the wealthy was slashed from 40 to 20 percent in 1926. Two years later, corporate taxes were reduced even more. Soon, the courts joined in the assault on the social legislation and **state intervention** of the World War I era. Several Supreme Court rulings clipped the wings of organized labour and restricted the application of anti–child labour laws.

state intervention: economic; the act of intervening in the economy by government.

At the same time that Coolidge adopted laissez-faire policies, his support of business involved the government in the private economy, and he in fact allied the federal government with big business. As the *Wall Street Journal* put it: "Never before, here or anywhere else, has a government been so completely fused with business."[3]

Some members of the Republican administration advocated limited government intervention in the economy to correct its faults. One such person was the Secretary of Commerce, Herbert Hoover. During World War I, he had earned a reputation as an expert administrator. After the war, Hoover sought methods to promote cooperation between government and business. As historian Ellis Hawley explained, "Hoover spoke for only one segment of the Republican administration, of course. His vision of governmental activism was not shared by such conservatives as Andrew Mellon and Calvin Coolidge. ... Yet the vision he set forth was clearly a major force in shaping public policy between 1925 and 1928."[4] As we shall see, this approach influenced the reformers who emerged in the wake of the economic collapse after 1929.

Focus

Why did Harding and Coolidge prefer government not to intervene in the economy?

The American Economy in the 1920s

What impact did these pro-business government policies have on the American economy in the 1920s? It is difficult to say what actually produced the prosperity that many Americans enjoyed during the 1920s—certainly these years were boom times for American business, and many Americans enjoyed the benefits of an improved standard of living. Per capita annual income went from $480 in 1900 to $681 in 1929. Real earnings grew, and many companies realized that working hours could be reduced without a loss in productivity. In fact, much of the economic growth and general affluence of the decade were due to dramatic increases in worker productivity, which often came as a result of new technology. For example, with the assembly-line techniques Henry Ford introduced, by 1925 a finished car rolled out of his plant every 10 seconds. At the close of the decade, almost 5 million cars were manufactured every year. Unlike in Europe, in America even families of modest means could afford a car, and there was about one car for every five persons in the United States at this time. As Henry Ford stated, "Machinery is the new Messiah."[5]

How does this automobile style of the 1920s differ from today's styles?

The popular mood went beyond a simple enthusiasm for new gadgets. A harsh new materialism emerged during the 1920s. As Coolidge put it: "Brains are wealth and wealth is the chief end of man."[6] Even those institutions that one might expect to be shielded from this obsession for worldly gain appear to have surrendered to it. Bruce Barton's book, *The Man Nobody Knows*, quickly became a bestseller in 1925 and 1926. The book was a biography of Jesus Christ that portrayed him as a gifted businessman! Some

Protestant pastors encouraged the salespeople in their congregations with the advice that they could make bigger commissions if they followed the Bible as their guide.

The general American public was in love with what one commentator has called a "business civilization." A wake-up call from Wall Street changed their mood quickly.

The Stock Market Crash of 1929

Although President Herbert Hoover declared that the American economy was "sound" when he was inaugurated in March 1929, there had been warning signs of danger from Wall Street, the heart of the U.S. financial district in New York, for some time. The stock market had grown rapidly for much of the decade, as Case Figure 11.1 illustrates, and thousands of Americans had invested in stocks hoping to get rich overnight. Many middle-class investors bought stock "on margin." This was done by making only a small down payment on the purchase of the stock and borrowing the rest from a stockbroker. If the stock rose dramatically, the investor easily repaid the loan. Of course, if the stock fell in value, the investor might have a difficult time paying off the loan.

Case Figure 11.1

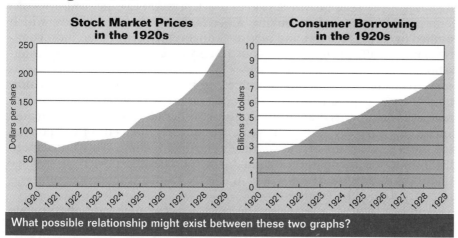

What possible relationship might exist between these two graphs?

Source: Paul Boyer et al., *The Enduring Vision: A History of the American People,* Vol. 2, 3rd ed. (Lexington, MA: D.C. Heath, 1996), p. 807.

Because very little of this process was regulated by the federal government, a tiny number of large investors was able to manipulate the prices of certain stocks in a manner that would have had them all convicted of insider trading today, but which earned them huge fortunes in the 1920s. This manipulation meant that the prices for many stocks were grossly inflated, and stock prices rose dramatically between 1925 and 1929.

Some sort of serious adjustment on the stock market was inevitable. It began in October 1929. October 29, "Black Tuesday," was the worst single day in stock market history. The average value of all stocks fell 37 percent in the next 30 days, and the plunge continued. With a Gross National Product (GNP) of about $104 billion, the United States now had to cope with a drop of more than $48 billion in the value of the country's stocks. As the decade drew to a close, the United States faced the worst economic depression in its history. Unemployment rose sharply, and wages and prices tumbled.

The Great Depression of the 1930s

The Great Crash of 1929 was not the only cause of the Great Depression that followed. Many other national and international developments contributed. During the 1920s, large corporations such as General Electric and General Motors instituted new management techniques that increased productivity and enabled them to produce ever-larger supplies of consumer goods. Farmers used improved agricultural machinery to expand the amount of land under cultivation and produce more food for the market. Wages, however, did not increase as rapidly as did productivity, and by the late 1920s, the demand for goods could not keep up with the increased supply. In addition, droughts in the midwestern states in the late 1920s ruined crops and forced many farmers into bankruptcy. Thousands of banks also failed, wiping out people's savings. The spread of the depression to other countries discouraged consumers from buying American manufactured goods, which resulted in closed factories and increased unemployment. When most countries raised tariffs on imported goods to encourage local production, international trade was cut in half.

Perhaps the most important problem in the U.S. economy was the enormous income gap between the rich and the poor. Large corporations had increased their profits dramatically during the decade, but had not increased employees' wages by nearly the same amount. Five percent of the population earned one-third of the country's personal income. This unbalanced distribution of income meant that the purchasing power of average Americans during the 1920s was dangerously low. Consumer spending was necessary to fuel the economy.

Another factor that explains the crash was the high rate of corporate fraud. As one Republican attorney general explained, "I am not going unnecessarily to harass men who have unwittingly run counter with the statutes."[7] Ironically, while laissez-faire beliefs had produced a situation that was harmful to the economy, many businesspeople opposed state intervention even when it would have made their sector of the economy more stable. Perhaps the best illustration of this short-sightedness was in American bank presidents' opposition to federal deposit insurance. If this program had been in place, scores of medium and small banks would not have gone under in the bank panic of 1932–33 because the government would have guaranteed people's bank deposits.

These people lined up for blocks waiting for their portion of potatoes and cabbages.

President Hoover probably intervened in the economy more than previous presidents, but it was not enough. Hoover hoped, at first, that recovery could be encouraged simply through informal cooperation between business and labour, and he asked companies not to cut wages or lay off workers. He also encouraged state and local governments to hire people for public works projects. But other developments (including an international financial crisis) destroyed what little good Hoover's modest measures accomplished. In the summer of 1931, Hoover turned reluctantly to more aggressive intervention, including financial help for banks, railways, and other businesses. But again, these actions were too little, too late.

Roosevelt's New Deal

If President Hoover had simply run out of ideas, Franklin Delano Roosevelt seemed willing to try anything to get the American economy moving again. Roosevelt radiated an upbeat, confident charm and easily defeated the gloomy Hoover in the 1932 presidential election. In the campaign, Roosevelt had criticized Hoover for spending more money than the government took in and promised to balance the budget. However, after a brief period of caution, Roosevelt moved boldly to confront the economic crisis. His understanding of economics was not strong, but the new president was an activist and he gathered around him a group of advisers who were committed to making sweeping changes to the relationship between the state and the private economy.

DEPICTING POVERTY

At the height of the Great Depression, one-quarter of the U.S. labour force was unemployed, and 28 million people were on some type of government support. Between 1929 and 1933, over 100 000 businesses went bankrupt and 5000 banks failed. Wages fell by 40 percent! Mere numbers do not adequately describe the everyday life of most Americans during the Depression. Millions of ordinary citizens swallowed their pride and wrote to the government for help. The following letter depicts the reality of the depression for millions of families.[8]

Philadelphia
November 26, 1934

Honorable Franklin D. Roosevelt,
Washington, DC

Dear Mr. President:

I am forced to write to you because we find ourselves in <u>a very serious condition</u>. For the last three or four years we have had depression and <u>suffered</u> with my <u>family</u> and little children <u>severely</u>. Now since the Home Owners Loan Corporation opened up, I have been going there in order to save my home, because there has been unemployment in my house for more than three years. You can imagine that I and my family have suffered from lack of water supply in my house for more than two years. Last winter I did not have coal and the pipes burst in my house and therefore could not make heat in the house. Now winter is here again and we are suffering of cold, no water in the house, and we are facing to be forced out of the house, because I have no money to move or pay so much money as they want when after making settlement I am mother of little children, am sick and losing my health, and we are eight people in the family, and where can I go when I don't have money because no one is working in my house. The Home Loan Corporation wants $42 a month rent or else we will have to be on the street. I am living in this house for about ten years and when times were good we would put our last cent in the house and now I have <u>no money, no home</u> and <u>no wheres to go</u>. I beg of you to please help me and my family and little children for the sake of a sick mother and suffering family to give this your immediate attention so we will not be forced to move or put out in the street.

<u>Waiting and Hoping that you will act quickly</u>.

Thanking you very much I remain

Mrs. E.L.

In accepting the nomination for president in 1932, Roosevelt declared, "I pledge you, I pledge myself to a new deal for the American people." The term **New Deal** was later used as the name for his economic reforms of the 1930s. In his first 100 days as president, Roosevelt pushed through Congress an impressive amount of legislation designed to save American capitalism from the deepening economic crisis. This first stage of the New Deal was primarily designed to promote recovery in the national economy. The president hoped to introduce improved management of the economy, especially of its productive capacity. He did not intend to do this through some sort of socialist economy, but by using the government to get business and labour to work together.

New Deal: the term used to describe U.S. President Roosevelt's economic reforms during the 1930s.

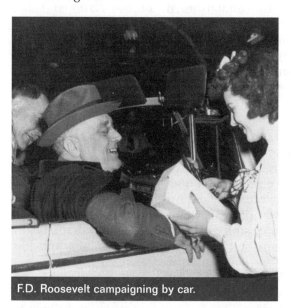

F.D. Roosevelt campaigning by car.

The cornerstone of the New Deal was the National Recovery Administration. The NRA was a government agency with sweeping powers. It oversaw a vast number of separate industry boards that were composed of representatives from employers, workers, and government. Each of these boards set production and price quotas and established other standards for a particular industry. Earlier legislation had attempted to outlaw or restrict this sort of collaboration or conspiracy among manufacturers, but Roosevelt felt that some cooperation was now permissible, indeed necessary—as long as government and organized labour were also at the table — in order to remedy the current economic mess. However, in 1935, the conservative Supreme Court declared the NRA unconstitutional.

Other programs in the first phase of Roosevelt's New Deal attempted to lower unemployment through public works projects. The Public Works Administration (PWA) spent millions of dollars in employing labourers on a wide variety of construction projects, from sidewalks to post offices. The Civilian Conservation Corps provided training for young people by employing them to improve the nation's forests and parks. Roosevelt also created the Securities Exchange Commission to regulate stock and bond markets and thus prevent another crash. The Federal Deposit and Insurance Commission guaranteed that people would not lose their savings if their bank failed.

By 1934, many federal policy-makers believed that the state had an important responsibility for the economic well-being of the country.

Focus

What was new about the New Deal?

welfare state: an economic system that is committed to the security of its population in the areas of income, health care, and job security.

However, not all Americans embraced this new interventionist view of the state, and conservative reaction to Roosevelt's programs (including the actions of the Supreme Court) prompted him to amend his approach. This second stage is often referred to as the *reform* phase of the New Deal. It included putting in place some of the essential building blocks for the American **welfare state**. The Social Security Act (1935), for example, established unemployment insurance and old age pensions supported by contributions from employees and employers. This act set the United States on the road that Canada and most European states had taken years earlier. In many ways, it represented a symbolic break with the fierce individualism and self-help philosophy of the past.

Another key change was the establishment of the National Labor Relations Board (NLRB), which outlawed unfair labour practices. Under the NLRB, organized labour became a key actor in the management of the American economy, and the number of union members rose steadily from 3 million in 1933 to 7 million in 1940. This, too, represented a significant departure from the laissez-faire economy of the past.

Evaluation of Roosevelt's Reforms

Clearly, some important changes took place regarding the role of the state in the private economy. Yet in several critical respects, the New Deal itself was a failure. Most historians agree that the New Deal did not end the Depression. Unemployment levels remained high. The New Deal also failed to reach many poor people. The economy did not fully recover until World War II production began. The war did what many in the government were reluctant to do — it introduced organized state planning and dramatically increased federal spending. The result was a booming economy and low unemployment.

We must remember that Roosevelt faced substantial opposition to his New Deal. After 1934, big business attacked most of his programs. At the same time, the Supreme Court viewed many of the measures as a threat to constitutional liberties. Although the Court's position softened, clearly Roosevelt had to reckon with strong opponents both within and outside the government. Compared with his predecessors, however, he was flexible and laid the foundation for an American welfare system on which subsequent presidents built.

The U.S. transformation that began in the 1930s was a profound and lasting one. As one analyst commented, "In the American mixed economy [of today], as in the private economy that preceded it, most of the important economic decisions are made by business executives. The difference now, a difference that grew out of the New Deal, is that other powerful players also help to determine the outcome of the game."[9] One indication of the government's growing power was the expansion of the federal civil service from under 600 000 employees in 1929 to over 1 million a decade later.

For the first time, the federal government acknowledged a responsibility to help the unemployed and the needy. Also for the first time, the government deliberately used deficit spending to stimulate the economy. The

United States, however, remained basically capitalistic — the profit motive and private property continued to be fundamental beliefs. Thanks largely to the implementation of unemployment insurance, social security, and other government programs, a depression as serious as that of the 1930s has not returned.

One of the many legacies of the New Deal was the widespread expectation that the government should take action in response to fluctuations in the business cycle. Roosevelt was not an economist; he was a practical politician who considered using deficit financing only as a last resort. The concept of stimulating consumer buying by pouring billions of government dollars into the economy, however, became the economic ideology of the post–World War II years. This theory, called Keynesian economics, held sway until the 1980s, when Ronald Reagan became president and adopted a new economic theory popularly termed "Reaganomics." Chapter 9 examines the theory behind these two economic ideologies. But before we explore the private enterprise system in more detail, it is important to study its major ideological rival, the centrally planned system.

BIOGRAPHY

BILL GATES, 1955–

Born to a relatively well-off family in Seattle, Washington, Bill Gates showed an early aptitude for both technology and business. By the age of 14, he was president of a profitable company, formed with several other young computer enthusiasts, that sold a traffic-counting system to municipalities (until the customers learned that the business was managed by high school students.)

After two years at Harvard University, Gates dropped out in order to form Microsoft Corporation with Paul Allen after they had devised the computer programming language BASIC for the newly emerging microcomputer. What happened next was a series of events that shaped the industry:

But the basis of Gates's great fortune was accidental. When his Microsoft venture was first formed in 1976, he wanted to concentrate on computer languages. The first time IBM people asked Gates for an operating system, he referred them to Digital Research. In a fine show of contempt that cost a fortune, Digital Research's chairman went flying the day the IBM team called. Enraged, IBM returned to Gates. Gates didn't have an operating system but was able to license one. He was still so uninterested that in 1980 he offered to let IBM buy DOS (disk operating system), as it became known. In one of the greatest business misjudgments of the 20th century, IBM rejected the offer. Gates bought DOS for a pittance.

IBM believed the future was in mainframes, hardware, and distribution. But a host of smaller companies were about to explode in the personal computer market while IBM was left stagnating. They all used DOS, and Gates made billions.[10]

Gates is a legendary hard worker (he took a total of only six days' vacation between 1978 and 1984), and unlike some of the other early computer leaders, he combined both technological and business skills. Microsoft soon dominated computer software, both in operating systems and applications. When Microsoft became a public corporation in 1986, Gates' 45 percent share made him an instant multimillionaire.

By 1992, 90 percent of the world's PCs used Microsoft operating systems, and the company had 44 percent of the world's software market. Microsoft's domination of the industry led to charges of unfair business practices. Gates responded, "It's not very complicated. We're not powerful enough to cause products that are not excellent to sell well."[11]

In his newspaper column, Gates reflected on the political potential of computers:

Personal computers hooked to interactive networks will empower citizens to participate in the democratic process and civic affairs with an ease and immediacy almost unheard of today.

The very nature of political dialogue will evolve as it becomes common for people to access public information and interact electronically with government agencies, as well as with each other.[12]

---

1 How does Bill Gates reflect important aspects of the economic system of private enterprise in the United States?

2 What are Gates' views on the relationship between information technology and politics?

Underlying and Emerging Issues

Give the reasoning and evidence that might be used to support different views or conclusions on the following issues.

1 Should governments increase their intervention in the economy in times of economic distress?

2 Should governments intervene in the economy to prevent inflation, recession, and depression?

3 Should governments increase public works projects to boost employment in difficult economic times?

4 Should governments pursue policies of full employment?

5 Does government intervention mean loss of freedom?

6 Is freedom from intervention more important than economic stability?

7 To what extent should private charity be relied upon to deal with the effects of poverty and unemployment?

8 Does the government have a responsibility for children living in poverty?

9 Should providing old age security and pensions be a responsibility of government?

10 Should everyone be entitled to such things as food, shelter, clothing, education, and medical care?

11 To what extent should government be responsible for the well-being of individuals?

12 Does capitalism allow large businesses to dominate the system at the expense of workers?

13 Does capitalism lead to domination of the political system by business interests?

14 To what extent are labour unions necessary and desirable?

15 To what extent should stock markets, banks, and other financial institutions be controlled by government?

16 To what extent should government try to create a climate in which business can flourish?

In your notes, clearly identify or define and explain the importance or significance of each of the following:

individualism	National Recovery Administration (NRA)
state intervention	Public Works Administration (PWA)
stocks	welfare state
insider trading	Social Security Act
Black Tuesday	Warren G. Harding
dividends	Calvin Coolidge
Great Depression	Herbert Hoover
New Deal	Franklin Delano Roosevelt

1 Describe the economic policies of each of the following U.S. presidents:

 a. Warren Harding

 b. Calvin Coolidge

 c. Franklin D. Roosevelt

2 What factors accounted for the boom in the American economy during the 1920s?

3 What factors led to the Great Crash of 1929?

4 In addition to the Crash of 1929, what factors caused the Great Depression?

5 How did the Depression affect ordinary people?

6 What were the main elements of Roosevelt's response to the Depression?

7 a. How did World War II affect the changes brought about by the New Deal?

 b. What were the main sources of opposition to Roosevelt's New Deal?

 c. What was the role of business after the New Deal?

Applying and Extending Knowledge

1 Write an essay in support of one of the following positions:

a. The New Deal was an unwarranted intrusion into private enterprise;

b. The New Deal was a legitimate response to an economic crisis;

c. The New Deal did not go far enough.

2 Interview someone who lived through the Great Depression. Write a description of how it affected that person's life.

3 Research and describe the impact of the Depression on organized labour in Canada and the United States.

4 Examine the more radical political responses to the Depression in North America. What groups offered solutions that were more extreme than Roosevelt's New Deal? How successful were these groups in attracting support?

5 Follow the business pages in the newspaper that list stock market quotations. Newspapers print a guide to reading the tables and graphs in this section; make sure that you use this information to help you understand the material. After one week, describe what you have learned about the stock market and the other markets (bonds, futures, commodities, etc.) listed in this newspaper section.

6 Find newspaper articles to illustrate some of the Underlying and Emerging Issues on page 311. Explain how the articles illustrate these issues.

CHAPTER *8*

Centrally

Planned

Systems

*H*OW DOES A CENTRALLY PLANNED ECONOMY operate, and what are its values, merits, and disadvantages? To answer these questions, this chapter describes the origins of central planning, evaluates the role of the Industrial Revolution in its growth, and examines the ideas of such early socialists as Robert Owen, Charles Fourier, and Louis Blanc. Karl Marx's ideas and contributions to central planning are outlined in considerable detail, and the chapter concludes with an analysis of the development of the Cuban economy from 1959 to the present.

Adam Smith, you will recall, stated that government should play only a limited role in the economy. The best way to ensure the economic well-being of a country, he argued, was for the government to stand aside and let the forces of the marketplace take control. At the other end of the spectrum is the idea of a **centrally planned economy**, in which the government plans every aspect of the economy and maintains constant control over it. This type of economy is also called "public enterprise" because of its reliance on public ownership of production and government decision-making on economic matters. This chapter examines the origins, ideals and values, advantages and disadvantages, and operation of centrally planned economies.

Origins of the Planned Economy

Planned economies go back a long way. More than 4000 years ago, the Sumerian society in the Middle East was state-controlled. In ancient Egypt, agriculture and natural resources were controlled and administered by the priesthood under the direction of the pharaohs. China has had at least three periods in its long history during which its rulers had tight control over the country's economy. Other examples include the Incas of Peru and several religious sects in the Middle Ages.

The idea that property is owned by an entire people, not by private individuals, is also very old. Some historians have traced this idea back to the Old Testament and to the writings of the Greek philosopher Plato. The first modern political movement that favoured common ownership of property, rather than private ownership, was an English group in the mid-seventeenth century called the Diggers.

Economic planning on a country-wide basis, however, was generally not possible until the Industrial Revolution of the eighteenth and nineteenth centuries. The invention of machines and the creation of the factory system made it possible to produce goods on a large and efficient scale. The economic advantages of mechanization, power-driven machinery, and factory production led to an unprecedented growth in output. For the first time in history it appeared that hunger and poverty could be eliminated. At the same time, advances in transportation and communications made it possible for industrialized countries to organize their economies on a national scale.

The early forms of capitalism created extreme income inequalities and deplorable working and living conditions. Capitalists were more concerned about making money than providing humane conditions. Since the capitalistic ethic preached that governments should not intervene in the economy, businesses were relatively free to do as they wished. Men, women, and children worked 12 hours a day, six days a week, or longer. Working in smoke-filled, cramped, and unsanitary rooms crippled or deformed many workers. Children were sometimes chained to machines, and those who did not conform to the harsh discipline of factory life were fined, beaten, or cast out to join the crowds of beggars in the city streets. Workers returned home at night to slum conditions of an appalling nature. Houses were severely overcrowded, badly ventilated, and poorly lit. Garbage and sewage were dumped in the streets; the smell was overpowering. Crime flourished, and drunkenness and prostitution grew at an alarming rate. The terrible conditions, combined with the tremendous increase in production, led to the emergence of communism as a major political force in the Western world.

centrally planned economy: an economic system in which the central government makes all the major economic decisions for the country.

FEMALE WORKERS DURING THE INDUSTRIAL REVOLUTION

Life in Russian Factories

The Industrial Revolution was fuelled by a large pool of available workers who had no choice but to accept low pay, long hours, and dangerous working conditions. Many of these labourers were women, as well as children as young as 5 years old. Eventually, the British government dropped its commitment to uncontrolled free enterprise and passed laws to forbid the worst abuses of industrialization. Although the Industrial Revolution came later to Russia, working conditions were no better; in fact, lacking democracy, they were worse. In the following selection, a Russian woman doctor describes factory conditions for women in 1913, four years prior to the Russian Revolution.

Fines are imposed for: late arrival, work which is not found to be up to standard, for laughter, even for sickness. If a worker is feeling unwell and sits down, a fine is incurred. … If an article is dropped, the fine is [levied and] … if the worker fails to "stand to attention" at the entrance of employer or foreman and until he leaves the room, she is fined. … At a well-known chocolate factory in Moscow the fine for laughing is 0.75 rbls. [roubles] and if a worker is 15 minutes late she is dismissed for one week. At another old established and famous chocolate factory in case of sudden illness a woman employee is instantly discharged. …

In the majority of factories where women are employed the working day is from 10 to 11½ hours, after deducting the dinner and breakfast intervals. On Saturday, in many factories … the work *sometimes lasts 16 and 18 hours per day. The workers are forced to work overtime on pain of instant dismissal or of transference to inferior employment, and in the case of children actual physical force is used to make them continue in their places. …*

The worst aspect of woman's factory labour is, however, the moral danger to which women are exposed from those in power over them. Immoral proposals from foremen and from their assistants are of general occurrence, and women who resist are persecuted in every possible way, and sometimes actually violated.

In a large tobacco factory in St. Petersburg the women workers who were asking for raised pay were cynically informed that they could augment their income by prostitution.[1]

Why did women accept such horrible working conditions?

How might such conditions have helped the growth of communism?

The Emergence of Socialist Ideals

The first response to the Industrial Revolution came from the **Utopian Socialists** (approximately 1770–1850). Moved by humanitarian ideals, Christian principles, and an optimistic view of human nature, they demanded that the terrible social and working conditions be improved.* Led by Robert Owen in Great Britain, Charles Fourier and Claude Saint-Simon in France, and Horace Greeley in the United States, the Utopian Socialists experimented with different forms of communal living that stressed cooperation, self-help, religion, and education. They thought that if the environment was improved, an ideal society could be established in which all people would be happy and prosperous. They also believed that these changes could be made possible through education and peaceful democratic methods, and they sought to convince businesspeople to adopt more enlightened practices. Robert Owen, for instance, attempted to set a good example for other industrialists. He reduced the workday for his cotton mill labourers from 12 hours to $10\frac{1}{2}$ hours, improved housing and working conditions, refused to hire children under the age of 10, and provided education for the young. Universal education, Owen argued, would eliminate crime and lead to prosperity for all. If other employers could be persuaded to adopt similar practices, the evils of industrialization could be ended forever. The Utopian Socialists did not want to destroy the capitalist system, they merely wanted to remove some of its more blatant evils.

Although some experiments in communal living flourished for a while, the Utopians were unable to win many converts, and by the mid-nineteenth century the movement had lost its vitality. The next step in the development of socialist thought was provided by Louis Blanc of France. He popularized the idea of large-scale **public ownership,** combined with labourers' control over the workplace, and the distribution of goods according to individual need. When this attempt at government-initiated socialism also failed, the stage was set for Karl Marx's more radical ideas.

Karl Marx

The impact of Karl Marx (1818–83) upon the socialist movement has been unparalleled. Marx was a brilliant scholar, economist, and philosopher. After studying law and philosophy in Prussia (now Germany), he became a journalist. His radical ideas led to successive exiles in Paris, Brussels, and finally London. There, Marx spent years reading, researching, and writing in the British Museum. With his close friend Friedrich Engels, he wrote the *Communist Manifesto* in 1848, followed by numerous other works, concluding with the three-volume *Das Kapital,* the last two volumes of which Engels wrote from Marx's rough notes and manuscripts. Although Marx did not invent socialism, he soon dominated the movement, and his theories came to be known as Marxism.

Utopian Socialists: a group of socialists (eighteenth to nineteenth centuries) who advocated peaceful and democratic methods to achieve more ideal societies, based on cooperation, planning, and communal approaches.

public ownership: government-owned and -operated industries.

---

* The term "utopian" came from a book written by Sir Thomas More in the sixteenth century that described his fantasy of a perfect society where everyone lived in harmony and mutual cooperation. When Marx used the word utopian to describe the socialists, he meant it as a derogatory remark.

Marxism: the economic and political theories of Karl Marx.

The term **Marxism** has different meanings for different people. It has been called the salvation of the future, the battle cry for revolutionaries, a religious dogma, and a harebrained scheme. To some people it is a system of ideas; to others it is a political movement. Although we are treating Marxism as an economic system in this chapter, you should bear in mind that it is both a political and an economic ideology that attempts to provide an overall philosophy of life.

Karl Marx (1818–83)

Marxist Thought

Like earlier Utopian Socialists, Marx was greatly moved by the inhumane conditions created by the Industrial Revolution. However, he disagreed with the Utopians' explanation of these conditions and with their solution to the problem. Life for the poor would never improve, he insisted, until the ruling class had been replaced by the workers.

The Industrial Revolution had spread from England to Belgium, France, and then Germany. Its abuses were even worse on the continent, and it was there that the young Marx first came into contact with the cruellest features of capitalism. *The Communist Manifesto,* urging the overthrow of capitalism, was the result of his observations. In 50 years socialist thought, spurred by worsening conditions in the cities, had moved from urging mild reforms in the system to advocating a complete overthrow of government.

According to Marx, all aspects of a person's life were determined by the individual's relationship to the **means of production**. Although the way in which a person made a living was not the only criterion in determining human behaviour, Marx believed that it was the most important factor. People's relationship to the means of production was the foundation upon which each society in history had erected its culture, laws, government, and artistic endeavours. The story of humanity, he wrote, was a history of class conflict between the owners of the means of production and the workers, between the exploiters and the exploited, and between the ruling class and the oppressed classes. In every case, the struggle was between classes that represented opposing economic interests. Each time, the struggle had resulted in the betterment of conditions for the majority—if only slightly.

means of production: land, tools, and factories; the factors required by people to engage in industry and agriculture.

In Marx's view, classes arose from their relationship to the means of production. The governing class owned the means of production, while the oppressed classes did not. In a nomadic society, for example, those who owned the most horses were the chiefs. In an agricultural society, landowners were the ruling class. As each new class achieved power, it gained control over the society's institutions (government, law, education, religion, art, media) and used them to justify and reinforce its dominant position in society.

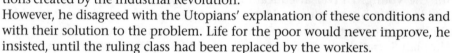

Focus

What are the major differences between Marx and the Utopian Socialists?

Figure 8.1: Marx's Theory of the Decline of Capitalism

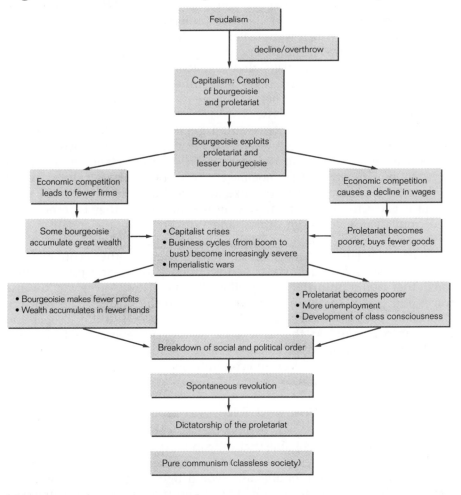

Marx and Class Antagonisms

The fundamental belief of Marxist thought was that capitalism was only a stage in the historical progress of humankind. Capitalism, said Marx, arose when the feudal medieval society became a hindrance to the economic growth of Europe's merchants and manufacturers. The new emerging class of traders and industrialists overthrew the existing agriculturally based economic structure and a new era of capitalism was born. The ideology of this new ruling class, which Marx termed the **bourgeoisie** (literally, town-dwellers), emphasized freedom from economic restrictions and freedom from the political domination of the old aristocracy.

According to Marx, the Industrial Revolution created two economic classes. The ruling class, or bourgeoisie, consisted of the owners of the means of production—wealthy financiers, large-scale merchants, and factory owners. The other class consisted of the workers, or **proletariat,** who were hired by the bourgeoisie. Without them the bourgeoisie could not survive.

bourgeoisie: according to Marxist theory, those holding a commanding position of economic power in a capitalistic society; the owners of the means of production.

proletariat: according to Marxist theory, the class of industrial wage earners whose only resource is their labour.

Focus

How was the Industrial Revolution important to the development of communist thought?

The central feature of the capitalist system, according to Marx, was that the workers must "sell" their labour to those who owned the means of production. The bourgeoisie exploited the proletariat by forcing it to create goods, the value of which was greater than the wages the workers received for their labour. It was this difference between the value of goods produced and the wages of the workers that enabled the bourgeoisie to become wealthier than the proletariat. Marx condemned both the profit motive and private property, which he believed were the major sources of conflict between the two economic classes.

The capitalist system exploited and degraded workers, Marx insisted. He believed that human nature is essentially creative and that the work people perform is an expression of themselves. Artists, for instance, fulfil themselves by making art, just as shoemakers do through making shoes. When workers have to sell their labour like an object and the creation of their labour is taken from them at an obviously unfair price, they become alienated from themselves, from others, and from their work. Capitalism thus prevented humanity from ever fulfilling its potential.

Marx believed that the capitalist system, like the other economic systems that had preceded it, contained economic, social, and psychological forces that would ultimately bring about its ruin. These forces would cause wages and profits to decline and would lead to the gradual emergence of class consciousness among the proletariat as the workers sank deeper and deeper into poverty. At the same time, some bourgeoisie would become wealthier as the means of production fell into fewer and fewer hands. These inevitable changes would lead to economic depressions, imperialism, wars, and finally to a revolution by the proletariat.

Marx: The Revolution and Afterwards

Ultimately, Marx believed, the exploited class would rebel as it had always done in the past. It was possible that the capitalist system would be so weakened by this time that violence would be unnecessary. It was much more likely, however, that the bourgeoisie would fight to retain its power and wealth, as had every other ruling class in history. Because the bourgeoisie controlled the police, the government, the law courts, and the media, violence was almost inevitable. It was not so much that the bourgeoisie as a class was selfish (although many individuals were), it was just that they were blinded by their ideology from seeing the injustices created by the capitalist system.

The revolution would be the final struggle between the exploiters and the exploited. Instead of creating a new form of class domination, as had all previous revolutions, the proletariat would establish a classless society. In fact, there would be only one class left—the workers—and class conflict would end.

Marx's writings on capitalism and its evils were very detailed and thorough, but on the post-revolutionary period he spoke only in vague and general terms. Following the revolution, Marx envisioned a brief period in which the many (the workers) rather than the few (the bourgeoisie) would control the government. This was to be a transitional period during which time both the bourgeoisie and the capitalist system would be converted to proper socialist behaviour. Under the dictatorship of the proletariat, the state would have the following characteristics:

- a centrally planned economy
- increasing economic production
- distribution of income according to work performed
- increasing economic equality
- a gradual disappearance of classes
- increasing desire to work for the good of society rather than for personal profit
- distribution of goods based on the motto "From each according to his abilities, to each according to his work"

After this transition period, Marx believed that the state would "wither away," poverty and crime would disappear, and "human history" would replace "class history."* In this final stage of pure communism, as Marx called it, not only class differences would disappear but also national differences. After a series of revolutions, capitalism would be eliminated, and all people would live in a voluntary and cooperative society. On the specific economic details of the communist state, Marx (who here concentrated on general principles rather than on specifics) was extremely vague. Society's production now would be distributed according to the motto, "From each according to his abilities, to each according to his needs." At first, individuals might tend to be greedy, but as they discovered that there would always be sufficient goods to meet their basic needs, such feelings would disappear. People would no longer go to work in order to survive and make a profit, as they did under capitalism. Instead, they would work because they wanted to work. In fact, according to Marx, human beings are dominated by the need to create and produce. Under communism, their creative abilities would be released, and the material and social accomplishments of society would prosper as never before.

In addition, there would be no need for a formal government structure because there would no longer be a ruling class and therefore no need to rule. Marx said that government would "wither away."

Lenin's Additions to Marxism

Vladimir Ilyich Ulyanov (1870–1924), better known by his revolutionary name Lenin, adapted Marx's ideas to conditions in Russia and established the first communist country. His views are often referred to as

---

* Presumably, Marx meant that the restricting powers of society would wither away, not that all government and administration would cease. In a classless, egalitarian society there would be no need to force people to do anything against their will.

"Marxist–Leninist." Unlike Marx, Lenin believed that strong leadership was necessary to bring about a revolution. Whereas Marx wrote that the role of intellectuals was merely to guide the working class, Lenin argued that a communist party should take the lead in cultivating class consciousness among the proletariat, rather than waiting for it to emerge on its own.

In 1914, Russia was the least industrialized country in Europe and there was no large, self-conscious working class. Rather than wait for the Industrial Revolution to create such a class, Lenin helped establish a small, dedicated group of professional revolutionaries to overthrow Russia's corrupt autocratic government and establish a Marxist state. Unlike the large, all-inclusive workers' party pictured by Marx, Lenin organized a small, tightly knit party of revolutionaries that sought popular support from peasants as well as from industrial workers. In this way, Lenin turned Marx's abstract doctrine into a revolutionary movement that seized control of Russia in 1917.

Lenin's other major contribution to Marxism was his belief that a country does not need to have a highly developed industrial and capitalist economy to experience a communist revolution. He proposed that a communist revolution could be used to create an industrial society. Lenin's actions once he took power are discussed in Case Studies 7 and 12.

···**The Ideal Marxist Society**

Marxist thought proceeds from an assumption that all people share certain minimum requirements—food, shelter, health, and physical and psychological security. Society should be organized to ensure that everyone's basic needs are met. At the same time, because all commodities are the result of a joint pooling of intelligence, skills, and labour, a country's resources should be shared to match the needs and interests of all the people. This does not mean strict mathematical equality, but enough for a decent standard of living, personal fulfilment, and self-respect for all. Individual differences would continue to exist, but they would no longer enable some people to amass enormous wealth while others lived in dismal poverty.

Economic production would be directed to creating a humane, democratic society in which everyone would have equal opportunity. The economy would be administered by people who would be elected periodically to collect information about everyone's needs and to decide what should be produced to meet those needs.

With private property and the profit motive abolished, and with the existence of a surplus of goods for everyone, crime and greed would not exist. Freedom from exploitation and economic insecurity would allow people to develop their creativity and cultivate their talents and interests. According to Karl Marx:

A being does not regard himself as independent unless he is his own master, and he is only his own master when he owes his existence to himself. A man who lives by the favour of another [his boss or employer] considers himself a dependent being.

The interests of the individual, many Marxists argue, are best served when the whole country benefits. Society should be based upon cooperation, not competition. Because they believe that self-centred, acquisitive people are developed and nurtured by such capitalist institutions as schools, media, law, and government, Marxists argue that the opposite type of personality can be developed by a "communist education." Individual attitudes and the economic basis of society must be altered to create mutual trust and an identification with common goals. Only then can the ideal society be achieved.

Central Planning

Since Marxism assumes a centrally planned economy, let us now turn our attention to how this economic system is supposed to operate. Because all economic decisions are planned rather than left to market forces, it may seem that this is a much simpler system. After the government (whether democratically elected or not) decides on its priorities, it appoints a committee of economic experts to ensure that these priorities are met. Making these decisions is a complex task in an industrialized economy.

As in any economic system, the law of scarcity (see Chapter 6) has to be addressed. Scarcity means that choices have to be made. The economic questions of what to produce, how to produce, and who gets what have to be answered. The difference between a market economy and a centrally planned economy rests on how these questions are answered. In solving the question of what to produce, a centrally planned economy's committee of economic experts must first decide on the overall

Table 8.1: Comparing Adam Smith's and Karl Marx's Economic Systems

	Smith	Marx
System	**Capitalism/Private enterprise**	**Marxism/Communism**
Works	*The Wealth of Nations*	*Das Kapital, The Communist Manifesto*
Ownership of means of production	Private property	Public ownership
Government's role in economy	No intervention	Government planning
Decision-making	Supply and demand	Society's decisions
Production/Profits	For individuals	Shared equitably
View of human nature	Selfish	Unselfish
Income	Based on ownership of resources	According to work or need
Classes	Yes	No

policy of the government. For example, if the government is concerned about an attack by a neighbouring country, it may decide to produce tanks rather than cars. If, on the other hand, the government is under pressure from the people to provide consumer goods, it may decide to produce cars rather than tanks. However, the government can only request that so many cars and/or tanks be produced. It cannot ask for 2 million vehicles if the resources (human, capital, and natural) can produce only 1 million vehicles. And if 1 million vehicles are produced, there will be less material (rubber, steel, and glass) for other products.

The central planning committee must also determine how these goods will be produced and what resources (human, capital, and natural) will be used. But again, economic and political forces will complicate the decision-making process. Politically, if the government decides that full employment is important, the committee might use human resources (labour) rather than machines, even if this method is less efficient. If the country lacks the needed natural resources, then more expensive imported materials will have to be purchased.

Who will receive the goods that are produced is the final decision to be made. Prices for goods may be set to achieve government goals rather than to reflect the forces of supply and demand. For example, if the goal is to pro-

Figure 8.2: Central Planning—What, How, and for Whom Goods Are Produced

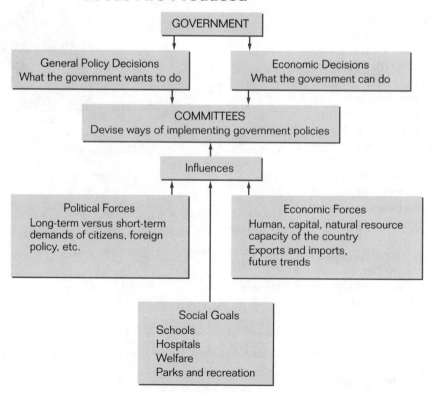

vide adequate housing for all citizens, then the government would have to set housing prices so that everyone could afford to rent or buy a house. However, by ignoring the actual housing costs, the government may create a serious economic problem. Charging a lower price for the lumber used in housing construction could hurt the economy if lumber is in limited supply. The law of scarcity should be reflected in how prices are determined, and if using up the forests creates a scarcity of lumber as well as problems of pollution from mills, then the country may eventually pay a price for having ignored economic reality.

The same principle can be applied to wages. If government policy decrees that everyone will be paid the same amount regardless of the type of work performed, this can be accomplished. However, some undesirable jobs may never be filled. The committee establishing wages may thus have to make some pay adjustments to provide an incentive for some people to take less desirable jobs. The following hypothetical case illustrates some of the strengths and weaknesses of central planning.

Corkscrews Versus Bottle Openers

You have just been appointed head planner of the third division in the western section of Ungawa. Your division is in charge of manufacturing corkscrews and bottle openers. Your first problem is to decide how many corkscrews and bottle openers should be manufactured this year. It soon becomes apparent that this decision is not nearly as simple as it seems. Your superintendent reports that last year people bought 10 000 corkscrews at $2 each and 5000 bottle openers at $1 each. But this still has not solved the problem of how many will be needed this year, especially as all the corkscrews and bottle openers were sold out in mid-October of last year.

To answer this question, you decide to ask the consumers. Your first idea to conduct a nation-wide poll is rejected by the central planning committee as too expensive, and your imaginative scheme of having every television linked to a giant computer is not yet feasible. It now appears that you will have to rely on last year's sales figures and the priorities set by the central committee. Because the government's plan is to reduce the amount of liquor consumed by the people, the planning committee has cut your supply of steel in half and has transferred 50 of your best factory workers to another sector of the economy. The best solution, it appears, is to manufacture 4000 corkscrews and 2000 bottle openers at last year's prices.

Less than a month later, trouble begins. When the government increases the price of wine in order to reduce consumption, wine drinkers switch from wine to beer. As a result, there are not enough bottle openers for sale, and most of the corkscrews are still sitting in the stores. By now, people are lining up in front of shops, and some merchants are reserving the bottle openers for their friends. As a temporary measure, you distribute ration coupons, but this creates a blackmarket ring that, it is rumoured, is selling bottle openers for $7 each.

What can you do? You are caught between the long-range goals of the planners and the immediate needs of the people. Your spouse suggests that

Focus

How would the price system "solve" this problem?

you raise the price of bottle openers and lower the price of corkscrews. Quitting your job is also an attractive option, yet this choice is not really acceptable because you remember the time when there was no planning and people were free to buy what they could afford—a time when a few individuals were rich and the rest were poor. If this was still the case, there would be no limits on the consumption of alcohol, except for its price. A country must have priorities!

There is a possibility of convincing the planning committee to give you additional steel supplies, but this means cutting back production in another area of the economy. Some workers are available in the midwestern section, but they do not have the proper skills, and your former bottle-opener workers have just learned their new jobs. Each sector of the economy is so interrelated that it is impossible to change one operation without affecting everything else.

The beer drinkers will just have to wait a couple of months until you can convert the corkscrew factories into bottle-opener plants. You can only hope that in the meantime they do not switch back to wine!

Advantages of Central Planning

Supporters of the centrally planned economy believe that this system is best designed to meet the needs of the people and the state. Whereas production in a private-enterprise economy reflects the businessperson's guess about future individual demands, the planned economy reflects government decisions about future national needs. If, for example, a country's priorities are to eliminate unemployment, pollution, poverty, and wasteful duplication of consumer products, this can be achieved by using the country's resources in a well-devised plan.

The principal assumption of the centrally planned economy is that government is capable of choosing suitable goals for the country and of selecting proper methods to implement them. The country's economic objectives and the methods employed to achieve these goals will therefore reflect the ideas of the country's leaders. Theoretically, a democratic government will design the economy to carry out the wishes of the elected representatives. The economic objectives and methods of a non-democratic country will depend on the desires of that country's leaders. Advocates of central planning maintain that the system failed in Eastern Europe and the Soviet Union because it was controlled by dictatorships that were not attuned to the people's needs and wants; combining central planning with democracy would solve this problem.

As our technology expands, particularly in computers, many of the technical problems associated with an overabundance of information can be overcome. In the past, planners failed simply because they were unable to exchange enough information to get the job done. Computers have the potential to handle the requests of millions of users so that fast, accurate, and efficient data can be used. This means that central planning, within an expanding advanced economy, is technically possible.

Disadvantages of Central Planning

Critics of the centrally planned economy believe that because such economic decisions as income distribution and the choice of employment are controlled by the government, the motivation of workers is reduced and their efficiency therefore declines. In addition, the emphasis on state planning and national goals unduly restricts individual freedoms and forces everyone to conform. The enlarged bureaucracy needed to manage the economy gives the government tremendous power over the lives of citizens. Without economic freedom, some critics believe, there can be no political liberty.

A more practical problem is the difficulty of coordinating the millions of interrelated decisions needed to carry out the central plan. Each economic decision affects other parts of the economy. In its efforts to solve one problem, a government may create another. The previous discussion of manufacturing corkscrews or bottle openers illustrates how an attempt to change one aspect of an economy through planning can have widespread economic effects. "Minor" changes can snowball, posing a serious dilemma for all planned economies.

Table 8.2: Central Planning: Advantages and Disadvantages

Advantages	Disadvantages
• Planning encourages high rates of economic growth.	• Planned economies are bureaucratic and inflexible.
• Planning helps to reduce wastage of resources.	• There is little incentive for efficient management.
• The distribution of income is more equal.	• The system stifles individual effort.
• Essential goods are produced before less essential goods.	• Freedom of choice is restricted.
• Planned economies do not suffer from unemployment and inflation related to business cycles.	• The quality, quantity, and variety of goods are limited.

The following discussion of the Cuban economy examines how one country uses central-planning techniques to answer the three basic economic questions. Case Studies 12 and 13 examine central planning in Russia and China.

The Cuban Economy, 1959–1996

As we saw in Case Study 8, Fidel Castro overthrew the repressive Batista government in 1959. Castro quickly set out to diversify the economy from its heavy reliance on sugar and to provide Cubans with the necessities of life. He divided the wealthy landowners' property among farmers; imposed price controls to ensure that everyone could afford the basic necessities of food,

Cuba at a Glance

Area: 110 860 km²

Population (1995): 10 093 000 (world's 64th-largest country)

Life Expectancy in Years (1994): Males 74, Females 79

GDP (1993): $13.7 billion (U.S.)

GDP per Capita (1993): $1959 (U.S.)

Doctors per 1000 People (1992): 1.89

Hospital Beds per 1000 People (1990): 5

Telephones per 1000 People (1992): 56

Televisions per 1000 People (1992): 203.4

Sources: John Robert Colombo, ed., *The 1996 Canadian Global Almanac* (Toronto: Macmillan, 1996); Marlita A. Reddy, ed., *Statistical Abstract of the World* (New York: Gale Research, 1994); *Statistical Abstract of the United States, 1995: The National Data Book* (Washington, DC: U.S. Department of Commerce, September 1995).

housing, and fuel; guaranteed employment to everyone; and raised the minimum wage. The new Cuban government also took control of the army, banned political parties, and established close economic and political ties with the Soviet Union.

In 1961, Castro declared to the world, "I must say with full satisfaction and full confidence, I am a Marxist–Leninist, and I shall be a Marxist–Leninist until the last day of my life" and nationalized all foreign companies, most of which were American, operating in Cuba. This naturally annoyed the United States, which sponsored an unsuccessful invasion of Cuba in 1961 (the Bay of Pigs invasion), stopped all trade with Cuba, and pressured its allies to do the same. By 1968, all private ownership in Cuba had been abolished, including corner stores and restaurants.

Castro wanted to create a society in which everyone was equal. He urged Cubans to work for the betterment of society rather than for personal gain, and awarded hard workers with such non-material rewards as pennants and honourary titles. Workers were urged to emulate the ideals of Ché Guevara (a leader of the 1959 revolution). To break down class distinctions, Castro asked professionals and urban workers to spend time as volunteer farm labourers.

Castro's centrally planned economy emphasized full employment, mass education, and free health care. He achieved these objectives through state control of prices and wages. By 1970, however, the economy was in turmoil. This was due to a combination of factors: the Soviet Union withdrew some of its economic support, sugar prices fell, and worker productivity declined. Castro had failed to convince the people of the benefits of working for society as a whole rather than for individual gain. Many workers quietly resisted by not going to work or by working slowly. In addition, the American boycott continued to cripple the Cuban economy.

Eventually, Castro retreated. Following the Soviet example (Case Study 12), Cuba introduced some features of the private enterprise system. Castro decentralized the economy, used profit incentives to encourage greater productivity, and manufactured more consumer goods, such as refrigerators and televisions. An anti-loafing law declared that work was an obligation, not the socialist right it had been earlier. Some farmers were allowed to cultivate private plots of land and sell their produce in the market. To encourage women to enter the work force, Castro granted equal gender rights in marriage, employment, earnings, and education. By law, men were to share in the housework if their wives worked outside the home. Free day-care facilities were provided, as was paid maternity leave. In 1986, however, Castro moved to cut back on his market reforms and the government reassumed greater control over the economy.

Cuba became the model for some developing socialist countries. The state bought farmers' crops at pre-set prices and either exported them or sold the goods in state stores at inexpensive prices. Rents were kept low and electricity was free. Cubans also had cradle-to-grave protection. Prior to the Cuban Revolution in 1959, Cuba's living standards were among the lowest in Latin America. Life expectancy was 59, pupil/teacher ratio in primary schools was one teacher for every 36 students, there was one doctor for every 1000 Cubans, one hospital bed for every 237 people, and for every 1000 births 32 children died in infancy. Thirty years later, the corresponding figures were life expectancy 76, one teacher per 12 students, one doctor per 300 people, one hospital bed per 136 Cubans, and 10 infant deaths per 1000 births.

Economic Problems

The collapse of Communist Eastern Europe and the Soviet Union between 1989 and 1991 devastated the Cuban economy. Over 80 percent of Cuba's trade had been with the Communist bloc. In return for sugar exports, Cuba purchased food, oil and gas, and manufactured goods. The Cuban economy contracted by 50 percent over the following four years, and imports fell by 25 percent.

The United States took this opportunity to put further pressure on Cuba's economy, hoping to topple Castro. For decades the American government had forbidden its citizens to visit or invest in Cuba. In 1990, the American anti-Castro lobby pushed through a bill to prevent American overseas companies from trading with Cuba. President Clinton successfully took advantage of Russia's need for foreign aid to pressure Russia to stop oil sales to Cuba. In 1994, Clinton stopped Cubans living in the United States from sending money home to Cuba. The following year, in an attempt to stop foreign investment in Cuba, the United States moved to punish foreign companies that used property Castro had taken from American businesses 30 years earlier.

Without Soviet support, and squeezed by the United States, Cuba experienced severe food shortages. Fuel, water, soap, gas, and medicine became scarce. Thousands of people fled the country for Florida on flimsy homemade rafts. Line-ups for food increased, and the average shopper spent 15 hours a week in food lines. According to Cuban historian Juan Antonio Blanco, the shortages in 1993 meant

hardship for every single Cuban. The food supply of the population has been dramatically affected because much of our food and animal feed was imported from the Eastern Bloc. The average Cuban today is getting around one-third of the consumer goods—food, clothing, etc.—that he or she received in 1989, although the social services like health care remain in place.[2]

The economic collapse forced Castro to concede some of his socialist principles. He denationalized some industries, encouraged foreign investment (under the slogan "Capital yes, capitalism no"), legalized possession of foreign currency, allowed self-employment, permitted farmers to sell their produce on the open market, and allowed government firms to lay off work-

F o c u s

How can Cuba's improved living standards be attributed to its planned economy?

ers. Although the state still provided the people with basic necessities, other prices were allowed to be determined by supply and demand, which Castro declared was "one of the elements of capitalism reality has obliged us to introduce for survival, even though we don't like it."

Despite American opposition, 25 countries signed economic deals with Cuba in 1995 alone, including Canada's mining giant Sherritt International, one of the largest single investors in Cuba. The opening of Cuba's tourist market brought in additional foreign money. In 1995, for example, $1.4 billion tourist dollars were spent in Cuba, and 54 planes a week flew between Canada and Cuba. Partly as a result of these reforms, the Cuban economy began to improve in 1995. Tourism, however, was not without its drawbacks, including increased prostitution, crime, black marketeering, and resentment on the part of Cubans, who were forbidden to use some tourist facilities.

In 1996, the American government tightened the screws on Cuba once again. The Helms-Burton Libertad law denied admission to the United States to top executives and their families of companies that used or invested in previously owned American properties confiscated by Cuba's communist government. The first executives to be banned from the United States were members of a Mexican telecommunications firm and Canada's Sherritt International Corporation. Although Canada, Mexico, the European Union, and the United Nations General Assembly denounced the Helms-Burton act as a violation of international law, Cuba's economy remained under attack from the United States.

How does this cartoon depict the effect on Canada of U.S. policy on Cuba?

Cuban Ideology: Castroism

To save Cuba's "socialist soul from the seductions of capitalism," Castro studied Russian, Chinese, and Eastern European market reforms, none of which particularly pleased him. He now says that he wants "socialism with Cuban characteristics." In 1993, Cuban historian Juan Blanco explained Castro's economic philosophy as follows:

What is the essence of socialism that we want to save? I believe that it is not a simple question of a planned vs. an unplanned economy, because there is a lot of planning in the West. ... The Japanese do more and better planning than the Russians or the Poles or the Czechs ever did. In the United States every major corporation has a strategic plan.

We do, however, have a different concept of the market. We don't believe blindly in the laws of supply and demand, we don't believe that market forces should determine if you have a right to have a roof over your head, if you have a right to see a doctor, if you have a right to a university education. There are things we believe should never be submitted to market forces. ...

The core of socialism is the question of how wealth is distributed, so we can be flexible in other areas, but we must keep the redistribution according to socialist principles.[3]

Communism and Change

Today, communism is enduring a great deal of turmoil. Until the late 1980s, approximately one-third of the world's population lived under a form of communist government. Communist countries in Eastern Europe, which seemed unshakable only a few years ago, have gone through major political and economic changes. Poland, the Czech Republic, and Hungary have moved toward forms of free enterprise. The former Soviet Union has moved away from the highly centralized economic system of Lenin, Stalin, and Khrushchev. Even in the former Soviet countries that have chosen reformed communist regimes, such as Lithuania, Bulgaria, and Romania, the economies are somewhat free, and non-communist political organizations are permitted. In China, vast regions have been opened up for Western-style capitalist development (see Case Study 13).

If it seems that central planning has not stood the test of time, it is important to note that many of the theories and ideas of Karl Marx have not been practised in any of the world's communist countries. Although it is impossible to fully understand contemporary communism without studying the central ideas developed by Marx, each communist state has interpreted his writings to suit its own specific economic, political, social, cultural, and military needs. The communism of the former Soviet Union can therefore be understood only by examining the ideas of Lenin, Stalin, Gorbachev, and Yeltsin.

It is thus inappropriate to speak of only one communist or Marxist ideology. There are many communist ideologies: Marxist–Leninist, Marxist–Leninist–Stalinist, Marxist–Leninist–Maoist, and so on. Toward the end of his life, when there were already many different groups calling themselves Marxists, Karl Marx wrote: "Of one thing I am certain; I am no Marxist." A good knowledge of Marx's ideas, however, is crucial to understanding the major economic and political issues of the twentieth century.

BIOGRAPHY

BEATRICE WEBB, 1858–1943

Born the eighth daughter in a wealthy and privileged British family, Beatrice Webb began as a young woman to question both her role and her society. "I feel like a caged animal, bound up by the luxury, comfort and respectability of my position," she wrote in her diary in 1883. She eventually rejected marriage to a wealthy and prominent politician, choosing instead to devote her life to social and economic reform.

As a social reformer and a historian, Webb had a profound impact on the twentieth century. Her marriage to fellow socialist Sidney Webb in 1892 was followed by their investigations into the roots of poverty in industrial Britain, and then into other social and economic issues. Their historical and social research resulted in an enormous literary ouput that continued throughout their lives.

The Webbs' biggest contribution was in the area of political action. Along with George Bernard Shaw, they played a crucial role in establishing the Fabian Society, with its emphasis on socialism through gradual democratic reform. Later they poured their efforts into supporting the British Labour Party.

Rather than exercising political power themselves, the Webbs attempted to initiate social change and to build up institutions that would have a long-term impact. They helped to found the London School of Economics and the *New Statesman* newspaper, and played a central role in promoting state-sponsored education and social security.

Beatrice Webb's life was not without controversy or problems. Her support for Communist Russia in the 1930s alienated some of her supporters, given her long commitment to democratic and evolutionary practices. She struggled with anorexia and depression, "but the world saw only her outwardly confident beauty, never her private agonies."[4]

George Bernard Shaw commented on the equality and completeness of the Webbs' marriage and partnership, stating that no one could completely separate their contributions or judge which was the more dominant or gifted partner. He concluded that Beatrice was "a great citizen, a great civilizer, and a great investigator."[5] A biographer described Beatrice as having "an epic life in which she proved how much can be accomplished by unwavering will."[6]

Webb's views are illustrated in the following excerpt from her work, *A Constitution for the Socialist Commonwealth of Great Britain:*

It is inconceivable that any intelligent Democracy should continue to permit the capitalist manufacturer, merely in order to increase his profits, wantonly to defile what is not his but our atmosphere with unnecessary and really wasteful smoke from his factory chimneys; to pollute the crystal streams that are the property of all of us by the waste products of his mills and dye-works; to annihilate the irreplaceable beauty of valleys and mountain slopes by his quarries and scrap-heaps; to leave a whole countryside scarred and ruined by the wreckage which he fails to remove when one of his profit-seeking enterprises has exhausted its profitableness, or becomes bankrupt. In so far as any industry is left to capitalist profit-making, the community must at least see to it that the greed for private gain is not allowed to rob the citizens of their common heritage in a land of health and beauty.[7]

1 How are Webb's views similar to and different from those of some of the early socialists?

2 Why would her biographer have described Webb as having had "an epic life"?

Underlying and Emerging Issues

Give the reasoning and evidence that might be used to support different views or conclusions on the following issues:

1 To what extent are problems in working and living conditions the result of industrialization or capitalism?

2 To what degree should governments regulate working conditions?

3 To what extent should governments be involved in public ownership?

4 Should the most important means of production be owned collectively?

5 To what extent do people have a natural tendency toward competition or cooperation?

6 To what extent can society foster values of cooperation and common goals through education?

7 Can societies bring out the best in people by improving their environment?

8 Are societies generally based on the exploitation of poorer groups by wealthier groups?

9 Does capitalism exploit and degrade workers?

10 Does capitalism create an unfair advantage for those who own the means of production?

11 To what extent are our governments, laws, and institutions dominated by wealthy people?

12 To what degree does "equality of opportunity" exist in our society?

13 Is our present society in need of radical change?

14 How effective are peaceful methods in bringing about meaningful change?

15 Does central planning provide a better way to meet future needs and national economic goals?

16 Does central planning lead to inefficiency?

17 To what extent might advances in information technology benefit central planning?

18 Is economic freedom necessary for political freedom?

19 How important is individual freedom as compared to meeting the needs of all people?

Focussing Knowledge

In your notes, clearly identify or define and explain the importance or significance of each of the following:

centrally planned economy	*class struggle*
Utopian Socialists	*proletariat*
bourgeoisie	*Marxist–Leninist*
public ownership	*central planning*
Communist Manifesto	*Louis Blanc*
Das Kapital	*Karl Marx*
Marxism	*Vladimir Lenin*
means of production	

Reviewing and Organizing Knowledge

1 How did early capitalism and industrialization contribute to the rise of communism?

2 What were the basic beliefs of Utopian Socialists?

3 Describe the main elements of Marx's views on

a. society and history;

b. capitalist society;

c. the Revolution and afterwards.

4 How did Lenin change Marxism?

5 In general, what are the key elements of an "ideal Marxist state"?

6 Describe how central planning answers the three basic economic questions.

7 Make a thorough list of

a. advantages/arguments in favour of central planning;

b. disadvantages/arguments against central planning.

8 a. What were the main elements of the economic system in Castro's Cuba?

b. What factors led to problems in Cuba's economy?

c. How did Castro change the economy in response to the problems?

9 What accounts for the variety of Marxist ideologies?

Applying and Extending Knowledge

1 Choose a Utopian Socialist (such as Owen, Fourier, St. Simon, or Blanc) to research, and write a critical analysis of that person's views.

2 Research the society of Peru under the Incas. To what extent were the various aspects of socialism reflected in Inca society?

3 Review the chart comparing the ideas of Adam Smith and Karl Marx (on page 323). Choose the three areas in which their views are most opposed, and describe the basis for their differences in terms of their assumptions about people and society.

4 Write a dialogue between Smith and Marx in which they react to the major developments of the late twentieth century.

5 Select articles from the newspaper that reflect aspects of central planning in Canada. Explain how the articles illustrate these elements.

6 Research the collapse of communism in Eastern Europe from 1989 to 1991. To what extent were the causes economic or political?

7 Examine Canada's reaction since 1960 to U.S. foreign policy regarding Cuba. Write an essay in which you take a stand on Canada's actions and policies in this matter.

8 Find newspaper articles that illustrate as many of the Underlying and Emerging Issues on page 333 as possible. Explain how the articles illustrate the issues.

9 Choose one of the Underlying and Emerging Issues, and list all the evidence and arguments on each side. Take a position, and explain why you concluded that the arguments and evidence supporting one view were stronger.

Economic Planning
in the USSR

Learning Outcomes

After reading this case study, you should be able to:

- describe how Lenin and Stalin sought to improve the Soviet economy

- compare the Soviet and Canadian economic systems

- evaluate the merits of central planning as practised in the USSR

- discuss Gorbachev's economic reforms

- hypothesize future directions of the Russian economy

*R*EMEMBER THE THREE BASIC ECONOMIC QUESTIONS? This case study examines how the Soviet Union managed those questions before and after General Secretary Gorbachev's assumption of power, and surveys the Russian economy after the fall of communism. Lenin's New Economic Policy and Stalin's First Five-Year Plan are examined, followed by an analysis of the merits and disadvantages of the Soviet economic system. The drastic decline in the economy that led to Gorbachev's policies of *glasnost* and *perestroika* and a description of the state of the post-Gorbachev and post-Soviet economy, and Russia's choices and prospects for the future, are considered.

Russia at a Glance

Area: 17 075 200 km² (world's largest country)

Population (1995): 149 909 000 (world's 6th-largest country)

Life Expectancy in Years (1994): Males 64, Females 74

GDP (1993): $775.4 billion (U.S.)

GDP per Capita (1993): $5190 (U.S.)

Doctors per 1000 People (1994): 4.69

Hospital Beds per 1000 People (1994): 13.8

Health Expenditures as Percentage of GDP (1990): 3.0

Telephones per 1000 People (1994): 160

Sources: John Robert Colombs, ed., *The 1996 Canadian Global Almanac* (Toronto: Macmillan, 1996); Marlita A. Reddy, ed., *Statistical Abstract of the World* (New York: Gale Research, 1994); *Statistical Abstract of the United States, 1995: The National Data Book* (Washington, DC: U.S. Department of Commerce, September 1995).

In a centrally planned economy there is no doubt about who makes decisions. The government, whether democratic or non-democratic, determines its most important goals for the future needs of the state and orders its economic planners to achieve them. Every aspect of the economy is regulated to carry out the government's overall objectives.

Article 2 of the Soviet Constitution stated proudly that "The economic life of the USSR is determined and directed by the state economic plan." Prior to the Gorbachev regime, economic competition, as we know it in Canada, did not exist in the Soviet Union. The state owned virtually all the land; controlled transportation, finance, industrial production, and international trade; and was responsible for over 90 percent of the country's retail stores. Although Soviet citizens owned as many clothes, televisions, automobiles, and other consumer items as they could afford, they could not open their own stores beyond a small retail level, own farms, or purchase stock (part ownership) in business enterprises. The Soviet economic system was a gigantic government monopoly that embraced the entire country.

The Economy After the 1917 Revolution

Following the success of the Communist Revolution in Russia, Lenin attempted to apply many of Marx's economic principles to the Soviet Union. He nationalized private property, factories, natural resources, and land. He gave the workers control over the factories, and he asked the peasants to give their surplus food to the workers.

These changes, which Lenin termed War Communism because they occurred during a period of civil war, failed to accomplish their purpose. Many peasants wanted their own land and refused to surrender their excess grain when they were offered little in return. When the government seized their grain, the peasants merely planted fewer crops, which resulted in a severe famine. In the cities, the workers were not educated or trained to manage the factories, and industrial production declined drastically.

The first major communist experiment in history seemed headed for disaster. Lenin thus devised a **New Economic Policy (NEP)** in 1921 to stimulate industrial and agricultural production. The state retained control over important industries, finance, transportation, and natural resources, but permitted small-scale private enterprises and allowed peasants to sell their crops to consumers. This new policy, which Lenin considered a temporary retreat, was a combination of private enterprise and state socialism. Lenin said it was like taking "one step back to take two steps forward."

New Economic Policy (NEP): an economic policy of partial return to private enterprise devised by Lenin in 1922 to stimulate industrial and agricultural production in the Soviet Union.

The Rise of Stalin

After Lenin's death in 1924, a split developed within the Communist Party between those who believed that the USSR should industrialize slowly and those who wanted to quicken the pace of industrialization and socialism. Leon Trotsky condemned the NEP as capitalist and called for a return to communist economic principles. In addition, he wanted to use the Soviet Union's resources to promote a communist revolution in Europe. Joseph Stalin believed the opposite. He wanted to strengthen the USSR before becoming involved in foreign affairs. Feeling threatened on all sides by capitalist countries, Stalin insisted on building socialism in his country first. He thus supported the NEP as a temporary measure. Stalin finally won this internal battle in 1928, forcing Trotsky into exile and defeating others who disagreed with him. As the unchallenged leader of the USSR, Stalin's next step was to improve the country's backward economy.

kulaks: prosperous peasant farmers who, under Stalin's regime, refused to sell their surplus grain at the government-set low prices.

At this time, the Soviet Union had approximately 25 million farms. Of these, 5 to 8 million peasant families were so poor that they tilled their land with wooden ploughs and had to rent farm implements and animals from rich farmers. These prosperous farmers (**kulaks**) numbered approximately 1 million. The state relied on *kulaks* to supply the cities with food, but they refused to deliver their surplus grain because of the low prices set for farm produce. Moreover, the government had very little money to import the machinery needed to industrialize farming, and Western countries refused to give the USSR financial help. The Soviet Union needed an agricultural surplus to pay for imported goods and to feed industrial workers. But most of the farms were so small (averaging 2.02 ha per family) or so poor that they were able to produce enough only for themselves.

The *kulaks* were the only people who could provide the necessary surplus for export, but they wanted higher prices for their produce and cheaper manufactured goods. However, Soviet industries were just getting started and were unable to manufacture a wide variety of inexpensive products. If the struggling country was to feed its workers and industrialize rapidly, more reliable methods of agricultural and factory production had to be adopted.

The First Five-Year Plan

In 1928, Stalin declared that the rate of industrialization had to be increased at all costs. This, he believed, would free the people from the bonds of poverty and would enable the Soviet Union to defend itself against Western European countries in a war that Stalin considered inevitable. Industrialization, he argued, was essential for socialism and for the country's preservation.

Five-Year Plan: an economic plan implemented by Stalin in 1928 to expand and improve industrialization to make the USSR self-sufficient.

The State Planning Commission prepared a **Five-Year Plan** to implement Stalin's policy. The fundamental aims of the plan were to expand the country's heavy industry sector so that it could provide industrial machinery, transportation facilities, and military weapons; to introduce modern technology; to eliminate privately owned farms and create state and co-operative farms in their place; to eliminate private enterprise; and to make the USSR self-sufficient.

Impact of the First Five-Year Plan

The plan was declared completed after only four years and three months, and a second Five-Year Plan was begun to continue the Soviet Union's drive toward industrialization. By the end of the 1930s, a firm industrial base had been created and the USSR ranked fourth in the world in terms of industrial output. Within four years, the number of industrial workers had risen from 3 to 6 million. By 1934, the Soviet Union was producing more pig iron and steel than Great Britain. During the first Five-Year Plan the production of oil doubled, electric power increased by 550 percent, machinery production grew by 400 percent, and such new industries as synthetic rubber, plastics, and aviation were established. The percentage of farmers on state and cooperative farms grew from 1.7 percent in 1928 to 61.5 percent in 1932, and to 93.5 percent at the end of 1938.

This tremendous industrial growth was achieved with great sacrifices. The concentration on steel, tractors, railways, and hydro-electricity meant that consumer needs were largely ignored. The production of shoes, clothing, and housing, for example, was left for a later date. Even food had to be rationed. Present shortages of consumer goods were justified on the grounds of future gains.

Nothing appeared to matter to Stalin as long as his plan succeeded. As a result, factory labourers were cruelly overworked, safety precautions were ignored, and housing conditions were miserable. Those who suggested caution and recommended more humane conditions were branded spies or saboteurs and were exiled or imprisoned. Factory managers feared for their lives if they failed to fulfil their production quotas. Private businesspeople were deprived of their civil rights, including housing, food, and medical services.

Most of the 3 million new industrial workers were created by forcing the peasants off their farms and into the cities. They were not prepared for this new way of life and frequently vented their frustrations by ruining machinery, working slowly, or breaking the law. To produce better workers and more social uniformity, Stalin relied on coercion and persuasion. Newspapers, radio, films, books, and posters publicized Stalin's goals. They praised the "heroes of the production front," exposed the poor work habits of "laggards," and told the people that it was their patriotic duty to work hard. Factory schools were created to teach good work habits and to improve skills. Stalin ordered the schools to emphasize such Communist "virtues" as devotion to hard work, conformity, sobriety, nationalism, and the infallibility of the country's leaders. Teachers were expected to indoctrinate their students, spread official information, and create efficient workers and managers. Those who refused to do so were dismissed.

Labourers who worked slowly or produced goods of low quality were punished—often brutally. More positive incentives included better food and accommodation and longer vacations. Such measures, the Communist Party believed, were essential in a country where the labour force was not used to industrial conditions. For many workers, however, the 1930s were a period of hardship and bitter experience.

JOSEPH (STALIN) DZHUGASHVILI, 1879–1953
Central Planning

Stalin's mother hoped that her favourite son would become a priest and achieve the economic security the family had never known. When Stalin was expelled from the seminary for reading forbidden literature, he abandoned Christianity for Marxism. Like many other revolutionaries, Stalin, which means "man of steel," suffered frequent imprisonment, and when the spring 1917 Russian Revolution began he was in prison in Siberia.

In the following 1931 speech to industrial managers, Stalin described his motives for introducing central planning.

Crises, unemployment, waste, poverty among the masses—such are the incurable diseases of capitalism. Our system does not suffer from these diseases because power is in our hands, in the hands of the working class; because we are conducting a planned economy, systematically accumulating resources and properly distributing them among the different branches of the national economy. ...

The superiority of our system lies in that we have no crises of over-production, we have not and never will have millions of unemployed, we have no anarchy in production; for we are conducting a planned economy. ...

It is sometimes asked whether it is not possible to slow down the tempo a bit, to put a check on the movement. No, comrades, it is not possible! The tempo must not be reduced! On the contrary, we must increase it as much as is within our powers and possibilities. This is dictated to us by our obligations to the workers and peasants of the USSR. This is dictated to us by our obligations to the working class of the whole world.

To slacken the tempo would mean falling behind. And those who fall behind get beaten. But we do not want to be beaten. No, we refuse to be beaten! One feature of the history of old Russia was the continual beatings she suffered from falling behind, for her backwardness. She was beaten by the Mongol Khans. She was beaten by the Turkish beys. She was beaten by the Swedish feudal lords. She was beaten by the Polish and Lithuanian gentry. She was beaten by the British and French capitalists. She was beaten by the Japanese barons. All beat her—for her backwardness: for military backwardness, for cultural backwardness, for political backwardness, for industrial backwardness, for agricultural backwardness. ... They beat her, saying: "You are poor and impotent," so you can be beaten and plundered with impunity.

Such is the law of the exploiters— to beat the backward and the weak. It is the jungle law of capitalism. You are backward, you are weak—therefore you are wrong; hence, you can be beaten and enslaved. You are mighty—therefore you are right; hence, we must be wary of you.

That is why we must no longer lag behind.[1]

Focus

Why does Stalin think communism is superior to capitalism?

What methods does Stalin use to encourage the managers to work harder?

Collective and State Farms

Industrialization was to have been financed by surplus produce from the farms. However, most peasants were too poor to produce a grain surplus, and the prosperous *kulaks* were unwilling to sell their crops for the low prices set by the state. Stalin's solution was to create large-scale **collective farms** where peasants would work together under state direction. Collective farms were created by combining a number of peasants' holdings into one large farm. The peasants were allowed to keep their homes, but all land, animals, and machinery were owned collectively by the group. An elected managerial board made all the important farming decisions about what to grow, what machinery to use, and how much money to put aside for future use. The remaining income was divided among the farmers in proportion to their property and to the work they had performed. Larger farms could afford to use modern machinery, which would help increase agricultural production. The mechanization of farming techniques would also release thousands of peasants to work in the newly developing industries in the cities. Collectivization would remove the well-to-do *kulaks*, whom Stalin viewed as a threat to the principles of communism. Finally, the collective farms had an important military objective: in times of war, they would provide the bases for organized resistance. Stalin also created **state farms** to test new agricultural methods. These farms were financed and operated by the government, which hired workers on a wage basis and kept the produce for state use.

At first, collectivization was voluntary. Lower taxes, easier access to government loans, and the use of tractors and modern machinery were offered to encourage the peasants to join the collectives. Because only the poorer peasants joined, Stalin concluded that the richer farmers would have to be forced into entering the state farms. In 1930, he began an all-out offensive against the *kulaks*. "We must smash the *kulaks*, eliminate them as a class," he proclaimed. "We must strike at the *kulaks* so hard as to prevent them from rising to their feet again."

Peasant was set against peasant. Committees of poor peasants were formed to denounce hoarders, and the government encouraged them to take the *kulaks'* machinery and livestock for the benefit of the collective farms. Soldiers went into the countryside to seize hidden supplies of grain. Villages that resisted were surrounded by soldiers carrying machine guns. The *kulaks* were forced to surrender. Some had the shoes taken from their feet, and their clothing—including warm underwear—confiscated. Men were sent to prison without any evidence that they had committed a crime. Some of the middle-income and poor peasants lost their belongings. Many rich farmers divorced their wives so that the women and children would be spared.

Rather than allow their property to fall into the hands of the state, many *kulaks* destroyed their machinery, burned their crops, and killed their cattle. By 1931, one-third of the cattle, one-half of the sheep and goats, and one-quarter of the horses in the USSR had been slaughtered. Agricultural production was lower in 1933 than it had been in 1928. Famine stalked the land in 1931 and 1932.

collective farms: large-scale, government-managed farms in the USSR, created by combining smaller peasants' holdings. The peasants were allowed to live on the farms and worked together to increase agricultural production.

state farms: government-owned mechanized farms created by Stalin to test new agricultural methods.

The number of deaths reached unimaginable proportions—estimates vary between 5 and 10 million. Tens of thousands of *kulaks* were deported to unpopulated regions in Siberia, thrown into prison, or sent to work camps. The Russian countryside glowed red as the flames of burning peasant huts lit the sky. The ground was darkened with the blood of slaughtered cattle. Much of the agricultural produce was seized by the government and used to pay for needed industrial machinery. The Russian people were forced to live on short rations while millions of tonnes of grain were exported to other countries.

Out of this chaos and destruction the collective farm system emerged. Huge state farms, averaging about 40 000 to 80 000 ha, were established on previously unused land. Thousands of tractors and combines were put into operation. Some 12 million ha of land were organized into state farms and, by 1937, over 90 percent of these farms were collectivized. The harvests of 1933, 1934, and 1935 were the largest in Russian history. For the moment, Soviet agriculture had been made more efficient—but at a tremendous cost.

World War II seemed to demonstrate the wisdom of Stalin's policy of forced industrialization. Once the USSR had recovered from the impact of the German invasion in June 1941, its new-found economic strength provided the weapons needed to defeat Hitler. The Soviet Union entered the postwar era with a prestige unimaginable in 1928. The next section examines how the modern world's first centrally planned economy worked.

Prices and Their Uses

Although Soviet consumers were free to buy whatever goods they could afford, demand only partly influenced supply. The Soviet government used its control over prices to help accomplish its goals. It set low prices on schoolbooks to promote education and on children's clothes to encourage large families. High prices were used to control the consumption of less socially desirable items, such as vodka.

Another objective was to reduce the gap between income levels. To do this, the government set low prices on such items as basic foods and clothing, which constituted a large proportion of the salaries of the lower-income groups, and fixed higher prices on luxury foods and cars that were more often purchased by people in the higher-income groups. In this way, the Communist Party influenced the buying practices of the citizens, based upon what it thought was in the best interests of the country. Soviet leaders were also discouraged from increasing the price of food and clothing because of the possibility that the people would go on strike.

Planning Stages Prior to 1985

The Soviet economy was controlled by an elaborate structure of economic plans. Long-term plans established general targets for up to 20 years in the future. Five- to seven-year plans set more specific goals. Annual, quarterly, and monthly plans were the most detailed. These plans underwent constant revision to provide for unforeseen circumstances. The purpose of the long-range plans was to point planners in the proper direction. They set down broad objectives for the economy by weighing social, political, international, military, and scientific goals. Every plan ranked its priorities from most to least important. This ranking system was determined by the Communist Party.

There were four stages to each plan. For the first step, planners used past performance to calculate how much of the country's physical and human resources would be needed to fulfil the requirements of the most important targets. Moving on to less important targets, they went down the list of priorities until all resources were exhausted. The **Gosplan** (the central planning agency) then informed the regional ministries, which were in charge of specific sectors of the economy, of which commodities were needed and in what amounts. Another planning body called the **Gossnab** determined how commodities were distributed. There were also separate agencies for determining prices, labour matters, technology, and foreign trade. In addition, each region and town had its own planning bodies.

In the second stage, the regional ministries and the larger firms determined whether they could meet these targets, drew up a list of all the resources (workers, money, equipment, natural resources) they required to fulfil these goals, and reported back to the Gosplan. In the third stage, the Gosplan coordinated all of these demands. Heads of the various ministries and large firms met with the Gosplan and from these negotiations, which often became quite heated, a detailed national economic plan emerged. In the final stages, each firm was issued orders detailing production quotas.

Gosplan: the central planning agency of the USSR that was responsible for informing regional ministries about which products were needed and in what quantities.

Gossnab: the planning body responsible for determining how commodities were to be distributed in the USSR.

Case Figure 12.1: Organization Chart of the Command Economy (1973–1991)

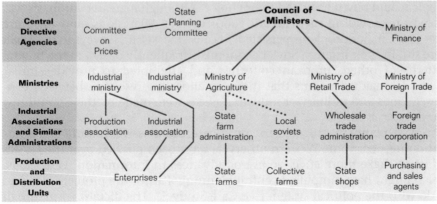

— Line of subordination in state sector
— Coordination and planning

•••• No legal subordination in collective sector but Ministry of Agriculture imposed procurement quotas and local authorities (soviets) had certain supervisory powers.

Source: Archie Brown, et al., *The Cambridge Encyclopedia of Russia and the Former Soviet Union* (NY, NY: Cambridge University Press, 1994), p. 422. Reprinted by permission.

Merits and Drawbacks of Central Planning

The Soviet economy never attained a perfect centrally planned economic system. Approximately 10 percent of the small retail stores were privately owned. More important were the tiny plots of land that farmers were allowed to do with as they pleased. Although these plots constituted less than 3 percent of the total arable land in the USSR, they produced approximately 30 percent of the country's food supply. In some items the proportion reached almost 90 percent.

The major advantage of central planning was that it allowed the government, rather than the market system of supply and demand, to determine which goods the country needed and who would receive these goods. If these decisions were poor, it was the fault of the political system, not of the economic system. It also allowed for the provision of more equality in distribution, since the state controlled distribution.

There were also disadvantages to central planning. When the planners made a bad decision, the effect could be disastrous because the plan was imposed on a national scale. Highly centralized plans were slow to respond to unforeseen changes. Because there was no effective built-in method of discovering consumer desires, huge inventories of unwanted goods often remained for years in warehouses or on store shelves. At the same time, shortages of desired consumer goods were a constant problem. Finally, when controls are highly centralized, individual initiative and innovation are frequently retarded. The Soviet Union, for example, imported foreign technology and established an underground smuggling network to acquire such items as computer microchips. It is partly because of this absence of initiative that the Soviet Union adopted a system of incentives (discussed in the next section).

In practice, planners found it difficult to determine exactly what items people would buy if they had their choice. Although a greater emphasis was placed on providing such luxury goods as cars, televisions, and furniture after 1960, major problems persisted. Because marketing surveys in the USSR were still in their infancy, Soviet economists frequently observed the buying patterns of other European countries and attempted to provide similar goods. All major decisions that involved allocating resources between consumer goods and military or industrial needs were made by the Communist Party.

Soviet planners struggled to coordinate the massive amounts of information needed. Some Western observers have been puzzled over the USSR's failure to make more effective use of advances in information technology, which might have simplified central planning. Part of the problem also had to do with the political system (see Case Study 7). The dictatorial nature of the regime meant that the economic system was also dominated by a political elite, which was not representative of the population, not in touch with their needs, and wished to protect its privileged position.

Use of Incentives Prior to 1985

The desire for profits is the major motivating force in a capitalist economy. Companies spend millions of dollars on research and development to produce products that will outsell those of their competitors. Individuals work hard to keep their jobs and earn higher salaries. Generally, the greater the production, the greater the profits. One of the most frequently heard complaints made by capitalists about government-operated industries is that there is no incentive for the employees to work hard or to ensure that the industry will operate efficiently.

Since almost all enterprises in the USSR were government-owned and -operated, almost everyone was a public employee. Soviet firms strove, above all, to fulfil the directives of the Gosplan. Profits, which went to the government, were incidental. The manager's goal was to fulfil the government's plans, not to adopt the best production methods. To solve this problem, the Soviet Union employed a wide variety of incentive plans.

Increased agricultural production from the collective farms was encouraged in two ways. On collective farms, the workers' incentive was sharing the profits. At the end of the year, each farm distributed its profits among the farmers according to their work record. Each farmer's contribution was determined by assigning a money value to every task, based on the difficulty of that task and the time needed to accomplish it. On state farms, the workers were paid wages and enjoyed few material incentives. The most frequently cited examples of state farm inefficiency concerned the case of tractor drivers. They were paid per hectare ploughed and received bonuses for fuel savings and avoiding mechanical breakdowns. Clever drivers dug many shallow furrows and collected large bonuses. This angered fellow workers, as the farm produced poor harvests in the following years and thus forfeited bonuses. Rural workers found it demoralizing that some people were rewarded for being tricky and performing shabby work, whereas the rest merely collected their guaranteed monthly salaries. Collective and state farms thus became symbols of economic stagnation and mismanagement.

Piece rates and bonuses were used to encourage greater efforts from factory workers. When the labourers' output reached a specific level, they received a bonus. Higher wages were given for dangerous and unattractive work to encourage people to take these jobs. Salaries were also based on expertise—the more skill involved, the higher the rewards. As a further incentive, when an enterprise fulfilled the government's plan, it received a share of the profits for its enterprise fund. Firms expecting to show a loss for the year received money for reducing the expected loss. Production in excess of the government's plan increased the enterprise fund, whereas underproduction decreased the size of the fund. The enterprise fund was used to pay annual bonuses to the workers and managers, to help needy employees, to improve working conditions, and to provide better housing.

Managers received bonuses for fulfilling the production goals set by the Gosplan. Other bonuses were given for introducing new technology and for producing consumer goods out of waste materials. Successful managers received better housing, theatre tickets, special vacations, and the use of cars, and were allowed to shop in prestigious stores that contained a wide variety of goods. Useful technological inventions were awarded with money, media coverage, and honours such as the Badge of Honour, the Order of Lenin, or a Hero of Socialist Labour.

As the following examples reveal, these measures were often not very successful. In the early 1980s, a Moscow newspaper reported that a factory manager in Ukraine had been reprimanded for having produced 13 000 pairs of sunglasses so dark that the viewer could look straight at the sun without seeing any light. Elsewhere, a fully loaded freight train left Moscow carrying concrete roof beams to construction sites in Leningrad; it passed a train with a similar cargo on its way to building sites in Moscow. One transportation firm moved carloads of water back and forth on the railway tracks to meet its quota of having moved a specific volume of water for the year.

A Stagnant Economy

The makers of the first Five-Year Plan would not have dreamed that 50 years later the Soviet economy would suffer from such problems. In theory, communism is supposedly better, more fair, and more productive than capitalism. It ignores the profit motive and emphasizes the need for social utility of goods and services. But centralization undermined economic efficiency in the USSR, and the system became so unwieldy that central planners in Moscow had difficulty keeping track of the complex operations of individual factories. The political system failed to ensure that the economic system responded properly.

In the early 1980s, the economy stagnated. The aging political leadership seemed incapable of solving agricultural mismanagement, stopping high-level corruption, and inspiring the demoralized work force. Cynicism, sloppiness, and shabby performance flourished. Ordinary citizens became unhappy with standing in endless lines for food and consumer goods while senior party members received luxury goods at discount prices in special stores.

The queue became a common feature of Soviet life. Citizens spent several hours each day lining up in stores. This was because the Soviet economy operated as a seller's market rather than as a buyer's market. Gosplan selected the consumer goods that would be produced, with little or no input from consumers. Thus, production became a hit-and-miss affair. Unpopular or defective goods lay unsold, while popular items were quickly snapped up. One queue for rugs lasted two days and totalled over 10 000 people! Not surprisingly, these problems of supply spawned an underground black market economy that dealt in blue jeans, nylons, fertilizers, and services such as plumbing and legal aid.

Several complicated factors account for the decline in the Soviet economy. First and foremost was the conservatism of the Soviet leaders. A country that is so vast in size, so varied in terrain and climate, and so culturally diverse needs innovation and imagination to prosper. Soviet leaders feared—correctly it now appears—that the smallest crack in the system would be fatal. Even minor innovations or variations from the ideological norms were rarely tolerated.

What is the message of this cartoon?

The economic situation was made worse by international factors. The United States under President Ronald Reagan launched a massive increase in military spending. When the Soviet Union increased its military expenditures in turn, its economy was put under serious strain. In addition, the USSR's war in Afghanistan that began in 1979 drained the country's resources and treasury.

Following General Secretary Leonid Brezhnev's death in 1982, Yuri Andropov attempted some reforms and tightened central control. He tried to scare workers and managers into improving their job performance. For example, he had loafers, drunks, and poor workers arrested and punished; he fired dozens of elderly and inept high-level bureaucrats; and he notified factory managers that their enterprises would be kept under close surveillance to monitor performance. This shocked the party into reluctant action.

After Andropov's death, Chernenko, the second Soviet leader in three years, failed to pursue his predecessor's tough policy. Most likely, the Central Committee desired a rest period. Life in the Soviet Union, as in Tsarist Russia, moved slowly and responded to the rhythms of old habits rather than to modern needs. Attempts by the authorities to make managers and workers toe the line through threats and intimidation produced sullen resistance and even industrial sabotage. Chernenko died after a short period in power and was replaced by Mikhail Gorbachev.

Gorbachev's Reforms: *Perestroika*

By the early 1980s, a consensus emerged among the Soviet elite that economic reforms were essential if the Soviet Union was to retain its position in the world. Some economists advocated radical changes. Siberian scholar Tatiana Zaslavskaia, for example, argued that the weaknesses of the Soviet economy were inherent in the system. She pointed out that this system had remained unchanged since Stalin and was the real reason for the poor standards of the labour force. This, she insisted, would change only when they enjoyed greater freedom in the workplace. She also criticized the overly centralized nature of economic decision-making and the weak development of the market forces of supply and demand.

Serious efforts at change came only after the election of Mikhail Gorbachev as General Secretary of the Communist Party in 1985. He was determined to revive economic growth by introducing imaginative production techniques, restructuring the economic as well as the political leadership, modernizing the economy, and eliminating the black market. Collectively, these reforms were known as *perestroika*, or restructuring. The bare outline of his reforms are sketched below.

- *Economy:* Decentralization of decision-making in such areas as prices, employment, wages, research, and sales. Plant managers, who presumably understood society's wants and needs better than government ministers, were to determine production plans. Factories that provided unwanted goods were phased out and many large state enterprises were made self-financing.

  Small, privately owned businesses were allowed, especially in the service sector. As a result, Soviet citizens opened a range of restaurants, repair shops, beauty salons, and other services.

- *Agriculture:* Decentralization of state-owned farms and strengthening of agricultural cooperatives encouraged limited private ownership of farms and allowed the sale of farm products on the open market.

- *Technology:* More resources were directed toward education and research in such high-technology fields as computers, robotics, genetic engineering, and space research. Joint ventures with Western companies were encouraged.

- *Consumption:* More high-quality consumer goods from the West were imported. "We are fully restoring the principle of socialism," Gorbachev wrote, "from each according to his ability, to each according to his work."

- *International trade:* Permission to trade directly with Western companies was encouraged. A **joint economic ventures** program, in which Soviet and international firms worked together, was designed to improve the USSR's export structure, to acquire foreign currency to fund modernization, and to fill the stores with high-quality consumer goods without having to rely on imports.

- *Democratization:* Decentralization of the Communist Party, the government, and the economy, and increased democracy in the workplace were coupled with greater freedom of political dissent.

- *Culture:* Increased freedom of expression was granted in speech, the press, literature, art, movies, and religion.

joint economic ventures: business undertakings that involve the companies of two or more countries.

Problems With *Perestroika*

Despite these measures, it soon became clear that Gorbachev had no overall and consistent plan in mind. His attempts to pacify the opposition of conservatives in the Communist Party led him to advocate contradictory policies. On some occasions he called for strengthening the authority of Gosplan, and on others he urged that greater autonomy in decision-making be given to individual enterprises. As a result, many managers were unwilling to risk taking their own initiative, and hard-line Communists resisted the reforms to protect their entrenched positions. Finally, bureaucratic red tape prevented some industries from reaping the benefits expected from their partnerships with foreign firms.

Consequently, the tentative measures of 1985 to 1987 merely complicated rather than revived the stagnant Soviet economy. By 1988 Gorbachev and his fellow reformers recognized the need for a more far-reaching and integrated program. They also realized that this could succeed only after political reforms broke the power of the conservatives within the Communist Party and government. By spring 1990, Gorbachev had transferred decision-making from the party to a state administration that he headed by virtue of his election to the powerful position of president.

Meanwhile, the economy continued to decline and empty store shelves and long line-ups remained the norm. Far from disappearing, the black market was expanding, as was the power of the Russian mafia. Hyperinflation reduced the value of the ruble from $1.75 to about $0.01. During 1990, labour productivity fell by 3 percent, GNP declined by 2 percent, and the economy as a whole shrank by 4 percent. Early in 1990, rumours that Gorbachev had the outlines of a plan for a new controlled market economy that involved abolishing price controls aroused widespread opposition. Once again, by trying to please both sides, Gorbachev ended up pleasing neither.

The stalled economic reforms probably were a major factor in the conservative coup of August 1991. In its wake, the Soviet Union disintegrated into its separate regional segments and the old centralized economic structure was left in fragments. Boris Yeltsin and many of the other new leaders recognized the looming disaster posed by the resulting disruption of long-established patterns of research and development, resource allocation, and production. Indeed, the new Commonwealth of Independent States (CIS) that replaced the old USSR was more an attempt to preserve these ties in a common market system than it was a political alliance.

Yeltsin also proclaimed a new era of the market-based economy in the Russian Federation. He permitted all enterprises with fewer than 10 000 employees to be privatized, as well as those involved in gas, oil, and pharmaceuticals regardless of size. Yeltsin also arranged for Western financing. Whereas the old Soviet Union had had only a handful of banks (one to look after people's savings, one to deal with foreign trade, and a few that dealt with different branches of industry), today's Russia has over 3000 privately owned banks. Over 95 percent of Russia's shops are privately owned, and on a relative basis, Russia has fewer state-owned businesses than does Italy. The basic institutions of a market economy appeared with astonishing speed.

Several hundred Western-style supermarkets, for example, were already in operation in 1994, and the stock market was flourishing.

However, these reforms stalled. Production fell, factories closed, prices rose, and the Russian mafia grew in strength. By 1995, Yeltsin had dropped most of the reformers from his government and seemed to be backing away from market reforms prior to the 1996 presidential election. At that time, only 3 percent of the Russian populace were considered rich and 10 percent "comfortable." As for the rest of the population, many were unemployed or, if they had jobs, had not been paid in months. Inflation made the pensions of old and disabled people virtually worthless. Not surprisingly, on the eve of the presidential elections of 1996 the economy was in trouble, popular discontent was high, and a revived Communist Party was once more a force of national significance. At the same time, some people were doing very well in the "new Russia," and the gap between rich and poor had increased dramatically.

What economic problems faced by President Yeltsin does this cartoon illustrate?

Conclusion

Russia's economic and political problems are enormous. Its government is seeking immediate solutions to quiet growing popular unrest. Should Russia adopt more private enterprise, and if so, how quickly? What balance should it seek between Western capitalism and the communist social safety net of the past? Should the government privatize all public enterprises? What social programs should be maintained, and how will they be funded? Should Russia stimulate economic growth by Keynesian or by supply-side economic measures?

The answers to these questions will determine Russia's economic and political future. At the same time, due to Russia's vast size, its wealth of natural resources, its 150 million people, and its military might, any economic changes will have a profound impact on the rest of the world.

EMMA GOLDMAN, 1869–1940

"Red Emma" was an impassioned anarchist rebel who devoted her entire life to the struggle for free speech, birth control, women's rights, and a just and peaceful society of equals organized in free cooperation rather than by a coercive state apparatus.

For her efforts, Goldman was alternately considered "one of the twelve greatest living women" (*The Nation*, 1922) or "the most dangerous woman in America," as her detractors called her.[2]

Born in Kovno, Russia, in 1869 into a lower-middle-class Jewish family, Goldman emigrated to the United States in 1885 to escape an arranged marriage. At her job in a clothing factory in Rochester, New York, Goldman experienced first-hand the shocking disparity between the ideal of the "American Dream" and the reality of the appalling conditions endured by immigrants in the sweatshops and factories.

News of the trial and hanging of the four "Haymarket anarchists" in 1886–87 for their alleged involvement in a bombing in Chicago prompted Goldman to join the anarchist movement. Over the next 30 years she became widely known as a powerful speaker, writer, and agitator. On one occasion she was jailed for a year for telling a crowd of unemployed workers that it was their sacred right to steal bread.

When Goldman helped to organize opposition to the military draft during World War I, she was deported to Russia along with 247 other Americans. Like so many other social activists of her generation, she had been inspired by the Bolshevik Revolution; however, what she saw in Russia was the opposite of everything she believed. Under War Communism, the Bolsheviks had clamped down on all dissenting views, even those supporting the revolution.

In March 1921, Goldman faced the ultimate disillusionment when the Red Army attacked the rebellious Kronstadt sailors and striking Petrograd workers, killing 18 000. The sailors had fought on the Bolshevik side in the October Revolution but were protesting the lack of freedoms and organized terror of the regime. In December Goldman left Russia, now inspired by a new cause—to tell the world the truth about social and political conditions in Russia.

When her book *My Disillusionment in Russia* was published in 1923, progressive Americans chided Goldman for not understanding that defending the world's first workers' revolution was important enough to justify harsh methods. But this reasoning did not satisfy Goldman, for whom the means used would always become part of the final purpose. For her, the "ultimate end of all social change is to establish the sanctity of human life, the dignity of man, the right of every human being to liberty and well-being." She remained a vocal opponent of the authoritarian brutality of the Soviet regime until the end of her life.

During the Spanish Civil War (1936), Goldman did all she could to support the anarchist cause, and was inspired by the brief life of the anarchist collectives and the workers' control of Barcelona. When the Republic was defeated in 1939, she came to Canada to build support and raise funds for the Spanish anarchist refugees. Tired but irrepressible, she died in Toronto on May 14, 1940, while working on the defence campaign of four comrades arrested for possession of "subversive materials."

During Goldman's time, not only conservatives and fascists but also progressives and socialists had abundant faith in the state as the guarantor of society's best interests. Goldman's plea for the spiritual freedom of the individual went largely unheard as the Cold War spurred support for one superpower state or the other. One wonders whether, had Goldman lived today, her message might have found more fertile ground.

In a letter published in *The Nation*, Goldman answered those who objected to her public criticism of the Soviet Union:

I cannot share enthusiasm ... [for] the "collective society" the Soviet government is attempting to create. I hardly need to emphasize my stand on private capitalism. I have fought it all my life. But collective slavery is nothing to be excited about or any improvement on the slavery created by the capitalistic class. It is merely a change of masters. ... It seems to me that liberals cannot consistently smooth over every outrage committed in the name of socialism, at the same time objecting to the suppression of liberal ideas at home.[3]

1 What aspects of her philosophy led Emma Goldman to reject the economy of the Soviet Union as well as Western capitalism?

2 Why would she be remembered by some as a hero and by others as a dangerous subversive?

Underlying and Emerging Issues

Give the reasoning and evidence that might be used to support different views or conclusions on the following issues.

1 To what degree was there equality of opportunity in the USSR?

2 Are public enterprise and central planning the most effective means for rapid industrialization?

3 To what degree does the welfare of the whole society justify sacrificing the interests of individuals?

4 To what degree does modern agriculture require large-scale enterprises?

5 Does central planning naturally lead to inefficiency?

6 Does central planning discourage innovation?

7 Does central planning provide a more just system of distribution?

8 Would public enterprise be more effective if it were combined with a democratic political system?

9 To what extent were the economic problems of the USSR the result of its dictatorial political system?

10 Did communism collapse more for economic or for political reasons?

11 To what extent do people need individual incentives to increase production?

12 Should Russia move rapidly toward complete private enterprise?

13 Should Russia seek a balance between private and public enterprise?

14 Should Western nations provide aid to assist Russia in moving to a private enterprise system?

Focussing Knowledge

In your notes, clearly identify or define and explain the importance or significance of each of the following:

War Communism   Gossnab

New Economic Policy (NEP)   incentives

"socialism in one country"   enterprise fund

kulaks   perestroika

Five-Year Plan   joint economic ventures

collective farms   Russian mafia

state farms   privatization

Gosplan   Leon Trotsky

1 a. What factors led Lenin to move away from central planning in 1921?

    b. How did Lenin seek to solve the USSR's problems through the New Economic Policy?

    c. Describe the split over economic policy that occurred after Lenin's death.

    d. What factors limited the effectiveness of Soviet agriculture during the 1920s?

2 a. Describe the main features of the first Five-Year Plan.

    b. According to Stalin's speech on page 340, what were the motives for central planning?

    c. What were the effects of the first Five-Year Plan?

3 a. What were the major goals of collectivization?

    b. Distinguish between state farms and collective farms.

    c. To what extent was force a main element of collectivization?

4 a. Describe the main elements of Soviet central planning.

    b. What were the advantages and disadvantages of central planning in the USSR?

    c. How did the political system limit the effectiveness of the economic system?

    d. How did the system use incentives before 1985?

5 a. What factors led to the reforms of the late 1980s?

    b. Describe the main elements of Gorbachev's *perestroika* program.

    c. Why were the reforms not more successful?

6 a. Describe the direction of the economy under President Yeltsin since 1991.

    b. What critical economic questions faced Russians after Yeltsin's re-election in 1996?

Applying and Extending Knowledge

1 Examine the USSR's economic system before Stalin. How did working conditions compare with those in Western Europe and North America at the time?

2 Research the famines in the USSR in the 1930s. To what extent does evidence support the view that the famines were deliberately created for political reasons?

3 Compare the reasons for the collapse of communism in the USSR to the situation in one Eastern European country. To what extent were the causes similar and different?

4 Compare the economic policies of Russia since 1991 to those of Hungary and Poland. Which country seems to have been most successful economically? What factors account for the differences?

5 Take and defend a position on the following statement: "Gorbachev's main contribution to the twentieth century was in destroying the political and economic system of communism."

6 Explain why Gorbachev is so highly regarded in the West but not very popular in Russia.

7 Research the economic policies in Russia since the 1996 presidential election. To what extent is Russia continuing to move toward private enterprise?

8 You have examined both the political and the economic systems of the USSR. Using what you have learned, write a paper on the following topic: "To what extent was the collapse of communism in the USSR due to political or economic factors?"

9 Making use of your work in Case Studies 7 and 12, take a stand on the following question: "If Russia had evolved into a democratic system after Stalin, would public enterprise and central planning have been retained?"

10 Select newspaper articles that reflect some of the Underlying and Emerging Issues on page 353. Explain how the articles illustrate the issues.

11 Choose one of the Underlying and Emerging Issues. Outline the arguments and evidence on the various sides, and explain why the issue is complex.

The Chinese Economy

Learning Outcomes

After reading this case study, you should be able to:

- understand the development of China's economy since the nineteenth century

- explain how the Chinese Communist Party controlled the country's economy

- detail Deng Xiaoping's strategy for modernizing the Chinese economy

- discuss some of the problems that have arisen in China as a result of Deng's reforms

- explain the relationship between Hong Kong and the growth of South China's economy

- debate whether China can sustain high rates of economic growth without changing its political system

CHINA'S ECONOMY HAS SHIFTED from a state-controlled communist economy to a system that combines socialism and market-oriented characteristics. Recent growth has been the result of the reform policies initiated by Deng Xiaoping in the late 1970s and early 1980s: China opened its doors to trade with the West, created special economic zones along its coast in order to encourage foreign investment, and began to deregulate many sectors of its economy. This case study examines the history of the Chinese economy since the nineteenth century and con-

China at a Glance

Area: 9 596 960 km²

Population (1995): 1 203 097 000 (largest population in the world)

Life Expectancy in Years (1994): Males 67, Females 69

GDP (1993): $2.61 trillion (U.S.)

GDP per Capita (1993): $2200 (U.S.)

Doctors per 1000 People (1992): 1

Hospital Beds per 1000 People (1990): 2.37

Health Expenditures as Percentage of GDP (1990): 3.5

Telephones per 1000 People (1994): 20

Televisions per 1000 People (1992): 27

Sources: John Robert Colombo, ed., *The 1996 Canadian Global Almanac* (Toronto: Macmillan, 1996); Marlita A. Reddy, ed., *Statistical Abstract of the World* (New York: Gale Research, 1995); *Statistical Abstract of the United States, 1995: The National Data Book* (Washington, DC: U.S. Department of Commerce, September 1995); *The World Almanac and Book of Facts 1996* (Mahwah, NJ: World Almanac Books, 1996).

cludes with an analysis of some of the problems facing the Chinese people today as they adapt to a Western-style economy.

Historical Background

China's recent economic growth has been phenomenal, especially considering the economic history of the country's past 200 years. When European traders ventured to China in the late eighteenth century, they encountered a country that had changed very little in over 2000 years. The emperor, or "Son of Heaven," ruled over hundreds of millions of peasants from his throne in the Forbidden City in Beijing.

Chinese society was governed by the principles of **Confucianism**, as ordained by the philosopher Confucius around 500 B.C. Confucius believed in a well-ordered, hierarchical society in which every citizen played a specific role. The emperor and the scholars ruled; the peasants grew food; the artisans made the tools and clothing necessary for existence. The merchants were the lowest class in society, as Confucius considered them to be little more than parasites who produced nothing. This negative evaluation of merchants and of commerce was an important element in traditional Chinese beliefs. Educated Chinese held merchants in contempt; no one with any ambition willingly became a merchant or trader.

> **Confucianism:** the beliefs of the philosopher Confucius.

Europeans came to China in the late 1700s to trade for its silk, porcelains, and tea. The ruling Manchu, or Ch'ing, dynasty confined Western merchants to the southern port of Canton (now Guangzhou) so they would not "pollute" Chinese society with their foreign customs. The British government quickly tired of the Chinese restrictions. In 1793, King George III sent Lord Macartney to negotiate a more open trading system with the emperor. Macartney brought examples of British goods, including fancy clocks, wind-up toys, silverware, and musical instruments. The Chinese ruler was not impressed with what he saw and refused to open his country further to Western trade. He denied the British requests that more Chinese ports be opened to foreign trade and that an official embassy be built in Beijing, the capital city.

The British returned to China in 1840, this time led not by ambassadors bearing gifts, but by marines firing guns. Great Britain and China were at war. The cause of this conflict (the Opium Wars) was the Chinese government's efforts to stop the illegal import of opium into their country. British merchants had been exporting thousands of crates of opium each year to Canton in an effort to balance their trade deficit with China. Since the Chinese did not want to purchase British goods, foreign traders turned to opium, which they obtained in India and traded with China for tea. When the Chinese authorities in Canton seized and destroyed millions of dollars' worth of British opium in 1839, the two countries went to war.

China lost this conflict and was forced to sign the Treaty of Nanjing in August 1842. This treaty not only opened China to foreign trade, it also ceded Hong Kong Island to Britain. For the remainder of the nineteenth century, China attempted to modernize its armies and economy, but these efforts were hindered by government corruption, foreign wars, poor communications, and the enormous size of the country. Following the unsuccessful attempt to drive out foreigners in the Boxer Rebellion of 1900, China increasingly fell under the control of foreign powers.

By the early 1900s, China's economy was still mainly based on agriculture. Some of the larger port cities, such as Shanghai, had modern factories and banks, but overall, the economy was still backward and most of the people were poor. The Chinese Revolution of 1911 ended the Manchu dynasty and established a republic. From the 1920s through World War II, China's new republican government attempted to modernize the country. The government built railways and factories, and made limited attempts at land reform. All of these efforts, however, failed due to government corruption, lawlessness, and the Japanese invasion in 1937. By the end of the war in 1945, the Chinese economy was in tatters. What modern industries the country had built were destroyed, and the peasants in the countryside were starving.

Since the mid-1920s, civil war between the nationalist government of Chiang Kai-shek and the Communist Party of Mao Zedong had devastated the country (see Case Study 8). A temporary ceasefire had been called during the war with Japan, but in 1947 it was forgotten, and the two sides fought for control of China. Despite massive American support for the government, the Communists gained the initiative and routed the Nationalist armies, which withdrew to Taiwan. On October 1, 1949, Mao Zedong announced the birth of the People's Republic of China. "China has stood up," he proclaimed, and most Chinese responded with enthusiasm. China was about to embark on a massive experiment with communism.

Chinese Communist leader Mao Zedong (1893–1976) became the ruler of mainland China in 1949.

···Mao's Reforms

Mao's political and economic strategies during the Chinese civil war were based on the importance of the country's peasantry. China had, and still has, a largely rural society, with over 80 percent of its population employed in agriculture.

After defeating the Nationalists in 1949, Mao sought to rebuild China's economy to cater to the needs of the peasantry, while at the same time fostering industrial growth. His economic policies were an ingenious blend of traditional socialist strategies, with an emphasis on industries such as steel and machinery, and new policies that were more suited to China's rural economy.

During the early 1950s, the Chinese government invited thousands of advisers from its ally, the Soviet Union, to help construct new factories and mines. Under Soviet guidance, China rebuilt its heavy industries and trained its people to be engineers and technicians. These new industries were state-owned and -managed. All private ownership was forbidden, and the state controlled the means of production. Mao launched his first Five-Year Plan in 1953. Based on Stalin's policies of the 1930s (see Case Study 12), Mao gave priority to heavy industry. Although this was a success, the peasants were unhappy with the low prices the government set for their products. The increasing split with the Soviet Union further complicated the situation after 1956.

In 1958, Mao began to reorganize farms into **communes**, in which people lived together and elected leaders to plan the local economy. These communes varied in size, but on average contained over 25 000 people. Each commune had its own factories, which were supposed to bring industrialization to rural areas. This plan worked well at first, but soon some commune leaders sought to outdo their neighbours in production. The government accepted the resulting exaggerated claims of production, which it then turned into national targets that became compulsory for every commune to match, but were of course impossible to duplicate.

Mao announced in 1958 that China would embark on a **Great Leap Forward** and predicted that China would overtake Great Britain in industrial output in less than five years. A deliberate attempt was made to overcome the "urban bias" of the previous years by giving priority to agricultural and rural development. Mao encouraged peasants to create self-reliant communes by building backyard furnaces to produce steel. In these primitive shelters, farmers throughout China began to melt whatever metal products they could find. Household items such as pots and pans, and even farm tools and railway tracks, were thrown into the furnaces. The result was disastrous: the steel produced was useless, and China suffered its worst famine in over 50 years as peasants were too busy making poor-quality steel to tend to their crops. The Great Leap Forward was really a huge step backward. Although during this time dams, roads, railways, mines, and factories were built, the Great Leap's ultimate failure weakened Mao's authority, undermined his alternative to the command economy, and destroyed the communes. The disgraced Chairman Mao was forced into semi-retirement.

commune: a community of people living and working together where responsibilities are commonly shared.

Great Leap Forward: a government program initiated by Mao Zedong in 1958 that was intended to bring China's economy in line with that of Western countries in only a few years.

The Cultural Revolution

China was increasingly on its own in the Communist world. Differences over ideology, leadership, and strategy led to a Chinese–Soviet split. The Soviet Union was alarmed at the excesses of the Great Leap Forward and withdrew its advisers from China in the early 1960s. In 1966, Mao regained political control with the help of his wife, Jiang Qing, and some of the more radical members of the Communist Party. The next decade, from 1966 to 1976, is termed the **Cultural Revolution**. It involved a rejection of intellectual or foreign elements to the point of xenophobia — fear of foreigners. Mao now encouraged a state of permanent revolution.

Cultural Revolution: a campaign launched in China in 1966 by Mao Zedong that aimed to promote radical socialist ideals at the expense of Western and traditional elements in China.

The Cultural Revolution had a profound impact on the Chinese economy. Universities were closed for most of this period, denying China a supply of educated technicians, engineers, scientists, and doctors. Engineers and managers were labelled political enemies of the people because of their education and social status. They were removed from their jobs and sent to the countryside for "re-education," including doing farm labour.

The rural communes again became the basic structure for the country's economy. Each commune developed light industries to supply its needs for consumer goods and technology. Although this saved on transportation costs and provided industrial growth in poor regions, most of the manufactured goods were of inferior quality and were more expensive than if they had been made in large-scale and better-equipped urban factories.

Dazhai, a commune in the northwest province of Shanxi, became the showcase of the Cultural Revolution. In propaganda pamphlets, Dazhai seemed to be a tremendous success. It produced agricultural goods far in excess of government quotas. What most Chinese did not know, however, was that Dazhai was a fake. Its leaders lied to the central government and claimed that their production levels had risen by over 500 percent in only two years. Mao was so pleased with these reports that in 1964 he urged all Chinese farmers to learn from Dazhai. He made a similar appeal to the industrial workers, urging them to follow the example of Daqing, the site of several rich oil fields in northern Manchuria. Daqing, however, was another bogus success story. When Mao died in the summer of 1976, bringing the last stages of the Cultural Revolution to a close, the Chinese economy was stagnant and in desperate need of major reform.

Post-Mao Economic Reforms

Deng Xiaoping emerged as China's next powerful political ruler. Deng and other moderate leaders instituted a series of economic reforms to update China's technologically backward economy. Universities were reopened, and graduate students and professors were sent abroad to learn from the West. The communes were dissolved, and farmers were allowed to sell their crops on the open market. Industry was also reformed, and factory managers and workers were rewarded on the basis of their productivity. In a speech to the Chinese people soon after he became premier, Deng remarked, "I don't care if a cat is red [communist] or white [capitalist], as long as it catches mice [makes money]." It is important to note, however, that Deng was not abandoning socialism, he was merely stating that the economy needed to be modernized and industries made profitable. The Communist Party maintained political control while loosening its hold on the economy.

The father of China's reforms, Deng Xiaoping.

China's new economic goals were based on the **Four Modernizations** — agriculture, industry, national defence, and science and technology. During the early 1980s, it was China's peasants who led the country's economic reforms. Freed from the commune system, many Chinese farmers quickly adapted to the new economic conditions and prospered. By the end of the 1980s, many rural households had televisions, tape recorders, radios, refrigerators, and washing machines. For the first time in recorded history, China's peasants were doing well.

Four Modernizations: four areas on which China focussed its reforms in the early 1980s: agriculture, industry, national defence, and science and technology.

Coastal Ports and Special Economic Zones

Deng realized that rural reforms would not be enough to stimulate country-wide growth. China needed foreign capital. In the early 1980s, therefore, he announced the opening of over a dozen coastal ports to foreign trade and investment. These ports and the surrounding regions were termed **special economic zones (SEZs)**. Foreign businesses were invited to build factories in cities such as Shanghai, Tianjin, and Canton. Billions of dollars of foreign investment poured into the Chinese economy as companies from Canada, Japan, the United States, and Europe competed to establish themselves in the growing Chinese market. These foreign firms founded **joint enterprises**, which were jointly owned by foreign companies and the Chinese government. Western companies provided the start-up capital and technical expertise in return for such economic incentives as free land and low taxes. The profits were shared by both partners. Throughout the 1980s and 1990s, thousands of joint enterprises were established in China, helping the country move toward a market economy while training Chinese people in modern business methods.

The southern Chinese province of Guangzhou, which borders Hong Kong, has been the most successful region in reforming and modernizing its economy. Taking advantage of the special privileges reserved for foreign investors, hundreds of Hong Kong companies set up factories in southern China, providing employment for local workers and huge profits for the par-

special economic zone (SEZ): part of a country that the government declares open to foreign enterprises and investment.

joint enterprises: companies jointly owned by two different parties, such as a corporation and the government of a country.

ent firms. The city of Shenzhen, for example, exploded from a small rural village in the early 1980s into a huge metropolis with a population of over 2 million.

Zhucheng Experiments With Privatization[1]

In northeastern China, the town of Zhucheng has become a laboratory for economic reform. The city is experimenting with privatization — it is turning over state-run enterprises to entrepreneurs and to the workers. *Before privatization began in 1992, two-thirds of the city's 282 state enterprises were either losing money or just breaking even. Now each of the city's 272 companies are making profits, some quite substantial.* The reforms have included leasing some enterprises, merging others, and allowing the hopeless ones to go bankrupt (which was once not allowed). But the main strategy has been to sell three-quarters of the state firms to their employees or to other companies.

One reason why the restructured companies have been successful is that the reforms have benefitted the workers. For example, prior to the reforms one electronic parts company made minimal profits and paid its workers an annual salary of about U.S. $241. In 1993, the government sold this company to the employees by issuing them stock. Both earnings and wages soared. Some economists believe that changes such as those in Zhucheng could mark the first step toward capitalist-style corporations throughout China.

Many experts on China believe that the economic future of south China depends on the smooth transfer of capitalist Hong Kong to Chinese rule. A British colony since the middle of the nineteenth century, Hong Kong has been guaranteed certain rights after its return to China in 1997. These rights might best be summed up by the slogan: **"One country, two systems,"** meaning that Hong Kong will officially be under the political rule of the Communists, but its economy will remain capitalist. Others have doubts and wonder what political and economic changes will emerge.

One country, two systems: the slogan that describes how China will remain communist while allowing Hong Kong to retain its capitalist system.

With Reform Comes Problems

Although Deng Xiaoping's reforms have helped to modernize China's economy, they have also created a number of social tensions and political problems. As China opens its doors wider to foreign trade and investment, Western ideas and values also inevitably enter the country. Many Chinese, especially the youth, are becoming less tolerant of the dictatorial nature of the Communist political system and are demanding political reforms. People are also annoyed at the scale of government corruption and the growing inequities between the rich and the poor.

Corruption

Government corruption in China is widespread. Children and relatives of high Communist Party officials are becoming a new class of wealthy entrepreneurs, and their success is often based not on hard work but on their connections to people with political influence. The Chinese term for this type of personal networking is ***guanxi***. Many people in China understand and accept that *guanxi* is a method of gaining employment or better housing, but many now say that such corruption has gone too far. The Communist Party is supposed to be the protector of common people, not an elite enjoying the good life.

In the mid-1990s, the Chinese government attempted to stop government corruption in an effort to win back the political support of its citizens. Hundreds of officials were arrested for accepting bribes, and some were even executed. This anti-corruption campaign, however, ended suddenly in the summer of 1995 when the state announced that all corrupt officials had been caught. Most Chinese believe that the reason the arrests ended was that the investigators had begun to target important politicians. It should be noted that this type of official corruption was one of the major issues of the student protesters in Tiananmen Square in 1989, which ended in the massacre of protesters by government soldiers.

guanxi: in China, a person's network of family, friends, and colleagues that can help them improve their material and economic conditions.

Case Table 13.1: Agricultural Production Purchased by the Government

Year	Percentage of China's agricultural products purchased by government ministries
1978	80.2
1986	38.2
1990	33.5
1991	32.9
1992	31.6

Source: Terry Sicular, "Redefining State, Plan and Market: China's Reforms in Agricultural Commerce," *China Quarterly* (December 1995), p. 1032. Reprinted by permission of Oxford University Press.

Case Table 13.2: State Ownership of Key Industries in China, 1994

Industries	Percentage owned by the Chinese government
Petroleum	100
Tobacco	97
Refining	91
Logging	89
Water	87
Electrical power	86
Iron and steel	71
Coal mining	67
Food processing	56
Beverages	54
Industrial machinery	52

Source: Barry Naughton, "China's Macroeconomy in Transition," *China Quarterly* (December 1995), p. 1090. Reprinted by permission of Oxford University Press.

F o c u s

How has the state's role in China's agricultural sector changed as the country has moved toward a market economy?

How might this change affect the prices of basic foods in China?

Over what sectors of the Chinese economy has the central government retained the most control? Why?

President Jiang Zemin attempts to weed out government corruption.

The Growing Gap Between the Countryside and the Cities

China's rural economy led the economic reforms of the early 1980s, and many peasants benefitted from the new market economy. However, as China's reform efforts shifted to developing the country's industrial sector, the countryside has been left behind. Peasants are again becoming impoverished as the central government imposes heavy taxes on agricultural products in order to raise the money it needs to build new factories, roads, ports, and communications networks. There is a tremendous shortage of housing and jobs in most Chinese cities, but overall, urban residents are not suffering to the same extent as are the farmers.

Inflation and the End of the Iron Rice Bowl

In a centrally planned economy, prices are set by the government, so inflation is not a concern. The government also provides jobs for workers. With the recent move toward a market economy, China is confronted with two problems: inflation and unemployment.

Although China's economy is growing at over 10 percent a year, the inflation rate is rising even more quickly, and in 1996 it was over 20 percent. Necessities such as housing and food consume almost 70 percent of many workers' incomes. While employees of new businesses receive regular raises and benefits, many workers in state-owned industries have found that their pay is not enough to cover their living expenses. The result has been the creation of a pool of millions of migrant labourers struggling to make ends meet. The **iron rice bowl**, the Chinese phrase for the cheap housing, food, and lifelong employment that state-run industries provided, is quickly becoming just a memory. As government businesses are forced to compete with new entrepreneurs and foreign-sponsored joint enterprises, many Chinese face the new phenomenon of unemployment. Educated and skilled workers are eagerly sought by factories and businesses, but for most unskilled labourers Deng Xiaoping's reforms have brought few rewards.

iron rice bowl: a Chinese term for the cheap housing, food, and lifelong employment that state-run industries used to provide.

Relations With the United States and the West

As China's economy continues to grow, the country will find itself increasingly tied to international markets and politics. Particularly important will be China's relationship with the United States. Although trade with that country accounts for only 10 percent of China's total foreign trade, the United States is an important export market and source of investment and technical expertise. Hundreds of American firms conduct business with China annually, bringing billions of dollars into the Chinese economy.

China also wants to retain its **most favoured nation (MFN)** status with the American government. This designation results in lower tariffs for Chinese imports to the United States. Since the 1989 Tiananmen Square Massacre, American administrations have granted MFN status to China only on one-year probationary terms, as they have been unhappy with China's human rights record. China has been accused of using convict labour in state-owned factories, forcing women to undergo abortions, and selling the organs of executed prisoners on the black market for transplants. Beijing has been annoyed by this condemnation and has accused Washington of meddling in China's domestic politics. However, if China hopes to enjoy continued economic growth and foreign support in the forms of investment and trade, the country's leaders will have to deal with the uncomfortable questions of human rights. This topic will also test how sincerely Canada, the United States, and other democracies value human rights in relation to the increasingly huge market China offers to capitalist investors.*

most favoured nation (MFN): a status conferred on other countries by the United States that gives those countries more favourable trade terms, such as lower tariffs on imports of their products.

HENG
LIANHE ZAOBAO

American President Bill Clinton attempts to tame the Chinese panda.

Focus

What does this cartoon imply about the balance of power between the United States and China?

---

* In 1992, the World Bank predicted that by the year 2020 China will have surpassed the United States as the world's largest economy.

SHEILA MELVIN
Living in Beijing

The following account of contemporary life in China's capital city Beijing was written in 1995 by an American who speaks Chinese and had lived in China prior to moving to Beijing to work for an international organization that had 15 years' experience in China. Many of the themes of this case study are echoed in Sheila Melvin's experiences. How many can you identify?

First, Chinese customs would not release the 10 boxes I airfreighted over here until another government agency gave me my work card. But, though I applied for it immediately after I arrived, the other agency needed two months to issue the card. Customs would have released my boxes for a $250 "payment," but I refused to pay the bribe. So I wore the same clothes for two months. ...

[After experiencing great frustrations with the bureaucracy in getting proof of her good health, Melvin was fined for being late in obtaining this certificate and was told to write a "self-criticism."] For a long moment, I considered quitting my job and returning to America. Then, I grabbed a pen to write the "self-criticism" in which I was supposed to lambaste myself for having shirked my responsibility by not extending my visa on time. The pen I pulled from my bag happened to be red, and when the officer saw it, she nearly jumped out of her chair.

"That pen is red!" she exclaimed.

"Yes, it is."

"It is not permitted to write with a red pen in China!"

"Not permitted?" I sputtered. "What is wrong with red? Isn't your flag red? Isn't red the color of communism?"

She glared at me, so I grabbed a black pen off her desk and scrawled a two-page "self-criticism" of the way the PSB [Public Security Bureau] had treated me, with a small apology tacked on the end, and paid the fine. ...

Electrical Shortages

Although my building is barely a year old, the paint is peeling, the hall windows are broken, and it generally looks like a poorly maintained, 20-year-old structure. The most annoying feature of this shoddy work is an inadequate electrical supply, which is due to wiring rather than shortages.

The power on my floor goes off daily: some days, it goes off as many as 10 times. Turning the power back on is usually just a question of going out to my floor's fuse box; even this, however, can be extremely annoying, particularly when it just flips right back off again. ... The silver lining is that nobody on my floor has ever received an electric bill. Even those who have lived here for a year have yet to receive one!

Why I Still Live Here

The hassles of living in Beijing are many and perhaps inevitable in such a rapidly changing city. On balance, the changes are far more positive than negative.

Focus

Why is having MFN status important for China?

It is much easier to make good friends with Chinese people than it was just five years ago. Lingering fears that associating with foreigners could be politically dangerous have vanished. The locals now seek foreign friends, and such friendships are easier to sustain. The common ground between urban Chinese and foreigners has widened considerably. When I lived in Shanghai five years ago, most of my Chinese friends had never been on a vacation — anywhere — and they lived on roughly US $13 a month. Now I have Chinese friends who have seen more of the United States than I have. ... Gone are the days when you had to eat cabbage all winter long, because no other vegetables were available in Beijing. Now supermarkets — which were nonexistent only three years ago — sell produce from southern China and around the world. ...

One of my favorite things to do in Beijing is simply to watch the strange and fascinating mix of ancient and modern ways that is a daily part of Beijing life. ... Although there are plenty of Mercedes Benzes in my neighborhood, there are just as many mule carts. It is this unique mixture of the present and the past that makes Beijing, to me, the most interesting place to live in the world.[2]

The Trade-offs

The People's Republic of China has one of the fastest-growing economies in the world. Despite Western outrage over China's use of military force against unarmed student protesters in Tiananmen Square in June 1989, foreign governments and companies continue to invest billions of dollars each year in China. Some economists predict that by the early twenty-first century China's economy will be the largest in the world. The average Chinese citizen has greater access to consumer goods, enjoys higher wages, and has more job opportunities than ever before. But there are also problems. The low prices for basic foods and housing that the Chinese government used to guarantee are gone. So too are many of the social services that the state provided, such as child care and old age security. China's adoption of many market-oriented practices raises many issues and choices, which has resulted in many trade-offs having to be made.

Population pressures have resulted in a state-imposed program of one child per family. As a result, parents who already have one child are pressured to abort any other pregnancies (abortion is legal in China). The one child per family policy has caused a shortage of marriageable women. In this society that favours male children, there are also reports of female babies being abandoned or killed.

China's experiences illustrate the trade-offs involved in making choices about economic systems. After 1949, the Chinese people achieved more equality and economic security, but at the cost of individual economic and political freedom. As they have moved toward a market economy, some people have become immensely wealthy and productivity has increased, but at the cost of increased inflation, unemployment, and insecurity. Political freedom is still withheld. Whenever countries make decisions about their economies, trade-offs are inevitably involved.

JIANG QING (CHIANG CH'ING), 1914–1991

One source characterized Jiang Qing as "the ringleader of the notorious Gang of Four, who gained great political power during the Cultural Revolution which her husband, Mao Zedong, launched in 1966."[3] Jiang played a central role in the time of Communist China's greatest upheaval as China's cultural dictator and as chief advocate of hard-line revolutionary policies.

In the 1930s, Jiang was a movie starlet in Shanghai, but was not content with the role. "Never forget," she was later to say, "that beauty is not as important as power."[4] After the Japanese invasion of China in 1937, she travelled to Yan'an, where she met and eventually married Mao Zedong after his divorce from his previous wife. The Communist Party reluctantly approved of the marriage on the condition that Jiang would not play a political role.

For over two decades as a wife and mother, Jiang remained in political obscurity. But Mao's struggle with the Party's moderates (or "revisionists") prompted him to assign a major role to his wife in 1963, and she quickly gained power and influence.

Jiang began by "reforming" the arts to ensure that they served the cause of the revolution. By the time the Cultural Revolution reached its peak, she was described as "the firebrand whose speeches and guidance inspired the massive wave of Red Guards which swept throughout China demanding a return to 'pure' Maoist revolutionary principles."[5] She became the first woman appointed to China's Politburo, the Communist Party's inner circle.

After the Cultural Revolution, as the aging Mao's influence declined, Jiang Qing became a central figure in the ensuing power struggle. She and her allies lost; within three weeks of Mao's death in 1976 she was arrested. At her "show trial" in 1980–81, she was defiant and unrepentant:

Fixing the bench with a baleful glare, she shouted at her judges: "You are revisionists and criminals."

And she insisted that her actions during the 1966–76 Cultural Revolution had Mao's approval and that of the party Central Committee as well. "The victim is I, Mao's wife, who for 38 years shared weal and woe with him," she cried. "During the war I was the only female comrade who stayed at the front beside Chairman Mao — where were you hiding at that time?"

The possibility of execution seemed to hold no terror for Jiang Qing. Observers present in court reported that after the prosecutor's remarks, she taunted Deng Xiaoping ("if you're a man") to execute her before a million people in Peking's Tian An Men Square. "Making revolution is no crime! It is right to rebel!" she shouted in defiance. And when perspiring officials finally ejected her from court she proclaimed, "I am prepared to die."[6]

Jiang Qing's death sentence was commuted in 1983 by Deng Xiaoping. She died in 1991, "by her own hand" after a long illness, according to the government. The *New York Times* concluded in an obituary that "few people have been so hated in modern Chinese history. She became a symbol of the excesses and brutality of the Cultural Revolution."[7] But biographer Roxane Witke reminded readers that, for a time, she was "the most powerful woman in the world."[8]

---

1 How does Jiang Qing's life reflect important issues related to communism in China?

2 In your opinion, how might she have reacted to developments in China during the last decade?

Underlying and Emerging Issues

Give the reasoning and evidence that might be used to support different views or conclusions on the following issues.

1 Do less-developed countries require different types of economic systems than more-developed countries?

2 How important is the goal of economic growth?

3 To what degree should less-developed countries emphasize the goal of rural development?

4 Should less-developed countries pursue policies of rapid industrialization?

5 Does central planning or private enterprise offer the best hope for economic growth in less-developed countries?

6 To what degree should less-developed countries seek a balance between private and public enterprise?

7 To what degree should less-developed countries pursue self-reliance, or integration into the global economy?

8 Is it necessary to give up individual freedom in order to ensure economic growth?

9 To what degree is foreign investment desirable and necessary?

10 To what degree do people need individual incentives in order to increase production?

11 How important are freedom and economic growth as compared with equality and security?

12 Is it more important to ensure a job for everyone, or to ensure economic freedom?

13 To what extent are economic freedom and political freedom tied together?

14 To what degree should a country's internal political affairs be considered in decisions on trade and investment?

15 Is economic cooperation more effective than economic sanctions in bringing about improvements in human rights?

16 Should Canada tie increased trade and investment to improvements in human rights in China?

Focussing Knowledge

In your notes, clearly identify or define and explain the importance or significance of each of the following:

one-child family	*Hong Kong*
Opium Wars	*"One country, two systems"*
People's Republic of China	*guanxi*
Confucianism	*iron rice bowl*
communes	*most favoured nation status*
Great Leap Forward	*trade-offs*
Cultural Revolution	*Mao Zedong*
xenophobia	*Deng Xiaoping*
Four Modernizations	*Jiang Zemin*
SEZs	*Jiang Qing*
joint enterprises	

Reviewing and Organizing Knowledge

1 What have been the trade-offs (what has been gained, and what has been given up) in China's move to a more market-oriented economy?

2 a. How did traditional Chinese society view commerce and merchants?

   b. How was China affected by nineteenth-century imperialism?

   c. Why did the Revolution of 1911 fail to solve China's problems?

3 What were the main elements of Mao Zedong's early economic policies after the Communist victory in 1949?

4 a. What were the main features of the Great Leap Forward?

   b. Why did this initiative fail?

5 a. What were the main aspects of the Cultural Revolution?

   b. What were its results?

6 a. What were the main elements of Deng Xiaoping's early reforms?

   b. What further reforms were put in place later to stimulate growth and obtain foreign capital?

   c. What problems have arisen as a result of Deng's reforms?

7 How has the question of human rights affected China's economic relations with other countries?

8 In what ways does Sheila Melvin's account reflect the impact of the changing economic situation in China?

Applying and Extending Knowledge

1 a. Make two lists titled "China Before Deng's Reforms" and "China After Deng's Reforms." Under each heading, list the positive and negative aspects of the economic system.

b. On the basis of this analysis, write an essay in which you describe the trade-offs involved in Deng's reforms.

2 Research the life of Deng Xiaoping, and write an explanation of how he was able to both survive and influence China through so many changes and regimes.

3 Write a dialogue in which Mao Zedong and Deng Xiaoping discuss the present situation in China.

4 Compare China's economic system with that of Cuba, Vietnam, or North Korea. To what extent are their systems and experiences similar and different?

5 Compare China and Russia in terms of changes to their political and economic systems over the last two decades. What factors account for any differences?

6 Write a position paper in which you take a stand on Canada's present policies regarding economic relations with China.

7 Examine and evaluate U.S. foreign policy regarding China since 1945.

8 Research the reasons why the United States has been willing to cooperate with the Communist government of China, but not Cuba.

9 Find newspaper articles that illustrate some of the Underlying and Emerging Issues on page 369. Explain how the articles illustrate the issues.

10 Choose one of the Underlying and Emerging Issues. Using China's experience as a basis, take a position on the issue.

CHAPTER 9

Mixed Economic Systems

Learning Outcomes

After reading this chapter, you should be able to:

- explain the influence of the Industrial Revolution in the growth of socialism and welfare capitalism

- evaluate the ideas of J.S. Mill, the Webbs, and J.M. Keynes

- discuss the differences between socialism and communism

- compare market socialism to welfare capitalism

- debate the merits of nationalization

- understand the origins and theory of Keynesian economics

- discuss the advantages of supply-side versus Keynesian versus monetary economic theories

EVERY INDUSTRIAL COUNTRY COMBINES at least some features of both private enterprise and centrally planned economies. Such "mixed" economies are the subject of this chapter. It describes the origins of democratic socialism, the role of the Fabians in its growth, the process of nationalization of key industries (and later their return to private enterprise), and the role of social democratic parties in Europe during the last 30 years. The chapter then outlines the origins of welfare capitalism and explains the contributions of the Great Depression of the 1930s and the ideas of J.S. Mill and J.M. Keynes, before analyzing the more recent Keynesian, monetarist, and supply-side (Reaganomics) economic theories.

We have examined the nature and values of both centrally planned economies and laissez-faire capitalism. You will have noticed that the Canadian economy does not fit into either category. It is not centrally planned—the existence of private companies is proof of that. Nor is it laissez-faire capitalism as the presence of public education and such enterprises as the Canadian Broadcasting Corporation (CBC) prove. Minimum wage laws, health and safety regulations, restrictions on tobacco advertising, taxes on alcohol, and meat and milk inspections are only a few examples of government involvement in the economy.

To understand the economic structure of our modern world, it is essential to know the basic concepts of private enterprise and planned economies, since it is from these concepts that most countries derive their economic philosophy. Nonetheless, in the real world, there are no economies that are either entirely centrally planned or completely laissez-faire. The economy of every major country is really a combination of the two systems—a mixed economy. In some, central planning is dominant; in others, the market system is more important. This makes it difficult to categorize contemporary economic systems. The problem is further complicated by the combination of different political systems with these economic variations.

One method of analyzing economic systems is to arrange them along a continuum, according to the extent of government involvement in decision-making in the economy. Figure 9.1 illustrates this distinction.

Figure 9.1: Governments and Economic Systems

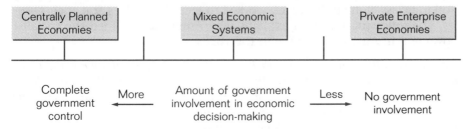

Centrally Planned Economies

Mixed Economic Systems

Private Enterprise Economies

Complete government control ← More — Amount of government involvement in economic decision-making — Less → No government involvement

··Origins of Democratic Socialism

Democratic socialism* had its origins in the Industrial Revolution. By the time Karl Marx died, many people realized that capitalism was not about to collapse. Legislation passed at the encouragement of liberal reformers in numerous countries helped to stabilize the capitalist system. As a result, several groups of socialists, influenced by the writings of Eduard Bernstein (1850–1932) and Jean Jaurès (1859–1914), returned to the Utopian Socialists' peaceful ideas that promoted gradual change. The ideas of these democratic socialists formed the basis for nearly every major non-Marxist socialist movement in existence today, from the powerful social democrats in Scandinavia, to the Labour party in Great Britain, to the New Democratic Party in Canada.

The Fabians

The specific ideas of democratic socialists vary from country to country. However, an analysis of the beliefs of Great Britain's social democratic offshoot, the **Fabian movement**, provides a good introduction to the theories of the early democratic socialists. In 1884, a small group of British intellectuals, led by Beatrice and Sidney Webb, George Bernard Shaw, and H.G. Wells, formed the Fabian Society. They rejected Marx's emphasis on class conflict and revolution and sought to change the system through gradual, democratic reforms.

Fabian movement: an elitist socialist group of the late nineteenth century that was determined to reform society through peaceful means.

---

*Most Europeans prefer the term "social democracy."

ANNA MAIER

Why I Became a Socialist

During the nineteenth and most of the twentieth centuries, middle-class women were not expected to work outside the home. Their job was to care for their children and husbands. Most men considered women to be physically and intellectually inferior to males, yet morally superior. Working-class women, however, worked to feed themselves and their families. The following selection explains why Anna Maier joined the socialist movement in Austria sometime in the 1890s.

When I turned thirteen my mother took me by the hand and we went to see the manager of a tobacco factory to get me a job. The manager refused to hire me but my mother begged him to change his mind, since she explained, my father had died. I was hired. When I was getting ready to go to work the next day, my mother told me that I was to keep quiet and do what I was told. That was easier said than done. The treatment you received in this factory was really brutal. Young girls were often abused or even beaten by the older women. I rebelled strongly against that. I tried anything that might help improve things for me. ...

Several years went by. The Women Workers' Newspaper began to appear and a few issues were smuggled into the factory by one of the older women. The more I was warned to stay away from this woman, the more I went to her to ask her if she would lend me a copy of the newspaper since I didn't have enough money to buy my own. At that time work hours were very long and the pay was very low. When my friend lent me a copy of the newspaper, I had to keep it hidden and I couldn't even let my mother see it if I took it home. I came to understand many things, my circle of acquaintances grew and when a political organization was founded in Sternberg, the workers were urged to join—only the men, the women were left out. A party representative came to us since I was already married by then. When he came by for the third time I asked him if I wasn't mature enough to become a member of the organization. He was embarrassed but replied: "When do you want to?" So I joined and I am a member of the party to this day.

I attended all the meetings, took part in all the demonstrations and it was not long before I was punished by the manager of the factory. I was taken off a good job and put in a poorer one just because I had become a Social Democrat. Nothing stopped me though; I said to myself, if this official is against it, out of fear to be sure, then it can't be all bad. When the tobacco workers' union was founded in November 1899, I joined and we had some big battles before we were able to make progress. Through these two organizations I have matured into a class-conscious fighter and I am now trying to win over mothers to the cause so that future children of the proletariat will have a happier youth than I had.[1]

Focus

Why did Maier become a socialist?

The Fabians placed great faith in the power of human reason and concentrated on preparing a series of pamphlets designed to educate the upper and middle classes in Great Britain about the benefits of socialism. Each pamphlet contained a detailed critique of the existing capitalist system, along with practical plans for correcting its evils. They knew that people could not be persuaded overnight and were prepared to continue their educational program until the public was converted. Reform, they believed, must come from within the democratic system, not through revolution. The Fabians sought to widen the franchise to include women and the working class, whom they believed would support economic and social reforms that would benefit the proletariat.

Like Marx, the Fabians were outraged at the capitalist system for creating both immense wealth and crippling poverty. Unlike Marx, however, the Fabians believed that the important conflict in the existing society was not between the bourgeoisie (the owners of the means of production) and the proletariat (the workers), but between a small group of bourgeois financiers and the entire community. The Fabians' solution was to gradually transfer ownership of the country's land and means of production (factories and equipment) to the entire community, not just to the proletariat (as Marx demanded). This could be achieved by **nationalization**. Slowly, as society became prepared for it, the government would take over the country's most important firms and trained experts would run them in the best interests of the community. When nationalization was combined with social welfare legislation and a taxation system designed to distribute wealth more equitably, humanity would be able to reach its true potential.

nationalization: state ownership and control of land and/or industries.

Nationalization

Although the Fabians were not immediately successful, many of their ideas were later adopted by the British Labour Party. Following World War II, the Labour Party was elected to power. It extended state welfare services; used income and estate taxes to redistribute income more equitably (and to pay for the welfare services); and began an extensive program of nationalization starting with the coal mining, electrical power, and railway industries.

Similar events occurred in a number of other European and Commonwealth countries after World War II. The degree of nationalization varied considerably from country to country and was determined largely by practical needs. In Great Britain, for example, the coal industry, which was vital to the country's welfare, was doing poorly. It was nationalized when it appeared to be on the verge of collapse. In France, the Renault automobile company was having financial problems and was nationalized, whereas the more economically stable Citroën company remained privately owned. In general, only those industries that were considered crucial to the economy—such as transportation, steel, energy, communications, and utilities—were taken over by the government. Most other businesses were left in private hands.

Nationalization was based on several arguments. Its supporters believed that state ownership would modernize backward industries and save dying companies, thus providing employment for the workers in endangered industries. Human welfare, not private profit, was the goal. Government ownership and planning, it was argued, could provide more orderly industrial development than the chaos of unrestricted capitalism. Finally, workers' morale (and therefore productivity) would presumably improve if the employees knew that the firm was managed for everyone's benefit.

The process of nationalization slowed in the 1950s. This was due partly to political opposition and partly to the mixed results of nationalization. In general, publicly owned industries operated no better than privately owned firms; some did better, some did worse. In addition, the economic theories of John Maynard Keynes (discussed later in this chapter) seemed to provide a method of regulating employment and economic growth without nationalization.

Ideals of Democratic Socialism

The fundamental belief underlying democratic socialism is equality, both political and economic. Democratic socialists believe that while everyone may not be born with equal abilities, all are equal as human beings and should therefore be guaranteed the basic necessities of life.

This means that the economic system should be operated in the best interests of society as a whole. If we believe that citizens in a democracy should control their political lives by contributing to political decision-making, then why should they not control their economic lives? Instead of relying on the profit motive to organize the economy, society should seek to define its goals and achieve them through rational planning. This planning would not be executed by self-appointed elites, but by a democratic government that is responsible to the people. Democratic socialists argue that elected representatives of the people should decide such questions as what industries should be nationalized and how the country's production should be distributed. The important fact is that the people have a say in their economy. Only in this way can the problems of poverty, unemployment, and terrible working conditions be solved.

Survey: Socialist Views

How disposed are you to the basic principles of socialism? Take the following survey and note whether you agree or disagree with each statement. There are no right or wrong answers; the questions are simply designed to identify your preferences in a general way.

1 Given the opportunity, we all have the potential and desire to act in a cooperative manner.

2 Poverty undermines one's basic humanity.

3 Without a competitive system, no one would have any incentive to work.

4 Our duty to others is limited to ensuring that no one starves.

5 The idea that anyone can succeed if they work hard enough is a myth—the system is structured such that some people can never get ahead.

6 Freedom exists when no one constrains your actions.

7 Society is divided into economic classes; the class into which you are born is usually the class in which you will die.

8 The free market may be imperfect, but a state-run economy would be much worse.

9 Nationalizing industry will reduce social inequalities.

10 Regardless of what we do, we will never achieve full equality; attempts to do so are futile.

Score one point for each "agree" on questions 1, 2, 5, 7, and 9, and one point for every "disagree" on questions 3, 4, 6, 8, and 10. Low total scores reflect little support for socialism; high scores indicate strong socialist leanings.

How Communism Differs From Socialism

It should be obvious from the preceding discussion that democratic socialism differs substantially from Marxism or communism. Yet democratic socialists are often associated with communists. Sometimes capitalist governments and business leaders encourage this belief in order to defeat socialist parties at election time. In other situations the misunderstanding is due to ignorance and to the wide variety of socialist parties and proposals. Socialists and communists have some beliefs in common: both favour public ownership and central planning (although socialists tend to favour a more limited amount of each); both dislike the profit motive and the emphasis on competition that is such a large part of capitalism; both sympathize with the working class; both desire equal economic opportunities combined with relatively modest differences in individual incomes; and finally, both believe that people must be taught to work in the best interests of society rather than solely for personal profit.

Despite such similarities, democratic socialists and communists have usually been archenemies. This has been especially true since the Russian Revolution of 1917, and each views the other as a major threat to its own future. Table 9.1 illustrates some of the major differences between the beliefs of socialism and communism.

Table 9.1: Socialism Versus Communism

	Socialism	**Communism**
Motto	From each according to ability, to each according to work.	From each according to ability, to each according to needs.
Source of beliefs	No guiding body of writing	The writings of either Marx, Lenin, or Mao
Method of gaining power	Democratic elections; peaceful persuasion	Violent revolution
Type of government	Multi-party democracy	One-party state
Degree of public ownership	Limited to essential industries	Extensive, if not complete
Means of acquiring public ownership	Nationalization with compensation (paying the owners for their property)	Nationalization without compensation
Private property	Most individually owned	None; state-owned
Dominant influence on human actions	Conscience and rational reasoning	The relationship to the means of production

Note: It is especially difficult to make specific statements about socialist beliefs, because socialists vary from country to country and from time to time. The beliefs listed here represent their most frequently held ideas.

Origins of Welfare Capitalism

Liberal reformers in Great Britain appeared at approximately the same time in history as did Karl Marx. Like Marx, they were horrified at the evils of the Industrial Revolution, but unlike Marx, they wished to preserve the basic institutions of capitalism. The views of John Stuart Mill (1806–73) represented a transitional period in the development of liberalism, in which the liberals abandoned their unconditional support of laissez-faire capitalism and began to advocate that the government take an active role in correcting the abuses of the free enterprise system. Initially, Mill had supported Adam Smith's ideas. However, as the abuses of industrialization multiplied, and as the industrialists showed little concern for the plight of their workers, Mill gradually came to believe that government should play a more active role in the economy. Mill sympathized with the desire of socialists for economic equality, yet he also admired the productivity of the capitalist system. Unlike Marx, he did not think that the market system inevitably led to class conflict. He felt that capitalism could be improved; as a result, he began to advocate government action to correct the abuses of capitalism without altering its essential features.

The ideas of Mill and his fellow liberal reformers influenced the passage of several factory acts and laws in Great Britain that improved working-class conditions in the nineteenth century. As the Industrial Revolution spread to the continent and to North America, so, too, did these reform ideas.

···Keynes Reforms Capitalism

As Case Study 11 discussed, the Great Depression of the 1930s changed the direction of capitalism. In the major industrial countries, one out of every four workers was unemployed, banks went out of business, farmers lost their land, and the world's economies declined drastically. Laissez-faire economists stated that the Depression was merely part of the inevitable business cycle, and that the only cure was to wait for the forces of supply and demand to bring recovery. After more than five years of waiting, however, it became obvious to many that something drastic had to be done. High unemployment and desperate poverty provided fertile ground for revolution, and people everywhere turned to the solutions offered by communism and fascism. The time was ripe for a change.

In 1936 the whole direction of modern economics was transformed by the appearance of a single book. British economist John Maynard Keynes' *The General Theory of Employment, Interest, and Money* became the most influential work in economics of the twentieth century. Keynes (1883–1946) diagnosed the patient (capitalism) as seriously ill but not beyond hope, and prescribed a remedy to restore its health. Although his ideas were controversial at the time, they soon provided the rationale for the economic policies of Western Europe and North America for the next 30 years or so.

Keynes argued that capitalism's problems were caused by extreme swings in the business cycle, with periods of recession or depression followed by periods of prosperity and economic expansion. He believed that the total amount of goods and services produced, and their prices, was determined by the demand for these goods and services. The greater the demand, the more manufacturers would increase their supply. Low total demand caused depression. To achieve a stable economy, there had to be a relatively close fit between the demand for goods and services and high productivity (supply). To increase demand during a depression, Keynes argued that governments should stimulate the economy by spending money (thus giving jobs and incomes to more people) and reducing taxes (so that people would have more money to spend).

Instead of attempting to balance the budget by reducing spending, governments should use **deficit financing**. When the economy improves, government can then reduce its spending and increase taxes. Keynes recommended that governments start public works programs to provide jobs and stimulate spending. Social welfare programs would also stimulate the economy. Unemployment insurance money, for example, would be used by recipients to purchase food and other consumer goods, and the increased demand for such items would prompt manufacturers to produce more goods, which would lead to higher employment and increased spending. Such "self-correcting" measures, Keynes stated, would remove the extreme highs and lows of the business cycle.

Keynesian economics thus required national governments to adopt an activist economic policy. The success of government economic planning in World War II (1939–45) strengthened Keynes' arguments. When most Western countries accepted his belief that governments should intervene in

deficit financing: the government practice of spending more money than it collects in revenue, through borrowing.

The Business Cycle

One problem with capitalism is the recurring depressions and unemployment that emerge as a pattern of economic changes. Economists analyze these economic changes by constructing charts that trace the progress of the economy. One method is to plot the total value of all goods and services (GNP) on a chart and compare the values over time. The resulting chart resembles a wave, which is often called the "business cycle." The four phases of each business cycle are recession, trough, recovery, and peak.

During a recession, the GNP declines. This reduced production usually causes high unemployment and lowers personal and business incomes. A particularly steep drop in the GNP is called a depression. The trough marks the point at which the economy bottoms out and begins to improve. During the recovery phase, production increases, worn-out machinery is replaced, and employment and incomes grow. Renewed business confidence pushes the economy to its peak, at which point the cycle begins anew. Unemployment, high incomes, and increased demand for goods and services strain the economy beyond its resources and plunges the country into a recession.

No two cycles are the same, as the peaks and troughs vary in height. The economy is said to be contracting when the peak has been reached and the cycle begins its downturn. When the cycle begins its upturn following a trough, the economy is said to be expanding. But the instabilities of the business cycle create serious problems for capitalism.

the economy to promote employment and stability, it seemed like the pure laissez-faire economics of Adam Smith had died.

These attempts to save capitalism from the destruction that Marx had predicted resulted in the creation of welfare-state economies in such countries as Canada, Japan, much of Western Europe, and the United States. These mixed economies attempted to correct the faults of the private enterprise system, provide a more fair distribution of income, and improve working conditions. The role of government in these mixed economies expanded to include responsibility for unemployment, economic growth, poverty, and health care. Because of its concern for greater equality, the mixed economy included a welfare system designed to aid poor, sick, disabled, and elderly citizens.

A complex maze of government regulations was passed to limit the activities of private enterprises. For example, individual firms had to conform to laws that prevented unfair business practices and dangerous working conditions. These regulations included minimum wages and maximum hours, anti-discrimination laws, anti-pollution laws, and advertising restrictions—the list was almost endless. The emphasis, however, was on regulation rather than on government ownership. Most property was still owned by individuals or private companies. Wealth was somewhat limited by taxation and other government policies, but huge fortunes could still be accumulated.

Figure 9.2: The Business Cycle

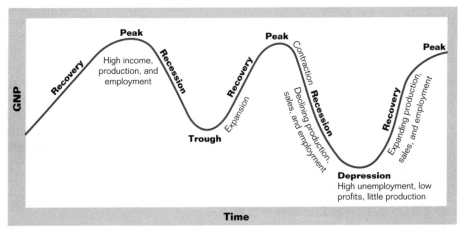

Fiscal and Monetary Policies

Such policies as altering the tax rate, increasing or reducing government expenditures, adjusting interest rates, and varying the supply of money in the country are strategies governments have at their disposal to influence the economy. Keynesian-oriented governments attempt to influence the economy by using fiscal policies.

Fiscal policies refer to the government's use of spending and taxes to influence the growth or decline in the demand for goods and services. They are the chief weapons in the government's economic arsenal. To stimulate a sluggish economy, the government will run a deficit (spend more than it earns) by spending money on such public works as roads and bridges, and by providing unemployment insurance and welfare payments. A budget surplus (created by raising taxes and reducing spending) is used to slow an economy that is growing too quickly.

Monetary policies refer to the government's regulation of the supply of money to influence the economy. In Canada, the Bank of Canada controls the country's money supply. When there is a large supply of money in the country, interest rates are low as lenders try to convince people and companies to borrow money. Because low interest rates make it relatively easy to borrow money, the economy, in theory, should begin to grow. The more it grows, however, the more likely inflation will occur. The Bank of Canada can reduce the amount of money available by increasing interest rates. This reduces borrowing, slows down economic growth, and stops inflation. The side effect, however, is increased unemployment. People who advocate reliance on monetary policies rather than fiscal policies are called **monetarists**.

Economist Milton Friedman is the leading proponent of monetarism, which has been a major tool of economic management during much of the second half of the twentieth century. Canada, the United States, and Great

fiscal policies: the government's use of taxing and spending to regulate and influence the economy.

monetary policies: the government's regulation of the supply of money to influence the economy.

monetarists: advocates of policies in which the monetary supply is used to influence the economy.

Britain are examples of countries that alter the supply of money to influence the economy. Friedman argues that if the government tried to alter the total demand for goods and services by increasing or decreasing government expenditures, or by increasing or decreasing taxes (both Keynesian policies), the national income would increase. This would raise the demand for money, which would cause interest rates to rise, and thus lead to a decrease in investments by private enterprise. The way to deal with inflation, Friedman believes, is for the government to expand or contract the money supply. Monetarists believe that increasing the money supply too much will cause inflation, whereas Keynesians state that when unemployment rates are high, increasing the money supply causes a decline in unemployment without creating inflation.

Supply-Side Economics

The near-universal faith in Keynesian economics (also called demand-side economics because its emphasis is on creating demand for goods and services) began to break down in the 1970s as government spending created high inflation, huge national debts, and increased taxes to pay for government expenditures. In addition to spiralling prices, governments continued to spend more than they collected, and the resulting national debt of such countries as Canada and the United States grew enormously. The deficit in the United States, for example, increased from $40 billion in 1979 to $366 billion in 1993 (the Canadian deficit will be discussed in more detail in Case Study 15).

neo-conservatism: an economic school of thought that opposes government involvement in the economy and emphasizes greater reliance on private enterprise; also called Thatcherism, Reaganomics, and supply-side economics.

During the 1960s, a **neo-conservative** economic school of thought emerged to challenge Keynesian practices. Its theories were subsequently adopted in the 1980s by Prime Minister Margaret Thatcher in Great Britain and President Ronald Reagan in the United States. More recent converts include premiers Mike Harris of Ontario and Ralph Klein of Alberta and Newt Gingrich of the Republican Party in the United States with his "Contract with America."

In general, supply-siders dislike government involvement in the economy and emphasize greater reliance on private enterprise. They praise the free market, dislike government regulations, and consider government-run businesses inefficient and wasteful. Their policies include cuts in social spending, lower corporate taxes, privatization, fewer government regulations, and a balanced budget. Supply-siders argue that if income taxes are reduced, everyone will have a greater incentive to work additional hours and to save more money. This increased incentive to work, save, and invest will spur the economy and result in greater tax revenues than a tax increase would produce.

What is the message of this cartoon?

Probably neither Margaret Thatcher nor Ronald Reagan ever imagined that their names would someday be used to represent an economic theory. What has commonly become known as **Thatcherism** or **Reaganomics** is an application of the economic theory previously known as supply-side economics. The following section compares the theories of the supply-siders and the Keynesian economists.

Thatcherism: a supply-side economic policy pursued by former British Prime Minister Margaret Thatcher.

Reaganomics: a supply-side economic policy pursued by former U.S. President Ronald Reagan.

The political relationship of U.S. President Ronald Reagan and British Prime Minister Margaret Thatcher helped to form a Western alliance and change economic policies.

How Keynesian Economics Deals With Recession

Keynesian or demand-side economics concentrates on the total amount of spending in the economy (as does monetarism). When consumers, businesspeople, and governments spend, they create demand for goods and services. This demand encourages business firms to increase production, which in turn creates employment. A drastic reduction in the amount of spending may cause the economy to enter a **recession**, which is just another way of saying that employment and production are greatly reduced. According to demand-siders, during a recession or **depression**, government should intervene in the economy by increasing its spending. This will increase the demand for goods and services, which in turn will encourage businesses to produce more goods and services, and employment will rise. As more people are employed, they will have additional money to spend. As spending increases, the cycle starts again.

recession: a downward trend in a country's economy.

depression: a deep and prolonged drop in the Gross National Product, with high unemployment.

Figure 9.3: The Keynesian Percolator—Solving a Recession

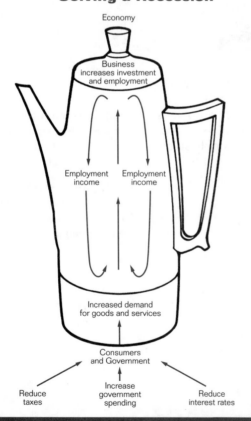

How could Keynes' theory be used to justify welfare payments to disadvantaged people?

How Supply-Siders Deal With Recession

Supply-siders insist that government intervention should be kept to a minimum. They emphasize the production side of the market (the producer). According to this theory, during a recession, government should stimulate the goods and services sector of the economy by reducing corporate and personal taxes.

Supply-siders argue that high taxes restrict productivity by discouraging work, personal savings, and business investments. Reducing corporate taxes creates more profits for business firms and acts as an incentive to others to enter business. A reduction in personal income taxes increases the public's incentive to work and provides more earnings to spend.

As the private sector produces more goods, employment levels increase. This results in additional spending and greater demand for goods and services. Supply-siders thus argue that increased production creates its own demand. They insist that increased demand for goods and services must come from the private sector, not from government spending.

Supply-siders believe that most forms of government regulation are harmful to the economy. Regulation may be minor, such as laws requiring fans in employee lunchrooms, or major, such as mandatory holidays. Reducing the number of rules and the amount of paperwork provides not only more cash to plough back into the company but also more flexibility in running the business.

Privatization removes "unfair" government competition with private companies and reduces the tax burden on the public (see Case Study 15).

Dealing With Inflation and Unemployment

Each year, a dollar seems to buy less and less. A situation of rising prices (or the declining value of money) is called **inflation**. Inflation arises when a country's total demand for goods and services increases faster than its production of goods and services. An increase in the price of a ticket to the movies does not by itself constitute an inflation. If, however, the price of transportation to the movie, the popcorn you eat at the movie, the clothing you wear to the movie, and so on all go up in price at the same time, this is inflation. In 1960, for example, a typical family spent $40 on food per week, whereas in 1995 the same amount and type of food cost $250.

In pursuing economic growth, governments must balance employment, inflation, productivity, and the **national debt**. Because it appears impossible to have the best of all these factors for very long, governments must constantly select which factors are most desirable at a particular time. The most common problem is selecting between high levels of employment and low levels of inflation. To reduce unemployment, Keynesians favour cutting taxes (to provide buyers with more money) and increasing government spending. Supply-siders support tax cuts (as an incentive to consumers to work hard and save), but argue against increases in government spending.

During an inflationary period, demand-siders suggest that the government remedy the situation by introducing such policies as reduced expenditures and tax increases. Supply-siders, on the other hand, believe that the unrestricted market will eventually bring inflation under control. Monetarists, on the other hand, argue that the money supply should be reduced.

privatization: the sale of government-controlled or -owned assets to the private sector.

inflation: a condition of generally rising prices owing to the supply of excess money over available goods.

national debt: the amount of money owed by one country to other countries as a result of deficit financing.

Figure 9.4: The Supply-side "Drip-Down" Theory

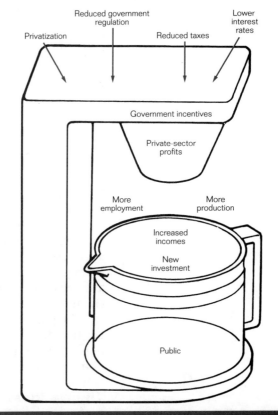

Supply-side theory states that if the private market is free to operate, then wealth will "trickle down" to the general public. What is your opinion?

Supply-Side Economics in the United States: Reaganomics

Reaganomics was a response to the economic problems of the United States in the 1970s, in which high inflation and unemployment and low productivity plagued the administrations of Richard Nixon, Gerald Ford, and Jimmy Carter. In the Kennedy/Johnson era of the 1960s, economic policymakers had been confident that they could use the government's fiscal and monetary tools to stabilize the business cycle and achieve low inflation and high employment. In the 1970s, this seemed no longer possible.

Conservatism was the dominant mood of the country when President Ronald Reagan was elected in 1980. Reagan claimed that he was elected to cut taxes, limit government spending on social programs, establish a stable money policy, reduce government interference in the marketplace, and balance the budget. Upon taking office, he immediately attacked the problems of the economy. Following the policies of supply-side economics, he reduced the federal budget by cutting billions of dollars from Medicare and Medicaid, food stamps, welfare subsidies, and inner-city school meals.

Reagan next reduced income taxes on wealthy individuals and corporations by $750 billion to stimulate saving and investment, the largest tax cut in American history. As prosperity returned, Reagan argued, corporate profits would trickle down to the middle classes and even to the poor.

Reagan claimed that he first understood the stupidity of high tax rates when he was making movies during World War II. At the time, the top personal income tax rate was 90 percent. He was shocked that top stars would make only four movies a year because getting paid for additional movies would have pushed them into the top tax bracket. Even in the middle of a world war, the stars refused to work for the government for 10 cents out of every dollar.[2]

Of all Reagan's policies, perhaps none have generated more controversy than those concerned with redistributing income. One of Reagan's first actions was to cut income tax by 25 percent across the board. This sounds like it would be a good move, but a 25 percent tax cut does not mean quite the same to everyone. Families earning less than $10 000 a year paid about $120 less in taxes, whereas families earning between $20 000 and $40 000 averaged about $800 less in taxes. Families earning over $80 000 saved an average of $15 000 a year in taxes. President Reagan himself, thanks to tax changes that he signed into law, saved $90 000 in income tax in 1982.[3]

The president's third major initiative was to reduce federal environmental, health, and safety regulations. These restrictions, he argued, were not only unnecessary, but also reduced business profits and discouraged economic growth.

The National Debt

national deficit: the amount by which government expenditures exceed revenues for a particular year.

Before further examining Reaganomics, we have to understand the **national deficit** and the national debt. Just like any household, a country must have income to meet its expenses. A country obtains its income through various taxes, whether they are direct (such as income tax) or indirect (such as tariffs on imports). When a government spends as much as it takes in, it has a balanced budget. If the government spends less than it takes in, it has a budget surplus, and if it spends more than it receives, it has a budget deficit.

Keynes suggested that a deficit was not necessarily bad during periods of slow economic growth. Increased government spending, he stated, would allow people to buy more goods and services. This increased demand would spur increased production and higher employment levels. Supply-siders argue against deficit budgeting. They support balanced budgets and consider deficit budgets inflationary and the cause of large national debts. If a country has a deficit, it must borrow money to pay its bills. The country must then pay interest on its loans, which is called "servicing the debt"; this in turn adds to inflation.

Although Reagan had some success in fighting inflation and unemployment, he failed to reduce his country's national debt. To reduce its debt, a government can either cut its spending, or increase taxes, or both. In his second term, Reagan had a choice of cutting the U.S. military budget of $1.7 trillion, increasing taxes,* or further reducing welfare and social programs. He selected the conservative option and cut welfare programs. However, largely because he increased military expenditures by 13 percent, the national deficit tripled between 1985 and 1988.

Reaganomics: An Evaluation

The controversy over the American experiment with supply-side economics persists.** Its critics claim that it has been a failure because Reagan left the American people with the highest debt in the country's history and his policies created an explosive social situation by dramatically increasing the gap between the rich and the poor. The critics also state that deregulated markets cause "boom and bust" cycles, and that Reagan's policies have led to the decline of the middle class, as well as the abandonment of the less fortunate in society.

Supporters of Reaganomics claim that supply-side economics has been successful in the United States. They argue that these policies have reduced inflation and unemployment while increasing production. They also claim that the fact that the rest of the world is moving toward freeing the private market proves the soundness of Reaganomics.

---

*It should be pointed out that although Reagan reduced the tax rate for the wealthiest 10 percent of the population, tax revenues from this group increased by 32 percent, thus providing support for the supply-side argument that tax cuts stimulate the economy and increase productivity.

**Many economists believe that President Reagan talked more about supply-side economics than he followed it. British Prime Minister Margaret Thatcher is generally considered to have adopted supply-side doctrines more rigorously.

···**Conclusion**

We have now examined the major economic theories. How well do they operate in practice? Case Study 11 explored the American economy between 1920 and 1940 and discussed why President Roosevelt decided that the government should play more of a role in the economy. Case Study 12 examined why the Russian economy went the opposite way, from total government control to an emphasis on the market forces of supply and demand. Case Study 13 discussed China's recent adoption of some aspects of private enterprise. The next three studies examine the mixed economies of Sweden, Canada, and Japan. For several decades, social democrats pointed to Sweden as an example of what proper government involvement could do and some economists considered Japan to have a model economy. Case Studies 14 and 16 explore what made these two economies successful in the 1970s and 1980s, and what has happened to them since. Case Study 15 studies Canada's economy and the debate over how much involvement the government should have in the economy. The final case study examines how two totalitarian dictatorships organized the economies of Fascist Italy and Nazi Germany.

BIOGRAPHY

GRO BRUNDTLAND, 1939–

The dominant figure in Norway's political system since 1981 has been Gro Harlem Brundtland, the country's first female prime minister, who has held the reins of government through much of the last two decades. During this time, her influence has spread far beyond Norway and Europe through her central role in the United Nations' actions on environment and sustainable development.

The daughter of a former cabinet minister in Norway's Labour government, Brundtland received a medical degree in Oslo and a master's degree in public health from Harvard University. She left medicine for politics in 1974, when she became Norway's environment minister. Brundtland was nicknamed "The Green Goddess" for her passionate commitment to the environment and a high quality of life for all citizens.

As prime minister in the late 1980s, Brundtland led Norway's mixed economy through a process of economic restructuring that resulted from a world recession and the falling price of petroleum, which was crucial to Norway's prosperity. She continued the main elements of Norway's social welfare system and economic health was eventually restored, but she was unable to convince Norwegians to join the common market of the European Community in a referendum in 1994.

Brundtland has systematically promoted the role of women in Norway's political and economic systems. She pushed her Labour Party to adopt a requirement for at least 40 percent of its candidates to be female. As a result, 34 percent of Norway's members of Parliament in 1986 were female, more than anywhere else in the world. (Her 1986 Cabinet had eight women and nine men.) In the 1991 election, the leaders of all three of the largest parties were women.

Brundtland's international reputation has come from her extensive work on global issues since 1983. She headed the United Nations' World Commission on Environment and Development, whose report *Our Common Future* called for "sustainable development" to deal with the interrelated problems of world poverty, population growth, and the environment. Brundtland described sustainable development in an interview with the *UNESCO Courier:*

We defined sustainable development as a system of development that meets the needs of the present without compromising the ability of future generations to meet their own needs. We then asked what exactly are the needs of the present and gave our answers in different chapters of the report. We made an integrated analysis which incorporates all the different aspects of human life and is rooted in an awareness of interdependence between nations.

What is fundamentally at stake is the question of human rights—not only those of people today but also those of their children and grandchildren. Since our children and grandchildren cannot take care of their own destiny we must do so on their behalf. In the past it was possible for each generation to leave the future to its successors, who when the time came would be able to assume their own destiny, find their own solutions, use new natural resources, develop different technologies and skills, enable life to go on, and perhaps even improve the human condition. But in our century massive population growth has led to increased exploitation of natural resources. Furthermore, it has caused pollution on such a scale that the Earth's atmosphere is being affected to the detriment of our common future. It is now that we must take the decisions that will enable people to live through the twenty-first century. ...

[T]he necessary political decisions have to be made by governments, not private industrialists. The market needs political direction. And governments are dependent on public opinion. If the argument for the future of humanity is convincing enough governments are bound to listen to it. In a sense there is no real choice; it's a question of how quickly and how broadly we tackle the problem. I have met no political leader who believes that we can continue "business as usual."[4]

Brundtland has recently focussed on the necessity of empowering women through education and inclusion in the political and economic systems in order to bring about world prosperity. The following selection is taken from her keynote address to the 1994 United Nations Conference on Population and Development in Cairo:

The final program of action must embody irreversible commitments toward strengthening the role and status of women. ... It cannot be repeated often enough that there are few investments that bring greater rewards for the population as a whole than the investment in women. But they still are being patronized and discriminated against in terms of access to education, productive assets, credit, income and services, inclusion in decision-making, and equal treatment in working conditions and pay. For too many women in too many countries, development has been only an illusion. Women's education is the single most important path to higher productivity, lower infant mortality, and lower fertility.[5]

---

1 To what extent does Gro Brundtland's view of sustainable development reflect the public-enterprise elements of mixed economies?

2 Why does she emphasize the importance of the role of women in changes to political and economic systems?

Underlying and Emerging Issues

Give the reasoning and evidence that might be used to support different views or conclusions on the following issues.

1 Do modern economic systems exploit or discriminate against women?

2 Can major economic change be achieved through peaceful and gradual measures?

3 How important is efficiency as compared with providing employment?

4 Does nationalization and public enterprise result in inefficiency?

5 Under what circumstances is public enterprise most effective?

6 Which economic activities are best conducted by government, and which are best left to private enterprise?

7 Should governments attempt to regulate economic decisions rather than engage in public ownership?

8 To what degree does an individual have a right to accumulate wealth?

9 Should governments attempt to redistribute income to achieve greater equality?

10 Should governments use fiscal and monetary policies to deal with the effects of the business cycle?

11 Should governments adopt policies of privatization and deregulation?

12 Does less government involvement in the economy mean greater disparities between rich and poor?

13 How important is it to control government budget deficits and debt compared with maintaining social programs?

14 What kinds of services should we expect from our governments, and how should we pay for them?

15 How should governments deal with monopolies and oligopolies?

Focussing Knowledge

In your notes, clearly identify or define and explain the importance or significance of each of the following:

mixed economy	neo-conservatism
democratic socialism	"trickle-down" theory
Fabian movement	deficit
British Labour Party	debt
nationalization	welfare capitalism
business cycle	recession
Eduard Bernstein	depression

Jean Juarès

Beatrice and Sidney Webb

inflation

John Maynard Keynes

John Stuart Mill

Milton Friedman

fiscal and monetary policy

supply-side economics

demand-side economics

Thatcherism

Reaganomics

Reviewing and Organizing Knowledge

1 Why is it difficult to classify economic systems as either "market" or "command"?

2 How does Anna Maier's situation reflect the ideas of the early democratic socialists?

3 a. What were the main elements of Fabianism?

b. What were the main arguments in favour of nationalization?

4 What are the fundamental ideas of democratic socialism?

5 a. In what areas do democratic socialists agree with communists?

b. In what areas do they differ?

6 What were the main elements of John Stuart Mill's views?

7 a. What ideas did Keynes contribute to the reform of capitalism?

b. To what extent were his views adopted?

8 What are the main features of supply-side economics?

9 Explain how each of the following would deal with recession: Keynesian economics, monetarism, supply-side economics.

10 a. How would Keynesian economists and supply-side economists deal with inflation?

b. How does each view deficit budgeting?

11 What are the main arguments for and against Reaganomics?

Applying and Extending Knowledge

1 Compare two early democratic socialists (such as Bernstein, Jaurès, the Webbs, Shaw, or Wells). To what extent were they similar and different in terms of motivation, circumstances, and policies?

2 Compare the operation of democratic socialism in Britain with the experience of another European country. To what extent were they similar and different?

3 Research the U.S. and British economies under Reagan and Thatcher. How similar and different were their policies and results?

4 Choose an industry that is publicly owned in Canada and in another country. Research and compare them in terms of operation and effectiveness.

5 Write a dialogue between one of the following pairs: Karl Marx and H.G. Wells; Adam Smith and George Bernard Shaw; John Maynard Keynes and Milton Friedman; Franklin D. Roosevelt and Ronald Reagan; Beatrice Webb and Margaret Thatcher.

6 Write a position paper in which you support the policies of either Keynes or Friedman. Explain the strengths and weaknesses of each, and why you chose one over the other.

7 Find examples of newspaper articles that are related to some of the Underlying and Emerging Issues on page 391. Explain how the articles illustrate the issues.

8 Choose one of the Underlying and Emerging Issues. Take a stand on the issue, and explain how you came to support the side you chose.

The Changing Face of Swedish Socialism

$\mathscr{S}$WEDEN HAS A UNIQUE BLEND OF PUBLIC and private enterprise in a democratic context. This case study discusses the similarities between Sweden and Canada before describing Sweden's form of democratic socialism in the 1970s. Although the Swedish government has left the production of goods to the marketplace, the state has had considerable influence over the allocation of these goods. The case study examines how Sweden initially succeeded in extricating itself from a severe recession, but then fell into an even deeper recession in 1990. It concludes by examining the role of Sweden's social welfare system in the country's economic problems and how the government is restructuring its economic and social policies.

Learning Outcomes

After reading this case study, you should be able to:

- discuss Sweden's major economic and social goals and approaches

- detail the strengths and weaknesses of the Swedish system

- debate the benefits of Sweden's economic system

- evaluate what Canada might learn from Sweden's experiences

- discuss the merits of currency devaluation

- decide how a country's economic competitiveness can be improved

- debate the merits of indicative planning versus central planning

- discuss the factors that act as work incentives

Sweden at a Glance

Area: 449 964 km²
Population (1995): 8 822 000 (world's 82nd-largest country)
Life Expectancy in Years (1994): Males 75.5, Females 81.2
GNP (1994): $194.7 billion (U.S.)
GNP per Capita (1994): $17 600 (U.S.)
Doctors per 1000 People (1993): 2.6
Hospital Beds per 1000 People (1993): 7
Health Expenditures as Percentage of GDP (1990): 8.8
Telephones per 1000 People (1994): 680
Televisions per 1000 People (1993): 470

Sources: *The World Almanac and Book of Facts 1996* (Mahwah, NJ: World Almanac Books, 1996); John Robert Colombo, ed., *The 1996 Canadian Global Almanac* (Toronto: Macmillan, 1996); Marlita A. Reddy, ed., *Statistical Abstract of the World* (New York: Gale Research, 1994).

An examination of the experiences of other countries can illustrate the strengths and weaknesses of different economic theories and policies. Sweden and Canada share many similarities. As a result, a study of Sweden's economic development can provide us with many useful insights. Each country has a northern location with a relatively small population compared with its land mass. Both are well-endowed with natural resources, including fish, farm products, forests, water power, and minerals (although Sweden is dependent on imported oil), and each relies heavily on exports for its economic growth. Both countries have high living standards and democratic governments.

There are, however, several important differences. Sweden has a history of low tariffs, whereas until very recently, Canada consistently placed high tariffs on most imported goods. Partly as a result of these different tariff policies, Canadian exports traditionally have been concentrated in the natural resources sector, whereas Sweden has diversified into manufactured products. In addition, Canada sells over three-quarters of its exports to one country (the United States), whereas Sweden's six major markets account for only half of its exports.

Politically, Sweden is a unitary state that is accustomed to peaceful and extensive consultation among government, business, and labour organizations. Canada's federal system and the frequent antagonistic relationship among business, government, and labour have tended to hinder the evolution of consistent economic policies. Unlike Canada, Sweden has an ethnically homogeneous society with only one official language. The only sizable ethnic group is the Lapps, a nomadic people in the north. Only about 7 percent of the population was not born in Sweden, and 95 percent of the people are Lutherans.

From 1870 to 1970, only Japan's economy grew faster than Sweden's. Swedish multinational corporations, such as Volvo, Ericsson, and Electrolux sold their products in every corner of the world. Sweden benefitted from a strong central government that helped to direct the economy, plenty of the right kinds of raw materials, and a well-educated population. By 1970, it was one of the richest countries in the world. Because Sweden had also developed a comprehensive social welfare system that protected its citizens from the cradle to the grave, many saw it as a "model economy." In recent years, however, the bubble burst. Unemployment rose to double digits, the national deficit mushroomed to alarming proportions, the banking system almost collapsed, and the GDP declined three years in a row.

What happened, and how is Sweden trying to solve its problems? The answers to these questions should be instructive to Canadians, as we face many similar problems.

A Brief Economic History to 1982

Following World War II, Sweden shifted its priorities from being primarily a supplier of natural resources to becoming a producer of manufactured goods requiring advanced technology and a skilled work force. It was a pioneer in

What are the advantages of living in a country that produces manufactured products rather than providing natural resources for the world market?

industrial technology, an innovator in labour–management relations, and a leader in social welfare policies. Inflation and unemployment were low.

Sweden's economy was such a complex blend of government and private enterprise that it is difficult to describe it in terms of socialism or capitalism. Although the production of goods and services was generally left to the marketplace, the state had considerable influence over their distribution. Income, but not production, was socialized.

Private Ownership

Agriculture was almost totally directed by private enterprise. Individual firms, which employed 90 percent of all industrial workers in Sweden, produced 95 percent of the country's manufactured goods. As in Canada and other Western countries, the industrial sector was dominated by a small number of very large firms. In fact, Sweden had more multinational firms *per person* than does the United States. These companies enabled Sweden to keep abreast of worldwide technological developments, and Sweden became one of the few net exporters of technology.

Government Controls

state monopoly: a commonly used economic policy whereby government owns, maintains, and operates vital facilities such as railways, airlines, postal systems, and similar facilities.

The Swedish government played an important role in the economy. This was especially true with regard to natural resources, transportation, and energy. Atomic energy was and still is a **state monopoly;** 25 percent of the country's forests, 50 percent of its water power, 85 percent of its iron ore, 95 percent of its railways, and 21 percent of its buses were publicly controlled. In addition, the government operated the telephone system and the liquor and tobacco businesses. Some of this nationalization was a direct result of social policy, in the case of atomic energy and telephones, for example. Others, such as the government takeover of the steel and shipbuilding industries, resulted from company bankruptcies and the desire to maintain high employment. Profit was not regarded as inherently bad—it merely had to be directed toward the common good.

Although relatively few industries were nationalized, the government exerted a strong influence over the economy through its fiscal and monetary policies (loans, interest rates, subsidies, and taxes), and by direct intervention. A good example of such intervention was the government's pollution regulations. Certain chemicals, such as DDT, were prohibited, limits were placed on polluting activities, and the state directed private research into anti-pollution equipment. Similarly, in housing, private initiative was hampered by building subsidies and rent controls. The government also decided how many homes would be built each year.

Government Planning

five-year plans: in Sweden, government economic projections for the future to assist industry in arriving at rational decisions.

The purpose of most government regulations was to allow free enterprise to run more smoothly. Sweden's **five-year plans** were a good example of this. Unlike some countries' long-term plans, they were not considered official government policy, but were forecasts or projections for the future designed to communicate information to private firms in every sector of the econo-

Stockholm, Sweden

my. The five-year plans provided guidance and helped to reveal problems in the market economy, but they did not fix production goals. There was less long-range planning in Sweden than there was in France, Norway, or Great Britain, but more than in Canada or the United States. The success of the Swedish plans was aided by voluntary cooperation among Swedish leaders of business, labour, and government. This method of indirect government planning, rather than providing incentives or issuing orders, is called **indicative planning** (in contrast to central planning in Marxist economies).

Indicative planning uses government targets to coordinate private and public economic decision-making. Individual companies may do what they wish, but are encouraged to meet agreed-upon economic targets. One approach to indicative planning is to ask firms to submit their investment and business intentions to the government, which then examines these plans for possible problems and attempts to resolve any possible difficulties through discussion. Another method is for the government to issue influential forecasts indicating the direction in which the economy is expected to go with the hope that companies will move in this direction. Indicative planning thus seeks to improve the flow of information in the market economy.

Direct government planning in Sweden was largely confined to social problems. The main goals were full employment and freedom from poverty for the Swedish populace. The state provided jobs for those who needed them, housing, adequate incomes, and medical care. The burden of raising children, for example, was to a certain extent transferred from the family to society as a whole. Mothers were given free prenatal care and a substantial family allowance for each child under the age of 16. Either parent was eligible for a year's maternity/paternity allowance. Nursery schools were free and higher education was funded by the government. The state also provided low-cost day-care centres for the children of working parents.

indicative planning: in Sweden, indirect government planning that uses targets as guidelines to coordinate private and public decision-making.

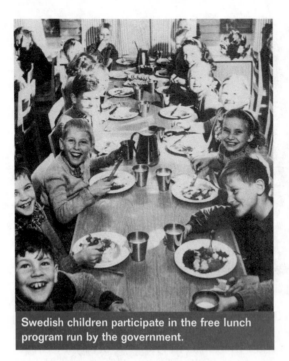

Swedish children participate in the free lunch program run by the government.

All employees were guaranteed five-week vacations. Old age pensions, which officially began at age 65, were tied to the cost-of-living index. Retired workers were granted two-thirds of the average salary of their most productive 15 years of work, thereby enabling older citizens to maintain their standard of living. Health was regarded as particularly important, and medical and dental care were almost completely free. The government provided free hot lunches to schoolchildren, and subsidized travel to and from work. Sweden's infant mortality rate was among the lowest in the world. Although there were large income differences in Sweden, there were no slums, no starvation, and little real poverty. As a result, Swedes had, and still have, one of the world's highest longevity rates.

Swedes believed that freedom could be achieved only in a proper social and economic environment. The better the social programs, the more freedom there was. Government thus assumed a position of watchful supervisor over all "significant" aspects of national life.

Union Participation

Over 80 percent of the Swedish work force is unionized. The goal of Swedish labour unions has been to abolish the negative aspects of capitalism without destroying the system itself. Instead of demanding public ownership and nationalization, unions emphasized social welfare policies in the 1950s and 1960s, leaving the management of industry to individual firms. During the 1970s, however, trade unions fought for economic as well as political democracy. The result was a series of reforms culminating in the **Co-determination Act of 1977,** which gave trade unions an important voice in the actual operation of Swedish industries. Union representatives received the right to sit on each company's board of directors and to participate at all levels of corporate decision-making. The employer's power to decide on matters of hiring, firing, and placing workers was abolished. In these situations, as in discussions on the nature and methods of production undertaken by each firm, all decisions are negotiated between the union and the company. In addition, the establishment of "wage-earners funds" gave employees shares in the ownership of their companies.

Co-determination Act of 1977: an act that gave trade unions a voice in the day-to-day operation of Sweden's industries.

Toys Я Us Versus Sweden's Labour Culture

The 1995 strike at the Toys Я Us stores in Stockholm, Malmö, and Göteborg, Sweden, illustrates both how powerful Sweden's unions still are and how North American business methods differ from those of Sweden. In May 1995, Toys Я Us refused to sign a collective agreement with the union, preferring to deal directly with the employees as it did in its other stores. But collective labour–management agreements are almost part of Sweden's soul. Such agreements cover everything from holidays and sick leave to working conditions, hours, and wages.

Other foreign firms, such as IBM and McDonald's, had collective agreements with the appropriate unions. Many Swedes believed that this giant American company, Toys Я Us, was trying to force its anti-union culture down the throats of Swedish workers. Most Swedish companies have few levels between top management and workers. Daily relations between management and labour are informal, and workers have considerable autonomy in decision-making. At Toys Я Us, the staff complained about the company's hierarchical management style. As one negotiator said, "It was a typical American set-up, no democracy. The boss tells you what to do, and you tell the next one down the line and he does it, and you don't ever think for yourself."[1]

The strike lasted three months. To some Swedes, it became a battle to protect their national values and traditions against the bullying management style of an American company. To others, however, it was merely another example of a foreign company that had been poorly advised about Sweden's labour culture.

Strikers formed picket lines outside each Toys Я Us store to discourage shoppers from entering. Soon other unions joined in: bank, transport, and dock workers supported the strikers; the printers' union refused to publish the company's advertisements in Swedish newspapers; one international union urged its 12 million members in 70 countries not to shop at Toys Я Us. Facing an international boycott, the company gave in and signed a collective agreement with the union in August 1995.

Focus

Do you think the tactics used by Swedish workers would be effective in Canada? Why or why not?

Economic Crisis and the New Industrial Strategy

In the 1970s, Sweden's economy began to decline, as did the economies of many countries. The national deficit rose alarmingly, inflation and unemployment increased, and the good relations among government, business, and labour evaporated. During this crisis period (1974–82), the government attempted to remedy the situation by increasing its control over the economy; it granted subsidies to firms that were in trouble, or nationalized ailing industries. Nothing seemed to work, and Sweden's ability to compete with other industrialized countries continued to decline.

In 1982, the Social Democratic Party of Olof Palme returned to power and embarked upon a new industrial program. Despite considerable opposition, the Palme government devalued the Swedish krona in relation to the American dollar; ultimately the krona was devalued to 50 percent of the American dollar. The government then adopted a plan designed to bring Sweden out of the depression by encouraging Swedes to save more of their incomes and to produce more goods per person (increased productivity). The socialist government discouraged the consumption of consumer goods and sought to persuade Swedes to invest their surplus cash in the country's economy. For the first time since World War II, the government reduced its spending. To further encourage industrial growth and investments, the government kept interest rates low.

Equally important, the Social Democratic Party reversed its earlier industrial policies. Instead of supporting chronically ailing firms with subsidies, the government gradually reduced its support to such businesses and adopted a new plan designed to promote industrial growth based on innovation and competitiveness with the rest of the world.

The devaluation of the krona lowered the price of Swedish export goods abroad, increased Sweden's national income, and enhanced the competitiveness of the country in world trading markets. To encourage industry, the government offered financial support and tax benefits to companies that were willing to invest funds in research and development into new products or to improve technology. It also generously subsidized the creation of new businesses. Palme created a more positive atmosphere for economic growth by reducing government regulations (deregulation) and "red tape," adopting a more cooperative relationship between government and business, and privatizing some industries.

Rather than using the traditional method of higher unemployment and reduced public expenditures to fight inflation, Sweden increased exports. This new industrial strategy restructured Sweden's economy. The emphasis on technology caused a decline in the number of labour-intensive industries, such as textiles, steel production, and shipbuilding, and an increase in knowledge-intensive high-technology industries. In other industrial sectors, such as pulp and paper, specialization and innovation allowed Sweden to capture a major share of foreign markets. Sweden became one of the largest developers of industrial robots, and its major exports now included cars, telecommunications equipment, electrical machinery, and pharmaceuticals. Sweden employed capitalist policies to maximize production, and socialist methods to redistribute wealth.

The results were spectacular. Exports of goods and services grew by 12 percent in the first year, and Sweden's trade balance rebounded from a deficit of 6 billion krona in 1982 to a surplus of 11 billion the next year. Labour agreements to limit wage increases to 5 percent further improved Sweden's international competitiveness, and by 1986, inflation and unemployment had been reduced to acceptable levels (3 percent and 2.7 percent, respectively).

Political conditions also played a part in Sweden's recovery. Rather than arguing over ideologies and personal benefits, various labour and political groups cooperated for the national good. Following the assassination of Olof Palme in 1986, the Social Democratic Party under Ingvar Carlsson enjoyed great popularity and growing public confidence. More willing to compromise than Palme, the new prime minister developed a spirit of harmony with industry and the other political parties. As a result, the pre-1974 society of shared values, cooperation, and stability was partially restored.

GUNNAR K. MYRDAL, 1898–1987

Testing Ideologies

Gunnar Myrdal was a Swedish economist who frequently challenged orthodox economic thought. In the 1920s, he criticized economists for defending the status quo and accused the profession as a whole of avoiding the economic problems of the real world. In the 1930s, Myrdal sought to widen the scope of economics by drawing attention to the importance of such social factors as education and health in economic decision-making. He and his wife Alva were active in reshaping Sweden's social and economic policies. In the 1950s, he described the vicious circle of poverty, ill health, lack of education, and unemployment that occurs in underdeveloped countries. Myrdal argued that economic aid from developed countries to developing countries was not in the latter's long-term interest. It was better to develop independently, he argued, rather than have restrictions placed on development.

Myrdal received the Nobel Prize in 1974 for his attempts to broaden the scope of economics. The following excerpt is from his 1968 book, *Asian Drama: An Inquiry Into the Poverty of Nations:*

An ideology can be studied from two different angles. One is its content of ideals and ideas. The ideology is then itself viewed as a "theory." It is tested in regard to its logical consistency, the adequacy to reality of its ideas about facts and about the causal relations between facts, and the significance and relevance of its ideals ... for practical conclusions and political action in the particular society. This approach is the traditional one for economists. In studying an ideology as a theory, an economist may dismiss it as untrue or irrelevant, or modify it and develop it into a more accomplished theory. ...

An ideology should also be looked on as a fact—as an aspect of the social reality from which policies emerge that, in their turn, influence actual develop-ment. Like other social facts it has to be explained in terms of its origins and its spread and influence. It is a guiding principle of this book that in studying underdevelopment, development, and planning for development in South Asia, the ideologies must be counted among the social facts.

We shall find that in these countries, policies develop in the context of totally different ideologies from those in the Western countries in their early stages of development. ... We are interested also in how the ideals expressed in ideologies compare with actual conditions in the South Asian countries and, even more, with the development of those conditions; and in the role of ideologies in the determination of policies.[2]

Focus

Why did Myrdal believe that economists should examine a country's ideologies?

Focus

Should wealthy people be allowed to move to other countries where income taxes are lower?

Social Policies

After being returned to power in 1982, the Social Democratic Party sought to revise the country's welfare policies. The financial burden of high taxes on the Swedish people had become crushing, especially with the downturn in the economy. As a result, many wealthy individuals, such as former tennis star Björn Borg, have left the country to avoid paying taxes.

Equally important was the growing unhappiness of Swedes with a system that controlled many aspects of their daily lives. The Swedish welfare state was designed for everyone, not just for the poor, so it affected everyone's entire life. Government-owned homes and apartments were drab and uniform because their occupants were not allowed to paint them without approval. The most publicized example of the government's intrusion occurred in the mid-1970s, when huge posters all over Sweden declared: "The Social Welfare Board wants us to eat 6–8 slices of bread per day." Few complained about the government's desire to have people consume the proper amount of fibre in their diet, but they did resent the fact that the government appeared to be commanding everyone to eat a set number of slices of bread. The posters were quickly removed, but this incident convinced many Swedes that the government had gone too far in trying to control people's lives.

Following the economic crisis of the late 1970s, the government began to emphasize self-reliance and place greater emphasis on reducing the costs of welfare programs. In several areas, such as kindergartens and medical practices, the government permitted private initiatives. Parents were now free to organize their own kindergartens, and doctors could establish their own clinics. Sweden thus began to re-examine some of its fundamental policies.

Case Table 14.1: Who Is Taxed the Most?

	Government Tax Revenues as a Percentage of 1992 GDP
Sweden	50.0
Denmark	49.3
Netherlands	46.9
Norway	46.6
France	43.6
Canada	36.5
Great Britain	35.2
Switzerland	32.0
Japan	29.4
United States	29.4

Source: © Organization for Economic Co-operation and Development, *Revenue Statistics of OECD Member Countries* (Paris: OECD, 1994). Reproduced by permission of the OECD.

Challenges to the Social Welfare System

Sweden's optimism was shattered in 1990 by a second economic crisis. Keynesian policies had reduced unemployment at the expense of government deficits and a growing national debt. The resulting recession was devastating: industrial production fell 18 percent between 1990 and 1993, reaching low levels not experienced since the Great Depression of the 1930s.

Unemployment increased from 2 percent to 9 percent and then to 14 percent. Compared with their Nordic neighbours, fewer new businesses were established in Sweden between 1984 and 1994. Such successful multinational corporations as Volvo and Electrolux thrived because of exports and foreign investments. The 25 largest Swedish companies had 75 percent of their employment, production, and sales abroad. At home, GNP per capita fell from $22 270 in 1990 to $20 550 in 1993.

According to many economists, these problems were linked to Sweden's generous welfare system and to the absence of competition in the public sector. In 1960, approximately one worker in eight was employed in the public sector. Thirty years later, this ratio had increased to one in three, and it was estimated that 70 percent of the population depended on the government for its livelihood. Although many countries reduced their expenditures on social welfare services in the 1980s, Sweden (in true Keynesian fashion) increased these expenditures. Employment in social services increased from 14 to 22 percent of the labour force, and health-care services employed 10 percent of the work force.

Case Figure 14.1: Changes in Swedish Public and Private Employment, 1950–1992

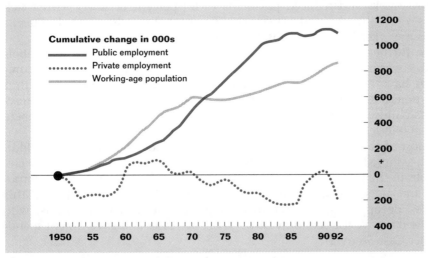

Source: "Slicing the Cake: The Rights and Wrongs of Inequality," *The Economist* (November 5, 1994), p. 20. © 1994 The Economist Newspaper Group, Inc. Reprinted with permission.

Reform of the welfare system had been on the agenda for many years, but the recession put it front and centre. The 1993 Lindbeck Commission recommended a complete overhaul to strengthen the country's economic competitiveness and to lower the deficit. Retirement policies, unemployment insurance, and sick leave benefits came under the most intensive attack and were subsequently modified.

In Sweden, citizens aged 60 to 64 can reduce their hours of work by up to 23 hours a week and be paid full wages for half of the missed time.

Approximately 13 percent of this age group takes advantage of the plan. Much of Sweden's social welfare expenditures go to those over 65 years old. With 17.5 percent of the population in this age category, Sweden has the highest proportion of older people in the world. In Canada, the proportion is 12.3 percent. Like Canada, Sweden plans to reduce future expenditures by increasing the age at which old age pensions begin, from age 65 to age 66.

Before the Commission's recommendations, people on unemployment insurance received 90 percent of their previous income starting on the first day they became unemployed and lasting for 14 months. To provide these people with a greater incentive to seek employment, the government reduced the level of payments to 80 percent and introduced a five-day waiting period before payments begin.

Paid leaves and injury insurance have also been reformed. Previously, sick or injured workers received 90 to 100 percent of their salaries. Parents were allowed 15 months' paid leave per newborn child; immigrants could apply for fully paid leaves to take lessons in the Swedish language; and workers could take time off to improve their education, participate in union activities, or care for sick relatives. These programs resulted in considerable absenteeism and low worker productivity. To correct this situation, the government decided not to commence sick pay until a worker had been absent for two weeks and reduced payments to 80 percent of salary. Other sick leaves were also reduced. These changes brought a dramatic decline in Swedish workers' notorious absenteeism.

To further promote efficiency, some government agencies were abolished, government regulations have been reduced, and over 50 state companies have been privatized. Competition has also been initiated within government agencies, including the option to contract out such social services as child care and elder care, and allowing private schools to compete with public schools for students.

Most of these changes were passed by the Moderate Party of Carl Bildt, which assumed power in 1991. This right-wing party stressed the need to create jobs in the private sector, slash government spending, and reduce corporate and personal taxes. In 1994, however, the people rejected this supply-side approach and returned to power the Social Democrats, who promised to save the economy through tax increases and government spending (see Case Study 2).

Conclusion

Sweden's economic system has evolved over time, illustrating once again that economic systems are dynamic. As circumstances change, so do our institutions, especially in the economic realm. Swedes, just like the citizens of other countries, must constantly weigh the trade-offs, costs, benefits, and values as they decide what type of economy they wish to have. The next case study examines the Canadian economy. What can Canada learn from Sweden's experiences?

Focus

Do you think Sweden's economic system will move closer to capitalism in the next decade? Why or why not?

BIOGRAPHY

OLOF PALME, 1927–1986

Sweden's dominant politician in the 1970s and 1980s, Olof Palme, played a central role in international affairs. While promoting democracy and social welfare in Sweden, he campaigned effectively for international peace, nuclear disarmament, and narrowing the gap between the world's rich and poor.

Born to a rich, conservative family in Stockholm and educated in private schools, Palme studied politics and economics at Kenyon College in Ohio. It was during this time that his upper-class beginnings were transformed into a lifelong commitment to democratic socialism:

> *Always a dedicated traveller, Mr. Palme after graduation hitch-hiked around the United States for four months, visiting 34 states on a $300 shoestring budget that took him into pockets of poverty in a land of plenty. It was a shocking experience for the young aristocrat.*
>
> *He recalled having seen "how poor some people were in the world's richest land." The adventure marked a turning point in his life, and the comment was virtually a theme for what was to become the socialist ideology of his political life.[3]*

After receiving a law degree in Sweden, Palme began his rapid rise in politics, first as president of the National Swedish Union of Students. After serving as personal secretary to the Social Democratic prime minister, he was elected to Parliament, became education minister in 1967, and prime minister in 1969. He served in that capacity until 1976, and again from 1982 to 1986. Palme was known as an idealist, but also as a supreme tactician. His personality and policies were summarized by *The New York Times:*

> *At home, Mr. Palme used high taxes to create a society generous with medical, educational, and recreational benefits. He scoffed at calls for tax cuts, more competition and less welfare spending as a prescription for a society of "egoism and sharp elbows."*

A slight, slender, blue-eyed man with a formidable intelligence and an eagerness for debate, Mr. Palme spoke fluent English, French, German and Spanish and some Russian, in addition to the Scandinavian tongues. He could inspire his followers with visions of Socialist life, but he also had a hectoring manner that many people took for condescension and arrogance.

"I was born in the upper class, but I belong to the labour movement," Mr. Palme once said. "I got there by working for the working class on its own terms, by joining the movement working for freedom, equality and fraternity among people."[4]

But it was in foreign affairs that Palme brought international attention to Sweden. He infuriated Americans with his unrelenting criticism of the Vietnam War, attacked apartheid in South Africa and dictatorship in Chile, and actively promoted nuclear disarmament and peace. He also played a central role in the Brandt Commission's actions to improve conditions in developing countries.

In 1986, as he walked home from a movie with his wife, Palme was assassinated by an unknown gunman. His death had a profound effect on the nation: "With his passing, Sweden seemed to shrink back into itself, to relinquish at least partially the role he had given it as 'the conscience of the Western world.' "[5]

---

1 Why would Olof Palme refer to capitalism in terms of "egoism and sharp elbows"?

2 How did his policies reflect the basic elements of Sweden's social democratic system?

Underlying and Emerging Issues

Give the reasoning and evidence that might be used to support different views or conclusions on the following issues.

1 To what degree should social programs be based on universality, and to what degree should they focus on those who are most in need?

2 Should Canada make greater use of indicative planning in its economic system?

3 Should government economic policies attempt to control distribution rather than production?

4 Should governments attempt to foster partnerships with business and labour?

5 Should governments support struggling industries in order to maintain employment levels?

6 To what degree should government provide support for families that are raising children?

7 Should government pursue policies of full employment?

8 Can people living in poverty participate fully in democracy?

9 Should governments make freedom from poverty a top priority?

10 What role should government play in supporting older citizens?

11 Should workers acting through unions have an important role in corporate decision-making?

12 Should businesses be required to promote employee ownership of shares in the company?

13 How can governments promote innovation and competitiveness?

14 To what degree should government social policies be based on promoting self-reliance?

15 Are effective government services worth high taxes?

16 What forms of taxation should governments use to obtain revenue?

17 What kinds of services should we expect from our governments, and how should we pay for them?

18 Should governments combat economic difficulties by moving to more private enterprise?

Focussing Knowledge

In your notes, clearly identify or define and explain the importance or significance of each of the following:

social welfare system	*boycott*
state monopoly	*devaluation*
five-year plans	*restructuring*
indicative planning	*Olof Palme*
Co-determination Act of 1977	*Ingvar Carlsson*
wage-earners fund	*Carl Bildt*
labour culture	*Gunnar Myrdal*

Reviewing and Organizing Knowledge

1 List the important similarities and differences between the economic systems of Sweden and Canada.

2 What were the major elements of Sweden's economic system after World War II?

3 What were the key characteristics of Sweden's economy before 1990 in the following areas:

a. private and public ownership?

b. government control?

c. government planning?

d. union participation?

4 How does the Toys Я Us incident reflect aspects of Sweden's economic system?

5 a. What was the Swedish government's initial response to the economic problems of the late 1970s?

b. How were social policies changed after the economic crisis of the late 1970s?

c. What approach to industry did the Social Democratic government take after 1982?

6 a. What were the effects of the recession in the early 1990s on the Swedish economy?

b. How did the Swedish government respond to these problems?

7 How does Sweden illustrate the dynamic nature of economic systems?

Applying and Extending Knowledge

1 Make a thorough list of all the elements of Sweden's economic system. Rate each element on a scale from 1 to 10 (where 1 is highly negative and 10 is highly positive). On this basis, select the four items that you found most favourable, then write an essay in which you describe your view of the extent to which these elements can and should be adopted by Canada.

2 Make two lists, one for the advantages of Sweden's economic system and another for the disadvantages. Write a description of the degree to which you think that Sweden's trade-offs are acceptable—that is, how the positives and negatives compare.

3 Do some research to compare Sweden's economy to that of Norway, Denmark, or Finland. In what ways are the economies similar and different?

4 Countries tend to develop economic systems that reflect their own specific circumstances. Describe the elements of Sweden's culture, history, or other factors that, in your opinion, most clearly account for Sweden's particular economic approach.

5 On the basis of your study of political and economic systems, write a report in which you act as a consultant to the Swedish government. How should Sweden change its economy, and what aspects of its system should it retain?

6 Find newspaper articles that reflect some of the Underlying and Emerging Issues on page 406. How do the articles illustrate the issues?

7 Choose one of the Underlying and Emerging Issues. Explain why the issue is complex by outlining the arguments and evidence on the various sides.

Canada's Mixed Economy

*H*OW INVOLVED IS THE CANADIAN GOVERNMENT in our economy? This case study outlines the areas in which the government intervenes in the economy, discusses the motives for this involvement, and explains the present demands for privatization, deregulation, and spending cuts. In an examination of the distribution of wealth in Canada, the wealthy people are identified along with the factors that determine why some people are wealthier than others.

Canada at a Glance

Area: 9 970 140 km² (world's 2nd-largest country)

Population (1996): 29 200 000 (world's 37th-largest country)

Life Expectancy in Years (1994): Males 74.7, Female 81.7

GDP (1995): $548.4 billion (U.S.)

GDP per Capita (1995): $18 800 (U.S.)

Doctors per 1000 People (1993): 2.2

Hospital Beds per 1000 People (1993): 5.0

Health Expenditures as Percentage of GNP (1990): 9.1

Telephones per 1000 People (1994): 580

Televisions per 1000 People (1992): 626

Sources: John Robert Colombo, ed., *The 1996 Canadian Global Almanac* (Toronto: Macmillan, 1996); Marlita A. Reddy, ed., *Statistical Abstract of the World* (New York: Gale Research, 1994); *Statistical Abstract of the United States, 1995: The National Data Book* (Washington, DC: U.S. Department of Commerce, September 1995).

Learning Outcomes

After reading this case study, you should be able to:

- evaluate the justifications for and against government-owned enterprises

- decide whether Canada has too much or too little government involvement in the economy

- analyze the reasons behind the growth of privatization

- understand the differences between relative and absolute poverty and the extent of poverty in Canada

- examine your own values regarding economic inequalities

- evaluate the importance of education, among other factors, to employment and high incomes

Most people acknowledge that capitalism has been extremely successful in promoting economic growth. Karl Marx, one of its harshest critics, wrote that capitalism "has accomplished wonders far surpassing Egyptian pyramids, Roman aqueducts, and Gothic cathedrals." It has, he said, "created more massive and more colossal productive forces than have all preceding generations together." As we have seen, the major stimulus behind this economic growth was the profit motive. Unfortunately, unrestricted competition among individuals struggling for the highest possible profits often created poverty, dangerous working conditions, and unhealthy homes for the "victims" of capitalism. It was largely to improve these conditions that governments intervened in the capitalist economy.

One of the most contentious areas of government involvement in the economy is the extent to which the state should control the policies and activities of individual business firms. Most businesspeople believe that they should be allowed to operate their companies with a minimum of government interference. They argue that competition among entrepreneurs is the best guarantee that consumers will receive quality goods at the lowest possible prices. Supporters of public enterprise disagree—the only way for the state to ensure that a just economy is created, they say, is for the government to operate the economy. Ultimately, this implies government ownership of the country's resources and businesses.

Canada's mixed economy lies somewhere between these two extremes. The actual amount and type of government intervention depends on a country's historical experience, form of government, objectives, and ideologies. Why and to what extent does the Canadian government intervene in the economy? Does it intervene too much or too little? To help answer these questions, this case study examines four areas in which the government intervenes in the Canadian economy—laws and regulations, government-owned and -operated companies, budget and financial policies, and income redistribution—and presents the arguments for and against each type of intervention.

Government Laws and Regulations

Regulation of economic activity is one of the principal functions performed by governments in all industrialized countries. The agricultural industry is a good example of the mixture of private enterprise and government regulation. In many ways, farmers are governed by the forces of supply and demand, and there is a high degree of competition within the industry. However, government-controlled marketing boards influence food prices by using crop controls and quotas to limit production. Food inspection, subsidies, and government-negotiated sales of wheat to foreign countries are just a few of the other ways that the agricultural industry is regulated.

In recent decades, concern over the environment, health, safety, and poverty has created thousands of pages of new rules and regulations. Pollution controls, minimum wage acts, safety standards, old age pensions, and food inspection are just a few such examples. In Canada, federal, provincial, and municipal governments all exercise a measure of control over the economy. For example, the federal government controls the money supply, establishes import duties, and regulates banks and trust companies. The provincial governments regulate the activities of lawyers, doctors, morticians, and many other occupations. City councils use their control over licensing to limit the number of taxis and pass laws regarding parking and transportation.

Government regulations allow businesses to remain in private hands while removing some of the worst abuses of capitalism. Health and safety controls ensure that children's toys meet safety standards, that food and beverages are safe to consume, and that restaurant kitchens are sanitary. Environmental restrictions protect endangered species and safeguard water and forest resources. Fairness laws prevent false advertising and discriminatory hiring practices. Cultural regulations restrict foreign ownership of certain industries and legislate how much Canadian content there must be in radio and television programs. Competition laws limit the growth of monopolies and attempt to discourage unfair business practices.

Case Figure 15.1 outlines the major reasons behind government regulations. Some laws are a direct result of the work of pressure groups and public opinion. Unions and women's organizations, for example, have been largely responsible for government regulations regarding safe working conditions and pay equity. In one example, widespread public outrage following the severe burning of several children wearing flammable pyjamas led to legislated changes in clothing materials for children.

Case Figure 15.1: Reasons for Government Intervention

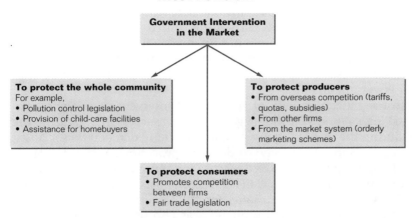

Source: E.D. Shade et al., *Fundamentals of Economics*, Vol. I, 3rd ed. Permission granted by McGraw-Hill Book Company Australia Pty. Ltd.

Most people accept the need to prevent unsafe working conditions, fraudulent advertising, and racial discrimination in the workplace. In arguing for **deregulation**, neo-conservative economists concentrate on criticizing economic regulations that involve production, pricing, hiring, and firing practices. By exposing businesses to competition, neo-conservatives believe

deregulation: a reduction of government restrictions on business enterprises.

that industry will become more efficient. So far, the Canadian federal government has made few such initiatives beyond financial services, transportation, and telecommunications. By law, for example, banks can sell stocks and mutual funds, but are not allowed to enter the insurance business. In 1996, the Ontario Conservative government of Mike Harris repealed labour laws that banned the hiring of replacement workers during strikes, ended rent controls, and made it easier for landlords to evict tenants. And Preston Manning's Reform Party promised to reduce the size of the federal government by eliminating waste, duplication, and red tape. To some people, government regulations are considered important to protect against the worst elements of capitalism. Other people think such regulations are an unnecessary invasion of their freedom. This long-running debate will continue as individuals ponder what type of society they wish to live in.

Government-Owned Businesses

The most controversial area of government involvement in the Canadian economy has been the creation (or nationalization) of government-owned and -operated businesses. Although public ownership is considered somewhat low in Canada compared with many European countries, there is more public ownership in Canada than in the United States. The reasons for this are not always easy to determine, but one explanation links Canada's greater preference for state-controlled companies to a long connection with Great Britain. The British government's practice of making important political and economic decisions for its colonies is said to have accustomed Canadians to the idea of government involvement in the economy and influenced the Canadian government to continue this practice. Also, because Canada had neither the immense sources of wealth of the United States nor a large population, individual companies could not finance such huge undertakings as constructing canals in the 1820s and 1830s, building railways in the 1850s and 1880s, or harnessing the power of Niagara Falls in the twentieth century without government aid.

The most significant growth of government intervention in the economy occurred after World War II. The government's success in organizing the economy during the war led many people, especially democratic socialists, to believe that it should continue to do so in peacetime. Socialists argued that central planning would make the economy more efficient and responsive to human needs. Some politicians and economists believed that **Crown corporations** would generate profits for the government. Control over such strategic industries as nuclear energy was also used to justify government ownership. In addition, Keynesian economists believed that the state could, and should, use its economic powers to create full employment and combat the ups and downs of the business cycle.

Sixty percent of Canada's public enterprises were created between 1960 and 1979; thereafter, government enthusiasm cooled. By the mid-1980s, there were about 300 federal Crown corporations, 230 provincially owned firms, and another 300 companies that were jointly owned by private indi-

Crown corporation: in Canada, a business enterprise owned by government and operated by a government-appointed management team.

viduals and governments. These enterprises were concentrated in the areas of electrical power, transportation, and communications. Some Crown corporations ranked among the largest companies in Canada.

Many public enterprises fulfil functions that private firms either will not provide or cannot be trusted to operate fairly. Privately owned railways, for instance, would not build branch lines to out-of-the-way areas of the country because there would be no profit in doing so. Control over such "natural" monopolies as electrical power, telephones, and drinking water could not be left to profit-motivated private firms because with no competition they could charge high prices for these vital services. The reasons for the growth of public enterprises can be divided into eight broad categories:

1 To control an area of the economy necessary for the general welfare;

2 To help stimulate regional development;

3 To produce goods vital to the country's security;

4 To provide services that private entrepreneurs are unable or unwilling to provide;

5 To earn income for the government;

6 To rescue a bankrupt firm that is essential to the economic well-being of a particular region;

7 To maintain and influence public morality;

8 To help stabilize the economy.

In most cases, the rationale behind public ownership includes several categories. The creation of Petro-Canada in 1975, for instance, was a result of Canada's desire to increase the country's energy supplies, to provide revenue for the federal government, and to limit foreign control over such an important industry. Petro-Canada has recently been privatized.

Hydro-Québec remains one of Canada's larger Crown corporations.

Case Table 15.1: Canada's Larger Crown Corporations, 1995

Company	Revenue (000) 1994	Employees
Ontario Hydro	8 730 000	22 590
Hydro-Québec	7 374 000	26 780
Insurance Corp. of B.C.	2 428 000	3 800
B.C. Hydro and Power	2 395 000	5 430
Canada Post	4 118 000	62 880
Canadian Broadcasting Corp.	1 374 000	9 120
Canada Mortgage and Housing	1 309 000	3 030
Manitoba Hydro-Electric Board	985 000	4 040
Export Development Corp.	844 000	590
Alberta Treasury Branches	666 000	3 210
Atomic Energy of Canada	465 000	3 920

Source: *Report on Business* (July 1995), p. 143.

Privatization

Privatization has been one of the major economic and political themes of the past two decades. Recall from Chapter 9 that privatization is simply the selling of state-owned companies to private industry so that they become a part of the private enterprise sector of the economy. Privatization of state-owned corporations first gained prominence in Great Britain under Margaret Thatcher's leadership. The idea quickly spread to the newly elected conservative governments in many Western democracies during the late 1970s and early 1980s, and by 1987, over 1400 state-controlled companies in some 80 countries were in the process of being privatized. Since then, developing countries have also embraced privatization, and the trend now appears to be worldwide.

The popularity of privatization can be attributed to several factors. During the 1970s it became fashionable to criticize the growing size of government bureaucracies and the alleged inefficiency of government-owned companies. The ideological climate also reflected a renewed faith in private enterprise. According to neo-conservatives, governments should stay out of the marketplace. More important was the drain on the government treasury that government-operated companies, many of which lost money perpetually, often entailed. Worries about inflation and mounting national deficits encouraged countries to sell their money-losing corporations. The airline business is an excellent example of the worldwide trend toward privatization. European governments sold part-ownership in Lufthansa, British Airways, Finnair, KLM, and Air France. Elsewhere, the airlines of Malaysia,

Singapore, Japan, Mexico, Argentina, Australia, and New Zealand have been completely or partially sold to the private sector.

In Canada, the Conservative government of Prime Minister Brian Mulroney followed the British example. Between 1984 and 1992, the federal government privatized 39 Crown corporations and other corporate interests, including Air Canada and CNCP Telecommunications. In the mid-1990s, Ontario Premier Mike Harris and Alberta Premier Ralph Klein initiated a round of provincial privatization. Premier Klein sold the province's retail liquor outlets, telephone company, and licensing services to private interests. Municipally, Edmonton sold its telephone system. Neo-conservatives argue that the forces of supply and demand will push these industries to perform more efficiently, while their opponents argue that privatization will increase the gap between the rich and the poor.

Do you think the government should be involved in the effort to ensure Canadian ownership of essential services such as air transportation?

Government Programs, Spending, and the National Debt

Government programs, especially in such areas as health, education, and welfare, constitute another major area of intervention in the economy. These programs are paid for through taxation. Each year, the government drafts its budget, which contains two key aspects: where it will spend money (programs), and how it will pay for its expenditures (taxation and borrowing).

In June 1958, Liberal Finance Minister Donald Fleming rose in the House of Commons to present the budget. His news was depressing: economic growth had slowed down, unemployment was rising, and foreign investments in Canada were falling. Fleming proposed using Keynesian methods to spend Canada out of the recession. He reduced taxes and poured money into the economy by initiating make-work schemes, increasing old age and veterans' pensions, and beginning a hospital insurance program. Of course, these policies would mean that the government would spend more money than it would earn (a deficit), but as Fleming said at the time, "Our desire for a balanced budget will not take precedence over the necessity to provide jobs for the unemployed." To finance the deficit, the government borrowed money by selling bonds at a set interest rate. Less than two years later, Fleming had turned a government surplus of $324 million into a deficit of $877 million.

Government deficits were not new. At Confederation, the national debt was $94 million. The costs of fighting World War I increased the debt to $2.4 billion. The Great Depression of the 1930s enlarged this figure to $5 billion, and by the end of World War II, the debt had expanded to $18 billion. But these were trivial numbers compared with the growth in the national debt from $38 billion in 1977 to $233 billion in 1987. In the early 1990s, high interest rates swelled the government's debt. This in turn caused investors to demand even higher interest rates to lend money to Canadian governments. By mid-1996, the national debt stood at $580 billion, which was equal to 70 percent of all the income earned in Canada that year.

Provinces and municipalities also have debts. The provinces' total debt was $250 billion in mid-1996. In 1995, Quebec and Newfoundland had the highest debt per person ($10 600), while British Columbia had the lowest ($5200).

Ask *Ideologies*

Q: What is the deficit?

A: It is the amount by which government expenditures exceed revenues for a particular year. If the government makes more money than it spends, there is a surplus. If it spends more money than it earns, there is a deficit. In 1992–93, the deficit of the federal government was $40.4 billion. Three years later, the government had reduced it to $28.6 billion.

Q: Why have our governments had continuing yearly deficits?

A: Governments need money to pay for such social programs as unemployment insurance and medicare, for civil servants' salaries, to run the government, to purchase major items such as submarines, and to encourage economic growth. When government revenues from taxes and other sources fall below these expenditures, a deficit is created for that particular year. Politically, it has often been more acceptable to run a deficit than to raise taxes or to cut programs. Reduced government earnings, either through tax cuts or when hard economic times decrease the amount of income taxes paid by individuals and corporations, also increase the deficit.

Q: What is meant by the national debt?

A: It is the total of all previous yearly deficits (minus years when there was a surplus), plus the interest on the money the government borrowed to pay these deficits.

Q: How large is the federal debt?

A: In 1995 the debt was $578 billion. This is equivalent to each man, woman, and child in Canada owing $19 300.

Q: Who is owed the national debt?

A: Individuals and companies lend money to the government by buying bonds, such as Canada Savings Bonds. In return, the government pays interest to the bondholders. Approximately 80 percent of the debt is owed to Canadians and to Canadian banks.

Q: Why has the debt grown so quickly?

A: The government must pay interest on the money it borrows. In times of high interest rates the debt grows very quickly. To determine how quickly it would take the national debt to double, use the Rule of 72. Divide the interest rate the government is charged to borrow money into 72. The product is how many years it will take the debt to double. For example, if the debt was $200 billion and the compound interest rate was 8 percent, the debt would grow to $400 billion in nine years (assuming no payments were made). In 1995, Canada spent over $45 billion just to pay the interest on the debt. These payments were more than three times what was spent on national defence.

Q: Why doesn't the government just print more money to pay off the debt?

A: This would cause inflation. Prices would rise, the value of the dollar would drop, and people would be reluctant to lend money to the government in the future.

Q: Why doesn't the government declare bankruptcy and avoid paying its debt?

A: This is dishonest, and no one would ever lend money to the Canadian government again.

Q: Why should we be concerned about the debt?

A: If the debt becomes too large, people will be reluctant to lend the government money unless they are promised higher interest rates. This means that the debt will then increase even faster. A large public debt means lower living standards and less money for social and cultural programs. Instead of spending money on these programs, the government must use the money to meet interest payments.

Reducing the Deficit

Prior to 1989 we rarely heard those nasty **d**-words. Now, the terms **d**eficit and **d**ebt seem to be everywhere. Every year for the past decade *Maclean's* has asked Canadians what they think are the most important issues facing the country. Ten years ago, only 6 percent mentioned the deficit. In 1995, over 25 percent said that the deficit was the most important issue facing Canada, and 66 percent thought that Ottawa had not done enough to reduce it.

The standard Keynesian method of fighting recessions is to cut taxes and increase government spending. When these practices stopped working in the 1970s, economists sought other solutions. Neo-conservative economists believe that the deficit problem is mainly a spending problem and recommend slashing social spending. This is the course several Canadian governments embarked on in the mid-1990s. The 1996 federal budget announced major spending cuts, and most provincial governments reduced their expenditures substantially. In the early 1990s, provincial governments believed that they could spend their way out of economic difficulties by stimulating the economy. They are now cutting back on spending, and as a result, government deficits in Canada have declined almost everywhere.

Neo-conservative policies, however, have their critics. Some people maintain that governments have a revenue problem, rather than a spending problem, because of the failure to effectively tax corporations and wealthy individuals. Others point to high interest rates as a major source of the problem. Although Alberta balanced its budget, it was done at the expense of closed hospitals, cuts in education and social programs, reduced salaries for civil servants, and 4500 fewer government jobs. In 1996, the federal government decreased old age pensions, decreased aid to the arts, reduced the budget of the CBC, and cut the civil service by 45 000 jobs. The 1995 Ontario budget trimmed $2 billion from the deficit by slashing welfare rolls and cutting back support to hospitals, school boards, arts organizations, and universities. Case Figure 15.2 shows the extent to which Canadian governments have reduced their spending.

Case Figure 15.2: Cutting Back: Government Reduction in Spending, 1990–1998

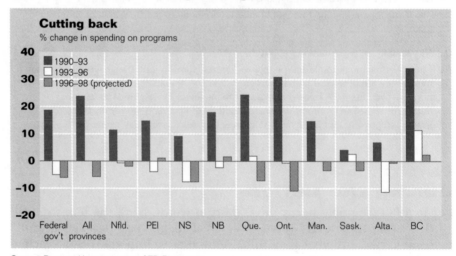

Source: Reprinted by permission of TD Economics.

Distribution of Income

In a laissez-faire capitalist economy, personal income is dependent on an individual's ownership of society's resources (land, labour, and capital). The value of these resources is determined by their supply and demand. The rich are those people who own valuable resources. The poor are individuals whose talents and resources are not in great demand, either because their skills are not considered important or because there is an overabundance of people with similar abilities and resources. In theory, those who contribute the most to what society considers essential will earn the most money.

In a planned economy, on the other hand, the state is responsible for distributing wealth. If one group is wealthier than another, it is because the state has placed a higher value on the contribution of that group. In theory, a planned economy aims at distributing the country's resources so that those who help to produce wealth get a fair share of it.

A mixed economy, such as Canada's, lacks a clear-cut theory of distribution. Since government and private enterprise are both involved in the production of wealth, how should wealth be distributed, and to what extent should the government play a role in redistributing income?

Throughout much of history, mass poverty had been generally accepted as inevitable. Following the Industrial Revolution, however, most countries in the Western world experienced sufficient economic growth to enable them to virtually eliminate mass poverty. Karl Marx's prediction that the modern labourer would become increasingly poorer did not come true in absolute terms. Since World War II, for example, Canadians' real incomes (incomes with inflation taken into account) grew at an average yearly rate of more than 2.5 percent. Beginning in the 1990s, however, this trend seems to have reversed.

As seen through the eyes of people in poverty-stricken countries, mass poverty has virtually disappeared in Canada. Many of those Canadians whom we describe as poor live infinitely better than the vast majority of people in such countries as Bangladesh, Rwanda, Haiti, and Nigeria. In the Philippines, for example, the average family spent 53 percent of its income on food in the early 1990s, whereas Canadians paid only 11 percent. In Mexico City, the average resident in 1993 had to work over seven hours to obtain the same basic food necessities that the average person in Ottawa could afford after working two and a half hours. In Ethiopia, in 1995, the average daily life expectancy was 50 years; for every 1000 births, 121 infants died; and the average daily kilojoule consumption was 7106 (in Canada, these numbers were 78 for life expectancy, 6.8 for infant mortality, and 14 630 kj). Canada has an average of more than one radio for every citizen, whereas in Pakistan, less than one out of every ten citizens owns a radio. It is true that some Canadians suffer from inadequate food, clothing, and shelter, but the total number of poor people in Canada pales in comparison to the widespread famine and poverty that characterizes some parts of the world.[1] At the same time, Canadians who do live in poverty (according to a Canadian definition) will not be comforted by the fact that some people in the world are poorer than them.

Should governments allow extremes of wealth to exist?

Relative Poverty

Poverty is often defined in relative terms. Simply, this means, "How much income do I earn compared with my friends, or with the entire population?" One method of determining who is poor is to construct an arbitrary "poverty line" based on the minimum amount of money needed to ensure adequate food, clothing, health care, and shelter. The National Council of Welfare, for example, declares any family to be poor if it spends more than 59 percent of its income on food, clothing, and housing. By this formula, in 1994 nearly 5 million Canadians, 17 percent of the population, fell below the poverty line.

Another method of measuring poverty is to compare the income of one group in society with the income of other groups. Case Table 15.2 illustrates the discrepancy between the wealthiest 25 percent of the population and the poorest 25 percent. If incomes were distributed equally, each group would receive the same amount. The extent of the difference between each group indicates the degree of economic inequality in Canada. To account for inflation, the figures are adjusted to the 1994 dollar.

Case Table 15.2: Income Distribution in Canada, 1980–1994 (average annual income)

Year	Lowest quarter	Second quarter	Middle quarter	Highest quarter
1980	7 260	14 690	25 770	40 820
1982	7 110	14 050	24 370	38 950
1984	7 000	13 530	23 390	38 120
1986	7 460	14 360	24 490	39 170
1988	7 950	15 020	25 140	39 410
1990	8 390	15 720	25 700	39 370
1992	8 160	15 210	25 450	39 210
1994	8 230	15 060	25 000	38 830

Source: Adapted from "Income Distribution in Canada, 1980–1994" from *Income Distribution by Size in Canada*, cat. no. 13–207, 1994. Reproduced by the authority of the Minister of Industry, 1996, Statistics Canada.

Focus

To what extent is there economic inequality in Canada, and how has it changed between 1980 and 1994?

VIEWPOINT

A DAY IN THE LIFE OF POVERTY

In 1970, a Special Senate Committee to examine poverty in Canada reported that poverty was the gravest social issue of our time and stated that unless something was done immediately, 5 million Canadians would continue "to find life a bleak, bitter, and never-ending struggle for survival." More than two decades later, this situation has changed very little.

The following excerpt from *The Canadian Fact Book on Poverty* describes the life of the poor in 1994. To update the cost of living figures to today's prices, add approximately 2 percent a year (compounded).

Aside from a small percentage of the poor population who are living at a bare subsistence level or below, most poor Canadian individuals or families suffer the effects of continual deprivation: a relentless feeling of being boxed in; a feeling that life is dictated by the requirements simply of surviving each day. In this way of life there is no choice, there is no flexibility and, if something unexpected happens—sickness, accident, family death, fire or theft, a rent increase—there is no buffer to deal with the emergency. Life is just today, because tomorrow offers no hope.

It is perhaps easiest to comprehend what a day in a life of poverty is like by converting a typical poverty income into a daily dollar amount. Survey information...indicates that, for an average poor urban family consisting of two adults and two children...the daily dollar amount available to each family member is $14.60 (amounting to $21 300 annually). Using daily per-person expenditure estimates based on the Department of Agriculture's Thrifty Nutritious Food Plan ($4.75), Canada Mortgage and Housing Corporation

data for shelter costs ($7.16) and Montreal Diet Dispensary estimates for clothing ($1.22), the daily cost of bare essentials for survival comes to $13.13.

Out of the remaining $1.47 per person per day, families need to pay for personal care items, household needs, furniture, telephone, transportation, school supplies, health care and so on. There is no money for entertainment, recreation, reading materials, insurance or charitable or religious donations.

The daily-dollar conversion makes it easy to understand why poor families must cut into their budget for essentials; why they must rent substandard housing; why they move often in attempts to save rent; why they purchase poor-quality food with little freshness or variety; why they must supplement their food budget with trips to food banks; why they own a minimum selection of mainly used clothing.

For the poor family, living on $14.60 per person per day is not an exercise in the imagination. It is reality, day after day with no relief in sight.[2]

Focus

Poverty is often described as a "vicious cycle." What does this mean?

Rich People in Canada

Before we examine who poor people are and why they tend to be poor, let us briefly discuss the rich. Among the wealthy of our society are those whose talents or resources are in great demand. The majority of society's wealthy citizens acquire only a fraction of their wealth through wages and salaries. Much of their income is derived from investments in stocks and bonds. Inheritance, royalties from inventions, and ownership of valuable land or companies also contribute to their fortunes. According to the *Financial Post*, in 1996 the corporate billionaires in Canada were Kenneth Thomson (Toronto, $8.2 billion), the Irving family (Saint John, $7.5 billion), Charles Bronfman (Montreal, $2.9 billion), the Eaton family (Toronto, $1.7 billion), Ted Rogers (Toronto, $1.4 billion), W. Galen Weston (Toronto, $1.3 billion), the McCains (Toronto and Florenceville, NB, $1.2 billion), and Paul Desmarais (Montreal, $1 billion). *The Toronto Star* reported that the cutoff figure to make the top 100 list of the highest-paid company executives in 1995 was $1.4 million. Frank Stronach, chair of Magna International, headed this list with $47 million for the year. This amount was equivalent to 1000 times the average salary of workers in the automobile industry. The heads of the Toronto Dominion Bank, the Bank of Nova Scotia, and the Canadian Imperial Bank of Commerce made approximately 150 times what the average bank employee earned.[3]

Case Table 15.3: Canada's Occupations: Incomes in 1993

	Average Yearly Salary
Chief Justice, Supreme Court of Canada	*$200 000
Prime Minister of Canada	*$157 600
Physician	$124 500
Provincial court judge	$110 000
Dentist	$106 750
Lawyer	$91 200
Chartered accountant	$68 000
Autoworker	$52 700
Coal miner	$48 800
Federal civil service manager	$42 500
Nurse	$38 000
Truck driver	$29 850
Car salesperson	$28 200
Bookkeeper	$27 700
Librarian	$21 500
Shoe salesperson	$14 600
Barber	$14 100
Gas station attendant	$13 400

*Actual salary
Source: Statistics Canada, Revenue Canada.

In general, people with high incomes say that they are happier than do those who are poor. Of course, it is not the amount of money that makes people happy—it is what they can do with the money. This includes eating well, getting a good education, travelling, and participating in cultural activities, as well as acquiring such material possessions as houses, clothes, and cars. A 1990 Canadian survey asked a random sample of people how they would rate their health. Three-quarters of wealthy Canadians reported their health to be either excellent or very good. This ratio decreased steadily as income levels dropped. Among the poorest group, only half the people were satisfied with their health.

Professional athletes and entertainers comprise another group of wealthy individuals. Their salaries are a product of people's demand to see them perform. They command high salaries because their talents are in scarce supply, and the demand for these talents is high. Golfers and tennis players capture millions of dollars annually in winnings alone (some athletes make more money in endorsements than they do from playing their sport). Blue Jay left fielder Joe Carter made approximately $7 million in 1996. Wayne Gretzky's salary for the 1995–96 hockey season was $6.5 million, not including endorsements. Rock star Bryan Adams earned an estimated $35 million in 1993 from record sales and concert appearances.

How Income Is Determined

What determines a person's income? According to a variety of statistical studies, it is related to such variables as a person's physical and mental capabilities, type of job, education, and location. Case Table 15.4 illustrates the close relationship between level of education and employment. A similar table would show the same connections between education and earnings.

Case Table 15.4: The Connection Between Education and Employment, 1994

Level of Education	Percent Unemployed
For Canada as a Whole	
Completed some high school	16.4
High school graduates	10.0
University graduates	5.4
For 15–24-Year-Olds Only	
Elementary school	28.7
Some secondary school	22.9
High school graduates	15.8
Post-secondary diploma	11.7
University graduates	9.6

Source: Reproduced by the authority of the Minister of Industry, 1997, Statistics Canada, *Canadian Economic Observer*, cat. no. 11–010, 1995.

As the economy became more complex and automated in the second half of the twentieth century, the demand for unskilled workers declined. Employers now require more educated employees. One study, for example, discovered that an automotive technician must be able to read over 90 000 pages of complex manuals in order to service the latest vehicles (the *Complete Oxford Shakespeare* contains fewer than 1500 pages). The average technical worker spends about 160 minutes per day reading memos, shipping orders, manuals, and other job-related materials. By contrast, the average high school student reads for less than 100 minutes per day. Since the volume of scientific knowledge is expected to double in the next 15 years, workers will have to be literate enough to undergo extensive retraining.

Focus

Disparities in wealth are usually attributed to ability, education, age, gender, discrimination, luck, inheritance, unique talent, motivation, unfair practices, hard work, occupation, and geographical location. Rank these factors from most to least important in determining disparities in wealth in Canada.

With growing global competition and technological changes, future workers will need to be better educated. Just a few years ago, entry-level jobs in the oil and gas industry required only a grade 10 education. Today, they need grade 12, and by the year 2000 industry experts estimate these positions will require 16 years of schooling. Employers are looking for people with good communication and interpersonal skills, and want the school system to graduate individuals who can read, write, think, and interact with people. As technology keeps evolving, one of the most important skills a person can have is the ability to learn.

Attitudes Toward Income Distribution

In the nineteenth century, upper- and middle-class Canadians generally ignored the plight of poor people because they believed that poverty was due to a failure of character—the individual's own fault. When help was provided, its purpose was to reshape character by providing the poor person with education, religion, discipline, and a belief in hard work and thrift. Anyone could become rich, it was thought, if he (women were expected to stay at home) had a good character and worked hard.

What is the message of this cartoon?

Source: Reprinted by permission of Bob Thaves.

By the turn of the twentieth century, however, liberal reformers had begun to argue that environment, rather than heredity, was the most important factor in determining a person's future economic success. This implied that poverty was not the individual's fault, and since the government was partly responsible for shaping the environment, it was the state's moral duty to care for the poor and to improve the environment.

These ideas grew stronger as the twentieth century progressed. World War I increased the extent of government involvement in society as the economy was adjusted to war production and income taxes were begun to help pay for the war. The Great Depression of the 1930s provided even greater stimulus to government involvement. In 1934, one out of every three adult Canadians was unemployed, and it was obviously not their fault. Reluctantly, the government acted to help the poor. It established relief and government-sponsored make-work projects out of genuine humanitarian sentiments, and because many government and business leaders feared a revolution if nothing was done to help unemployed people.

Finally, the tremendous growth of government involvement in all aspects of life during World War II led to the beginning of present-day government welfare programs.

Welfare Capitalism

Today, the concept of **welfare capitalism** is under attack. As its name implies, welfare capitalism conforms to most of the theories of free enterprise capitalism, but adds the belief that government should take responsibility for the well-being of its citizens. In the last 50 years (before recent changes), the Canadian government adopted numerous policies designed to make life more bearable for the poor. These programs can be divided into four major categories:

Demogrants are grants to people in specified population groups who might need financial help. At one time, for instance, all Canadians 65 years of age and over received money under the Old Age Security program, and families with children under 18 years of age received family allowance payments.

These grants were universal, which means that everyone received them when they were eligible to do so. To reduce the deficit, and for ideological reasons, the age at which people collect their old age pensions has been increased recently, and more wealthy people will not receive this pension at all. Also, families must now earn less than a specified family income to qualify for family allowance.

Social-insurance programs include employment insurance, welfare payments, mothers' allowance, veterans' pension, and workers' compensation. Their major purpose is to protect people against a total loss of income.

Many of these programs have come under recent attack by neo-conservatives, who think that welfare and unemployment insurance destroy people's incentive to work. Governments are cutting back on these programs, both for ideological reasons and to save money. In 1996, for example, Premier Harris of Ontario announced plans to reduce income taxes, close some hospitals, end junior kindergartens, and substitute work-for-welfare for the existing welfare program.

The **transfer program** bases its grants upon the recipient's needs. Examples include aid to people with disabilities, help for Aboriginal people, and grants to underdeveloped and depressed areas of the country.

In recent years, in an attempt to balance the budget and to relinquish some powers to the provinces, the federal government reduced its grants to less prosperous areas of the country such as the Maritime provinces.

Taxes are the fourth category of welfare policy. Economic inequality has two basic sources: unequal earnings and inheritance. **Progressive taxes**, such as the graduated income tax, are meant to deal with unequal incomes by deducting more money from the rich than from the poor. The larger the income, the greater the proportion of the tax that is deducted. Neo-conservatives argue that higher tax rates on wealthy people discourages them from expanding their business endeavours and thus results in fewer jobs and lower incomes for many workers.

welfare capitalism: capitalism that is based on the belief that government should take responsibility for the well-being of its citizens.

demogrants: grants offered by the Canadian government to population groups who might need financial help.

social-insurance programs: financial programs offered by the Canadian government to protect people against a loss of income.

transfer program: a federal financial plan designed to relieve the poverty of individual groups, based on the recipients' needs.

progressive taxes: taxes that are proportionately higher depending on a person's annual income.

Conclusion

When the Canadian economy was booming following World War II, governments spent billions of dollars to provide Canadians with the social programs they wanted. During the 1990s, governments, burdened with massive debts and annual deficits, no longer felt able to spend such large sums of money. The problem that now confronted Canadians was how to reduce the debt while still retaining the country's important social programs. There are no simple answers. Should the government balance the budget by increasing taxes, by cutting programs, or both? Who should be taxed? What programs should be reduced—hospitals or employment insurance, day care or education? Each choice involves trade-offs; something is gained and something else is lost. In the end, the choice is a matter of values, judgments, and ideologies.

BIOGRAPHY

JOHN KENNETH GALBRAITH, 1908–

An "unapologetic liberal to the end," Canadian-born Harvard professor John Kenneth Galbraith has always argued for "an economy that is more caring than conniving"[4] in a career as an economist that has spanned more than six decades. During that time Galbraith authored more than 50 books, was personal adviser to every Democratic candidate for the U.S. presidency from Roosevelt to Johnson, and served as U.S. ambassador to India during the Kennedy administration. But his main interest always has been as an educator, in translating economics into terms that ordinary citizens can understand—and in advancing his own views in the process.

Galbraith describes his formative boyhood experiences in an agricultural community of Scots in southwestern Ontario in his book *The Scotch*. He said he inherited "his liberalism, his interest in politics, and his caustic wit from his father... 'the leading Liberal of the community.'"[5] Galbraith began accompanying his father to political rallies when he was 8 years old.

In keeping with his rural upbringing, Galbraith studied agriculture in college, but soon began to enjoy the debate and stimulation of academic life. He received a PhD in agricultural economics in 1934, taught at Harvard and Princeton universities, worked as an economist for the U.S. government in World War II, and returned to Harvard as a professor of economics in 1949. His travels and activities in diverse countries and settings have been anchored by a secure base in Harvard and in his marriage since 1937 to Catherine Atwater Galbraith.

Much of Galbraith's writing has centred on examining the human impact of economic policies and decisions, and a concern for "the very real human and social costs of allowing market forces, such as they were, to dictate what goods and services would be available to whom and at what price."[6] A long-time admirer of economist John Maynard Keynes, Galbraith challenged conservative and supply-side economists, deploring "the American obsession with the overproduction of consumer goods," and "public squalor amidst affluence." He advised Americans "to readapt their values by stressing genuine needs, such as cleaner air, decent housing, and adequate support for the arts, rather than focusing on such unnecessary consumer goods as bigger and faster automobiles."[7]

In his 1996 book *The Good Society: The Humane Agenda*, Galbraith rejects neo-conservative trends and defends an activist role for governments. He favours the goal of full employment over zero inflation: "Society cannot relegate some parts of its population to idleness, social distress and economic deprivation in order to achieve price stability." He also rejects tax cuts ("There is no certainty that the funds released by tax reductions will be invested or spent") and the obsession with deficits ("Similar borrowing in the private sector of the economy is both accepted and wholly approved").[8]

The authors of *Thinkers of the Twentieth Century* characterize Galbraith as "a tireless reformer bent upon improving rather than overthrowing the free enterprise system" and conclude, "In the course of his career [he] has established himself as one of the most preeminent and persuasive writers of the twentieth century...and influenced the thinking of countless generations."[9]

---

1 On what subject has much of Galbraith's writing been centred?

2 What are the main elements of Galbraith's rejection of neo-conservativism in economics?

Underlying and Emerging Issues

Give the reasoning and evidence that might be used to support different views or conclusions on the following issues.

1 To what extent should Canadian governments pursue policies of deregulation and privatization?

2 Under what circumstances is public ownership justifiable or desirable?

3 How important is it to deal with government deficits and debts?

4 To what extent are present Canadian financial problems due to excess spending or inadequate revenue?

5 To what extent should governments use Keynesian policies, monetary policies, or supply-side policies to deal with financial problems?

6 Is it more important to maintain social programs or to reduce taxes?

7 Do neo-conservative policies benefit the rich at the expense of the poor?

8 To what extent is poverty a relative concept?

9 To what extent are people living in poverty responsible for their own situation?

10 To what extent are extremely wealthy people responsible for their own situation?

11 Is there too much of a gap between rich and poor people in Canada?

12 To what extent should governments attempt to redistribute income?

13 Does everyone have a right to education and medical care?

14 To what extent should the education system be based on meeting the needs of business?

15 To what extent does the Canadian economic system need to be changed?

Focussing Knowledge

In your notes, clearly identify or define and explain the importance or significance of each of the following:

regulation	interest payments
deregulation	neo-conservative economics
poverty	absolute poverty
Crown corporations	relative poverty
income distribution	privatization
poverty line	Keynesian economics
demogrants	progressive taxation
national debt	deficit

Reviewing and Organizing Knowledge

1 Why do governments vary in the degree to which they intervene in the economy?

2 Construct a chart in which you compare government involvement in Canada's economy in four areas—Laws and Regulations, Government Ownership, Budget and Financial Policies, Income Redistribution—on the basis of the following:

a. extent/nature of the intervention

b. arguments in favour and arguments against

3 What is the difference between absolute and relative poverty?

4 What factors affect income distribution in Canada?

5 Describe the four categories of programs designed to reduce poverty in Canada.

Applying and Extending Knowledge

1 Make a list of all government interventions in Canada's economy. Rate each item from 1 to 10 where 1 is "highly negative" and 10 is "highly positive." On this basis, write a paper in which you describe your views on the three most important and three least important types of government economic intervention in Canada.

2 Write a letter to your Member of Parliament in which you outline your views as a citizen on

a. the preferred role for government in the economy;

b. the changes that are necessary.

3 On the basis of your study of political and economic systems, take and support a position on the following question: "How should Canada's governments deal with the issues of deficit, debt, and social welfare programs?"

4 Write a position paper on the topic "How should Canada deal with poverty?"

5 Research the life of one of Canada's wealthiest people (see page 422). What factors account for the person's wealth?

6 Are the high salaries of some professional athletes justified? Take a position, and support it with arguments and evidence.

7 Research and present your conclusion on the question "How effective have the government's policies on income redistribution been?"

8 Contact a representative of each of Canada's political parties, and ask for his or her position on the role of government in the economy. Which party's position comes closest to your own?

9 Compare Canada and the United States in terms of government involvement in income redistribution and social programs. What factors account for the differences in the two systems?

10 Select newspaper articles that illustrate some of the Underlying and Emerging Issues on page 428. How do the articles illustrate the issues?

11 Choose one of the Underlying and Emerging Issues, and explain in detail why Canadians might come to differing conclusions on the issue. Take a stand, and explain why you came to that conclusion.

The Japanese Economy

$\mathcal{A}$T THE END OF WORLD WAR II, Japan was bankrupt, many of its cities and factories had been destroyed by American bombing, and its citizens were demoralized. In the last 50 years, however, Japan has rebuilt its economy to such an extent that it now rivals that of the United States. This case study explores the reasons behind Japan's success and concludes with an analysis of the problems facing Japan in the 1990s. After 1945, the Japanese economy benefitted from a combination of American aid and domestic economic strategies. The Japanese government played a significant role in managing the economy by providing incentives to business, encouraging research and development, and protecting the domestic market from international competition. Other important factors in the Japanese economic miracle included the *keiretsu*, or business groups; the educational system; the relationship between employers and employees; and the emphasis on discipline, hard work, and sacrifice for the benefit of the group.

The Achievement

Although the Japanese economy has experienced a recession during the 1990s, it is still the second-largest economy in the world. Japan is the largest creditor country, with foreigners owing its banks more than $250 billion. This small island country, with roughly 2 percent of the world's population, controls over 12 percent of the world's economy. In 1995, 10 of the world's 15 largest companies (by sales) were Japanese (see Table 5.2 on page 256). Nine of Asia's 10 largest banks are Japanese,

Japan at a Glance

Area: 377 835 km² (roughly half the size of Alberta)
Population (1995): 125 506 492
Life Expectancy in Years (1993): Males 76.3, Females 82.5
GDP (1993): $2.55 trillion (U.S.)
GDP per Capita (1993): $20 400 (U.S.)
Doctors per 1000 People (1993): 1.7
Hospital Beds per 1000 People (1993): 15.8
Health Expenditures as Percentage of GDP (1992): 6.5
Telephones per 1000 People (1992): 555
Televisions per 1000 People (1992): 610

Sources: *The World Almanac and Book of Facts 1996* (Mahwah, NJ: World Almanac Books, 1996); John Robert Colombo, ed., *The 1996 Canadian Global Almanac* (Toronto: Macmillan, 1996); Marlita A. Reddy, ed., *Statistical Abstract of the World* (New York: Gale Research, 1994).

and Tokyo is quickly becoming the financial capital of the world. With the Pacific Rim emerging as the key economic centre of the world, Japan appears poised to play an important role in the global economy well into the twenty-first century.

Historical Background

Japan's economic expansion in the last five decades has been spectacular, but it would be a mistake to think that this growth is only a postwar phenomenon. The origins of Japan's economic success go back to the middle of the nineteenth century, when the country first confronted the West. At that time, Japan had essentially a feudal society. The samurai, or warrior class, dominated the country's peasants and merchants. Japan was closed to the outside world, as the ruling shoguns (Japan's military and political rulers) forbade foreign merchants and missionaries from landing on their shores. In 1853, American naval commander Matthew Perry and his "black ships" arrived in Tokyo Bay. Commodore Perry threatened that if Japan refused to open its doors to trade, he would destroy the capital. In this way, Japan was forced into the modern world.

In 1868, a group of young samurai reformers overthrew the shogun's government. The **Meiji Restoration** marked the beginning of Japan's modern era, and the people rallied behind the new rulers to strengthen the country in order to protect it from exploitation by Western imperialists. The Meiji leaders sought *Fukoku-kyōhei*, which translates as "a wealthy country and strong army." To achieve these aims and modernize its society, Japan built dockyards, railways, telegraph lines, factories, and mines and created a modern army trained in Western methods of war. The new rulers also attempted to Westernize some aspects of Japanese society. Traditional styles of dress were discouraged, a modern constitution was drafted, and European foods, music, and fashions were imported into the country.

Meiji Restoration: the introduction of wide-ranging reforms of Japan's economic, political, and social structure.

Early Industrial Growth and Expansion

As the traditional Japanese economy was based on agriculture, most Japanese lacked the necessary funds to build modern factories. The Meiji government established new industries such as textile mills and shipyards. The government used these model companies to train the Japanese people in Western business methods. During the 1880s, however, the Meiji government found itself short of cash and was forced to sell these companies— often to close friends of prominent politicians.

This was the beginning of Japan's **zaibatsu**, huge financial and industrial combines that were dominated by a single family or clan. The *zaibatsu* soon controlled Japan's new finance, mining, transportation, and manufacturing sectors. Two of the most powerful of these companies were Mitsui, founded by one of the most successful merchant families in Meiji Japan, and Mitsubishi, owned by a former samurai clan. By the end of the nineteenth century, Japan was the most modern and industrial country in East Asia. So successful was its modernization program that its business and military leaders began to expand beyond Japan's borders, by commercial treaties if possible, but by force if necessary.

Japan had few sources of natural raw materials. In particular, it had no iron, coal, or copper. The *zaibatsu* leaders, together with Japan's military, controlled the country's weak government and pushed for overseas expansion. In 1894, less than 30 years after it began to modernize, Japan went to war with China and won. Ten years later, Japan defeated Russia in another war. Both of these conflicts were the result of Japan's modernization and its desire to secure raw materials for its growing industries. (During the nineteenth century, the United States and many European countries had followed similar imperialistic policies.) The war with China was fought for control of Korea, which for hundreds of years had been under Chinese domination. Similarly, Russia and Japan fought for control of Manchuria's raw materials.

World War II mirrored these earlier conflicts. Japan wanted to secure control of the raw materials that its home industries required. These materials were found in China and in the European and American colonies of Southeast Asia. Again, the concerns of the *zaibatsu* and military commanders won out over the more peaceful desires of Japan's democratically elected politicians. The Pacific War lasted from Japan's invasion of China in 1937 to Emperor Hirohito's surrender after the United States dropped atomic bombs on Hiroshima and Nagasaki in August 1945. During the final years of the war, Japan's economy was severely damaged by American B-29 bombers and by the American naval blockade that prevented Japan from acquiring such important raw materials as steel, rubber, and oil. By the end of 1945, when the American Occupation forces arrived in Japan, the country's cities and factories lay in ruins and its citizens were starving.

zaibatsu: Japanese monopolies, each industry dominated by a single family, that jointly controlled the industrial life of Japan prior to and during World War II.

Modern Tokyo.

VIEWPOINT

WOMEN IN JAPAN

During the nineteenth century, Japanese women were regulated by the Confucian "three obediences." These guidelines demanded that women obey their fathers before marriage, their husbands after marriage, and their sons after their husbands died. Although women's social status was clearly subordinate to that of men, Japanese women performed important roles in the fishing, farming, and silk industries.

Women's status changed very little during the Meiji era. The image of the ideal woman remained someone who was submissive, obedient, graceful, and devoted to her family. With increased industrialization, however, Japanese women began to leave the countryside for work in the growing cities. In fact, women made up the majority of Japan's industrial work force prior to World War I. During the 1930s and 1940s, Japanese women played a key role in wartime industries, taking over jobs that had previously been reserved for men.

The following account by a Japanese woman indicates that the status of women in Japanese society has improved considerably since World War II.

Once it was women who were chained, responsible for family and household while men were free to pursue power, wealth, and adventure outside the home. But now men have become increasingly chained to the institutions they have set up with their commit- ment to long-term employment and the promotional ladder rigged to seniority. Their wives, on the other hand, have been set free by the development of home appliances. ... Not only can they work outside the home, but they have great freedom to decide how, where,

*and under what terms they will work.
...*

Women's freedom is enhanced by their husbands' tendency to entrust them with everything from control of the family finances to the children's upbringing and education ... and anything else that they find bothersome. One reason is that men spend so little at home. Some wives who see their hus-bands very little (because they work long hours) refer to them as "boarders."

I believe that women, through their sheer determination to change what they can around them and with their concern for social issues like preserving the environment, may be the hope for tomorrow's Japan. Now, it is men's turn to change.[1]

Focus

To what extent is the status of women in Japan different from that in Canada? Why?

Postwar Government Strategy

Despite being defeated in World War II, Japan possessed the elements necessary for recovery and renewed economic growth. The country's industrial and transportation infrastructures were still in place, although they needed a great deal of repair. More importantly, three other factors combined to shape Japan's economic recovery: America's decision to rebuild Japan and create a stronghold against communism in the Pacific, the economic strategy of the Japanese government, and the desire of the Japanese people for economic growth.

In the months immediately after the war, General Douglas MacArthur and the other American officers who commanded the Occupation forces in Japan attempted to democratize the country and remove its militaristic tendencies. The Americans in charge of **SCAP**, the Supreme Command of the Allied Powers, supervised the drafting of a new constitution and dismantled the *zaibatsu* monopolies, which they believed had helped to lead Japan into war. Japan's new constitution guaranteed women's rights and universal adult suffrage, limited the emperor to a symbolic role in politics, and stated that "the Japanese people forever renounce war as a sovereign right of the nation." The constitutional reforms also provided a cornerstone for rebuilding the economy.

Cold War tensions between the Soviet Union and the United States, however, altered American policy in Japan. The Cold War blew into the Pacific when Mao's Communists assumed control of China in 1949. American attention now focussed not on democratizing Japan, but on turning Japan into a capitalist ally in the Pacific. The final years of the American Occupation thus saw the return of many of Japan's wartime business leaders to positions of power. The Americans also allowed the *zaibatsu* to return, although in a slightly altered form. These business groups, now called **keiretsu**, were clusters of companies formed around one dominant firm. They were composed of a diverse range of enterprises that included manufacturing and financial businesses. Since the 1950s the *keiretsu* have flourished, and now most of the country's business and banking is dominated by approximately a dozen of these conglomerates.

Yoshida Shigeru, prime minister from 1946 to 1947 and from 1948 to 1954, was one of the most important figures in the early postwar period.

SCAP: the U.S. Occupation forces in Japan following World War II.

keiretsu: successors to the *zaibatsu*, which dominate contemporary Japan's business life.

Yoshida Doctrine: policies from the mid-1940s through the 1980s favouring the development of Japan's industries and an alliance with the United States.

Yoshida had opposed the military leadership in Japan during the 1930s and 1940s. His policies, commonly called the **Yoshida Doctrine**, favoured the development of Japan's industries and an alliance with the United States. Although reconstruction was essentially completed by 1953, these policies continued in force until the end of the 1980s. The Japanese government actively sought to develop Japan's economy. The means of production were left in private hands, but the businesses themselves were guided by government suggestions and support.

Case Figure 16.1: The Sumitomo Group

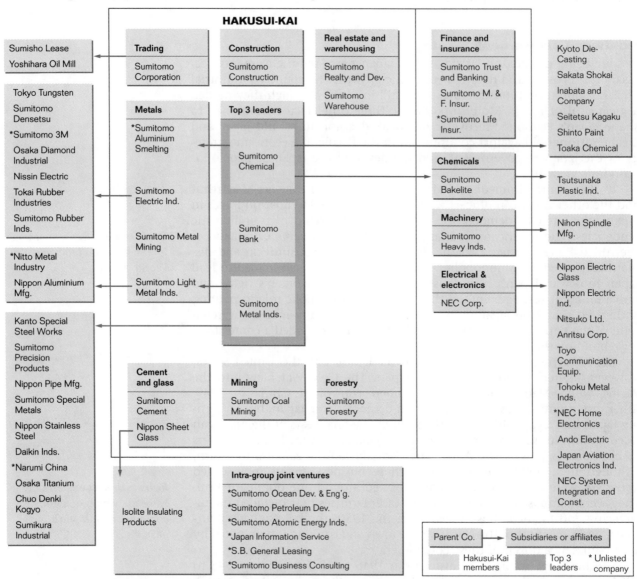

Souce: Dodwell Marketing Consultants, *Industrial Groupings in Japan*, rev. ed. (1986/87). Reprinted by permission.

How the Japanese *Keiretsu* Operates

The keiretsu has at its core a commercial bank and usually one or two other firms, including a trading house. ... Clustered closely around these core firms are other large companies from a wide cross section of industries. The Mitsui Group, for example, includes companies in fibre and textiles; foodstuffs; construction; retailing; finance and insurance; chemicals; pulp and paper; mining; steel and metals; transportation and warehousing; electricity and machinery; and automobiles.

Financial control remains closely held within the "family." Firms affiliated with a group may borrow widely, but their main banking relationship is always with the bank at the group's core. Both the bank and other firms within each group also own shares of the other member firms.

The members of each group ... conduct the bulk of their business activity within the group. For example, they procure their supplies and materials where possible from other members of the group, and they market their products through the group's trading company. It is estimated that as much as 50 percent of the business transactions conducted by group members is with other affiliates of the same group.

Most importantly, the keiretsu co-ordinates planning and strategy formulation among its member firms. ... In particular, the CEOs [chief executive officers] of the companies near the centre of each group meet periodically to discuss matters of common concern and to co-ordinate their business strategies.

It is difficult to overemphasize the importance of these meetings, at which the CEOs discuss candidly such matters as new product developments, competitive strategies and governmental policies. They may decide to provide ... assistance to member companies that are launching new products [or] entering new markets.

It is largely these stable networks of business and financial relationships that enable Japanese firms to benefit from long-term planning. ... In contrast with competitors elsewhere, Japanese managers need not pay excessive attention to short-term earnings. In a recent study in which American and Japanese managers were asked to indicate over what time period their performance was measured, 59 percent of American managers responded that their performance is measured in periods of less than one year; only 2 percent of the Japanese respondents said that their performance is measured in a span of a year or less.[2]

Source: Reprinted with permission of *Business Quarterly*, Published by the Richard Ivey League of Business, The University of Western Ontario, London, Canada, Autumn 1989 issue.

The Ministry of International Trade and Industry (MITI)

The Ministry of International Trade and Industry, MITI, has been a key element behind Japan's postwar economic miracle. MITI coordinates government, business, labour, and research according to centrally planned policies and national goals. MITI assists Japanese businesses by providing them with foreign exchange, technology, low-interest loans, and tax incentives. It also discourages companies from venturing into what it believes are non-growth areas by withholding licences, transferring personnel and research resources to other sectors, and lobbying executives to follow its directives.

MITI was established in 1949 to rebuild the country's heavy manufacturing and chemical industries. Many Japanese politicians and American planners initially opposed this strategy as they believed that Japan's economy should have been based on light industry and agriculture. By the early 1950s, however, MITI's policies were accepted and Japan began to build steel mills and chemical plants. The outbreak of the Korean War in 1950 ensured that Japan's decision to concentrate its efforts on heavy industry was a success. The United States needed a cheap source of military equipment, aircraft, and machine tools for its war effort. Japan became the factory for the United Nations forces in Korea, and the profits derived from supplying military goods laid the foundation for Japan's economic growth of the 1960s.

Throughout the 1960s, MITI supervised the development of Japan's shipbuilding, electronics, and steel industries. MITI also kept the Japanese

Focus

How does a Japanese firm differ from a Canadian company?

currency, the yen, at an artificially low value so that Japanese exports would be less expensive on the international market. Throughout this period, the Japanese government spent very little on defence and social services and instead concentrated its investments in developing new industries, the most successful of which was the automobile industry. In 1960, Japan produced only half a million cars a year, but by the end of the decade it was the second-largest car producer in the world after the United States.

In 1973, Japan faced an economic crisis caused by the rise in the price of oil due to the unstable political situation in the Middle East. Since Japan had no oil resources of its own, MITI realized that Japan should not concentrate its economy in industries whose profits were linked to low oil prices. As a result, MITI promoted the development of Japan's electronics and computer industries. By the 1980s, companies such as Sony, Toshiba, and Hitachi were leaders in high-technology development and production.

MITI has created a harmonious relationship among Japanese industry, labour, and government. This has enabled Japan to concentrate its efforts on specific sectors of the world economy: steel and heavy industry in the 1950s, automobile manufacturing in the 1960s and 1970s, and electronics and computers in the 1980s and 1990s. The government actively fosters the growth of exports. Imported foreign-manufactured goods, however, are discouraged by high tariffs and quotas. Thus, while Japan's domestic market is protected from outside competition, Japanese companies concentrate on selling their products overseas.

Japanese business works more closely with government than do companies in most other democratic nations. The closeness of the relationship has prompted some economists to suggest that Japan (and other countries such as Taiwan and South Korea) represents a third approach—neither capitalist nor centrally planned. In Japan, the government guides the economy using information received from the business community. According to Japanese specialists Coates and Holroyd, "This tight relationship between business and government differs substantially from the Canadian model. ... The Canadian focus on short-term economic considerations, company profits and political imperatives has largely prevented the country from establishing long-term objectives and priorities like those in Japan."[3]

Education and Industry

The education system in Japan reflects the order and planning that characterize the country's economy. Japanese schools teach the skills and attitudes necessary to assist industry. Employers extend this schooling with a systematic training program that teaches the skills related to their particular business. Japanese workers are engaged in a process of lifelong learning, as they are constantly attending classes on new technology and production techniques.

In Japanese primary and secondary schools, students have to master a difficult curriculum as well as learn the importance of obedience and hard work. Japan's school system is among the most effective in the world, as demonstrated by a 1992 government census that recorded a literacy rate of

100 percent. Japanese students are required to assist in cleaning their class-rooms and to participate in daily calisthenics. These practices not only help to foster a healthy population, but also promote feelings of responsibility and group membership.

Developing an industrious attitude is accomplished by a long school day (8:30 a.m. to 4:00 p.m.) and school week (half-day classes every second Saturday), as well as a rigorous homework load. The attitude that school is a place of hard work intensifies in the higher grades. The future is determined by success in university entrance examinations, so competition is fierce.

The top universities are the recruiting grounds for Japan's most important companies. If students want to get a good job with Mitsubishi or Toyota, for example, their university grades count for less than which university they attend, and this is determined during their final year of high school, commonly referred to as "examination hell." To prepare, many students supplement their classroom schooling by attending "cram schools" at night. These classes add another two or three hours to each school day. The end result of this education system is a highly literate and disciplined population. Critics, however, claim that the emphasis on rote memorization tends to restrain imagination and initiative.

Other Factors Affecting Success

Japan has borrowed extensively from the West in its efforts to modernize. Western technologies and business methods were adopted early on by the Meiji leaders in their desire to industrialize the country. Western music, fashion, and even political ideas were also imported. Despite this borrowing, it would be wrong to conclude that Japan is little more than a transplanted Western country in Asia. The Japanese have always maintained their national identity and have transformed what they borrowed from the West. It has been this innovative, or adaptive, element in Japanese society that has enabled the country to continue to prosper. Japanese companies are excellent at observing new technologies and then improving them. The government and individual companies spend billions of dollars on research and development, and employ research scientists and engineers to ensure that their products remain competitive in the international market.

The Goal to Strengthen the Country

Since the middle of the nineteenth century, the Japanese people have rallied behind the country's efforts to modernize. They were acutely aware that they were latecomers to the modern era, and Japan's economic and technological backwardness in comparison to the West dominated their national consciousness for more than a century. When viewed in this framework, Japan's economic success since the end of World War II can be seen as the final phase of a project of national development. While other non-Western countries have been aware of their economic backwardness, few have been so driven to improve as the Japanese. By the late 1970s, Japan had become a formidable economic power.

Japanese Culture

Japan's culture played an important role in achieving this goal. Japan has a homogeneous population, which enables the country to enjoy a strong sense of nationalism and purpose. Going back to the days of the samurai, the Japanese have had a tradition of respect for authority, obedience, social discipline, and national solidarity. These factors have enabled the Japanese government and companies to demand levels of hard work and self-sacrifice that would be impossible to achieve in the West. By constantly adapting Western knowledge and technology to fit its own social and economic structures, Japan has met the challenges of a changing world.

Employer–Employee Relations

Large Japanese companies such as Mitsubishi, Mitsui, Sony, and Toshiba have done much to foster industrial growth and economic stability by nurturing a well-trained work force. Japanese workers are trained to work together in teams and to be multi-skilled, and they are often involved in helping their companies develop new production techniques. In Japan, the division between management and workers is less obvious than in the West. Japanese managers have had to work their way up the corporate ladder by experiencing every aspect of the production process. Even graduate engineers and management trainees begin their company careers performing menial janitorial jobs and working on the assembly line. This ensures that managers understand how their company functions. It also improves morale, as workers see their future bosses performing the same jobs that they do. In many ways, Japanese companies are like families, with everyone working together to guarantee success.

The relationship between unions and businesses is far less confrontational in Japan than it is in the West. Union leaders and managers have traditionally cooperated in planning their company's future and determining production. Although lifetime employment is no longer a reality in Japan, this policy did much to foster growth and stability in the 1960s and 1970s. Only recently have workers been faced with layoffs. Wages in Japan are quite good, with bonuses awarded to workers who exceed their production quotas or who suggest ways of improving a manufacturing process.

Japanese companies have benefitted from the high productivity of their workers. Japanese workers tend to be more productive than their Western counterparts; they work longer hours and make fewer mistakes. The result is that Japanese goods are often priced lower than similar products made in North America and Europe. This difference in pricing, however, has diminished since the late 1980s as Western companies (copying Japanese techniques) improved their methods of production, and as the high exchange rate of the Japanese yen increased the cost of Japanese goods.

An Alternative Explanation for Japan's Success

In the following quotation, Paul Johnson suggests that there might be another explanation behind Japan's economic success. In what areas does he agree with the above discussion, and where does he differ?

There was nothing miraculous about this miracle. It was a straightforward case of Adam Smith economics, with no more than a touch of Keynesianism. ... Moderate taxation. Low defence and government spending. A very high rate of personal saving, efficiently channelled into industry through the banking system. Shrewd import of foreign technology. Very fast replacement rate of existing plants, made possible by remarkable wage restraint, with productivity running well ahead of wages. Labour was ... exceptionally well-educated and skilled because Japan geared the educational expansion ... closely to industrial needs. ... The Japanese government provided a degree of external protection and export support. But its chief contribution was to erect a framework of intense internal competition, on an Adam Smith model, and a climate of benevolence toward business.[4]

The Price of Success

Japan's rapid economic growth has not been achieved without costs. It is a difficult process for any country to industrialize its economy while at the same time modernizing its society. Only a little more than 100 years ago, Japan still had a feudal society that depended on farming for its survival. Today, Japan is the most technologically advanced country in the world, and its citizens enjoy all the political rights and freedoms that are found in the West. This said, it is also clear that social, economic, and political tensions exist. With success has come greater expectations, and now that Japan's economy is a world leader, new problems and issues must be confronted.

Domestic Problems

Japanese born after World War II are beginning to question the values of their parents' generation. In the 1950s and 1960s, self-sacrifice for the greater good was required. The Japanese economy needed obedient and dedicated workers. These workers, having lived through the horrors of war and the hardships of the early postwar years, were happy to obey. Today, however, this attitude is much harder to support, as Japan has one of the world's strongest economies. Although most people continue to be hard-working and diligent, some are asking if there is more to life than work. Not only are they beginning to question the Japanese work ethic, but many young people, accustomed to a middle-class standard of living and imported Western values, are no longer willing to accept what they deem to be low-class jobs. The "three Ks," *kitanai*, *kiken*, and *kitsui* (dirty, dangerous, and strict), include such jobs as those in steel manufacturing, chemicals, and assembly plants. Many younger Japanese have no desire to enter these occupations. They want to be **salaryman**—what Westerners call white-collar workers.

salaryman: Japanese term for a white-collar worker.

To recruit good workers for their factories, Japanese companies must offer attractive wages. However, high wages mean lower profits. The result has been the establishment of branch plants in other Asian countries where wages are much lower. Dozens of major Japanese corporations now assemble most of their products elsewhere, particularly in China.

Some critics argue that Japanese companies have been successful at the expense of their workers. Japanese managers, the salaryman, are especially subject to what, by Western standards, seems unnatural workloads, often in excess of 60 hours per week. The stress of such jobs has affected the health of many of these managers, leading to heart attacks and strokes. The Japanese call this *karoshi* (death from overwork).

Japan's industrialization has also taken its toll on the environment. Mercury poisoning was a terrible problem during the 1960s and 1970s, when people in the city of Minimata unknowingly ate fish that were contaminated with toxins. In Japanese cities, air pollution was a major health hazard, and some citizens had to wear masks.

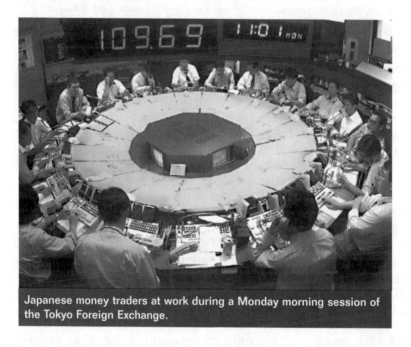

Japanese money traders at work during a Monday morning session of the Tokyo Foreign Exchange.

International Concerns

Japanese banks have faced tough times in recent years. During the mid-1980s, when Japan's trade surplus was reaching record levels, MITI encouraged Japanese to invest overseas. Although Japan is now the world's largest creditor country, its banks have been dangerously tied to economic conditions beyond the control of the Japanese government. After investing heavily in North American real estate in the 1980s, Japanese banks lost hundreds of millions of dollars when property prices fell. More significant than these international losses were the bad loans Japanese banks made to domestic businesses in the past decade. Many of Japan's major banks granted risky loans to Japanese companies that needed capital for investment during the recession of the early 1990s. Since the economy has been slow to recover, many of these loans are now in default and Japanese bankers are scrambling to minimize their losses.

Just as the oil crisis of the 1970s affected the Japanese economy, so too has the worldwide recession of the 1990s. Japan may be a leading economic power, but it is not above global developments over which MITI has no control.

The most serious threats to Japan's economic stability are the high value of the Japanese yen and the tensions that exist with its Western trading partners, particularly with the United States. Japan's export trade has suffered throughout the 1990s due to the high foreign exchange rate of the yen, which makes Japanese goods more expensive than they were in the past. One method of getting around this problem is to open branch plants in other countries. Japanese companies with factories in Canada include Mitsubishi, Toyota, Honda, Nissan, Mazda, Suzuki, Sharp Electronics, Sony, and Yamaha.

Countries such as Canada and the United States are now demanding that Japan end its protectionist policies and open its domestic market to foreign goods. In the mid-1990s, Japan finally opened its doors to some Western goods, but foreign governments continue to complain that big-ticket items, such as American cars and electronic products, are being kept out. The possibility of a major trade war between Japan and the United States continues to be of concern to Japanese politicians, although they remain reluctant to end the tension by opening the country's doors to freer trade.

Japanese–Canadian Trade

In the last decade, trade between Canada and Japan has increased rapidly. Canadian exports of manufactured goods to Japan, for example, expanded from $432 million in 1991 to $708 million in 1995. Japan is Canada's second-largest trading partner after the United States, with a two-way trade of $23.9 billion in 1995. Traditionally, Canada shipped raw and semi-processed materials such as lumber, coal, wood pulp, fish, canola, and copper to Japan in exchange for such manufactured items as cars, computers, telecommunications equipment, and electronic goods. This pattern began to change in 1995, when Canada exported considerable quantities of prefabricated homes and computer software. Following the disastrous Kobe earthquake in 1995, Japanese buyers purchased North American–style homes for their stronger construction and better insulation. Using the following graph, determine which regions in Canada benefitted the most from trade with Japan, and hypothesize reasons for this success.

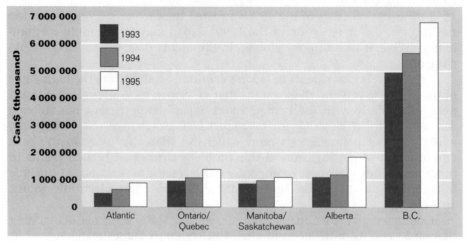

Case Figure 16.2: Canadian Exports to Japan by Regions 1993–1995

Source: From *Canada–Japan Trade Perspectives by James Tiessen* published by the Canada–Japan Trade Council, 1996. Reprinted with permission.

The 1990s: End of an Era

With the end of the Cold War, many Western countries have begun to demand that Japan assume responsibility for its own defence, which had been guaranteed by the United States. This would mean a substantial increase in Japan's military spending. If Japan increased its military budget to only 3 or 4 percent of its GDP, it would have the third-largest military force in the world. Understandably, many Asian countries oppose such a move, remembering the Pacific War. There is also considerable domestic opposition to rearmament. Japanese businesses do not want to see increased government spending on armaments, as such a move would result in higher taxes. More importantly, many Japanese are committed to international peace and cite Article 9 of their constitution, which forbids Japan from having a military force of any size for external use.

The world of the 1990s is much different from that of even 20 years ago. For Japanese politicians this means that the old Yoshida Doctrine of concentrating the country's efforts on building the economy while allowing the United States to defend peace in the Pacific is outmoded. Japan has achieved its goal of catching up to Western industrialized countries and now needs to define for itself a new national purpose. Perhaps this purpose will be to play an increased role in international affairs.

In 1986, a report by MITI concluded that "Japan cannot expect to grow or prosper unless the rest of the world grows and prospers." Not only will Japan have to find ways of encouraging economic growth in other countries, but it likely must also begin to take a more active and responsible role in the United Nations and other international organizations. Although domestic

Seven Prerequisites for Industrial Growth

1 A large pool of money available for investment;

2 A large, inexpensive, and well-educated work force;

3 Accessible and cheap natural resources;

4 Domestic and foreign markets;

5 Enterprising people;

6 A modern transportation and communication infrastructure;

7 A stable and favourable political climate.

and foreign pressures may keep Japan from developing its military, there is evidence that many non-Japanese leaders would support Japanese leadership in economic and non-military ventures. One hundred and fifty years ago Japan was forced into the world economy. Now, as we enter the twenty-first century, it may find itself playing a leadership role in this same arena.

Focus

Which of these prerequisites does Japan possess? How has Japan compensated for the prerequisites that it lacked in the twentieth century?

Lessons, Trade-offs, and Choices

When the world began to take note of the growing Japanese economy in the 1970s, some people believed that the West could learn much from Japan's example. A sociologist from Harvard University wrote a book called *Japan as Number One*, in which he argued that countries such as the United States had to copy Japanese industrial and economic practices and strategies.

Before other countries can decide whether to adopt Japan's methods, they must consider the following question: To what extent are Japan's methods and accomplishments the result of its geographic location, unique situation, and culture? A second question involves trade-offs and choices: What did Japan give up to achieve its present situation? An examination of these issues is essential before deciding what can be learned from Japan's economic success in the second half of the twentieth century.

AKIO MORITA, 1921–

Sony, one of the world's most powerful multinational corporations, was founded for about $500 and operated out of a burned-out department store building in war-torn downtown Tokyo. The driving force behind the group, 25-year-old Akio Morita, went on to become Chairman of Sony and, according to *World Press Review*, "one of the century's top 10 tycoons."

As the eldest son of a wealthy family, Morita was expected to take over the *sake* (rice liquor) brewing business that had been in the family since the late 1600s, but his fascination with electronics led him to convince his father to allow his younger brother to run the brewing company. Morita earned a bachelor's degree in physics in 1944 and served briefly in a non-combat role at the end of World War II in the Japanese navy, where he met engineer Masaru Ibuka. Their friendship developed into a lifelong business partnership; in 1946 they founded the company that was to become the international giant Sony.

Morita's early success came from buying the rights to an American company's miniaturized electronic circuit, the transistor. "Sony used it as the core of a wave of products such as tape recorders, radios, television sets, and videocassette recorders that swept the world."[5]

Morita was convinced that Sony (and Japanese business in general) needed to concentrate on international markets, especially the United States. He faced the task of reversing the prevailing American perception of Japanese goods as cheap imitations of American products, so he took the unusual step of moving his family to New York and developed marketing strategies suited to North America. As a result, Sony created an American subsidiary, the first Japanese corporation listed on the New York Stock Exchange. By the end of the 1960s, sales of Sony televisions eclipsed those of American giants such as RCA and Zenith, and Morita became spectacularly wealthy. Today,

70 percent of Sony's sales come from outside Japan.

Although he has had some failures (Sony's technically superior Betamax format for videocassette recorders lost out to the less-expensive VHS format), Morita has continued to lead the way by "his dedication to staying two steps ahead of the competition in the development of new products."[6] His creation of the Sony Walkman resulted in the sale of 20 million units in the two years before the opposition could catch up. His approach to marketing is quite distinctive: "Our plan is to lead the public with new products rather than ask them what kind of products they want. The public does not know what is possible, but we do."[7] Sony's $2 billion purchase of CBS Records in 1987 and its promotion of compact discs continued its pattern of development and innovation.

Morita also fostered a management approach that emphasizes encouraging and valuing employees: "Those companies that are most successful in Japan are those that have managed to create a shared sense of fate among all employees. ... In the long run, your business and its future are in the hands of the people you hire."[8]

Morita's retirement after an illness in 1994 ended a career that is summarized in a journalist's assessment: "More than anyone, he can be said to have put Japan and Japanese goods on the international business map."[9] In his autobiography, *Made in Japan: Akio Morita and Sony*, Morita offered an assessment of the global economy:

The world economic system has slipped out of our control; increasingly, our economies are at the

mercy of financial opportunists. Entire companies have become objects of exchange for the money traders, and great, old businesses are eating up their own assets in pursuit of quick profits. Some nations are crushed under debt burdens they cannot hope to liquidate. And as some industrialists invest in the money trading game instead of the future, the ability of some countries to produce their industrial necessities is diminishing rapidly. None of this activity is helping to create the better, more stable world we say we want. ...

I believe there is a bright future ahead for mankind, and that future holds exciting techno- *logical advances that will enrich the lives of everybody on the planet. Only by expanding world trade and stimulating more production can we take advantage of the possibilities that lie before us.*[10]

---

1 What factors contributed to Akio Morita's success in business?

2 How does Morita's career reflect important elements of Japan's postwar economic system?

Underlying and Emerging Issues

Give the reasoning and evidence that might be used to support different views or conclusions on the following issues.

1 Is promoting efficiency and productivity more important than ensuring competition?

2 Should corporations emphasize long-term development over short-term profits?

3 What policies should governments employ to promote economic growth?

4 What should be the relationship between government and business?

5 What should be the relationship between employers and employees?

6 Should corporations promote lifelong employment and a "family" atmosphere for employees?

7 To what extent do employers have a responsibility for the quality of life of their employees?

8 Is it necessary to protect domestic markets from outside competition in order to establish industries?

9 To what extent should the education system focus on employment skills, and to what extent should it promote the development of the potential of each individual?

10 To what extent should education emphasize responsibility and group membership?

11 To what extent should the education system promote creativity and imagination?

12 Should corporations pursue higher profits by moving production to countries where wages are low?

13 How should industrial economies deal with the question of rising unemployment due to increasing economic globalization?

14 Should countries focus on export markets to achieve economic growth?

15 How important should be the goal of gender equality in the economy?

16 Has industrialization resulted in unacceptable trade-offs in its impact on the environment and society?

17 To what extent are Japan's successes due to cultural factors?

18 To what extent can Japan's economic approaches be implemented in other countries?

Focussing Knowledge

In your notes, clearly identify or define and explain the importance or significance of each of the following:

samurai

Meiji Restoration

zaibatsu

keiretsu

Yoshida Doctrine

Ministry of International Trade
   and Industry (MITI)

Sumitomo

salaryman

Reviewing and Organizing Knowledge

1 What evidence is there that the Japanese economy has been successful?

2 What factors promoted Japanese economic growth before 1945?

3 How did each of the following contribute to economic growth in Japan after 1945: American Occupation policies, the Cold War, economic strategies of the government, *keiretsu*, Ministry of International Trade and Industry (MITI), the education system, cultural factors, employer–employee relations?

4 What is the basis for Paul Johnson's assertion that the key factor in Japan's success was "Adam Smith economics"?

5 What are the trade-offs, problems, or issues that have arisen as a result of Japan's economic growth, in each of the following areas: domestic problems, workers' lives, social and environmental concerns, the role of women, international involvement?

6 What issues should countries consider before they make decisions about adopting aspects of Japan's approach?

Applying and Extending Knowledge

1 List all the factors that have contributed to Japan's economic success. Choose the four factors that seem most important, then explain the basis for your selection in an essay.

2 Write a position paper on the following topic: "To what extent is Japan's economic success due to actions by its government?"

3 Write a position paper in which you take a stand on Paul Johnson's contention that the basis of Japan's success was "Adam Smith economics."

4 Describe the similarities and differences between Japan's "guided capitalism" and Mussolini's "corporatist state."

5 Take a stand on the following statement: "Canada should use Japan as a model for its economic system."

6 Research the economic situation of a less-developed country in Africa, Asia, or Latin America. On the basis of what you have learned in your study of political and economic systems, write a report in which you act as a consultant on the question, "To what extent should this country attempt to imitate Japan's approach to economic systems?"

7 Compare Japan's economic system with that of China. Describe the key factors that led these two countries to such different economic systems.

8 Collect newspaper articles on Japan for a period of two weeks. To what extent do the articles reflect important aspects of Japan's approach to economic systems?

9 Write a position paper in which you take and support a position on one of the following topics:

a. Japan should assume more responsibility for leadership in the world.

b. Japan should eliminate its trade surplus by encouraging imports.

10 Select newspaper articles that reflect some of the Underlying and Emerging Issues on page 448. Explain how the articles illlustrate the issues.

11 Choose one of the Underlying and Emerging Issues. Describe the relative strengths of the various sides, then take a position and defend it.

Fascism and Nazism as Economic Systems

*T*HIS CASE STUDY EXPLAINS how Benito Mussolini, the Fascist leader of Italy, and Adolf Hitler, the Nazi leader of Germany, organized their countries' economies to achieve national goals. Mussolini created the illusion that he could cure his country's relatively backward economic system and heal the world's economic woes. His methods included manipulating Italy's working and lower-middle classes and befriending Italy's wealthy landowners and capitalists. This section of the case study concludes with an assessment of whether Mussolini's corporatist experiment was indeed a "third economic way." The section on Hitler's Germany illustrates how Hitler catered to big business and the armed forces in preparing Germany for war during the 1930s and how the Nazi Party combined private enterprise and government direction to fight World War II.

Learning Outcomes

After reading this case study, you should be able to:

- understand the economic problems of post–World War I Italy

- analyze the methods that Mussolini used

- explain the theory and the reality of the corporatist system

- discuss the motives behind Hitler's economic system

- evaluate the success of the Nazi economy

- compare the Fascist and Nazi economic approaches

Fascism as an Economic System

To be understood, fascism must be viewed in the context of the events of the twentieth century. In the 1920s and 1930s, fascism and communism were often seen as the two main alternatives to the liberal capitalist democracies of the West. The impact of the Great Depression of the 1930s convinced many people to consider adopting fascist or communist economic principles. Although these two ideologies are often considered to be polar opposites, occupying the two extremes of the ideological spectrum, in practice they share many similarities.

In fascism and communism, economic power is subservient to political power. Although in theory both ideologies exert almost complete control over the economy, they differ in several important respects. In Fascist Italy and Nazi Germany in the 1930s, economic planning and government ownership of the means of production for non-military purposes were minimal. When these countries attempted to plan economic matters it was almost solely for military reasons. Attempts to limit imports, for example, were to make the country self-sufficient during wartime. Economic decisions were made to benefit members of the ruling party and the industrial elite rather than the workers. The ultimate goal of communism, on the other hand, was to construct a new economic and social order. To achieve this revolution, the state operated the economy as if it was one large business firm and attempted to reshape the people's habits and attitudes to create a new way of life.

Fascism was based on a clear rejection of both capitalist democracy and Marxist communism. According to Benito Mussolini, fascism would bring order to capitalism without imposing the inefficiency of state ownership. "It is no longer the economy aiming at individual profit," Mussolini stated, "but an economy concerned with collective interests." Fascist Italy's government under Mussolini sought to introduce a "third economic way"—an economic system that would reduce the freedoms of capitalism, and eliminate the repression of individual freedom under Marxism.

Origins of Italy's Fascist Economy

corporatist system: in Fascist Italy, an economic system developed by Benito Mussolini that combined aspects of the medieval guild system and syndicalism.

Mussolini's **corporatist system** was a combination of a variety of practices and ideologies. Foremost among his models was the ancient European medieval guild system, in which each occupation in a town created its own organization, or guild. The elected guild leaders controlled all the affairs relating to the guild, including product quality, prices, distribution, pay scales, and discipline. Mussolini liked the idea of joint employer–employee involvement in the guilds and sought to extend guild-like control from individual towns to the entire country. Mussolini also wanted to add representatives of the Fascist Party to each guild.

syndicalism: a political and economic approach developed by George Sorel in the late 1800s that envisioned trade unions governing society.

The second aspect of Mussolini's corporatism was **syndicalism**. Swiss social philosopher Georges Sorel, who conceived syndicalism at the end of the nineteenth century, wanted trade unions to govern society. To this idea, Mussolini added representatives from employers and the Fascist Party. In theory, the three participants (employers, employees, and government) would work together. In practice, employers and government cooperated with each other and dominated the workers.

The Corporatist State

Mussolini wanted to modernize Italy's backward economy. Corporatism, in Mussolini's view, would discourage workers from joining communist organizations and encourage rich industrialists to share their profits with the poorer members of society.

Corporatism had begun on a modest scale prior to Mussolini's assumption of power in 1922. As the leader of the Fascist Party, Mussolini had established six experimental "corporations" to serve as alternatives to socialist and Roman Catholic trade unions. Each corporation contained representatives from labour and owners. The Fascist Party supervised them to ensure fair settlements. However, the workers and the employers were reluctant to surrender their independent, separate status, and the corporations met only occasionally.

Mussolini was nonetheless impressed with the potential of corporatism, and in 1925 he forced the industrialists' and the workers' organizations to bargain with each other on all economic matters. These corporations negotiated wages and working conditions. All agreements, however, had to be approved by the government. The next year (1926), the government outlawed strikes and lockouts, and created six nation-wide corporations for industry, agriculture, banking, commerce, transportation, and the merchant marine. Associations of soldiers, police, government officials, and professors were prohibited. Every adult was required to pay dues to the appropriate corporation. The Fascist government appointed the corporation officials, who had to be members of the Fascist Party. The **Ministry of Corporations**, with Mussolini as its first minister, had veto power over all decisions. Immediately below this ministry were the 12 corporations (6 each of employers and workers), which met to conduct negotiations.

Each corporation was governed by a council composed of equal numbers of employers, workers, and Fascist Party members. These corporations provided the vehicles by which the government controlled the economy. As Mussolini declared, "We control the political forces, we control the moral forces, and we control the economic forces."

Ministry of Corporations: in Fascist Italy, a government ministry that controlled nation-wide "corporations," or associations of workers and managers in various industries.

VIEWPOINT

BENITO MUSSOLINI, 1883–1945

Fascism

It takes more than rhetorical skill and charisma to win the support of a country. A successful leader must also have an ideology or a set of objectives that is appropriate to the period and to the people. Mussolini's set of ideas (confusing as they sometimes were) was called fascism.

"Our program is simple," stated Mussolini, "we wish to govern Italy. They ask us for programs, but there are already too many. It is not programs that are wanting for the salvation of Italy, but men and will

Benito Mussolini gives the Fascist salute as he reviews detachments of the Italian military police.

power." He saw life as a struggle in which positive action and discipline were needed for success. Democracy and socialism were too passive and sentimental to survive in a world of conflict and struggle. Democracy was flawed because it glorified the individual and did not admit that most people are irrational. Majority rule therefore meant that the country was reduced to the level of the lowest common denominator.

Individuals, according to Mussolini, were first and foremost members of a nation to which they gave all their loyalty and love. In his view, the whole was greater than the sum of its individual parts. Only by subordinating themselves to the will of the state could people reach their fullest potential. This appeal to nationalist ideology gave many Italians a sense of belonging, security, and self-worth. They were part of a larger whole that Mussolini promised would become one of the most powerful nations in the world.

Fascism also glorified the leader. People owed absolute obedience to their immediate superior. Just as there were some classes in society better able to rule than others (that is, the Fascist Party), only one person, Mussolini stated, was qualified to govern the Italian nation. Since this leader knew the real needs of the state, he (it was assumed that the leader would be male) had to be given total obedience. In a moment of vanity, Mussolini once declared: "Fascism is Mussolinism ... what would Fascism be if I had not been?" Every high school had a portrait of Mussolini hanging on the wall, and school textbooks praised his knowledge of economics and politics and stated that corporatism was the ultimate solution to the world's economic problems.

The following excerpt is taken from an article signed by Mussolini, but written by Italian philosopher Giovanni Gentile in 1932, titled "The Political and Social Doctrine of Fascism."

Fascism combats the whole system of democratic ideology. Fascism denies that the majority, by the simple fact that it is a majority, can direct human society. It denies that numbers alone can govern by means of periodical consultations. It affirms the inequality of mankind. ...

Fascism uses whatever elements in Liberal, Social, or Democratic doctrines that still have value and rejects all the rest. Given that the nineteenth century was the century of Socialism, of Liberalism, and of Democracy, it does not necessarily follow that the twenti-eth century must also be a century of Socialism, Liberalism, and Democracy. Political doctrines pass, but humanity remains. It may be rather expected that this will be a century of authority, a century of fascism. If the nineteenth century was a century of individualism, it may be expected that this will be the century of collectivism, and hence the century of the State. ...

Fascism conceives of the State as an absolute, in comparison with which all individuals or groups are relative, only to be conceived of in relation to the State.[1]

···The Fascist Economy in Practice

Almost as soon as the corporatist system was established, Mussolini ignored it. To a large extent, the corporations had little effect on economic life and remained advisory in nature—a façade that made for a good public image. However, as the economy worsened during the Great Depression of the 1930s, Mussolini revived the corporatist system, increasing the number of corporations to 22. These units occasionally met in the newly formed **National Council of Corporations** to discuss general economic concerns.

In 1938, the government abolished the Chamber of Deputies (similar to Canada's House of Commons) and replaced it with the Chamber of Fasces and Corporations, some of whose members were elected directly by the corporations. The Fascist Party selected the remaining members. Mussolini thus substituted representation by occupation for individual and geographic representation.

Corporatism created such an excellent impression worldwide that during the height of the Depression some liberals outside of Italy were willing to try this system, even if it meant the loss of some individual freedoms. This foreign support was hardly surprising. Corporatism had a respectable pedigree, it enjoyed the support of the Roman Catholic Church, most Italians favoured it, the system appeared on the surface to be an inventive and courageous attempt to defeat the Depression, and, most importantly, all other methods had failed to end the Depression.

In reality, corporatism failed to solve Italy's economic problems. In practice, the 22 corporations had only limited authority. Fascist Party members exercised most of the decision-making power, and they, in turn, received their orders from the Fascist leaders. The corporations were merely window dressing for the benefit of domestic and foreign observers. In fact, these corporations did little more than rubber-stamp the decisions reached beforehand by the Fascist Party.

The corporatist system also worsened class relations. The wealthy classes retained most of their power in Fascist society. Trade unions, on the other hand, had been outlawed in the 1920s, and their leaders had been killed, jailed, or silenced through threats and intimidation. As a result, the employers won most negotiations, and fascism revealed itself as the defender of big business. The corporatist system thus failed to improve the lot of ordinary Italians. The extensive network of administrative agencies was run by faithful Fascist Party members and their families, which led to bribery and widespread corruption.

Almost from the start, Mussolini favoured the business class, which had brought him to power. This is one reason why fascism appealed to some industrialists in other countries. Fascism, unlike democracy, seemed to protect capitalism from the threat of communism. Corporatist Italy included high tariffs, low corporate taxes, and generous government contracts for big industrial firms. The Depression strengthened the government's links with capitalism, as Mussolini rescued financially unstable large-scale businesses while allowing smaller firms to perish. Under these conditions, monopolies increased quickly, while the working classes lost most of their earning power.

National Council of Corporations: a council comprising 22 corporations in Fascist Italy.

Mussolini knew the political importance of creating the impression that the country's leader was intelligent and confident. Thus, although he had little understanding of or interest in economics, Mussolini invented the story that as a youth he had studied under expert economists and that his economic decisions were now "almost infallible." The Italian press was instructed not to mention the country's economic hardships, and to emphasize that Italy's economy compared favourably with that of the most prosperous countries. To ensure such beliefs, economic figures were falsified and Mussolini bragged that the efficiency of the Italian railway system was the envy of Europe. In fact, the previous government had already modernized the country's rail system and it was a myth that under fascism the trains invariably ran on time.

Mussolini's public works programs and extravagant projects created some employment, but they could not conceal the fact that Mussolini supported the industrialists at the expense of the workers. After being ousted in 1943, Mussolini admitted that his betrayal of the working classes had been his most serious error. But in the interwar years, many people saw Mussolini's program as a "third way" between communism and capitalism.

The Economic System of Nazi Germany

In many aspects, Nazism was a variety of fascism, although it was more racist and totalitarian. Adolf Hitler came to power 11 years after Mussolini and learned from the Italian leader's example. But in other ways, Hitler's National Socialism had distinctive features, especially in its anti-Semitic doctrines.

Hitler's Early Economic Promises

On the eve of the Nazi revolution, Germany's economy was in ruins. Unemployment had risen steadily from 1.4 million in 1929, to 3.1 million in 1930, to 5.7 million in 1931, and finally to 6 million in 1932.* Many other people had only part-time work. Millions of Germans were without food and shelter. Many of these people blamed their suffering on the harsh peace terms that the victorious Allies had imposed on Germany at the end of World War I and on their new democratic government (the Weimar Republic), which had signed this peace treaty. Communist supporters pointed out that while German workers were suffering, the Soviet Union had made a miraculous economic recovery under Joseph Stalin. In 1928, he had launched a Five-Year Plan that had eliminated virtually all unemployment in the Soviet Union and had established free social services.

As a result, many Germans began to look to the Soviet Union as a model. Germany's elite, consisting of the still-powerful army officer corps, the Protestant and Catholic clergy, most intellectuals, and wealthy businesspeople, feared the rise of communism in Germany.

---

*Germany's population was approximately 65 million. By contrast, France, with a population of 40 million, never exceeded 850 000 unemployed people, and Great Britain (population 60 million) had approximately 3 million unemployed people.

At first, Hitler wanted to gain the support of the working people. The name of his party, the National Socialist German Workers' Party, reflected this fact. Throughout the early 1920s, the Nazi Party aimed its propaganda against Jews, communists, the Allies, the Weimar Republic, and capitalists. These policies brought the Nazis only moderate support from the working classes, and alienated a large segment of the remainder of the German electorate. The failed Munich *Putsch* (uprising) of November 1923, which was an illegal Nazi attempt to seize the local government, convinced Hitler that he could gain power only through semi-democratic means. To attract the more conservative segments of German society, Hitler toned down his attacks against capitalism, as Mussolini had done in Italy.

At the onset of the Great Depression of 1929, Hitler made numerous promises to Germans to win their electoral support. He promised the farmers that they would not lose their lands to foreclosures. To attract the clergy he pledged to restore the Christian churches to their earlier position of influence. He swore to support Germany's war veterans. He vowed to overturn the hated Versailles peace treaty through peaceful means if possible, but by force if necessary. Hitler courted Germany's industrialists by promising a strong, productive, and prosperous Germany that would extend its economic power throughout the world. He especially stressed the need to acquire Eastern Europe, long believed to be Germany's major economic hinterland. Finally, Hitler offered direct, if brutal, action against communists and Jews.

Although Germany's major industrialists were uncertain whether or not to trust Hitler, they were sufficiently impressed by his promises not to oppose him in the January 1933 election. Even with their passive consent, and despite terror tactics, Hitler won only 43 percent of the votes. However, he managed to gather a majority of 52 percent by forming coalitions with right-wing and conservative parties. Thus the Nazis came to power mainly through semi-democratic means. After Hitler consolidated power in his own hands by dismantling Germany's democratic institutions, the way was clear for the Nazis to shape the economy in any way they wished.

Germany's Economic Objectives

Pragmatism is the best word to describe Hitler's economic policies. Unlike Lenin and Mussolini, Hitler never claimed to possess a systematic economic ideology. Instead, he pledged to stick to practicalities. Hitler had no formal training in economics, but he was clever enough to understand that political and military decisions would affect Germany's economy in a major way, and vice versa. Consequently, he exerted considerable influence on Nazi Germany's economy.

pragmatism: practicality over ideology.

Hitler was convinced that although Germany's economy should be guided by the Nazi Party's overall goals, the actual direction of the economy should be controlled by the capitalists. This scheme allowed no room for organized labour, and labour unions were outlawed in May 1933 with the enthusiastic support of Germany's industrial class. Hitler also promised the leading industrialists that he would keep employee incomes low, offered tax concessions to large businesses, and held out hopes of large government contracts.

Early in 1933, Hitler began to rearm Germany in violation of the Versailles Treaty in order, he claimed, to jump-start the German economy. He also promised to introduce conscription and to return the armed forces to their earlier position of honour and power. These decisions gained the enthusiastic support of the country's military officers' corps, and the following year they swore personal allegiance to Hitler as their commander-in-chief. As a final step to ensure the support of the military and big business, Hitler awarded huge government military contracts to the industrialists.

In June 1933, Hitler proclaimed Germany's first Four-Year Plan and established a public works program that emphasized building superhighways for civilian as well as military purposes. Thousands of young men were kept busy for the next six years constructing 7000 km of highways (the Autobahn). The Four-Year Plan also included tax concessions and government subsidies to private businesses; these were designed to revive industrial production and consumption. The plan was highly successful. Within one year, the number of unemployed people had declined from 4.8 million to 2.7 million, convincing many domestic and foreign observers that the Nazi Party had a master plan for solving Germany's economic crisis. Hitler began to portray himself as an economic expert; in fact, he had no master economic plan, and he lurched from one economic scheme to the next.

rearmament: rebuilding of a country's military system.

Rearmament was the priority in Hitler's economic program. Even unemployment took a back seat to the demands for weaponry. When, in February 1933, Cabinet discussed the urgent need for a reservoir in Upper Silesia, Hitler ended the project by demanding priority for the armed forces during the next four to five years. Between 1933 and 1938, government expenditures on defence rose from 9 to 43 percent of the total budget.

Financing the Government

Financing Hitler's rearmament plans required extraordinary financial strategies. Hjalmar Schacht, the head of the Reichsbank (similar to the Central Bank of Canada), was a financial genius. Schacht provided unlimited financial credit to the government, despite Germany's massive national debt of nearly 1 billion marks (about $250 million, a huge sum in those days) that Nazi Germany had inherited from the Weimar Republic.

Mefo-bills: a form of currency based on a dummy corporation that Germany's Nazi government used to finance at least 20 percent of its rearmament costs.

Schacht succeeded in fooling not only the international banking community and the German public, but also most of Germany's financial experts. He created a dummy corporation and printed bills, called **Mefo-bills**, based on the company's supposed profits. Mefo-bills served as a form of money and were accepted by government contractors and banks. About half of these bills were used to pay off contractors—all of them munitions firms. The other half were sold to the German public at 4 percent annual interest. The German government took infinite care not to reveal even the approximate value of the total bills circulating at any given time and lied about the true intention of these bills. Nobody was permitted to discuss them in public, and all pertinent documents were treated as top secret.

Germany repaid the Mefo-bills, plus interest, after 1936. By this time, inflation had lowered the real value of the German mark. In other words, Germany financed at least 20 percent of its rearmament costs at virtually no expense to itself.

The local Jewish business community was another important source of income for the government. On November 9, 1938, called *Kristallnacht* (the night of the broken glass), the government acted against the Jewish community, using the assassination of a German diplomat by a Polish Jew as an excuse. The Nazis shattered Jewish shop windows, burned places of Jewish worship, and terrorized Jewish businesses and individuals. The government then closed all Jewish businesses and seized their assets. The government also fined the Jewish community 1 billion marks for the assassination, and pocketed 6 million marks in compensation for damages that the Jewish proprietors would have received from insurance companies. The government gave some of these former Jewish enterprises to non-Jewish German middle-class businessmen, and distributed the rest among high Nazi officials and large corporations upon whose good will and support the government depended. These dramatic events distracted ordinary citizens from the country's economic problems.

Gaining Self-Sufficiency

In 1936, Germany began to run short of certain strategic raw materials. The more deeply Germany became involved in rearmament, the more sophisticated became its needs for vital supplies, such as oil and rubber. Germany had no oil, but Soviet Russia and Romania did, and Germany was dangerously dependent on these two countries for its fuel resources. In March 1936, the Soviet Union and Romania refused to sell Germany any further fuel supplies unless they were reimbursed in gold or in American or British money.

This incident highlighted Germany's critical weakness and prompted Hitler to launch his Second Four-Year Plan (1936–40), which was designed to achieve self-sufficiency. German scientists were challenged to invent artificial sources of foods, discover alternative fuels to replace oil, and devise synthetic rubber substitutes to keep the German armed forces on the move. The appointment of Hermann Goering, a trusted and ruthless Nazi official, as commissioner of raw materials in April 1936 ushered in the period during which the Second Four-Year Plan placed Germany on an offensive war footing.

To gain control of the economies of Eastern Europe, Germany began to strangle the economies of its Eastern trading partners. It promised to pay these countries higher than prevailing world prices for their agricultural products. This was the bait that Germany used to separate these countries from their Western customers and to persuade them to expand their agricultural production to suit Germany's requirements. When these countries accepted Hitler's offer, Germany soon held them within its economic grip.

After 1937, Germany insisted on selling guns in exchange for grain. By then, Germany had effectively switched over to producing offensive weaponry, and needed a market in which to dispose of its unwanted defensive armaments. The East European countries had no choice but to accept these weapons at vastly inflated prices. On the eve of World War II, Germany's economic position was still precarious. But six years of intense efforts had created a mighty offensive arsenal and a huge army to match it. As of 1938, Germany had the capability to strike against the small countries to the east that had purchased German-made obsolete defensive weapons.

Germany's War Economy

During World War II, German factories produced enormous numbers of tanks, planes, cannons, and shells, despite the devastating destruction caused by Allied bombings that began in 1942 and continued until the Allied victory in May 1945. This success in production can be explained mainly by one word: organization. In March 1940, Hitler appointed Fritz Todt as the Minister for Armaments and Munitions. To improve the economy, Todt established a series of committees, each headed by an expert that he appointed. These committees recommended improved uses of raw materials and better distribution to the various war industries. These recommendations were relayed to another committee that controlled Germany's war plants and had the power to force every industry to share its know-how, resources, staff, and machinery. Because this committee had access to the inventory and production data of all factories, it could introduce improved production methods in each plant, including purchasing new machinery and transferring equipment from one plant to another.

From the point of view of efficiency, the Todt plan was a success. To cite but one example, Todt's efficiency experts discovered that the consumption of raw materials, use of machinery, time taken to complete orders, and the quality of the final product varied from plant to plant by as much as 300 percent. Todt's reforms improved production and helped the German armaments industry make enormous profits. Most importantly, since this system preserved the entrepreneurs' freedom of action and allowed them to earn profits, the business community generally participated eagerly in war production. Despite being encircled by the armed forces of nearly the entire world, Germany came perilously close to winning World War II.

Albert Speer Replaces Todt

In February 1942, when the economy was encountering serious problems, Todt was killed in an airplane crash on the Russian front and Hitler appointed Albert Speer as his successor. Speer had been responsible for staging the dramatic and highly effective Nazi Party rallies. These efforts brought him to the attention of Hitler, who recognized his genius and entrusted the young man with increasingly more difficult and prestigious tasks. Speer turned out to be an even more effective manager of Germany's war effort, and dealt quickly with the problems that Todt had been unable to solve.

Todt's achievement record was impressive, but under Speer's direction, war production increased more rapidly, even though Germany was under withering around-the-clock attacks by Allied heavy bombers. The Speer regime was an improved version of the Todt method of production. Unlike Todt, Speer held regular conferences with Hitler, who supported him in the face of all opposition. At these meetings, which continued almost to the end of the war, decisions on strategy and the general economic situation were reached. In February 1942, Hitler enthusiastically approved Speer's designs for increased war production at the expense of civilian goods. So strict and meticulous was Speer that any committee head over the age of 55 had to have a deputy not older than 40, to ensure the uninterrupted flow of production in the event of a death.

In every respect, Speer "tightened the screws." He made adjustments to the economy without disturbing its capitalist basis. He created more factory floor space, employed more workers, and designated certain industries as "vital," such as the production of certain metals, oil, powder and explosives, chemicals, power, and railway boxcars. Essential workers were exempt from the draft. Between January and March 1942 alone, an estimated 244 000 men were designated key workers. Speer went so far as to eliminate all army influence over economic decisions. But in the end, Germany's economic efforts were not enough to stave off defeat.

Some Conclusions

An important factor to consider in Nazi Germany's economic system is the fact that, apart from maintaining a relatively free capitalist system in a totalitarian state (an accomplishment in itself), the Nazis engaged in a giant game of on-the-spot improvisation, which nonetheless followed a certain amount of rational planning. For example, the chief problem before the war was how to raise the funds to establish and equip a huge army without unleashing a war prematurely, without bankrupting the country, and without causing the worst inflationary spiral in world history.

At the same time, the war brought Germany more heavily into economic planning. However, the war also forced the Allied countries to resort to greater national economic planning. It is tempting to speculate how the Nazi economy might have operated in the absence of war. However, militarism and rearmament were so central to the Nazi ideology that perhaps the question is not, in the end, very relevant.

BIOGRAPHY

ALBERT SPEER, 1905–1981

As "Hitler's architect" and Minister of Armaments, Albert Speer played a critical role in the Nazi regime during World War II. But his life and actions raise fundamental questions about both the appeal of National Socialism and the issue of responsibility for Nazi acts.

Born in Mannheim, Germany, to wealthy parents, Speer spent his youth in comfortable, upper-middle-class surroundings. Showing considerable potential at school, he was sent to Munich to study architecture. After graduating in 1927, he was hired as head assistant in one of Germany's most respected architectural firms.

As a young man, Speer had no interest in politics. However, he underwent a radical transformation after his first encounter with Adolf Hitler at a rally. Hitler's impact on Speer was immediate and overwhelming, changing him from a disinterested observer into a direct participant in German government and society. "I was carried away," Speer later recalled, "on the wave of enthusiasm which bore the speaker along from sentence to sentence. It swept away any skepticism, any reservations. Here, it seemed to me, was hope. Here were new ideas, new understanding, new tasks."[2]

While he seemed to have abhorred both the brutality and the racism of the Nazis, it is clear that Speer was much taken with some aspects of their ideology. In particular, he saw their program as an antidote to the helplessness, poverty, and decay of Weimar Germany.

After joining the Nazi Party in 1931, Speer quickly rose through the ranks of the organization, becoming its official architect in 1934. Among his early successes were his designs for the enormous Nuremburg Party Congress of 1934 (captured so dramatically by filmmaker Leni Riefenstahl in *Triumph of the Will*—see Case Study 9), the German Embassy in London, and the German Pavilion at the 1937 World's Fair. Plans for even more grandiose buildings and monuments (Hitler wanted a triumphal arch 50 times as large as the Arc de Triomphe in Paris) were scrapped with the outbreak of World War II in 1939.

Speer's power and prestige rose exponentially in 1943 with his appointment as Minister of Armaments and Production, despite his protests to Hitler that he had no experience in such matters. The results of his efforts were remarkable. Within a year of his promotion, Speer increased the production of fighter aircraft by four times, tanks and ammunition by five times, and weapons by seven times. Many historians feel that, even by conservative estimates, Speer's skilful management of the German economy allowed the country to remain at war for up to two years longer than it would have under the previous minister (a point that provides Speer's many critics with considerable ammunition).

The basis for this success stemmed from Speer's intelligence, organizational abilities, drive, and use of slave labour. By 1944, it appears that Germany was relying on as many as 10 million prisoners to provide the labour necessary to keep the war economy moving.

After the fall of Hitler's regime in 1945, Speer was arrested and forced to stand trial alongside 24 high-ranking Nazis at Nuremburg, the scene of his former triumph. Speer alone entered a guilty plea. At the trial, he stated, "Who else is to be held responsible for the course of the events, if not the closest associates around the chief of state?" While the Russians pressed for the death penalty, Speer's relatively humane treatment of the prisoners in his charge saved him from execution. The court also was influenced by testimony regarding Speer's break with Hitler near the end of the war, including his refusal to implement Hitler's "scorched earth" policy.

The court spared Speer's life but found him guilty of using slave labour, and sentenced him to 20 years' confinement in Spandau prison (a term that he eventually served to the hour). While in prison, Speer read voraciously, learned English and French, and secretly wrote his memoirs. Upon his release in 1961, he published his book *Inside the Third Reich*, which became an international bestseller. In the following excerpt from this work, Speer attempts to address his responsibility for his actions in the Nazi regime and the war:

> *Today, a quarter century after these events, it is not only specific faults that burden my conscience, great as these may have been. My moral failure is not a matter of this item and that; it resides in my active association with the whole course of events. I had participated in a war which, as we of the intimate circle should never have doubted, was aimed at world dominion. What is more, by my abilities and my energies, I had prolonged that war by many months. ... Nor was it only symbolically that Hitler dreamed of possessing the globe. It was part of his dream to subjugate the other nations. ... Although I never actually agreed with Hitler on these questions, I had nevertheless designed the buildings and produced the weapons which served his ends.[3]*

1 How does Speer's life reflect the appeal that National Socialism held for some people?

2 Why is Speer considered a controversial figure?

Underlying and Emerging Issues

Give the reasoning and evidence that might be used to support different views or conclusions on the following issues.

1 To what extent should people divide into national societies based on common features?

2 Are the interests of society as a whole more important than the interests of any one individual?

3 What are the legitimate boundaries between public interests and private interests?

4 Do we need strong governments in order to transcend the narrow self-interests of individuals?

5 Is fascism preferable to communism?

6 Does capitalism provide too much freedom?

7 Should government attempt to guide the economy rather than engage in public ownership or central planning?

8 Should government attempt to bring employers and labour together?

9 To what extent should workers play a role in decisions in industry?

10 Do all workers have a right to independent unions?

11 To what extent should workers have the right to strike?

12 Is it worth giving up some freedom to get economic stability and order?

Focussing Knowledge

In your notes, clearly identify or define and explain the importance or significance of each of the following:

"third economic way" *rearmament*

corporatist system *Chamber of Fasces*

guild system *and Corporations*

syndicalism *Georges Sorel*

Reviewing and Organizing Knowledge

1 How have fascism and communism been linked in the twentieth century?

2 In terms of their economic systems, how were fascism and communism

a. similar?

b. different?

3 To what extent did fascism represent a "third economic way"?

4 How was Mussolini's corporatist system based on

   a. the medieval guild system?

   b. syndicalism?

   c. cooperation with the Roman Catholic Church?

5 a. What were the main features of the early corporatist state?

   b. How was the system expanded in the late 1920s and 1930s?

6 a. Why did corporatism appeal to some people outside of Italy?

   b. What were the main criticisms of the corporatist system?

7 Why did fascism appeal to industrialists and other wealthy people in other countries?

8 How did Hitler's Nazism differ from Italian Fascism?

9 a. What factors contributed to the success of Nazism in Germany?

   b. How did Hitler gain the support of industrialists?

10 a. Describe the main features of the economy of Nazi Germany before World War II.

   b. How was Hitler able to finance his economic plans?

   c. Describe the main elements of Hitler's drive for economic self–sufficiency.

11 Outline the key concepts of Germany's wartime economy under

   a. Fritz Todt;

   b. Albert Speer.

Applying and Extending Knowledge

1 Both Mussolini's Fascism and Hitler's National Socialism made attempts to include limited elements of socialism to broaden their appeal. Describe the ways in which the democratic socialist parties of the 1920s and 1930s differed from fascism.

2 Read biographies of Mussolini and Hitler. To what extent were the factors that led them to fascist ideologies similar and different?

3 Research one of the other countries that adopted fascist elements during the 1930s. To what extent was the country's economic system similar to and different from that of Fascist Italy?

4 Research fascist movements in Canada and the United States during the 1920s and 1930s. Why did fascism not gain the acceptance in North America that it did in Europe at the time?

5 Find newspaper articles that reflect the presence of fascism in countries today. Explain how the articles reflect specific aspects of fascist political or economic approaches.

6 Examine the rise of neo-fascism in the 1980s and 1990s. How are these movements similar to and different from those of Mussolini and Hitler?

7 Combine the results of your study of the fascist economic systems with your work on fascist political approaches in earlier chapters and case studies. Write a description of the main elements of these systems in an essay on the political and economic systems of fascism.

8 Select newspaper articles that reflect some of the Underlying and Emerging Issues on page 464. Explain how the articles reflect the issues.

9 Choose one of the Underlying and Emerging Issues. Outline the arguments and evidence on the different sides, then take a position and defend it, explaining why you see this side as stronger.

CHAPTER 10

Citizens and Societies

*I*N CHAPTER 1, it was suggested that for a democratic country to operate effectively, its citizens must understand not only how its institutions operate but also their limitations. Throughout this book you have analyzed different ideas, evaluated opposite points of view, and judged issues as you have examined the major political and economic ideologies of the past. You now need to come to your own conclusions about the types of political and economic systems you favour. You must also decide what role you will take in the years ahead in supporting or changing Canada's political and economic systems.

As citizens and decision-makers for the twenty-first century, you have important choices ahead, including the question of how involved you will become in influencing the world around you. This concluding chapter puts these questions in the context of some of the major changes that are affecting our decisions about ideologies as a new century and millennium begin. Is the nation-state as we know it doomed to become obsolete? If so, should it be replaced by some form of international body, or by a host of smaller states based on ethnic solidarity? On the economic level, such developments as the rise of **globalization** and multinational corporations also pose fundamental questions related to the traditional economic and political ideologies of the twentieth century.

Many of the questions and issues examined in this book have revolved around the relationship between the individual and society: What are "reasonable limits" to individual freedom? How much power should our governments have? Which needs should we fulfil for ourselves, and which are better met through collective action? Which val-

Learning Outcomes

After reading this chapter, you should be able to:

- understand the importance of recent global developments in making decisions on ideologies

- recognize the role played by factual and value judgements in coming to conclusions on issues

- appreciate the need for individual citizens to make informed decisions on current issues

- apply what you have learned in coming to individual decisions on competing ideologies

globalization: the increasing interdependence of countries and economies that is making national boundaries less relevant.

ues are most important? What are the most effective, efficient, and humane ways of achieving our goals?

Clearly, these are not abstract, idle questions—their answers will have a crucial bearing on how we will live our lives, and on the nature of our societies in the years to come.

The Impact of Emerging Developments

In view of the developments of the late twentieth century, the questions posed above take on a new sense of urgency. Changes in the role of women in Western societies have clearly challenged traditional male dominance of political and economic systems. Earlier assumptions of continued growth and prosperity in the developed Western economies have been called into question by rising unemployment, debts and deficits, and cutbacks in public services. People in many countries in Africa, Latin America, and Asia have witnessed enormous changes in their political and economic systems. People in the countries that once made up the Soviet Union and its empire face fundamental transformations in their ways of life.

International factors such as the increasing globalization of the world's economic systems, environmental issues, the end of the Cold War, and massive changes in information technology have affected people everywhere and have called into question the very suitability of our political and economic systems. These conditions force us to re-examine the existing roles of individuals in society and of citizens in government.

The Future of the Nation–State

Is our present political structure, which is based on the nation-state, consistent with the realities of the global economy? Some observers point to the impact of the changes resulting from globalization, information technology, and the increasing power of multinational corporations and argue that the nation-state is becoming obsolete. Others see the need for cooperation. Prime Minister Gro Brundtland of Norway suggests that just as tribal communities gradually realized the need for a common system, nation-states must now surrender some of their traditional national authority and share responsibility with other nations for dealing with problems that are global in nature.

Another issue related to the future of nation-states is the rise of nationalism, particularly in its more aggressive and exclusive forms as described in Case Study 10. Canadian writer Michael Ignatieff, in his book *Blood and Belonging*, draws a distinction between **civic nationalism**—the view that the nation should be composed of all those who accept the nation's shared set of political practices and values, regardless of such factors as race, colour, gender, language, or ethnicity—and **ethnic nationalism**—the view that nations are made up of people with common inherited factors based mainly on ethnicity. This rising tide of ethnic nationalism is clearly evident in those nation-state structures that collapsed with the former Soviet Union.

civic nationalism: nationalism based on shared political practices and beliefs.

ethnic nationalism: nationalism based on cultural, linguistic, religious, or racial factors.

People in the midst of political and economic uncertainty looked to those of their own ethnicity for support. One of the dangers of this shift from civil to ethnic nationalism is the potential threat to the civil liberties of minority groups within the society.

The Gap Between the World's Rich and Poor

"The world's most halting statistic has come in the 1996 United Nations' Human Development Report. Take it in slowly: the total wealth of the world's 358 billionaires equals the combined incomes of the poorest 45 percent of the world's population—2.3 billion people."[1] These figures draw attention to some people's concerns over the growing gap between the world's wealthiest and poorest people and countries.

Obviously, market economies produce winners and losers. The trend toward more market-based economies was accelerated by the success of some Asian economies and by the collapse of communism in the Soviet Union. The **International Monetary Fund (IMF)** and the **World Bank** promoted capitalism in developing countries by tying loans to policies of privatization, deficit reduction, and a reduced role for government (often referred to as **structural adjustment** policies).

Despite the advance of such Asian market-oriented economies as Hong Kong, Singapore, Taiwan, and South Korea (which together represent less than 2 percent of the population in developing countries), the contrast with some other countries is stark. According to Eric Hobsbawm, "the belief ... that unrestricted international trade would allow the poorer countries to come closer to the rich, runs counter to historical experience as well as common sense. A world economy developing by the generation of such growing inequalities is, almost inevitably, accumulating future troubles."[2]

The Citizen and Society

The magnitude of such issues as the rise in ethnic nationalism, the increasing globalization of the world's economic systems, or the inequities between the world's rich and poor causes some people to retreat from attempting to solve them and to focus only on their own situation. However, although the questions that we face seem to relate to us only as individuals, many of our personal decisions are affected profoundly by our political and economic systems. Our career paths may be affected by the decisions of businesses and governments. Individual decisions about postsecondary education may well be altered by decreased government support and increased tuition fees. Transportation, cultural and recreational facilities, housing, public safety, crime, and pollution are all shaped by local, national, and international forces that seem well beyond our control as individuals.

Yet, in a democratic society we have the opportunity to shape this larger political and economic context through our actions as citizens. To a con-

International Monetary Fund (IMF): a branch of the United Nations that is concerned with international financial matters such as promoting monetary cooperation among states and stabilizing exchange rates.

World Bank: a branch of the United Nations whose aim is to raise the standard of living in developing countries through financial and technical assistance.

structural adjustment: policies that reduce the role of government in the economies of developing nations.

siderable extent, our society will continue to be shaped by the collective decisions of millions of individuals.

Views on the role of the citizen in a democracy are often shaped by one of two approaches. The first focuses on the role of the citizen as an individual. It emphasizes "inalienable" individual rights and their protection by the state. The second approach flows from the view that citizens inevitably function as part of a larger society and stresses the citizen's actions as a member of the community. These two approaches present citizens with further choices.

Citizenship and Decision-Making

The number and complexity of the major issues that face the world might lead some people to the conclusion, "Let's just leave it to the experts." This is a tempting solution, but the immediate problem becomes, "*Which* experts?"

A compelling illustration is the argument over economic approaches, between monetarists and Keynesians, as reflected in the decades-long debate between Milton Friedman and John Kenneth Galbraith. Both men have PhDs in economics, teach at prestigious universities, have been economists for over half a century, have published numerous books, have acted as consultants to governments, and have wide followings. They are both experts— but they come to opposite conclusions on some key issues. If the experts cannot agree, how can we expect "ordinary" citizens to come to wise conclusions?

In part, the answer is related to why the experts disagree. Sometimes they differ on issues that require factual judgements (will tax cuts lead to increases in production?), but often their opposing conclusions stem from differing value judgements (is it more important to promote full employment or to eliminate inflation?). The fact that experts often disagree does not change the need for us to make informed decisions based on our own values and judgements. In addition, neither Friedman nor Galbraith would advise "leaving it to the experts." They argue that it is absolutely essential for individual citizens to examine the issues carefully and to decide for themselves. Each individual has the opportunity to make decisions. Out of our debates and disagreements and differing conclusions and judgements come society's overall decisions.

To effectively fulfil this essential role of decision-maker, we should have a solid knowledge of political and economic systems, an understanding of the factual and ethical aspects of particular issues and choices, and a commitment to making informed decisions. This book was designed to provide the key elements of the necessary "solid knowledge" in political and economic systems. But it is only a base, which will be quickly eroded or outdated if it is not used and enhanced.

Political and economic systems are dynamic—they constantly change. Citizens must keep up-to-date by following important events and issues on a regular basis. The decisions facing the people of Russia in the late 1990s are dramatically different from the decisions of a decade earlier. The questions related to health care in Canada have changed substantially with the federal government's funding cutbacks and the provincial commitments to balanced budgets. Most occupations require constant updating; being a citizen is no different.

When citizens "opt out" of their responsibilities, the inevitable result is that small but well-organized groups gain a disproportionate share of power. In other words, even if we choose not to participate, others will—and *they* will make the decisions.

Some people believe that as long as they vote, they are effective citizens. But a decision merely to cast a ballot every few years is only marginally better than non-involvement. Citizens need to be committed to making informed decisions about current issues. Modern democracy is based on the assumption that citizens will come to conclusions on the important issues of the day and that they will communicate their wishes to their representatives. Effective involvement gives people more power over what affects their lives, and society benefits from the collective decisions of an informed citizenry.

As Canadians begin a new millennium, they face profound questions about what courses of action to follow, both as individuals and as societies. This book is an attempt to provide you with a foundation for decision-making by introducing the various approaches to political and economic systems and the trade-offs associated with the various alternatives. As such, it is "the end of the beginning"—the decision about future involvement as a citizen rests with you. But if there is one conclusion that we can reach with confidence, it is that our interests will be best served by committed citizens making conscious, informed decisions on current issues.

Underlying and Emerging Issues

Give the reasoning and evidence that might be used to support different views or conclusions on the following issues.

1 How should political and economic systems respond to changes in the role of women?

2 To what extent are growth, progress, and prosperity possible in the modern world?

3 To what extent has the move toward market-based economies widened the gap between rich and poor people and countries?

4 To what extent have political and economic changes in Eastern Europe improved people's lives?

5 To what extent are our present political and economic systems consistent with emerging global realities?

6 To what extent is the nation-state system obsolete?

7 Do we need to create stronger international institutions to deal with global problems?

8 Is increasing ethnic nationalism a threat to human rights and democracy?

9 To what extent do the lending policies of international institutions result in the loss of social programs?

10 Has our present society gone too far in emphasizing individual self-interest over the common good?

11 To what extent are decisions about individual goals affected by local, national, and international forces?

12 How can ordinary citizens make decisions on complex political and economic issues?

13 Do citizens in Canada need to become more involved in making informed decisions and communicating them to their elected representatives?

14 To what extent should you become actively involved in political and economic issues as a citizen?

Focussing Knowledge

In your notes, clearly identify or define and explain the importance or significance of each of the following:

globalization

Michael Ignatieff

civic nationalism

ethnic nationalism

International Monetary Fund

World Bank

"structural adjustment"

citizenship

Reviewing and Organizing Knowledge

1 Identify the central theme of *Ideologies* and explain how the questions related to that theme are relevant to individuals.

2 Which late-twentieth-century developments have affected key questions related to political and economic questions?

3 a. Give examples of the ways in which individual choices are affected by the broader context of political and economic systems.

b. How can individuals have an impact on the larger political and economic context?

c. Describe the two basic approaches to the role of the citizen in a democracy.

4 a. In a democratic society, why can we not simply leave decisions to "the experts"?

b. Why are debate and disagreement essential in a democracy?

c. Describe the factors that are necessary to effectively fulfil the role of citizen.

d. Why is it essential for citizens to stay up-to-date on important issues?

5 a. What are the consequences of not being involved as a citizen?

b. Why is it not enough to simply vote?

c. Describe the advantages for the individual and for society of effective citizen involvement.

Applying and Extending Knowledge

1 On the basis of your study of political and economic systems, make two lists: first, a list of changes that you would recommend regarding Canada's political and economic approach; second, a list of the characteristics of Canada's approach that should remain the same. Choose the three most important points in each list. On the basis of these points, write a position paper on the topic "Canada's political and economic systems: necessary change and continuity." Send a copy of your position paper to your MP, and invite his or her comments.

2 Write a position paper entitled "My Ideology" in which you outline your conclusions on the central questions raised in your study of ideologies.

3 From each of Canada's political parties, obtain information on the party's basic approaches to political and economic systems. Compare this information with your own positions, and decide which party comes closest to your views.

4 Read *The Unconscious Civilization* by John Ralston Saul, or *Jihad vs. McWorld* by Benjamin Barker. How do they contribute to your understanding of the role of a citizen in modern democracy?

5 Outline your view of how you intend to act as a citizen. To what extent and in what ways do you intend to be involved? What factors led you to this position?

6 Choose one country, and research its particular combination of political and economic systems. Describe the nature of these systems and the ideology that seems to underlie them. Why do you think the country developed this particular ideology and approach? Support your conclusions with specific information wherever possible.

7 Write an evaluation of your experiences during your study of ideologies. Choose the three things that had the most important impact on your thinking during this study, and explain why you chose them.

8 *Ideologies* featured biographies of 25 individuals. Identify the two individuals to whom you responded most positively, and the two that you responded to most negatively. Explain the basis for your selections.

9 Choose 2 of the 25 people featured in the biographies who had sharply contrasting views (for example, Milton Friedman and John Kenneth Galbraith, Beatrice Webb and Ayn Rand, or Jiang Qing and Emma Goldman). Write a dialogue in which the two individuals debate their views.

absolute power: the doctrine or system of government that bestows unlimited control on a ruler.

anarchy: the absence of a system of government and law.

apartheid: a political system in South Africa under which blacks had to live in segregated Bantustans, or townships, where they were supposedly permitted to develop their own culture. Apartheid was abolished in 1993.

authoritarian government: a political system in which those in power are not controlled by the people but rather dictate to the people.

authoritarian personality: a personal trait in which people are governed by the need to dominate everyone with whom they interact.

authority: the power or right to command, enforce obedience, or make final decisions.

autocrat: a person who rules as an authoritarian.

backbencher: a Member of Parliament who is not a member of Cabinet or one of the leading members of an opposition party.

Balkans: a large peninsula in southeastern Europe.

bandwagon effect: joining what appears to be the winning side in a political campaign.

belief: a conviction that something is true without certain proof.

bicameral legislature: a legislature that consists of two houses of parliament.

bourgeoisie: according to Marxist theory, those holding a commanding position of economic power in a capitalistic society; the owners of the means of production.

bureaucracy: a system that administers the affairs of a government or business enterprise through employed officials; in government, this is also called the civil service.

caucus: the plenary (full) meeting of the elected representatives of a political party in which party policies are discussed and approved, often by consensus.

centrally planned economy: an economic system in which the central government makes all the major economic decisions for the country.

charismatic; charisma (n.): having the ability to capture the attention and gain the support of people through the force of one's personality.

checks and balances: a system of government in which the executive, legislative, and judicial branches of government are constitutionally vested with the right to check one another's actions in order to prevent concentration of power.

civic nationalism: nationalism based on shared political practices and beliefs.

civil liberties: the lawful freedoms of action and belief enjoyed by citizens of a democratic state.

classical (traditional) liberalism: the early-nineteenth-century version of liberalism, which opposed almost all government intervention of any kind, including social welfare measures.

coalition government: a government that stays in power by combining with another political party or parties to form a majority.

Co-determination Act of 1977: an act that gave trade unions a voice in the day-to-day operation of Sweden's industries.

collective farms: large-scale, government-managed farms in the USSR, created by combining smaller peasants' holdings. The peasants were allowed to live on the farms and worked together to increase agricultural production.

command economy: an economic system in which the basic questions of what, how, and for whom to produce are resolved by the government, which makes all major economic decisions.

commune: a community of people living and working together where responsibilities are commonly shared.

competition: rivalry among entrepreneurs engaged in the same business enterprise, each of whom is trying to capture as large a share of the market as possible.

Confucianism: the beliefs of the philosopher Confucius, who preached a well-ordered, hierarchical society in which every citizen played a specific role.

Congress of People's Deputies: a government body, introduced by Mikhail Gorbachev to wield full authority in the USSR.

conservative: a person who favours the retention of traditional values, especially in government, economics, religion, and morals.

constituency: an electoral district used to elect members to parliament.

constitution: a legal document that outlines the basic rules for government and assigns different functions to each governing body of a country.

corporatist system: in Fascist Italy, an economic system developed by Benito Mussolini that combined aspects of the medieval guild system and syndicalism.

coup d'état: an attempt, whether successful or unsuccessful, to overthrow the government of a state.

crisis theory: the political science theory that all historical events in human society are triggered by various crises, such as war and economic depression.

critical thinking: the ability to subject ideas and situations to a sound estimate of the problems involved.

Crown corporation: in Canada, a business enterprise owned by government and operated by a government-appointed management team.

Cultural Revolution: a decade-long campaign launched in 1966 by Mao Zedong that promoted continuous revolution and radical socialist ideals at the expense of Western and traditional elements in China.

deficit financing: the government practice of spending more money than it collects in revenue, through borrowing.

demand: the relationship between the various possible prices of a product and the quantities of the product that consumers are willing to purchase.

democratic centralism: a Soviet political approach under which issues are discussed from the bottom up, then resolved by the party congress with the expectation that all party members will obey the policy.

demogrants: grants offered by the Canadian government to population groups who might need financial help.

depression: a deep and prolonged drop in the Gross National Product, with high unemployment.

deregulation: a reduction of government restrictions on business enterprises.

dictatorship: absolute rule by one person or by a small elite.

direct democracy: a state in which all political decisions are made directly by qualified voters.

economic system: an organized approach to producing and distributing goods and services.

efficiency: maximizing the amount of output obtained from a given amount of resources or minimizing the amount of resources used for a given output.

electoral process: the system of organizing and administering the voting process.

electorate: the body of citizens that has the right to vote.

Enabling Act: the act passed by Adolf Hitler in 1933 that gave him absolute dictatorial powers in Germany for four years.

equality: treating people the same in terms of human and political rights.

ethnic nationalism: nationalism based on cultural, linguistic, religious, or racial factors.

Fabian movement: an elitist socialist group of the late nineteenth century that was determined to reform society through peaceful means.

fascism: a political ideology characterized by an extreme right-wing view and support for totalitarian government, with a corporative economy.

fact: an actual occurrence, or a piece of information, presented as having reality.

federal system: a political system under which legislative and administrative powers are divided between national and regional governments.

first-past-the-post: selection of the winning candidate by the largest number of votes (not necessarily a majority).

fiscal policies: the government's use of taxing and spending to regulate and influence the economy.

Five-Year Plan: an economic plan implemented by Stalin in 1928 to expand and improve industrialization to make the USSR self-sufficient.

five-year plans: in Sweden, government economic projections for the future to assist industry in arriving at rational decisions.

formal democracy: term applied by communists to the ideas of freedom of speech, freedom of the press, freedom of association, and equality before the law.

founding myth: the underlying "story" that explains how/why a government came to power.

Four Modernizations: four areas on which China focussed its reforms in the early 1980s: agriculture, industry, national defence, and science and technology.

Führer: "Leader" in German. Specifically, Adolf Hitler.

fundamentalism: the belief that the words of a holy book (such as the Bible or the Qur'an) are the words of God and therefore should be taken literally.

glasnost: a policy of openness that allowed increased freedom of expression of political opinions within the Communist Party and the USSR under Mikhail Gorbachev.

globalization: the increasing interdependence of countries and economies that is making national boundaries less relevant.

Gosplan: the central planning agency of the USSR that was responsible for informing regional ministries about which products were needed and in what quantities.

Gossnab: the planning body responsible for determining how commodities were to be distributed in the USSR.

government: a system of ruling or controlling the affairs of a specific geographic area.

Great Leap Forward: a government program initiated by Mao Zedong in 1958 that was intended to make China's industry as productive as Western countries in only a few years.

"Great Man" theory: a theory that perfect government demands rule by a man possessing extraordinary abilities.

Greenpeace: an international environmental protection agency that uses various methods to influence governments and private companies.

Greens: political activists who are functioning in many countries to save the environment.

Gross Domestic Product (GDP): the total income generated within a country.

Gross National Product (GNP): in economics, the sum total of a country's annual economic production.

Gross National Product (GNP) per capita: the average amount of goods and services produced each year by every individual in a country.

guanxi: in China, a person's network of family, friends, and colleagues that can help them improve their material and economic conditions.

guerrilla warfare: small-scale fighting, mostly hit-and-run raids, by small groups of often non-professional combatants.

guest workers: people from poorer countries who legally settle in a richer country in order to work, but who have no possibility of gaining citizenship in the new country.

hereditary monarch: any ruler who inherits the right to rule a country, based usually on family (dynastic) affiliation.

human rights: the rights of all people to enjoy certain basic freedoms and protection against such dangers as hunger and disease.

Il Duce: Benito Mussolini, "The Leader" of Fascist Italy between 1922 and 1945.

indicative planning: in Sweden, indirect government planning that uses targets as guidelines to coordinate private and public decision-making.

individual freedom: the constitutional or traditional right of individuals to be protected against illegal actions launched against them by their government.

individualism: an ethical, economic, or political theory that emphasizes the importance and responsibility of individuals over groups.

individual's rights: the natural or lawfully delegated power of an individual to enjoy certain privileges or powers.

Industrial Revolution: the transformation, which occurred first in mid-eighteenth-century England, of a traditional agricultural economy into an urban, factory system of production.

inflation: a condition of generally rising prices owing to the supply of excess money over available goods.

interdependence: in economics, the need for individuals and business firms to interact with one another for the mutual benefit of all parties involved.

interest group: an organized or informal group representing a specific political, social, or economic position in society.

International Monetary Fund (IMF): a branch of the United Nations that is concerned with international financial matters such as promoting monetary cooperation among states and stabilizing exchange rates.

invisible hand: the expression used by Adam Smith to explain the fact that the selfish economically governed actions of all individuals of a society ultimately combine to benefit all of society.

iron rice bowl: a Chinese term for the cheap housing, food, and lifelong employment that state-run industries used to provide.

jingoism: a nationalistic attitude that favours an aggressive foreign policy.

Johann Gottfried von Herder: an eighteenth-century German philosopher who advocated the preservation of native language from foreign influence.

Johann Gutenberg: a mid-fifteenth-century printer noted for pioneering movable type.

joint economic ventures: business undertakings that involve the companies of two or more countries.

joint enterprises: companies jointly owned by two different parties, such as a corporation and the government of a country.

junta: an oligarchy controlled by the military.

keiretsu: large enterprises (successors to the *zaibatsu),* which dominate contemporary Japan's business life.

kulaks: prosperous peasant farmers who, under Stalin's regime, refused to sell their surplus grain at the government-set low prices.

Kuomintang: Chinese political party that was founded by Sun Yatsen in the early twentieth century. After losing power to Mao Zedong's communists in 1949, the Kuomingtang has dominated the government and politics on the island of Taiwan.

left: political groups representing the radical or liberal wing of socio-political reform parties.

liberal: a person who favours reform, especially in government, economics, and religion, and who prefers democratic or republican forms of government in a constitutional state.

lobbying: a form of direct or indirect communication with government members designed to influence public policy.

lobbyist: usually a paid employee of various economic and political groups or business firms whose task is to influence governmental action or legislation.

Long March: the 9600 km journey of Mao Zedong and his Red Army to their eventual base in Yenan.

market: any arrangement for bringing buyers and sellers together.

market economy: an economic system in which the basic questions of what, how, and for whom to produce are resolved by the interaction among buyers and sellers.

Marxism: the economic and political theories of Karl Marx.

means of production: land, tools, and factories; the factors required by people to engage in industry and agriculture.

Mefo-bills: a form of currency based on a dummy corporation that Germany's Nazi government used to finance at least 20 percent of its rearmament costs.

Meiji Restoration: the introduction of wide-ranging reforms of Japan's economic, political, and social structure during the latter half of the nineteenth century.

Mein Kampf: My Struggle, Adolf Hitler's autobiographical and philosophical book, which outlines his objectives.

mercantilism: an economic system widely practised in Europe until the end of the eighteenth century, in which private enterprises were permitted to function only by submitting to detailed intervention and supervision in their business activities by the government.

Ministry of Corporations: in Fascist Italy, a government ministry that controlled six nation-wide "corporations," or associations of workers and managers in various industries.

minority government: a government in which no one party has the majority of the seats in the legislature.

mixed economy: an economic system that combines the market and centrally planned systems;

private enterprise is subject to some government regulation.

moderate: a political middle-of-the-roader, who believes in neutrality or compromise.

monetarists: advocates of policies in which the monetary supply is used to influence the economy.

monetary policies: the government's regulation of the supply of money to influence the economy.

most favoured nation (MFN): a status conferred on other countries by the United States that gives those countries more favourable trade terms, such as lower tariffs on imports of their products.

multi-member constituency: a political subdivision from which more than one person is elected.

multinational corporation (MNC): a business organization that functions on a global basis and so is not subject or loyal to any particular government or state.

multi-party system: a system in which more than two parties dominate politics and legislation, usually by means of coalition governments.

National Council of Corporations: a council comprising 22 corporations in Fascist Italy.

national debt: the amount of money owed by one country as a result of the accumulation of deficits.

national deficit: the amount by which government expenditures exceed revenues for a particular year.

nationalization: state ownership and control of land and/or industries.

natural rights: a political theory, according to which all people are born with certain inalienable privileges—rights that cannot be taken away.

natural state: a condition under which people are not organized under a social contract.

Nazi Party: the National Socialist German Workers' Party that governed Germany under Adolf Hitler from 1933 to 1945.

neo-conservatism: an economic school of thought that opposes government involvement in the economy and emphasizes greater reliance on private enterprise; also called Thatcherism, Reaganomics, and supply-side economics.

neo-fascist: a term used to describe contemporary movements or persons advocating white superiority and racial purity.

New Deal: the term used to describe U.S. President Roosevelt's economic reforms during the 1930s.

New Economic Policy (NEP): an economic policy of partial return to private enterprise devised by Lenin in 1922 to stimulate industrial and agricultural production in the Soviet Union.

Nuremberg Laws: the laws passed by Adolf Hitler in 1935 that took away German Jews' citizenship rights and prohibited Jews from marrying non-Jews.

oligarchy: an authoritarian government conducted and controlled by a relatively few influential members.

One country, two systems: the slogan that describes how China will retain its communist system while Hong Kong retains its capitalist system, for a transition period of 50 years.

one-party system: a system in which only one political party wields all the constitutional power.

opinion poll: a survey conducted by a public opinion firm or political party to test the public's attitude concerning certain events, conditions, or leaders.

parliamentary (constitutional) monarchy: a political system in which the head of state is a king or queen, but political power resides in an elected parliament.

party discipline: obeying party decisions, which is a stronger feature of Canadian politics than loyalty to constituents or a politician's personal views.

party loyalty: the obligation of elected members of a political party to cast a vote in the legislature in their party's favour, even if they disagree with the party's position.

party platform: a plan of action or statement of policies and principles of a political party.

passive resistance: the systematic, non-violent refusal by individuals or groups to obey the laws and regulations of a state, and their refusal to cooperate with government officials and their representatives.

perestroika: a program of economic and political restructuring introduced in the USSR by Mikhail Gorbachev in 1985.

Platt Amendment: a United States law of 1901 that made Cuba an American protectorate. It was abolished by the Cuban Treaty of 1934.

plebiscite: a direct ballot by all qualified voters on an issue of national importance.

pluralism: a theory that states that diversity of ideas and competition among interest groups allows citizens greater control over government decisions.

polis: in ancient Greece, a city and its surrounding countryside.

Politburo: the supreme executive agency of the Communist Party in the former USSR that was responsible for making and enforcing policy.

political system: an organized way to make, carry out, and interpret laws and rules.

pollster: a person employed by a public opinion firm or political party to canvass public opinion.

pragmatism: practicality over ideology.

pressure group: a group with a special interest that is aggressive and activist in its efforts to achieve a certain objective.

price system: the mechanism that coordinates the multitude of economic decisions carried out in the marketplace.

privatization: the sale of government-controlled or -owned assets to the private sector.

productivity: in economic theory, the rate of labour output by individual workers and machinery.

profit motive: the desire of business entrepreneurs to accumulate capital by engaging in a commercial venture.

progressive taxes: taxes that are proportionately higher depending on a person's annual income.

proletariat: the class of wage-earning labourers.

propaganda: systematic attempts to manipulate opinions or beliefs, often through the mass media, to maintain control over or to intimidate a populace.

proportional representation: a political system under which parties gain their seats in the legislature based on the percentage of votes they receive in an election.

protective tariff: a tax imposed on imports to protect domestic producers.

Protestant Reformation: the sixteenth-century religious revolution that resulted in the splitting of the Roman Catholic Church.

public order: a state in which law and order are maintained by governments either by law or by extraordinary powers vested in them.

public ownership: government-owned and -operated industries and services.

puppet dictatorship: a dictatorship in which the leader is under the control of a person, group, or country.

Putsch: *a coup d'état*, loosely translated into German.

quality of life: the standard of living of a country measured in terms of not only income, but also available education and health care, political freedom, life expectancy, and other such factors.

radical: a political extremist

reactionary: a person who favours a return to narrow, traditional values, especially in government, economics, religion, and morals.

Reaganomics: a supply-side economic policy pursued by former U.S. president Ronald Reagan.

rearmament: rebuilding of a country's military system.

recall: the ability of citizens to replace one elected representative with another through a by-election.

recession: a downward trend in a country's economy.

referendum: the submission of a planned law to a direct vote of the people.

Reichstag: the lower legislative chamber of Germany's Parliament in the Weimar Republic.

representative democracy: a state in which the legislative powers are delegated by qualified voters to their representatives in a legislative body, such as a parliament, senate, or congress.

republic: a political system in which the head of state is a non-hereditary official, usually a president.

resources: in economic theory, the basic items (land, labour, and capital) used in all types of production.

responsible government: a system of parliamentary government in which the executive functions at the will of the legislative body.

right: political groups representing the conservative or reactionary wing of socio-political parties.

Riksdag: the Parliament of Sweden.

run-off system: an election system in which, if no candidate receives a majority of the votes, the top two vote-getters are placed on another ballot and a second election is held to determine the majority winner.

salaryman: Japanese term for a white-collar worker.

SCAP: the U.S. Occupation forces in Japan following World War II.

scarcity: in economic theory, the limited availability of resources and goods; the excess of wants over resources.

Secretariat: the supreme administrative agency of the Communist Party which managed the daily activities of the Party.

secular: worldly or non-religious.

separation of powers: a political system in which the executive, legislative, and judicial powers of government are distinctly divided.

sexism: the intentional or unintentional refusal to practise gender equality.

Shiite Muslims: an Islamic sect that broke away from Sunni Muslims in the late seventeenth century, largely on doctrinal grounds.

single-member constituency: an electoral district in which one person is elected to represent the citizens of that district.

social contract: the theory that a government cannot wield its authority by force alone but must have the tacit or written consent, such as a constitution, of the governed.

Social Darwinism: the misguided adaptation of Darwin's biological theories to aspects of human society.

social-insurance programs: financial programs offered by the Canadian government to protect people against a loss of income.

socialism: an economic system that involves state ownership of the means of production, equitable distribution of incomes, and centralized economic planning.

sovereign: a person who exercises supreme (but not necessarily unlimited) power; to be independent of any other authority; free.

special economic zone (SEZ): part of a country that the government declares open to foreign enterprises and investment.

squadristi: in Mussolini's Italy, groups of young Fascist paramilitary men sent into the streets to combat the communists.

standard of living: the relative level of material goods, comfort, and well-being in a society.

state farms: government-owned mechanized farms in the Soviet Union, which paid wages to workers.

state intervention: the act of intervening in the economy by government.

state monopoly: a commonly used economic policy whereby government owns, maintains, and operates vital facilities such as railways, airlines, postal systems, and similar facilities.

Storm Troopers: a paramilitary force of Brown Shirts, also known as the SA, who were the Nazis' private army.

structural adjustment: policies that reduce the role of government in the economies of developing nations.

subsidiary: a company that is more than half owned or controlled by another company.

suffrage: the right to vote in an election.

supply: the relationship between various possible prices of a product and the quantities of the product that businesses are willing to supply.

Supreme Court: the highest court of appeal; the final authority in the interpretation of laws.

sustaining myth: the underlying "story" that explains why a government continues in power.

syndicalism: a political and economic approach developed by George Sorel in the late 1800s that envisioned trade unions governing society.

system: an orderly combination or arrangement of parts, elements, facts, or concepts into a whole.

Thatcherism: a supply-side economic policy pursued by former British Prime Minister Margaret Thatcher.

theocracy: a system of government in which God is recognized as the supreme ruler and religious laws are regarded as the laws of the state.

Third Reich: the name given to the period in Germany of 1933–45 by the ruling Nazi Party.

tolerance: permitting, although not necessarily condoning, particular actions or beliefs that differ from or conflict with one's own standards.

totalitarian: relating to a political system in which the ruler or ruling body has established total control over all aspects of society.

traditional economy: an economic system largely practised by people in a pre-industrial stage of development, based mostly on agriculture or fishing and on a division of labour decreed by custom and tradition.

transfer program: a federal financial plan designed to relieve the poverty of individual groups, based on the recipients' needs.

two-party system: a system in which two political parties dominate the politics and legislation of a country.

tyranny of the majority: a condition under which the ruling majority oppresses minorities of any type.

unitary system: a political system under which all geographic regions are governed directly by the central government.

universal suffrage: a political system that grants the right to vote to all qualified citizens, regardless of political or religious beliefs, gender, race, or ethnic affiliation.

Utopian Socialists: a group of socialists (eighteenth to nineteenth centuries) who advocated peaceful and democratic methods to achieve more ideal societies based on cooperation, planning, and communal approaches.

value: a subjective standard, such as a philosophy or principle, that is deemed valuable or desirable.

Weimar Republic: the republican type of parliamentary democracy, with its capital located in Weimar, that ruled in Germany from 1919 to 1933.

welfare capitalism: capitalism based on the belief that government should take responsibility for the well-being of its citizens.

welfare state: an economic system that is committed to the security of its population in income, health care, and job security.

World Bank: a branch of the United Nations whose aim is to raise the standard of living in developing countries through financial and technical assistance.

Yoshida Doctrine: policies from the mid-1940s through the 1980s favouring the development of Japan's industries and an alliance with the United States.

zaibatsu: Japanese monopolies, each industry dominated by a single family, that jointly controlled the industrial life of Japan prior to and during World War II.

Chapter 2
1.   This summary is an abridged and modernized vesion of the major ideas Hobbes proposed in *Leviathan*, published in 1651.
2.   This is an abridged and modernized version of John Locke's ideas on government as presented in his *Two Treatises of Civil Government*, published in 1690.
3.   This is an abridged version of Rousseau's ideas. His ideas are difficult to summarize because his two major works, *Discourse on the Origin of Inequality* (1754) and the *Social Contract* (1762), contain many conflicting, or at least contradictory, statements.
4.   Aristotle, *Politics*, trans. T.A. Sinclair and Trevor J. Saunders (New York: Penguin Books, 1981).
5.   *Current Biography 1973*, p. 34.
6.   Deborah Felder, *The 100 Most Influential Women of All Time* (Secaucus, NJ: Citadel Press, 1996), p. 55.
7.   Roland Turner, ed., *Thinkers of the Twentieth Century* (Chicago: St. James Press, 1987), p. 175.
8.   Simone de Beauvoir, *The Second Sex* (Alfred A. Knopf Inc., 1980), pp. xxix and 689.

Chapter 3
1.   Preston Manning, *The New Canada* (Toronto: Macmillan, 1992), pp. 324–27.
2.   *Amnesty International Report* (New York: Amnesty International Publications, 1993).
3.   The Gallup Poll, Vol. 56, No. 33 (May 2, 1996).
4.   Albert Camus, *The Rebel* (New York: Vintage), p. 75.
5.   Will Durant, *The Story of Philosophy* (New York: Pocket Books, 1961), p. 432.

Case Study 1
1.   Joseph Wearing, "Is the Prime Minister Too Powerful—No," in Mark Charlton and Paul Barker, eds., *Cross Currents: Contemporary Political Issues*, 2nd ed. (Scarborough, ON: Nelson, 1994), pp. 161–62.
2.   *Saturday Night* (July 1985), p. 19.
3.   *Canadian Human Rights Advocate* (February 1990), pp. 3, 5.

Case Study 2
1.   *Scandinavian Review* (Winter 1994), p. 23. In November 1994, 53.2 percent of Swedes voted in favour of joining the European Union.
2.   John Hiemstra, "Getting What You Vote For," in Mark Charlton and Paul Barker, eds., Cross *Currents: Contemporary Political Issues*, 2nd ed. (Scarborough, ON: Nelson, 1994), p. 289.
3.   *Swedish Election Guide* 1994, p. 11.
4.   Cited in Olga S. Opfell, *The Lady Laureates*, 2nd ed. (Metuchen, NJ: The Scarecrow Press, 1986), p. 92.
5.   *Current Biography* (January 1996): Bok, Sissela.

Case Study 3

1.   The following discussion has been abridged and adapted from Jack Lively, *Democracy* (Oxford: Basil Blackwell, 1975), pp. 44–49.
2.   *The Chronicle-Herald* (Halifax) (April 23, 1996), p. C1.
3.   *The Toronto Star* (December 30, 1995), p. B4.
4.   Robert J. Jackson and Paul Conlin, "The Imperative of Party Discipline in the Canadian Political System," in Mark Charlton and Paul Barker, eds., *Cross Currents: Contemporary Political Issues*, 2nd ed. (Scarborough, ON: Nelson, 1994), pp. 203–4.
5.   Maclean's (April 4, 1996).
6.   Ibid.
7.   Ibid.
8.   Sheila Copps, *Nobody's Baby* (Toronto: Deneau, 1986), pp. 191–92.

Case Study 4

1.   Reprinted with permission from *When Freedoms Collide: The Case for Civil Liberties* by Alan Borovoy, published by Lester & Orpen Dennys Ltd., copyright © 1988 A. Alan Borovoy.
2.   The Gallup Poll, Vol. 55, No. 44, 1995.
3.   Martin Luther King, Jr., *Why We Can't Wait* (New York: HarperCollins, 1991), p. 88.
4.   Nelson Mandela, *No Easy Walk to Freedom*, ed. Ruth First (New York: Basic Books, 1965), pp. 163–68, 180–81, 184–89.
5.   Chris Wood, "Showdown," *Maclean's* (September 11, 1995), pp. 27–29.
6.   Deborah Felder, *The 100 Most Influential Women of All Time* (Secaucus, NJ: Citadel, 1996), p. 63.
7.   Rosa Parks, *Rosa Parks: My Story* (New York: Dial Books, 1992), p. 150.
8.   Ibid.

Case Study 5

1.   Quoted in Richard V. Ericson, et al., *Negotiating Control: A Study of News Sources* (Toronto: University of Toronto Press, 1989), p. 175.
2.   Reprinted with permission from "TV Debates" by Rupert J. Taylor, *Canada & the World Magazine* (November 1976), Oakville, Ontario.
3.   *Time* (February 26, 1996), p. 22.
4.   Stephen Brooks and Andrew Stritch, *Business and Government in Canada* (Scarborough, ON: Prentice-Hall, 1991), pp. 237–38.
5.   James Geary, "The Man Who Keeps the Eco-Warriors in Control," *Time* (June 10, 1996), pp. 42–43.
6.   Peter C. Newman, *Maclean's* (October 1993), p. 14.
7.   *Maclean's* (September 11, 1995), p. 30.

Case Study 6

1.   *Farmer's Advocate & Home Journal* (June 10, 1910).
2.   *The Manitoba Free Press*, January 28, 1914, quoted in Catherine L. Cleverdon, *The Women Suffrage Movement in Canada* (Toronto: University of Toronto Press, 1975), p. 59.
3.   Ibid., p. 105.
4.   Maryka Omatsu, *Bittersweet Passage* (Toronto: Between the Lines, 1992), pp. 34-38.
5.   *Current Biography Yearbook* (1995), p. 554.
6.   Jerry Buckley, *International Wildlife* (September/October 1988).
7.   Ron Wideman, *David Suzuki* (Toronto: Fitzhenry & Whiteside, 1988), quoted in *Current Biography Yearbook* (1995), p. 557.
8.   Current Biography Yearbook (1995), p. 554.
9.   David Suzuki, *Time to Change* (Don Mills, ON: Stoddart, 1994), pp. 118, 213.

Chapter 4

1.   Quoted in Eugene Weber, ed., *The Western Tradition*, Vol. 1, 5th ed. (Lexington, MA: D.C. Heath, 1995), pp. 511–12.

2. Quoted in T. Hoy, ed., *Politics and Power: Who Should Rule?* (New York: Putnam's, 1968), pp. 254–55.
3. The examination of totalitarianism is derived largely from Reo. M. Christenson, et al., *Ideologies and Modern Politics* (New York: Harper and Row, 1981), Chapters 3, 4.
4. Hannah Arendt, *Eichmann in Jerusalem: A Report on the Banality of Evil* (New York: Penguin, 1963), p. 33.

Case Study 7
1. V.I. Lenin, "What Is to Be Done," *Collected Works of V.I. Lenin* (Moscow: Progress Publishers, 1974), pp. 373, 400, 464.
2. *Current Biography 1988*, p. 534.

Case Study 8
1. Quoted in Alfred Andrea and James Overfield, eds., *The Human Record: Sources of Global History*, Vol. II: *Since 1500* (Boston: Houghton Mifflin, 1994), pp. 453–56.
2. *1992 Current Biography Yearbook* (New York: H.W. Wilson Co.), pp. 27–31.
3. Ibid.
4. S. Fragin, "The Passion of Suu Kyi," *New York Times Magazine* (January 7, 1996), pp. 32–37.

Case Study 9
1. Adolf Hitler, *Mein Kampf* (Munich: F. EherNachfolger, 1927) as found in Alfred J. Andrea and James H. Overfield, eds., *The Human Record: Sources of Global History*, 2nd ed., Vol. II: *Since 1500* (Boston: Houghton Mifflin, 1994), pp. 401–2.
2. Jeremy Noakes and Geoffrey Pridham, *Documents on Nazism, 1919–1945* (London, UK: Jonathan Cape, 1974), p. 292. Reprinted by permission of the Peters Fraser & Dunlop Group Ltd.
3. Ibid., p. 273.
4. Ibid, pp. 273, 275.
5. From *22 Cells in Nuremberg* by Douglas M. Kelley. Copyright 1947 by the author. Reprinted with the permission of the publisher, Chilton Book Company, Radnor, PA.
6. *Hitler: A Study in Tyranny* by Alan Bullock (first published by Odhaus Press), reprinted by permisson of Paul Hamlyn Publishing, part of Reed International Books Ltd.
7. Noakes and Pridham, p. 335. Reprinted by permission of the Peters Fraser & Dunlop Group Ltd.
8. Joachim Remak, *The Nazi Years: A Documentary History*, pp. 87, 88. Copyright © 1969 by Simon & Schuster, Inc. Reprinted by permission of Simon & Schuster, Inc.
9. Hitler, *Mein Kampf*, as found in Andrea and Overfield.
10. William L. Shirer, *Berlin Diary, The Journal of a Foreign Correspondent, 1934–1941* (New York: Knopf, 1941), pp. 18–19.
11. George L. Mosse, *Nazi Culture* (New York: Grosset & Dunlop, 1968), p. 278.
12. Ibid.
13. Ibid, p. 241.
14. Ibid., p. 357.
15. Hitler, *Mein Kampf*, as found in Andrea and Overfield, pp. 401–42.
16. Bruno Bettelheim, *The Informed Heart: Autonomy in a Mass Age* (Macmillan, 1960).
17. Mosse, p. 275.
18. Richard Corliss, "Riefenstahl's Last Triumph," *Time* (October 18, 1993), pp. 91–92.
19. R.M. Barsam, *Filmguide to Triumph of the Will* (Bloomington, 1975).
20. David Guston, "Leni Riefenstahl," *Film Quarterly* (Fall 1960), p. 4.
21. Albert Speer, *Inside the Third Reich* (New York: Macmillan, 1970), pp. 72–73.

Case Study 10
1. George J. Church, "The Forgotten," *Time* (October 9, 1995), pp. 28–29.
2. James O. Jackson, "Master Giver," *Time* (July 10, 1995), p. 30.
3. Ibid.

4.   Ibid., p. 32.
5.   George Soros, "For Once We're All in Sync...It's a Worldwide Upswing," *Business Week* (October 3, 1994), p. 105.

Chapter 5
1.   Jonathan Power, "Who Will Get the Peace Dividend? Make Civilization, Not War," *World Press Review* (June 1990), pp. 21–22.
2.   Quoted in Roger Gibbins and Loleen Youngman, *Mindscapes: Political Ideologies Towards the 21st Century* (Toronto: McGraw-Hill Ryerson, 1996), p. 169.
3.   *The Annual Obituary 1989* (London: St. James Press, 1990), p. 362.

Chapter 6
1.   P. Saunders, L. Silk, and A.H. MacDonald, *The World of Economics*, 2nd Canadian ed. (Scarborough, ON: McGraw-Hill Ryerson, 1979), p. 24.
2.   *Statistical Abstract of the United States, 1995* (Washington, DC: U.S. Department of Commerce, September 1995), p. 855.
3.   *International Living*, Canadian ed., vol. 15, no. 9 (January 1996).
4.   R.D. Francis, et al., *Destinies* (Toronto: Harcourt Brace, 1996).
5.   "The 100 Most Important Americans of the 20th Century," *Life*, vol. 13, no. 12 (Fall 1990), p. 32.
6.   "Good Guru Guide," *The Economist* (December 25, 1993), p. 23.
7.   "100 Most Important Americans," p. 32.
8.   Peter Brimelon, "Interview with Milton Friedman," *Forbes* (August 17, 1992), pp. 42–46.

Chapter 7
1.   Adam Smith, *An Inquiry Into the Nature and Causes of the Wealth of Nations* (1776).
2.   Samuel Smiles, *Self-Help: With Illustrations of Conduct and Perseverance* (London: John Murray, 1897), pp. 1–3.
3.   Samuel Smiles, *Thrift* (New York: A.L. Burt, n.d.), pp. 6, 14, 18–21.
4.   This section is adapted from J.P. Wogaman, *The Great Economic Debate* (Philadelphia: Westminster Press, 1977), p. 78.
5.   Milton Friedman and Rose D. Friedman, "Free to Choose: A Personal Statement," (Florida: Harcourt Brace Inc., 1980) pp. 148–49.
6.   Milton Friedman, *Capitalism and Freedom* (Chicago: University of Chicago Press, 1962), pp. 65–67.
7.   *1982 Current Biography* (New York: H.W. Wilson Co.), p. 332.
8.   Ayn Rand, *Atlas Shrugged* (New York: Random House, 1957), p. 1069.
9.   Quoted in "Good Guru Guide," *The Economist* (December 25, 1993), p. 26.

Case Study 11
1.   Quoted in William E. Leuchtenburg, *The Perils of Prosperity, 1914–1932* (Chicago: University of Chicago Press, 1958), pp. 96–97.
2.   Ibid.
3.   Ibid., p. 103.
4.   Ellis W. Hawley, *The Great War and the Search for a Modern Order: A History of the American People and Their Institutions, 1917–1933* (New York: St. Martin's Press, 1979), pp. 83–84.
5.   Quoted in Leuchtenburg, pp. 187–88.
6.   Ibid.
7.   Quoted in Leuchtenburg, p. 190.
8.   Robert S. McElvaine, *Down and Out in the Great Depression: Letters from the Forgotten Man* (University of North Carolina Press, 1983), as quoted in Robert D. Marcus and David Burner, eds., *America Firsthand: From Reconstruction to the Present*, Vol. II, 3rd ed. (New York: St. Martin's Press, 1995), pp. 189–90.
9.   Thomas K. McCraw, "The New Deal and the Mixed Economy," in Harvard Sitkoff,

ed., *Fifty Years Later: The New Deal Evaluated* (New York: McGraw-Hill, 1985), p. 37.
10. Louise Mooney, ed., "The Century's Top Ten Tycoons," *World Press Review* (February 1996), p. 24.
11. *Newsmakers 1993* (Detroit: Gale Research), p. 161.
12. Bill Gates, "Billionaire Bytes, askbill@microsoft.com," (The Vancouver Sun, July 17, 1996) p. C16.

Chapter 8
1. Quoted in Marvin Perry, et al., eds., *Sources of the Western Tradition*, vol. 2, 3rd ed. (Boston: Houghton Mifflin, 1995), pp. 214–15.
2. Juan Antonio Blanco, "Cuba: Crisis, Ethics, and Viability," in *Latin America Faces the Twenty-First Century: Reconstructing a Social Justice Agenda*, eds., Susanne Jonas and Edward McCaughan (Boulder, CO: Westview Press, 1994), p. 186.
3. Blanco, "Cuba: Crisis, Ethics, and Viability," p. 190.
4. Carole Seymour-Jones, *Beatrice Webb: A Life* (Chicago: Ivan R. Dee, 1992), p. 321.
5. Ibid., p. 322.
6. Ibid., p. 322.
7. Tony Benn, *Writings on the Wall* (London: Faber and Faber, 1984), p. 120.

Case Study 12
1. Joseph Stalin, "The Tasks of Business Executives," quoted in Alfred J. Andrea and James H. Overfield, eds., *The Human Record: Sources of Global History*, 2nd ed., Vol. II (Boston: Houghton Mifflin, 1994), pp. 397–98.
2. Ruth Ashby and Deborah Gore Ohrn, eds., *Herstory* (New York: Viking Press, 1995), p. 7.
3. Richard Drinnon, *Rebel in Paradise* (Chicago: University of Chicago Press, 1961), p. 254.

Case Study 13
1. The information for this section was derived from "Zhuckeng Tests Privatization" by Kathy Chen, *The Wall Street Journal*, as reprinted in *The Globe and Mail* (June 10, 1996), p. B5.
2. Sheila Melvin, "Life in Beijing: A Search for the Elusive Middle Way," *International Living*, Canadian ed., Vol. 15, No. 8 (December 1995), pp. 1, 12–13.
3. *Britannica Book of the Year 1992* (Chicago: Encyclopedia Britannica, 1992), p. 68.
4. Ward G. Chua-Eoan, "Woman Devoured by History," *Time* (June 17, 1991), p. 23.
5. *Current Biography 1975* (New York: H.W. Wilson, 1975), p. 77.
6. "I Am Prepared to Die," *Newsweek* (January 12, 1981), p. 41.
7. *New York Times* (June 5, 1991).
8. Roxane Witke, *Comrade Chiang Ch'ing* (Boston: Little, Brown, 1977), p. 4.

Chapter 9
1. Adelheid Popp, ed., *A Commemorative Book: Twenty Years of the Austrian Women Workers' Movement* (Vienna, 1912), pp. 107–9, quoted in Eleanor S. Riemer and John C. Fout, eds., *European Women: A Documentary History, 1789–1945* (New York: Schocken Books, 1980), pp. 94–95.
2. *Newsweek* (December 26, 1988).
3. *Canada and the World Magazine* (February 1984), pp. 18–19.
4. "Interview: Gro Harlem Brundtland," *UNESCO Courier* (September 1990), pp. 4–9.
5. "Empowering Women: The Solution to a Global Crisis," *Environment*, Vol. 36, No. 10 (December 1994), pp. 18–20.

Case Study 14
1. Quoted in Nicholas George, "Don't Toy With Us: Swedish Unions vs. U.S. Giant," *Scandinavian Review* (Winter 1995), p. 33.
2. Gunnar Myrdal, *Asian Drama: An Inquiry into the Poverty of Nations*, vol. 2 (New

York: The Twentieth Century Fund, 1968), pp. 707–8.

3.   Robert McFadden, "Olof Palme, Aristocrat Turned Socialist, Dominated the Politics of Sweden," *The New York Times* (March 1, 1986), p. 4.

4.   Ibid., p. 4.

5.   *Britannica Book of the Year 1987* (Chicago: Encyclopedia Britannica, 1987), p. 507.

Case Study 15

1.   *Statistical Abstract of the United States, 1995: The National Data Book* (Washington, DC: U.S. Department of Commerce, September 1995).

2.   David P. Ross, E. Richard Shillington, and Clarence Lochhead, *The Canadian Fact Book on Poverty—1994* (Ottawa: The Canadian Council on Social Development, 1994), pp. 3–4.

3.   *The Toronto Star* (July 20, 1996), pp. A19, E3.

4.   David Olive, "The Galbraith Principles," *Report on Business* (August 1996), p. 7.

5.   *Current Biography* (1975), p. 151.

6.   Roland Turner, ed., *Thinkers of the Twentieth Century* (Chicago: St. James Press, 1987), p. 273.

7.   *Current Biography* (1975), p. 152.

8.   John Kenneth Galbraith, *The Good Society: The Humane Agenda* (Boston: Houghton Mifflin, 1996).

9.   *Thinkers of the Twentieth Century*, p. 273.

Case Study 16

1.   *Japan Times* (January 16, 1994).

2.   Adapted by permission of *Business Quarterly*, Vol. 54, No. 2 (Autumn 1989), pp. 20–24, published by the Western Business School, the University of Western Ontario, London, Ontario, Canada.

3.   Carin Holroyd and Ken Coates, *Pacific Partners: The Japanese Presence in Canadian Business, Society, and Culture* (Toronto: James Lorimer & Company, 1996), pp. 89–90.

4.   Paul Johnson, *Modern Times* (London: Phoenix, 1992), pp. 733–34.

5.   "The Century's Top 10 Tycoons," *World Press Review* (February 1996).

6.   *Newsmakers 1989* (New York: Gale Research, 1989), p. 345.

7.   Ibid., p. 347

8.   Akio Morita, *Made in Japan: Akio Morita and Sony* (New York: E. P. Dutton, 1986), p. 131.

9.   "The Century's Topc 10 Tycoons," World Press Review (February 1996), p. 24.

10. Akio Morita, *Made in Japan: Akio Morita and Sony* (New York: E.P. Dutton, 1986), p. 309.

Case Study 17

1.   Benito Mussolini, "The Political and Social Doctrine of Fascism," *International Conciliation* no. 306 (January 1935). Published by the Carnegie Endowment for International Peace.

2.   *The Annual Obituary 1981* (New York: St. Martin's Press, 1981), p. 557.

3.   Albert Speer, *Inside the Third Reich* (New York: Macmillan, 1970), p. 618.

Chapter 10

1.   *Edmonton Journal* (July 28, 1996), p. F2.

2.   Eric Hobsbawm, *Age of Extremes* (London: Abacus, 1994), p. 571.

page 21 From *Mindscapes* by Roger Gibbins and Loleen Youngman, 1996. Reprinted by permission of McGraw-Hill Ryerson Ltd.; **page 25** Aristotle, *Politics*; **page 37** From *The New Canada* by Preston Manning published by Macmillan Canada, 1992. Reprinted by permission of Preston Manning; **page 41** From *Amnesty International 1993 Annual Report, Index No. POL 10/01/93*. Reprinted by permission of Amnesty International Secretariat, 1 Easton Street, London WC1X 8DJ; **page 50** Reprinted with the permission of Simon & Schuster from *The Story of Philosophy* by Will Durant. Copyright © 1926, 1927, 1933, 1954, by Will Durant; **page 60, 79** From *Cross Currents: Contemporary Political Issues*, second edition, by Mark Charlton and Paul Barker. Used by permission of ITP Nelson Canada; **page 80** *Swedish Election Guide 1994*; **page 93** The Canadian Press; **page 95** From *Cross Currents: Contemporary Political Issues*, second edition, by Mark Charlton and Paul Barker. Used by permission of ITP Nelson Canada; **page 99** From *Nobody's Baby* by Sheila Copps. A woman's place is in the House (of Commons); **page 103** From *When Freedoms Collide: The Case For Civil Liberties* by Alan Borovoy, published by Lester & Orpen Dennys Ltd. © 1988 A. Alan Borovoy. Reprinted by permission of Key Porter Books; **page 111** From *No Easy Walk to Freedom* by Nelson Mandela, Basic Books, 1965. Reprinted by permission of Heinemann Educational Books; **page 115** From *Rosa Parks: My Story* by Rosa Parks with Jim Haskins. Copyright © 1992 by Rosa Parks. Used by permission of Dial Books for Young Readers, a division of Penguin Books USA Inc.; **page 120** From *Canada and the World*, November 1976. Reprinted with permission of Canada and the World, Waterloo, Ontario; **page 127** From *Business and Government in Canada* by Stephen Brooks and Andrew Stritch, 1991. Reprinted by permission of Prentice-Hall Canada Inc.; **page 129** © 1996 Time Inc. Reprinted by permission; **page 130** *Maclean's*, October 1993. Reprinted by permission; **page 132** *Maclean's*, September 1995. Reprinted by permission; **page 138** *Farmer's Advocate & Home Journal*, June 10, 1910; **page 149** From *Bittersweet Passage* by Maryka Omatsu, 1992. Reprinted by permission of Between the Lines; **page 151** From *Time to Change* by David Suzuki, 1994. Reprinted by permission of Stoddart Publishing Co. Limited; **page 158** Jacques Bossuet, *Treatise On Politics: Based on the Very Words of Holy Writ*, 1678; **page 168** "The Accused, pp. 21-35", from *Eichmann in Jerusalem* by Hannah Arendt. Copyright © 1963, 1964 by Hannah Arendt. Used by permission of Viking Penguin, a division of Penguin Books USA Inc.; **page 174** From a pamphlet titled *What Is to Be Done* by V. I. Lenin, 1902; **page 201** From *Masterpieces of Chinese Fiction*, published by Foreign Languages Press, 1983; **page 210** Reprinted by permission of Ellen Levine Literary Agency. Copyright © 1996 by Claudia Dreifus; **page 218** From *Mein Kampf* by Adolf Hitler, translated by Ralph Manheim published by Pimlico, 1943; **page 219** (bottom), **220** (middle), **221** (bottom) From *Documents on Nazism, 1919-1945* by Jeremy Noakes, 1974. Reprinted by permission of the Peters Fraser & Dunlop Group Ltd.; **page 221** (top) From *22 Cells in Nuremberg* by Douglas M. Kelley, 1947, published by Chilton Book Company; **page 222** (top) From *Mein Kampf* by Adolf Hitler, translated by Ralph Manheim published by Pimlico, 1943; **page 222** (bottom) From *Berlin Diary* by William L. Shirer published by Alfred A. Knopf, 1941. Reprinted by permission of Don Congdon Associates, Inc. Copyright © 1941 , renewed 1968 by William L. Shirer; **page 223** (top, bottom), **224** (top), **225** (bottom) George L. Mosse, *Nazi Culture*, Grosset & Dunlop, 1968, and Shocken Books, New York, 1981. Reprinted by permission of the author; **page 224** (bottom) Reprinted with the permission of The Free Press, a division of Simon & Schuster from *The Informed Heart: Autonomy in a Mass Age* by Bruno Betttelheim. Copyright © 1960 by The Free Press; copyright renewed 1988 by Bruno Bettelheim; **page 227** Reprinted with the permission

INDEX